Liberationists

a story

Liberationists
a story

Xun Yuezang

Copyright © 2017 by Xun Yuezang on behalf of the author

All rights reserved. No part of this publication may be reproduced, stored in a retrieval system, or transmitted, in any form or by any means, electronic, mechanical, photocopying, recording, or otherwise, without the written prior permission of the author. For such permission, please contact liberationistsstory@gmail.com

Published in the United States by Pema Press

Grateful acknowledgment of permission to reproduce the painting, "Böhmen liegt am Meer" © Anselm Kiefer (1996; oil, emulsion, shellac, charcoal, powdered paint on burlap; 74 ¼ in. x 18 ft. 5 in. [191.1 x 561.3 cm]) as cover image, and of permission from the Metropolitan Museum of Art to use the digital image.

For permission to reprint excerpts, grateful acknowledgment is made to the following publishers: Profile Books for *Occupation Diaries* by Raja Shehadeh; W.W. Norton for *The Life and Death of Democracy* by John Keane; Oxford University Press for *The People's Republic of Amnesia: Tiananmen Revisited* by Louisa Lim; Palgrave Macmillan for *Tiananmen Exiles: Voices of the Struggle for Democracy* by Rowena He; and Princeton University Press for *Two Cheers for Anarchy* by James C Scott.

Every reasonable effort has been made to contact copyright holders of material reproduced in this book. If any have inadvertently been overlooked, the publisher would be glad to hear from them and make good in future editions any errors or omissions brought to their attention.

ISBN-13: 978-0-9972385-0-1
LCCN: 2016913456

To

*all who seek liberation
their own and others'
especially those who do so
at great personal risk
in China and elsewhere*

*Alem
and all forsaken
children of the world*

*Mayren
who struggled so long
to be free*

Y and Z

As Ivan Klima prefaced <u>Love and Garbage</u>:

None of the characters in this story—and that includes the narrator—is identical with any living person.

The only exceptions are people who are well-known public figures, such as Xu Zhiyong, Ilham Tohti, Cao Shunli, and so on, though the last is, alas, no longer amongst the living.

And as Li Xiaojun prefaced <u>The Long March to the Fourth of June</u>:

I publish this book under a pseudonym. This is because I have to be cautious not only for my own and my family's sake, but for that of my colleagues and friends, especially those who have helped me.... Accordingly, I cannot say who I am or what my work is.... In present-day China it is not possible to write and publish a book like this without consequences: I have written it because I wish China to become otherwise.

epigraphs

Bohemia lies by the sea

If houses here are green, I'll enter a house.
If the bridges here are sound, I'll walk on solid ground.
If love's labor's ever lost, I'll happily lose it here.
If it's not me, it's one as good as I.

If a word here borders me, then I'll let it border.
If Bohemia lies by the sea, I'll believe in seas again.
And if I believe in the sea, then I'll hope for land.

If it's me, then it's anyone as much as I.
I want nothing more for myself. I want to go to ground.

To the ground- that means to the sea; there I'll find Bohemia again.
In the ground, I'll wake quietly.
From the ground up now I know, and I am unlost.

Come, all you Bohemians, seafarers, port whores and ships
unanchored. Don't you want to be bohemian, all you Illyrians, Veronese
and Venetians. Play the comedies that make us laugh.

And that make us cry. And err a hundred times over,
as I erred and never withstood the trials,
though I have withstood them, time and again.

As Bohemia withstood them and one fine day
was pardoned to the sea and now lies by the water.

I still border a word and another land
I border- and how very little- everything ever more,

a Bohemian, a vagrant who has nothing, who holds nothing
gifted only, by the sea, which is contentious, at seeing the land of my choice.

—*Ingeborg Bachmann, translated from the German, "Böhmen liegt am Meer"*

Debbo riperderti e non posso.

—First line of the poem series, "Mottetti", Eugenio Montale (I must re-lose you and cannot)

What I meant with the word *ripensamenti* doesn't have much to do with the time one has, or one hasn't, for oneself; it has more to do with the fact that, at our age, life is characterized by second thoughts, changes of mind about the things one would have liked to do, paths one would have liked to take, instead of the paths one took. We find ourselves living a life that is only in part, in a very small part, the life we have chosen; and what we have chosen doesn't seem to be what would be best for us —as if our lives were modelled on images shaped by someone else.

—from a friend, in correspondence about looking back on life from the middle of it

The important thing is not to believe that [the occupation] will end any time soon. Mother's hope that she would see the end before she died was folly, and it is unlikely that I will see it either. The important thing is not to give up.

—Occupation Diaries (p 33), Raja Shehadeh in reference to the continued occupation of the Occupied Territories

Wishful thinking—the longing to bend the present world into a different and better future—is often mocked, but the plain fact is that it is a regular feature of the human condition. Whenever we refer to the world around us in language, we habitually allude to things that are absent. We conjecture, we say things that miss the mark, or that express yearnings for things to be other than they are. We live by our illusions. The language through which we speak is an unending series of short little dreams, in the course of which we sometimes fashion new ways of saying things, using words that are remarkably apposite, and strangely inspiring to others. The feminine noun *demokratia* was one of those tiny terms that sprang from a little dream, with grand effect. It was to rouse many millions of people in all four corners of the world—and give them a hand in getting a grip on their world by changing it in ways so profound that they remain undervalued, or misunderstood.

— <u>The Life and Death of Democracy</u> (pp ix-x), John Keane

Darkness always hates the light. Ugliness always hates beauty.

—Xiao Guozhen commenting on the treatment of Song Ze, an advocate for poor petitioners in Beijing who was kidnapped by the Partystate under the pretext of draconian Article 73

Il n'est possible d'aimer et d'être juste que si l'on connaît l'empire de la force et si l'on sait ne pas le respecter.

— "L'Iliade ou le poème de la force," Simone Weil (It is not possible to love and be just without having known the empire of force and how not to respect it.)

[The soldier, Chen Guang] did not believe this about-face [on the part of Beijingers from supporting nonviolent demonstrators to siding with their killers] was motivated by fear, but rather by a deep-seated desire—a necessity even—to side with the victors, no matter the cost: "It's a survival mechanism that people in China have evolved after living under this system for a long time. In order to exist, everything is about following orders from above."

— <u>The People's Republic of Amnesia: Tiananmen Revisited</u> (p29), Louisa Lim

When I was forced to remove my black armband [in memory of the massacred] in 1989, I thought that would be the end of it. Bodies had been crushed, lives destroyed, voices silenced. They had guns, jails, and propaganda machines. We had nothing. Yet somehow it was on that June 4 that the seeds of democracy were planted in my heart, and the longing for freedom and human rights nourished. So it was not an ending after all, but another beginning.

— <u>Tiananmen Exiles: Voices of the Struggle for Democracy in China</u> (p182), Rowena He

Twenty-five years have gone by, we have all grown old. But Tank Man in these pictures is still so young. From far away, his white shirt looks like a lily in summer, pure and unblemished. Tanks stopping in front of a lily. A historical moment, a poetic moment.... You are made of steel, I am flesh and blood, come on down, shithead!

— Liao Yiwu paraphrasing Tank Man

Yes, there is beauty and there are the humiliated. Whatever the difficulties the enterprise may present, I would like never to be unfaithful either to one or the other.

— "Return to Tipasa," Lyrical and Critical Essays (pp169-170), Albert Camus (trans. Ellen Kennedy New York Knopf 1968)

In a free country I would happily spend my life in the library doing research. But I live in a country where I cannot in good conscience merely live such a life. I feel that I have no alternative. I have to voice my criticisms of our messed up social reality. Otherwise I would be uneasy. I would not be able to sleep well.

— Ran Yunfei, as cited in "China Releases Dissident Blogger, With Conditions", Andrew Jacobs; New York Times; August 10, 2011

But almost always, during the initial stage of the struggle, the oppressed, instead of striving for liberation, tend themselves to become oppressors, or "sub-oppressors." The very structure of their thought has been conditioned by the contradictions of the concrete, existential situation by which they were shaped. Their ideal is to be men; but for them, to be men is to be oppressors. This is their model of humanity.

— Pedagogy of the Oppressed (p45), Paulo Freire

I think the Russian problem is not just the president as a person, the problem is that our citizens in the large majority don't understand that their fate, they have to be responsible for it themselves. They are so happy to delegate it to, say, Vladimir Vladimirovich Putin and then they will entrust it to somebody else, and I think that for such a big country as Russia this is the path to a dead end. Which, in a particular fashion, is where we are now. You have to explain, "Hey, guys, if you want to live in a democratic country, you have to change the system."

— *Mikhail Khodorkovsky after his release from prison, from "Q & A with Mikhail B Khodorkovsky," Alison Smale;* <u>New York Times</u>; *December 22, 2013*

To think of humans as freedom-loving, you must be ready to view nearly all of history as a mistake.

— <u>*The Silence of Animals*</u> *(p58), John Gray*

Freedom is a pretty strange thing. Once you've experienced it, it remains in your heart, and no one can take it away.

— *Ai Weiwei in the film, "Ai Weiwei: Never Sorry"*

Freedom is a gift inside one's soul... you can't have it if it isn't in you.

— *DH Lawrence, as cited by Geoff Dyer in* <u>*Out of Sheer Rage*</u> *(p138)*

.... And the world will not discourage you from operating on your default settings, because the world of men and money and power hums along quite nicely on the fuel of fear and contempt and frustration and craving and the worship of self. Our own present culture has harnessed these forces in ways that have yielded extraordinary wealth and comfort and personal freedom. The freedom to be lords of our own tiny skull-sized kingdoms, alone at the center of all creation. This kind of freedom has much to recommend it. But there are all different kinds of freedom, and the kind that is most precious you will not hear much talked about in the great outside world of winning and achieving and displaying. The really important kind of freedom involves attention, and awareness, and discipline, and effort, and being able to truly care about other people and to

sacrifice for them, over and over, in myriad petty little unsexy ways, every day. That is real freedom. The alternative is unconsciousness, the default setting, the "rat race"—the constant gnawing sense of having had and lost some infinite thing.

— *commencement speech of David Foster Wallace to graduating class of Kenyon College*

Every young soul hears this call by day and by night and shudders with excitement at the premonition of that degree of happiness which eternities have prepared for those who will give thought to their true liberation. There is no way to help any soul attain this happiness, however, so long as it remains shackled with the chains of opinion and fear. And how hopeless and meaningless life can become without such a liberation!

— *Schopenhauer as Educator: The Third Untimely Meditation,* Friedrich Nietzsche

The condensation of history, our desire for clean narratives, and the need for elites and organizations to project an image of control and purpose all conspire to convey a false image of historical causation. They blind us to the fact that most revolutions are not the work of revolutionary parties but the precipitate of spontaneous and improvised action ("adventurism" in the Marxist lexicon), that organized social movements are usually the product, not the cause, of uncoordinated protests and demonstrations, and that the great emancipatory gains for human freedom have not been the result of orderly, institutional procedures but of disorderly, unpredictable, spontaneous action cracking open the social order from below.

— *Two Cheers for Anarchism* (p141), James C Scott

Certainly those determining acts of her life were not ideally beautiful. They were the mixed result of a young and noble impulse struggling amidst the conditions of an imperfect social state, in which great feelings will often take the aspect of error, and great faith the aspect of illusion....

> Her full nature [. . .] spent itself in channels which had no great name on the earth. But the effect of her being on those around her was incalculably diffusive: for the growing good of the world is partly dependent on unhistoric acts; and that things are not so ill with you and me as they might have been, is half owing to the number who lived faithfully a hidden life, and rest in unvisited tombs.
>
> — *closing words of <u>Middlemarch</u> (p896), George Eliot*

> ... for anyone who has not suffered a Communist disaster..., what I have gone through is an overwhelming disaster. However, for those who have suffered at the hands of the Communist regime, it is very trivial.
>
> — *introduction to <u>My 1,000 Days Ordeal</u> (pXVI), Ching Cheong*

> Hello my dearest Nima. Writing a letter to you my dear Nima is so very difficult. How do I tell you where I am when you are so innocent and too young to comprehend the true meaning of words such as prison, arrest, sentence, trial, injustice, censorship, oppression versus liberation, freedom, justice, equality?
>
> How do I explain that coming home is not up to me, that I am not free to rush back to you, when I know that you told your father to ask me to finish my work so I can come back home? How do I explain that in the past six months I was not afforded the right to see you for even one hour?
>
> My dear Nima, in the past six months, I found myself crying uncontrollably on two occasions. The first time was when my father passed away and I was deprived of grieving and attending his funeral. The second was the day you asked me to come home and I couldn't come home with you. I returned to my cell and sobbed without control.
>
> —*Nasrin Sotoudeh's letter to her three-year-old son, written on tissue paper from Ward 209 (reserved for political prisoners and run by the Intelligence Ministry), Evin prison, Tehran, May 2010, nine months into her imprisonment*

To know and not to act is not to know.

— Wang Yang-ming, as cited in <u>Burger's Daughter</u> (p213), Nadine Gordimer

What, in the end, is politicization? Is it when you recognize that things are wrong and unjust in the world, or is it when you understand how powerful the powers are that seek to prevent you from changing anything?

— "The Long Road to Angela Davis's Library," Dawn Lundy Martin; <u>The New Yorker</u>, December 26, 2014

I hate the indifferent. I believe that living means taking sides. He who really lives cannot help being a citizen and a partisan. Indifference is apathy, parasitism, cowardice, not life. That is why I hate the indifferent.

Indifference is history's deadweight. Indifference operates with great power on history. It operates passively, but it operates. It is fate, that which cannot be counted on; it twists programs, ruins the best-laid plans; it is the raw material that ruins intelligence. What happens, the evil that weighs upon all, happens because most people abdicate their will, allow laws to be promulgated that only revolt can nullify, allow men to rise to power whom only a mutiny can overthrow. Between absenteeism and indifference few hands, unsupervised by any control, weave the fabric of collective life. The masses are ignorant because they don't care, and then it seems as if it is fate that runs over everything and everyone: It seems as if history is nothing more than an enormous natural phenomenon, an eruption, an earthquake of which all are victims, those who wanted it and those who didn't, those who knew and those who didn't, those who were active and those who were indifferent. Some whimper piously, others curse obscenely, but nobody, or few ask themselves: If I had tried to impose my will, would what has happened have happened?

I hate the indifferent also for this reason: their whimpering protest of eternal innocence annoys me. I hold each of them accountable for how he has dealt with the task that life has given him and gives him every day, for what he has done, and especially for what he has not done. And I feel I am able to be merciless, to not squander my compassion, to not shed tears for them.

I am a partisan, I am alive, I feel already pulsing in the conscience of those on my side the activity of the future city that they are building. And in this, the social chain does not depend on a few; in this, everything that happens is not coincidence, fate, but the intelligent work of the citizens. Nobody in this is standing at the window watching while the few sacrifice themselves. I am alive, I am a partisan. That is why I hate those who don't take sides, I hate the indifferent.

— Antonio Gramsci, Città futura, 11 February 1917

If we have faith—and faith in what we do—then every one of us can really sail very far in life.... They'd say, What does he think he's doing? We have 200,000 soldiers watching him here, over 1 million soldiers all over Poland watching him. We have nuclear arsenals. And he wants to topple them with leaflets?! As an opposition activist, I asked the leaders of the world—prime ministers, presidents, even monarchs—if we could beat Communism. Not one of them gave us the slightest chance. It had been drilled into all of us that only a nuclear war could change anything.... We realized how many of us there were. It wasn't true that there were only a few of us. We began to recognize our strength....

— Lech Walesa in "Three Short Films about Peace," Errol Morris

"Man is by nature a political animal," declares Aristotle in the first book of his "Politics." "Nature, as we often say, makes nothing in vain, and man is the only animal whom she has endowed with the gift of speech ... the power of speech is intended to set forth the expedient and the inexpedient, and therefore likewise the just and the unjust." Aristotle here means that humans fully realize their nature in political participation, in the form of discussions and decision making with their fellow citizens about the affairs of state. To be barred from political participation is, for Aristotle, the most grievous possible affront to human dignity.

— "Is the United States a Racial Democracy?" Jason Stanley and Vesla Weaver, New York Times; January 12, 2014

Power in China lacks all legitimacy. After 60 years in control, how can you still not let people vote? When you disassociate yourself, without trust or credibility, any other talk has no meaning.... We may try to jump from the western frame to measure what China is. But what China really is, is a society which lacks the very most fundamental basis for a real social structure.

— Ai Weiwei in "An Artist's Duty: An Interview with Ai Weiwei", En Liang Khong, Open Democracy; January 6, 2014

When life is unfair, the people on the losing side spend a lot of time worrying about what they are doing, questioning themselves. And the people on the winning side don't think at all. They don't have to.

— Anne Enright, The Believer interview, Conan Putnam, January 2014

The great majority of men and women, in ordinary times, pass through life without ever contemplating or criticising, as a whole, either their own conditions or those of the world at large. They find themselves born into a certain place in society, and they accept what each day brings forth, without any effort of thought beyond what the immediate present requires. Almost as instinctively as the beasts of the field, they seek the satisfaction of the needs of the moment, without much forethought, and without considering that by sufficient effort the whole conditions of their lives could be changed. A certain percentage, guided by personal ambition, make the effort of thought and will which is necessary to place themselves among the more fortunate members of the community; but very few among these are seriously concerned to secure for all the advantages which they seek for themselves. It is only a few rare and exceptional men who have that kind of love toward mankind at large that makes them unable to endure patiently the general mass of evil and suffering, regardless of any relation it may have to their own lives.

    These few, driven by sympathetic pain, will seek, first in thought and then in action, for some way of escape, some new system of society by which life may become richer, more full of joy and less full of preventable evils than it is at present.

But in the past such men have, as a rule, failed to interest the very victims of the injustices which they wished to remedy. The more unfortunate sections of the population have been ignorant, apathetic from excess of toil and weariness, timorous through the imminent danger of immediate punishment by the holders of power, and morally unreliable owing to the loss of self-respect resulting from their degradation.

To create among such classes any conscious, deliberate effort after general amelioration might have seemed a hopeless task, and indeed in the past it has generally proved so. But the modern world, by the increase of education and the rise in the standard of comfort among wage-earners, has produced new conditions, more favorable than ever before to the demand for radical reconstruction.

— Introduction to <u>Proposed Roads to Freedom</u>, Bertrand Russell

Deep in your hearts, you are terrified — terrified of having open trials that citizens can freely attend, terrified of your names appearing on the Internet, terrified of the free society that is coming.... We are citizens, the masters of this country, not its subjects or lackeys, rabble or a mob.

— *Xu Zhiyong addressing Chinese leaders in the closing statement at his trial, a statement he was not allowed to finish delivering. It was subsequently released by his lawyer.*

I have realized that I don't have too many good days ahead of me... Therefore, I feel that it is necessary for me to leave a few words behind before I no longer have the ability to do so.... I am currently very healthy and do not have any illnesses.... If I do pass away in the near future, know that it is not because of natural illness and it certainly will not be suicide.

— *Ilham Tohti in a statement to Radio Free Asia before his enforced disappearance*

Our impact may be large, may be small, and may be nothing. But we must try. It is our duty to the dispossessed and it is the right of civil society.

— *Cao Shunli*

Q: *In 2007,* Time *magazine nominated you as one of 'the one hundred men and women whose power, talent and moral example is transforming the world'. It said of you that: 'By blogging truth to power, she is planting the seeds of a new—and true—cultural revolution.' In your view, what does the expression 'speaking truth to power' mean in China today?*

A: If it's up to me, I'd just go by 'speaking the truth'. I don't intend to oppose the regime, to become the other side of the coin. To me, speaking the truth transcends party politics and power. It is how people should naturally behave in a normal society. Speaking truthfully does not mean that one wants to be oppositional. It is an attitude we are born with. Of course, in reality, speaking the truth offends those who suppress the facts, and people who normally stand for 'power'. In today's China, 'speaking the truth' first of all means giving up the benefits to be gained from being ambiguous. First, becoming a Communist Party member brings benefits: you get opportunities for promotion, if you're at fault your punishment is mitigated and you also receive financial benefits. But you don't believe in Communism. So do you join the Party or not? Second, in Chinese society, relationships and connections are important. They bring all kinds of little advantages and conveniences. Can you forego these rewards and be independent of all these 'mutually beneficial' social relations? Third, there is the situation of bearing witness. It is often costly for you to speak out about what you have witnessed. The extent to which you tell the truth depends on the cost you are willing to bear. At the very least, you should keep silent and adopt a stance of passive resistance when you are unable to speak the truth. One can only ask oneself how one would behave in these three situations.

— Zeng Jinyan in "An Interview with Zeng Jinyan 曾金燕," Elisa Nesossi, <u>The China Story</u>; May 27, 2012

In the daily lives of most men and women, fear plays a greater part than hope; they are more filled with the thought of the possessions that others may take from them, than of the joy that they might create in their own lives and in the lives with which they come in contact.

It is not so that life should be lived.

Those whose lives are fruitful to themselves, to their friends, or to the world are inspired by hope and sustained by joy: they see in imagination the things that might be and the way in which they are to be brought into existence. In their private relations, they are not preoccupied with anxiety lest they should lose such affection and respect as they receive: they are engaged in giving affection and respect freely, and the reward comes of itself without their seeking. In their work, they are not haunted by jealousy of competitors, but concerned with the actual matter that has to be done. In politics, they do not spend time and passion defending unjust privileges of their class or nation, but they aim at making the world as a whole happier, less cruel, less full of conflict between rival greeds, and more full of human beings whose growth has not been dwarfed and stunted by oppression.

A life lived in this spirit—the spirit that aims at creating rather than possessing—has a certain fundamental happiness, of which it cannot be wholly robbed by adverse circumstances. This is the way of life recommended in the Gospels, and by all the great teachers of the world. Those who have found it are freed from the tyranny of fear, since what they value most in their lives is not at the mercy of outside power. If all men could summon up the courage and the vision to live in this way in spite of obstacles and discouragement, there would be no need for the regeneration of the world to begin by political and economic reform: all that is needed in the way of reform would come automatically, without resistance, owing to the moral regeneration of individuals. But the teaching of Christ has been nominally accepted by the world for many centuries, and yet those who follow it are still persecuted as they were before the time of Constantine. Experience has proved that few are able to see through the apparent evils of an outcast's life to the inner joy that comes of faith and creative hope. If the domination of fear is to be overcome, it is not enough, as regards the mass of men, to preach courage and indifference to misfortune: it is necessary to remove the causes of fear, to make a good life no longer an unsuccessful one in a worldly sense, and to diminish the harm that can be inflicted upon those who are not wary in self-defence.

— <u>Proposed Roads to Freedom</u> (pp139-140), Bertrand Russell

They never forgot
That even the dreadful martyrdom must run its course
Anyhow in a corner, some untidy spot
Where the dogs go on with their doggy life and the torturer's horse
Scratches its innocent behind on a tree.

— from "Musée des Beaux Arts," WH Auden

I am giving away my body as an offering of light to chase away the darkness, to free all beings from suffering, and to lead them—each of whom has been our mother in the past and yet has been led by ignorance to commit immoral acts—to the Amitabha, the Buddha of infinite light. My offering of light is for all living beings, even as insignificant as lice and nits, to dispel their pain and to guide them to the state of enlightenment. I offer this sacrifice as a token of long-life offering to our root guru His Holiness the Dalai Lama and all other spiritual teachers and lamas.

— *Lama Sobha, who set fire to himself on January 8, 2012, in his final testimony, found after his death on a tape cassette wrapped in his robes; cited in* <u>Storm in the Grassland</u> *(p16), International Campaign for Tibet*

Goodbye, May Kasahara.... You looked great in a bikini.

—*the protagonist at the bottom of the well speaking to the very same May Kasahara who has pulled the ladder up from him and is about the seal the top of the well,* <u>The Wind-up Bird Chronicle</u> *(p589), Murakami Haruki*

Untitled

Is it a tree?
It's me, alone.
Is it a winter tree?
It's always like this, all year round.
Where are the leaves?
The leaves are beyond.
Why draw a tree?
I like how it stands.
Aren't you tired of being a tree your whole life?
Even when exhausted, I want to stand.
Is there anyone with you?
There are birds.
I don't see any.
Listen to the sound of fluttering wings.
Wouldn't it be nice to draw birds on the tree?
I'm too old to see, blind.
Perhaps you don't know how to draw a bird at all?
You're right. I don't know how.
You're an old stubborn tree.
I am.

— Liu Xia (Translated from Chinese by Ming Di and Jennifer Stern)

Liberationists

1

When you disappeared, I thought of the long conversation we'd had, lasting weeks, perhaps months. You had a choice between two jobs. It was, for you, an agonizing choice. Whenever you threw up your hands in despair at how difficult the decision was and said neither choice was perfect, each had its benefits and disadvantages, I would reply, At least you have a choice, between two good things no less; two different organizations want you. Then you would laugh. It was true, after all. That conversation came back to me in the moment when I realized you had disappeared because I felt a sharp pang of guilt. Guilt at the advice I had given you. Wasn't it largely my fault you had disappeared?

I often said you were a rising young star in your field. Few had your combination of talent, intelligence, skills, experience, work ethic, and, crucially, moral conviction. That last quality was sometimes regarded—when regarded at all—as the least indispensable; it could even be seen as a liability, a hindrance to "professional" objectivity. But the reason I loved you—one of the many—was that you knew what was right and did it—often, it must be said, against your own inclination, against everything in your culture and society that suggested in a constant, steady low-voiced thrum that it was always wiser to play it safe. And playing it safe rarely involved standing up for what you believed. Doing what was right was not easy for you. It was often agonizingly difficult, coming with real costs and sacrifices. That made the fact that you did all the more admirable.

But it wasn't because of your moral conviction that you were in demand. People wanted you for what you could do for them.

You had ideas about how to make things better, ideas that to me seemed pretty obvious but were new to many others. From the start, we shared a world view, on top of which, we had been together so long that our ideas echoed and mutually reinforced one another. It was easy to forget how far out of the mainstream they were. It was one of the best things about being together: We saw things—HK, China, the world—the same way. That was what made it possible for me to face the world at all.

And now, you were gone.

•

You had accepted the new position and taken up the job just a few months before your disappearance. You'd already been working there on a temporary contract for a year. You'd taken a sabbatical from your own permanent position with the blessing of your boss, a gracious gesture on her part, considering how important you were to her small organization.

When, at the end of that temporary year, the person you were filling in for took another position, you were offered the job, presenting the dilemma: Accept it or return to your own position, from which you'd been on leave?

That was the organization where you'd gotten your start. You owed it a lot, and more precisely, its founder and director, your boss, for all you'd learned, the many opportunities it had afforded you, all of the people you had gotten to know. Most importantly, you believed in the organization, the way it worked. It had the right strategy, the right way to work on human rights in China.

It was axiomatic that change in China, progressive change, towards a more rights-respecting, democratic society, would, if it came at all, come from within, from the Chinese people themselves. Your organization was a collaborative effort between people inside China and exiles. Inside China, the organization was underground, by necessity, and made up of a loose network of activists working in various rights areas with a very small number of people at its hub. The purpose of the deliberately few people outside of China—for the lion's share of resources was to be invested in the country directly—was to support those inside of China in their work. This meant many things; for instance, getting word out to the world beyond about the situation in China, especially when a rights defender was being persecuted; also, helping those inside to improve their skills, to *build their capacity*, in NGO lingo. You found that the people's strength was heart, courage, the experience and ability to resist and withstand enormous pressure from a force, the Partystate, that was much more powerful than themselves, willing and able to wear them down, make them crack, destroy them. They knew how to *chi ku*, to eat bitterness, to suffer, and to persevere even when their goals seemed impossibly distant. But often, living and working under such persecution, they had few opportunities to learn, neither from each other nor from abroad, and so their *methodologies*, again to use NGO lingo, could often be rough, arguably ineffectual. They tended to be more effective in working with their natural constituencies at the grassroots than at research or documentation or advocacy or simply presenting their work and making others aware of its value. Those were the areas where you helped, gaining a vast network of contacts in virtually every area of rights work in the country, work that functioned like an underground, and often clandestine, stream flowing just beneath the surface of the society.

And what the organization was doing seemed to be working, at least to the extent that such a small, loosely knit organization could have an impact in the biggest country in the world, which also happened to be ruled by the world's most powerful dictatorship. The Chinese "rights defense movement", as it had been labeled, was growing and spreading. Internationally, your organization continued to attract attention and funding. Many in the know considered it amongst the most effective in working on rights in China. The theory, practice and objectives of the diverse and multifarious rights defense movement were arguably humble, in contrast to, say, revolutionary aspiration, and its push for change incrementalist in nature. Taking on the government directly, challenging its monopoly on power, had been tried and failed in 1989, and there seemed to be little appetite amongst the populace at large to try that again any time soon. Instead, the theory went, work on improving rights in the interstices, in the cracks and spaces afforded by the Partystate's stated interest—whether genuine or not (I thought not)—in developing rule of law and by the new freedoms brought on by economic development and social change. Such work could contribute concretely to the improvement of people's rights and lives and perhaps even to gradual political liberalization. The effects of dictatorship were felt at virtually all levels and in all places of Chinese society, not only as abuses of rights but also in terms of the corruption, cultural and spiritual degradation, and environmental pollution, all of which infected the country in epidemic proportions. It was these issues, with their tangible effect on people's lives, the sorts of things ordinary people noticed, rather than political ideology, that motivated people to act on a local level. If China could change slowly, from the ground up, so to speak, when the next opportunity arose for substantial political change, it would be better prepared to take advantage of it and the risk would lessen of lurching into the apocalyptic chaos that Partystate propaganda incessantly warned against.

Of course, this was merely one calculation among many. The Partystate was an altogether new beast. The most powerful, wealthiest dictatorship that had ever existed, it put massive resources into maintaining and strengthening its grip on power. In size and scale, no other organization or even coalition of organizations— which were, anyway, prevented from coalescing— could compete. The Partystate's grip on power could last for a long time to come, and in the meantime, it was having a greater influence on the world beyond its borders.

To put it simply, the future was China, but no one knew what that future might be. The country could go in any number of directions, some quite bad. And as China went, so went the region, the world. If China became more democratic and rights-respecting, that boded well for the world, and if it continued as it was, the world could easily become a less democratic, less rights-respecting place. To put it more starkly, China was the key element of a global battle between democracy and neo-authoritarianism. The stakes were high.

And in the meantime, the Partystate continued to corrode society and culture. Even if the Partystate ever fell, it would take the country decades to recover from the harm it had caused, simply to people's thinking, morality and treatment of one another in everyday life. Just to take one example, its modus operandi reinforced the basic premise that it was the most powerful who should decide. Another was that you could tell any lie you wanted as long as you had the power to enforce it (which included preventing others from contradicting it and punishing them for doing so). A third was that power conveyed the right to benefit from one's position however one saw fit. A fourth was that the language of one of the oldest civilizations on earth had been so damaged by Partystate-speak that it had lost its ability to discuss and debate publicly, rationally, logically. And so on.

In the larger scheme of things, then, there was only so much the organization could do, but to the extent that there could be a solution, it was part of it, and at the grassroots, it had the effect of simply making people aware of their rights vis-à-vis the Partystate and showing them various ways that they could fight for their rights (though not and never without risks). This was a new way of thinking, a new culture, an antidote to Partystate culture, and perhaps—perhaps—one day its effect would take hold.

You never knew what could happen. That was what I always told myself. In that sense, I was much more hopeful than you, somewhere between you and the Chinese rights defenders. They were prone to hyper-optimism: It's only a matter of time before the regime falls, they would say, whereas we believed it was wiser to operate on the assumption that the Partystate could monopolize power indefinitely. Nothing was foreordained. If people didn't bring about the Partystate's fall, it wouldn't happen by itself. Indeed, the arguably more persuasive argument was that the Partystate was becoming more powerful all the time.

You disappeared around the time Mandela died, at the ripe old age of 95. Tributes poured in from around the world, as well as reminders of how things used to be. In Mandela's waning years, the historical verdict was pronounced: Apartheid was bad, the great evil of its day. Anyone could see that, as clear as black and white. And, no question about it, Mandela was a hero, a saint. But in the seventies, the eighties, that consensus was distant. The apartheid regime appeared solidly in place and had international support from business and rightwing politicians in democratic countries. It was only due to sustained campaigns both within and outside of the country that a faction in de Klerk's party calculated the status quo was unsustainable, a way out had to be found. The reformist faction of the ruling party gained the upper hand, much as in the Soviet Union. Nothing of the sort appeared to be happening in China, and the Partystate was not vulnerable to the same pressures, either internally or externally.

Still, was not the message of Mandela's example, as well as those of so many struggles, that one never knew, one simply never knew? *It always seems impossible until it is done.* And was not that alone a cause for hope, or at least an opportunity to hope? And should one not take whatever opportunity to hope presented itself? Or was that merely an invitation to delusion?

Each nonviolent revolution not only had similarities with others but also set its own precedent. The cognoscenti always told me, The Partystate is more powerful than any dictatorship ever. And they were right... until the day they might turn out to be wrong. I was reminded of Walesa reflecting that in his Solidarity days, not a single Western leader gave his movement the slightest chance.

●

At that time, it seemed all the best people doing the best work were connected to the organization. It was an inspiring place to be, at the center of the action. Journalists and in-the-know China watchers knew it had the inside track. Why would you go on sabbatical let alone contemplate leaving such an organization? It wasn't every day that opportunities of this sort came along in your line of work. They had to be appreciated. You should have considered yourself lucky to work with people you liked and respected, doing something worthwhile and influential, history in the making no less.

But the work had become stale, and you'd become bored with your role, performing more or less the same tasks over and over again, bored with the lack of "growth opportunities" as they say in the job world. You were frustrated with not being heard. It wasn't for lack of trying. You'd always been naturally the sort who was good at looking at problems and finding pragmatic solutions. But you were disheartened by your boss's constant response of no to whatever good idea you had. The organization suffered from some of the problems often found in small organizations run by their founder—an oversize presence with a clear sense of the organization's agenda and not much room for anything else. That was definitely Jeanette. She knew priorities; she wasn't good at sharing them. They stayed in her head. And sometimes they may not have been all that formulated or rationalized there: She had an intuitive sense of the direction she wanted things to go, a sense that, if forced to, she would find difficult to explain. When you came with ideas, Jeanette's excuses were multiple and shifting: there were not many resources; it was people inside China who had to drive the organization and determine its direction, they were the ones to take the lead. Whatever the case, you had come to something of a dead-end; you could contribute much more than you were allowed to.

You felt very grateful to Jeanette for all that you had learned from her, for the many opportunities the work had afforded. We were both very fond of Jeanette. She was a good leader and a good person—wise, kind, generous, experienced, down to earth, approachable, modest, well-connected, well-liked, selfless, with no need to draw attention to herself. And she'd managed, collaborating with people in China, to put the organization together from scratch. Now it was growing by leaps and bounds, becoming ever more effective. This made the decision to go on sabbatical followed by the dilemma of whether or not to return at the end of that year all the harder. And through the whole process, Jeanette had been gracious, patient, understanding. One could do much worse, to considerably understate the matter.

You were also fed up with being a young woman working in a Chinese cultural environment. In the organization, within China, men did all the talking, women all the doing. Most of the men in decision-making positions were middle-aged or older.

They were kind to you, well-disposed, but had the tendency to treat you as an assistant. They were largely unaware of your capacities, ideas, talents, experience, or of the fact that on many relevant matters, you were better educated and more knowledgeable than they. Of course, there were things you couldn't beat them on: their courage, their hard-won experience. But still, you thought there was room for new voices in the organization, and a lot of what you heard was heavy on rhetoric, on theory, on ideals, and light on pragmatism and innovation. It was hard, in a Chinese context, to come up through the ranks and be recognized based on merit rather than age and sex. You became ever more impatient with the sort of sclerotic hierarchical assumptions that seemed hard-wired in Chinese culture. You were always impressed with the women activists, who, while a minority, were doers, had much less time for theoretical discussion or highflown denunciations of the government. They were good at figuring things out. And hardworking. And unassuming. Perhaps too much so, going along with the tacit agreement to remain invisible, to cede the limelight to the men. (Actually, in a context as dangerous as China, that was a pretty savvy move.) At any rate, you were a little tired of struggling to escape being thrust into the role of eternal assistant. Indeed, as you never failed to point out, in the private sector, your skills and hard work would have been much more recognized and rewarded, at least in terms of monetary compensation.

•

When it came, your year's sabbatical from the small organization, during which you took up the temporary position as a researcher at the big international human rights organization, was a welcome relief. There, the level of competence was much higher, as could be expected at a place where, unlike in China, people had had the freedom to obtain the skills needed. With international recruitment, the organization was able to choose the best of the best from around the world, and it showed. It was an extremely well-run, trim, efficient outfit, highly productive, with uniformly high-quality research and also quite effective advocacy within the narrow parameters of its strategic imperatives (that is to say, lobbying elites, governments, placing op-eds and getting covered and quoted in the mainstream media). You found it inspiring and educational to be surrounded by colleagues who were "at the top of their game". At the same time, you felt valued as a professional, an expert in your area, China, even though China was huge and there was so much of it, so much of the human rights situation there that you were patently not an expert on, indeed, knew virtually nothing about (though, when you set your mind to it, you were one of the best, fastest, sharpest learners I'd ever known). You were often consulted; this, in spite of your age, in spite of the fact that there were many who knew more than you did, who were more accomplished, more experienced. Whereas at the small organization, you felt that what you knew and what you could do was often not recognized or acknowledged, at the international organization, you sometimes felt you were masquerading, that colleagues assumed you knew or could do much more than you believed you could. You had to "raise your game", a much welcome challenge. As a researcher, you had much more autonomy in your work. Indeed, you could pretty much decide what to focus on and how to spend your time.

Of course, there were aspects of the organization you found less appealing, compared to which, the small organization was better. The "professionalism" cut both ways: On the one hand, the people were much more skilled, had had elite educations, had worked for elite organizations. On the other, it could at times seem a little dry of passion, and some of the people struck you as a little too polished, ambitious, a little too good at presenting themselves, a little too articulate and well-spoken, a little too anxious to be recognized; in a word, too slick. It seemed at times that some people had their own agendas, as separate from the mission of the organization, which involved furthering their careers. It wasn't as if their objectives were in direct conflict with those of the organization; usually, the two conveniently dovetailed; it was just that you sensed people were "casting their eyes about," fixed somewhere on the horizon not necessarily of a world free of human rights abuses but of their own individual careers, looking for the next big thing. You sometimes found the atmosphere a little chilly, not to mention a little white and Western, with not a single person in the leadership team coming from a different background. And the elitist strategy and outlook bothered you too. These were people used to flying high; they were not from the grassroots, didn't even hang with them. All very nice people, you said, but "small potatoes" they're not.

It wasn't just in your colleagues' backgrounds that you noticed the elitist streak, but also, more significantly, in the organization's way of working. It did great research, and on the basis of that research, targeted its advocacy efforts at elite audiences, in particular, Western governments and mainstream media. The thinking went that this was the way to reach people in positions powerful enough to do anything about the abuses the organization documented so well. Over the course of its three-decade history, the method of operation (for it seemed as much that as a strategy) was certainly very successful, simply in terms of raising awareness about human rights not only in the upper echelons but across wide swathes of many Western societies. And it was partly due to the work of large international human rights organizations based in the West such as this one that human rights had been cemented in place as a key policy concern, at least in some parts of the world, namely, the West, where arguably the situation of human rights was already better than most other places. But apart from what one might see as its neo-colonial aspects, that method of operation had perhaps increasingly diminishing returns in a world in which Western governments were less powerful than before and prioritizing human rights less, while other governments, such as China, with less respect for human rights, were more powerful. This was a situation the organization itself recognized. Only recently, it had announced that a billionaire financial speculator had donated $100 million with the express purpose of expanding research and advocacy efforts in countries and regions where it had insufficient presence, Brazil, India and South Africa mentioned in particular, China also name-checked (rather strangely given that having an open presence, let alone lobbying the government, in the country was simply an impossibility), in recognition of this newly emerging "multi-polar" world. But though it did appear the organization went on something of a hiring spree (its publically stated target was to increase the size of its staff by about a third), overall, it was hard to discern much of a shift in its methods of operation, especially in advocacy. At root, I thought, was the inertia of institutional culture: Even institutions that saw the need for change and wished to change found it hard to do so because, of course, it was people who made change and the people were the same and had to change themselves (or leave and be replaced by others) in order for strategic changes to be more than cosmetic.

Indeed, it was the desire for the sort of change announced at the time of the $100-million donation that was one reason they were interested in you. You knew China, knew how the country worked, its dynamics, and, most importantly, knew the people on the ground who did the work. Amazingly, you were the first Chinese national the organization had ever hired, at least to conduct research on China. This was partly for fear of compromising security by hiring a spy, a fear your previous organization had as well, which is why it was so wary of hiring Chinese nationals outside of China, even though all of the people who worked for it inside of China were obviously Chinese. It was also because of concerns about the safety of a Chinese-national researcher, given that the Partystate had a record of treating its own citizens more harshly than foreigners. Having a foreign passport, especially if you were not ethnically Chinese, afforded some protection in case of trouble with the Partystate, a constant, looming prospect in that field of work. The organization had had excellent researchers on China, though they always operated at something of a distance.

You were critical of the organization's fixation on influencing elites, especially when it came to China. Its approach there was not substantially different from how it worked on the rest of the world, but China was different. Remarkably, there were few similar countries left in the world. Yes, there were plenty of unfree countries, plenty of dictatorships, but there were not so many full police states where the regime had the means, the finances and the desire (or, more accurately, the Nietzschean will to power) to surveil, monitor, censor and control virtually every aspect of life that it chose. One of those frequently-trotted-out statistics was telling: the Partystate spent more on what it called "stability maintenance" (basically, internal security) than it did on defense. One way to interpret that was the regime saw its own people as its greatest threat, its greatest enemy. When researchers from all over the world gathered for your annual retreat, you enjoyed the company. You liked the people and admired their work and their commitment to it, and to an extent, being with them made you feel less alone in your work. But hearing them speak of the challenges they faced also made you feel quite apart, since there were only a handful of countries—Iran, perhaps; Vietnam certainly; North Korea of course; Russia to an increasing degree, though the organization still had an office there— in which researchers faced the sorts of challenges as in China, first and foremost, the impossibility of working openly, the necessity of doing everything secretly, the threat of arrest for your work. Indeed, the organization had recently even opened an office in Rangoon, something that would have been unthinkable only a few years earlier.

Your views on how to work effectively on rights issues in China developed during your time at the small organization. And you applied them in the first major report you did for your new organization, on insufficient access to education for children with disabilities. Indeed, even the subject of the report was part of the strategy. Because of your specific security concerns as a Chinese national, you and your fellow China researcher, a foreign national, had made an informal pact that he would focus on the more "sensitive" rights issues, the ones that the Partystate did not even acknowledge as issues at all, the ones that, if you worked on them, made you instantly a persona non grata, a hostile element, while you focused on issues which, in theory at least, the Partystate regarded as actual issues, even if it did not exactly view them through the lens of human rights or prioritize them. Access to education for children with disabilities was one such issue. The idea was that, even though there was no chance of lobbying the government directly, it might be the sort of issue that some government ministries and departments could be interested in improving on, and therefore, the report might have an impact. In short, this was the rights defense approach, the same taken by your old organization and the generation of rights activists who had come of age in the nineties and noughties. Your method of researching the issue involved organizations in China that worked with children with disabilities, primarily though not exclusively by providing services to them. In turn, the hope was that the report could play a supportive role in the advocacy work of such organizations, not only when they interacted with government agencies responsible for education and disability issues but also to help them identify issues they could work on as well as how to work on them. For example, one conclusion of the report was that families of children with disabilities often didn't know what rights their children were entitled to, what options were available to them, or how to advocate for themselves and their disabled loved ones. They often regarded themselves as subjects rather than citizens and were grateful for any services their children received, whether useful or not, whether needed or not, whether effective or not, whether appropriate or not, whether discriminatory or not. One lesson of the report was that civil society organizations had to do more outreach work to educate families of children with disabilities about what they could get out of the system, how to negotiate it for the benefit of their children, and how to advocate for their children's rights. At a deeper level, this method of work played a role, however small, in gradually bringing about the sort of paradigm shift that had to occur if the country was ever to become rights-respecting; namely, it helped people understand themselves as citizens with rights and legitimate demands, ideally even one day as bosses of their own government, rather than as subjects who could at most petition, as if on bended knee.

While the large international organization was simply the best when it came to placing op-eds and getting the issues it covered into the establishment international press, it had few connections in national, non-English-language media. You made sure that an ever-increasing number of Chinese journalists working at the peripheries of the state-owned media which dominated the news and propaganda landscape in China were aware of the report, and some used it to write about the issue, though they could not actually cite the report or the organization or even characterize it as a rights issue, simply as a story about disabled children's education. There was an official propaganda response to the report, mostly to trumpet how superbly the Partystate was doing in educating children with disabilities. Many took the simple fact the government felt the need to say something (not exactly respond or rebut, for it would not officially acknowledge the existence of your report, though everyone working in the area knew about it) as a sign that the report had been heard, even within the corridors of power, and there were people in the Partystate bureaucracy receptive to and influenced by some of its ideas.

You surmised that your work was not well appreciated or understood by your superiors. All that mattered, it could often seem, was sound bites in *The New York Times* and its ilk—something that you said definitely did not matter in China. Just getting something like an e-newsletter in Chinese sent out required a lot of effort within the organization—people couldn't see the point. So, when it came down to it, however great the working conditions were, however strong the feeling that you'd "made it", you did not always feel you fit in so well there, neither in terms of your background—grassroots—nor in terms of your thinking about the most effective ways to work. When it came to China, you thought the small organization you'd just left had a more effective strategy and method of operation. The large organization could be, at most, a kind of support or backstop for people working on the ground. Indeed, in general, that was perhaps the main utility of large international human rights organizations—they were conservative, they insisted on international human rights law, and in doing so, they helped people in countries where abuses were occurring fight for their rights. So, at the end of the day, as welcome as the sabbatical was, you also felt rather far away from the action and torn between two worlds. You missed your old colleagues, the salt-of-the-earth types.

•

Apart from those reservations, at the end of the sabbatical year, at the end of your one-year contract, when it became clear that the researcher you were replacing would not be returning, thus rendering the permanent position vacant, and when you were asked to apply for it and then were offered it, the big sticking point was the requirement of going to China, the mere thought of which was enough to send your already high level of anxiety shooting through the roof. There was a protest t-shirt against the 2008 Beijing Olympics in the face of unaddressed human rights abuses. The t-shirt featured the games' mascots, five hideously kitschy and cuddly figures named Beibei, Jingjing, Huanhuan, Yingying and Nini (one of which was, by the way, your alias on the human rights radio show we hosted on a pirate radio station in HK). The first syllables of their names together spelled out the message, "Beijing welcomes you". But on the t-shirt, rather than being cuddly and smiling, they were on the verge of tears, behind prison bars. That was how you imagined you would end up looking one day, like those sad mascots, the same glum expression on your face, far from your child, whom you had brought into the world, and who, in turn, had converted you, through love, to motherhood.

During your year at the organization, you had entered the mainland three times. On each trip, extensive security precautions had been taken, and a trustworthy companion accompanied you. Each trip went off without a hitch. There was no sign of being followed or monitored, no dangerous incident. While one might think that record would allay fears, in a place where the

Partystate is by definition above the law, arbitrariness casts a long shadow; nothing can be taken for granted. (Indeed, that was a crucial mechanism of control: In a world in which anything's possible, they can do to you whatever they want, you are kept guessing and must constantly calculate risk, weigh the dangers. From the Partystate's point of view, this will make you less likely to act in any way it might perceive as threatening; it is always safer not to.) Not only that, but it was one thing to know that you had to visit the mainland over a limited period of time—upon each return, you heaved a huge sigh of relief and looked forward to the end of the one-year contract—, and quite another thing to take a permanent position that involved travel there on an indefinite basis. The time before each trip felt like a storm front approaching—the rise in barometric pressure was palpable in the house and became nearly unbearable as the date of departure neared. And then you went, you returned, and the return was like a new lease on life: You could breathe again—how wonderful to be alive, to be free.

On top of that, the situation on the mainland had gotten substantially worse ever since the new capo had taken the helm. A broad crackdown on virtually all sectors of civil society continued unabated, with no end in sight. The apparent intended end was the destruction of the fragile, incipient civil society, its complete dissolution or co-optation by the Partystate.

We discussed the job's requirement of entering the mainland while sitting next to each other on the pink sofa, the faded, fading, dirty pink sofa, night after night for what seemed like weeks on end, that pink sofa I called our raft through the night, inherited from the previous tenant with whom we'd had a dispute. He left it there to spite us. We adopted it. Usefully, it folded out into a bed. Many a person escaping mainland persecution had spent many a night there, our home a safe house and most likely under constant surveillance for that reason alone, if not for the work we did as well. We sat on the pink sofa and talked after having put Z to bed. It was the thought of that little girl sleeping in the room on the other side of the door that was foremost in your mind, the prospect of being abducted, of being deprived of seeing your child, of your child being deprived of her mother.

This was what you'd always feared, the root of all your anxiety. You were anxious about many things. You were an anxious person. Sometimes it seemed the chief enterprise of your day was to find ever more reasons to be anxious, and if one looked, there were always plenty to be found. But beneath them all, there was this, the fear of being abducted, and, even worse, stolen away from your daughter, from your daughter's childhood. This was what I imagined crossing your mind at the very moment of abduction—what you had feared most had now come to pass.

Did I downplay the danger? The job was a great opportunity for you, I said. It was deserved recognition of your talents. Yes, the requirement of going to the mainland was a complication, but we'd deal with it as it arose, cross that bridge when we got there.

During that period of deliberation, you consulted many others. There was an interesting breakdown of responses: The Chinese said, No problem; the non-Chinese said, No way. The Chinese were so used to dealing with the risks associated with such work that they thought of it as normal that anyone advocating for rights should be oppressed simply for doing so. The abnormal was their norm. And so it was hard for them to regard the risk you would face as particularly consequential. It just came with the game. It was not that they courted trouble, not in the least—most did everything they could to minimize the risk of attracting the unwanted attention of the dreaded security apparatus—, but they realized there was only so much you could do, and they thought that the fact that you were working for an international organization would provide some degree of protection, since the Partystate would prefer to avoid the negative international attention that was bound to accompany kidnapping the employee of an international organization, even if the person did happen to be an "anti-China" Chinese national. In this respect, I seemed to be more Chinese than non-Chinese. Or maybe I was just more reckless, or more willing to put my wife's security at risk. The non-Chinese—and those you consulted were very knowledgeable about China—simply saw the risk as not worth taking. For them, choice was the norm, so why choose to take the unnecessary risk of losing one's freedom?

We had gone to Beijing together in late 2008, after the security clampdown for the Olympics the previous summer. You were working for the small organization at the time. How cold it had been; we both got sick from being under-prepared, under-dressed. In HK beforehand, it was hard to imagine how cold it could be in Beijing at that time of year, even though we saw the temperatures in the weather forecasts; we suffered for our lack of imagination. Looking back, I was struck by how easy it had been to meet people then. I remembered a big banquet with an array of the more prominent human rights lawyers. The atmosphere was free and easy, the lawyers confident, unconcerned. In subsequent years, many of those same lawyers were stripped of their license to practice law. Some were detained and tortured. Some had been intimidated into silence or reckoned it best to lie low for a while. It would be hard to imagine a similar banquet taking place in the current atmosphere.

In 2009, a rights defender peripheral to the small organization was detained and interrogated. After his release, he reported that, among others, he had been asked about you, not about your real name but about your pseudonym. After that, we decided that for a good long time, it was best for you not to cross the border. I spent the summer of 2009 in Beijing. You had planned to accompany me, but after we got word of the interrogation, we decided against that.

And so nearly three years passed. In the space of that time, serial crackdowns occurred, some dating back to the Beijing Olympics, others related to various campaigns of repression of Tibetans and Uighurs, another related to the release of Charter 08, one associated with the anonymous internet call for a "Jasmine Revolution" inspired by the Arab Spring uprisings. Then came the crackdown related to the awarding of the Nobel Peace Prize to Liu Xiaobo, and the most recent one on anti-corruption campaigners and the New Citizens Movement. The nearly incessant series of crackdowns hardly allowed you to catch your breath—and those were only the major ones. Arguably, they all amounted to just one big on-going crackdown, though all agreed the situation had become worse overall and Partystate tolerance of civil society activism had clearly decreased. Aside from those systematic crackdowns, there was the routine persecution of individuals all over the country for their rights work, just one example being Ye Haiyan, the advocate for women, children and sex workers, who was serially evicted from several homes. It just went on and on. China was a double reality. To many, it could seem an ever more "normal" country, one like any other, and as long as one stayed far away from a whole range of issues which the Partystate considered sensitive, one could be quite confident the "other reality" would not become one's own, but if you trespassed, whether wittingly or not, upon the prerogatives of the Partystate at any level, or happened to simply be amongst one of the many oppressed groups, there was a panoply of ways and means to make you suffer beyond the point of endurance.

There was also a history of ethnically Chinese HK residents having suffered at the hands of the Partystate in ways big and small. Your "home return permit" could be confiscated, which had happened to some you knew, both human rights workers and pro-democracy activists. There was the possibility of being detained once having crossed the border, the fate of several HK businesspeople accused of economic crimes—detentions often arising from business disagreements with adversaries who had political connections. There was the notorious case of Ching Cheong, the HK journalist abducted, kept in solitary confinement in an undisclosed location, and then convicted of "endangering state security", a case which served as a warning to all. And then there were cases like that of our friend, D, who had often crossed the border to investigate factory working conditions, and had been detained and abused on several occasions, most recently for mourning the suspicious death of long-time dissident Li Wangyang in the town where he'd died. But her detentions lasted for no more than two or three days each. Also, D worked for a local HK organization, with little pull or clout, and the HK government was notoriously poor at advocating for its own residents, since it was essentially appointed by the Partystate to do the latter's bidding. You, on the other hand, now worked for one of the most renowned and reputable international human rights organizations in the world. The Partystate had detained mainland Chinese working for major international media organizations and refused renewal of visas of foreign journalists it considered "hostile", but I couldn't remember a case of a human rights worker for a large international human rights organization having been detained. Still, you never knew, and the fact that, unlike many ethnically Chinese HK permanent residents, you had no foreign passport was a source of concern.

As an HK permanent resident (there was no such thing as citizenship in HK, presumably because one was technically a citizen of the PRC although that conveyed few privileges or rights and had many potential drawbacks), you were virtually as unprotected, as without remedy or recourse, as a mainlander.

When, after the 2009 interrogation of your distant colleague, we did cross the border again, it was to visit your father's home village to show off Z, a year after her birth. We thought crossing the border with your parents would give us cover. We went on a Friday and returned the next Monday. Up to then, we had resolved that, in case of the necessity of entering the mainland, only one parent at a time would go, so as to avoid the possibility of both parents being detained. Rather than at Shenzhen, we crossed at Zhuhai, having taken the ferry from HK. Your mother's home return permit had expired and had to be renewed. Long after all other ferry passengers had passed through immigration and gone their separate ways, we were still in the no-man's-land between ferry disembarkation and the other side of the row of booths of immigration officers waiting to check travel documents. It made you nervous that we were singled out, all eyes of the bored immigration officers upon us, but more than suspicion, the humid air hung heavy with their impatience to go to lunch. Eventually, the renewed permit was issued, and we proceeded without problem.

So, during the one-year contract with the international organization, you became slightly more confident that you could enter the mainland. You enlisted Opal as your sidekick. As you yourself said, Opal, a fellow HKese, was much more courageous than you. She was up for anything, not least of all, a little fun and adventure. She was a free spirit, a true grass-roots radical, an entrepreneurial activist, full of inspiring if farfetched ideas she was constantly trying to realize, the sort who wouldn't take no for an answer. Most recently, she had started an unregistered lesbian hostel in a remote HK village for women from across East and Southeast Asia. She was best known for having been arrested by the HK government for assault. During a demonstration outside the Central Government Liaison Office to celebrate the awarding of the Nobel Peace Prize to Liu Xiaobo, Opal inadvertently sprayed champagne from a bottle she opened on a Liaison Office security guard standing nearby, thus "assaulting" him. After much negative publicity, eventually the HK government dropped the absurd charge against one of the most physically non-threatening people imaginable. Opal was so short she was often mistaken for a child. She looked like a little boy, a mischievous little boy. I remembered once riding with her in a taxi from the Geneva airport to a session of the UN Human Rights Council. Opal got in the front. The driver said that in Switzerland, there was a law against children sitting in the front of taxis. She was constantly looking for true love and went through an endless string of girlfriends. Each seemed the right one, if only for a short time, but for that short time, it was forever, so much so that she convinced me it was written in the stars, in spite of her history, and so the next time I saw her, I never failed to be surprised that the former true love was not in the picture any more and had been replaced by a new one. You had helped Opal get a job at the small organization, for which she now did all the grunt work, with aplomb, without complaint—it beat the string of precarious and alienated employments with, for example, credit card companies she'd had up to then. While your heart fluttered at the prospect of crossing the border, Opal's did not so much as skip a beat. She was the perfect chaperone. Indeed, there were few people I would have trusted as much as Opal to help to keep you safe, at least in terms of right intention and right motivation, though perhaps not always right judgment. Her attitude when first "invited to tea" by the Partystate secret police was, Why not? I talk with everybody.

Afterwards, you said to her, *But don't you realize that you could have compromised the security of the organization or endangered someone associated with it?*

Oh, yeah, said Opal, *maybe you're right; I hadn't thought of that.... But I didn't tell them anything about the organization, not even that I worked for it.*

On the mainland, when someone was "invited for tea", it was an offer that could not be refused. The invitee's calculation invariably was that much worse could happen if the "invitation" was rejected. There was no use provoking the suspicions and hostility of the security apparatus, which was, after all, composed of individuals and whose very nature was arbitrary; yes, it was a monolith, but a monolith with distinctly human faces that it was wiser to appease than rebuff. It was better to show you had nothing to hide, easier that way to hide whatever it was. In this way, millions of people in China "consented" to being monitored, were aware they were under surveillance, a strange dance. In HK, it was not necessary to "consent"; there were no levers to compel, or punish. Opal should have avoided the "invitation". She said one reason for meeting them was to get a sense of what they already knew about her, about her affiliations and connections—monitor the monitors, as the move was called, a dangerous game. She came back with snatches: It appeared a workshop she had organized and held in HK for mainland HRDs had been infiltrated, though by whom and how was unclear, and there seemed to be some awareness that she was making money transfers to various people on the mainland; again, how, who knew? All of this news was in itself alarming and pointed to fuller awareness and surveillance of not only Opal but affiliated individuals. After that, an intern returned home to Sichuan to visit and was also "invited to tea" and asked about her connection to and awareness of the organization, a surveillance trail that could in all likelihood also be traced back to the workshop infiltration, yet another indication that the noose might be tightening.

You and Opal first crossed the border together at Shenzhen to visit Opal's father. The day-long trip, which something like 300,000 people made every day, went off without a hitch—no problem at the border, no sign of being followed. It was used as a dry run to establish security protocol. You left me a long list of telephone numbers, in the order in which they were to be called, of people to contact in case of trouble. You called me right before crossing the border, immediately after crossing the border, and every two hours over the course of the day. If I didn't hear from you, and if you didn't answer my call made after not hearing from you, I was to sound the alarm. It was the pattern followed on subsequent trips.

The next trip was to Guangdong, in connection with a research report you were working on. The destination was an out-of-the-way place that was not considered "sensitive" (such as the capital or any area where some kind of "mass incident"—the Partystate's term for a demonstration—had occurred). And you had back-up: your host, a rights activist, was well-known and well-connected in the area; some of his relatives were in the police. Again, the trip came off without a hitch. You had sharp antennae for signs of surveillance but detected none. There was one time you didn't call exactly when planned. All kinds of thoughts ran through my head, but they were washed away by relief when your call eventually came.

You hired mainlanders to conduct interviews and surveys in other places in the country where it was more likely that your presence would attract the attention of the Public Security Bureau or other elements of the Partystate security apparatus. Overall, the project went so smoothly we wondered whether or not we had simply been paranoid. But we kept reminding ourselves one could never be too cautious, one should never let one's guard down; indeed, it might be the tactic of the Guobao to lull us into a false sense of security, a suspicion which, again, might sound paranoid, but paranoia, or heightened vigilance, depending on your point of view, was the price to pay for doing such work in a police state.

That is the catalogue of visits during the period of the sabbatical/one-year contract. Your research report was published, and considering that it was not a hot-button topic, it got quite a lot of coverage outside of the country, and a lot of support and approval within from the activist community in general and from rights advocates in particular. All in all, you had pulled it off remarkably well, in trying circumstances, with many challenges in both the country and the organization. This was the situation at the time of the decision you faced.

With the small organization, you collaborated with Chinese counterparts and didn't have to cross the border yourself. You connected via internet and occasionally met at workshops outside of China. The lack of requirement to enter the mainland weighed in the small organization's favor. In addition, Jeanette, your boss, had upped the ante. The organization had been considering establishing a presence in HK, among other reasons, to signal clearly that it wasn't a "foreign" organization but a Chinese one. It had held a workshop in HK to test the waters. The fall-out from the workshop was considerable. It appeared to have been infiltrated by informers, if not secret police themselves, and many people who had attended had subsequently been called in for questioning. The next time a workshop was held, in Geneva, nearly two-thirds of scheduled participants had been stopped at the border or even before they got there and not allowed to leave the country. It was suspected that the secret police had so infiltrated the organization as to have obtained a list of workshop participants in advance, and that the infiltration had its origins in the HK workshop.

(One woman, Cao Shunli, was abducted by the authorities at Beijing airport as she sought to depart for Geneva. For five weeks, no one knew what had become of her, though she was presumed detained. Then her family received an arrest notice. She was charged with "picking quarrels and making trouble". Her "crime" appeared to be that she was part of a group that had requested that, in compliance with international law, citizens be allowed to participate in the Universal Periodic Review of China to be conducted at the upcoming session of the UN Human Rights Council. The authorities took the opportunity of her attempt to leave the country to participate in a training session on UN human rights mechanisms to detain her. Her detention was the beginning of an ordeal that was to end most tragically.)

One person in the organization was strongly opposed to any official presence in HK. The place was simply overrun with spies; it was far too easy for the Partystate to monitor whatever went on there, and that posed a risk not only to the people in HK but to all others associated with the organization. But Jeanette was nothing if not stubborn once she got an idea into her head, and she persisted in the attempt to open an office in HK. To entice you to return after your sabbatical, Jeanette offered to create a new position for you, Director of HK Office. The position would come with not only research and capacity building responsibilities, as before, but, in addition to those, responsibilities for running the office and coordinating and conducting related activities. It seemed the organization was ready to make a defiant stance in HK, the only place under current PRC control where such an office could exist. There was something about that defiance I appreciated, relished; one had to be up for a fight, especially in this day and age when it seemed few were willing to stand up to the Partystate. (But there I went again, underestimating the security concerns, which should always be paramount. Dictum number one was, Do not endanger others, do not endanger, especially without their consent, those with whom you work.)

If you had known nothing of the organization previously, had had no previous history with it, you might have been tempted. Even taking into account your history with it, you were tempted. You missed the friends and colleagues, the mutual solidarity, the common understanding of the dangers and pressures faced. You missed working at the grassroots with people you naturally had greater sympathy and affinity with than the elites with whom you currently hobnobbed. But you just couldn't imagine Jeanette changing, couldn't imagine being perceived and therefore treated as anything more than a bright subordinate, couldn't imagine the dynamics changing, and you remembered how stifled and frustrated you had felt, hampered in taking initiatives, trying out new ideas and approaches.

So there it was and there it stood: Two good choices, each with strong cons: At the small organization, potentially a situation like before; at the international organization, struggling against an ineffectual strategy, at least as far as China was concerned, and even more crucially, having to go into China.

I'd said to you on numerous occasions, there was nothing perfect in this world, and you were far more fortunate than the great majority of workers in that you had options, good options, good if imperfect options.

I tended toward the international organization, not without regret, in such great esteem did I hold your current employer, with such great fondness and respect did I regard Jeanette. I thought the international organization would give you more opportunities to grow and improve and meet people, become more well-rounded, more effective in your work. If you wanted to, there might be a chance to return to the small organization at a later date, and then, maybe, you would be treated with more respect, if for no other reason than that you would be older.

It was your decision to make. We often laughed about how indecisive you were, a person who found it hard to decide what to wear, what to have for dinner.

It was lucky our daughter was an accident; otherwise you would have spent the rest of the years of fertility trying to decide whether or not to have children, and there would have been no Z. Maybe it was better to let life make decisions for you, sometimes at least. But the problem here was that life couldn't decide between these two options; you had to.

Several evenings of discussion ended with you asking, tentatively, *Well, then, we've decided, haven't we?*

I would respond, *What have 'we' decided?*

And you would say, *I'm not sure, but we have, haven't we?*

And the next evening, the discussion would recommence, and we would pour over the same considerations as we had already several times before, reaching similar conclusions. You swung between wanting to be your own person, defiantly declaring your independence, and wanting decisions to be made for you, by fate, if possible, or circumstance. Up to now, whatever you'd done, you'd half fallen into it. And now here was a decision that could not be avoided.

●

I mentioned at the start the guilt I felt at your disappearance. It had been my fault. I had encouraged you to leave the small organization and go to the big one. But this guilt was irrational: As far as I was able to find out in the aftermath of the disappearance, it was most likely related to a decision you had made without even telling me, a decision you might well have made if you had stayed with the small organization instead of moving to the international organization, and almost certainly didn't have to do with that organization's requirement to travel to the mainland—the big organization was as clueless about what had happened to you and what you had been doing before your disappearance as I.

It took me some time to understand that my feeling of guilt had to do with something much broader, a sense of being at fault for all that had come before the disappearance, and, in turn, the feeling that all that had come before had somehow mystically lead to your disappearance. I think that even if I could confidently rule out every possible way in which I might have been at fault for your disappearance, I would still feel responsible for it. For, at the end of the day, every bad thing that might happen to you was my fault, if not because I caused it, then because I failed to prevent it from happening; and even if I neither caused it nor prevented it, I was existentially at fault, res ipsa loquitur, a bit like Josef K in *The Trial*—Kafka must have been inspired by the absurd concept of original sin.

My analysis told me otherwise—indeed, told me that the case was quite nearly the opposite—but the guilt was a feeling I couldn't shake.

●

Looking back at the time before the disappearance, I was struck by the constant stress we had been living under. I wondered at the toll it took, psychologically, spiritually, and how and why I had not seen it more clearly then. I did see it, but in the sense that I never acted on my awareness, I did not. For while I was well aware of the pressure, I never had the sense to say, We must stop living this way. We must do something else. At the very least, we need a break. Let's go away. Let's get far away from here. Or actually, now that I thought of it, we—especially you—said things like that rather often. We just never acted on them.

In this way, I believed my errors of judgment, my passivity and acts of omission had certainly a part to play in bringing about your disappearance, even if, as I say, as far as I could find out, it seemed to stem most directly from a decision you had made without so much as letting me know, a decision so unlike your cautious self I wondered whether it was possible you had taken it under duress, or at all.

The stress we lived under became, through habit, the norm. It came with the work. We assumed we were monitored, and we acted accordingly. It may not have been the case that we were—though there was plenty of evidence—, it was simply the safest assumption upon which to operate. Based on it, we acted so as to never put anyone else at risk. We did it so often, it became almost an automatic process, deciding what could and could not be said in our home, what we had to exit the house and enter the free air to communicate to one another, what could and could not be said to whom, what could never be said to anybody, and generally hiding much of our lives from others.

You had multiple pseudonyms, aliases and backstories, and sometimes pseudonyms within pseudonyms. It was difficult to keep straight who knew you as what. Each was associated with a different role in a different organization or context. Your most recent was an in-joke. It said, I am that which cannot be caught or grasped, least of all by the long tentacles of the Chinese despots, for I do not exist, I have no essence. That winking wit suggested a dashing figure, a fantasy superhero about as far from your actual style—steeped in humility, caution, uncertainty, dark premonition, fear—as one could get.

I thought of Gandhi, a real superhero, who had no pseudonyms, no use for them. He believed in doing everything out in the open for everyone to see, based on the premise that one had nothing to hide, nothing to be ashamed of in this kind of work. Truth and justice were on his side and he would stand up for what he believed. The dastardly deceit, clandestine activities and lies of the powerful adversary had to be consistently, resolutely opposed by openness, directness, honesty, a different way of doing things. I had always admired that stance, that way of operating, but we couldn't be more different; we justified our shell games on the grounds of keeping others safe. I wondered sometimes how Gandhi would deal with oppressors like the Partystate, how they would deal with him.

Every once in a while the abnormality of our life lived nearly underground came into stark relief and something within us rebelled. On a day I happened to be gone, Anna, the woman who looked after Z, came scurrying home in a fright, pushing Z in her stroller. They were being followed, she claimed. By whom? you asked. Anna did not know, but she described three frightening men, paunchy, in polo shirts and tan pants. It sounded like Partystate internal security types to you—they looked the same, dressed the same. Anna had noticed them for the first time the day before but hadn't given it much thought. They were snooping around the house. She took them for prospective property buyers. Then, that day, Anna had seen them at the market. She was not the sort who was on the lookout for being spied on, so it was hard to believe she had simply imagined it. She became suspicious and kept an eye on them. They followed her and Z wherever they went, at a discrete but perceptible distance. When Anna turned into the road where we lived—a strictly residential area where few people who didn't live there came—, and the men pursued her, she became alarmed. She turned the last corner, peaked over her shoulder and saw them turn the corner behind her, then broke into a run, hoping to get home before they caught up with her. You went out to have a look around but saw nothing. You called me, and I told you to stay in the house and call the police. I didn't think the police would do anything, but at least it would signal to the pursuers that we knew they were around and were prepared to do something about it. HK wasn't like the mainland where they could harass without constraint.

This was at the time of Chen Guangcheng's dramatic escape. There was a period of several hours when no one, including the Partystate, knew where he was. It had become clear that he'd disappeared from his home, where he and his wife and children had been living under illegal house arrest, the house surrounded by rings of dozens of thugs paid by the local government, but it hadn't yet become clear that he'd managed to enter the US embassy in Beijing. The Partystate was frantically looking everywhere for him. I surmised they suspected people associated with you of somehow being involved and maybe they were staking out our house to see whether there was any link to Chen Guangcheng. Of course, the very fact they were indicated they knew where we lived, which in itself was hardly reassuring.

Why had they been so obvious? Did they think Anna was too stupid to know? Were they just bumbling? Had they meant to let us know we were being watched, followed? Perhaps we were paranoid about the Guobao stalking Z but since we couldn't be sure, we had to assume they were. And how low could you go, stalking a child? Especially in a country where it was not uncommon for children to be stolen, where there were periods of epidemic child theft. The day before, in HK, a kidnapping attempt had been made on a little girl whose mother was a billionaire. It was foiled by the girl's driver and grandparents, who reported they'd heard the would-be kidnappers—who got away—speaking Putonghua. But it was their job to be low, to act worse than anyone thought possible, so as to convey the message that anything was possible, that there was no limit to the depths to which they would stoop, in order to strike fear.

From that moment on, whenever Z was inside, the door was locked. If she was outside, even in the yard, someone always had to be with her. She could not be let out of sight, not even for an instant. Of course, these were precautions many parents would take with young children these days, but we felt we had to be extra-vigilant against a potentially malevolent force.

The incident made you shake with anger whenever you thought about it. You wanted to lash out, kill somebody. It wasn't hard to see how they could get to you- by targeting your child.

That episode and others like it wore you down. You wondered whether you really wanted to do the work. You could easily see yourself doing something else, leading a different kind of life, or so you said, with increasing frequency. Why, you said, should you even bother when it seemed the majority of Chinese were not prepared to fight for their own freedom, indeed were not even aware that they were not free? Why take any risk on behalf of people who didn't care? You would often say, *I should stop this and do something more fulfilling, become a pre-school teacher or a gardener.* There were plenty of things you loved to do, were good at, believed in, without any of the ambivalence you felt towards your actual work.

You became increasingly alienated from the "normal world out there". You'd recently gone to your secondary school reunion. When you returned, you said, *They're such nice people. I'd forgotten how wonderful people can be, how wonderful they are, and they're even more wonderful now, they've matured, become even kinder, more generous than they were before. And yet, their lives are so different from ours, they seem to live in an entirely different reality. I hadn't the energy to try to tell them how we live. In the end, being there amongst all those good people made me feel very alone.*

We sometimes dreamed of the quiet life. When the housing crash hit the US and prices tumbled, we thought of buying a nice little house in a nice little second-tier city at a bargain, settling down in a diverse mixed-income, mixed-ethnicity neighborhood, with neighborly neighbors, a good local school, a park, a café. We would move there first and then figure out how to make a living. But we never did. The dream was no more than that. However much you might have thought that was what you wanted, I imagined you would quickly get bored with the quiet life, experience a crisis of loss of meaning and purpose, feel you weren't doing anything useful or important with your life—the real action was elsewhere, important things were happening elsewhere while you just looked on, an observer, a spectator.

After all, where we were was where things mattered. The future of the world over the next century or so would to a great extent be determined by events where we lived. Perhaps those events could be influenced to some small degree by our actions. Perhaps we could help to tip the balance in the right direction. You never knew, and if you could do anything about it, even if just a very little, was it not worth fighting for? And as a Chinese person who cared about democracy, cared about human rights and freedom, could you think of any better place to be, any better way to lead your life?

The flipside of that outlook was your inherent, incessant, grueling, grinding, maddening pessimism, a pessimism I could not blame you for, as you were born into it—it was part of your inheritance: Nothing ever works so why even try? Just maintain yourself. Life is a matter of physical survival: Eat well, sleep well, leave the rest to fate. Don't try to control matters beyond your power. It is not for us to make decisions regarding the wider context of our lives, but to accommodate ourselves to the decisions made by others far away, and if we do that with savvy and cunning, we might even get ahead, make a tidy profit. Life hovered above one big abyss; the best you could do was protect yourself and your family from the worst. In such an environment, it was easy to become jaded about something as pie-in-the-sky as human rights—why waste your life on something whose outcome could not be assured, something so insubstantial and distant, when there was money to be made right here right now, when indeed money had to be made to get by, to support your family? To do anything less was irresponsible. There were only so many years you could earn. You should not let them pass you by in fruitless effort, in unprofitable activity. Coming out of that environment, the miracle was that you had come to believe in the importance of freedom, democracy and human rights at all.

Your pessimism had its benefits, justification, persuasive power and even attractions, but in the long run, I found it exhausting. It stood in stark contrast to the outlook of many of the people you worked with. Their optimism could often seem quite poorly aligned with "the objective facts", as the Partystate liked to put it. It was, one could argue, a necessary attribute for the sort of work they did. It fortified like faith; without a belief that things would get better, how could one keep on? Where would one find the motivation and courage to do the sort of work they did, against such odds, in such danger, with the largest dictatorship in the world towering over them, ready to crush them like ants, and tamp down their graves with the same lies about history it had been telling ever since it came to power, angels transformed to devils, devils to angels?

These people never got around to telling others about their extraordinary circumstances and the courage it took to do the work they did because 1) they were too busy doing it to talk about it, 2) it entailed security risks, drawing as it would more attention to themselves, and often their work depended upon a certain degree of anonymity, even secrecy, and 3) it wasn't something they recognized as worth telling about, as it was something they all experienced as normal (like the stories of Tibetan refugees or your own father—they never recognized their extraordinary stories of suffering caused by the Partystate as worth telling; they saw them as commonplace—everyone else they knew suffered the same way, what was there to tell?).

They would say, *The regime is bound to fall, in two years, three years, five years, ten years; it is only a matter of time.* You were more focused on the many pitfalls, challenges, obstacles. Your innate skepticism was part of what made you such a good analyst: you looked at things with a cold eye, even things that affected you emotionally.

Ultimately, the question was, Who was wearing down whom? Was the slow rise of civil society gradually eroding the power of the Partystate? Was the Partystate so corrupting society that the efforts of a weak and constantly embattled civil society were no more than an inconsequential drop in a bucket? The reality was hard to discern, seemed to flicker from day to day, moment to moment even, to depend on the angle from which you viewed it.

Why was it that some people put up with it, persevered in the face of what often looked like no progress at all, in fact often its opposite, when it seemed they were constantly fighting rearguard actions to stave off the worst rather than positively working toward an ideal? Why did you, at the end of the day, why did we?

The words of MLK echoed in my ears: *…And if a man happens to be 36 years old, as I happen to be, some great truth stands before the door of his life, some great opportunity to stand up for that which is right. A man might be afraid his home will get bombed, or he's afraid that he will lose his job, or he's afraid that he will get shot, or beat down by state troopers, and he may go on and live until he's 80,* but he's just as dead at 36 as he would be at 80, and the cessation of breathing in his life is merely the belated announcement of an earlier death of the spirit. He's died... **A man dies when he refuses to stand up for that which is right. A man dies when he refuses to stand up for justice. A man dies when he refuses to take a stand for that which is true....** I sometimes found myself repeating them, like an incantation, a prayer. I liked them because they were matter-of-fact, practical, non-idealistic: What else could you do? they said. It was either that or lose your soul.

When I thought of you, your attitude toward your work, what came to mind were early Renaissance depictions of the Annunciation. In the ones I adored, especially Simone Martini's and Beato Angelico's, Mary appears decidedly reluctant, perturbed, resistant, fearful, or simply far from pleased, bending away from the angel approaching her on aggressively bended knee: *Hail, Mary, the lord is with thee, blessed art thou among women.* Good news, a gospel that is a fait accompli, an offer you can't refuse. In the Beato Angelico, her hands weakly placed over the stomach and slightly slumped posture seem to say, *I think I'm about to be sick* (though there is a certain stiff formality about her figure, and what Angelico probably intended was a gesture of reverence and humility). In the Martini, the physical aversion is depicted more emphatically with a turning away and a facial expression of displeasure: Please, don't bother me, don't touch me, don't come anywhere near me. Even by the high Renaissance, the ambivalence remains: In Botticelli, the hands say, No, please don't.... as if to pre-empt the annunciating angel before he has a chance to open his lips—whatever you have to say, it's nothing I want to hear. As if the hands simply by their grace could push away a fate suddenly thrust upon her.

No one, so far as I knew, had actually called upon you, unlike Mary, to fulfill any particular mission, but it was as if there were a force field around you, a gravitational or magnetic pull. MLK depicts the proposition facing him as self-evidently, unavoidably righteous; Mary's reaction is to the absurd, to an idea never previously thought possible, this divine rent-a-womb, and to the prospect of her life being sacrificed to a greater cause not of her choosing, pitching her into the unknown. Who is this person who has barged into my life, making me an offer I can't refuse, announcing the incredible will be performed upon me, whether I like it or not, accede or not? Can I not rewind time and make this person disappear? Your doubts about the strategy and effectuality of your work, your tirades against Chinese people who did not seem to want freedom and rights enough to fight for them themselves, your far from firm conviction that you were on the path of righteousness and not simply doomed to fail, the fears and anxieties that chronically beset you, the strained look on your face.... That one should work to realize basic freedoms and rights in a country that had virtually never seen such, for a people that often seemed amongst the most cynical, against the most powerful political force in the world that spent more on "internal security" than defense.... a fool's errand, surely; insistence upon a miracle.

Your black views reminded of John Gray's tirades against simple-minded assumptions regarding the inevitability of human progress. They were an important reminder, a corrective, an antidote. Yes, people should beware of being mesmerized by the idea of progress, that it was inevitable or would simply happen naturally, without anyone really trying, or that there was an inevitable trend toward human perfectibility, or that economic growth or material prosperity was an indubitable, conclusive, definitive sign of progress, or that in order for progress to occur or continue, economic growth had to be infinitely constant; yes, one should beware of assuming that just because one was working on some kind of progressive, world-improving cause, one was contributing, progress was being made, one wasn't actually doing harm. And on a day-to-day basis, one could be forgiven for thinking that it didn't seem anything would ever improve; maybe a sounder, less deluded basis for action was the belief that things would never improve.

And yet, if one looked back over the last century, as far as human rights was concerned, couldn't one say that things had improved, in most places, for most people, in quite a few different and substantial ways, and couldn't one, further, say that this was due to the efforts of a great many people fighting for human rights in a great many places in the world, often in obscurity, often at enormous risk, even to their lives?

●

With you taking the job, we were stuck in HK for the foreseeable future. Apart from the fact that it doomed you to chronically high anxiety and, at best, semi-happiness, or fleeting moments of happiness, there was nothing wrong with staying. HK was as good a place as any other, as far as I was concerned. Your career, which was going well, came first, should come first. There wasn't much for me to do in HK, much I wanted to do, but I didn't mind—there was Z to raise, and that was about halfway to being enough for me, and the other half could be filled with, what? Well, I would figure that out. I had come to an age, or maybe more accurately, a stage in life at which there was no imperative to be any particular place, geographically, professionally or otherwise. Being nowhere, or anywhere, was fine. I was the sort who was happy just about anywhere, and happy even when unhappy.

You, on the other hand, I often said, had never learned how to be happy. By that, I meant that happiness was a learned habit, a skill, a solid foundation of appreciation for life, people, and out of that appreciation, joy, love, thankfulness, even at times of misery and depression. Indeed, appreciation overlaid by misery made life all the more beautiful, if at times painfully so.

(Anyway, I always thought that happiness was over-rated, if what was meant by that was some kind of constant contentment, equilibrium, equanimity, for was it not offensive, nearly immoral, to be "happy" in that sense when much of the world was not? No, rather than happiness, give me meaning, purpose, perseverance, an anchoring in a life's work, accomplishment, though only if internal, invisible, unrecognizable except by the self. As Freud apparently said, the pursuit of happiness is a distraction from living.)

And this, this... what? Blessing? This great appreciation for all that befell me came easily, mostly because I'd spent so much of life in the company of people far less fortunate, obviously, shockingly so, and could in contrast recognize my fortune as well as all of value in life; perhaps that could be said, in a sense, to be the gift of others' suffering.

You, on the other hand, seemed permanently jittery. You reminded me of those souls in Canto V of Dante's *Inferno* whose fate it was to be continually blown back and forth by the winds of a violent storm. There, in the second circle of hell, though, the sin is lust, while in your case, it would be the inability or refusal to just relax, in spite of it all. Outwardly, you were far more social than I, far more talented at enjoying yourself, enjoying life, enjoying company, and much better at having fun. I, as you never tired of reminding, was a real stick in the mud—what people seemed to generally regard as fun, I did not find fun at all. But I made up for my lack of talent for fun with a propensity for calmness no matter what was happening around me. That's rather obscene in the face of your disappearance, isn't it? But then the disappearance challenged all that.

Recognizing in yourself the propensity to unhappiness, you were intent on raising Z differently from how you had been raised. *I was so deprived*, you often said. *We never did anything. It was too dangerous to go outside, so we never did, not even to the playground. My mother had so much to do, so many children to look after. My father was always working, never around. They were never exposed to any ideas about how to raise children except those from their own background, and many of them were negative. They always meant the best, and dedicated themselves to raising us, but they knew nothing of the resources available to them, or, really, there weren't many resources available to them. It was mostly a grim struggle to get by.* While pregnant, you read *Raising Happiness*, a primer for parents. It was a revelation, not because it said anything you didn't already know or think, but because it articulated your own concerns and ideas, put words to what had inchoately been swirling within you. It was only when you left home at the age of seventeen that you realized you had been depressed for much of your upbringing. You didn't want the same for your child—a childhood, a youth of incessant competition, struggle, criticism, negative comparison to others, a paucity of values. But the first rule of *Raising Happiness* was that the parent had to be happy herself, for how could you raise a happy child without being happy yourself? That was the most difficult requirement for you to meet. Not being raised happy, happiness did not come naturally. But *Raising Happiness* gave you hope: It was a reminder there was another way to bring up a child.

At any rate, whatever good might have come of the decision to stay in HK, to continue to work on human rights in China, it proved corrosive of the relationship. It was not really the decision itself, but the anxiety brought on by the work, the location. That anxiety came out, as they say, in inappropriate ways. And now that we were staying in HK indefinitely, it came out chronically. Perhaps saying so sounds like letting myself off the hook, blaming difficulties on you, but the difficulties were part and parcel of the shouldered burden. Any time one saddles oneself with a mission, a lot of undesired baggage accompanies it. What else should one expect?

But, I can hear you answering, it was HK that made you unhappy. It wasn't until you came here that you began to self-destruct. You felt unfree. You could not be whoever you wanted, as you felt you could elsewhere. You felt all sorts of pressures, from parents, culture, to be a certain way, and you perceived Chinese culture, Chinese society as massively unfree, at times as little more than a conspiracy to deprive the individual of freedom. You attributed your depression for much of your upbringing not only to familial, social and cultural pressures but also to the educational system. You believed it robbed children of their childhood, turning them into office drones at an early age. It was highly competitive, and you had been one of those who had succeeded, parleying your achievement into scholarships to foreign secondary school, university and graduate studies. But, you believed, at the price of destroying your capacity for happiness, your creativity, your imagination. Leaving HK was a liberation; returning years later, a tribulation. You wanted to be closer to your parents, and, of course, you were working on China and it made sense to be as close to the mainland as possible. But HK was still the undemocratic place you left, the people suffering from an apparently terminal colonial mentality, used to the big decisions about their lives and society being made elsewhere, by others. And it had become even more unequal than when you left, with one in three elderly—the people who had built the city—and one in four children living in poverty. You knew yourself what that meant, since you were one of those who had escaped poverty, having grown up in a 350-square-foot room with your parents and brothers. You were aware from a very young age that your family was poor, and it infused you with a deep sense of the inherent insecurity of life, something you felt to this day. Indeed, that sense was re-enflamed by the return to HK. In short, for you, returning to HK was a great emotional, yes, even spiritual challenge, and sometimes it was hard to see any pay-off in return.

We had moved from London. You looked back nostalgically on our time there as an oasis of dark light and freedom, the first place we lived together after getting married, a wonderful time even though in terms of work, it was tough. Life was not so difficult for those around us, which made it easier for us to enjoy ourselves. And there was much to enjoy in that dark light. There was an ease, a lightness to the relationship. It flowed on its own, of its own accord. There were no questions, no problems, just the two of us, together.

Our us-against-the-world way of seeing the world took us to live in seven countries on four continents in five years. A romantic sweep. Now we'd already been five years in HK, the longest I'd ever lived anywhere in my adult life with the exception of that Northern Paradise (eight years, before expulsion). Far from paradise, HK was for us a symbol of being stuck with the way the world was, with ourselves, our decisions, a symbol of having come to a dead end that might (or might not) be a new start. Up to now, there had always been a way out. Now there was no way out, none that made sense, none that could be taken with integrity, with a belief that we were doing what was best and not just running away. We often thought of leaving, but the question we kept confronting and could not answer was, Where to?

From your point of view, the romance had ended. HK was a dead end in that sense as well. Don't all relationships reach their dead end? The real problem was recognizing one when you saw it. Wasn't it even a good thing, getting past the romantic period? OK, now we can put that aside and just be a couple, see each other for what we really are, nothing more, nothing less. There was much beyond romance, much that was better. I was content, but maybe that was because I was boring or undemanding or had low expectations. Whatever the case, I knew being with you was what I wanted. Or, at any rate, this was the way it was, and that was o.k. You were more doubtful. You wondered whether you had made the right choice, or the right choice had become the wrong choice. Had things changed irrevocably for the worst?

I would answer, *Well, of course things change: We have a kid now. It changes the dynamics, makes us relate to each other differently. I mean, when she's around, we can't even have a conversation without getting interrupted about once every sentence. Your idea of a relationship has to change with reality.*

To which you would respond, *No, it started to change even before Z —you wanted me less; I could tell.*

How could I make you understand that I was a middle-aged man with a reduced sex drive, and it was nothing more or less than that? These divergent views of the relationship made me wonder whether we lived in parallel realities. Was one of us deluded? And that was what made me saddest: Whereas before we were in it together and saw things alike, now our views were irreconcilable—both of them could not be true. I often thought the problem was that you didn't know how to control your anxieties, your stress, your fears: They just bled into everything. Or, to put it another way, you took them out on me.

Except in your dealings with me, you were selfless. You were always working. Or looking after Z. You never had time to do anything for yourself, shop for clothes, for instance. Whenever you had to dress to go out and look respectable, you sighed, *I don't have any clothes.* And it was true. Your underwear (I knew, for I did the laundry; once when I was gone, you called to ask me how to turn the washing machine on) was worn, frayed, stained, holey, the elastic waistband flimsy. Your tights had holes. You had one pair of scuffed slip-on shoes that didn't go with most of your outfits and that you wore in all weather. And the outfits themselves were old. You couldn't find clothes that matched, and so you would end up with the strangest combinations, which in themselves, I thought, constituted something of a style, and because you looked so good, the clothes looked good on you. Whenever you did find any time to do anything except work or look after Z, you were invariably shopping for Z, or planning Z's next educational activities and making the materials that accompanied them. Whenever I went out, you gave me a long list of things to get, almost always either things for Z or food.

And you were a dedicated mother, constantly ensuring that Z was exposed to art—dance, music, painting, drawing and reading—, taking revenge on your own childhood, your own education. (*I had no inspirations. No books, no art, no anything.*) You spent evenings after Z went to bed coming up with new activities, rearranging the shelves where the materials for the activities were placed, cutting out and laminating flash cards with the laminator you'd bought expressly for that purpose. After your disappearance, I tried keeping up with your efforts, poorly of course, and my shortcomings only went to show how dedicated and painstaking you had been.

Your office, at the back of the house already the darkest room, was like a cave, desk piled high with books, papers and bags, teacups full of moldering old tea bags, sometimes halfway full with a curdling layer of milk forming on the surface of the tea, the floor around the desk so crowded with bags that one could hardly walk into the room without tripping over them. It looked like the room of a hoarder, but it was the room of someone so busy she never took the time to put things away, and for the most part, the bags were full of things for Z, fabrics of old clothes, materials to be made into "learning activities", art supplies. Even in earlier, more harmonious times, messiness was my chief complaint against you, and I often imagined you like the Peanuts character, Pigpen, except that instead of a cloud of dust trailing after you, it was a swirl of objects. But the messiness had of late been compounded, and my only strategy was to segregate it in that back room. Whenever I looked through the door, my first thought, which I tried to keep to myself, was, How could anyone live like this? But that was how you lived. And live you did. Better than I, in fact.

You, the most unreligious of souls, experienced motherhood as a kind of religious conversion. When you found out you were pregnant—we hadn't been trying—, your immediate response was, *Oh, no, that's the end of my freedom!* But now being a mother was the center of your life. You went from being ambivalent about the idea of having children to thinking that anyone who didn't was missing out on something essential in life. Indeed, before your disappearance, you had for some time been lobbying for a second child. I wasn't absolutely against having a second child, especially if you ardently desired it, but I did notice a certain resistance within me that had to do with several factors.

The first was that our life was unstable. We rented a small place in one of the most expensive cities in the world and would probably continue to do so for the foreseeable future, your work more or less obliging us to remain in HK. In recent years, I had dreamt, as I never had before, of owning a place, a comfortable place, a spacious place, a place to call our own. I was tired of being so transient and living in places that were good enough because we weren't going to be there that long anyway. Our quarters were so cramped where we now lived—not so cramped by HK standards but cramped compared to elsewhere in the world—that we didn't have a room for Z, let alone for a second child.

My second reservation had to do with the fact that you didn't have all that much time to spend raising the child. You seemed to like the vision of having two children, but I wondered how you would find the time for it. I didn't mind that most of the child-rearing responsibility fell to me, but I wanted you to be involved.

But the deeper fear was that desiring a second child was greedy, and greed was punished by the gods. Any time I saw an autistic child, a child with Down syndrome, a disabled child I felt a deep hurt within myself and wanted to look away, as if that child had something to do with me, with us. It is hard to describe the anguish. The child was like a warning and a cry. I had dark premonitions of which I was ashamed because they seemed superstitious. I hardly felt myself up to raising one child, let alone another who would require love and attention and commitment beyond my capacity, or my desire. Something deep within me said, One should not ask for too much, one should be satisfied with what one has. Z felt like a blessing, and to want another was tantamount to not recognizing the magnitude of that good fortune. I wondered, wherever you were now, whether you still thought of having a second child. I imagined, when you returned, you would want a second more than ever, it would feel all the more urgent to you.

And the kicker was that I couldn't understand how, in one moment, you could speak fervently about your desire for a second child, and, in the next, with just as much conviction, about our relationship falling apart. How could you want to have another child with someone who, you said, you didn't want to be with?

I was stunned at how badly you treated me at times. You said absolutely venomous things I could never imagine saying to someone I was together with, no matter how angry I might be, things no one had ever said to me before. You were the first person to say to me, *I hate you*, seethingly, in a luxury mall, amidst overpriced children's clothing and toys. *I am tired of being with you. It just can't go on. This just isn't working.* The outbursts, the invective reverberated in me, as if my body were a tuning fork that had been struck by them. They were hard to get over, left me feeling damaged. It wasn't as if I held a grudge, but I couldn't shake them. They had gotten inside of me and I didn't know how to get them out. I kept telling myself I let them affect me far more than I should, granting them more significance than they deserved, taking them out of proportion, not allowing that you said such things only when you were very upset, but there it was. And what had I ever done except be myself? No bad habits, no drinking, no gambling, no adultery, no irresponsibility— I might not be great, but one could do much worse, I sometimes thought.

You said we'd gotten together when you were too young. You hadn't had a chance to lead enough of life on your own, to try out different ways of living, without having to constantly refer to me, work things out with me. Our relationship had cramped your style, arrested your development. We were simply very different people, and our differences were irreconcilable, corrosive rather than complementary.

I didn't agree, but I said, *OK, but you've been saying that for ages; either get over it or act on it, but stop being stuck on it.* To me, at the end of the day, such complaints were what someone made a lot out of when they were just plain unhappy with one thing or another and so they latched onto explanations that sounded more like excuses, or magnifications of what were really quite small and eminently manageable problems.

Your accusations were insistent, repetitive. Though never said in so many words, you thought I was boring, stuck in my ways, unwilling to try anything new. That was why you kept repeating yourself, you said, because nothing ever changed. You'd given me many chances to change, but the problems remained the same.

The attacks deadened me. Without intention, I avoided eye contact. We united over Z, sometimes discussing her, but otherwise not communicating more than a few words. Nights were spent sleeping on different sides of the mattress, without touch. Was that what falling out of love was like? The level of stress sometimes became unbearable. It was as if it emanated from you. It was exhausting just being in your presence. What appeared to me a relatively minor matter would stoke that anxiety, enflaming it to a conflagration.

You were vivacious, multitalented (human rights research, photography, gardening, cooking, dancing), incessantly curious and inquiring, fun-loving—how did I, Mr stick-in-the-mud, end up with someone like you for so long? Over a short time, what had seemed permanent suddenly was something that just couldn't last. Days before your disappearance, you had said you couldn't live with me anymore; you had to know what it was like to be with someone else.

Most of your accusations were correct: I confessed to being boring, if what was meant by that was that I found uninteresting what many people considered fun or entertaining. (I didn't even get the idea of entertainment. What was entertaining, or fun, was one's work, one's chosen relationships, a deep engagement, a deep concentration that subsumes self.) I sometimes felt I had conspired to ruin your life, to make it as boring as mine when it could have been bigger, better, beyonder. I seemed to be at an age when character became fate. And so my time with you was tinged with regret, which only deepened after your disappearance, and was another reason why I felt guilty—you would have never ended up in a position like that if you hadn't have been with me, if I hadn't strongly encouraged you to pursue that vocation.

You were a great dancer. You loved to dance. And when you danced, something in you came alive, or what was alive in you became more apparent, accentuated in the dance. Joyful life radiated from you. You had a spontaneity about you, a love for simply and fully enjoying yourself, that passed me by. One of your favorite dances, and the one you were best at, was salsa. You had danced it for years. And you had tried for years to get me to dance it with you. It was, after all, a dance that required a partner, and what better partner than one's life partner? Whenever I attempted, you said things that made me miserable—oh, you were such a bad teacher, I told you repeatedly, so discouraging. You'd already gotten it in your head that I couldn't or wouldn't dance, and so you were trying to teach me what you believed I would never learn. In fact, when I was younger, before you, long before you, I danced quite a lot, and enjoyed it, and considered myself perfectly o.k. at it.

I told you in any couple, there are things that one person enjoys and the other doesn't. Not only is there nothing wrong with that, different interests are to be encouraged. The two halves of a couple shouldn't smother one another, extinguish each other's individuality. Both should have the freedom to pursue their own interests, separately at times. You agreed, and yet it always made you sad I had never learned salsa, had never been your partner. You asked so little of me, after all, and even that little was apparently too much.

One image I recalled with the intensity of irredeemable absence. It was evening, just after dark. I was cooking dinner in the kitchen. I heard salsa and turned to look. You had rolled back the rug, put on your dancing shoes, and were dancing, perfectly poised, graceful, with unmoving shoulders, your back towards me, looking at your reflection in the blackness of the sliding glass door. I could see your expression in the dark glass—a smile of pleasure, contentedly lost within yourself. Looking at you, I felt deeply ashamed, terribly inadequate. At such moments, it hit home with full force what a terrible bore I was, how miserably I had failed you (though the dinner was good).

After your disappearance, on some evenings, after putting Z to bed, I would find myself mimicking your steps in the dark greyness of the one big room in the flat, without any conscious purpose, though perhaps unconsciously practicing for your return. I hoped you were dancing the steps, wherever you were, using them to keep sane. I imagined the two of us dancing the same steps, in tandem, at the same time, you in a cell, I in our dark flat.

I took commitment seriously. How could you talk so easily about being tired of me, tired of the relationship, of it not working, just not working, of how you couldn't imagine it would ever work, of needing something else? Of course, I thought, there would be low points, but the low points were not exit points. Once you made a decision to marry, it wasn't in order to be happy, it was absolute; in this sense, the traditional wedding vows were exceedingly wise, or, to put it another way, I was surprised at how traditional I was.

Tender as was the moment of dancing in the dark and hoping you were as well, at other times, just remembering—even after the disappearance—some of the things you said could nearly make me spit. *Well, then, go try something else, why don't you?* I said to the empty air. And you had, hadn't you?

For some time after your disappearance, with no information about what had happened to you, the thought would occur from time to time that perhaps you had willed it; perhaps it had been your decision to disappear; perhaps you had simply run away.

Ironically, I had never been better in a relationship, never so loving, faithful, devoted, constant, and yet never had such a difficult time. It was the longest relationship I'd ever been in as well; perhaps that was part of the problem. Karma, I thought:

In previous relationships, it had been my partner who was the better half, the better behaved, the more virtuous, the more dependable. I was most at fault for their demise. And here: *I hate you!* What had I done to deserve that? Past lives, past relationships come back to haunt.

At moments, during your absence, it was as if we'd never been closer—whatever we had to go through, we would go through arm in arm, step by step; nothing could break us; the oppression made us stronger. At other moments, I would tell myself, You are deluded; it is all an illusion. Desolate memories emerged from the depths.

A walk along a lake in a northern place, a place where you could breathe because it was free and there were no dangers but also because it happened to be one of the first cool days of autumn. The sky was overcast and spat rain. The lake was one gray wide empty expanse. We pushed sleeping Z in the stroller, hood pulled down, a blanket wrapped around her. An uneasy sleep, like most of her naps out in the open; she was never an easy sleeper. She was sick, poor girl—the things she put up with from her parents.

We had visited my mother, in chronically poor and deteriorating health, in an ineluctable downward spiral and acute pain. There were open wounds on her spindlethin legs. She wasn't even aware of how bad they were because she couldn't bend down to see them. You were the one who pointed them out to her: *M,* you said, *you have open wounds on your legs.*

Oh, she replied, *is that what that is?*

She had just moved from the home where she had lived for forty-five years into a flat in an apartment building for the elderly. Materially, it was comfortable, but she called it a "warehouse for old people".

I tried to engage her in conversation to distract her from her pain. Also, aware she might not be around much longer, I tried to mine her for information that, once she died, would disappear forever. Did she remember the address of where they lived when I was born? She thought she did, but she wasn't sure. The street was right; she was less certain of the street number. It was nothing special, a low-rent apartment complex surrounded by other nondescript buildings. How grim was childhood seen in retrospect! I was born there, but my younger brothers were born in a different apartment. Then when the youngest was only eight months old, the family moved to the house that she had just vacated after forty-five years, the first and last home she and my father ever owned.

They were so young then, my parents, I gasped to myself, so desperately, tenderly young. Their lives held such promise, such hope, opening out before them, stretching wide to the horizon. And now my father dead, my mother chronically ill, in constant pain, housebound in the warehouse for old people.

They then are we now, I thought, except that I am older than they were when they had a child the age of Z, and neither our lives nor the world look so uncomplicatedly hopeful as theirs did. There is no way I can ever provide for my child the way they provided for me, I thought.

As mother and I spoke, mass was being broadcast live on the television she had on all waking hours. (It drove me crazy when I visited, the commercials, the jingles, the jingoism, the uniformly wretched quality. I always thought of my mother as so much more intelligent than that—why did she put up with it?) The reading was the story of the prodigal son. It was one of those dream-like moments when the stars aligned in such a way that everything in the external world was about me: "gathered all together, and took his journey into a far country, and there wasted his substance with riotous living," except that I did not live riotously but instead wasted it on unattainable dreams and ideals while my parents built things up slowly, surely, practically, concretely; their gains were real and assured. "For this my son was dead, and is alive again; he was lost, and is found." The words choked me up; I could hardly conceal my emotion in front of my ailing mother, nor would I have known how to explain it if she had noticed and inquired. Everything passes, all is in vain. Where shall we, you and I, be four decades from now? And Z? Everything dies, everything dies, and everyone. Everyone and everything.

And then we went for the walk. In the face of unrelenting, uncontrollable change, Z sick, mother sick, I felt inadequate to the challenge, lonely, friendless. I'm in that period of life, I thought—grihastha the Hindus call it, the householder stage—, when I spend all of my time taking care of others. I had to be strong but didn't feel strong. Lakeside, I turned to you: *I need a hug.* You walked away, and kept walking, in the opposite direction. You rounded a bend and disappeared from sight. I was pretty sure you would return, but still, the reaction stung—one in a litany of failures on your part, a litany I had to struggle with myself to resist totting up. Whatever it might be, a relationship was not a form of scorekeeping. People failed in small and big ways in relationships all the time. So what? You couldn't hold it against them, not if you hoped to continue.

It was an unusual request on my part. You always accused me of needing nothing, of being far too self-sufficient, self-contained, and therefore, closed, cut off emotionally. You complained of how I never opened up, but now I was so lonely I did, and you left me alone pushing the stroller with the sick, sleeping child along the bleak grey lake. That was too much for you. You snapped. Everything is bleakness, I thought.

You later returned. And apologized. We hugged. It was no problem, I said. And in one sense, it wasn't, but in another, it was: Why else would that memory return in the wake of your disappearance? This time, you walked away and didn't come back, even if it was because you were prevented from doing so.

We continued as before, pretending to be a family taking a walk along a lake, pretending to be what we were. Z woke up, played on the playground, we left the lake and walked to the coffee shop, then to the bookstore. We kept trying and trying because we really did love each other, and because we had a child to raise who was as yet so very small.

Tenderness and exasperation, and, maybe, beneath it all, a hardness that despite my best efforts wouldn't entirely go away, not even, it must be admitted, after the disappearance, though, for me, the hardness was not a sign of demise, more a sign of life being tough, accept it, get on with it, deal with it, don't dismiss it or wimp out, or run away from a commitment for what? a lark, and it was clear that underneath even that hardness that indeed always threatened to corrode, was the tenderness, and the tenderness in turn was based not on all the wonderful times, but on all of the times wonderful and horrible mixed together and passing through my bloodstream: On Saturday you and Z make pancakes, Z standing on a rickety collapsible stool at the kitchen counter helping you mix ingredients, then watching the pancakes fry in the pan, the air just starting to turn cool at the end of another oppressively muggy summer; later, the day would still become uncomfortably hot, so we take a walk early, after pancakes, to beat the heat, Z on my shoulders, you with your camera.

At times, it seemed as if something had snapped in you. You had entered a period in life, a place, where I could not accompany you. You wanted to go out, to dance, to forget things, to be free and easy, to spend time lightheartedly with friends. Not long before your disappearance, you went on a work trip to NYC. Beforehand, you had dreaded being away from Z for so long—more than two weeks. I constantly had to convince you it was both necessary and o.k. to go, that Z would be fine, would be here when you returned. You went and had the time of your life, so much so that it made you sick. You spent your nights drinking and dancing and having fun, seeing old friends and making new friends, your days working, and the time in between getting bronchitis so severe that you had to visit the doctor. It reminded you of how life was before you met me, of how free you felt back then. It was the life you were planning to lead before I came along. When you returned, you were restless. More than once, you became very upset and said the sort of terrible things you had a penchant for: *It's just not working. I can't see how we can live together anymore.* In the evenings, after putting Z to sleep, we had two or three hours before I collapsed in exhaustion, and when you weren't working. You sat on the pink sofa bored, distant.

Every time you raised the prospect of leaving me—the eruptions were periodic, and then afterwards, it was as if you had forgotten what you'd said, and just when things seemed "back to normal", another would occur, keeping me on permanent edge—, I imagined what that might actually be like. The hardest was the question of what would become of Z, where Z would end up. The worst was that I might find myself in a situation in which I was cut off from Z much of the time, but even less bad situations were almost unbearably painful to imagine. However unlikely the scenario, I imagined living with Z in the place we now lived, you having moved out. The vision left me desolate: How would I be able to stand it? How would I live on? How would I make a living? How would I raise Z by myself, or if not by myself, as the primary caregiver, the person with whom she lived? And now, of course, after your disappearance, that was exactly the situation, and the only partial consolation was the high probability that you didn't intentionally leave us, or, to be more precise, leave me. When you were still around, it had gotten to the point that I thought, In other relationships, they would have given up long before now. In response to the question, Why stay together?, sometimes I could find only two good answers: Because I said I would, and, For the sake of the child.

Ultimately, I regarded your outbursts as symptomatic of a general deterioration of spirit, an erosion caused by your work, that manifested itself not least of all in you physical health. Ever since I'd known you, you had been a "connoisseur of ailments". I had trouble keeping track of them all. Prior to Z's birth, you characterized yourself as a hypochondriac. We joked about the condition. You'd inherited it from your father. But the hypochondria by and large ceased at Z's birth, as if having Z had "cured" you. All of your health concerns were displaced upon the child, your own health, by comparison, being of little import.

But in the months before your disappearance, your health concerns began to increase again, almost as if your body, or your psyche, could sense the impending event, a kind of barometer. You had been plagued by migraines off and on throughout your life. The first time was in primary school. You remembered touching your nose: Your nose could feel the touch but not your fingers. Then a flash- objects changed color. By the time you got home, you vomited, had to lie down for hours. Years would pass without any migraines at all; then, one day, another would come upon you, the initial signs as recognizable as the face of an old unwelcome acquaintance. The series of migraines that descended upon you in the months before your disappearance were so severe they caused concern. You were diagnosed with anemia and prescribed iron supplements. When you took the tablets, your hair started falling out. Before Z's birth, hair loss had also been a problem, but it was something about the hormonal changes brought about by pregnancy and motherhood that put an end to that. Now, with the iron tablets, the hair loss had returned. Your long black hairs carpeted the flat. Long after your disappearance, long after the house had been cleaned and cleaned again many times over, Z and I still found "mommyhair". What used to annoy me now made me mournful, joyful—yes, something of you still does exist here.

You felt a dull pain in the abdomen that came and went. You thought it could perhaps have to do with the IUD, but when you finally got around to visiting a doctor, you were told it was in the wrong place to be that and there was no way of determining whether or not some problem was there without a CT scan. I accompanied you to the hospital. We had to wait for hours, sitting on a bench, you in a hospital gown tapping away at your smartphone. You received a message requesting advice from a former research assistant. The assistant had received a query from a person saying she was a professor at the Chinese Academy of Social Sciences: Did the assistant know anything about how the project she had worked on with you was done? Who and how many carried out the research? You said intelligence people often posed as CASS researchers, so frequently in fact that it was a standing joke: Oh, CASS? Must be Guobao. You wrote back to tell the assistant not to respond at all to the query. So annoying, you said, just when you were about to embark on another big project, the constant reminder they were lurking, as if just around the corner. After hours of waiting, the scan took a matter of minutes. You went back the next day to meet the doctor, who told you there was nothing there. Perhaps, he suggested, grasping at straws, the pain had something to do with posture. Perhaps, I wanted to say, its roots were in your soul, your spirit, your heart and art and practice and life. As we left the hospital, a question you had frequently asked before Z's birth returned: *Am I going to die?* you asked in a little girl's voice. *Yes*, I said, as I always had. *Everyone does. But probably not any time soon.*

2

When you disappeared, I was in London. Of course. Of course, I was; where else could I have been? It was as if fated that I would let you down, be in no place where I could be of any help at all just when you needed me. In the wrong place at the wrong time. Not that there was much that I might have been able to do anyway.

The London trip had been planned for weeks. Then, a matter of days before my departure, it was decided you had to go to China. Something had come up, an opportunity to scout out a potential research project on domestic violence against women and determine whether or not it was feasible. Some reports indicated that upwards of one in four Chinese women had been victims of domestic violence; a statistic that, if accurate, pointed to a problem of epidemic proportions. There was a conference coming up at which many of the major players battling domestic violence would be present, including academics, lawyers, women's organizations and NGO people who provided services to victims. There would probably be more than a few Partystate types lurking about as well. Since it was in Shenzhen, just on the other side of the border, the idea was to go over for the weekend of the conference and then return—a quick trip, in and out, easy as that. The details of the trip were never exactly clear to me, or maybe I wasn't paying close enough attention, but in retrospect, I might have taken the fact that they had somehow passed me by as the first sign that things were perhaps somewhat other than they initially appeared.

You'd been fretting over the project for some time. Independent human rights research of any kind in China involved headaches one would not encounter in a free society. The normal procedure would be to start off contacting experts in the field and getting their read on the situation, then tracking down their leads, before eventually interviewing victims of domestic abuse directly. But to contact the experts, the question arose, should you use a new pseudonym (ie, different from the usual pseudonym under which you normally worked) or not? If not, they might be too afraid to speak to you because you worked for a human rights organization and you might attract the attention of the security apparatus to them, but if under pseudonym, then it could be hard later to build the sort of network you envisioned and use the report to support these people in their work, since you'd already, effectively, misrepresented to them who you were, hardly a solid foundation of trust for a work relationship. If anyone learned where you really worked, they would be most guarded in allowing you to use their contacts and gain access to interviewees. Then, whether you went under an alias or not (recalling that even your "real identity" was a pseudonym), there was always the chance that someone you contacted would be an informant and report you. That could essentially put a stop to your research because if you tried to pursue it, you would be prevented, interrogated, even detained, or you would be followed, thus potentially endangering those with whom you came into contact. You would explain the ins and outs to me in excruciating detail, mapping out the dizzyingly complex options, scenarios and potential consequences. I did not know how to sort them out.

So when the opportunity to attend the conference arose, you jumped at it, even though you knew the risk of surveillance at a place where so many gathered to discuss a single (potentially "sensitive") issue would be high.

Should I still make the trip to London, then, or postpone it?

Go, you said. *You've had it planned for so long. And we can still follow the security protocol, whether you're in London or HK.*

When you said those words, the first thing that came to mind was how similar they were to what my father had said when he was terminally ill. I'd come to visit, had been with him for weeks, and was planning to stay on indefinitely, but I followed his advice. It turned out to be the last time I saw him.

Still, to London I decided to go.

Later I would recall an explanation by Takna Jigme Sangpo, formerly Tibet's longest serving political prisoner, for how he could have assumed he would get away with hanging posters in Lhasa calling for Tibet's independence: *The Chinese have a tactic to make people think everything is normal so they will relax but all the time they are watching and waiting for the opportunity to make arrests.* That must have been it: We, or I, had been lulled into a false sense of security by a relatively quiet period coupled with several trips to the mainland during which nothing untoward had occurred. But with the Guobao, it is advisable to be paranoid, to assume the worst, even in the absence of any immediate, clear evidence.

You did not say, Do not go. You were far too stiff-upper-lip and I-want-you-to-lead-your-own-life for that. But should I not have been able to detect something in your eyes, your demeanor, a gesture or mood that was a plea, whether conscious or not?

Perhaps I was just jaded and needed a break from you, from Z, from family life? I ended up being better cut out for it than anyone, including I myself, could have ever imagined, but still, there was a person in me that would not go away and wanted to have a life of his own, retain some corner of himself reserved for himself, not totally consumed, infused, pervaded, occupied by being a husband and father. I had indeed been looking forward to the trip. There were work-related reasons to go, but they were not urgent, and beneath them were the other reasons: I wanted to be alone for a while, to break free, to see old friends, to be inspired by new stimuli and impulses, to return to the place we had lived before coming to HK, a place I had not been since, a place we had loved, where we had been happy and carefree.

The primary security protocol would be handled by someone else, a Japanese woman in your organization who was based in Tokyo. I didn't know her; we'd never met. Even though the Japanese woman was formally and officially responsible for security protocol, I had asked you to keep directly in touch with me. That would mean phone calls in the middle of night in London. So, my conscience could attest, I wasn't entirely negligent.

As on previous forays, you enlisted Opal to accompany you. And Opal, as ever, willingly, enthusiastically, bravely, matter-of-factly agreed to go. The woman was game for anything.

•

Amasis and Shanti's beautiful Peckham homestead felt like a refuge from all the craziness of the world, with its warm blood and ochre walls, bright in dark November. Since I'd last been there, they had built a conservatory out back, now too cold to use but beautiful to look at nonetheless. I stood on the warm side of the sliding glass door, savoring the sort of life that could be lived in such a place, a sense of deep security—here I am safe. Amasis and Shanti are all embrace and greeting, even in the midst of their busy lives. Nothing can touch me here, I think, and breathe. Nothing can touch me here. I can breathe.

They had bought the place years before. Even then, the real estate boom in London was already well underway, but Peckham was still considered a dump, so the place came cheap, relative to everywhere else. It was new when they moved in, part of an initial re-development of the area, and they were its very first occupants. A home, a real home, I thought. How long it had been since I'd been in a real home, a place its residents took care of, a place that exuded their personalities, the lives lived there, because they had it made it their own.

I thought of all the full-page ads in HK newspapers for new luxury apartments in London, which was still in the midst of a building boom while much of the rest of the UK was still in the post-financial crash doldrums. The subtext of the ads was clear, targeting as they did the rich of HK: Gain a foothold elsewhere while you can; you never know what will happen in HK, but London will always be safe. And indeed, London had become one of those places where the wealthy from elsewhere parked their assets, driving up prices for the locals. I thought of the ragged, toothless maintenance worker I met on the bus to Amasis and Shanti's, on his way home from work, still wearing the fluorescent orange outerwear with silver reflecting stripes, telling me where to get off, pointing me through the dark park where the tennis courts shone under floodlights. Where did that man live? How did he get by? How did he afford to live here?

It had been five years since I had last seen them, since I had last been in London, since you and I had left, knowing even then that we were leaving something good for something probably not as good. As different as they were from us, I thought of Amasis and Shanti as our other halves, our doubles. They didn't think of themselves that way or know I thought of them that way, but I did. Different backgrounds, contexts; similar beliefs, commitments, convictions, values. An attempt to coherently put them into practice in their lives that in many cases went far beyond our own often inconsistent, tentative steps. It was inspiring, fortifying to see them, to spend time with them, to be in their presence. Even just knowing they were somewhere out there in the world living their lives had in the intervening five years been a comfort. But all the more powerful tonic to now see them in the flesh. He a social worker, she an NGO worker— the human rights organization where we met; later, Save the Children, now Oxfam—, though their jobs were just the tip of their activism iceberg, which included, beneath the surface, seats on the Southwark Council adoption board and the board of directors of Cambridge House, a community anti-poverty organization. Londoners born and bred, they had never really lived anywhere else, though their parents were immigrants, his from Martinique, hers from Gujarat, his businesspeople, hers academics. Quintessential Londoners, then, second-generation immigrants. For various reasons, all of their parents had refused to attend their wedding or bestow their blessings on the marriage. It wasn't just the beautiful blood-and-ochre walls of their home that conveyed the message, You are safe, you are understood, you are not alone, but they themselves, what they said, what they did, how they lived, despite being half a world away and the fact that Shanti, so engrossed in her life, was, like most of the people I knew and longed to hear from, a poor correspondent. Indeed, there were large blank spaces in my knowledge of their lives over the last five years, much to learn about what had happened in that time.

And that first evening, I could see in Shanti's eyes—troubled or just tired, I did not know which—, in the dark circles beneath them, that something had occurred. I'd met her at her front door, she having just returned from her new job, a four-hour round-trip daily commute to the development NGO. She looked like she needed a hug, but was an angel, always taking on the caring, giving roles expected of her and playing them impeccably. Her goodness could be easily taken advantage of, so fervently did she wish to see the best in everyone

Over warm tea on a cold night in that cozy blood-and-ochre-walled room, I lost no time in conveying to her my dogmatic position on the development industry. Without firm commitment to democracy and human rights and functioning institutions to realize and protect them, international development aid consisted not only of largely pouring money down the drain but distorting and corrupting the societies where it was invested, making true, sustainable development even harder to bring about. Nothing new in that view, but I had come to it through long experience, seeing it up close in places like East Africa where the dysfunction of development aid was rampant. Name one place that had developed largely through infusions of development aid. Most that had developed owed their success to organic economic development great enough to benefit a large proportion of the population to one degree or another, à la China and its East Asian precursors, Japan, South Korea, Taiwan. To my democratic sensibility, it was regrettable that it was in a dictatorship that such massive improvement in the standard of living was brought about, contributing to the largest and fastest decrease in absolute poverty ever seen. Not least of all, this was due to the Partystate hardline on sovereignty of all sorts, including economic sovereignty, as well as a commitment in the early decades of Partystate rule to widespread provision of basic education and health care. Its timing also happened to be fortunate, its own economic liberalization dovetailing with neoliberal globalization at a time when corporations were looking for a cheap place to produce their goods. Be that as it may, it had a record of economic growth no other developing country could rival. Whereas Western development aid? At best, its effects were palliative. Yes, save people when they needed saving, but beyond that, stay out of their lives, out of their way. They've got to do it themselves, to fight for their own rights, to build their own democratic institutions, and to the extent that they need aid, solidarity with them in their pursuit of democracy and human rights was most effective.

What a trip to lay on someone who had just returned from a four-hour commute to an organization, one of the best of its not-so-impressive kind, engaged in work I was writing off as ineffectual and wrong-headed at best, harmful at worst. Shanti was as gracious as ever at my lack of tact and manners. She reminded me of my priest friend, about whom I said, If all priests were like him, I'd revere the religion.

If Shanti had verbalized what I imagined she felt at that moment, it might have been in the words of rebuff from an imagined woman in "The Love Song of J Alfred Prufrock": *That is not it at all, / That is not what I meant at all.* What she really needed, I grasped after my formal denunciation of the development aid industry, was to pour out all that she had experienced, all that she had endured, and be heard. I shut up and listened.

In the past twelve months, she said, *I've been to twenty countries, most of them not very pleasant places, at least the parts in them where I found myself.* Shanti usually spoke in the politically correct language of "appreciation of other cultures", but you could see she thought the places she'd been were shitholes, through and through, awful places where people lead awful lives and it was hard to see any way out.

Her story didn't flow from her. She didn't want to talk, at least not too much. She didn't want to draw attention to herself. She was used to being semi-visible. She was the one who got things done behind the scenes while others talked, the one who did the things for which others, superiors usually, took the credit. If I could select an infinitely reliable and resourceful team to work in an impossible situation, I would want her on it. But she wasn't a talker; she unconsciously assumed her story wasn't worth airing, or didn't recognize which parts were, or what, for her own good, she had to get off her chest. Even if her story deserved telling at least as much as any other, were there not many others—all of those she worked with, after all—who were in situations far worse than her own, situations they could not escape while she just traipsed in and out? No, her stories did not emerge smoothly, seamlessly, effortlessly. They came in scraps and patches. They had to be drawn out. Slowly. With questions, requests for elaboration, the kernel of something much larger listened for, detected. It was not that she was deliberately hiding something or even reluctant to talk, more that once someone gets into the habit of not talking, it is hard to undo, hard to start to talk.

The next morning, long after Shanti had left before light for her two-hour commute, Amasis confided over breakfast that he'd been "neglectful" of Shanti over the course of the past year. He didn't entirely understand at the time what she was going through and the toll it was having on her, especially as she wasn't the sort to advertise or dramatize her "internal difficulties". That word of his, neglectful, struck me: It sounded like negligent and mournful put together, mournful for being negligent. He'd been busy with his own thing, a full-time job and a full-time Master's degree program in social work. He alluded obliquely to marriage difficulties that sounded not dissimilar to ours. *I did not care for her properly*, he said, *and she didn't ask, so it was easy to overlook when she needed me. The time has taken its toll*, he said. And he repeated it. *The time has taken its toll.* I thought of the dark circles under her eyes I'd noticed the night before, and an aspect that seemed not just fatigue but something more like grief. Who says whatever doesn't kill you makes you stronger? What a strange idea! All that I had ever seen suggested that life could simply grind you down, indefinitely, into a fine powder, with no redemption, no redemption whatsoever. *It is good you are here*, Amasis said. *She tells you things she's never told anyone else, even me; she opens up.* He didn't mean Shanti hid things from him. She would tell him things but stop short; the detail did not crack open to reveal the universe within. Over the days of the visit, much trickled out slowly.

She'd written to me of relationships with friends having changed. Even when I asked her to expand, it was hard to get to the bottom of what she meant. What I gathered was that she had had experiences that were difficult to communicate with old friends, and she was put off by some off-hand, perhaps unintentionally dismissive or ignorant responses. She felt alienated.

They were understandably focused on domestic concerns. The rest of the world was far away. I'd lamented that while the world was in a period of advanced globalization when it came to production, trade, finance, the consciousness of its citizens was nowhere near as globalized. We wore the sneakers made by the Chinese factory worker but otherwise didn't give a thought to his situation.

She'd been treated badly by her employers. That was my summation; she couldn't bring herself to say it. Perhaps she didn't see it that way, or not entirely; but I did. In the human rights organization where we'd met, after I'd left in disgust, she filed a harassment and bullying grievance against our immediate supervisor, a woman I knew full well was capable of the behavior of which Shanti accused her. The process reached no definitive conclusion, and at the end of it, the woman was still Shanti's supervisor, an impossible situation. Yet she hung on until she could abandon ship and leap to another job at one of the largest international development organizations. Run like a corporation, it was continually in the process of "restructuring". Her job got phased out, but she hung on with one short-term contract after another, undervalued, doing the grunt work of an organization that was supposed to do good for others but couldn't treat its own employees decently. Now she had that impossible commute to another development job on a fixed-length contract of eighteen months.

And still without child. Amasis said Shanti was focused on work; she gave all to jobs that didn't reward the effort with recognition of her value, and whose impact was debatably negligible.

Her situation reminded of yours: Young talented right-minded women doing important work, facing challenges, stressed, coming to the end of their tether. Similarly, I imagined the marriage difficulties Amasis obliquely alluded to had to do with the stress of her work bleeding into the relationship, infecting it. Also being at risk, in danger while finding little immediate evidence of the impact of her work.

There were two trips in particular, both to conflict zones, one the Colombian department of Nariño, the other Gaza, trips that Amasis later referred to as near-death experiences, though Shanti rolled her eyes at what she considered her husband's exaggeration.

She was in Bogota to conduct a workshop and was asked to accompany a fact-finding mission to a remote indigenous village high up in the mountains of Nariño. Afterwards, the head of security at her organization, based in Washington, scolded her for ever having agreed to go along and criticized the in-country staff for having set off at all on such a poorly planned mission. But once she was there, there was little she could do but go through with it. The staff had heard the villagers didn't have enough food and wanted to check out the situation of the children there. The idea behind having Shanti along was that she could witness the situation first-hand and then bang out a report in English, thereby circumventing a lengthy translation process and hopefully drawing more immediate international attention to an urgent situation.

The in-country staff weren't from the area and didn't know it well. In fact, they were city people themselves. They were told by a local guide it would be two hours up the mountain, shorter down. But just looking up, Shanti could see that was an underestimate. She was annoyed that people weren't more precise; then they would know how to pace themselves properly. The rain was torrential, unceasing. Every step sunk into the earth, a slog. The area was mined. They were lead by the guide, but at points he was uncertain, as the paths, which had been marked out so as to avoid the mines, had shifted due to the rain. Paramilitaries in the employ of narcotraficantes as well as FARC guerrillas were invisibly present. It was a place, she said, where she felt invisible eyes watching her. Under no circumstances were they to be out after dark, when the risk of attack increased. Her organization had a good reputation in the area and a relationship of mutual understanding with the combatants; as long as they wore their red t-shirts, they were known, safe, left alone and would not be attacked. But in the pouring rain, Shanti shivered in her drenched red t-shirt, despite the tropical heat, and yet couldn't put anything warmer over it for fear of not being recognized. The footing was so bad, and they were so much slower than the guide and the locals that they hired donkeys. Shanti hadn't done anything remotely equestrian since she was little, and she struggled to stay mounted on the uneven and steep path.

They got up to the village, saw what needed to be seen, carried out their grim assessment. Of course they're hungry, who wouldn't be hungry in these conditions—caught between the rains, the guerrillas, the mines, the narcotraficantes, the military—, they're used to being hungry, they're in better shape than we are, Shanti muttered to herself madly. Now that they had found out what was known all along, confirmed it with their own eyes, they could file a report and somehow, the food would come, at which point the villagers would have somehow found food for themselves anyway, though the extra food would surely be welcome to supplement the children's diets, poor in even the best of times (they looked stunted, and not because they were stocky mountain people by nature).

The ascent had taken so long, it would be tough getting back down before dark. There was nowhere to stay in the village, which anyway wouldn't be safe, since it was vulnerable to attacks, especially if the presence of strangers was known. All there was to eat was meat. When she told people she was a vegetarian, they would roast an ear of corn or two for her, but that was all she'd had to eat for several days. She felt weak, light-headed, physically overwhelmed. They headed down, in the rain, going as fast as they could. Shanti was amazed that despite her weakness, she was ahead of everyone else but the guide. She got so desperate to beat the darkness, she started heading straight down the mountain, leaving the zigzag path. She kept thinking, I can't get down the mountain I can't get down the mountain I'm not going to make it I'm not going to make it I want to give up I can't. Military helicopters buzzed overhead, presumably looking for FARC. If they were put to useful purpose, Shanti thought, they could simply airdrop food into the village, and the whole miserable reconnaissance mission wouldn't even be necessary. If the military were really all about protecting the people, why wouldn't they do that? She could only contemplate the absurdity of the whole escapade as she reached the foot of the mountain.

She was stuck in Gaza during the Israeli Defense Forces' bombardment, Operation Pillar of Cloud (not to be confused with Operation Returning Echo, carried out eight months previously, or with Operation Cast Lead, some three years and two months before that—how many bombs had dropped there in recent years! she found herself thinking, as the bombs dropped). She had been in Ramallah, in the West Bank, and had crossed over to Gaza to hold a series of workshops. Even though she worked with a recognized charitable organization, the crossing was difficult due, she believed, to her Muslim-sounding surname and her dark skin. It wasn't terribly dramatic, she said; she was just stuck for several days while rockets fell all around her. It was not so much frightening as nerve-wracking, and somehow, she felt, she was not in particular danger. That was most certainly not the case for the inhabitants of Gaza, and to the extent that she did feel terror, it was on their behalf, a feeling that seeped into her by osmosis. During the whole bombardment, she couldn't leave the safehouse in which she'd been lodged by her organization's local staff. She was "grounded" less to protect her from bombs— the IDF, at least in theory, knew that that building housed international NGO workers—than from various Palestinian groups that might have designs on kidnapping for ransom. Indeed, even if the bombardment had not occurred, such security precautions would have been taken, although she would have been allowed to go out during the day under the protection of security hired by the organization. At the end of the bombardment, she got out of Gaza. Besides herself, the only others trying to cross the border that day were elderly Palestinians who had received Israeli permission to exit Gaza for medical reasons. Even though they had permits and there was no one else at the otherwise closed crossing—a spooky atmosphere, Shanti said— they were still made to wait for hours and then, in spite of their poor health, walk hundreds of meters under the hot sun in the no man's land that separated the Gaza exit from the entrance to the corridor in Israel proper that would conduct them to the West Bank. They still got through in quicker time than Shanti, who was made to wait eight hours for no given reason. This time, she suspected, it had less to do with her Muslim-sounding surname and more with punishment for being part of an organization that was aiding the enemy. It was irrational, she thought, given that her organization focused on helping children, but it was very much her sense that at least within the military, there was a perception that anything Palestinian was the enemy, including sick old people and children.

Not long after that, she was made redundant, or, to be precise, her position was discontinued as part of the latest restructuring. She survived the cut by creating a new position for herself, itself short term, and getting it approved, thereby extending her stay for a number of months and buying herself time to find a new job, which turned out to be the one she'd just started and was working at now, the job of the four-hour commute.

I, to whom the maxim was self-evident that the apolitical risk being politically co-opted, manipulated, exploited, complicit, always noticed that Shanti didn't express much of a political opinion about her experiences or really anything else for that matter. Though she spent her life dealing with political matters, she wasn't a political person, at least in my sense of the term. I often found such people frustrating, for they recognized many of the issues of justice on a personal level but couldn't or wouldn't see how these were related to larger social and political issues. It was as if it just didn't interest them, or they couldn't be bothered; they couldn't bring themselves to regard "big politics" as real. I tended to perceive such people as eternal children in adult guise: They wanted someone else to deal with, take responsibility for those larger matters. I didn't feel that way about Shanti, though. After all, she was fully committed (if anything, over-committed) to the cause of justice, of helping the disadvantaged, the unfortunate, the oppressed. Perhaps for that reason, I found the apolitical inclination even more puzzling. Yes, when she encountered something like the punitive act of making elderly people in need of medical treatment wait hours at the crossing and then walk hundreds of meters under the hot sun, she despised it, but that was more a reaction, almost a visceral reaction, to a particular circumstance than a political judgment. I supposed that her withholding of judgment was part and parcel of her willingness to continue working in the development industry despite its poor track record. She was willing to put up with too much, I sometimes thought—strange for someone with such high standards for her own work. Perhaps she just thought people were infinitely fallible—what else could you expect? And anyway, what was the point of stating the obvious?

I had lived in places where people faced the prospect of unnatural death, of sudden and violent death, or death from easily preventable causes. They were not nice places. The question was how it affected you. I recognized the guilt that Shanti felt for being able to come and go while others were stuck. Beyond that, you find your own way. Mine, which seemed to come naturally, was that you accepted it as the way things were, at least for now, in those places. That was what the people there did. Since they couldn't get out and were powerless to change their circumstances (usually because all of their effort went into the struggle for survival), they had no other choice. And so you found that, at least on the surface, people were phlegmatic, philosophical, apparently brave, while somewhere beneath the surface, sometimes far far beneath the surface, they were a mess. But allowing yourself to fall apart was not an option; that occurred only if you lost control, and then, of course, you were lost. Being able to come and go, I found, gave at least the illusion that nothing truly could touch me. I could be philosophical while at the same time letting emotions affect me, feeling them without being submerged by them. But it was a trick. Perhaps part of it had to do with incorporating the experience into my general worldview. But as I say, it just came about that way; it was not a plan I devised and executed. And at a certain point, I decided I didn't want to spend time in such places anymore, largely because, when I was there, I felt I was doing little useful, and certainly nothing indispensable; I had no power to change the basic circumstances that made the people have to face death in its various guises close up and personal on a regular basis, so what was I doing there? Yes, a witness serves some purpose, but only if he can come out and affect those circumstances, and that meant political action, at a higher level. In Shanti's case, it appeared she thought she shouldn't really let it bother her, so she didn't, but it did. Others had it much worse; it was on them the focus should stay. But as a result, she overlooked herself. And you could tell. You could see it in her eyes.

•

Shanti and Amasis had bought their place in Peckham back in the day when housing, especially in that part of the city, was, if not cheap, still within the realm of affordability for ordinary people. It was in one of the first redeveloped areas in South London. Now it seemed all of Southwark was under redevelopment, one big construction zone. I had been a dedicated North Londoner. I'd ended up living there by pure accident coupled with the consideration that it was most within striking distance of my workplace at the time, but once I moved there, I was hooked, identified with that part of the city, spent most of my time there. As a result, I hardly knew South London, had hardly given it a thought, and only visited on a number of occasions, not least of which was to see Shanti and Amasis. Apart from that, I didn't know it at all. Staying with them gave me the chance to get to know an almost entirely new part of the city. They were away at work during most of my visit. I saw them only evenings and one weekend. The rest of the time, I was on my own.

I loved to be alone, and I loved to walk, just walk and walk and walk, especially in cities. It was fortunate I had somehow come to have some obligations and relationships to others; otherwise, I would have just ended up spending my life doing nothing but walking. Wherever I went, I could walk for hours and hours, experiencing nothing in particular, discovering nothing in particular, seeing nothing in particular, just walking and walking and walking. It felt like being cleansed of problems, not running away from but walking through them, persistently, step by step, doing my best to be a worthless, superfluous human being, someone who does nothing for others, gets in nobody else's way, just comes and goes, comes and goes, like the wind and water and rain, someone who exists just to exist, with no add-ons, no pretensions, no vain ambitions. And in that time, I had to admit, to walk, to do nothing else but walk, was bliss.

There in South London, when I had to go to a different part of the city, I walked up to Elephant and Castle (one of those urban areas that is so unsightly it almost seems like a joke), each time by a different route, and took the tube from there. If the destination was anywhere in the center of the city, I walked there, crossing the Thames by one bridge or another (the Thames had never really been a part of my life when I lived in the city, was always simply just there, a vague bordery notion). And when I had the time, I walked aimlessly, not out of South London, but within it, or, on a couple of occasions, I made my way up to the landmarks on the river, the Tate Modern and the London Bridge area, with Borough Market and the recently opened Shard.

During my walks, I thought of Amasis, of things he had said, things he had told, conversations we'd had. He was a great monologuist, the very opposite of Shanti, who had so much to say but withheld, or struggled to get it out. Few people had helped me more than Amasis to understand the city, how it worked, and in particular those for whom it didn't work. This was his turf. Unlike Shanti, who flew off to the other side of the world to risk her life engaging in the sometimes necessary but largely superfluous work of the development industry, Amasis's mission was in his own neighborhood. He walked to work, or, on days when he had to visit people, his "clients" as he called them, he biked. He was a social worker for Southwark Council, his caseload—young adults aged eighteen to twenty-five who had recently ceased being wards of the state upon attaining majority—statutory, his job, therefore, about as secure as you could get, the counterweight to Shanti's on-going job insecurity in the international NGO world. (I was struck at how much the employment practices of the international NGO world resembled those of the neo-liberal economy, especially the in-built precariousness.) He'd come to the work because he was good at it; he'd never gotten a degree. Over the past year, he'd been studying part-time for a Master's in social work. The degree would give him opportunities for promotion to positions that required degrees. As it was now, he knew more than most any of his superiors but wasn't rewarded for it. During the day, he worked; during the evening, he studied. That was partly why, as he put it, he'd been "neglectful" of Shanti through the difficult period—he had virtually no free time.

On the walks, I imagined some of the people I passed were Amasis's clients, or like Amasis's clients. Most of those former wards of the state had spent their childhood in foster homes, usually from a very young age. Most had been forcibly removed from their biological parents, who had been found by the state to be incapable of raising them, often due to drug problems or mental illness or mental disability or because they were serving long prison sentences, or to some combination of the above, or because they had abused the child, in some cases having committed such heinous acts that it took some stretch of the imagination to understand how anyone could do that to another person, especially a defenseless child, let alone one's own. Amasis was full of stories of people who had kids for no other reason than to collect welfare or because they simply knew no better, people who had had five, six children and more, each of whom was removed by the state. These, the clients, were the *disgraziati*, the unfortunates whose only sin was to be born to their parents, falling outside of the grace of god, the gods, any god, any higher power, except, of course, the state. Amasis had come to believe, through his work, that there was no worse fate that could befall you than to become a ward of the state. For that reason, he served in a voluntary capacity on the council adoption oversight committee, the body responsible for ensuring the council was following the law and its own procedures throughout the long process of removing children from their biological parents and finding adoptive parents for them. He wanted to prevent as many children as possible from entering into the system, from becoming wards of the state, from turning out like his clients, who, removed from their parents at a young age, ironically ended up in situations quite similar to their parents'. Many had criminal records, had spent time in and out of juvenile detention facilities, and now in and out of prisons, had not finished school, had difficulties getting and keeping a job, to the extent that they were even motivated to look and capable of looking for one. They had personal problems, relationship problems, psychological problems, drug problems. The gamut. Few came through unscathed. Amasis' term for them was "damaged individuals who came from damaged individuals".

The work of the council, as overseen by Amasis' committee, could be regarded as ripping children from their parents' arms (setting aside for a moment the fact that in more than a few cases, the parents didn't really want the children), but on this point, Amasis was clear: Sooner rip the child from the arms of an unfit biological parent and put her in the arms of a permanent adoptive parent who will love her and take good care of her than allow the child to remain or enter into the limbo of years of foster care. It was the best way to break the cycle, however extreme it might seem to the uninitiated (ie, to those who had never seen his clients up close and personal, seen what the effects of unfit parents and/or years of foster care were). Amasis had recently returned from the committee's monthly session drained but gratified. Virtually all of the children up for adoption were under the age of five. Prospective parents weren't interested in adopting children older than that. If you didn't place them by that age, they were almost certainly doomed to become wards of the state. That evening, two sets of adoptive parents had been approved: a gay couple living in the gentrified London Bridge area who had just bought another house in Hackney and had a third in the south of France, and a Nigerian-British couple of modest means who had already been matched to a child born to a developmentally disabled Nigerian woman who had apparently had the child primarily in the hope that it would help her to obtain permission to remain in the UK.

The *disgraziati* were everywhere, my walking feet thought. Who would you rather be? A victim of violence in a conflict zone, a victim of a dictatorship, a member of the seemingly permanent underclass in a rich democracy? Take your pick.

•

South London, my walks confirmed, was still agreeably down at heel enough to be real, with plenty of housing estates, rundown terraced homes which it was easy to imagine were originally built to house workers in some long-ago-torn-down nearby factory, lots of new construction projects, strips and patches of gentrification, creative renewals of old housing stock, places in which, beforehand, it was hard to see the possibilities, and afterwards, you said wow.

In stark contrast to all that low-rise human jumble, one walk took me—inevitably, it seemed in retrospect, as if by force of gravity—to the Shard, a place that could have just as well had a sign above the difficult-to-find entrance that said *No disgraziati allowed*, as if there weren't a multitude of other means of conveying that message, of preventing access to the undesirable, the undesired. Seeing the Shard, a phenomenon of early twenty-first century global capitalism, an utterly material phenomenon, through and through, right down to its architectural pretensions, was an almost mystical experience—not for just anyone, certainly, but for me, because of its associations. It could be seen from just about everywhere in the city, so obtrusive was it upon the otherwise flat skyline of that end of town. And I quickly got in the habit of looking for it just about anywhere I was, seeing it from all different vantage points and angles. But it was first one chilly afternoon I found myself out front, having wandered up to it through the gentrifying, hip London Bridge neighborhood, where, I recalled, the well-to-do adoptive gay couple lived. And there I was, suddenly standing in front of it, hardly even noticing I was there after days of staring at it from afar.

During its construction, right up to its completion, many had railed against the building: It destroyed the skyline. It was a symbol of the rising inequality of the city, of the worst excesses of global capitalism, of the prerogatives of the wealthy and unelected. While "Shard" aptly described its shape, "1% Tower" captured its socio-economic profile. It was 95% owned by the Qatari government, its interiors a combination of office space for hedge funds and financiers, a luxury hotel, ten residential flats going for anywhere from 30 to 50 million pounds. *Tapered faceted form referencing London's history of spires and masts... broken apex... cut diamond reflecting the city on all sides... top of a broken beer bottle... can't help but think of the Tower of Babel* (comments of a South London preacher)...., it stood complete, stationary, inert in the sky, who knew for how long to come (decades, centuries?), and still mostly empty, I'd heard—the impact of the financial crisis was difficult to overcome even for economy-defying iconic structures like that.

As far as that kind of building went, this one impressed me in spite of my prejudice against the skyscraper, all the more so for being set apart from all the others, the only tall building in the vicinity, and it had a kind of lightness, an airiness to it that both made it stick out (compared to the heavy exteriors of brick and other solid material darkened through the centuries) and blend in, but not to the ground, to the air, its reflecting glass façade more sky than earth.

Architects seemed willing to jump into bed with just about anyone—when it came down to it, form trumped function. If someone wanted to throw money at them to realize the structure of their dreams, who were they to say no? Looking up at the Shard, I thought of the CCTV Tower in Beijing, another highrise protruding from cityscape, another landmark whose commissioners were autocrats. That was Rem Koolhaas building the headquarters of the biggest propaganda organization in the world run by the biggest dictatorship. "Big boxer shorts", the *laobaixing* called it; others said it was a woman (why not a man?) on her hands and knees waiting to take it up the butt, a symbol of the relationship between subjects and ruler. Or between media and Partystate; or architect and patron, for that matter. What had Rem Koolhaas been thinking? I wondered. Presumably no more than that it was a great opportunity to build a cool building. From a strictly formal point of view, it might be great (though I couldn't see its greatness, as I could with the Shard), but still, talent in service of the oppressor was utterly dispiriting. Nothing new about that, though, from the pyramids to the cathedrals, down through the ages. If you wanted to make a big building, you couldn't be picky about who financed it.

The Shard was Renzo Piano. Another Renzo Piano. Renzo Piano was cool. Renzo Piano was everywhere these days. If you just abstracted the building from its whole context—the financing, the politics, the socioeconomics, who used the building, what for, who was included, who was excluded— it did look pretty cool. But how could he have done something like this? Couldn't pass up the chance to make his mark, I suppose. Architects' jewels were extravagant territorial markings in world cities. Someone tells you, we'll give you free rein on this prominent site right at the heart of something or other. Your name down in history, your building in the heart of the city for generations to come. Who could say no? What ambitious architect would reject such an offer?

But then wasn't that how most urban landmarks got built, by money and power, for money and power? Everything these days seems a fait accompli, I thought, standing there in front of that fait accompli, staring up at it. In the face of it, in the face of the immensely powerful forces that created it, in the face of so many forces these days, what use were words, thoughts, consciousness, morals, ideals, how powerless am I, are we? The accomplishment, yes, that was impressive: Look at what we have accomplished, and you have not, the stolid towering façade said. While you go on pounding your head against the wall, we have built a wall, a big wall, all four walls rising high into the sky. Compare yourself and what you have done in your life to this and see how truly small you are. The fait accompli elicits apathy, passivity, resignation—it's already done, whatever, what's the use?

I wondered how Tatyana saw it, having been at the heart of the project; Tatyana, Piano's assistant, his shadowy genius, standing in the wings, the invisible presence hovering over every last detail, determining that contour, this curve, this graceful shape, marking the difference between the ordinary and the sublime. She'd always had an AynRandian (or was it Nietzschean?) side to her—the world is for the masters of the universe, those of superior intellect, talent, will, mental strength, ambition (of which she was most definitely one, possessing all of those attributes in spades). I'd found that side of her intimidating, not being one of those masters myself. In her presence, I felt I would eventually be swept aside, "overcome"; I kept wondering when she would realize I wasn't a master like herself. And wouldn't she just as easily brush aside egalitarian teeth-gnashing? We'd bitterly disagreed about some things, especially the wars in former Yugoslavia (about which, to this day, I still believed I was right and she was wrong, even though it was her family getting bombed... so maybe I wasn't right even though I was—how can you argue with the bombed?), but on most, I usually came around to seeing her side. I was sure as far as the Shard was concerned, I'd end up seeing it however she saw it. I'd believe her and agree. She was one of the few I'd ever encountered who could co-opt my contrarian nature. It was something to do with the combination of her passion for what she did and her emotional vulnerability, the latter having, I imagined, decreased over the years. Would she be better or worse for it, having steeled herself, to the world, to others? When I knew her, she was all raw nerves; it was part of what made her beautiful (and terrifying), that and her surface disdain for politics, social duty, soppy moral concern, progressive activism that believed it was fighting for "the people", for a "better world".

From street level, it was as if the building didn't exist. It was camouflaged, just something gigantic and in the way. It was meant to blend in to the transport infrastructure of London Bridge station, and so was hardly visible, in spite of its size, both there and not there, as if floating in the air for the select few. There was no clear entrance, but instead, an alienating bus terminus, lots of stops all jumbled together, not much different from elsewhere, just newer. (Would it age better than the hilariously depressing Elephant and Castle? I wondered).

In a gesture of goodwill or to keep on the good side of local politicians, the Shard offered employees of Southwark Council free admission to the observation deck on the sixty-eighth to seventy-second floors, with what was supposedly the best view of the city, before it opened to the public. As soon as he received the email invitation, Amasis leapt at the chance, immediately clocking out of work and cycling up to the Shard. He was thrilled by the view he had the privilege of enjoying before most everyone else. He spent a whole afternoon staring at the city, a city he didn't take for granted though he had lived there his whole life, his city nearly all to himself as far as the eye could see. He studied each known element from that perspective on high; he was the angel of his city. He thought of "Wings of Desire"—everyone, now, could be an angel hovering above the city, overhearing the secrets of people's lives. It was like a meditation, he said, and hardly a soul was there besides himself—he couldn't figure out why: Were his colleagues so crazy to be so dedicated to their work as to not take time off for this?

But standing in front of it, I couldn't bring myself to search out the entrance in order to go up. It was the price, yes: I was cheap and it was expensive—what was it? Twenty, twenty-five pounds for entry to the observation deck? Something outrageous. If it were free, I might have gone in. But those people don't need my money, and there are a lot of other people who do. What else could twenty-five pounds go towards? How might it help to make the world a better place? If I want a view of London, I'll go to Alexandra Palace or Parliament Hill. But it was more than the price; it was as if a force greater than miserliness or principled spending was preventing me. I should have, though; I really should have. I regretted that I didn't. Because of Tatyana, if nothing else, to see what she'd made, to pay my respects. We hadn't been in touch for years. It was a project she'd been responsible for, ushered to completion, taking up the whole early half of her career, nearly a decade, while everyone else was doing other things, things with less enduring results than the tallest building in western Europe.

So I turned and walked away. It was with only a little satisfaction, wistful, Pyrrhic satisfaction, or the Nietzschean ressentiment of the weak, that I recalled being told that none of the luxury apartments had yet been sold, and only one of the office spaces rented, and the luxury hotel's opening kept getting postponed, the latest opening date targeted for over half a year thence. As a symbol, it worked much better as an empty shell, a beautiful gleaming empty shell, a very expensive empty shell; that was how I liked it best.

For days after that, the rest of my time in the city, I had dreams of Tatyana seeking me out, I who rarely dreamt, or, if I did, rarely remembered that I had dreamt. The dreams were intensely vivid. When I awoke, it took more than a moment to recognize where I was, and that what I had dreamt had not really occurred, and that, rather than having seen her again, another night had gone by, adding to years and years of nights when I had not seen her, more than a dozen now since we'd last seen one another. And yet there she was, in a fashion.

It was like a visitation, as by those ancient Greek gods who found means to possess their objects of desire, often in disguise. And she had a specific purpose. It was a business matter. She wanted to have a child with me. She had been too busy, making her career, building masters-of-the-universe buildings, leading her life, to bother to do anything as prosaic as finding a mate and breeding, but now, before it was too late (and how strange it was to think of her already in her thirties; in the dream, she had hardly aged), she wanted to be sure to leave behind progeny, at least one. She had not found a stud of any higher quality than I to provide the necessary ingredient. This was, as she presented it, not a matter of sentiment but of reason. Like that last time in B, she was in firm control of her emotions.

I would have loved for something tangible to exist, a product, a sign, a consecration, a monument to us having known one another, however briefly, a child, yes, half of each, going out into the world. Otherwise, it was as if it had never existed, I had made it all up, it was a figment of my imagination, just like the dream. Could I be involved in the child's life? I had asked. Awake, I couldn't recall whether or not she had answered that question, or if she had, what she had said. I could only guess that the answer would probably be no. The child would never know her father, at least until majority was attained.

What would have happened, how would life have turned out, if I had contacted Tatyana after Solveig left? Why hadn't I tried? One would have thought those were questions I would have given much consideration to, but before that time of the vivid dreams, although the question had occurred to me, in the midst of a busy life I had skated over it, and for years, forgotten it, even while almost every day Tatyana crossed my mind. Perhaps if I had contacted her, she would have been entirely over me by then, uninterested, now that I was finally, for the first time since we had come to know each other, single. But the question remained: Why hadn't I even tried to reach her? I couldn't remember exactly why, couldn't even remember if there was a reason. I was simply living too fast, was what I concluded now, living in remote places where I rarely had access to means of instant communication that would have allowed me to act on emotional impulse.

Such dreams occur, such thoughts cross one's mind when travelling alone. Only after returning to HK did the dreams cease, somewhat to my regret. They were brought on by the solitude, the distance from the familiar, from ordinary life. The whole time in London was dreamlike; the dreams fit the surroundings. And the idea lodged that there was some causal relation between the dreams of Tatyana and Y's disappearance.

I had always endowed Tatyana with supernatural powers. Yet more to feel guilty about.

•

You called. My poor old phone, 2G, ancient, a Nokia I'd bought used at a market in Kampala—I could hardly hear you. My ears strained, first one and then the other as I transferred the phone between them, trying to get the best sonic glimpse of your voice. You were in IKEA, getting things for Z. Z was there with you. *Yes, yes*, I said. How had you managed to call, and speak, I wondered, accompanied by Z, in that swarming store? You must have been desperate. Usually you would call from the quiet of an empty room after putting Z to sleep. The pressure was building. You would depart at the end of the week. It sounded as if, mid-store, you'd come down with a panic attack at the prospect of crossing the border, your voice tense, distraught: *Do you think it will be o.k?*

Everything will be o.k., I said. *Of course, everything will be o.k. Don't worry about it. You've planned well. There's nothing to worry about. You've planned as well as you can. You've taken into account every eventuality. You've made your contingency plan. There's nothing to worry about.*

What else could I say, especially at that distance, and with such a bad connection? Of course, I had no idea whether or not everything would be o.k., and you knew I had no idea. You just needed to hear from someone, someone who knew the situation entirely—and that could only be me, or so I thought at the time—that it would be o.k. You had a tendency to mentally compound your troubles, starting with, I'm worried about the upcoming trip, and going to, Maybe this isn't the right job for me, maybe I should be doing something else, what is the point of life? "Keep it manageable" was my message, even if it wasn't manageable, even if there was a lot that was out of our control.

And then we did what we always did at that point (this type of conversation having an almost rehearsed quality to it, so many times had it been repeated in one variation or another), the point where it didn't seem there was anything else to say: We started talking about some case or other, usually the case closest to hand. We transferred our fears and doubts about ourselves, our lives, our situation to others, to theirs. It was a safety valve. The other alternative, which unfortunately all too frequently occurred, was to take out on each other the anger and frustration which could not be directed toward its real target, the dark powers safely sequestered in their lair at Zhongnanhai, and to direct our frustration toward one another was an exceedingly self-destructive way to live, which we both knew, though we sometimes seemed powerless to stop it.

You told the story of a woman you'd just spoken with. The woman was the sister of a man on death row. Her lawyer had put you in touch. The defendant in this case had been convicted of murder eight years before. Just the fact that he had not been executed was in itself a small miracle since capital punishment was usually carried out swiftly after the sentence was imposed, a miracle attributable to the persistence of his lawyer and sister who had repeatedly appealed his case at every opportunity. The prosecution's case was so flimsy that in any country under rule of law, it would have been thrown out long ago, but all the lawyer and sister had managed to achieve at this point was to indefinitely stave off execution. The conviction was based entirely on a confession that the sister and her brother said had been coerced through torture. Besides that, there was no substantial evidence connecting the defendant with the death of another man. The sister and lawyer were getting a toxicologist to run some tests in the hope of eliciting an expert opinion that could be used to exonerate her brother. You marveled at both the sister and the lawyer. Tough women, she said, but what a case! And after listening to them, you felt helpless: what could *you* do? You put them in touch with a sympathetic journalist at one of the largest papers in the world, since they thought some international press coverage might be useful.

I just listened.

Later, you sent me a photo of Z pushing a mini-shopping cart around the store, wearing a paper crown on her head.

A couple of days after the IKEA phone call, I got a letter:

Dearest,

It's grey, grey and grey here. Probably just as grey as London. When HK is like that—grey and a bit cold—there is something heartbreaking about the place. Perhaps it's just the approach of the end of the year, Christmas decorations all over the place, that makes me feel a bit sad. It's not like we've wasted a year, but the thought of the end of it approaching makes me feel sad that time is passing.

I went out yesterday afternoon to meet T. He told me that the HK NGO people who participated in the UPR have been repeatedly approached by people who work for the C government. People who purportedly do 'research', who asked friendly but very nosey questions. This is the first time I have heard this, I wonder what they asked about.

I did some shopping afterwards. I got some embroidery frames to make dressing frames for Z, so she can learn how to zip up clothes, button and so on. Then I went to a Montessori school to look at the materials they sell. The woman whom I spoke with was rather condescending. I left without buying anything. I walked to an art supply shop. On the way there I saw lots of bored maids with children, who instead of interacting with the kids were playing with their cellphones. It makes me sad—that as Z grows up, we have to entrust her to strangers who might not possess the qualities and attitudes we'd like them to have.

The art supply shop was a lot of fun though, and I got a lot of materials for Z. I bought some wooden tablets, and some poster paint. In the evening I made color tablets for Z to match and learn colors. They look good. I really hope she learns to love art. I certainly wish I had had more exposure to all that. I had a classic education that not only under-stimulated me in every way but also a home environment that was anything but inspiring. When you're back, we have to talk about her music education (!). I have some ideas. And in general, we should take her out more often for performances, activities and other things.

As you can tell from this message, I'm feeling a little down. I keep finding myself 'tilting'—like losing center. Part of it is you being away, part of it because of the trip, and part of it just general anxiety that has been going on since moving back here. Yesterday when I was waiting for the bus home, I thought, Why am I not feeling well? Then I realized that I hadn't had lunch. My mind keeps obsessing about one thing or another and never rests. Certainly not really focusing on the here and now. I really need to do something about it. These days I find myself full of directionless anxiety. Or has it been years?

Painting those wooden tablets was calming. I think I'll try to learn to paint. I like working with colors, and painting is therapeutic. Or just some activities where I use my hands to create rather than my head.

I hope your trip to Paris goes well. We'll try to call you in the morning. But in case we don't reach you, please give me a call when you are in Paris. Say hi to W and her boyfriend from me. I hope you had a good day in London and are sleeping very soundly now. S sent me a picture of you holding Z's new Arsenal *shirt. Very very cute. I miss you. Time is crawling, but we will see you soon!*

Love,

Y

It was your last written communication before your disappearance.

During all our years together, we spent substantial periods apart, separated by countries if not continents, and always we had corresponded, communicating, I sometimes thought, even better, more freely than when we were together in the same room with each other.

After you disappeared, I noticed the effects of the years of correspondence: In the absence of your voice, in the silence, not only did I continue sending you my thoughts, but my thoughts became like a ticker compulsively writing your correspondence to me. Perhaps you were writing me mental letters that couldn't be sent; whether or not that was the case, you were writing me letters in my own mind.

I read your letter just before boarding the Eurostar bound for Paris at beautiful St Pancras station. When we'd lived in London, I used to pass by there every day on my way to work and back, about twice a week to buy sourdough bread from my favorite bakery. I rarely had time, but when I did, I would go to the cavernous train hall just to stand and look up at the translucent ceiling held up by its skeletal black cast-iron beams, the enormous clock on the brick wall, the tracks and platforms.

I was going to Paris to see Wangmo. In retrospect, it was a strange coincidence that the visit happened to occur right before your disappearance, since the reason for going was that I had feared my sister had herself disappeared. It had been a long time since I'd last been able to reach her—unusual since she'd always been good at keeping in touch. Not even when I wrote her repeatedly to tell her I would be in London and would like to come over to visit did she respond. I had begun to suspect that something dastardly had befallen her. Only once I'd arrived in London did I hear from her. Now I was going to Paris to see for myself that she was alive and well.

At the bakery, as much for old time's sake as due to actual hunger (I'd be in Paris before lunchtime), I got two spelt quinoa scones and a mozzarella baguette for the trip, a coffee too. I felt shop attendants should have recognized me somehow—I was an old customer, after all—, and I smiled at them the way one does to someone one hasn't seen in some time, a smile of recognition. But this was the big city, and staff turnover was high. I didn't recognize a soul; why should they recognize me? Probably no one there now had been there back when I last came regularly. They must have found my faint smile slightly mad.

Wangmo and I had adopted one another during my time in Dharamsala over a decade ago. She was a refugee from Tibet and, when I met her, a secondary student, though already beyond ordinary secondary age and just about to fail Indian state exams corresponding to O-levels that would allow her to continue to study and obtain a school-leaving degree. It was no surprise she struggled at school, having received no formal education in Tibet. She had no one else in the world, especially after she was deserted by a boyfriend she'd planned to marry. She had not been in touch with her family since the age of thirteen. They were poor nomads in a remote area of Tibet and sent her to Lhasa to work as a domestic servant for distant relatives who mistreated her. She escaped and fled by foot over the Himalayas to India, where, under the protection of the Dalai Lama, she hoped to receive the education she'd been denied in her homeland. After failing her exams a second and final time, she moved to McLeod Ganj and for years worked as a clerk in a shop for tourists, selling t-shirts and souvenirs. I'd visited her several times, but the last visit had been already four years previously. In the meantime, she'd met a man from France. It was not unusual for young Tibetan women to get together with foreign men—or vice-versa, Tibetan men with foreign women—in that tourist town. In fact, it was kind of a cliché, and when I first heard of the relationship, I inwardly rolled my eyes, Oh, no! I was nervous and protective: There were many stories of foreigners making romantic promises to Tibetans that they did not keep.

Wangmo persuaded Tenzin, the Frenchman, who'd adopted a Tibetan name, to take her to France. Shortly after their arrival, they decided Wangmo should apply for asylum on the grounds of persecution in her homeland. Again, I was skeptical: If they wanted to be together in France, why didn't they just marry? Not only that, she'd been living in exile for years: If she were to tell her real story, she could hardly show that she had suffered persecution or was at imminent risk in India. Not long after her arrival in France, I ceased to hear from her. No phone calls, no emails, no replies to mine. Never in all the years I'd known her had we gone so long without being in touch. Fueled by frustration, my imagination got carried away: Had Tenzin done something horrible to her, murdered her perhaps, chopped her into bits, disposed of the corpse, in a place where she knew no one, where no one would notice she was missing or miss her? After all, I hardly knew the man. And Wangmo had known him for less than a year in India before coming to France. Perhaps he had lured her into his lair. Her first reports had been reassuring: It was Christmas and cold, but warm inside his mother's house (such a contrast to Dhasa, where there was no indoor heating and you shivered inside concrete walls). His mother was kind to her, though they had no common language. It was so silent in Tenzin's hometown. Then nothing. With each month that passed, I grew more worried and also guilty that I had not done more to protect her, to ensure her safety. Her whole life long, everyone else had failed her, and now I.

The last I had heard, they had moved from Tenzin's hometown in the provinces to Paris to make it easier for Wangmo to apply for asylum. The day after I arrived in London, she sent me an email, apologizing for having been out of touch and inviting me to visit. I immediately rearranged my schedule, cancelling long-planned meetings, and booked a Eurostar ticket. I was so busy, I could afford to stay for no longer than twenty-four hours.

I spent the ride categorizing the Tibetan self-immolations — number of women, number of men, ages, occupations, monk or lay, locations. I should have memorized all the names and chanted them like a mantra. I'd been asked by a website to write an article about them few would ever read. My main thought while sitting in that comfortable Eurostar to Paris was, 123 people had set themselves on fire, and it made virtually no difference to the rest of the world. What did the self-immolators, all 123 of them, wish to say? Theirs were not acts of despair, at least not in the sense of, say, Mohamed Bouazizi's self-immolation in Tunisia. Bouazizi had been slapped by a policewoman, his wares had been confiscated because he had no vendor's license. It was not the first time he'd been abused by the police. He set himself on fire in desperate protest at his treatment. No stories had emerged from Tibet of self-immolators having been personally targeted or abused by Chinese officials. Their acts could not therefore be regarded as acts of personal despair, though they might be considered acts of national despair: They did it because the point had been reached at which the scope of action for the average Tibetan in advocating for the basic rights of her people had been narrowed to close to zero, the Partystate having shut down just about every avenue, Tibetan areas having become run ever more oppressively according to principles of military occupation and omnipresent surveillance. Even promoting Tibetan language and culture could get you imprisoned. Apart from that, the self-immolations could be regarded as symbolic acts. To take your life for a symbolic purpose might normally seem a poor use of it, but Tibet was not a normal place. The Partystate had already labeled the self-immolations acts incited by the Dalai Lama and decided that its response, as on most every other occasion in its dealings with Tibet over the last twenty-five years, was to clamp down hard.

Who was the self-immolators' intended audience? To the Partystate, the acts were a cipher. As long as it continued to deny the voice of the other, as long as it continued to deny Tibetans the right to express themselves freely, it had no interpretative framework with which to understand the act. The world beyond recorded the self-immolations when they were reported—in itself a feat since restrictions on journalists in Tibet were so tight that the only reports that leaked out almost invariably came through the exile community in India who were in touch with the people in Tibet—, and a great many people the world over sympathized, but governments had taken no action apart from issuing rote statements of concern, asking the Chinese government to ensure religious and cultural freedoms of Tibetans, freedoms that had been missing for a long long time. It seemed the primary audience of the self-immolations was Tibetans themselves. And the message was this: We are all Tibetans. We must stay united in the face of our oppressors. This was something that almost all Tibetans felt deeply, and the self-immolations were an emphatic iteration of it. It was possible that some of the first self-immolators may have wished to set off something bigger. They may have been inspired by Bouazizi and thought an uprising similar to that in Tunisia could be sparked in Tibet. They may have hoped to rekindle the uprising that occurred in 2008. But now, after so many self-immolations had occurred without leading to a general uprising, it was improbable that people were self-immolating with the hope of starting something larger. For now, the uprising seemed to be occurring in Tibetans' hearts.

To light yourself on fire....

A little girl not much older than Z was happily chattering to herself in the seat across from me. I couldn't make out her words, just heard her sing-song voice. I thought of a small piece of paper I'd rediscovered recently when I opened John Ashbery's *Selected Poems* to re-read "Self-Portrait in a Convex Mirror". It was a Starbucks receipt I had been using as a bookmark. On the back I'd written in blue ink row after row of Z's name in Chinese and Tibetan, alternating—one row of Chinese characters, one row of Tibetan, neat and earnest as a schoolboy with an endearing belief in the future, determined to do his best, practicing his handwriting painstakingly, with great care, as if it all mattered, as if everything mattered, every last detail, copying the same characters over and over again. I could still remember the exact details of the receipt: an espresso doppio purchased for seventeen dollars, a fifty-dollar note proffered, thirty-three dollars returned in change, on the seventeenth of June two-thousand eleven at fifteen thirty-seven, a week and eight hours after Z was born. When I re-found it, I showed the receipt to you. Then, after re-reading the poem (which I hadn't read in years), I put the receipt back in the book, wondering how much more it would yellow, cheap receipt paper that it was, how much more the print of the receipt would fade (the characters, I believed, would not considerably—they were in bold, thick blue ink). I wished I could open the book in front of me in just that moment and see the characters again.

You go under a wide body of water and come up in another country. How easily one may cross the border between former enemies! So easily one may not even notice, hardly different from taking the Tube. My SIM card wouldn't work here, the currency was different, but apart from that....

The border you were about to cross separated two parts of supposedly the same country, but one was a place ruled by law, the other a place ruled by force, brutal force: Abandon all rights, you who enter here, the sign above the entrance echoing Dante (*Lasciate ogni diritto, voi ch'intrate*).

Or the tremendous effort to cross the border between our world and the world of the 123 self-immolators. That was why they burned themselves to death, the borders that sealed them in a country-size concentration camp.

•

No one was there to meet me at Gare du Nord. I had no way of contacting Wangmo. I hoped she had understood me correctly. It was cold, colder than London. I stood outside a café at the end of the train platform. I would just wait.

After about fifteen minutes, I saw at a distance a figure approaching, recognizable but older, heavier. When she looked up and met my eyes, I noticed thin lines across her forehead, around her eyes.

A short young woman named Dechen accompanied her. Dechen had herself arrived in Paris from India just three months earlier, she told me. Dechen had gone to Suja, the school where I'd taught, famous in the exile community as the first home in India for many child refugees. We calculated that she was in primary while I taught secondary there, some ten years before.

Wangmo was a bumpkin in the big city. She told me Dechen had had her wallet and other belongings pickpocketed from Gare du Nord and asked me to beware. For them, Paris was not a place of beauty or culture (not once while I was there did I hear them express any admiration for the architecture, cityscape or anything else) but of danger, fine margins, alienation. Though I didn't know my way around Paris at all and could have said nothing about the city's layout or how to get from one place to another, my familiarity with European cities gave me a more intuitive sense of orientation than Wangmo, who had been there for many months, and, as became clear, had during that time had to make her way to many different parts of the city. We would come up from the underground, or find ourselves at an intersection or in the train station, and she would pause, look around, go clearly the wrong way, and I'd pipe up unprepossessingly, *I think it's this way.* And why wouldn't she be like that? She came from the back of beyond in Tibet, a place that, when she left, didn't even have roads. Then she had been living in a small hilltown in northern India, the entirety of which could be crossed by foot in a matter of minutes and had not a single traffic light. And suddenly she found herself in a metropolis and a culture vastly different from her own. From Gare du Nord, we took the Metro to the place she was staying. Upon arrival, Wangmo and Dechen realized we'd taken a roundabout route.

Just a few days earlier, Wangmo told me, after almost exactly a year in France, most of that time in Paris, her application for asylum had been granted. She was safe now; she couldn't be deported. She was on her way to becoming French. She told me the good news in a voice so low I had to bend down to hear. Had I heard her right? I'd been skeptical of her chances: On the surface, her case was weak. And now it had happened so easily, almost as a matter of course—you fill out the form and there you go. In the back of my mind were all the horror stories of rejection, deportation, waiting for years, getting caught in the maw of indifferent or even hostile bureaucracy.

Wangmo and Tenzin obviously knew more than I. What they'd heard about France being a relatively soft touch proved correct.

She sheepishly told me she'd had to lie, testifying that she had very recently escaped from Tibet to Nepal. I wondered whether she had avoided contacting me all those months to be on the safe side: If the French authorities ever bothered to dig a bit, her mere association with me would disprove her story. I also recalled that not long after arriving in France, she'd deleted her Facebook account, another discovery that, at the time, I took to be suspicious—had it not been the murderer Tenzin who had done that? I'd found myself speculating. If she had told the truth—that she had been in India for many years—she almost certainly would not have received asylum. Lots of Tibetans were doing the same in those days, Wangmo said. Her interview had been perfunctory, lasting little more than ten minutes; not a single tough question was asked. She'd prepared by reviewing the different denominations of Chinese currency, in case they tried to trip her up by asking what a particular one looked like (they all have Mao on them! I thought, you couldn't answer incorrectly), but no, nothing like that.

Life in Paris was tougher than what Tibetans imagined, Wangmo said, she herself included, even though Tenzin had warned her. In a place with chronically high unemployment, especially among young people, jobs of any kind, let alone the few that Tibetan refugees with poor French could get, were very hard to come by. A cruel irony was that many ended up working illegally in Chinese restaurants, often as dishwashers. They worked very long hours, much longer than allowed by French law, and it was not uncommon that their employers did not pay them for all of the hours worked. Since it was black work, they dared not seek legal redress for exploitation. They had successfully escaped the Chinese only to find themselves working for them again in poor conditions, in a place of refuge, a supposedly free society with the sorts of rights protections longed for back in Tibet.

In addition to lying on her asylum application, Wangmo also had to ensure that the authorities could, if they chose to investigate (which apparently they did not), find no trace of her relationship with Tenzin. How remiss could the immigration officials be in their work? I wondered, given that Wangmo had initially entered the country on a tourist visa, based on a letter of invitation from Tenzin's father. Maybe I just had a grim view of immigration people as preternaturally suspicious if not hostile; perhaps all this approving was being done in surreptitious solidarity with Tibetans; it was nice to think so.

From the time she'd arrived in Paris from Tenzin's hometown until very recently, they'd lived apart. When Wangmo told about that time, I understood why I hadn't heard from her: She had lived in the city's netherworld. There were no specific provisions for refugees in Paris. If they couldn't find and pay for their own housing, they were considered homeless and had to call 115, the city's hotline for the homeless. They were then assigned a place to stay, some cheap hotel or boarding house or other, which had made an agreement with the city to fill otherwise vacant beds, more often than not in remote outskirts and hard-to-find locations far from the city center. They often could stay only a single night, meaning that they had to move from place to place to place and spent much of a given day just making arrangements for accommodation and travelling from one place to another. At one point, she was able to get a place on a houseboat for refugees moored on a river in Paris (not the Seine, she said, but she couldn't remember the name—Wangmo's hopeless Paris geographical knowledge again). One part of the boat was for men, another for women. Amongst the women were nineteen Tibetans. There were divisions between those from India and those who really had recently come from Tibet. A fight broke out between the two groups, and as a result, all were kicked off the boat and had to resort to calling

115 again. One night, Wangmo simply couldn't find the place to which 115 had referred her, and in desperation, she ended up knocking late on the door of some Tibetans she knew and was given a place to sleep on the floor. More recently, she and Tenzin moved into a room in the rented flat of a Tibetan family. The family had been in France for six or seven years. Their flat was near the Tour Eiffel. Indeed, from Tenzin and Wangmo's fifth-floor window, which looked down on a ever-shadowed courtyard, the very top of the Tour could just be seen above the building opposite, lit up in different colors at night. Strange to be at the heart of everything and yet so invisible, I thought. Now, at least, the two of them were living together.

Tenzin worked long hours at a bar in the Place dauphine near the law courts, on Île de la Cité, just a few blocks away from Notre Dame. He found the job when he came to Paris, had never worked at a bar before. He made 1,400 euros a month, which he considered a fairly good wage. Wangmo got 300 to 400 euros a month in refugee support from the French state. That's what they survived on. Wangmo and I took the RER to meet Tenzin at the bar. We got lost along the way. Then Wangmo noticed police vans parked near the quay, recognized the courts, and knew the bar must be nearby. Many reporters were waiting outside the courts. The day before, an unidentified gunman had walked into the offices of *Libération*, opened fire, and then escaped. Television crews were awaiting news of the citywide manhunt. Tenzin's bar was quiet, though there was a steady stream of customers. Tenzin said working at the bar in winter was easy because there weren't many customers, just people from the courts, lawyers, their clients, regulars. The rest of the year, many tourists came. It was rainy, windy, raw. One wanted to be inside, protected from the weather. There were empty chairs and tables out front on the sidewalk. Tenzin said they filled up in summer. The customers looked like lawyers. They exuded cultured prosperity. Another capital, another metropolis, like London, with wealth beyond compare, wealth that made one wonder, How do they do it, how do they manage to accumulate? From the outside looking in, it seemed mysterious, alchemical. One could easily feel as if staring at the banquet from the other side of the window. But Tenzin and Wangmo did not see it that way. They hardly even noticed the disparity. They had their own goals that had nothing to do with Paris. Paris was simply a means to an end. Now that Wangmo had asylum, they wouldn't be staying much longer.

Tenzin ran the bar with one other young man. I'd seen Tenzin in photos, had talked with him once on the phone. This was the first time I'd met him in person. He exuded youth, health, physical vitality, optimism. He looked younger than Wangmo, *was* younger by about three years. In comparison to him, standing side by side, Wangmo looked worn and weathered beyond her years, diminutive as well. Even to the casual observer, I imagined she looked like someone who had lived a hard life. The extra weight she'd put on was a good thing, as she'd frequently struggled with poor health, especially a chronic stomach ailment that I'd always suspected was psychosomatic. For years, she'd taken Tibetan medicine to treat it. Since she'd come to France, it had largely disappeared. But the extra weight made her look formless and blocky. As a physical specimen, she didn't compare to Tenzin. Was she somehow his pity project? What were the prospects for their relationship? She was of course—as I'd never ceased reminding her, ever since she first told me of the relationship—in the infinitely more vulnerable position.

Tenzin enlisted in the army in his early twenties, for idealistic reasons, to serve his country. (Tenzin seemed earnest to the point of incredulity, the sort who made me question my own skepticism about people's views and motivations, only to decide I was right in most cases but in a few, Tenzin's for example, perhaps I was not.) He was dismayed by how poorly run his army unit was, and dissipated: He became incensed when he saw that those like himself who worked hard and lived clean were overlooked for promotion in favor of those who went along with the general culture of drinking, drugging and visiting prostitutes. He complained about the rule-breaking, which didn't make him popular amongst his superiors; indeed, his superiors refused to act, so he asked to be released from the army. Receiving no reply after many attempts to get an interview with the officer to whom he'd written his request for permission to leave, he left; that is to say, he deserted.

He'd seen a video about Tibetans fighting for their freedom that affected him deeply. Knowing nothing else, he decided he had to offer his help. Off he flew to India. On the plane, he met two Tibetans who showed him the way to Dharamsala and introduced him to their son, with whom he ended up living for some time. That was his introduction to the Tibetan community. Over time, he ingratiated himself with his willingness to fit in. He learned Tibetan and now spoke it with impressive fluency. It was the main language in which he and Wangmo communicated, even as she struggled to learn French. He helped people whenever and however he could. His encounter with Tibetans seemed a kind of religious conversion, a cause in which he could believe, to which he could apply himself. The moral dimensions of the Tibetan struggle and the many admirable people he met who were engaged in it must have stood in contrast to the soft corruption and general lack of purpose and idealism he encountered in the French army. He had found something. Himself. He took a Tibetan name, not for religious reasons, which I had originally imagined, but simply because Tibetans couldn't pronounce his French name.

And then he found Wangmo. Wangmo was not easy to win over. She had seen far too many bad relationships between

Westerners and Tibetans and was skeptical. On top of that, he had had a Tibetan girlfriend before; she was suspicious that he just wanted a Tibetan, a fetish that more than one Westerner in McLeod had. But she heard about Tenzin from many people who all said he was a solid, dependable young man. So she decided to trust him. Not long after they got together, she began speaking of going to France. Tenzin initially tried to dissuade her. *It's tougher than you think*, he said. *Life is not necessarily so happy there, and it will be very difficult for you to fit in and get used to it. There are not many Tibetans. Life is not so bad for you here in India. At least you have the Tibetan community and your friends.* But Wangmo persisted, and he eventually said, *All right, if you insist, but don't say I didn't tell you so.*

While we waited for Tenzin to get off work—he'd arranged with his colleague to leave early, as soon as the bar cleared out, but new patrons kept arriving in small groups of three and four—we had coffee, I warm apple pie with ice cream, Wangmo chocolate cake. *Was he right?* I asked Wangmo. She nodded, a little embarrassed. *Yes, he was*, she said. *Things are difficult here.*

Wangmo was enrolled in free French classes provided by the state and went three times a week, but she had learned little French, especially given that she'd been in the country a year and had had to survive alone on the streets of Paris in recent months. She spent most of her time with Tibetans, and with Tenzin she spoke either Tibetan or English. I took up a newspaper hanging on a rod near the door. The night before, the French national team had a dramatic comeback victory over Ukraine to qualify for the World Cup. It was the cover story. We read the headlines. Then we read the weather forecast on the back page. I remembered from being her teacher years before how hard learning came to her. As she tried to make out what to me with my basic French seemed easy words, phrases and sentence, I thought, This is not going to be easy, living here, learning the language.

While Tenzin and Wangmo prepared to go to France—a long process that entailed collecting the many necessary documents from Tibetan government-in-exile and Indian authorities, not the most solicitous or service-oriented of types—Tenzin's father was helping back at home to get his military status resolved. Eventually politician friends prevailed upon the military, arguing that the officer in charge had acted improperly in not even responding to Tenzin's requests for discharge, and the military issued Tenzin an honorable discharge. This made it possible for him to return to France without facing charges of desertion. Their plans now were to remain in Paris until Wangmo was issued travel documents that would allow her to travel anywhere but China (the country from which she was a refugee, according to official documents—she hated that her country of origin on all documents related to her asylum application was Chine) and then to go to Tenzin's hometown. There, Tenzin planned to buy a small bar where they both could work. That would be their life. They were not city people and did not feel at home in Paris, not to mention the fact that it was very difficult to get by there on their low income. They felt more at home in the mountains. The only disadvantage of leaving Paris was that at least there was the Tibetan community. Their presence was the source of a lot of support. In Tenzin's hometown, there were no Tibetans.

When Tenzin finished work, we thought of touring the city, but the weather was so miserable, we just went back to their place. Tenzin and Wangmo often ate with the family they lodged with. When they found out I was vegetarian, the mother of the house with the help of Dechen prepared aloo momo (Tibetan dumpling with potato filling, nouvelle Tibetan cuisine that came out of its meeting with Indian cuisine) for dinner.

I was often impressed by how well Tibetans had dealt with sixty-plus years of occupation, destruction of their society and culture, genocide, oppression and exile. They had reconstructed in India parallel institutions to those destroyed under Chinese occupation and educated their children as Tibetans in the diaspora. They had maintained a strong sense of their own identity within Tibet in the face of constant attempts by the Partystate to destroy their way of life. They could often appear strikingly well-adjusted in the face of all of the suffering they had endured, but the family Tenzin and Wangmo stayed with reminded me of the high price paid for all that struggle and strife.

The family were rural, salt-of-the-earth Tibetans; the parents had very little education. The father was thin, unhealthy, ghostly pale, drunk. Just looking at him, I thought, A person like that can't live too many years. In the evening, he left the house. I could hear the mother crying in her room—she had been unable to prevent him from going out drinking. He'd promised he wouldn't, but in the end, he did; he couldn't stop himself. He had not had a job in the seven years they had lived in France, nor had the mother; they survived on government assistance. They spoke only rudimentary French. The first time I glanced into the bare main room dominated by a flat-screen television on one wall, I saw the father hugging someone and crying. The father's face streamed with tears, his arms around the other person's broad back. I assumed he was blubbering a maudlin drunken goodbye to an old friend who had come to visit. Later, I realized he had been hugging his son, their eldest child, who was severely mentally and physically disabled. He could not walk or speak. Wangmo told me he slept with his mother, who had to carry him, a heavy boy, a teenager, wherever he needed to go, including the toilet. The two younger children, a five-year-old girl, Dolma, and nine-year-old boy, Norbu, loved to play with Wangmo and Tenzin and spent much time hanging out in their room. They were especially attached to Tenzin, with whom they could speak French, their best language. Norbu was a baby when his family arrived in France; Dolma was born there. They could hardly tell their parents what they had done at school, since French was the natural language in which to narrate and their parents wouldn't understand, so they waited for Tenzin to come home from work and told him. The two children were inseparably good friends. In a tone of strong disapproval, Wangmo told me they already spoke back to their parents, telling them they were stupid and knew nothing.

Wangmo had mentioned there were four children. I had been too preoccupied to notice the discrepancy between that and the number I'd met. The next morning, I asked who usually stayed in the room where I'd spent the night. It was only then that Wangmo told me about the eldest daughter, now eighteen. The room looked like a teenager's, with school textbooks and pop culture artifacts. Wangmo said the father had heard from other Tibetans the girl had fallen in with a bad crowd, *spending time with Africans*, as Wangmo put it. When he confronted her, she rebelled, he hit her, corporal punishment of children being habitual in Tibet. The girl ran away and reported her father to the police. She had not returned since. A post-it note on the wall, presumably written to herself, reminded of an upcoming appointment, suggesting it had been very recently that she'd left. After Wangmo told me this story, I looked at a stack of papers on the desk in the girl's room. They were official letters from Lycée Condorcet, demandes de justificatif d'absence of Noryang Dekyi Namgyal from la responsible de la vie scolaire, Mme PELISSIER. Where had I heard that name before, Lycée Condorcet? Some time later, it occurred to me that Condorcet was Proust's lycée. Strange to think of this Tibetan refugee girl and Proust having attended the same school, even if over one-hundred years apart. Later I looked it up: It had to be among the most illustrious French lycées; alumni included Raymond Aron, Henri Bergson, Pierre Bonnard, Henri Cartier-Bresson, Serge Gainsbourg, Claude Levi-Strauss. It had produced an enlightenment, a culture all of its own. Now it was a school of the underclasses, the newly arrived, from the farthest peripheries of the culture, not even having French as their first language. I doubted Noryang was aware of her lycée's heritage, its pedigree. I wondered, for that matter, how aware she was of her Tibetan heritage and identity. Had her parents ever seen the letters from Mme PELISSIER? If so, had they understood them and responded? (The letters required a response from a parent in order for the student to be formally excused for the absence.) I imagined the girl intercepted them, or the parents had received them and had to trust the girl to tell them what they said. The parents must wonder what had hit them, their eldest daughter slipping away into a world they didn't know or understand, and now even the two much younger ones recalcitrant.

Wangmo showed me a photograph of an essay written by her cousin. He had sent it to her via WeChat, the Chinese app, and then immediately deleted it. The essay was written in perfect Tibetan script—the cousin was clearly making an effort with his handwriting. Its content was run-of-the-mill, calling on Tibetans to not smoke, not drink, not gamble, to only speak Tibetan, pure Tibetan, to teach proper Tibetan to their children. I had seen similar calls in recent months and years. They were an assertion of national identity and a call for self-preservation and cultural regeneration in the face of the threat of Chinese and China. Wangmo showed me another photo that had been sent to her and immediately deleted. The photo depicted the main square of her hometown, a very remote place in Kham, or eastern Tibet Autonomous Region according to Chinese-imposed geography. The recent photo showed the town square full of Chinese troops, even in that out-of-the-way place where nothing ever happened. It had been left untouched by the demonstrations across the Tibetan plateau in 2008 and by the recent self-immolations. Such a large military presence even there showed just how concerned the Partystate was to exert total control. Although the Partystate had managed to establish total physical control over the land and the institutions of government, the sort of mind control to which it aspired continued to prove elusive. I often joked about how some requests the Dalai Lama made of the Tibetan people left them torn. One of these was his call to eat less meat. On the one hand, Tibetans loved meat and it played a central role in their diet and culture. On the other, they wanted to do what the Dalai Lama asked of them. Wangmo told me that in her hometown, lamas had told people to eat less meat out of respect for the Dalai Lama and indeed, that was what the people were doing. That was the sort of influence the Dalai Lama exerted even in remote corners of Tibet which might appear all but cut off from the outside world. It was remarkable first that the Dalai Lama's pronouncements even filtered down to such a remote area and second that all there attempted to live up to them. That was what drove the Partystate crazy and made it constantly accuse the Dalai Lama of all sorts of malevolent plots, the accusations further steeling Tibetans against it. The Partystate could fill every square of every remote area of Tibet with troops, but it could not as easily occupy the minds or the hearts of the people. This was impressive resistance that wasn't even resistance per se so much as Tibetans simply attempting to stay true to who they were. And yet at the same time, the price the Tibetans had paid was huge and could be seen at the level of the family, in nearly every family in one way or another, whether simply separation, as in the case of Wangmo, or outright dysfunction, as in the case of the family with whom she and Tenzin lodged.

Wangmo and Dechen took me back to the Gare du Nord. We arrived early and went to a café across the street to wait for my train. What would become of these people? I wondered. Of their struggle? In twenty years, His Holiness would almost certainly have died. Where would people like Wangmo and Dechen be? Dechen had a degree in English literature from a university in Delhi. She was relatively well-educated. Why did she come to France? I asked. All there is in the Tibetan community in India is schools and monasteries, she said. If you didn't want to be a teacher, there were few other opportunities. There must be more to life, she thought, and if she didn't go now, when would she? We talked about what it would mean that so many Tibetan young people were not settling for India, not content to remain in the Tibetan communities there, but were spreading out around the world, especially to Europe, North America, Australia. Would it lead to dissolution of Tibetan identity and weakening of the struggle? Or would these people continue the struggle in a different way, further internationalizing it? None of us knew. It would depend on people like them, I said.

Just as they had picked me up the day before, Wangmo and Dechen saw me off, and I was gone as quickly as I had arrived. The flash visit reassured me, I told Wangmo. I was relieved that her asylum application had been approved, that she could stay in France and one day become a French citizen. I had met Tenzin and seen that he was earnest, reliable, not a psychopathic murderer, and apparently committed to Wangmo (though I still could not understand why they had not gotten married). She was in good hands, and even if she wasn't, she had the papers that would allow her to live independently. As we hugged goodbye, I said to her, Who could have imagined when last we met in McLeod, the next time would be in Paris?

•

That evening, you departed. It was late in London, morning in HK. Opal and you were due to make your way up to the border around nine, one in the morning in London. I got the first call from you a little after. You were at the border and about to cross. You would call when you got to the other side. I waited five, ten, fifteen minutes. It was possible the immigration queues were long. I tried to call both your HK and mainland numbers—you bought a new mainland SIM card each time before crossing. No answer. I waited another fifteen minutes, tried again. Again, no answer. By this point, more than a half hour had transpired. You must surely have crossed by then—why no answer? I waited fifteen minutes more and called. Again, no answer. This time I also called Opal's HK and mainland numbers. No answer at either of those.

I got a message from the Japanese woman, the one whose responsibility it was, according to the security protocol, to receive periodic communications from you confirming your safety. *There's been a problem*, the message simply said. I called her. She didn't have more to tell than that, simply that she hadn't heard from you either and couldn't reach you.

OK, I said, *what's to be done?*

She replied, *I'll contact others in the organization.*

Will you get back to me? I asked.

Yes, of course, she said.

OK, I'll wait before doing anything else. There are a lot of people to contact. I had a long list, including lawyers in China, others in HK, HK government offices in Beijing and HK that dealt with matters pertaining to HK residents on the mainland, the US embassy in Beijing and US consulate in HK, the Shenzhen procuratorate and central police station, potentially journalists.

Yes, I know, she said. *I have that list too.*

I waited. It was now the middle of the night. While waiting, I called the airline and changed my return flight. There was nothing available the coming day until very late. Perhaps I should have just discarded the ticket and found a flight on another airline, but then, once up in the air, I'd be out of contact for a dozen hours, during which many things could occur- was it not better to remain on the ground for some time in case something occurred or the picture became clearer? I didn't know what to do. I booked the flight near midnight the coming day.

Toward morning, the head of your division called. *There's been no word*, he said. *No one we know has been able to find out anything. We have to assume she and her companion have been detained. We're going to go ahead and contact people. We have our usual list as well as the list she filled out on the protocol form. About contacting relevant government officials in China directly, we've decided to hold off on that for now, as it might blow her cover. If they get confirmation she's one of our researchers, it might actually make things worse for her; she could be accused of being a spy or entering the country under false pretenses. But we will ask US and HK government officials to contact their counterparts in China and enquire. We can't be sure how much the US will do for her, though, given that she's not a US citizen. We will emphasize that this is a US-based organization whose employee has gone missing and is presumed detained. In the past, State Department people have been quite helpful, but you never know. We might ask you to come forward and speak to them as well. We'll hold off on contacting the media for the time being, and I strongly advise you to do the same. It's best to see if, in the first instance, the matter can be dealt with quietly and out of the public eye. Of course, what we want to find out first and foremost is what happened to her. Just getting confirmation on whether or not she is in custody is an important first step.*

Remember, I said, she was accompanied by another.

Yes, he said, *we're aware of that. Unfortunately, her companion is neither a US citizen, nor employed by us, nor working in an official capacity for us, so it makes it hard for the State Department to justify advocating on her behalf. But she certainly will be mentioned to all.*

So Opal had even less protection than you. She must have known that would be the case, but knowing her, she probably didn't even think of that. She was too brave.

By the way, he asked, *do you know what she was doing there?*

Well, yes, she was doing legwork for a potential new report; she was going to attend a conference on domestic violence.

Yes, that's true. It's just that we also have had some indication that she may have been involved in something else as well. That's why I ask. I just want to be sure I have the full picture. It's not very good to advocate on someone's behalf and then find out later you don't know something that can change the way the case looks.

No, I don't know anything else, I said. *If I did, I'd let you know. If I do find out anything, I'll let you know. What is it you're referring to?*

I don't want to say anything more now because I don't know how accurate what I've heard is. That's why I'm trying to check it out.

But please do let me know whatever you do. It's important.

Yes, of course, I will. We'll be in touch soon again to let you know if anything arises and report on contacting these other people.

They seemed to have the situation under control, as much as it could be, all the more reassuring given how little I could do, there in London. Then again, even if I were in HK, there wasn't much I could do. When the largest dictatorship in the world abducted someone, these days there wasn't much leverage.

I contacted Opal's organization. Unsurprisingly, Jeanette knew nothing of the trip. She was alarmed and, I suspected, peeved—it was irresponsible of Opal to just cross the border without letting her know, even if it was on her free time. She said she'd see what she could do, then hesitated. I sensed she was trying to decide whether or not to tell me something. She wasn't the sort to freely divulge.

You do know, she said, *that BY has disappeared?*

No, I said, *I didn't know that. Do you think there's any connection?*

I don't know. I suspect Opal was quite upset by the disappearance.

That was all she said. I could tell she was thinking that maybe Opal and you had decided to undertake a "rescue mission". Was that what your division head had been referring to when he said he'd heard you might be up to something else besides attending a conference on domestic violence? You had been missing only a few hours, and already I had the distinct sense that others knew, or suspected, things I didn't. I did not like that sense.

I had no contact information for any of Opal's family, not even her friends. I felt bad. I wondered whether anyone had told them. I hadn't even thought to ask you about Opal's security precautions. Knowing Opal, there weren't many, and given that Jeanette, Opal's boss, knew nothing, it was safe to assume that was the case with virtually everyone else. There was so much one realized one should have done only after disaster struck.

I got dressed. Upon arriving from Paris, I'd returned to Shanti and Amasis' home. Shanti had already left for work that morning. I'd heard her getting ready and thought of saying good morning and goodbye but figured she was in a rush and didn't want to disturb her. Anyway, I didn't feel like telling her. I don't know why not; she would have been sympathetic. Amasis was still asleep. I went out. Spent the day walking. There was nothing I wanted to do, nothing I wanted to see. I could think of no one to call. It was a lonely day. There was no one to spend it with.

I went over the details of the situation, but there was only so much to think about, given the lack of information. So the mind kept churning the same bits again and again, obsessively, hoping to uncover something previously overlooked, until I told myself it was just as well to try to think of something else. But what? I spent a lot of time just telling myself to keep calm. Was it possible that something else could have occurred besides abduction by the Partystate? Of course, it was, but it was hard to imagine what, especially given that both your and Opal's phones went dead right there at the border.

I thought of other cases of HK residents kidnapped by the Partystate. The most notorious was that of Ching Cheong, a journalist for the Singaporean newspaper, *The Straits Times*. He had covered China for many years, had for a long time worked for an HK paper that was all but a mouthpiece of the Partystate, and had been what I considered a well-meaning but gullible "patriot". It was quite a stretch for the Partystate to see him as a threat. After over one-hundred days under "residential surveillance" (effectively a form of state kidnapping, consisting of being held without charge in solitary confinement at a secret location, denied sleep and interrogated repeatedly—Ching later called it the equivalent of mental torture), he was charged with stealing state secrets and passing them to Taiwan, then inevitably convicted. After he served a total of nearly three years in prison, he was released and returned to HK. The imprisonment had turned him into a vocal critic of the regime, something he had not been previously. He wrote a book detailing the experience, but he refrained from describing the circumstances of his initial abduction, presumably to protect certain people who could be put at greater risk by certain revelations. For that reason, rumors still swirled as to what he was up to, and the one that rose most frequently to the surface was that he was about to receive a trove of recorded interviews with Zhao Ziyang, the deposed Partystate leader who had been under house arrest since 1989. The rumors were credible insofar as nothing was more sensitive to the Partystate than information about top leaders.

Then, more recently, the story of Yao Wentian had emerged. The man was elderly, and when his case was made known to the public, he had already been under detention for nearly three months. He had lived in HK for many years and worked as a publisher but was originally from the mainland. At the time of his detention, he was about to publish a book by well-known Chinese writer in exile Yu Jie that purported to debunk mainland myths and propaganda about Xi Jinping. According to his wife, he'd been lured over the border on an errand to deliver paint to a friend in Shenzhen. He was kidnapped, arrested on a charge the police initially refused to divulge but was later revealed to be smuggling, and had spent most of the time incommunicado in a medical detention center due to health problems. I found it strange that it had taken three months for the news to appear. Even those in HK who paid attention to such things knew nothing about it. Presumably, Yao's wife had wanted to keep a low profile, as the head of your department was advising me to do, and had only gone public when it became clear that the low-profile approach was getting nowhere. She had been made to pay 60,000 yuan to Shenzhen police in order to be allowed to see her husband in medical detention, her one and only visit in three months to the old, frail man. Eventually, at the age of 73, he was convicted of smuggling industrial chemicals with a value of over ten million yuan and sentenced to a whopping ten years in prison.

In both Ching Cheong's and Yao Wentian's cases, there was essentially no recourse. Pressure brought to bear by concern groups and establishment figures in HK did probably lead to an early release in the Ching case. He was well-known and well-established and knew many people, including some close to the Partystate, and that helped. But Yao was an outsider. There were few lobbying for his release, and none with any power or clout in Beijing.

Would your disappearance remain low-key? If it burst into the public domain, it was hard to imagine you would receive as much support in HK as Ching Cheong, but that might be compensated for by more international support. Hard to say, though.

The whole day I couldn't avoid the awareness that I was doing nothing while something terrible was probably happening to you. At that very moment. And the next. And the next. As I safely walked down the street. As the rest of the world went about its business because it didn't know what had happened, and even if it did, it wouldn't matter; it had things to attend to; there were lives to lead.

In the evening, I went to a panel discussion I'd planned to attend before the disappearance. I had nothing else to do—London—the world, for that matter—had become one big waiting room. I arrived early and sat in a café down the road waiting. I had been walking the cold London streets all day and was tired.

It was WZ who had invited me. He was one of the members of the panel. The deliberately provocative title of the discussion was, Is the Dalai Lama bad for the West? The Prime Minister of the UK had just been in China and paid obeisance after having been scolded by the Partystate for having met the Dalai Lama some time before. He and his government had decided in the meanwhile that trade, the prospect of trade, trumped everything else. That was the prompt for the discussion, the idea that Western leaders would increasingly be avoiding the Dalai Lama, and by extension, the whole Tibet issue, in order to not "complicate" relations with the Partystate. Tibet, human rights in general were issues, they calculated, they could do no more than pay lip service to without significant political consequence.

I wasn't particularly interested in the discussion. You could predict virtually everything that would be said. The panel was made up of the usual suspects. These discussions were periodically held, the same old arguments rehearsed, and afterwards everyone went home, no better or worse off than before. It was more to see WZ, and to have something to do, to take in the scene of Tibet supporters I had known so well when we lived in London, that I went.

I sat in the back of the room, by myself. I waved and smiled across the room to people I knew. I always had a compulsion to make myself as unobtrusive as possible at such events, to become the chair upon which I sat. The son of Robert Ford was present, the recently deceased former radio operator for the Tibetan government who was captured by the People's Suppression Army upon their invasion of Tibet, spent years in Partystate prisons as a spy, and upon his release, went on to become a decades-long supporter of the Tibetan cause. Why it should matter to me that his son was there I didn't know, but it did matter; it was somehow heartening.

Before going to Paris, I had had dinner with WZ and his wife, Sofia. WZ was a former student leader in the 1989 demonstrations in Beijing, who, after being released from a spell in prison, escaped to HK together with Sofia, eventually making their way to Sweden, where they applied for and received political asylum. They had been sent to a small town above the polar circle while awaiting a decision on their application, and it had given them a bad impression of the country. As soon as they were granted asylum, they headed for London. They had lived there ever since, in mild, sustainable poverty, he a PhD student, she an artist, both committed activists. We had much to discuss. I considered them great friends, comrades. Sofia had started a new period of oil paintings. Her pictures were amazing—fugitives, passersby, people waiting for visitors, people riding on trains, sitting in lobbies, waiting in waiting rooms. She often focused on those absent in-between moments, was good at capturing their atmosphere. People spent a good deal of their lives waiting, going from one place to another, zoning out, daydreaming, or being stuck in-between.

At dinner, they seemed distant, but I figured I was just imagining that. They were curious about your work. I told them what I could. A big con, I said, was the necessity of travelling to the mainland. You, I said, were planning a trip very soon, and I briefly described the many fears and precautions.

As I sat and listened to the panel, I marveled at how pleasant it felt to be in that warm room listening to people speaking intelligently about something that mattered, even if what they said would have virtually no effect. At the very moment of gratitude for that feeling of physical well-being, a thought suddenly struck me, nearly jerking me out of my seat: Was it WZ and Sofia who gave you away?

It had been indiscrete, to say the least, to mention that you would soon be travelling to the mainland, even if it was friends I was speaking to. Was it possible that they had passed that information on to state security? Were they informers? The idea was absurd, I immediately told myself. That the thought even occurred to me was a sign of how paranoid I had become, suspecting WZ and Sofia. Their dissident credentials were impeccable—they had suffered much. But for that very reason, they would make great informers, the other voice in my head answered. If you had been detained, state security must surely have been on the lookout for you, and how had that occurred? Had it been alerted that you might soon be crossing the border? If WZ and Sofia had informed, then it was essentially my fault that you had been detained. The train of thought made as much of a physical impact on me as the general feeling of well-being a moment before. Panicked, I got up and tiptoed out of the room, closing the door as quietly as possible behind me. Through the small window in the door I looked back at WZ: No, he had not noticed I left, and no, in that moment, he didn't look guilty.

I had to walk, just to keep moving, as if that would shake off the panicky feeling. Walk and walk and walk. Without hardly any forethought, I found myself taking the Piccadilly Line north, like a migratory animal with a certain route preprogrammed into it. It was the line home, our home when we lived in London, which we didn't anymore, of which I had to remind myself now. I got off at Manor House, our old stop, and only at that point said, Well, I might as well. Might as well make my way to our old home, which wasn't our home anymore. We had no ties to it at all, though I might have knocked on the door of our landlords, who lived in the flat directly below our old flat. I didn't though. I just crossed the dark park, the exceedingly dark park, no light in sight in that corner of it—was it that dark when we'd lived there? I couldn't recall—, taking the path I'd always taken to go home, and upon exiting the park, back into the glow cast by the streetlights along Endymion Road, I stood on the pavement on the far side of the street and stared up into our flat on the top floor of 31. The light was on in the window, but I could see nothing besides that. The light was on in our landlords' flat too on the floor below. Hanging on the wall was the mirror with the ornate, thick golden frame above the no-longer-functioning fireplace. The mirror had been there when we lived there, on the floor above. I remembered when I first peered into their flat thinking that mirror overthetop, too obtrusive, though it made the space look bigger, more airy and spacious than it was.

So it was I who had advised you to take the job, I who had assured you that somehow everything would be all right crossing the border, I who had revealed the trip to WZ and Sofia. Was there no end to my culpability? Knew my carelessness no bounds? Had I not sent you, my wife, my love, straight into the jaws of the monster?

I'd thought of you a lot while in London, even before the disappearance. It was a place that meant something to both of us, to our sense of the two of us together. You called our time there our "honeymoon" since we had never had a proper honeymoon and that was where we lived right after formally, legally tying the knot. But what you meant was more than that: You remembered that flat, our lives there, enchanted, without stress, carefree. We were just living, enjoying ourselves, enjoying each other, enjoying our time together, doing simple things. By comparison, now life seemed more complicated, duty-filled, risky, anxiety-inducing, less safe, even before the disappearance.

During my stay, I'd collected things to bring back to you, anything that reminded me of you, of us, of our time there. The "buy one get one half price" books at Waterstone's, an offer we had taken advantage of so often during our years in the UK, going back to your time at university, reading one book after another aloud to each other, a practice that had decreased and then all but ceased during our subsequent life in HK. I availed myself of the offer for old time's sake, getting *The Red House* and *Philomena*, not least of all because both struck me as quintessentially English (ok, Philomena was Irish, but she lived most of her life in England and the writer of the book was a UK journalist). The quadruple chocolate chunk cookies at Sainsbury's that tasted as if made to be eaten with milky tea. Yellow gingko leaves I'd found on the pavement, fallen from a tree above, reminding of the leaves I'd collected from the gingko out front of the department where you'd studied. I pressed them in my London A to Z, itself a relic of bygone times that I'd fished out of a pile of old books before the trip.

I imagined I looked suspicious, standing on Endymion Road staring at the house across the way. I wandered back through the dark dark park, then down along the wasteland of Seven Sisters Road flanking the park, a stretch I'd always avoided when I lived there, so painfully unlovely was it, past the tangle of streets and railway lines and fastfood joints around Finsbury Park station, circling around the mosque and the Arsenal store there, remembering how I would always lose my sense of direction in that tangle and begin heading down the wrong street, and then down Blackstock Road, past Gillespie Road which used to take you straight past the old Arsenal stadium, and if you continued down to the end of it would now convey you to the new one, then past the border where black and brown suddenly turned to white, and then Highbury Park, upscale surroundings, fancy pubs, an organic shop with vegetables displayed like objects in a museum.

The whole walk took place as if in a dream in which, rather than self-locomoting, I was being transported, carried along. At that point, I suddenly realized how tired I was, having hardly slept the night before and walked most of the day up to then, so tired I felt as if I could fold down into the pavement. It was cold, and I wore a beautiful and very warm and long blue scarf a friend had leant me because I hadn't packed enough warm clothes. I'd forgotten how gloomy London could be at that time of year, the temperature hovering just above freezing, the trees having mostly lost their leaves, the days short, darkness descending soon after four. The air was saturated with moisture, such that it was hard to tell whether or not it was actually raining; it was not quite drizzle but there was something in the air. I stopped frequently and gazed up at streetlamps to see if I could discern the fine lines of rain passing through their beams of light. I opened the umbrella, then some time later, stuck my hand out from beneath it to feel whether or not it was raining, then closed the umbrella, only to repeat the process again later. Spitting air. This was the sort of weather, the sort of time of year, the sort of darkness, the sort of night that inspired the phrase, "dark night of the soul", and it felt like that, mine, yours, China's. I could have been in Amasis and Shanti's warm, well-lit den, with good friends, waiting to return to HK and face the fact of your disappearance. But instead, I was walking in the spitting cold. Why prefer the dark night of the soul to the company of good friends?

I passed down through Highbury Fields. I had often passed there walking northward on my way home from work, on days when I forsook the Tube. I'd often imagined us living there, in a flat in one of the beautiful houses bordering the park. It was a vision of safety, security, of being in a place where we could stay and not be at risk. I imagined Z growing up there, playing in the park, going to a school nearby. We would be wealthy enough to live there and to afford Arsenal season tickets. Z and I would walk to the home matches.

Only a few days before, Amasis, Shanti and I had walked through the park briskly, looking for a pub showing the Southampton match. The park was dark except for islands of light over certain areas such as the tennis courts off in the distance. We heard a concerted cheer erupt out of the darkness, emanating from the stadium only a few hundred meters away. Amasis said, *Arsenal must have gotten their second.* We walked faster, to find out what we were missing. On the other side of the park, we found the Highbury Barn televising the match. A strange atmosphere in that upscale place, not your ordinary football crowd, young professionals and so-called creatives, some of whom were more interested in their smartphones than the match. As it turned out, the cheer was for a fine save by Szczesny; the second goal came later, we saw it there in the pub, scored by Giroud from the penalty spot to seal the victory.

I'd never been inside the stadium, though I'd lived nearby all that time. I'd seen many matches televised in pubs no more than a few hundred meters from where they were actually being played. Every game was sold out. Tickets on the secondary market went for over one-hundred pounds. I could never justify paying that kind of money to watch football, even if it was Arsenal.

Amasis had been to the stadium on several occasions. His brother-in-law had season tickets just like his father before him. When Highbury was torn down, they purchased their seats, the actual seats. I wondered what they'd done with them. The brother-in-law sometimes invited Amasis to the matches, who, though a Liverpool fan, appreciated the opportunity, so impressed was he by all that Arsenal did. He marveled at the new stadium (as he did at the Shard) not only as an architectural structure and a venue to watch football (on both counts, he said, it couldn't be beat)—entering that huge space and seeing the perfect green pitch spread out before you as if entering a different world, a perfect world, leaving that other world out there behind—, but also the financial planning genius of which it was a part, a long-term strategy for the club that was in the process of being realized. Yes, Amasis said, Arsenal had to tighten its belt for a number of years in order to make the financing possible, and had gone those years without a trophy, but now it was coming to the end of the lean era and would be reaping the benefits of its earlier decisions, as its current place at the top of the league indicated. Given that he was a Liverpool fan, I thought Amasis very magnanimous.

I suspected Amasis' optimism about the team's prospects on the pitch (as opposed to at the bank) was shallow or premature. Years without a trophy did that to you, made you resist getting your hopes up no matter how good things might look. You knew the ground could always fall out beneath you; it had so many times before. Still, it was not just Amasis's natural optimism, but something in the air—there was a change about the club. It was by far the most likeable collection of players since I'd started following them back in my London years. It was the first time I could remember liking the team as a whole as well as every individual player: Arteta, Wilshere, Ramsey, Özil, Cazorla, Koscielny, Szczesny, Mertesacker, Sagna, Flamini, Giroud, Rosicky, Podolski, Walcott, Oxlade-Chamberlain, Gibbs—genuinely nice guys, the lot of them, hard-working, great team spirit. You wished them well. And they played well together, supporting one another, and also, crucially, winning. They were far from a great team. They were rarely top notch, but they managed to eke out results match after match, surpassing, up to that point of the season, teams that had spent literally hundreds of millions of pounds on player transfer fees. It was strange to think of a bunch of young millionaires as underdogs. You used to be able to recite the starting eleven, but towards the end, you couldn't care less, got annoyed when I asked you to. Of course, you were never interested, but at least once upon a time you humored me.

I had just bought Z her first Arsenal jersey; in fact, the whole kit, with shorts and socks. It was for three-to-four-year-olds; it would fit her like a tent now, but she would grow into it. I'd had difficulty deciding what number to put on the shirt. Of course, it had to have Z's name, not some player's. For the number, I chose eight. I liked the shape. I'd never worn it myself. It was the luckiest number to Chinese. Z always forgot it when counting to ten—one, two, three, four, five, six, seven, nine, ten. (When I'd bought the kit, I could hear her voice counting clearly in my head, and again as I remembered it.) Having eight on her back might act as a reminder. And it was Arteta's number, Arteta the rock of the midfield, responsible for breaking up attacks before they reached the back four, coming out of the back distributing the ball around the field with metronomic consistency, steady, reliable, unflappable, understated, dignified, unprepossessing, the sort who almost invisibly made the team work, drawing no attention to himself except for his black Lego hair that magically stayed in place over the course of ninety minutes. When he came to Arsenal he was an attacking midfielder, the creative playmaker, who got his share of goals as well. He arrived in the midst of a crisis and was converted to a defensive midfielder because that was where there was a gap in the team (one of several at the time). He managed the change well, becoming one of the best at what he did, if largely unsung outside of his fan base. He always did his duty for the team. I was yet to hear of any cringeworthy doings off the pitch or stupid statements of which footballers were so infinitely capable (in contrast to Theo, for example, a very good but gullible guy—when the Chinese Olympic torch came through London in 2008, he was one of the last torch bearers, much to my chagrin; he did it because, being a good gullible guy, he wanted to oblige and enjoyed the "honor" of carrying the torch—a highly dishonorable act under the circumstances—, and because he was entirely naïve about the geopolitical implications of the act, that it was part of a Partystate propaganda exercise, something that he should have at least found out about because of the thousands out protesting against the torch that day, myself and you included; Oh Theo, Theo! you would say, in exasperation, though truth be told, you didn't expect much from footballers). If anything, Arteta was the king of bland, and there was something about that I liked as well. I wondered if he had any opinions on anything not related to football. I was confident that once Z knew who Arteta was, she'd be proud to wear his number on her back.

Now at the south end of the Fields, nearing the Highbury and Islington station, a memory occurred, made piercingly painful—I had to stop to breathe—by the circumstances: In HK, you had come to resent my spending two hours a week watching football. In London, we'd gone to the pub together, and although you were hardly a football fan, you enjoyed the atmosphere and could name the starting eleven, Sagna, Fabregas and Rosicky being favorites. In HK, you became entirely uninterested and went beyond that, resenting me for my time spent watching men kick a ball on a screen, petty, I thought, considering how little time I actually spent doing things on my own (virtually none).

And then I scolded myself: What was I doing anyway at that moment, thinking about anything else but your plight? How frivolous I was, unable to keep focused on the urgent issue at hand, like Hamlet, who one moment resolves that he will think of nothing else but avenging his father's murder...

> *Remember thee!*
> *Ay, thou poor ghost, while memory holds a seat*
> *In this distracted globe. Remember thee!*
> *Yea, from the table of my memory*
> *I'll wipe away all trivial fond records,*
> *All saws of books, all forms, all pressures past,*
> *That youth and observation copied there;*
> *And thy commandment all alone shall live*
> *Within the book and volume of my brain,*
> *Unmix'd with baser matter*

... and the next moment is already bemoaning his fate....

> *The time is out of joint: O cursed spite,*
> *That ever I was born to set it right!*

...thereafter never seeming to follow through on his mission, until, of course, it's too late and all is lost, including his own life. At least, when he got lost in his ruminations, he was thinking tobeornottobe, not Arsenal. I identified with him in his sense of powerlessness as well: What revenge had we for those wrongs done to us, or worse, to those we loved? If anything, the wrongs just showed how powerless we were.

Then again, as long as I could remember, even when people not related to me, people I didn't know personally, suffered some catastrophe such as disappearing down the rabbit hole of the Partystate, I felt guilty for enjoying myself, for lying in my bed at night, having gone to bed when I wanted, knowing I could wake up when I wanted and plan my day in freedom, while they could not.

It was at that moment, now heading south along Upper Street, yuppified, highly commercial, bustling even then in the late evening, that I recalled you had disappeared once before, a kind of practice disappearance, a foreshadowing. Ironically, it occurred in that Northern Paradise, safest of all countries, where nothing ever really seemed to go wrong, a place far away from the risks faced simply as part of doing the sort of work you did in the part of the world where we lived. We arrived in its second city, pretty, orderly, quaint, with a population that would hardly qualify it as a town in China (the whole population of the Northern Paradise would hardly qualify as a city in China!). We were jetlagged from two flights that had already brought us from HK, and hadn't reached our destination yet. We had to wait in that town for a ferry for the final leg of the journey.

We were in its large main square, where a small children's fair was going on, with activities and events of the sort that was inconceivable in HK, where the child, as well as anyone else who could not pay, seemed eternally squeezed out of the cityscape. HK was for capital first, people second. Throughout our stay we were reminded of how the society was one of the few that truly was designed around the child, the family. It seemed so civilized, such a good place to raise a child. Still, there was something a little sad about the place; it was a little too quiet, too peaceful, too perfect, a melancholy paradise. As I'd often heard you say, The problem with paradise is that it's boring.

You were feeling ill, a combination of anemia and a heavy period, on top of which there was the jet lag and a cold coming on. For weeks, you had been looking forward to buying strawberries, real strawberries—the best in the world in our humble opinion—, which you had remembered so fondly, strawberries whose flavor was intense because they ripened so slowly in the cool summer weather. The first thing we did upon reaching the city was to buy them at the open-air market, little red jewels near the end of the growing season. But you felt too ill to eat more than one or two, and even those without the zest you had anticipated. Z, on the other hand, made up for you. All of us were ragged with exhaustion. We had to wait all afternoon for a ferry that would take us further north. Coming from unbearably hot and muggy HK, and having been in airplanes and airports for nearly a day, the cool fresh air was welcome if bracing and seemed to, if anything, make us even sleepier, more in need of a bed, a place to lay our heads.

You said you were going to look for something to drink and asked us to wait for you at the children's fair on the square. Z was stacking giant soft building blocks into a tower, then knocking them down. After some time, she asked, *Where is mommy?* I said, *She's gone to look for something to drink.* By then, you had been gone about a half hour, far longer than it would normally take to find something to drink. Z began to ask, *Where is mommy? Where is mommy?* over and over, the question accompanied by ever more plaintive, louder cries, until I held a sobbing child in my hands who wanted no more than to see her mother again. I had to admit that I did not know where mommy was or when she would return. Given that you were ill, I began to imagine that you had fallen unconscious, had been found and transported to hospital, with no way of telling the people about us or where we were. Our mobile phones didn't work, so you couldn't just call me, nor I you.

I carried Z to the convenience stores around the square to look for you, without luck. I faced a dilemma: Did I search further afield or stay where you had left us in case you returned? What if I went and you returned and couldn't find us? I couldn't believe that you had done this to us—so thoughtless, so insensitive, so utterly lacking in empathy. I had a palpable fear you were gone, accompanied by a feeling of helplessness all the more forlorn for the fact that I held in my arms a small child who was crying for her mother.

And how could you, out of all the dangerous places we'd lived and all the dangers we'd come through, disappear in that safest of all countries? I was reminded of a former student, a Saharawi who had grown up in the refugee camps on the Algerian side of the border with Western Sahara. The refugees' lives consisted of sitting and waiting in the forty-degree heat of the desert, one of the most inhospitable climates on the planet, their history one of outrageous injustice and dispossession, massive violence and expulsion. My student came to that Northern Paradise to tour summer camps of youth wings of political parties in order to publicize the situation of Saharawis and hopefully further their cause in one of the countries that was most sympathetic to them. At the very first youth camp she visited, a lone anti-immigrant terrorist killed 69 people. She hid behind a rock, heard people being shot right on the other side of it, and eventually escaped unscathed. From one of the places on earth most seared by violence, she came to one of the safest, only to come closer to death than ever before. (As a result of being a survivor of the massacre, she was given a spot in the university's Master's in Public Health program. Leave it to that Northern Paradise: It turned a nightmare into a dream come true.)

After about an hour, you reappeared. You had gone to several shops looking for one where we could get cash from buying something with a credit card, as none of our bank cards had worked in ATMs since we'd arrived. Rather than relief at your return, I felt anger and lashed out: How could you do that? How could you not think of us? Why had you not come back and told us that you would be away longer than it took to pop into a convenience store? Did you understand how much you had upset Z? I surprised myself by the intensity of my anger.

Now that you had actually disappeared, now that it was not simply a case of having taken too long to find what you were looking for, I recalled my reaction. And now there was no anger, just desolation, a deep sense of vulnerability, shame.

I passed Bunhill Fields. Blake territory. The ground where Blake was buried, somewhere, no one knew where, amidst the jumbled layers of corpses piled up down through the centuries. It had been a burial ground for "dissenters", "nonconformists", those outside of the Church of England. The ground was closed at that hour. I paused briefly and looked through the gates: So dark within. I had been there many times. I kept coming back to Blake, a touchstone in HK more than London. In London, Blake was history; in HK, the present. I frequently found myself absent-mindedly reciting "London" in the streets of HK: *I wander through each chartered street near where the chartered Thames does flow and mark in every face I meet marks of weakness marks of woe. In every cry of every man, in every infant's cry of fear, in every voice in every ban the mind-forged manacles I hear.*

Was it really so? Did most people really lead lives of quiet desperation? In London, in HK even, things were better than in the early industrial revolution, no?, when conditions were at their worst and exploitation at its most brutal (child labor, chimney sweeps and all). True, the majority of people did not look too happy. But even if happiness were perhaps too much for most people to hope for, there were, were there not?, moments of happiness, high points, small pleasures, creature comforts, such as holding a warm cup of coffee in one's hands, consolations, entertainments, diversions and distractions, enough perhaps to patch together a semblance of a life that rises above misery.

And the mind-forg'd manacles? Blake was a Buddhist in that sense, and yes, the Buddhists were right as ever—most suffering was self-inflicted, mental, though also directly related to social and political situations—that was Blake's genius in "London", seeing the connections between those spheres. Most people worked not very exciting or interesting or rewarding jobs, and far too many people worked shit jobs, almost all of them in undemocratic workplaces doing stuff which, when all was said and done, was of negligible utility, necessity or meaning and could actually be harmful, and yes, there were discomforts and sufferings both physical and mental, and social inequalities that produced misery and were simply unjust, and dysfunctional relationships, and relationships that caused more unhappiness than happiness, and the litany could go on and on, but you could still watch Arsenal, no? And there was art and music, in fact a great deal of it here in Blake's city, including his own room at the Tate Britain. And the museum was free, no less. And one did have one's freedom, to a certain extent. One could go home in the evening, and make of one's home a place of refuge from the cruel world out there. And most people did not have loved ones who had disappeared, who they were powerless to bring back. So, weren't the marks of misery marks of woe, though still true today, only part of the story?

But maybe that was the point: If all there was, was the divertimenti to make up for the essentially unfulfilled life one lead, then what was the point? Life had to be more than just being gradually ground down with a divertimento or two thrown in now and then for alleviation. At any rate, was London now not the sort of place where, for most people, there was sufficient freedom that there was some chance, more than before, of leading the sort of meaningful life that wouldn't leave you with perpetual marks of weakness, marks of woe. More so, no?, than in many places, such as HK, where a relentless turbo-capitalism, without sufficient countervailing, ameliorating cultural and political forces and values, pervaded, saturated people's lives, making it one of the most unequal societies on earth and turning a large number of people into little more than a stock of captive labor. "London" felt real in the streets of HK, looking into the faces of the people, though perhaps rather than outright woe what was most striking was what Thoreau called "quiet desperation", or a sort of zombie-like impassion, a lack of spontaneity, which I associated with the unlearning of joy from an early age, reminding of what you always said: The purpose of an HK education was to kill the child and replace it with an office drone who could be "productive in society". I remembered a Japanese friend who visited. At the end of her stay, she was asked her impressions of the city. *People don't seem very happy here*, she simply said, which rang true. If your parents were posed the question, Are you happy?, they would not know how to answer it. It wouldn't compute. They had spent their lives trying to survive, from paycheck to paycheck, raising their children, who now had substantially better material lives. There was no time to dwell on such questions as happiness. To ask oneself such a question would be a kind of luxury they could not afford, or felt they could not afford. To consider happiness was decadent, self-indulgent, could make them soft in a hard world. Little in their environment, in their culture, in their society would encourage them to ask such a question or to see the ideas implied by it as valuable. One did, simply, what one had to do. A question like, Have you eaten? Or, Are you full? was more concrete, made more sense. Oh, I sighed, at the sudden thought: How would those poor parents take news of your disappearance? Should I not have phoned immediately to let them know? But then, what would have been the point—there was nothing they could do. And maybe, just maybe, by the time I got back, you would have resurfaced, and then there would have been no need to dismay them in the first place.

When I got back to Amasis and Shanti's, they were sleeping. I let myself in. I thought, *This is the last night of knowing nothing*, though I knew there was likely much more of knowing nothing left to come. I took my suitcase and left, without saying a proper goodbye. Amasis helped me out the door, in a rush to get to the airport—the long ride on the Piccadilly Line I had taken so many times before.

The head of your organization called. He'd made the phone calls to the necessary people, who said they'd look into the matter. All counseled silence, not going to the press just yet, at least until it could be determined what had happened to you, the both of you. Even that early in the game, I thought to myself, In such an untransparent system as China's, it was hard to make any progress at all; the only chance was to make the relevant authorities calculate that they stood to gain more by revelation than concealment, by release than detention. After the call, I felt there would be no simple solution, no moment when you magically reappeared and made the nightmare seem no more than a bad dream. No, it was going to be a long slog.

The endless uneventful flight back to HK, over the largest landmass in the world, the Eurasian—brown and brown and brown in various shades and striations thirty-thousand feet below; now over Iran, now Afghanistan, now Pakistan. One could only imagine the various tyrannies and illiberalities that lay below.

I thought of when I tried to make it in time to see my father before he died—the mis-relationship with time: You need to do something fast, but things can only go so fast. You are held in a static force field: Something is occurring elsewhere; all you can do is wait until you get there and hope it hasn't happened before you arrive. Travelling halfway around the world in half a day is spectacular speed, but it feels interminably slow while it's happening. I arrived at the airport, the last stopover on a trip that had already taken me through three other airports, and called my mother from a pay phone. She told me father had died early that very morning, but, she added, perhaps by way of consolation, he'd been unconscious for two days prior to that. In the case of your disappearance, I felt the need to return as fast as possible, but it was illusory, since it didn't really make much difference, did it? What would I do when I got back to HK?

●

What amazed me most was that nothing had changed. After such an occurrence as your disappearance, one expected that nothing could ever be the same again, even if, rationally, one told oneself otherwise. And indeed, people just went about their business, as they had always done, oblivious. But how could they know? There'd been no news. Of course, even if they had known, I wouldn't expect it would affect their daily actions much—it wasn't their loved one and there was nothing they could do. One couldn't simply shake the world by its lapels and say, Wake up! While you go about your business like an automaton, there are injustices occurring. You could do something about that! You could! You really could!

On the Airport Express, the lines from "Musée des Beaux Arts" came to mind as I watched insipid infomercials on the television monitor:

About suffering, they were never wrong,
The old Masters: how well they understood
Its human position: how it takes place
While someone else is eating or opening a window or just walk-
ing dully along;
How, when the aged are reverently, passionately waiting
For the miraculous birth, there always must be
Children who did not specially want it to happen, skating
On a pond at the edge of the wood: They never forgot
That even the dreadful martyrdom must run its course

> *Anyhow in a corner, some untidy spot*
> *Where the dogs go on with their doggy life and the torturer's horse*
> *Scratches its innocent behind on a tree.*

The lines were superimposed on the scene passing outside the window like sub-titles on the infomercials. I turned my head from infomercial to landscape and back, the water on one side, green mountains on the other, then the tunnel, the high-rises, the port. Both the lines of the poem and the landscapes by Breughel that inspired it—winter landscape with bird trap, dark snowy Flemish ca 1550—palimpsested blinding South China Sea sunlight of the early twenty-first century. I used to teach the poem, knew it nearly by heart. The students couldn't love it as much as I; I laughed at their indifference to a poem about indifference. ... *the torturer's horse / Scratches its innocent behind on a tree*, I would think to myself (and sometimes mutter aloud) while staring at their faces, behind which were dreams of... well, what exactly? Video games, facebooking, being out running around, hanging with friends, anywhere else but there. *Children who did not specially want it to happen.* How hard it was to concentrate on anything these days! And why should one, anyway? But most of the students were good, were willing to try. They wanted to care. But wasn't it expecting too much, to expect people to care? The world went on, no matter what happened. The poem asked whether indifference and ignorance were culpable or just the way things were. I thought of Havel's words, something to the effect of all of us being infinitely responsible for everything in this world, responsibility being *that fundamental point from which all identity grows and by which it stands or falls; it is the foundation, the root, the center of gravity, the constructional principle or axis of identity.* Yes, I thought, that we were—responsible for all, for everything. But what could that possibly mean, in practice? Most people in this city, I thought, again looking out the window where, at the moment, no individual people could be easily discerned, everything just a forest of high-rises, they were just struggling to get by, could hardly keep their head above water. How could they save someone else from drowning, or really play any sort of constructive role in the larger world beyond their immediate concerns?

And by the way, when was I going to get my head out of the clouds? Instead of theoretical speculation, I should be going over carefully all of the steps I had to take, all of the people to call, in which order, what needed to be done the moment I stepped in the door in order to find out what had happened to you, and, of course, to attend to Z's needs. I should be thinking about embracing her, putting her first. Yes, I would do that, of course, all of it.

But there was part of me that was resigned. The case would take its due course, and at the end of the day, I feared there was not much that could be done, especially when dealing with an unknown entity, or, to be more precise, a despotic regime that was an unknown entity because everything depended on secrecy. It wasn't a society governed by rule of law. It wasn't like playing a board game with clear rules that everyone followed. No, the whole point of the game was that it was skewed by the people who made it up, and only they knew the rules, if there were any, and even if there were, they could break or change them any time they wanted and didn't even need to let anyone know, because no one knew what the rules were to begin with.

Of course, I would do everything, leave no stone unturned, but at the end of the day, what was there to do?

Approaching HK Station, I thought, People roll in here every day. It's so efficient, so clean, tragically, dreadfully so.

I'd left the students with a question: Is Auden implicitly decrying this state of affairs, suffering here, indifference and ignorance there, or is he just making a comment: This is simply the way it is, whether you like it or not? My problem, I thought, as the train came to a slow halt in the basement station and the doors opened, coughing travellers out into the city, was that there always had been inside of me a loud vicious little man, not too different from a crybaby, who wouldn't accept the way things simply *are*.

Z had made a sign for me, a kind of collage. White hearts on black construction paper. At the top, in yellow and orange, Welcome home baba. After it was written, she smeared the letters, making it just barely legible, a stroke of genius that made it look all the cooler. She remembered she and I would make such signs whenever mommy came back from her mainland trips. Z might have sensed just how relieved I was to see you upon your return, without knowing the reason why. You had helped Z to make the sign before departing for Shenzhen, expecting to be by Z's side when she gave it to me.

After Z went to bed, I opened a book, Gordimer's *Burger's Daughter*. It happened to be lying on top of a shelf, where it had been since before I'd gone to London, a sign of the constant disarray of our home, perpetual action, perpetual motion, perpetual mess. It was a library book, probably overdue. Before London, I had been trying to get through the book, reading it in fits and starts in between other books, which in itself was not unusual as I was typically reading five or six books at a time, like a halting juggler who somehow just managed to keep things aloft. It was admirably well written, imposing, a clear accomplishment, an edifice, but like taking medicine, so disciplined was it, so diamond-hard, so adamantly not about what it was about, so stringent, severe in its strictures against sentimentality. I happened to turn to a page I had already read, a certain passage that even upon first reading had caught the eye: *Even animals have the instinct to turn from suffering. The sense to run away. Perhaps it was an illness not to be able to live one's life the way they did... with justice defined in terms of respect for property, innocence defended in their children's privileges, love in their procreation, and care only for each other. A sickness not to be able to ignore that condition of a healthy, ordinary life: other people's suffering.* Taking the words in, I felt a bit like those believers who think that in time of need, you need only open the Bible to a random place and find the message from God that was meant for you. Then again, the epigraph to that part of the book seemed to suggest the opposite: *To know and not to act is not to know*, from Wang Yangming, Neo-Confucian scholar/philosopher, Chinese no less.

3

Even a few days after the disappearance, I could still, if I so chose, continue to doubt that you had gone. Well, not exactly that—you *had* gone, you were not there; that much was clear. The doubt was that you had been abducted, for there was no sign of what had become of you.

And half the time I did so choose to doubt, but the other half I thought there was no use deluding myself. She is gone, most likely abducted—I repeated this to myself, to try to convince of what would, I imagined, be obvious to any objective observer.

I thought of wives of sailors and fishermen who in ages past waited for their husbands to return from sea. At what point, if ever, did they just *know* they weren't coming back? There would have almost certainly been some who refused to let hope die under any circumstances: At what point would they have been considered deluded?

In our case, there was still hope you would return. You were not swallowed up by the sea but, most likely, by the largest dictatorship in the world, which, whatever its multitude of evils might be, had reason to keep you alive. So I chose to believe. The belief was based on its recent track record: It had gone out of the business of flash extrajudicial executions, and the number of out-and-out terminal disappearances had also decreased in recent years.

That said, short of a bullet to the head (and one should not forget it had been the world leader in judicial murders for many years now), the Partystate had a large catalogue of methods of inflicting horrors large and small. As a suffering-infliction machine, it was well-tuned, well-calibrated, hard to beat.

So there was hope. And worry. Plenty to hope for, and worry about.

In the absence of any information at all, I found myself even thinking that perhaps you had engineered the disappearance, had run off, a possibility the rational side of me discounted but that existed nonetheless. It wouldn't have been like you even if Z were not part of the equation. It was hard enough to imagine you running off from me, even if that was what you wanted to do, but virtually impossible to imagine you abandoning Z. But then again, anything was possible, and the non-rational voice was loud, often persuasive. Perhaps you were somewhere far away beginning to lead the life you had always wanted to lead. Perhaps you had gone off with another. People do crazier things.

I thought of other relationships in which pre-existing tensions were exacerbated by persecution, separation, detention. Nelson and Winnie. Hu Jia and Zeng Jinyan. Neither relationship survived the release of the incarcerated half, or, to the extent it had, in a much different form. After Hu Jia got out of prison, Zeng Jinyan moved to HK and took their daughter with her. The house arrests and harassment had simply gotten too much for her. Was it too much to expect that at least the child should be able to lead some semblance of a normal life? There were too many things she wanted to do that proved impossible in a life circumscribed by forcibly restricted movement and constant surveillance. The escape to HK was to give their daughter the chance to grow up freely but also so that Zeng Jinyan could pursue interests other than being the wife of a persecuted activist. She was still young; she wanted to do things with her life.

The regime allowed her to leave. While Hu Jia remained under house arrest, she started a PhD program in HK and her daughter went to school. They were relatively free but their life remained topsy-turvy. I recalled one incident: It was Hu Jia's fortieth birthday. He wanted to see his daughter. Somewhat surprisingly, the regime allowed him to travel to Shenzhen. Jinyan sent their young daughter across the border to see her father and attend his birthday celebration. Her presence was his best birthday present. Several relatively prominent and active citizens (I hate the word "dissident". See Havel's "The Power of the Powerless" for a critique of the term) organized a dinner in his honor.

The police and Guobao agents raided the party and detained the celebrants, including the birthday boy himself, but made no arrangement for his daughter. She ended up being looked after by a friend of a friend who managed to get her back across the border to her mother. Hu Jia was released soon after and returned to house arrest in Beijing, having seen his daughter for no more than an hour.

In both Mandela's and Hu Jia's cases, it was the one outside prison, the woman, who drifted away, who ended up displaying what seemed from afar a faithlessness when the other half needed her most. But I'd seen enough of the havoc wrought by the Partystate on families to know better than to judge anyone affected—the story was always complicated. One of the clearest patterns amongst victims of persecution was the enormous strain it put on families, and indeed, the Partystate had a tried-and-tested technique of making the family suffer for the "sins" of the individual.

My mind, almost like a homing device, continually searched for precedents, points of comparison, to gain traction on an uncontrollable, unknown reality.

For the first time in my life, I had difficulty sleeping. I would lie awake, next to sleeping Z, thinking about you, wondering where you could be, what had happened to you, how I might be able to get you back, but the thoughts went round and round in circles, never coming to any conclusion. I only hoped my insomnia wouldn't affect Z, seep into her, so to speak.

Then there was the panic at now being a single parent, left alone with Z. That was the least rational reaction given that, for a long time, indeed most of Z's life, I had been the main caregiver, the one who filled in when you were too busy. Even when you felt the most alienated from, angry at, exasperated by me, you would always acknowledge I was a good father. Z herself was Exhibit A testifying to her father's indispensability, with her constant, *I want baba*. Well, now she had him, and only him. But then, however irrational that panic at being the sole provider, it was as if the irrational was taking over me; I felt invaded by my emotions. It was all I could do to hold them at bay. And I was hardly one of those men who never allowed himself to feel anything; if anything, I'd always chided myself for being too governed, too influenced by emotion.

And then how to explain to Z her mother's disappearance? Nothing prepares you for explaining to a young child why her mother is not there.

I kept it vague and simple, explaining that mommy loved her and wanted to be with her, but would be gone for some time. She would come back, hopefully before too long.

Z picked up a bread cookbook and said, *This is the bread book for mommy, this is for making bread for mommy*. She studied it as if by doing so, she would divine just how it was done, as if there was a magic recipe for bringing mommy back—if she made the bread, mommy would come. Mommy had always made bread for baba and Z; now Z was making bread for mommy.

●

Soon after returning to HK, I awoke one morning very early, before Z, and stared at two photos of you.

In one, you are shirtless, in profile. It was taken the day before Z's birth. You look pale and exhausted, your back bent forward in a posture that looked certain to be painful if maintained for any length of time, pulled that way by the weight of the huge stomach. The photo was my idea: I wanted to remember what you looked like right before giving birth, and so I asked you to stand in profile to emphasize the largeness of the stomach. You posed grudgingly, in the apprehension that the photo would be perhaps not the most flattering. But that was what I wanted: the exhaustion of pregnancy preserved for posterity. The image was of poor quality—I had always been a poor photographer, unlike you, whose images were always well composed, technically adept. The day after the photo was taken, you walked to the ferry pier, took the ferry, went to the hospital, and gave birth.

The other photo was framed and hung on the wall of your office. It was the only human image of any kind displayed in the flat. There, too, the belly was featured, the belly with Z inside. You sit on the rock beach out front of our old house, the one from which we were expelled two months later. It was not long before the birth. You are wearing a black tanktop, light tan linen trousers. The stones on which you sit, and which surround you, are a lighter shade of tan, some tending to white. And round, sea-polished, so round, round like your belly, as if in sympathy with it. You are turned full face toward the camera. I am about to be a mother, the expression says, and just as the other photo showed the way that pregnancy could wear a woman down physically, this one showed its beauty, its grace, its dignity and calm.

I felt a flood of tenderness: The images recalled to me why we were together, which was no reason, for they were themselves the clinching argument in divine court in the case of the relationship's legitimacy, its raison d'être. Yes, they said, we have counted for something in this world, in spite of it all. The shared joys, all that we had endured as accomplices and companions, perseverance in itself a victory over the elements, against the odds, over the hostile gods. Why should it not continue to be so, I asked myself, even in the new dispensation? That person, I thought, that person is gone.

You had been scrubbed clean from reality, drug down to the netherworld. Your organization, Opal's organization, other human rights NGOs, the US embassy in Beijing and its HK consulate, the HK government—some of these entities working with much greater motivation and determination than others—had together managed to find out nothing. Nor had the media picked up any trace, even though there were some pretty good China reporters with their noses close to the ground, people who often found out things before we did. All Partystate elements contacted through various connections had nothing to say, nothing to divulge. That was expected; they were contacted only in order to cover all the bases, and to signal to the Partystate that the US and NGOs were aware of the situation. I assumed the HK government had done the same, though maybe not, so normally prostrate was it before its master. If there was a choice between searching for one of its citizens most likely kidnapped and avoiding the displeasure of the Partystate, I had little doubt which the average HK official would opt for.

Then Opal was released.

Her mother had notified me beforehand. I had been the first to tell her of her daughter's disappearance, days after it had occurred. Of those few who knew, no one else had thought to, no one else had bothered. And now she called me, in the middle of the night, because she had been called, in the middle of the night, anonymously, and told to go to the Lo Wu border crossing the next day. No time. Just the next day. So, along with her mother and friends, I met her there, nearly two weeks after the disappearance.

When I got Opal alone, she was able to tell me, well, if not much, at least something, something that excluded some remote possibilities and sent me down a track, however faint, where previously there had been no track at all.

Opal had been hooded and led out of her place of detention. She didn't know where she had been detained but assumed it was a secret detention facility run by the Guobao and used exclusively to detain those under "residential surveillance". Once in the center of Shenzhen, she was unhooded, escorted to the border by security agents, expelled. But strangely, her home return permit (the travel document allowing ethnic Chinese HK permanent residents to enter and exit the mainland) was not confiscated. It was standard Partystate practice to strip "disloyal" HKers of the document, thus preventing them from entering the mainland. There was no recourse if that occurred, and you didn't know if you'd ever have a chance of getting one again. Had the Guobao simply overlooked cancelling the home return permit, or was there some dark intention behind the omission?

In her typically phlegmatic way, Opal explained that nothing much had happened in detention—the usual, she said: sleep deprivation, solitary confinement, constant interrogation, though even that seemed pro forma, as if the interrogators were just going through the motions.

The interrogators' questions kept circling back to your connections, not Opal's, even though Opal was just as well if not better connected, often with the same people. Opal suspected they didn't really want to get much out of her, and were not interested in her per se; the main reason she was being held was so that she could not immediately alert anyone to your disappearance. She was not surprised by her rather quick release.

Opal took it all in stride. She was only worried about you. She wanted to go in search of you immediately. She still had her home return permit in hand, after all; she could set off that very day. I restrained her. Let's just reconnoiter a bit more first, I said.

There was no one looking out for Opal, no big organization, no network of established people with any pull. She was on her own. The Partystate could have held her indefinitely, and the rest of the world would have hardly raised a finger; she was the proverbial nobody. She was fine with that. She liked it that way. She didn't expect anything else. She came from small potatoes, she was a small potato, she was proud of that, it was her strength. Of all the people I knew, she was amongst those I admired most. Integrity, courage, honesty, conviction: There didn't seem many these days who possessed those qualities.

It was on such nobodies, I thought, the future of the world depended, the deceptive sing-songiness of Dickinson's poem in the back of my mind—*I'm Nobody! Who are you? / Are you—Nobody—too?* Others, though skilled and useful, were too intent on enhancing their reputations, furthering their careers, guarding their gains, middle class, middle of the road, content with the lives they lead. There was room for that, a need, but it was not from there that the impetus for progressive change would come. At most what that establishment could do was play a supportive role for the small potatoes like Opal, when (or, more accurately if) they ever decided in sufficient numbers to take matters into their own hands, to stop being molded by others, for the benefit of others. Regardless of what the other small potatoes would do, Opal would not be molded by anyone except herself. I wasn't confident she would win. I didn't doubt her ability; I doubted the propensity of a critical mass of people from her background to become enlightened enough to act as she did, to become active citizens asserting their rights.

One could argue whether it was out-and-out torture or simply "other cruel, inhuman or degrading treatment", but any way you looked at it, Opal had been abused by the Partystate. It had made perfectly clear to her that she was entirely at the mercy of an entity not known for its mercy, and she was no worse for wear. At least on the surface. One could never be sure beneath that. Victims of the regime bore their scars in all kinds of ways, some more manifest than others. She was a grounded person. She grounded me. When my imagination threatened to embark on a flight of fancy, my emotions to get the best of me, she brought me back to earth, just by being there, being who she was. She never reprimanded me, but the way she looked at me said, *Get your act together.*

She seemed reluctant to divulge, as if to do so was to betray you, or reveal something she had promised to reveal to no one, and she did so only because she felt pity for me, also perhaps because she thought it might help to obtain your release. And after all, I was your other half, and even if you had not told me yourself... but why had you not told me yourself? I could see this line of thinking zipping through Opal even as she composed her speech to me. She was a bit taken aback at how little I knew, and she wondered why. You had told her the mission was top secret but apparently not just how restricted knowledge of it was.

It was disconcerting to discover that, even though you had not run off with someone, you had most likely been keeping things from me. What I learned showed you in a much braver light than you usually painted yourself. You constantly characterized yourself as unfit for this sort of work, having fallen into it, a case of mistaken identity. You admired your colleagues across the border who were really taking risks and suffering for their commitment and said you could never do that, even before having a child, and now, as a mother, you were even less inclined to. But here you were, and why?

And why the need to withhold, deceive (if indeed, you had)? And why? And why?

What Opal told me: You and she went through immigration together in the same queue, you directly in front of Opal. You'd thought of going into separate queues, to avoid any appearance of being together, but then decided to stick together, still making sure that once you were in the same queue, you didn't speak to one another or give any other indication that you were together. You just wanted to keep an eye on one another. Up to that point, Opal said, there wasn't any more than the usual nervousness about crossing the border. In fact, you seemed optimistic, if anything, that things would go fine. Then again, Opal was such a cool cucumber, she may not have been the best judge of your anxiety level. I imagined that, if it was as usual, you could hardly contain yourself, even if you might have appeared perfectly composed. As you stood at one window, Opal, behind you, went up to the one next to it. Opal kept her eye on you and saw that a group of four immigration officials approached the window and lead you away. She followed you with her eye until she could see you no more, her view increasingly blocked by the hordes of other border-crossers, but it looked to her as if you were being lead in the direction of a series of rooms resembling offices, or perhaps interrogation rooms. At that point, she began to think something had gone wrong, or was about to. When her home return pass was handed back to her by the mainland immigration official, she actually tried to wheel back in the direction of HK. At that point, as if by magic, her path was blocked and she was surrounded by a group of, well, she couldn't be sure, immigration officials or police or officials from some other security entity. Some of them were plainclothes. She was encircled, lead away. She remembered having the distinct impression, These people know what they're doing; they're well versed at their art. She wondered what would happen if she put up a struggle, made a fuss. She said, in Putonghua, something to the effect of not wishing to cross the border after all. But she was being firmly guided. She felt the eyes of the crowd upon her. I knew that stare, I'd seen it—the un-shy gawking that was pure curiosity without a shred of empathy. It's not, We're on your side but can do nothing about it, but, Oh, how curious! Something to entertain us in the midst of our dreary day, like an animal in a cage at the zoo. But Opal's was a relatively hushed procession amidst the general hubbub and commotion of the crossing point (she wondered whether she should have shouted and tried to gain attention), and it was only those in the immediate vicinity who enjoyed the mildly entertaining distraction—something just vaguely out of the usual (...*How everything turns away / Quite leisurely from the disaster..*, coming back to "Musée des Beaux Arts")—from their wait.

And then she was in a room, and it was, she knew, too late. Strange the mechanisms of apprehension: *It was the sort of thing*, she said, *where, if you imagine it, or before it happens, you think you will be able to avoid it, to deal with it effectively, but when it comes upon you, it is just there. One moment you are free and the next, you are not. In that split second, regret for what you might have done but did not sets in. And it's a regret that, depending on what they do to you, could last a lifetime.*

She was, to be precise, apprehended even before she'd crossed the border and entered the mainland. I did not know if there was any legal distinction to be made there, but it seemed there should be. Was she technically kidnapped from HK? From no man's land? From what was officially designated a "Frontier Closed Area"?

From this point onward in her story, she no longer spoke of herself, her experience, her predicament, unless prompted to do so by a question I had for her, but instead, speculated about your fate.

You see, she said, *that was the last I saw of Y, when she was lead away from the immigration window. So, of course, I assume she was taken into custody, but I can't say I actually saw that occur with my own eyes. I mean, what else could have happened to her, especially considering what happened to me? I was taken into custody, no doubt about that, no doubt about that at all. Where she could have been taken, I don't know, but I imagine it couldn't be far away. I wasn't taken far away. But you never know. She might have been more important* than me. People have been known to have been whisked off as far away as Beijing. It all depends on exactly who took her into custody and what for.

I was interrogated there, briefly, just, you know, what are you doing in China, who did you come with, where are you going to stay, for how long? I had an alibi. My dad lives in Shenzhen, with his mainland wife—you know he totally deserted my mom and me, disowned us to all intents and purposes—and I'd arranged to stay with him, he thought I was coming. Call my dad, I told the officers. They just stared at me. I still don't know whether or not they ever called my dad. My dad wouldn't have liked that! To hear from the Guobao! He would have blamed me for it. They later said they had and that he wasn't expecting me at all. Knowing my dad, he could have been scared when he heard from them and denied ever knowing me, ever having had me, let alone that I was intending to visit, but he isn't such a nob that he wouldn't have been worried about me at all. So who knows what he actually told the Guobao. He might have told them the truth and they just lied to me. I haven't tried to call him since I was released. I don't know if I will. I supposed I will, some time. I wonder if he wonders what happened to me. He doesn't have any contact with my mother and never called her while I was away.

Anyway, they took me from there to a nearby police station in a van. And that's where the hood came out, and I thought they transferred me to another van, probably one without windows you can see in, and I guess it must have been a half hour to an hour we drove from there. I imagined I was in some place on the outskirts of the city, or some place surrounded by villages. Anyway, the whole time I was there, I was in a room without windows, and I could hear no sounds outside, so I never had any sense of where I was—that was the point of course, to disorient you. They just asked the same questions over and over again in different ways. And for a long time didn't let me sleep any more than a few hours at a stretch. It was painful. They told me what I've always heard they tell people in situations like that: You'll never get out of here unless you confess. You're so predictable, I thought. Confess what? I said. You know, they said. Know what? I said.

But I have to say, being in a situation like that, well, it does rattle you a bit. (A bit, I thought. Only Opal: a bit!) You know, it's almost a physical effect on your body; it dislodges you from your right mind. They put you in a situation where you want to do anything to please them. I think just knowing a lot of people who've been in a similar situation helped; I knew what to expect, I knew what those people are like and how they operate. I wasn't taken by surprise. But it still has an effect on you. But anyway, what could I tell them?

Here, Opal smiled her sly smile that said there was something else she could tell them (and me) but didn't (and wouldn't?).

They wanted to know the usual, what we were doing, where we were going, where we were staying, who we were planning to meet. So they just assumed we were together, though I never told them that, which means they must have got that from somewhere. They also wanted to know what my relationship with my organization was—it seemed they weren't certain whether or not I actually worked for them. The only thing I gave away was that Y and I were travelling together. I hope that wasn't too much. I hope it didn't contradict whatever Y said when they asked her. Knowing her, she might have wanted to protect me and denied we were. But we'd agreed a story in advance. We were going to a conference about domestic violence in Shenzhen that weekend. We wanted to find out more, and we wanted to meet people working on domestic violence and talk to them. No more, no less. I was going to stay with my dad, go to the conference, and come back to HK at the end of the weekend.

Yes, I said, *that's what she told me.*

O smiled her sly smile again. Well, she said, *there you go.* And then, resuming her tale, Round and round it went, she said, *in that way, the same questions over and over again.*

It was funny and terrifying and sad how much they knew. They knew everything about the 'champagne assault'. I used that to my *advantage. I just claimed I was a grassroots HK activist and through that, had met people like Y. Who else did I know? they asked. Just the usual suspects in HK, I said. They didn't get much out of me. That's the advantage of always appearing up front, ready to talk. You know, you all criticized me for 'going to tea' in HK with those Beijing thugs when they requested it. You said I was under no compulsion to do so and just drew attention to my work and maybe the work of others, perhaps putting them at greater risk. But hey, they know me as someone upfront, with nothing to hide, and that makes it easier to hide things,* she said, with her sly smile. *They didn't get much out of me, I say. I think they figured out pretty quick that I didn't have much to tell them, and the only reason they kept me for so long was so that I couldn't sound the alarm about Y. Even when I was there, I strongly suspected it was Y they were really after. They had something on her, or thought they had.*

So, I said, finally asking the question I'd been waiting to ask: *What was it you were really up to?*

Without hesitation, as if she'd been waiting for the question, Opal responded, *We were headed to Hebei.* She looked around, then leaned toward me, her shoulders hunched, her voice dropping, a caricature of someone with something to hide. Surely, if we were being monitored, this would be the point where the spies would crane their ears. But then, after the initial revelation, she seemed uncertain, uneasy, reluctant about how to proceed. Perhaps you had told her to not tell even me, though by Opal's bewilderment at how little I seemed to know, I guessed you hadn't.

Hebei?! What for? Hebei wasn't just around the corner; it was way up north, abutting the capital. One would have normally taken a plane to get there, not crossed the HK land border.

We were going to take a train, an overnight train, all the way up there.

Yes, and...?

We were going to try to find BY.

At the sound of BY's name, things began to fall into place. But Opal could surely tell from my face that I was still perplexed.

Yes, I'm not surprised you don't know. Hardly anyone knows yet. BY's disappeared.

BY?

You didn't know, right?

Well, Jeanette mentioned it to me when I told her Y had disappeared.

The few who did didn't want to tell anybody else until we could figure out what had happened. That's why we went.

I had met BY twice. She came to visit us once on the island together with three other women. They were passing back through HK on their way home from a workshop abroad. One was a tough-as-nails veteran Shanghai petitioner with a deep hoarse voice who'd been in and out of detention for years. I wondered what she had been like before her numerous confrontations with the regime, which, I imagined, had hardened her considerably. But BY was just the opposite, quiet, sensitive, modest and deferential, though the monster had done much to break her as well. She had that older-than-her-years look of many of the citizens who'd been persecuted, but there was also something girlish about her, young and innocent and kind, open to the world. We took the four women to the beach. They rolled up their pant legs and waded in the warm surf. BY said it was the first time she had ever been to the sea. It was easy to see from the look on her face what a special feeling it was for her, the thrill, the wonder, feet pressing into the soft wet sand, water washing over ankles and calves—sun, sand, water and fresh air offering a hint of freedom, release.

BY's history in the struggle went way back. A student demonstrator in eighty-nine, she married a man who was a student leader. He was imprisoned for his role. After he got out, he continued with activities that angered the Partystate, and before long, found himself back in prison. Thus started a pattern of imprisonment, sometimes for years at a time, and release. In addition to his political activities, BY's husband was also a well-known poet. Over the course of the serial imprisonments, BY stood by her man, but the stress of the experience eroded the relationship, and shortly after one of his more recent releases, they divorced, more at his initiative than hers, though I had always sensed something in her was relieved. In spite of the divorce, whenever the husband was subsequently imprisoned, it was BY who visited him, delivering requested items, and arranged his legal defense. They had a daughter, and because of his long absences due to imprisonment, BY was all but left to raise her alone. After the divorce, the daughter continued to live with BY, and her father played ever less of a role in her life. BY dedicated herself wholeheartedly to raising the girl.

By virtue of running in similar circles, she came into contact with the network of human rights defenders for which you worked, and within a relatively short time, due to her competence and reliability, the same qualities she had shown throughout the years as the wife of a branded "dissident", she gained its trust, to the extent that she became one of the few communications hubs between its discrete elements. She threw herself as wholeheartedly into the work as she did into raising her daughter. She was a great logistician and fixer, the sort who figured out how to make things work in difficult if not sometimes impossible situations. She never lost heart, even at desperate moments. Her ex-husband's imprisonments proved good training in courage. She kept her head low, trying to remain as invisible as possible, since invisibility was key to her effectiveness—she was a facilitator, making things happen for others. She was humble, low-key, dedicated, loyal, selfless—she never let her own needs or desires get in the way of the work. She was the sort of person every organization needs, especially one operating on such few resources in such a risky, hostile environment.

You had a saying about the active citizens of China: The men talked, the women got things done. This was especially true of those of the older generation, the so-called eighty-niners, who got their start as students in the Beijing demonstrations and then, after their imprisonments, persevered. The men were the "theoreticians", the women the doers. You often found yourself rolling your eyes at the men's long-windedness, their need to be the center of attention, their lack of practicality or creative thinking about how to actually accomplish what they talked about. And BY was your exhibit A. That didn't mean she never attracted the attention of the authorities. Indeed, she was at particular risk because, on the one hand, she knew so many others and, on the other, she was so unknown herself. Due to her husband, she'd always been monitored, but the Guobao's suspicions of her probably grew in connection with its latest crackdown on the New Citizens Movement.

Whether because of her own work or her husband's, her daughter was prevented from attending university, even though her gaokao score qualified her for a relatively competitive place. That was a clear warning signal to BY, who had been saving up for her daughter's university education for years. She took her savings and borrowed from others in order to send her daughter abroad to study. Though she missed her terribly almost from the moment she left and suspected it was the end of her daughter's future in China, the beginning of her life elsewhere, she was relieved to get her out of the country. She had always feared the Partystate would make her daughter pay for her parents' "sins". Now, with her daughter out of harm's way, she had, as she saw it, nothing to lose.

You had immense respect and affection for BY. In a way, the two of you had been the organization's most indispensable workers, the one inside, the other outside the country. But you never forgot who was at greater risk. When you decided to leave the network and go to the big prestigious international human rights organization, the hardest thing to say goodbye to was the close and excellent relationships with colleagues you admired, BY more than anyone else. It wasn't hard to imagine that when you heard BY had disappeared, you felt personally responsible to her.

Well, what do you know? I asked Opal.

Basically, BY played a much more central role in the NCM than anyone suspected. And the NCM was larger than anyone suspected, the people who got the most attention being just the tip of the iceberg. And we think the Guobao figured this out. We think somehow they pieced it together from all of the NCM people they'd rounded up and interrogated, rather roughly, I imagine. Somehow, some trail, probably several, lead back to her.

But what were you planning to do once you got there? I asked. I'd been afraid the story was much bigger than it first appeared. I wasn't sure whether that was a good thing or not for your situation.

We just wanted to find out what we could. You see, up to that point, no one knew anything, and even up to now, no one's heard. We just wanted to see what we could find out. We hadn't been able to come up with anything; nobody knew anything. No one else was working on the case. No one else in the country dared to get near it, and no one outside of the country knew about it. Y feared BY was at substantial risk. She disappeared without a trace. No one had been notified of her detention, as required by law. Her detention had not been confirmed in any way. You know, it is often these lesser-known figures who simply disappear without a trace in the system. The better known figures, especially those known abroad, have some protection since the Partystate doesn't want to treat them so badly, especially physically. But people like BY, if they want to, the Partystate can disappear her without a trace and no one will know, no one will care, at least, no one who can speak up for her.

Opal's answer made sense but was also unconvincing. I wondered whether they'd been up to something more than Opal was letting on. Heading up to Hebei might have been in keeping with Opal's predilection to rush in, but you were cautious, analytical, not prone to the headstrong impulsive act. You could have gotten other people already in China to check things out, like whether or not neighbors had seen BY getting carted away, anything to substantiate the suspicion she'd been kidnapped by the Partystate. Maybe there was just no one close you trusted; maybe it had gotten to that point, the network had been so decimated by the recent crackdown. Still, something didn't add up.

I don't know what happened, Opal continued. *Maybe they got it into their heads that the NCM's 'puppet masters' were outside the country, that maybe Y was one of them. Absurd, yes, but the paranoia is extreme. You know how they like to label 'black hands', claim that 'the people' have been mislead by a few evil masterminds pulling the strings behind the scenes for nefarious purposes. And it's even better if they can blame any trouble on 'foreign influence' or 'foreign interference'. Y isn't foreign, but she works for a foreign organization, so she's a foreign agent, right? Or maybe they are just lashing out wildly at anyone.*

That didn't make entire sense to me either; the crackdown appeared calculated, specifically targeted. After all, they'd let Opal go. And then I wondered about what always passed through people's minds when one person was released and another continued to be detained: Had Opal done a deal? Had she talked? Had she been turned? Was she spying on me in that moment? For a split second I felt nearly the same panic I'd had in London when it suddenly struck me that Sofia and WZ might have passed on the information I'd given them that you would soon be crossing the border. I immediately dismissed the possibility, wondering whether my face had betrayed the thought to Opal, but the flavor or it lingered. If nothing else, it made me realize how desperate I was in the position I was in—I had to trust someone, and had to get information out of whomever I could. I hated being suspicious, or feeling I had to be suspicious, of everyone, even those I considered friends. Still, I wondered, had they gotten information about Y and O crossing the border, or were the two (or the one or the other) simply on some watch list and were flagged on the immigration officers' computers? Did they have information linking Y and O to BY before the detentions?

Maybe, Opal said, *BY was just bait: They used her to lure Y. This idea makes me sick to my stomach, that we have been successfully deceived. I have to get Y out. It's up to me.*

What? You think this is some kind of CIA rescue operation?

No, I just won't rest until we get her out.

And how are we going to go about that? We don't even know where she is or what happened to her.

I don't know. I don't know.

The thing was, it wasn't even your responsibility to figure out what had happened to BY. You didn't work for her organization anymore. Opal did, but Opal had been following you out of loyalty to you and BY; in fact, neither your nor Opal's organization knew anything ahead of time about what the two of you were planning to do. It was a case of sister solidarity. I could see the thinking: Someone had to do something; who's better placed than us? It was the thinking of the grassroots environment of the network; it was not "professional" thinking.

Your current organization was highly professional. The culture was one of sticking to professional responsibilities, following protocols, processes. One acted professionally to guarantee quality, objectivity, also security, safety. One performed one's role to the best of one's ability, entirely above board. This was the best way to further the cause. You didn't go out on a limb, you didn't go solo, off-road, renegade, with no cover. From that point of view, you had gotten in over your head, confused personal emotions and obligations with your professional role, not to mention had probably not been entirely forthright with the organization about what you were really up to. If this was true, it was so unlike you, unlike the way you liked to characterize yourself as lily-livered, trepidatious.

Y's organization surely knew nothing about this? I said.

Nobody knew anything about this, besides us. Not even you knew anything about this, Opal laughed.

Ha ha. Yes. Very funny. The question is, did the Guobao know anything about it? Through previous interrogations, your names had probably at one time or another come up in connection to your organization, maybe even to BY, but could they have known in advance what you were on about crossing the border now?

Probably not, but they didn't need that. The link with the organization was enough to excite suspicion, especially at this point in time.

Should I share what Opal told me with your new organization? Would it help them to work on your behalf, or disincline them to, given that what it appeared you had been engaged in at the time of your disappearance was, strictly speaking, not part of your work for the organization, that you had not received authorization to do that work, that indeed, in a sense, you had deceived the organization about what you were really up to? Assuming, that is, that Opal was telling me the full story, and that, in turn, you had revealed all to her.... Then again, if I wanted them to help, I had to let them know what I found out, didn't I? And maybe they too knew more than what they had revealed to me.

●

Maybe you were more involved in the New Citizens Movement than I knew, but if so, it was hard to imagine how. We'd both kept a close watch on it, but we were observers, onlookers, supporters, cheerleaders. Ever since Xu Zhiyong's fake trial, conviction and sentencing to four years in prison for "gathering crowds to disrupt public order", you had been thinking of writing a short history of the rights defense movement. You saw Xu's trial as the end of an era for the movement. The movement's main tactic had been to take the Parystate at its word when it said it wished to "strengthen rule of law". The movement's efforts were intended to do just that. But even assuming the Partystate sincerely wished to "strengthen rule of law" up to a point, it would not countenance any perceived threat the rule of law might pose to its rule. And lately, it had made that more abundantly clear than ever. So, you said, Xu's trial marked the end of illusions that working on specific rights cases would lead to strengthening the rule of law. It was a strategy that had run its course, depending as it did on the Partystate allowing lawyers and other rights advocates room to maneuver, room that had been of late ever shrinking. The New Citizens Movement was the culmination, and, ultimately, the end of the strategy.

I thought the book you had in mind was a great idea. I kept encouraging you to write it: You were well-placed, knew all the key figures, had insights nobody else had and could synthesize them. But you kept saying you were too busy and didn't know when you would ever have time. Those who know and can, do. Those who don't, write books. You weren't really the book-writing type. The point of your book was to emphasize that the period of the rights defense movement was a discrete era in recent history, with certain events, actors and techniques that characterized it and distinguished it from what came before and whatever was to come next. Xu's trial was a convenient marker of the end of the movement since Xu had been part of what many considered the first great victory of the movement.

His New Citizens Movement was an outgrowth of the broader rights defense movement, which had begun a little more than a decade before with a campaign by Xu and other young, idealistic lawyers to end a detention program called Custody and Repatriation, according to which authorities detained people for not possessing a residence permit of the place where they were found and "repatriated" them to the place where they had a residence permit, often first detaining them before eventually doing so. It was a system that had been in place for two decades and seemed particularly out of keeping with a period in the country's history in which hundreds of millions of people were migrating from the countryside to the city for work. Apart from that, it was an obvious abuse of the right to freedom of movement, and it was a system rife with abuses and entirely lacking due process. The apprehended had no recourse to judicial authorities and there was no judicial supervision. The issue had come to a head when a young student rounded up under the authority of Custody and Repatriation was beaten to death. Xu and the other young citizens were able to use the notoriety of the case to draw attention to the program's systematic abuses. Eventually, Custody and Repatriation was abolished, and its abolition was regarded as a new kind of victory for a new kind of civil society.

People in the rights defense movement came from many walks of life, and there was some debate about the extent to which it could really be accurately characterized as a coherent movement at all, so diffuse and diverse were the many manifestations and without any clear organization, which would have been fatal to the movement, so hostile was the Partystate towards citizens organizing outside of its control, especially for quasi-political purposes. If it was not a movement, it was a spontaneous burgeoning. What the various actors had in common was that they were trying to work within the framework of the system, however unjust it might be, to change it gradually, to make it more rights-respecting, more receptive to citizens' demands. They worked piecemeal, on discrete issues, deliberately avoiding posing any direct political challenge to the Partystate, though of course virtually every issue they took on had at its root the problem of the monopolization of political power by the Partystate. For that reason, even though the people involved never did anything that could remotely be construed as illegal under true rule of law, there were frequent crackdowns. Indeed, at times, the crackdowns appeared so unrelenting that we joked about how abused through overuse that word "crackdown" was; essentially, we said, the crackdowns bled into each other such that it could be said there was one big on-going crackdown, in which case, the way the country was run amounted to a constant crackdown, even if there appeared to be periods of heightened persecution, often related to a certain event such as the Beijing Olympics or calls for a Jasmine Revolution, periods during which the regime appeared especially concerned about "security". Along the way, virtually everyone we knew had fallen foul of the Partystate in one way or another, at one time or another, to one degree or another, one after one, and suffered retribution, restrictions and punishment of various kinds, even though these people tended to be eminently moderate, the kind whose energies and devotion, if the Partystate were truly interested in "strengthening rule of law", it would harness, but instead, it simply couldn't tolerate them. Just recently, Cao Shunli, Guo Feixiong, Wang Gongquan. The list went on and on. Liu Xia, Liu Ping, Wei Zhongping, Li Sihua. And most recent of all, Pu Zhiqiang. It was hard for even the well-informed to keep track of them all. At the same time, they had managed to push some boundaries and expand awareness about some rights issues. Now that Xu, one of the movement's defining and longest-surviving figures had been tossed in prison on spurious charges, you argued, that era had come to an end.

Whether it had won more than it lost would be a question your book posed. It would give the movement the credit it was due and show its limitations when it came up against a Partystate that refused to relinquish control over the judicial system or virtually any other sector of society. Since you said you were too busy to write it, we had planned to collaborate, you conducting the interviews with the many main actors we knew (at least, the ones who were not yet in prison and dared to talk) and doing the primary research, and me doing the actual writing according to an agreed outline. It was one of the many projects we never got around to. And now you had apparently fallen victim to the on-going crackdown you intended to write about.

Xu, I thought, must have certainly known from the start of the New Citizens Movement that he was pushing the envelope. If there was one thing the regime would not countenance, it was any form of independent organization outside of its control, even though NCM was the loosest, most diffuse sort of movement, mostly involving discussions, debates, and circulation of views and ideas— precisely the sort of thing for which dictators have low tolerance. Xu and others tried to make the movement as non-threatening as possible to the Partystate's vested interests, often taking up issues which the Partystate regarded, rhetorically at least, as legitimate, issues like the rights of rural migrants in cities, and in particular, their children's right to education, their right to enroll in urban schools where they lived and to take the gaokao in the place where they were educated (the city) as opposed to the place of their residence permit (their home village, where they often had not lived for many years). Basic common sense and decency stuff, essentially demanding that the authorities iron out the discrepancies caused by the inability or unwillingness of the Partystate to keep up with the rapid changes that had taken place in the society and that had made it all the clearer that rural people were second-class subjects ("subjects" as opposed to citizens, as there were no true citizens in China, in the modern sense of people formally politically in charge of their own destiny and working freely to shape it). NCM also promoted gatherings across the country to encourage people to discuss what they considered to be the most pressing social issues and petitioned the National People's Congress (the fake legislature) to ratify international human rights conventions. In other words, it was "acting as if", to use the Havelian phrase—acting as if a truly independent civil society organization could operate freely and without persecution. And in that sense, however mild it was, its effect was to dare the Partystate: Either accept us and recognize that society is evolving or crack down.

The thing that pushed NCM beyond the invisible line that the Partystate's subjects learned to sense deep in their bones from an early age was its demand for public disclosure of officials' wealth and assets. In theory, the demand dovetailed with the Partystate's anti-corruption campaign. But this was just the problem: The Partystate could not countenance citizens speaking up on the issue, stealing its thunder, perhaps manipulating the issue towards their own ends. The Partystate had no intention to get to the root of corruption (that being monopolization of political power) but just to appear as if it was doing something about it. The new General Secretary intended to use the issue to consolidate power and destroy the power of rival factions within the Partystate, which certainly wasn't about to disclose officials' assets. To do so, and to allow reporting on that, could lead to its downfall. Because, at root, the Partystate *was* corruption; there was no difference between the two.

After the Partystate ditched ideology (Communism, Maoism), it had nothing to ensure the loyalty of the tens of millions of members and supporters needed to keep it in power besides allowing them to profit from their positions. The country had become one large racketeering enterprise. The new General Secretary had called corruption an existential threat to the Partystate, but actually, rooting it out was an even greater threat. Killing corruption would have been tantamount to committing suicide—what other attraction could the Partystate—an organization which at root stood for little more than power and profit—possibly hold for its tens of millions of members, collaborators, hangers-on, colluding business elites and other beneficiaries? Its elaborate system of patronage would collapse. But the fact that the emperor had no clothes couldn't be so obvious; his nakedness couldn't be televised nationally, couldn't even be discussed on the internet. Thus, the official campaign, and thus, the crackdown on NCM. The NCM could not have trod upon a more "sensitive" issue. Xu had to have known that as well. So, essentially, under the guise of lawful moderation, NCM was a radical attack on the heart of the regime, as any real, principled and consistent adherence to rule of law ultimately couldn't fail to be.

Xu's trial and those of other NCM members (at least eighteen people in all had been detained; three had already been tried without verdict), happening within days of one another, were even more farcical than political trials of this sort tended to be. Foreign media broadcast footage of their reporters and camera crews getting hounded and roughed up by government-hired thugs outside, and in some cases blocks away from, the courthouse. The reaction was shock: This was an ever so brief and slight glimpse of the netherworld that was the country's reality, of the way the regime treated its subjects. Of course, it was a shock to journalists, even those seasoned in covering China, and viewers, as it had to be to those who lived in civilized places where they were regarded as citizens, to have in such plain view the utter incivility which was the basis of the relationship between Partystate and subjects in China. The Partystate didn't much care what the rest of the world thought; still, the public relations disaster of the coverage of the trials must have surely given it pause... for a very brief moment.

Countless times I replayed the scene: The police arrive at Xu's home and present his newly pregnant wife with the arrest warrant. He was at that point, if I recalled correctly, the twenty-fourth to have been arrested in the crackdown in the last three months. Ever since the others, the "small fish", started getting hauled in, people had been waiting for the foot to drop: When would they be knocking on the big fish's door? It seemed they were using the previous arrests to gather evidence to arrest Xu as the "black hand" behind it all.

Not that evidence was needed; the will of the regime was sufficient to determine any judicial outcome. It was strange dealing with a power which often took great care to maintain the appearance of compliance with the law for entirely nefarious, extra-legal purposes. At other times, as in the cases of BY and you, but certainly not only your cases (think Gao Zhisheng), even the pretense of adhering to the law was dispensed with. How could one argue with the arbitrary? It is whatever it says it is. And whatever it says is, is. By definition. Strange to live in a country where reality was determined by a bunch of venal old men—what did it mean that a billion people were willing to put up with their continual theft of power?—and anyone who challenged that reality, who presented to the public a different vision for society (think Charter 08) was constantly threatened with the full force of their vengeance. What did it mean to have a nation where the official version of reality differed so greatly from the lived reality of the people, who were prevented from entering into the public discourse?

I remembered the faces of the NCM members who'd been detained. How very ordinary they looked, this person a stockbroker, that a student, this one employed by the state railway, that one a bus driver, an entrepreneur, a lawyer, a teacher, a factory worker, from all walks of life. It was this that incensed the Partystate: They were Everyman, the real superhero, no threat to power at all in their exceedingly low numbers, but a potential threat if their numbers were allowed to grow in a country where it was hard to find someone who would not complain about corruption. What the Partystate feared was not those people per se but the possibility of an idea, a cause around which the resentments of many, if not the majority of the people could coalesce and find political voice. In fact, the NCM were pitifully few, but what they represented was the threat of bringing the wealthiest, most powerful regime in the world crashing down.

How far had the country come in the twenty-five years since the eighty-nine demonstrations? Back then, one of the key demands of the demonstrators was an end to official corruption, and twenty-five years later the regime was still sending people to prison for calling for an end to official corruption, which had increased exponentially. The difference, perhaps, was that the Partystate had become more sophisticated, co-opting and monopolizing the anti-corruption discourse, which was why NCM peeved it so—how dare they?!

I always marveled at the dual and paradoxical nature of the society: On the one hand, China was one of the fastest-changing places in the world—whole cities were physically unrecognizable from the places they had been just a few years before; and yet on the other hand, it seemed frozen in time—the basic contradictions, deficiencies and problems of the society could not even be openly discussed let alone addressed because to do so threatened the Partystate's monopoly on power.

The question, ultimately, was whether its brand of political "management" was the past or the future. It was hard to tell. Indeed, at base, that was what was at stake, not only the sort of place China would be in the future, but Asia and the wider world as well. I often said, As China went, so went the world. There was a lot worth fighting for; how sad, then, that it often seemed so few were fighting. It was easy to understand: Even if you saw there was a lot to fight for, it seemed, on the surface, there was so little to be gained, and those who tried were, therefore, fools, perhaps noble fools, but fools nonetheless.

And now Fool Xu faced four years in prison for his foolishness. For thinking that China could peacefully, gradually change—ha! And he hadn't even ever seen his daughter, his first and only child, who was born on the Monday of the week before his trial began, nine days before, to be exact. His wife, who had received his arrest notice when she first got pregnant, had petitioned the court to allow him to see his own child, but the court had rejected her request. The girl would not know her father for the first four years of her life. When he came out, he would be a stranger to her.

Xu being forcibly separated from his own child affected you deeply, as it did me. You remembered your friend, Wu Jie, sentenced to ten years in prison when his daughter was nine. She would be nineteen when he came out. At least he got to know his daughter, she got to know him, before he was sent away, and she would have some idea of what having a father meant. The same could not be said for Xu's daughter.

How this all wore you down—the steady drip-drip-drip of seeing friends, acquaintances, colleagues, fellow rights defenders one by one going down. That was, of course, the intention of the Partystate: If you persist, we will crush you. Every season, every new crackdown brought new personal tragedies.

I thought of the ghostly videos of Liu Xia surreptitiously taken under her house arrest and smuggled out. There was something otherworldly about them, unearthly: Was this taking place on earth, in this world? It was like seeing, before your eyes, someone get crushed slowly beneath a rock. I thought of the controversy a few years back when videos appeared online of skimpily clad women crushing kittens to death by sitting on sheets of glass placed over the tiny creatures. The videos provoked outrage, indignant uproar, and the response of human flesh search engines vowing to hunt down and punish the offenders vigilante-style. Why didn't the same occur when the same was done, however metaphorically, to human beings? Only the most egregious abuses, like mentally disabled children being kidnapped and forced to work as slaves in brick kilns, provoked any outrage at all.

Perhaps your reaction to BY's disappearance was simply, Enough is enough—something must be done. Righteousness—potentially one of the most dangerous and foolish emotions.

●

Was it really all those New Citizens Movement interrogations that lead to BY? Was BY really as central as Opal believed? Opal had been known to exaggerate—as you'd said, Opal was a fighter, not a researcher. Or was BY's disappearance entirely unrelated to the NCM crackdown? One could not say for sure, though the timing suggested a connection. But then why was she completely disappeared, as opposed to criminally detained with notification of family, as in the case of the other NCMers? At least with them, there was confirmation they were in the system. But now, first BY and then you simply disappeared.

Being all too aware of the panoply of techniques your probable captors were used to applying, I hated to think of what could be happening to you both.

At the time, I was getting cryotherapy for a large wart on the bottom of the big toe of one foot. The operation was not medically necessary. Two doctors had told me the wart, which had been there for years, posed no health risk. But you, an inveterate visitor to doctors, had been bugging me to get it removed, and as long as I was insured, through your organization's family plan, I figured I might as well attend to a problem I'd meant to fix for years, even though doing so went against my basic principle of steering as far clear of the medical establishment as possible, a principle which the fortune of my heretofore good health had allowed me to stick to.

And so there I found myself prostrate, once a month for several months, on a dermatologist's examination table, my toe getting sprayed with liquid nitrogen. It was the closest I'd come in some while to having insight into the experience of being tortured. Each session was more painful than the last; the doctor, disappointed with the effects of the previous surgery, kept increasing the dosage in an attempt to produce a better result. The pain became so intense that I wanted to run away from it but could not because it was part of my own body. And the pain, throbbing, endured for days after the session. The last two sessions in particular had been excruciating. Discomfort escalated to pain, and then, just when the pain was at the point of becoming unbearable, the doctor relented, turning off her liquid nitrogen gun. Was it supposed to be that painful? When I asked, the phlegmatic doctor, female, said that women bore pain better than men.

Feeling the pain, I imagined the torturer crossing the threshold from inflicting bearable to unbearable pain. The doctor, however effectively, was trying to heal me, and in doing so, caused pain, whereas the torturer was trying to cause pain; his purpose was to hurt the object of his torture. The surgery reminded me, not for the first time, that I would almost certainly be among the first to yield to torture.

Once I'd said as much to you. You'd told me that your research had lead you to conclude that in China, quite often, the torturer tortured for no other reason than for the sake of torture; infliction of pain was an end in itself. Or, rather, one could say, torture was emphatic, intended to make it entirely clear to the tortured who had control, the representative of the Partystate demonstrating his (you had yet to come across a female torturer) and, by extension, the regime's power over the victim. Or torture was to break the victim, to render her an irreparably damaged person, to change something in her personality, that part of her that made her do whatever she had done to provoke the Partystate's, the torturer's reflexive desire to inflict pain in the first place. The torture was to render her harmless to the Partystate. I didn't doubt you were right, but of course, the purpose of torture, practiced as systematically as it was, was often more instrumental—to get the victim to confess, and an exceedingly high number of convictions—studies suggested over 90%—had as their primary if not often exclusive evidence the confession of the defendant, a great number of those confessions coerced. In this sense, it wasn't stretching things much to assert the whole criminal justice system was built on torture.

Now, for all I knew, you could very well be undergoing if not actual physical torture, then torture of the psychological kind that Ching Cheong said had been inflicted on him simply by virtue of being held incommunicado in solitary confinement in a room with no windows and no natural light for months on end. I could hardly bear the thought. My mind kept running away from it but then turning back; I couldn't look at it and couldn't look away.

I considered the recent case of the father of Xue Mingkai, a young man who had been imprisoned after a conviction on the notorious charge of "subversion of state power" (itself a "new, improved" version of the old charge of counter-revolution). After Xue's release, he had spent long periods under house arrest but had recently evaded authorities and snuck away to some undisclosed location. His parents were then taken into custody, probably in an effort to pressure Mingkai to return. Authorities claimed his father had committed suicide while in detention by jumping from a high floor of the procurator's office. That explanation was highly suspicious; more likely, many said, was that he had been killed by interrogators while under detention. Whether by design or accident, the torturers had gone too far. There had been many recent cases of suspicious deaths under detention.

During the last session of wart removal, I had, for the first time in my life, something resembling a vision, or an out-of-body experience. It started as a conscious decision to think of something to take my mind off the pain, but then it was as if I was hovering over the table, over myself lying upon it, and, before long, over the entire country. Lying there, staring down at Dr Mak blasting my toe with liquid nitrogen at the end of the table, I thought of all the people getting tortured across China right at that very moment, and the country took on the aspect of one big torture machine. The vision expanded, going back in time, across decades of bodies that had been damaged and destroyed, sacrificed to the Partystate's consistent objective of staying in power, the country's history strewn with the broken bones and corpses of those with the foolish yearning to be free.

Not long before your disappearance, you had been conducting research to get an overview of the torture situation in the country. Torture was one of those things that everyone knew took place systematically, but the country, especially the security apparatus, was still so closed that it was very hard to gather information systematically; most was anecdotal, usually from victims of torture. Several reforms had been announced in recent years with the stated aim of preventing torture in custody, such as CCTV cameras in interrogation rooms, and you wanted to find out whether or not the incidence of torture had decreased as a result. Of course, it hadn't. With the impunity that existed and the wide latitude and powers of prosecutors and police, and, beyond that, the fact that they were the underlings of a Partystate that was above the law, the same old problems still persisted. If anything, torture had proliferated in ever newer forms.

There on the operating table, particular cases swam through consciousness. A former policeman now in prison. In a surreal touch, you were able to call him since, even though he was a prisoner, he was allowed to keep a mobile phone because he'd been given an unofficial position guarding other prisoners. He was a member of a nationwide group of ex-policemen with grievances against the government for mistreatment. He had gotten on the wrong side of a higher-up who found an opportunity to frame him. He was tortured into confessing and was serving eight years. You'd been trying to find police, or ex-police, willing to discuss torture. He laughed at your question about its pervasiveness. Of course, he said, everyone does it, all the time; it simply comes with the territory. Had he ever done it? you asked. Of course, he laughed again, you could hardly be a police officer and not do it. There were all sorts of techniques. Most officers were proficient, well-versed. Had he ever thought it could happen to him? Another hearty laugh. No, he said, never. It was a culture in which, as a policeman, you always believed you were above the law.

Then there was the family in Shaanxi, peasants, people used to things happening to them, to fate raining down from above, used to being without recourse. Their twenty-year-old son was now a vegetable for life. He had been working in an internet cafe where a fight broke out. The police took him away. The family heard nothing for weeks and did not even know where he was. Then they were contacted by the police and told he was suspected of involvement in the fight, but they were not allowed to see him or know where he was being held. Then, many weeks later, they were told by police that he had contracted meningitis and was being transferred to a hospital. When they saw him again in a hospital bed, he was unconscious, and so, they were told, he would ever remain, with massive head injuries. Though they could not put this in their official report, hospital employees confided to the parents of the young man that the source of his injuries was "external", that he did not have meningitis or any other disease. The family was certain the son's injuries were incurred through torture. He had visible wounds on his forehead and feet. The family suspected the police kept him so long without notifying them so that the most obvious signs of torture had a chance to disappear. It was probably just a case of a couple of officers getting carried away, a frequent occurrence, and then once the damage was done, there was no undoing it; all that remained was to cover it up. A dime-a-dozen case, one of the many that never came to the attention of anyone who might be able to work for a modicum, a slim modicum, of justice. One of the nobodies that nobody cared about, except his parents. All over the country, the mangled bodies of nobodies.

What compounded the sadness, I thought to myself, still horizontal, as the session was about to conclude, the pain about to reach its climax, was that most of the victims and their families to whom you spoke believed their cases were anomalies, aberrations. Otherwise, the system worked; they were just unlucky. They had no idea that torture was systematic, no idea that their case was part of an enormous problem, an enormous scandal, an enormous injustice. That was the result of an unfree press. To think of all those people living in isolation, fear and grief across the land... imagine if all of them united and demanded justice.

After all those sessions, the wart, though diminished, was still there. How hard could it be, I wondered, to remove a simple wart?

The apparatus of oppression and persecution extended far beyond torture. Through decades in power, the Partystate had developed a highly refined tool kit. I imagined a huge laboratory-cum-thinktank whose purpose was to conduct research in order to hone its methods, a kind of factory of evil; I also imagined the ordinary blankfaced people who worked there. I was a poor cataloguer—I never took the time to stop and document—but living in the country and working on human rights had lead to a notional taxonomy of brutality, abuse, intimidation, harassment, surveillance, incarceration and general persecution practiced on a regular basis by the Partystate.

The regime's full arsenal was much more finely calibrated than the old blunt Maoist "off with the counter-revolutionary's head" approach, but it was still rather arbitrarily not to say incoherently and unevenly applied. As long as people stayed off the radar of the security apparatus, they could slip between the cracks and do quite a lot. Even once you were in their tracking system, what actually happened to you depended to a great extent on the reaction of particular bureaux or officials which might or might not be in communication or agreement with other entities in the security apparatus. There were hundreds of thousands of ordinary people whose only contact with the massive security apparatus was invitations to tea, at which they were expected to give an account of themselves and, perhaps, of others they knew. That said, the overall deployment of massive resources, human and other, to neutralize perceived enemies was a definite strategy that came from the very top. The umbrella term for the full panoply of operations was *weiwen*, or "stability maintenance", an amusing euphemism for maintenance of Partystate monopoly of power. The budget for it (something in the vicinity of 700 billion yuan) exceeded that for national defense. Another way of putting it was that, in terms of budgetary priorities, the biggest "security threat" to the regime was its own people, as opposed to any external entity.

The arbitrary nature of the system was deliberate: The message was, Anything can happen to you at any time, depending entirely on what we think, so be careful, you are at our mercy. Then again, it was fairly rare these days that they just killed you. Some people took that as a sign of improvement. If detained, though, the chances of being tortured were very high. A systematic combination of physical abuse, medical neglect and poor conditions meant that many people left prison with their health destroyed or permanently damaged. The face and figure of Ni Yulan came to mind, a disbarred lawyer who was left paralyzed by the torture she'd endured in prison. Her crimes had been to defend Falun Gong practitioners and fight the enforced demolition of her own home and neighborhoods in Beijing. Once she came to HK, and you pushed her wheelchair through the streets. You said it made you realize how unfriendly HK was to the wheelchair-bound.

Besides torture, some of the more widely practiced other methods of control included:

Low-grade harassment, intimidation and surveillance, including invitations to "tea" for a "chat" by the Guobao; following and monitoring; tapping your phone and hacking your email; ensuring that you have no way of using modern communications infrastructure to get your message out to the world, blocking or deleting Weibo accounts and taking blogs off-line; pressuring landlords to evict you from your home; warning potential landlords against renting to you; confiscating and never returning your possessions including papers and computers; harassing your family members including your children and denying them opportunities for employment and education.

Many active citizens in China took this treatment as par for the course; they would be surprised if some combination of these things didn't happen to you.

House arrest, not infrequently the fate of the better known active citizens. The authorities couldn't pin even trumped-up or entirely invented criminal charges on them, or for whatever other reason they preferred to not formally put them in prison, but they still had to be controlled and couldn't be allowed to simply roam free—house arrest was the solution. In most cases, the house arrest was wholly extra-legal. Often, thugs surreptitiously hired by the Partystate enforced it. Hu Jia, Liu Xia, Chen Guangcheng and Hada were all recent high-profile cases of house arrest. Less well-known people were also placed under house arrest for shorter periods of time amounting to a few days or weeks, usually in relation to "sensitive" events such as the anniversary of June 4. There were degrees of house arrest, from being virtually cut off from the world, including having internet and phone lines disabled, to just not being allowed to leave your house or being allowed only under certain conditions, for example, to shop for groceries or visit relatives or the hospital, usually accompanied by guards or followed by the Guobao.

Detention without charge, often referred to as "residential surveillance". The justification for detaining people without charge for an extended period of time up to several months was to investigate a suspected crime. In most cases, you were held incommunicado at an undisclosed location. Often, no one, not even close family members, knew where you were or had even confirmation from the regime that it had detained you. It was a sort of black hole into which you disappeared at the regime's convenience. Often you were roughed up or otherwise mistreated without being out-and-out beaten. You were interrogated constantly, deprived of adequate sleep, and often made to understand in no uncertain terms that no one knew where you were and anything could be done to you without anyone finding out. Even those who had not been physically assaulted while under residential surveillance often described it as a form of psychological torture. Often, the regime just wanted to show you what it could do to you; at other times, it wanted a confession of some sort to wrong-doing, whether tax evasion or stealing state secrets. In cases that did not lead to actual criminal prosecution, the detention was meant as a stern warning of what could happen to you in the future—far worse—if you didn't shape up. The message was, Stop what you're doing; it's not worth the price. We can ruin you, body, wallet and soul, and not just you but your family and friends. This usually happened to relatively well-known or "respectable" types, persons of a certain stature, such as Ai Weiwei or the Beijing rights lawyers who were rounded up in the wake of calls for a Jasmine Revolution even though they had absolutely no connection to that.

Re-education through labor camp. If you didn't have that stature, they might just as well unceremoniously throw you in a re-education through labor camp for up to three years. This was a form of extrajudicial detention since it wasn't the result of being convicted of a crime by a court of law but an administrative decision taken by the police with virtually no judicial oversight. You had no opportunity to defend yourself. It was often used to lock up suspected prostitutes or drug offenders, but also suspected members of Falun Gong, pesky petitioners or others suspected of having wrong political beliefs or having committed political offenses. After speculation lasting a decade, it was announced in 2013 that re-education through labor camps would be abolished, though the details of how that was to occur were unclear, and many feared they would simply be replaced by another form of detention under a different name, much as the crime of "counter-revolution" was replaced by "subversion or incitement to subversion of state power". Recent reports had indicated that new forms of extrajudicial detention were emerging, apparently as replacements for the supposedly abolished re-education through labor camps. They were being called "reprimand centers" and officials had been quoted as saying that they were intended to provide "warning and education" to "abnormal petitioners". Other reports had claimed that drug users and others who would have previously been sent to re-education through labor were being forcibly incarcerated in drug rehabilitation centers, again extrajudicially. It was less clear what would replace re-education through labor for Falun Gong practitioners and petitioners who needed to be kept under control or punished.

Black jails, another form of detention without charge, existing wholly outside of the legal system, indeed, in secret—thus, the name. These were places where people considered the no-account riff-raff of society, such as petitioners, were dragged off, to keep them from being an annoyance to someone in power. They were often run by provincial or municipal government authorities who wanted to keep people from complaining to higher levels of the Partystate about their supposed misdeeds. People were often held in them for short periods of time before being forcibly transported back to their home area. Police either connived or looked the other way. The Partystate denied that they existed, though their existence was well documented.

Prison. Increasingly, this option was being reserved for the "incorrigibles", people who had been warned through other methods amongst those listed above and for whatever reason just didn't get the message, people who persisted in "living as if" they lived in a free society where their rights were respected, the rights guaranteed in the country's constitution, which the Partystate paid little heed to because it stood above it. It was often meant for those whom the government perceived as clearly having crossed the invisible line of the permissible, often by doing something that either implicitly or explicitly challenged its power. Liu Xiaobo was the classic example here, in his connection with Charter 08. In most cases, the charges against the defendants, or the ways in which they were applied, were patently ridiculous, simply an excuse to put them behind bars. For example, even if Xu Zhiyong had organized a demonstration that did not have the requisite permit (something that was all but impossible to procure anyway), what civilized society would put him behind bars for four years for doing so?

Disappearance, both quasi- and entire, judicial and other. This could happen to those like Gao Zhisheng who refused to bend or were too defiant or who dealt with far too sensitive issues such as Falun Gong. It had also been used to some extent to deal with inconvenient religious figures such as the boy Panchen Lama and Catholic bishops who swore fealty to the Vatican. In this day and age when the regime preferred to paint a legal veneer over persecution, it had become a technique somewhat restricted in its usage. In cases where it occurred, Gao's being perhaps the most well-known, it seemed that the victim had somehow personally crossed a powerful figure, or that a powerful figure in the regime had a personal animus against him, or that the regime just couldn't help it itself—perhaps it had tortured someone so badly that he was scarred and maimed and therefore had to be hidden away, at least until the visible manifestations of his abuse sufficiently healed. It could also happen to those who were unknown or considered nobodies—people no one would miss. And it happened more often in legal black holes, especially regions such as Tibet still under totalitarian rule.

Bishop Shi was first imprisoned not long after the Partystate seized power and spent most of the next 60 years in detention facilities of one kind or another. During one of his brief periods of release in 2001, already aged 80, he was kidnapped from his home never to be seen or heard from again. If he was still alive, he would now be 94. Recently, a great-niece reported having been told by an official that Bishop Shi had died, but when the family went to collect his remains, they were told that the official who told them he was dead had been drunk. So had he died or hadn't he? There was no way to find out. Indeed, since he had been disappeared in 2001, the Parystate had not so much as confirmed it had him, and during that time, his family had heard from him not even once.

The Panchen Lama had, of course, been kidnapped as a boy along with his whole family and was never heard from again.

Stories like those haunted the dark corners of my mind. But then, you weren't a bishop or a reincarnated lama were you?

What was I forgetting? Surely something. The list went on and on. There was shuanggui, the entirely extralegal detention system, but that was reserved for Party members or others who were found to have somehow violated Party "discipline." Basically, when you fell into the clutches of the Partystate, it could do whatever it wanted to you. All of the methods and techniques listed above of depriving people of their freedom or otherwise abusing their rights could be considered forms of the old strategy of cutting off the head of the monkey to scare the chickens. These people were to be made an example of: This is what happened to you if you defied the Partystate.

Perhaps you had feared the worst for BY, that she had been entirely disappeared, and that was even more worrying given that she wasn't a well-known figure.

And now, it seemed, the same had happened to you.

Sometimes China could feel a world apart from international trends. In recent decades, much work had been done internationally to expressly outlaw enforced disappearances, culminating in the International Convention for the Protection of All Persons from Enforced Disappearance, which entered into force in December 2010. So far, 93 countries had signed the convention, and 42 had ratified it. Many of the countries that had spearheaded the effort were, unsurprisingly, Latin American, whence the original impetus for the treaty came, in response to the systematic practice of enforced disappearance by right-wing military regimes in that region during the seventies and eighties, and Europe, which always seemed to be in the forefront of respect for human rights. Few Asian countries had signed it (seven) and only one, Japan, had ratified it, even though—or more likely, because—, these days, Asia had the highest incidence of enforced disappearance in the world.

China, of course, had neither signed nor ratified the convention. In the international discourse on enforced disappearances, China was hardly ever mentioned, even though it was a highly problematic country in this respect. Your organization had put out a report on black jails and a bulletin in response to the disappearances of Ai Weiwei and prominent rights lawyers in the wake of calls for a Jasmine Revolution, and a statement of concern was made by the UN Working Group on Enforced or Involuntary Disappearances, again in response to the Jasmine Revolution crackdown. China also excited quite a lot of attention when it included in its proposed revisions to the Criminal Procedure Law provisions that would essentially legalize, or at least provide a legal veneer to, enforced disappearances, allowing law enforcement agencies to hold people without charge or notification in undisclosed locations for up to six months in cases related to terrorism or state security, terms which were applied in a highly elastic manner in China (for example, a poet was recently accused of endangering state security in one of his poems).

When the changes were eventually adopted, some of the worst language had been excised, but according to the infamous

Article 73, while law enforcement agencies did have to notify relatives within twenty-four hours of detention, they did not have to disclose the whereabouts of the detained and could hold them for up to six months without access to a lawyer. As ever in China, the real question was not what the law said but how and to what extent it would or would not be followed and enforced by those charged with the responsibility of enforcing it. Recently, your old organization had documented 3,833 cases of arbitrary detention in one year, certainly the tip of the iceberg.

Some would argue that what most often occurred in China didn't really constitute "enforced disappearance" according to the originally intended definition of that term, since the model came from cases in countries where the regime would simply abduct and kill a person, disposing of the corpse and not notifying anyone of the occurrence. In China, rarely did that occur. But what had happened to BY, you and countless others certainly fit the definition in the Convention: *the arrest, detention, abduction or any other form of deprivation of liberty by agents of the State or by persons or groups of persons acting with the authorization, support or acquiescence of the State, followed by a refusal to acknowledge the deprivation of liberty or by concealment of the fate or whereabouts of the disappeared person, which place such a person outside the protection of the law.*

When I had to advocate on your behalf to others, I always made sure to use the term "disappeared" with its international legal definition in mind. I never said you had disappeared, as if that had just magically happened, but that you had been disappeared, employing "disappear" as a transitive verb. I wanted to emphasize that what we had here was a kidnapping outside of legal procedure, a kidnapping in all likelihood performed by the state.

I had had a vague awareness of the Criminal Procedure Law regarding detention and of international law on disappearance and had heard about many abuses, but in China, human rights abuses were so numerous they became a blur, hard to keep up with. It was only when you disappeared that I became something of an amateur expert on enforced disappearances, in China at least.

•

O and I went up to Lo Wu, the border crossing where you had disappeared. We were scouting for Opal's potential trip. It was just a short train ride from the center of the city. Very convenient: These days people could get disappeared without having to travel great distances. So strange, I thought: The moment you exited the relatively safe zone of HK, you entered straight into the maws of the Partystate; a matter of meters separated the two. The crossing point was almost emphatically non-descript, and very busy, with hundreds of thousands crossing every day, the vast majority without hindrance or delay, apart from the long queues, ever-increasing in recent years, as more and more mainlanders entered HK. As ordinary as it appeared, to people like myself the crossing had over the years taken on an almost mythic, magical aura, the point of transition from one dimension of reality to another, one world to another.

Not even the hordes—40 million mainlanders had crossed the border the previous year, ten times more than a decade before—that now passed through could tamp down its history, its ghosts. People flooded over the border to escape the Partystate takeover in forty-nine, resulting in a nearly threefold increase in HK's population over two years, from around 750,000 to over two million. The steady increase of the ensuing decades, with a spike during the years of Partystate-inflicted famine, especially in the early sixties, was due to people sneaking over the border, HK growing by about one million a decade up to 1980. The colonial authorities implemented a so-called touch-base policy in 1974, according to which, if you managed to sneak across the border and enter the center of the city to reunite with your family or report to a police station, you had "touched base" and were allowed to remain, but if you were picked up in the closed frontier area near the border, you were immediately repatriated, a cruel act, as well as an egregious contravention of international law. The policy failed to halt the flow of people and was abolished in 1980, replaced by simply outlawing "illegal" immigration. Since then, the population had increased by another two million in a territory with one of the lowest birth rates in the world. HK was an immigrant city par excellence, the vast majority having fled the mainland within the last few generations.

Then came the Tiananmen massacre of eighty-nine. In the ensuing crackdown, thousands of demonstrators went underground, and many of them tried to escape the country. HK supporters set up Operation Yellowbird to smuggle them over the border. Colonial authorities looked the other way, on the tacit understanding that the escapees would keep their heads down and not "cause embarrassment" or diplomatic complications. The authorities preferred them to discretely make their way to another place as soon as possible. Few decided to stay, among other reasons because they had no confidence that they would be safe in HK in the long run, for even if the colonial authorities continued to offer them protection, they feared that they could be apprehended after the handover in ninety-seven. (One I had met said he arrived in HK and was hidden in an apartment with curtains drawn and told not to go out. He still remembered the view from the narrow space between the opaque curtain and the window frame peering down into the street in this strange new place called HK; it was virtually his only view of the city—I came to HK, he said, and that was all I saw! He ended up in

France.) Hundreds of people were rescued, including over a dozen of those on the regime's most wanted list. The operation's name came from the Chinese saying, The mantis stalks the cicada, unaware of the yellowbird behind. It was made possible by the cooperation of human rights workers, crime syndicates and professional smugglers, foreign diplomats, and in some cases even sympathetic mainland officials and police, as well as financing by HK businesspeople and celebrities. It was one of those few shining moments when very diverse elements of society united to achieve a common just aim.

Nowadays the main smuggling that went on was not of people but of milk powder, and that in the opposition direction, from HK to the mainland. In the wake of the melamine milk powder scandal, mainland parents were desperate to get milk powder they could be confident was safe to feed their children, and many of those 40 million border crossings from the mainland every year were made by small, so-called parallel traders who would come and go several times a week, each time taking the maximum limit allowed by mainland customs officials of milk powder or some other product on the mainland that was hard to come by, or more expensive due to import duties. And there was also something unheard of before: Much migration in the opposite direction, with HK people, like Opal's father, starting businesses and building homes much more spacious than anything they could afford in HK, as well as older people going there to retire, the cost of living being much lower.

Ultimately, when I looked at the crossing, I thought of the plot of the regime and its minion, the HK government, to gradually and invisibly assimilate HK into the mainland, to flood it with people, with Putonghua, the language that one heard ever-increasingly floating through the air in many areas of the city. Eventually, long before forty-seven, when the fifty-year grace period of the so-called "one country, two systems" arrangement after the handover was officially scheduled to end, the border would be so blurred as to make it disappear and HK would be virtually a mainland city just like any other, culturally and politically.

The trip up to the border was a pilgrimage to a site of horror, even though, quite literally, there was nothing to see, at least nothing that had to do with your abduction, no evidence whatsoever; it was just like any other place. I stood there and dumbly stared. I did not know where you were, or what had happened to you, and this trip brought me no closer.

Opal had decided to attempt to cross over again to test how the authorities would react. The pretext was a visit to her father in Shenzhen. He lived less than three kilometers from the border. They hadn't been in touch since her disappearance. I questioned the wisdom of the foray, coming so soon after your disappearance, but Opal insisted. What could become of her? The Guobao wouldn't take her; they wouldn't dare. If they wanted her, they would have kept her. So she said. She thought of the trip as a kind of reconnaissance mission; if all went well, perhaps she would follow up with a trip to find you.

And then Opal disappeared, across the border. Only to return two days later. The trip had gone smoothly, she reported. She had stayed with her father. She was neither prevented from nor delayed in crossing the border either way. But, she did point out, she was trailed constantly by security people who followed her in the street and lurked outside her father's apartment building. She suspected she was allowed to pass so that the Guobao could see whether or not she would lead them to anyone else.

●

Then there were your parents to tell. What could I say to them? "Your daughter's disappeared"? Yes, that I could say, had to.

But how? How did one tell parents their child has disappeared? After you had gone to the mainland and before I returned from London, they had taken care of Z. From the very beginning, they had been a big part of her life. Wonderful grandparents, devoted, even if you worried about all the ways they were too Chinese, constantly directing and controlling the child, telling her she was naughty, criticizing her, neglecting to praise her for what she did well, overdressing her, constantly giving her made-in-China crap plastic toys that you feared were toxic and tried to discretely disappear.

Your parents knew almost nothing about your work. They knew you had a job, which was good, but it was hard for them to believe it was a real job: You didn't have an office to go to, after all. They knew it had something to do with human rights in China. And they knew that was dangerous. And perhaps a bit embarrassing. Why couldn't you have a normal job like your brother, who was an accountant, and not only supported his own family but gave more than double the amount of money to your parents that you did? They never asked you about yourself, how you were doing, about your work. That wasn't because of the kind of work you had; it was just something that didn't occur to them to ask. Don't Ask Don't Tell was the practice. Their philosophy of life was unarticulated but firm: Keep your head low, don't anger the powerful, don't even attract their attention, for it can bring nothing but harm in the end. Stay out of the way, lead your small life, scratch what you can out of it, don't think too much.

I didn't tell them until I returned from London. I didn't even tell them I was coming back early. I just showed up, and there they were, in our small flat on the island, taking care of Z. And then I waited until Z went to bed. And then my poor Cantonese was actually an advantage. I could keep it short and simple; I had to; linguistically, I had no other option. *Keuy set je jong—she has disappeared.* And then to make sure it was clear: *Your daughter has disappeared.* And just to be sure: *My wife has disappeared.* They nodded but looked blank, uncomprehending, vaguely distressed. *Keuy set je jong,* I repeated, then added, lapsing into Putonghua, *zai Zhongguo—in China.* They stared at me for a moment as if assessing whether or not I meant to say what I had just said, whether or not I had made a language error, but it was the "in China" bit that seemed to make them conclude between themselves without any exchange of words that I had not, that what I had said was what I meant to say.

Disappeared in China? your father asked.

Yes, I said, *that is all I know, no more.*

What'll we do? their expressions seemed to say. They didn't know how to take the news; what parent would, especially sprung upon them like that, out of the blue, while they were looking after their daughter's daughter? They didn't know what to do either; they were not people with their hands on the levers of power, the movers and shakers of the world. There above the surface of the pond is no place for us; we dwell here below. We accommodate ourselves to reality, have no expectations that reality should accommodate itself to our needs or desires, or that we have any influence upon, any say in anything beyond our immediate sphere. We work we eat we sleep we stay out of trouble. This is the way it's been for centuries, the tradition of us small potatoes. The very foundation of Chinese tyranny is that we stay in our place. So when hardship hit, even if it was the disappearance of their very own daughter, all they could do was hope for the best and persevere.

That was that. Being the generous, devoted, selfless people they were, they immediately volunteered to take up the childrearing slack. I thanked them. *I will have to spend some time looking for Y,* I said. In the time to come, they would spend a lot of time looking after Z. I was grateful to them for that.

●

It was New Year. Z and her grandparents got white orchids and a helium-filled purple dolphin balloon at the New Year's market. You loved white orchids. Z loved the balloon. She tied it to her play stroller in which she strapped her stuffed baby penguin, and she took the two of them, penguin and dolphin, for walks, until the latter lost its helium, becoming day by day ever more crumpled, floating lower and lower over the stroller. In the days after she got it, I warned her that if she let go of the string, it would sail up into the air, goodbye forever. She took that very seriously, wrapping the balloon around her wrist and having me tie it there. There was no fear of that now from the drooping balloon. *Poor dolphin*, Z said. The flowers prospered, though I did nothing to take care of them. I knew nothing about flowers in general, about orchids in particular, about growing plants at all, and I had no interest. I liked plants, I liked having them about, I liked leaving them alone. The orchid sat outside in a pot, in a shady place beneath a palm.

You had once grown orchids, when we first came to HK. Eventually, they died. You blamed yourself. Stopped growing them. Z kept calling them "Mommy's flowers"; she couldn't remember "orchids". She would say to a visitor, This is my dolphin and these are Mommy's flowers. Orchids, I'd say. Orchids, she'd repeat. And then the next time she'd revert to Mommy's flowers.

On the first day of New Year, she wore the light blue brocaded Tibetan jacket lined in thick white wool that Wangmo had sent. It was the image I would always remember from that first New Year without you: Z in that jacket zooming around the vertigo-inducing balcony-corridor on the twentieth floor of Tin Wan House on her scooter, slowing down and making sharp turns at each of the corners of square courtyard that, if you looked over the railing, seemed to never finish receding below. The first time I'd come to Tin Wan House, I had made to cut across the courtyard at ground level and you had pulled me back to the perimeter path that I later noticed everyone else stuck to. Watch out for falling bodies, you said.

Z zoomed past the rooms of the poor on one side, their chicken coops, from which they were released during the day to serve their masters for subsistence wages, and the red railing on the other, the abyss beyond that. Z's grandparents watched her tear around the courtyard terrace from their room, where they had lived since you were a little girl of Z's age. The first time I visited, the white upright piano you played as a kid was still there, pushed against a wall, your ledge of a bed jutting out from the wall directly above it. It was the only luxury your parents ever allowed themselves, and it was for you. They kept the piano for many years after you had grown up and gone away. Then they gave it to another little girl, a decision your father still regularly lamented, though no one had played it for years and it took up precious space in the cramped flat. They originally thought they would get out of there once their children were working and could support them, but here they still were, all these many years later, paying HKD 1,200 a month for 350 square feet.

I followed Z around and peered into other rooms where families hunkered down over their New Year's feasts. Occasionally a face peaked up to see what the commotion was out in the hall, a blur of a little girl flying past. City kids didn't learn to ride scooters like that. She was a wild child. You would have had her hair in neat pigtails. I never managed that. Now halfway down her back, her hair flew behind her in the scooter breeze. The year before, we'd still commented on how bald she was; her hair had come late and fine. Now, in your absence, it hung in her face, and she was constantly brushing it aside with her hand.

Your parents had taken to occasionally bringing Z to their place to stay the night; to give me a break, they said. Before that, Z had never spent a night apart from us. You couldn't bear it, or you thought Z wouldn't. Z wasn't very pleased at first, but she got used to it, and she liked being with her grandparents, who after all gave her all the attention she desired. I often reminded her to not take advantage of them. *I want to go home*, she would always say in the end. *I want daddy.*

We had a thing between us. Even when you were around, it was always *I want daddy*. After you disappeared, I thought that if it had to be one of us, better you, at least as far as Z was concerned. And then I scolded myself for thinking that. It was a stupid way to think about things, wasn't it? Of course, Z missed her mother greatly, even when she wasn't aware of it; you were irreplaceable.

You'd worked so hard to escape that room on the twentieth floor of Tin Wan House. You forced yourself to succeed on others' terms, in ways valued by people who had money and power. As a result, you earned their scholarships to secondary school abroad, then one of the world's top universities, then a master's program. And now Z, your daughter, the daughter you wanted to have all of the things of which you were deprived, to avoid all of the childhood-killing forces you'd faced, spent the night there where you grew up, though, as became apparent watching her whiz about on the scooter, it was arguable that she brought more life to the place than was sucked out of her.

That New Year, while eating the New Year's meal with your parents on the twentieth floor of Tin Wan House, I recalled how tense the previous New Year had been. The trigger was tiny, finding out that the travel agent had not booked seats on a complicated series of flights we had to take over the coming months, but it nearly pushed you over the edge. You feared that Z and I would have to sit in middle seats on one flight, and on the return to HK, when we were all together again, we would not be able to sit together, no three contiguous seats being any longer available. It was one of those proverbial straws that broke the camel's back. You couldn't take HK anymore, you said, you couldn't stand it.

This came on the heels of HSBC summarily closing our bank account. When you questioned the bank's representatives, underlings all, functionaries, none of whom was responsible for the decision, you were told it was an "administrative decision", and no other reason or further explanation was given. Amongst people working in human rights, there were rumors of a task force of HK and mainland security personnel monitoring the human rights community in HK. HSBC had a bad reputation for easily acceding to demands of Partystate officials, having recently ceased placing ads in the only pro-democracy daily newspaper in the city even though it had one of the largest circulations. We'd never had a financial problem of any kind, had never been behind in a payment, never been in debt, were always exceedingly financially responsible, so we suspected our account had been closed because we had ended up on that task force's black list; there was simply no other reason or explanation we could think of, and the bank wasn't giving us any. It was true that we transferred small amounts of money to active citizens on the mainland, especially when they were in trouble with the authorities and had had their bank accounts frozen, a common action undertaken by the Partystate against its perceived enemies, but we'd never used our own account to do that. Perhaps the Partystate had discovered these "illicit" transfers and decided to punish us by asking HSBC to close our account. Whatever the case, treatment like that meted out by the bank was so unfair, it simply drove you crazy. It left you thinking, We live in a society, in a part of the world, without recourse. We shouldn't have had an account with HSBC anyway, so bad was its reputation, but it had a nearly monopolistic hold in HK and if you wanted to transfer or receive funds from other accounts without exorbitant fees, HSBC was the easiest, since everyone had an HSBC account. It was a long, complicated process to extricate our money from the account.

Your aggravation was understandable. This rights work was an exercise in anger and paranoia management. If you didn't watch it, it all turned inward; the anger, the hate, the resentment could seep into every crack, saturate every pore, infecting yourself, your relations with others, your daily encounters. I found myself on a number of occasions berating functionaries though they served no other purpose than to act as gatekeepers, preventing me from gaining access to those truly responsible for one cowardly, unjust act or another. I was embarrassed, ashamed of my behavior. So, too, I believed, much of the friction between us was caused by emotions that seeped into the relationship from the work.

The bank account closure and then the confusion about seats on upcoming flights—you'd had enough. You wanted to live in a sane place. You had to get out of HK, out of this kind of work.

But that's exactly how they want you to react, I said.

Yes, and it's how I react, you replied.

Could it take so little to make you cave? I knew better than to say those words aloud, but they were what I thought.

In a concatenation I couldn't quite remember, that brief exchange metamorphosed into an attack on me for not understanding you, not sympathizing with you, not appreciating you, not understanding the risks and pressures of your work, and ended with the emphatic declaration that I remembered very clearly a year later: *You don't understand me. What's the point of being married?*

How could you go from irritation at a travel agent forgetting to book seats and consternation at the unjust closing of the bank account to *why be married?*

A few days before, you had sighed, *If I ever get detained, I will miss you both so much. You won't leave me will you? You'll stick with me?*

Real Jekyll&Hyde stuff.

No matter how often the eruptions occurred, I was always taken by surprise. I didn't know how to respond to them. Anything I said or did (or didn't say or do, for that matter) just seemed to make matters worse. I would inevitably allow myself to be provoked, and it would end in a stand-off, with you threatening to end things and going to bed and me thinking, Where in the world did that come from?

We talked and talked about going away to a saner place, but we never did. We continued doing the same thing, leading the same life. You blamed me for everything, including getting into that line of work, having that particular job, for everything you didn't like about your life. It was all my fault, an accusation that at the time seemed preposterous, but, a year on, looking back, seemed right.

Such were my musings that night over New Year's dinner. I was very quiet, lost in thought. In summer, your parents place was always cool, there on the twentieth floor, with the breeze blowing through the two open doors on either side, between the balcony and the courtyard. In winter, though, it was a concrete refrigerator, and no matter how warmly I dressed to go there, I shivered.

In the late evening, Z and I left for home. She loved traffic, since she didn't get to see it on the island. Loved sitting on my lap on the mini-bus, looking out the window, watching the taxis, cars, buses, trucks. She was placidly engrossed, tired, silent for longer than usual, and eventually, when we got home, half-asleep. I carried her heavy body up the long steps from the ferry pier. She was happy to go to bed that night.

●

The bedtime routine varied little. We took a bath, read books and brushed teeth. I warmed up the milk. We got into bed, usually with her baby penguin. We turned on the turtle, which, depending on which button you pushed, cast dim green, blue or orange stars and a slim crescent moon onto the walls and ceiling from its shell. While she drank her milk, she requested stories, which I duly told. When she finished, we talked about whatever happened to be on her mind. Then I said, *OK, it's time to go to sleep. Sleep well. Sweet dreams. Love you.* It would usually take a while, and several reminders from me, for her to stop talking and settle down. Then the room would go silent. I waited for her to drift off to sleep, staring up at the ceiling or at her face, barely discernible in the dim light of the glowing turtle.

Sometimes—usually just before midnight, at which point she had already been asleep three or four hours—, she would awake in a fright, as if from a bad dream. I went to her side, bent down to where she was lying on the mattress in the open-sided crib, and placed a hand on her back. *It's o.k., sweet Z, go back to sleep.* She stuttered through her sobs—it often took time and effort to understand what she was saying—, *Is mommy still awake?*

A difficult question to answer. At that moment, wherever she was, mommy might still be awake. But then, that wasn't really what the child was asking, was it? She was disoriented, half asleep, not recalling mommy was not at home, or hoping that, waking in the middle of the night, mommy might magically reappear. And anyway, no matter what the import of the question, was it not more urgent to provide a placating rather than truthful answer? You wanted the child to go back to sleep, after all. "Mommy isn't here now; remember?" just wouldn't do at midnight. If I said, Yes, mommy is still awake, then she might ask, Where is she, can I see her? She wanted to hear her voice, to sense her physical presence. Usually, I resorted to saying, *Mommy is fine, let's go back to sleep*, and hoped that would do.

It almost always did. She was a remarkably resilient child. Perhaps that was a quality many, if not most, children possessed, the ability to bounce back. What else were they to do, the powerless? Amazing that they did so with such grace, hope, humor, and—perhaps the most indispensable ingredient—obliviousness. Still, Z reminded me constantly, by example, that resilience had a power all its own, the power of the powerless.

Baby penguin was sometimes parked in the play stroller at the foot of the bed, or sometimes Z brought baby penguin into the bed and she rested by her side. As often as she would call for mommy upon suddenly awaking in the middle of the night, she would call for baby penguin. She'd seen a short video clip that showed penguin chicks being fed by their parents. In the opening, the fathers are sitting on the chicks to keep them warm, hundreds of to-human-eyes identical-looking fathers and chicks clustered on a wide icefield. The fathers have almost no food left to feed the chicks; both chicks and fathers are hungry. The mother penguins return from a long hunting trip. They approach from a distance, waddling across the icefield, and then begin calling for their partners and chicks amidst the hubbub. Once reunited, an exchange is performed: the baba shuffles the chick out from under him and the mommy gathers the chick under her. The operation must occur quickly in order to avoid the chick freezing to death. As soon as the chick is under the mother, it sticks its beak into its mother's and hungrily gobbles a gooey-looking substance. Meanwhile, the fathers head off on a hunting trip of their own, alternately waddling and tobogganing on their stomachs over the icefield to its edge, where they slide-dive into the black water to swim far far off in search of food.

Something about the solicitude of the parents, especially how they sit upon the chick that would otherwise freeze to death and feed it out of their mouths, coupled with the chick's vulnerability, made an impression on Z. She especially liked the image of the mother penguins walking with the chicks between their legs and she imitated them with baby penguin between hers. Up to then, she'd had no special stuffed animal, doll or security blanket, no soothing ritual such as thumb-sucking, but had acquired several "friends" from our many trips. She'd already flown around the world twice and collected a friend from each location, Uma, a girlchild from Berlin; Knut, a sheep from Norway; Elk, a wolf from the northern U.S. But after seeing that video multiple times upon request ("one more time, one more time!"), she adopted baby penguin as the creature for which she had special responsibility, of which she took special care. She went to bed with her (for it was a "she"—baby penguin is tired), brought her to the table to eat (baby penguin is hungry), pushed her around in her play stroller, and took her along in a pink backpack with white stars whenever she went out, whether on a short trip down the main street of the village to the playground or a longer trip on the ferry to the city. Baby penguin she'd gotten on a visit to a local aquarium, where she'd first seen penguins in the flesh. At about the time of the video, she had been reading night after night a Curious George story about George visiting an aquarium and saving a baby penguin that had fallen into the water while no one was looking and could not yet swim. Even the small had within them a voice that said we must look out for the small, a simply empathetic voice that said we must care for the world around us, especially creatures smaller than ourselves that have less power; I must use my greater power to that creature's greater good.

New Year was a dark time, cold and rainy. With that chilly damp on the skin, it was hard to remember what most of the rest of the year was like. Lying there in bed as Z drifted off to sleep, a process that usually took upwards of an hour, I thought of her great capacity for joy. I remembered the mid-summer sea, the brightness after days of rain, the sun floating out over the water, its surface stretched out before us, the distant island so piercingly, vividly sharp, as if sky, clouds, mountains, sea were there to break my heart, the brightness all the more blinding in contrast to the dark days that had come before.

Already, back then, she was so much younger. At that age, aeons are traversed in a matter of weeks, the change so fast. The image of her then was already slipping from memory, overlaid by her image in the present. An image even better than previous ones. How could she just keep getting better? All the time, better and better.

While the rain came down, it was hard to imagine it would ever cease, the constant splatter splatter on the flagstones out front of the house, the softer pitter patter on the roof, and in the background, the thud thud of raindrops hitting the leaves, especially the big banana leaves, a sound not much different from the wind blowing.

Z stood at the sliding screen doors, staring out, singing over and over a trancelike medley: It's raining, it's pouring, rain rain go away rain rain go away. In fact, she liked the rain, liked putting on her green froggy rainboots and matching green froggy rainjacket with white polka-dots, taking her childsize umbrella your parents had given her and heading out into the rain to look for puddles to jump in. But when it rained as heavily as that, just to be dry, to be in a dry place, to have shelter was a blessing, a mercy. Count your blessings, count your blessings, the rain insisted. I do I do, I replied, but also sorrows. One must count them both to recognize either, no? That was my medley, a counterpoint to Z's. But the rain listened to neither.

And then, just when it seemed as if it might go on forever, it stopped. The clouds disappeared. The clarity of the air snapped the lulled senses to attention. Due to smog and humidity, the view was usually murky at best, the distant islands no more than smudged outlines against the horizon. But that moment, all came into focus. And we did what we always did when the rain stopped: We went to the beach. A still, nearly silent day, braced, expectant yet placid, as if listening for something, a day formed by the undulations of the sea, so small and inconspicuous one could not deign to call them waves, they in turn formed by the day, day and waves, waves and day, Z in her inflatable ring bobbing up and down up and down on the barely perceptible waves—peaceful, as close to peace as we could come. Before she had the ring, how tightly she had clung, her chest pressed against my chest, her cheek against mine, another form of joy, the sensation of skin touching water, skin touching skin.

This was something Z loved, to bob tranquilly up and down up and down in rhythm with the sea, as much as she loved the big crashing white waves, loved to feel herself floating freely over their tops in her inflatable plastic ring (cheap plastic madeinchina by exploited labor not feeling nearly so free at that moment or perhaps any other, not to mention her synthetic swimsuit, red with strawberries, cuteascanbe and made in the same place—ah, yes, every freedom is illusory, or based on someone else's unfreedom, no?, everything inflected through and through) just when it looked as if they would come crashing down over her, floating freely, independent of me or anyone else in her floating ring, independent of everything except the waves, the enormous sea, that tiny figure in the enormous sea, over the top of one wave and down into the trough of the next.

That sensation of freedom, I thought, watching her, that came from floating on the waves was in fact dependent on them, on taking oneself away from what and whom one depended on to something else, a larger kind of surrender and giving over to a force much larger than oneself. Is that not the opposite of freedom; is it not utter subjugation? Or is it paradoxically the key to freedom, and the gate through which one must pass? But for Z, it was not meditation, just sensation, pure sensation, coursing through the body. That was the freedom, then, to revel in pure sensation, in the moment, the present, not anywhere else but here and now, the here-and-now itself not being time but sensation.

And teased from that freedom, that sensation, a presentiment of the infinite fragility and contingency of all life, a presentiment that through love became its own sensation. Imagine that upon this placid scene came a tidal wave, a tsunami, and everything was swept away at once. We would be gone when you got back. You would have nowhere to return to, no one to return to. You would wish you had never returned and could go back to where you had come from, not back to captivity, if indeed that was where you were, but back to before any of this had happened, back to where all remained unbroken, undestroyed.

Strange that it was I having such thoughts of sudden disaster. You were the one who always feared the impending catastrophe that lurked around every corner. My role was to play down your fears, tell you to calm down, be at peace, scold you for your inability to manage your anxiety, warning it was corrosive. It was a feeling that pervaded your whole being: Life is uncertain; dangers lurks around every corner. You are small, unimportant, flotsam on the sea of life—the joyful freedom that Z felt at being alive rendered as helplessness, her clement universe no more than the indifference of the powers that be to her fate and all others'. All you can do is try to protect yourself, keep your head down, take infinite precautions, foresee every danger. Calm down, I said again. And then you disappeared.

I remembered the moment I first put Z in the floating ring, a ring her mother had bought: I walked out into the water and placed the ring on the placid surface. I held Z up high and lowered her feet into the middle of the ring, draping her arms over it. Then I let go. Discovery passed over her face, jolted her whole body: Floating, floating on one's own, independently, without baba or anyone else holding her up, floating in the wide sea, that immensity of water that stretched far beyond imagination, and she, that tiny creature in the midst of immensity, she laughed, and giggled, and smiled, and tensed her body, and kicked her legs. Pure joy, I thought. Contagious pure joy. Nobody in her presence could fail to be affected by it. Pure joy, pure physical joy at the sensation of being alive. This is what pure joy looks like, I thought, unadulterated, uncut, a joy I recognized, was inspired by, but cut off from. I felt joy too, probably more often than most, but it was measured, tempered, constant, moderate, a grieving joy, arising from awareness of suffering, mine and others', precious but different from hers, fully present, in the moment. I marvelled at it, that great capacity for joy.

The passage at the start of *To the Lighthouse* came to mind: *...he appeared the image of stark and uncompromising severity, with his high forehead and his fierce blue eyes, impeccably candid and pure, frowning slightly at the sight of human frailty, so that his mother, watching him guide his scissors neatly round the refrigerator, imagined him all red and ermine on the Bench or directing some stern and momentous enterprise in a crisis of public affairs.* A description of the child, James, a premonition of what he would grow up to be.

No, not Z. How unlike that she was. No severity at all. And nothing that presaged a particular future. Just sorrow or joy. Mostly joy. In fact, my fear—to the extent that I had any, for part of me felt that any way she turned out was just fine, as long as she turned out, as long as she survived—was that she would become as I: Rather than dressed in red and ermine or directing some stern and momentous enterprise (for at least then you could say you had accomplished something), the eternal opt-out, not by choice but predilection, through taking one small decision after another that resulted in *this*, the person I was for better or worse but did not wish her to become. Part of me wondered how I might be able to set her on a track to accomplish something, anything. So that she could one day look back and say, I have done that. Indisputably. Instead of, What have I accomplished, what have I to show for all these years in the service of abstract ideals? I wasn't even sure how I would continue to support her financially until she could support herself—which reminded me: I wasn't even sure whether your organization had continued to pay your salary after you had been disappeared—something to check. She loved to do household chores, to wash dishes; I joked that a lot of tourist restaurants on the island were looking for help. Some severity, some disdain, like James', for human frailty might come in handy, might be an ingredient in the recipe for success.

I was an o.k. father, as fathers go, but the weight of raising a child on my own, the prospect of being a single parent for an indefinite, perhaps lengthy period of time, made me fear she would turn out too much like me. Not that she hadn't already shown sufficient sign of being her own person, from birth in fact, regardless of influence; indeed, I was quite confident she would be, though certainly with inflections from those with whom she spent the most time.

It was just exhausting to be with her all of the time. Physically exhausting, mentally exhausting. I found myself constantly thinking, How do people do this? How do they manage? How do some not only manage but thrive, prosper, get their children to thrive, prosper? And I've got just one; many have more.

The more people I could share her around with, the better, the more chance of tiring her out too and not just me. The more impulses, the more stimuli, the more different types of people she met, the richer her life. Having just me to turn to seemed a rather impoverished upbringing. Even before having a child, I felt inadequate unto myself, and now I was to be a resource to another?

In fact, people lived with whatever they had, whatever the circumstances, whatever the gods, the fates had dished up. And from that angle, the remarkable thing was how adaptable children were: they could put up with most anything short of flat-out abuse and come out the other end, often come through it well even. You had to work hard to damage them. That was some consolation. At times.

There was that other line from *To the Lighthouse*, much later in the book. How did it go? Something about waves.... *All that in idea seemed simple became in practice immediately complex; as the waves shape themselves symmetrically from the cliff top, but to the swimmer among them are divided by steep gulfs, and foaming crests.... Down in the hollow of one wave she saw the next wave towering higher and higher above her.* We were down in the hollow of a rather large wave, and I kept trying to imagine the scene from above. I often ran along the high ridge of the island; from there, you could look down on the beach far below. It was not hard to estimate the size of the waves because I knew from experience what the waves actually felt like when I was in them, could distinguish a big wave from a small wave. Perhaps that one wave in whose hollow we were would not even be visible from the ridge. And if so, then there was a problem too, for the wave did indeed exist, even if it appeared trivial or eminently surmountable from a distance, from above.

Z had now climbed out of the ring and was clinging to me tightly, her chest pressed against my chest, her cheek against mine. Our chins touched the surface of the calm water. The islands far across the wide stretch of water were so sharply visible, it was as if binoculars much stronger than the naked eye had screwed them into focus.

Unmystical I felt a mystical feeling at this power of sight, of seeing far, of the bright blue sky above punctuated by enormous white shifting clouds, of the flatness of the sea stretching out and connecting to those islands way over there and much else beyond. If one stared intently, intensely enough, one might penetrate some secret or answer to a precious question hidden in the air, in its very crispness and clarity. It seemed too sharp to be just for itself, an end in itself. On the distant islands, every contour, every detail, every tree, every building, every person going about his business could be discerned; indeed, if one peered long enough, hard enough, one might even be able to look straight into each heart. That's how sharp the visibility was, the air like an envelope, the eye following its smooth surfaceless surface, seeking the crease to pry it open. And if opened, what would one find?

All those stories that had to do with entering alternate dimensions, "The Wizard of Oz", *The Chronicles of Narnia*, *Alice in Wonderland*, *The Wind-up Bird Chronicle*, Orpheus and Eurydice pace Ovid. Most, though not all, were for children: At the very least, did one not need a child-like faith in the possibility of the seemingly impossible? These stories' premise was that the solution could not be found in this reality but lay in a dimension not usually accessible to us mere mortals since we did not know about it and even if we did, could not get there on our own. Whatever their particular wonders and attractions, whatever their aesthetic pleasures, I never much appreciated the alternate realms. This world and all its wonders and sorrows, I thought, are more enough for me. But I understood the impulse, the need, especially for children who felt powerless, whose imagination was restricted in this world, really for all people who felt powerless, people who came up against the thick wall of injustice in this world, who wanted more than to be mere eggs cracked against its surface. How did you pass through it, or circumvent it, to the other side, where problems would be solved, redress rendered, desires fulfilled?

Someone disappears just like that. Shouldn't there be some just-like-that way to get her back? But what is it? Especially when that someone has been spirited away by a power much greater than yourself, behind some dark impenetrable curtain? And in a way, you hope she has; it hurts less than the possibility that this someone has taken herself away of her own volition, for her own mysterious reasons. The unknown marks disappearance as its fundamental element. There's no one to ask, nothing is clear. It's like losing someone to a larger-than-life natural force, the tsunami, the earthquake, the avalanche, the storm, except at least there, the cause is clear, even if the exact moment of demise is forever inaccessible, the corpse unrecoverable. You want to imagine every moment of that disappearance, to know everything that that precious person experienced right up to and including the last moment, to, in a way, experience it all with her, to relieve her of the loneliness of experiencing it all alone, or perhaps even more to relieve yourself of the loneliness of her absence, of not knowing what occurred, of the guilt at not having been able to prevent it or at the very least to experience it at her side, and yet, you don't, you turn away from it too, fearful it will overwhelm, swallow you as well.

Most children's stories having to do with alternate dimensions resolved the problem in those dimensions and then returned the protagonist safely to the world from which she originally came. The adult stories of katabasis, of descent to the underworld, usually ended tragically: Just as Orpheus is about to succeed in miraculously rescuing Eurydice from the Underworld and bring her back to the land of the living, he turns back and … all is lost.

I was especially troubled by Plato's take on the story. To Plato, couched in the voice of Phaedrus in the *Symposium*, Orpheus was a selfish coward because he did not choose to die in order to be reunited with his beloved but instead resorted to going to Hades and seeking to return with her: *But Orpheus, son of Oeagrus, [the Gods] sent back with failure from Hades, showing him only a wraith of the woman for whom he came; her real self they would not bestow, for he was accounted to have gone upon a coward's quest, too like the minstrel that he was, and to have lacked the spirit to die as Alcestis did for the sake of love, when he contrived the means of entering Hades alive. Wherefore they laid upon him the penalty he deserved, and caused him to meet his death at the hands of women.* For Plato, then, the refusal to see that there was no other alternative to a tragic ending, and thereby to recognize that full self-sacrifice was necessary, the false belief that the situation could somehow be rescued and return to at least some approximation of what it was before, was a form of cowardice. He compares Orpheus negatively to those who sacrificed their lives for their beloved, such as Achilles who sought to avenge the murder of Patroclus: *...whereas Achilles, son of Thetis, [the Gods] honored and sent to his place in the Isles of the Blest, because having learnt from his mother that he would die as surely as he slew Hector, but if he slew him not, would return home and end his days an aged man, he bravely chose to go and rescue his lover Patroclus, avenged him, and sought death not merely in his behalf but in haste to be joined with him whom death had taken. For this the gods so highly admired him that they gave him distinguished honor, since he set so great a value on his lover.*

How stately the rhetoric of Phaedrus/Plato, how authoritative, and how puny I appeared in his shadow. Plato's mocking words echoed in my mind: *for he was accounted to have gone upon a coward's quest, too like the minstrel that he was*—ouch!, even if, at the end of the day, my rational self judged him wrong or at least simplistic, death's romanticist. Phaedrus' judgment appeared in the context of a discourse on love: *So there is my description of Love—that he is the most venerable and valuable of the gods, and that he has sovereign power to provide all virtue and happiness for men whether living or departed.* Essentially, Phaedrus/Plato is saying

Orpheus' love of Eurydice was weak, that it was actually a kind of self-love masquerading as love, and his fate proves it. That reading played on my own guilt: the beloved disappeared, I had not (yet) ventured into the murky underworld of the largest dictatorship in the world, where power was all and I had none, where you almost surely had disappeared at the hands of the seemingly omnipotent, in order to confront the monsters and rescue you; instead, I preferred, when push came to shove, to protect my own skin, even if I could credibly justify the act of self-preservation with two arguments in my defense: 1) There was little I could do, not knowing where you were or who had you, and my efforts would simply be ineffectual and possibly even self-defeating, counter-productive, while at the same time I could be putting myself in danger for no good reason, which was related to the second argument: 2) Without her mother around, someone had to look out for Z—shouldn't that be my first priority, perhaps even above finding you? But oh, Phaedrus/Plato, however sound my arguments might appear, your claws still dug deep!—willingness to die for a cause, for the beloved, for anything higher than yourself, however futilely (for who can know in the short run what shall prove truly futile and what not?), was greatest. My heart was a sucker for the argument; was that alone not enough to prove it false?

The brightness of the sun glittering across the wavy surface of the water filled up the vision. All became glittery bright, as if a reflection of Z's joy. When you were not in the water, the sun was oppressive, pounding down on you. You wanted to take shelter. While living in that far Northern Paradise, dark half the year, raining over two hundred days a year, I was a sun worshipper. It was hard to imagine being a sun worshipper here. Here, you wanted the sun to go away. Except when in the water. Then, one's perspective shifted, and one thought, Yes, everything in the world is in its place, the sun is not oppressive, it is just there in the sky, for us, even, and we are enveloped in a world of brightness. Everything else vanishes; even disappearance.

At home, on the bookshelf, pressed between the pages of Montale's *Tutte le poesie* were the sonograms of Z while she was still inside of you, at different stages of the pregnancy, three in total, as well as the letter you wrote to Z on her first birthday, to be opened when she was old enough to read it and understand. Why did I stick them there? It would be nice to say because they would be at home surrounded by the poetic beauty, but more because the volume was large enough to contain them, and I so seldom opened the book that I could be confident that the sonograms and letter would remain undisturbed, pressed flat, protected, hopefully for years to come, from the HK humidity that curled paper almost before your eyes. Holding Z now, looking at her, I thought of those sonograms, that letter, her mother, a superb photographer and documentarian wishing to preserve every moment of her daughter's life, the prospect that in her mother's absence, so much would now go unrecorded, slip from my fallible grasp, escape memory, disappear into oblivion. At this age, Z was too young to remember much, if anything; it was almost heartbreaking to think that when she was older, she would have virtually no memory of this time in her life, we would be her only memory, we and these records, mementoes, the photos, the words. Or, if for some reason, you were never to return, Z would have no memory of her mother.

Z said, *Big waves.* She was remembering a recent day at another beach, on the other side of the island, when the waves rumbled and crashed upon the shore with what seemed almost intentional drama (indeed Z called them "drama queens", something I'd recently called her when she was whining and making a scene for a reason I couldn't recall). Most were not so big that they crashed on top of us, but instead lifted us onto their tops and carried us. Z found it a thrill and shrieked in laughing anticipation at each approaching wave, having learned to estimate the amount of time it would take to arrive. Now she said, *Big waves*, and then paused as if reflecting. She meant to contrast them with the stillness, the calm of the sea on this day. Perhaps she was a little disappointed by today's waves, whose placidity I greatly enjoyed. I said, *Today the waves are small. Sometimes the waves are big; sometimes the waves are small.*

She considered this a moment and replied, *Sometimes pink biscuits, sometimes green biscuits, sometimes orange.* She had newly grasped the concept of "sometimes" and enjoyed applying it. She was reminded of a nursery school she attended twice a week in a small room on the village main street. A snack was served each time, the lack of nutrition of which had been a constant if low-grade complaint of yours. When Z mentioned the pink, green and orange biscuits, I imagined you rolling your eyes in exasperation at the lack of nutritional knowledge of the well-meaning, good-hearted woman who ran the group. Other snacks were marshmallows and what you referred to as "toxic" raisins from Xinjiang. Z didn't seem to mind. She liked the sugary biscuits, much to her mother's chagrin. *Yes*, I replied, *exactly: sometimes big waves, sometimes small waves, sometimes pink biscuits, sometimes green biscuits, sometimes orange biscuits.*

●

Z loved to run naked on the beach, scurrying about and stopping now and then to pick up rocks, shells, handfuls of sand that she gleefully cast into the air, some of it landing on her head. (When I bathed her in the evening, her fine hair was full of fine-grained sand.) *This beautiful difficult child.* No more difficult than most. Difficult as children were wont to be; difficult because a child. Even before your disappearance, I had been ever more feeling the need of a break from Z, from the strain of being a parent. Much of the effort of the first two years I had welcomed, embraced, with zeal, commitment, and something I liked to think of as love. And those years disappeared in a haze, giving as nothing else in my life to that point—including the many dangerous and life-threatening situations in which I had been, the many people I had seen die—a deep feeling of life's transience. But recently, something like burnout seemed to have set in, a heaviness that went through the night and continued into the day, like living in perpetual haze, that descended into going through the motions. It seemed every moment of every day and night was tied to Z's needs and desires. *This grueling luminescent beauty* was the phrase that kept coming to mind in regard to the experience of being a father. I had started to dream of taking short trips alone, just to get away, to have a break. I had checked airfares, made enquiries. The desire seemed both frivolous and necessary. I needed more fortitude, I told myself, greater endurance. I needed to hang in there.

The typical day. Wake at 6:29 after being awakened during the night at 2:31 and 5:42 by plaintive calls for *nainai*—milk. Z had never been a particularly good sleeper. She had become better, going down most nights around 8, waking between 6 and 7 in the morning, but with usually two disruptions during the night. What this meant for me, who might go to bed around midnight, was that I never felt well-rested. I had never needed much sleep, but now whole days I could spend in a semi-stunned state, never quite waking up. Sometimes I thought that parenthood and age had made my mind duller than ever before, and parenthood had accelerated the aging process, wrought havoc on fitness. Sometimes the sheer monotony wore me down, and it felt as if my soul were being eroded. Sometimes it was as if I could see myself aging before my eyes. In the mirror, my face looked more angular, wrinkles were spreading in creases from my eyes, and was I just imagining that my face appeared more lop-sided than ever, with a weaker chin, was I just imagining that each day my hair was a little greyer than the day before?

Crying fits and tantrums became more frequent. While it was tempting to ascribe them at least partly to her mother's absence, it was more likely that it had to do with that particular stage of development, as I heard reports of similar behavior from her friends' parents. One time, though, it was clearly her mother's absence that was the cause: Having gotten all ready, put on the swimsuit, sunscreen, gathered the beach toys, packed towel and snacks, we went to the beach, and just as we were about to descend the stairs from the path to the sand, she said, *I want mommy, I want to go home.*

Mommy's not home, I said, *she's not here right now. Can't we just go to the beach and enjoy ourselves?*

But she was not open to persuasion and did not calm down until we started heading back home. I felt dejected, down-trodden, impatient, angry, resentful, but in the next moment thought, Look at yourself: who needs a sullen father?

We ate breakfast at the table in the yard before anyone else in the neighborhood woke. In the stillness, each small noise we made seemed to fill the air, the sky. Yogurt, bread—which Z and I made together, continuing a practice of yours, in your honor—with marmite for Z, peanut butter for me, watermelon, muesli (mostly raisins, Z's favorite) with soy milk. The leaves of the banana tree at the edge of the yard were ever-encroaching; it was producing more bunches than I thought possible, and with each bunch came the blossoms wrapped in thick petals looking like red elephant's skin, which attracted bees that otherwise never came around. On the ground next to the table were the fallen red elephant skin blossoms swarmed by intoxicated bees.

After breakfast, we watered the plot you had planted before your disappearance, digging up a corner of the lawn that was already more weeds than grass. I did not even know what was there, since you had planted it together with Z, and nothing yet had grown sufficiently for me to recognize it. At this point, Z was naked. I'd taken off the diaper she wore at night, along with the pajamas, which were more often than not damp from urine perspiration. She was busy in the yard, riding her tricycle, playing in water, including two portable plastic bathtubs in which we'd bathed her in her first months of life and a large half-broken bucket, climbing the ladder to inspect the bunches of bananas. When I could manage to get her attention, I dressed her and put her hair up, something I was never very good at. You put it in pigtails, your mother braided it; both styles were beyond my ability, so she now wore it in a scruffy ponytail.

We visited her friend, Ramona, who often wasn't at home, in which case we descended the steep stairs near her house to a narrow strip of sand, where Z threw stones in the water. From there we went to a little cove where villagers kept their beat-up fishing boats, and in the sand from which the tide had receded we stepped over boat lines and looked inside the boats. Then we went to the library and checked out books. After that, we went to the organic store, where we talked with Gavin, the man who ran it and had a child the same age as Z. We had a snack, usually an orange, in the back of the store where there was a self-serve café that faced out onto the harbor. We went to the concrete football pitch to practice riding the purple scooter that I often pulled Z around on. I rarely carried her anymore, and when she insisted, I said that she was too big and heavy; she had to either walk or ride the scooter. By this time, the football pitch and adjoining playground were baking in the sun. Z sat on a bench beneath a shady awning and read a book she had checked out of the library. I shot goals with an old, slightly warped ball I'd found in a corner of the pitch.

Part of me wished Z was more interested in balls. Whenever I had one, she momentarily showed interest, gave it a kick, picked it up and tried to throw it, and then wandered off to something else. Perhaps she was still too young. But other children her age were more interested, and already becoming more adept.

I was surprised how long she let me take shots undisturbed as she sat reading in the shade. Reading—that was something she liked. And if I had to choose between ballplay and reading, I suppose I'd choose reading. We went home and read the other books she got from the library, *Curious George* and *This is not my hat* (*A fish has stolen a hat. And he'll probably get away with it. Probably.*), plus two bad Chinese books, one called *I love my family*, the other called *Brushing my teeth* (you always complained that there were no good children's books in Chinese—they all moralized or were overly didactic; on the other hand, we were always struck by how many amazing children's books there were in English).

We had lunch, after which I put Z down for a nap. That usually took a while. We had a discussion about parents, sons and daughters because I had been telling her who was whose parent, who was whose son or daughter on the island, and what the difference between a son and a daughter was. She got up to go to the potty, and while sitting there, recited to herself a largely unintelligible monologue about who is whose parent, who is whose son or daughter. After I finally got her to sleep, I luxuriated in the silence, the wonderful space created by her absence. I didn't do much; I just listened to it, enjoyed it. I often heard of other parents who did so many chores, who accomplished so much, even writing, while their children slept. I couldn't quite understand how they managed; it was all I could do to keep from collapse. Sleep time for her was recovery time for me. Lately she'd been sleeping better during the day, an hour and a half, sometimes two hours, and sometimes I'd even have to wake her from a nap that went over two hours. She was sleepy, bleary-eyed, sometimes a little weepy, and we went to the kitchen and cracked open a cold coconut, blinded the shell in one of its two eyes with a knife, and inserted a straw. Z drank the juice. Or sometimes it was a popsicle of yogurt, banana and spinach (one of the ways of smuggling greens into her diet, another one of your clever inventions). She laughed that she could bite the rock-hard popsicle straight out of the freezer while I couldn't; it made me shiver just to watch her.

We went to the beach, played in the water, played in the sand, went to the garden beyond the beach where there were pineapples, a big long-an tree, pumpkins growing on high trellised vines above our heads, and inspected the progress of the fruits and vegetables through the season. Z became adept at recognizing a wide range of plants. On the way home, she ran barefoot along the main street through the village, looking like a ragamuffin, a savage. She dressed in an oversize t-shirt she chose herself from our last visit to that distant Northern Paradise. I'd warned her at the time of purchase that it would be long before it would fit her properly, but that didn't matter. It went down nearly to her knees, pink, with four pictures of an identical moose face in different colors. Z pointed out to me that in fact the moose faces were not identical—each had a different expression, something I hadn't noticed.

In the evening, we had a simple dinner, a good dinner but less elaborate than when her mother was around. Pasta, rice, edamame or other beans, vegetables. Often Z sat on the kitchen counter and watched me make breakfast and dinner. She enjoyed being in the kitchen, enjoyed when I let her help me, especially enjoyed washing dishes (I let her wash all the plastic cups, bowls and plates), standing on her black wooden stepstool pushed up against the sink. After dinner, we had a bath, both of us naked in the bathtub, facing each other, and after that, read books, brushed teeth, went outside to look at the moon. She had long been interested in the moon, and just recently, we'd been talking about the difference between a crescent moon, a half moon and a full moon and noting each evening whether it was waxing or waning. While she looked at the moon, I held her and looked at her face in the moonlight inches from mine, eyes turned upward, full of wonder, reverence. Then a bottle of milk in bed while I put on diaper and pajamas. Then a demand, *Stories!*

I said, *What do you want a story about?*

And she said, *About... a frog, a snake, the windmill*—referring to the only windmill on the island, the only one in the whole city, to which we'd occasionally hike, lying down under it and staring up, watching the blades whoosh down towards us and then bend upwards again—, *VVs*—the "village vehicles" that raced around the carless island making deliveries, carting trash away, and so on.

Then I improvised. She was a tough audience. If she didn't like a story, she would say, *I don't like that story*, or, *That's not a story, that's just a tell!* and make me start again with a new one. It took upwards of forty-five minutes of storytelling and lying next to her before she would fall asleep. We had just hung a dreamcatcher from the top bar of the crib after some deliberation about the best place to put it. It had been given to Z by grandma the last time we visited her. She had gotten it from a school for Indian children she supported. It was probably made in a Chinese factory. I had forgotten to unpack it from the suitcase we returned with, and only recently, upon opening the suitcase, refound it. Z repeated, *My dreamcatcher is catching dreams.*

Yes, your dreamcatcher is catching dreams, I said in response.

Only a few nights before, toward morning, but still dark outside, she had awaken, apparently from a bad dream, crying and saying over and over, *I have too much stuff to carry, I have too much stuff to carry.* The dreamcatcher, I said, would catch that kind of dream before it reached her. Then she would fall asleep, and I would rise up as quietly as I could out of the bed next to her crib, drape a light blanket over her legs and belly, and sneak out of the room. Then the wonderful silence, when I felt too tired to do much of anything and sat on the worn pink sofa reading and thinking of you.

This, all of this, upon the pale surface, the skein of the day, all of these mundane acts sacred. It was hard to explain their significance. Within each was an essence, a history, memories trailing back, associations spreading outward, a joy and a melancholy. We were pals, inseparable. And when separation occurred, for even a few hours, it was accompanied by sobbing, lamentation, arms wrapped viselike around my neck, chest pressed against mine. The intimacy was precious but made me wonder about the fine line between it and addiction, for it was perhaps not entirely but amongst other things a reaction to another separation in her life, one that was truly traumatic because indefinite and unknown, as well as most likely caused by violence. And each period of her life—periods in a life so young were measured in weeks—seemed more beautiful than the last, so that when I looked back on only a few months before, what seemed so beautiful then paled in comparison to the present.

●

When you disappeared, when it hit me that you were gone, one of my first thoughts was, I am Z's only parent, her sole source of sustenance. Could I do it? Could I raise her on my own? Even with you, I had been plagued by a sense of parental inadequacy, of not being up to raising the child, of not having sufficient inner resources. I could hardly manage myself, and yet here I was supposed to raise another? After Z was born, the adage, It takes a village to raise a child, took on new meaning. Yes, at least a village, I thought, at a bare minimum.

And where was our village now? I felt lonely and burdened, though it was not true that I was alone. Far from it.

Those who did not live on the island, with whom we only occasionally were in touch, did not know of our new situation. I did not go out of my way to tell others. The only ones who knew, apart from your parents, were those on the island whom we were accustomed to seeing on a daily basis. Many reached out in that time of distress. Of course, there were also those who didn't. Many offered their condolences and went their way. One couldn't blame people. They had their busy lives, they had many other pressing matters to attend to. I probably would have done the same. Others acted as if we had the plague, as if we were cursed, and stayed as far away as possible—the trouble might rub off on them. Perhaps they thought we must have done something wrong if such a fate had befallen us. Of course, we didn't know many people on the side of the Partystate, and so there were hardly any who distanced themselves from us for political reasons. Overall, especially amongst those close enough to actual do anything tangible or practical, the reaction was heartening.

Of course, there were your parents, Z's devoted grandparents, Gong-gong and Po-po. Even before your disappearance, they had been a big part of Z's life. They were more than ready and willing to help in any way they could, and they directed even more energy toward Z, these grandparents who had waited years to become grandparents, who regarded grandparenting as the main vocation of their last years. They increased the number of weekly visits from one to two, and sometimes would peak around unannounced another one or two times a week, often bringing some item, usually food, they thought we needed. It was all well-intended. They were indeed a help, an enormous help. And Z appeared to appreciate their increased presence. But it felt intrusive as well, and I in turn felt guilty for feeling invaded. Thus, a paradox: I, on the one hand, felt lonely and overburdened, while on the other, felt people pressing in on me on all sides, and often wanted only for them to go away.

The paradox extended beyond your parents. I faced the same challenge with others we knew.

Your disappearance meant that we had to "come out" to some degree. Few of those we knew on the island had been privy to our circumstances. Your disappearance rendered clear what had been easy for even me to forget: We had been living secret lives. None but a handful of people had much idea of the work we did, the challenges we faced, and even most of them only knew a small portion of the whole. If they were ever to be brought together in a room, they might be able, through swapping information, to piece together more or less the whole story, but even then, first they would have to realize they were even speaking of the same person, given that, at the point of your disappearance, you had so many pseudonyms, not that many people even knew you by the same name, and I had to constantly be on my toes to refer to you by the correct name depending on the company I kept.

Some of those who knew at least surmised the gravity of the situation and were willing and eager to do what they could to help, especially the parents of Z's friends. I often referred to the island as the Republic of Fertility, so many children were there, a much higher percentage than found elsewhere in the city where the birth rate had recently dipped below one child per woman, so challenging, so unappealing was it to have children there, with paltry maternity leave, no comprehensive system of child care, and a cityscape generally unfriendly if not downright hostile to children, to families. Our island, by contrast, was breeders' paradise. Many brash, ambitious young people came to the city in their twenties to work long hours in the financial industry and party hard. Eventually, they hooked up, decided to "settle down and have a family" while continuing to work in finance, and suddenly their cubbyhole-sized flats in the center of the city seemed cramped. Our island was one of the few places in the city where their children might have a modicum of the sort of childhood they remembered having in those green, democratic countries far away where they had grown up—space, nature, not as much as what they had had, but much better than elsewhere in the city. Through Z, you and I had entered into a new social circle, parents of children born within a few months of her, of which there were perhaps a couple dozen on the island. These were not close friendships, centered as they were around the children, but there was a sense of solidarity amongst the parents, and it was reassuring to have others to consult about common challenges. They often came around with food or offered to take Z for an afternoon; she could hang out with their kids.

Most of them had Filipinas helping to look after the children, all of whom, in turn, knew Z. When Z and I walked down the village main street, above which we lived on a steep hill, many people greeted her, many of whom I myself did not know, not only parents and "helpers", as they were called, but also shopkeepers and others—that "village to raise a child": The Tibetan-Buddhist barber, the former organic herb farmer who had had a falling out with his partner and now managed the organic shop, in the back of which was the small self-service café where Z and I often stopped to eat an orange or drink a bottle of soy milk (warm in the winter, cold in the summer). Sometimes the shopkeeper's son was there as well. The boy was one month older than Z and had been born in the exact same delivery room at the gargantuan hospital on the hill the ferry passed on the way to the city. The boy's name contained the character for "sun" (and the parents had given him the infelicitous English name, Sonny, or did they spell it Sunny?)

because when he was born, the sun was shining bright outside the upper-floor maternity ward delivery room window. I remembered well the view from that window, an expansive view of the sea. Z had been born in the morning, just as the sun was rising on what would be a hot, clear summer day. Out the window, the sky was perfectly clear, blue, the sea was placid, blue, ships of various kinds speckling the water. Across the channel, the largest island in the territory could be discerned. It was like a modern version of a traditional Chinese seascape. Looking at it, moments after Z had been born and was resting on her mother's chest, drinking milk, I thought, How could anything be but o.k. in this world?

Then there was the twice-a-week nursery school run by simple village Christians, the one that fed the children snacks of dayglo biscuits. You disparaged it—it was not only the snacks but the "art" projects, most of which involved painting and decorating toilet paper rolls or paper cups, plates and bowls. Even much of that the children couldn't do by themselves but was done by teacher and assistant, the children having little freedom just to explore and do what they wished and were capable of. But Z loved it—they sang, they danced, they ate nice snacks, they played with toys. And Z liked teacher. I credited the place with giving her positive associations with school.

On top of that, the mothers of Z's friends organized a weekly playgroup, to which you'd always brought Z before your disappearance, something I now continued to do in your absence. Week by week, we saw the children grow up together. It had become a tradition. And of course, Z saw her friends often at the playground, in the village, elsewhere during the course of the week.

So there was the village it took to raise a child. And Z grew up less isolated than children elsewhere in the city who spent a lot of time cooped up in cramped apartments in the care of helpers, who had to watch out for traffic whenever they went out on the street, who were lucky to see a bit of nature every now and then. Compared to them, Z ran free, she knew a lot of people, and a lot of people knew her. She loved to be outdoors; she was a nature child. Her time was spent at the beach, at the playground, on main street, in the company of others.

In spite of all of those people, that village, that support, at the end of the day, after your disappearance, it was Z and me—me who put her to bed every night, woke up with her every morning, comforted her during the night when she woke up and could not sleep. Indeed, I spent endless hours trying to get her to sleep both for her nap during the day and for the night. If there were any hours with her that I could retrieve and spend in some other way, it would be those. But then, as soon as I said that, I thought again—no, those hours were precious too, and if they were taken away from me, I would mourn their loss.

I lie next to her, my face to hers, inches away. Her eyes are closed. I stare into her face and feel like I could do this forever. Sometimes she is upset about her mother's absence. I stroke her hair and whisper, *My brave little girl, my brave little girl*. Her anguish subsides. Her features become softer, the breathing more regular. (Why is it that her breath never smells bad? in fact, just the opposite—I love to smell it.) And even after it is clear she has fallen asleep, I continue to whisper, or really, mouth, *My brave little girl, my brave little girl*.

As a single parent—for that was what I was, wasn't I? hopefully temporarily, in your absence—, I felt intensely inadequate. I woke every morning thinking I was not up for the challenge. But I had to be; there was no choice.

However else things might have been between you and me, I'd always been impressed with how well we complemented each other as parents. You were good at projects. Z and you cooked, made bread and pancakes, made playdough, painted, drew, made beads, cards, wrapping paper, gardened, planting seeds, watering them, tending the plants. You had a clear philosophy, which you applied as consistently as you could, a philosophy of love, freedom, confidence, creativity, wonder for the world and for life. You were a mother par excellence, in every part of your body and mind. And with your own child, you wanted to make up for all that you had never had yourself in your own childhood, and you knew it would take study, research, conscious thought and effort.

Indeed, the logical conclusion of your search for the childhood you wanted for your daughter was to start our own preschool, so much did you dread handing Z over to HK's meatgrinder of an educational system, a system you despised and resented, having been damaged by it yourself. You wanted your child to be free; your child *was* free, and you wanted it to stay that way. Through your research, you'd become enthused by the Montessori and Reggio Emilia approaches to childrearing and early childhood education. You wanted to start a cooperative preschool inspired by those pedagogies with other parents of children Z's age. You remade our home into a mini Montessori/Reggio Emilia center. After your disappearance, I carried on with your Montessori/Reggio Emilia home scheme. You had many great ideas you'd never had the chance to follow through on due to preoccupations with your work and the constant emergencies that arose in China. Whenever you set aside time for Z's education, something else would come up. You frequently expressed the wish to leave your line of work and become a full-time mom and/or preschool teacher, so much more interest did you at times profess in early childhood development than human rights in China, so much more confident were you in the impact of your efforts in the former field compared to the latter, where, you often felt, futility reigned. You were always telling me, Read this book, that manual, look at this website, none of which I ever seemed to get around to. You would then berate me and insist that I didn't care. I said, *What do you mean I don't care? The reason I don't get around to reading all of that is that I'm busy looking after the kid. Then when she goes to sleep, I'm too tired to do anything but sit there and stare.*

After your disappearance, I ordered a set of free-standing open shelves and, to make room for it, disposed of the two-seater sofa that had taken up the whole center of the main room though it was hardly ever used except as a place to put Z's "friends", her stuffed animals. I assembled the shelves, and Z and I put many of her belongings on them. With the shelves, it was much easier for her to take out and put away her things. I also got an easel, and I put a magnetic strip on the wall above her table from which cup-like bowls of her art supplies—crayons, pastels, markers, paint brushes, scissors, glue, tape—could hang. Z became an avid painter. Previously, she had mostly seemed to enjoy painting her own body. I implemented a bit of discipline—she had to paint on the butcher-block paper we taped to the easel. Over time, she built up quite an impressive portfolio. I took the paintings down from the easel and rolled them all up chronologically, dating each one, so that when you returned, you could look at them and see how your daughter's painting had developed. I supposed there was the tendency in every parent to think the child a genius, but I did marvel at Z's skill as an abstract painter. I thought it had to do with starting each painting, each stroke from scratch, without preconceptions, whereas every stroke of mine was predetermined, I had some grand idea in my mind I was trying to reproduce. I got a small futon mattress for Z and put it on a straw mat on the floor, so that it was easy for her to get into and out of bed and to make her own bed. I erected a row of hooks on the wall near her mattress for her to hang her clothes, and put her most frequently worn clothes in baskets near her bed. I got a new dining table that folded in half, to create more space in the main room. In the middle of it, where it folded, there were a number of small drawers for Z's utensils, bowls and plates, snacks, washcloths and bibs, all of which she could get out herself. At each step, I thought how pleased you would be with me; if and when you returned, you would hardly recognize the place.

One day, long after your disappearance, Z found a mommy hair in the playdough she and her mother had made together. Rather than becoming sentimental—which was my tendency, sentimental at what used to annoy me, finding hair all over the place—, Z got upset, first at its appearance and then at the fact that she could not remove it. I came to the rescue and extricated the long strand from the playdough. Though probably entirely unrelated, later that very same day, unbeknownst to me, Z took the considerable amount of purple playdough that was the very last she and her mother had made together not long before the disappearance and put it in a bucket of water out in the yard. When I discovered it there at the bottom of murky purple water, it was nothing but sludge, and it was my turn to become upset, the purple sludge seeping from between my fingers as I picked it out in clumps from the bottom of the bucket. I was anyway the sort who cried over spilt milk. Sometimes it seemed to me, orderly, tidy, perhaps to a fault, that Z's days consisted mostly of losing, breaking, spilling and ruining. But this was a keepsake, this purple playdough, something she had made with her mother, and to treat it so carelessly! I couldn't stop myself: *You know, you and mommy made that together, and now you've ruined it, now we have to throw it away, and mommy's gone, so you can't make any more. Why did you do this? You have become so careless. Can't you be more careful? If she knew, mommy would be very sad you did this. She liked making playdough with you so much. This makes me so sad.*

Z lowered her head, listened, did not respond. She was sad too now, but not sad about the playdough, sad that I was angry—there was nothing that could make her sadder, except perhaps your absence—and a bit embarrassed at my inability to control myself. I marveled at her emotional intelligence. She detected instinctively that my reaction was not primarily against her or her action; it was sadness about her mother. When she did speak, she said in a soft voice, *It's ok, baba, it's ok*. Something in her wanted to comfort me, even though I had scolded her with greater vehemence than on any but a few other occasions, even though it was *her* mother who was missing. I scold her, and she consoles me. Now who's the more psychologically insightful, the more emotionally mature there?

I did not probe her thoughts and emotions about her mother's absence. That is not to say she did not express them occasionally, or act in ways that lead me to believe that she felt and thought what she could not or simply did not express. For example, on those few occasions I was away a few hours, she experienced my absence as abandonment, and her reaction was a sign of the trauma attached to a parent's disappearance, however briefly I was gone. Who knew, after all, whether when that person walked out the door he would ever come back? It wasn't even entirely up to him, was it? That is not to say we did not discuss her mother's absence; indeed, she was entering an age at which she was much more aware of her mother not being there than she would have been before, and she was adept at articulating what she felt about that and how much she missed her. I had no doubt it was a difficult time for her, no matter how well-adjusted, how happy and content she almost always appeared. The therapeutic lay in being together, just that, sharing each other's company. We took turns being disconsolate.

Though I attempted the coherent, holistic approach to raising Z with the focus on developing the abilities to be happy, responsible, free that you had advocated and with which I certainly agreed, I didn't have that sort of wholeheartedness, initiative, commitment, skill, nor a child's imagination, nor the flexibility to forsake my own imagination and attempt to enter freely and willingly into the domain of the child's. We just hung out. I followed her lead. We didn't do anything in particular. We stayed at home, we played in the yard, we went to the playground and the beach, we wandered about. We didn't wake up thinking, What shall we do today? We just ended up doing things. Z and I had a certain bond; I had a better feel for her, her moods, her dreams, imaginings and inclinations, her sense of time, how to deal with her in difficult situations and put her to sleep than you did; mine was, I liked to think, a kind of instinctive mindfulness. Z and I just liked each other and got along. I was grateful to her for liking me, experienced her affection as a kind of mercy, but then, I thought, she hadn't much choice, did she? But still, I did not regard myself as a natural caregiver, whatever that might be, perhaps someone who seemed wholeheartedly dedicated to the task of raising a child, who "lived for it", who had found his life's calling in that function, that gesture of giving over and relinquishing, wholeheartedly, without reservation, qualm, second thought. I saw parents on the island, in most every case mothers, who were like that. They were stupifyingly meticulous. They paid attention to everything that mattered, down to the smallest detail. My admiration for them was ceaseless, but it was like admiring a creature you knew you could not become; you hadn't the speed of the leopard, the strength of the gorilla, you never would, but my god, watch it streak across the plain, swing from limb to limb with that amazing combination of both strength and grace, grounded in the air!

Though I had not planned it that way, the fact that I'd had Z in my forties—late in life (ah, to think that I had come to an age when the phrase "late in life" sounded accurate!)—was a fortune, insofar as I was at my least selfish. By that age, though I had not really succeeded at anything, at least not in any definitive sense that was clear for all to see, I had at least had a chance to do most everything that I might otherwise have felt having a child would hinder me from doing. I could imagine ambivalence in my twenties and thirties at the prospect of fatherhood; my life was for me, and a child would just complicate matters. Now I was ready, at least as ready as I would ever be, to dedicate myself to being a parent.

And yet, in the daily grind, I often found myself bored with playing with her, attending to her, and with the many errands associated with her that filled up the day. I was surprised at how much I yearned for time on my own, but given my eternal predilection for solitude, I should not have been; how much I yearned to concentrate on my own projects and interests and thoughts, however inchoate and ill-defined (indeed, illusory) those might have been. My selfishness was stubborn, tenacious. There was neither the interest nor the inclination of the natural caregiver. Nor, in many respects, the capacity, though most of the time I could act as if, I had learned to be a reasonable facsimile. I often experienced parenthood as a strain. Deep down, I lacked the patience and that ability to faithfully deliver myself to something larger. And I found myself at a great distance from the child's spontaneous joy and wonder, as if exiled to a greyer, sadder country from which there was no chance of return, as if viewing life through a thin but impermeable screen. I revered that joy and wonder but stood apart from it. It was Z herself, her way of being that inspired me most to stick at it, this business of parenthood, to really stick at life generally in that period, the period of your disappearance.

In previous times of life, I had spent considerable time and effort trying to do good for others, do the right thing, which meant improving their lives in some way, leaving them better than before I came. I tried to do so consciously, regarding my efforts through an ideological lens that stressed compassion, equality, justice. But those efforts were pedagogical, or political, or social, or economic, at a certain remove, limited in scope and responsibility, obligations that I could ultimately walk away from without the enterprise collapsing, the people succumbing. I felt more comfortable with that certain distance. The doing good one to one, face to face, in the same room, constantly, without fail, forever, with complete and ultimate responsibility, this creature's life being given over into my hands, rubbing her back as she lay on her stomach, thinking she is so small so small when she was ill or tired but couldn't fall asleep, there she is, lying there, a reality, an unblinking incessant reality that won't go away, that I can't quite ever get over really exists—that sort of doing good came hard to me, it required constant practice, and maybe the only reason I did not escape was that there was no way out, not to mention that much of the time was everything the clichés said, profoundly meaningful, a deep form of love; if life had no other meaning, at least it had this. It wasn't transcendent; the time, the effort, the experience evaporated into thin air, into oblivion, but it did exist.

Sometimes having a child seemed a kind of radical unfreedom, not only in the sense that nearly every moment of the day was given over to being with the child, caring for the child, running the many errands that went hand in hand with having a child, and not getting around to the many other things, from frivolous to substantive, that I could imagine otherwise spending time on, but also in the sense that it felt like a kind of invasion of the bodysnatchers. I was dispossessed of myself, even physically. When Z was ill, or afraid, or feeling insecure, all she wanted to do was to cling to me. She cried whenever I tried to put her down; I could do nothing else but hold her. (Actually, I learned to do quite a few things *while* holding her.) My life had become hers. It was as if every thought had been sucked out of me, and what spun through my head was old regurgitated thoughts or reminders of errands I had to run on her behalf. I was reminded of a comment made by a mother on the island in reference to the experience of raising her young child: *My brain has turned to mush.* There was nothing left over. I couldn't remember the last time I was able to go to the bathroom or look in the mirror or comb my hair or shave my face without interruption, without that small creature standing there, watching me, talking to me, that constant presence. *What are you doing?* she asked, even after I had answered her question several times. *Can I clean the toilet when you are done?*

As for my intense loneliness, I upbraided myself, thinking of Z's best friend's mother. She and daughter lived only a few hundred meters away in an old fishermen's village on a high promontory overlooking the sea. Approaching forty and not having found anyone she wanted to spend her life with, she had chosen to have a child as a single mother. She was a universally popular woman with a strong social network. Few children had more toys than her daughter had, though she rarely bought anything for her and as a physiotherapist earned less than most two-parent, two-income families. That was because so many people gave her hand-me-down toys. Before your disappearance, I laughed when we commiserated about how difficult it was raising a child, thinking of how well Hannah did it all on her own, without ever complaining or drawing attention to the fact that she was a single parent.

In contrast to Hannah, I was bad at socializing, had little to no social network, had neither the skills nor the desire to build one and did not reach out to others when I needed help; in fact, just the opposite: I tended to isolate myself, even at the best of times, and needed to remind myself that that tendency was not necessarily in Z's best interest. Your absence magnified my deficiencies. You were more like Hannah, social by nature, adept at using your network as a resource. While you were around, Z was well plugged into whatever occurred on the island involving children. You were constantly on the lookout for opportunities for Z like swimming, art and dance classes and playgroups and got her out of the house and into social situations with other children on a daily basis. Plus, there was the mommy link, which was strikingly difficult for a father to penetrate; the mothers just had a natural rapport with one another. When you disappeared, I realized I didn't even have the phone numbers of most of the mothers, so much had I depended on you to make arrangements of that sort. After your disappearance, Z and I spent much of our time alone, just the two of us, something I hardly even noticed at first. Neither of us seemed to mind. Being alone together had a pressurizing effect; it was very intense, both for better and worse.

It wasn't that I had no social skills whatsoever, more that I took no pleasure in employing them. I wasn't attracted to others, with few exceptions, and in those cases, it was intense, sometimes to the point of impropriety and beyond. As I got older, I liked people less, found them less interesting. From a distance maybe, but not close up. That worried me. I sometimes wondered whether I hadn't lost faith in the idea of community, the possibility of community, the power of community, that imprecise and overused concept. The prospect that I had was difficult to face, since the idea of community had a key place in my vision of the world and how to improve it. Solidarity and cooperation were crucial, but they were hard to realize without people actually knowing each other, being in touch with each other, establishing ties, trust, faith not only in each other but in the idea that they were more powerful in cooperation than acting alone. Upon that foundation could organization and mobilization occur. Or perhaps more than having lost faith, I had simply lost interest, had come to the end of the road: Community used to be my thing but now it was something other people "did". I was glad they did it; it needed to be done; but it was increasingly distant from whatever I was, whatever I was doing. Maybe this was nothing new, just traits age accentuated; I'd always been too much of an individualist, a solitary, a solipcist, a narcissist, not wishing reality, the way people really were, to intrude on my imagination, where I could construe and organize them as I wished. The latent misanthropist had always lurked within. It was indeed true that there were few people whose company I really enjoyed or who I wanted to get to know. I read all the time about people who sounded interesting but rarely met any myself. Better to read about them, I thought. Sometimes it was nice to be surrounded by other people, to have them in one's midst, to feel the warmth of human feeling, but for the most part, they were more trouble than they were worth. If I was becoming more misanthropic with age, what kind of model was that to Z, who thrived on the company of others, who went stir crazy at home and wanted to be out and about? Was she already beginning to learn my bad ways? Without you—who were everything I was not socially, were in your element surrounded by others, had no particular need for solitude and would always opt for company, enjoyed other people immensely and returned from social occasions with a glow—, she would have no one to counteract my negative influence. In the sometimes prayerful silence of late-night solitude, the words formed, Please don't let her turn out too much like me!

•

Then there was Anna. Or had been Anna. That there would be again looked unlikely.

Anna had looked after Z on weekdays ever since Z was three months old. With both you and me working full-time, and you getting only ten weeks of maternity leave, the HK maximum, we needed some help. But the city had no system of childcare. The de facto childcare system of foreign domestic workers that had come about was an option only for the middle to upper classes, those with the ability to pay. There were more than 300,000 "helpers" (I found the term weird and patronizing) in HK, about half from the Philippines and half from Indonesia, in a territory with a population of a little more than 7 million people. Helpers made up about 4% of the population. The vast majority were women. If you did not have enough money to pay their minimum wage of HKD4,010 per month, tough. Poor families were faced with the prospect of one of the parents having to forego remunerated work outside the home in order to look after the children, a perfect way of keeping poor people poor in one of the most unequal societies in the world, where one in six people, one in four children, one in three elderly lived in poverty and upwards of 50% of the population lived in government-subsidized housing, unable to afford shelter at market rates.

Setting aside the issue of HK people's lack of access to child care, I never ceased to be astounded at the essential craziness of the system that had emerged: Women from significantly less prosperous countries leave their own children behind and go far away to look after other people's children, whose parents leave them behind to go to work. The imported women obviously couldn't go home to their own children at the end of the day. By law, employers had to pay for them to go home once for a minimum of two weeks per every two-year contract. That meant the imported women might see their own children for no more than two weeks out of every two years, and that was the case with most. There had to be enough in it for everyone—employer and employee—for the system to continue to exist, and indeed, it was often said that with the wages they earned in HK, helpers could support their whole family, often extended family, at home, and, over the years save up enough to build a house for themselves, making much more than they could nursing or teaching back home. OK, fair enough, maybe, though I still felt I lived in a warped reality. Hiring women from abroad to leave their own children behind when alternative systems were possible just seemed, well, exploitative. On top of this, the helpers were legally discriminated against, on visas different from those issued to other foreigners, which forced them, effectively, to leave the territory every two years and then reapply for a new visa in order to continue to work in the city, even if for the same employer, whereas other foreigners, once resident in the territory for seven consecutive years, could apply for permanent residency, effectively putting them on an almost equal legal footing with all others in the territory. This route was never open to helpers, though many of them remained in HK for decades. They were condemned to second-class status. These women were not licensed, the way child-care providers in other developed societies were, nor were they regulated. So, essentially, you did not know who you were inviting into your home, or whether or not she was qualified to look after a child or do the many other possible chores a helper was assigned. All she had to do was "help", and for that, there were no qualifications, or, to put it another way, everyone was essentially qualified. Many helpers found their work, their situation lonely, boring, oppressive, humiliating. For others, it was a liberation from the home culture, and they would hate to contemplate going back to a place where they could no longer be themselves.

HK was like most societies in that it paid lip service to the idea that "children are our future", but the gap between, on the one hand, the oft-professed cliché and, on the other, deliberated, coherent child- and family-friendly policies that would guarantee that future was the best possible was immense. I'd always been struck by the hypocrisy created by the gap between the rhetoric and the reality, which, as I say, was hardly exclusive to HK. I was reminded of a recent visit to that distant Northern Paradise, the most perfect society on earth, a place where I'd once lived and had left, forever after to feel as if exiled from a cold Eden. We walked into the bank, and in the corner there were a child-height table and toys. At the pizza place, there was an enormous jungle gym complete with a labyrinthine system of tunnels, nets and slides, not to mention a whole separate dining room for families with children. There was year-long parental leave. It had the only sort of patriotism I could stomach, its national day essentially being a children's day, featuring a children's parade. In the capital, the royal family stood out on the balcony of the palace to receive the children, who paraded up to it. A whole country, a society designed around children, like something out of a fairy tale, a place that took a slogan like "children are our future" seriously, one of perhaps only a handful.

In HK, by contrast, children like everything else were sacrificed to the eternally profit-seeking turbo-capitalist maw, which included the exploitation of foreign labor to look after the children so that the adults could serve out their lives as office drones, whether at higher or lower levels of the rigid corporate hierarchy, working amongst the longest hours in the world. Children were just groomed to replace their parents once the system had used them up and spat them out. They were fodder. A recent survey found that the average father spent less than five minutes a day with his child. I found that hard to believe, but that parents had insufficient time to spend with their children was undeniable. The society had one of the lowest birth rates in the world and people wondered why, but what were the incentives to have children? Indeed, it seemed a daunting prospect.

I didn't want anything to do with a system like that, but what were the alternatives? Having a child meant almost by definition having to settle for imperfect situations and solutions, your own principles and values at times in tension with the immediate interests of the child, such as having someone to look after her. It made you get down in the dirt of the society; there were fewer inconveniences and injustices that you could simply avoid, or rise above, or turn away from. Our compromise was that whomever we hired had to have either no or only grown children. At the very least, we didn't want someone looking after our small child while her own languished in a country far away.

Anna had six grown children. All of them had grown up during Anna's twenty-some years in HK. One daughter was now, in fact, herself a helper in HK. And though they were adults, it emerged from Anna's stories, which formed a litany of travails, that she still supported most of the family. Anna said her relationships with her children had suffered due to her long-term absence. How could that not be the case? I wondered. Her intention was to work a few more years in HK, until her children were entirely finished with their education and had all found work themselves—something I imagined unlikely given what she'd told me about her children and the lack of employment opportunities for educated youth in the Philippines—and she had enough money to retire, and go home.

By law, helpers had to live with their employers, but on the island, most helpers "lived out". We paid Anna a housing allowance on top of her salary. But even though she did not live with us and only came during the day, and however helpful she was (in a practical sense, far more helpful than anyone else), and even though she got along well with Z and took good care of her, I felt crowded out of my own home, a small space to begin with. It would have been for me well-nigh psychologically impossible if she had had to live with us, the case in many cramped middle-class homes across the city, with helpers often sleeping in woefully small makeshift spaces.

So Anna came on weekdays. You had worried whether she and Z would hit it off, whether she would be good at looking after Z. By all evidence, they had a good rapport, and Anna, an infinitely patient woman, a way with little kids. That had been a relief.

Anna was a farmer by background, and she had a farmer's stolidity, thickness, physical there-ness. She was a very kind woman but not what one would call an "initiative taker", much to your exasperation. If you spelled something out for her, she did it; if not, she didn't. Maybe this was a survival technique she had developed over years of working in HK: It was better to err on the side of caution, of omission rather than commission. The best way to get by, the safest, was to take no initiative for which you could later be criticized because you did something you hadn't been told to do, to hide yourself, to show none of yourself, to not make the mistake of appearing, of being a person in your own right amongst people who could potentially take it as an affront. It was as if she were a piece of wood drifting along the currents of time, dressed in non-sequitur t-shirts. (The one I found most striking was "VODKA: connecting people", a play on Nokia's slogan, this covering the torso of a teetotaler Christian of the more conservative variety.) While I understood it as possibly a survival technique, her learned deference at times irritated me. It was hard to relate to her as an equal. And I could never get over the fact that she was older than both of us and yet in a subordinate position. Everything about it, that we had a helper at all, that she was older yet deferred to us, just seemed all wrong, but there we were, getting used to a situation I could not have imagined being in but a few years before.

We'd hired Anna shortly before getting kicked out of our previous residence. As with the closure of the bank account, we suspected the long arm of the Partystate in the eviction, but as with the bank account closure, there was no smoking gun, no way to get to the bottom of the motivations behind the act. These things "just seemed to happen" to us.

The new apartment we found had, unusually in HK, a yard, a small yard to be sure, with a lawn not much bigger than a living room rug. Anna being a farmer, we wondered how she would fare caring for it. The answer was not well. The longer we lived in that place, the more the yard deteriorated. Anna rarely had the time, most of it being taken up caring for Z—a prioritization we'd requested and for which we were grateful—, and what she had beyond that was dedicated to preparing dinner. Our small flat as well as the yard outside were in a perpetual process of deterioration nearly from the moment we moved in. Doors fell off of cupboards, lights came loose from the walls and ceiling, the green lawn turned brown and weed-choked, the bushes and trees grew wildly in all directions, the two wooden gates fell apart, piece by piece. Anna, unfortunately, had a high tolerance for clutter (I imagined the grounds of her farm in the Philippines to be cluttered with all manner of junk not so much collected as accumulated over the years), like my co-habitants who produced it proficiently. If I had lived alone, I would have lived like a Zen monk, minimalistically, sparely, tidily, with everything in its right place. I kept telling myself that all-falling-apart-around-me was the natural state of things—everything decays, dies; all is change—and I should appreciate the constant reminder right before my eyes. You cannot control things, you cannot stop change, accept it, let it be. On top of that, this was the price you paid for living with others, in this flat, in this world: Not all could be to your liking, and you should not try to place all within your control.

In one corner of the untended garden were grapevines on a wooden, chest-high trellis. Whose strange idea had it been to put them there? The vines bore hard green grapes. Even when a few managed to turn reddish purple, they were inedibly sour. But Z loved them and thrilled to the fact that you and I didn't, chasing us teasingly about to offer some that she had just picked. Unpruned, the vines had snaked their way up into a neighboring tree so that, in amongst its leaves could be seen tight green bunches of the sour grapes. And then the bougainvillea went everywhere, pink and purple and red and beautiful and invasive, tendrils crawling through trees and bushes, along the grass, the dead grass, the grass I couldn't figure out how we'd killed, the grass that seemed to come a bit back to life after a rain, with patches of green, but for most of the year was gray and tan.

The place spoke of efflorescence, not quaint and hopeful, not tractable, but of the sort that would eventually take over everything, leaving little trace of our presence or anyone else's. The island was dotted with old skeletal concrete structures, roofs collapsed, over which banyans and less sturdy plants crept, as if eating them alive. Efflorescence and thunder, more often than not distant, a nearly perpetual summer soundtrack, symbolic of the turbulent nature of the place, the city, the country, that part of the world (maybe even the wider world, except for the fact that I had experienced many peaceful places too, sequestered in those faraway countries with a modicum of prosperity, rights, democracy, rule of law, seemingly insulated from the chaos and violence beyond, and because temperate, not even nature seemed so marauding). It was not a place where one could rest and relax, even if the island where we lived was restful and relaxed relative to the rest of the city. Or, to put it another way, it was a place where *we* could never, and never did, relax. Life there seemed continual contention, with our own anxieties and worries to begin with, and spreading out to mild but real dangers and threats, brazen injustice, and cruelty and brutality disguised as the-way-things-were. It was what we had chosen, wasn't it? Or had it chosen us?

The most dominant feature of that ragged yard was the banana tree, a ragged tree. After she'd gone, whenever I looked at it, I thought of Anna. It seemed to embody her. I sometimes had an intimation that her spirit had taken up residence in it (and, tellingly, withstood the most recent typhoon, whereas a typhoon had knocked down its predecessor right before our arrival). The banana tree, so unlovely, with its frayed splayed leaves, resilient, able to grow in almost any soil, make use of so little to produce so much.

I couldn't help but compare it to the totemic tree of our previous home, situated in the middle of a forest on a steep hillside. That tree was a giant bamboo. Epic, mystical, awe-inspiring, its thick multiple poles jutting out of the dark earth dwarfed the house, casting the corner where it dwelled in perpetual half-darkness. When the wind blew, the stalks of the bamboo creaked loudly like the unoiled hinges of a giant door perpetually swaying back and forth. The banana, by contrast, was prosaic, nothing to get worked up about, apart from its fruit.

Anna knew a lot about banana trees, prolific on her farm, and she educated me. What a strange creature! Not really a tree at all but, technically, a giant herb. Not woody but starchy, its trunk really no more than the bases of many leaf stalks. It needed no fertilizer. It needed no pesticide. It could grow in shallow soil. It flourished anywhere wet and warm. I thought the fraying of leaves occurred to prevent the plant from catching enough wind to blow it down, given its short, shallow roots, but that was only surmise. Funny leaves, not much good at all as shade from the sun.

Besides Anna, the tree reminded of Basho, whose pen name meant banana tree. His disciples gave him a house, a hut really, and outside of it, a banana tree grew. That was his first permanent home. Up to then, he'd been a wanderer (or so I liked to imagine; I did not know this for a fact). It seemed apt that his disciples planted a banana tree outside his hut, given his placelessness, his restlessness, his seeming inability to settle down, which, to me, the tree's general raggedness and appearance of impermanence symbolized: Nothing lasts. (The giant bamboo, on the other hand, said, I have been here forever and always will be—I am pre- and post-historic, will outlast you, into the age when insects rule the earth.) And so it was as if prophesied: the hut Basho's disciples had given him burned down within a year or two, and not long after that, even though they built him a replacement hut, he set off wandering again, thinking he might never return, given the danger of travel in medieval Japan. So began the pattern of the last fifteen years of his life—alternation between wanderings and sojourns at huts, three altogether, if I recalled correctly, provided by disciples. His final haiku (actually, it was not his final haiku but his penultimate, even though it was widely thought to be his final):

falling sick on a journey
my dream goes wandering
over a field of dried grass

One was not to read haiku symbolically, but I couldn't help myself: The journey was life, and all of us were on that journey. Even the seemingly most settled amongst us were in fact wanderers. And what was Basho's dream? Was it a dream of all he wished to realize, all that he wished the world might be? Did that dream then outlive him, or did the fact that the dream went wandering mean that it would never be realized?

So we settled here, in our unsettledness, beside the ragged banana tree that had now survived several typhoons, an altogether unsettled settlement. Rather than receiving the place from disciples, we rented it from greedy landlords, never having owned a property, never having had a place to call our own, moving from place to rented place, in a place that neither you or I wished to settle, or could afford, given the inflated housing prices, a place we often despised, railed against, where we would never find peace, where there was much to fight for though the battle was uphill, perpetually, and the fight was defensive, seeking to prevent the worst from happening as opposed to assertively struggling for the best. For better or worse, our lives were here, and so we remained here, with our lives, ready to be unrooted by the next storm as the years passed, but the years passed and the tree remained rooted strangely miraculously mundanely.

I was never especially fond of the banana tree, never regarded it as my friend, and now it looked as if this place, the place of the banana tree, might be where I lived the longest in my life so far. Precisely because I was not fond of the tree, a fondness grew. The tree did not try to charm or awe, did not try to do anything but grow fruit, it just was—the very definition of stupid: This stupid tree is living here too. With this stupid person. Not unintelligent stupid but thick, stubborn. Withstanding, I thought, required a certain Annalike bananatreelike stolidness. Banana trees were not majestic; they muddled through.

Z, unencumbered by such thoughts, liked to climb the ladder and peer up between the large tattered leaves to where a bunch of green bananas ripened ever so slowly. From the stump of the banana tree blown over by the typhoon just before we moved in, a new tree had emerged, and now its first bunch, which had appeared before your disappearance, was about to ripen. Anna had been monitoring it all along.

Its harvest day glowed, virtually sepia-soaked in pre-emptive nostalgia, the sort on which I thought, how could a childhood be any more perfect? (Apart from the bit about the missing mother, of course.) Yes, said the day, said the moment, we were providing this child with a great childhood, in spite of our worst propensities, our obvious weaknesses and failings. A moment that could make your heart break, in such concentrated form did it hold the commingled truths of time passing and the precious joy of life. Anna noted that some of the bananas had already turned yellow. She'd said previously that the bunch should be harvested when the bananas were still somewhat but not too green; otherwise, they would be eaten by birds and insects. And that very day was the day to hack them down. We wanted Z to see that. She spent much of the day at the beach with her grandparents, other children, their caregivers. While she was gone, Anna cut down some foliage preventing her from getting to the bunch. Then we tied one end of a rope to it and the other to another tree because the bunch hung over a sheer drop to the backyard of the house below ours on the steep hillside. If one were just to hack it off, it would fall ten meters into the yard below.

When Z returned, it was already late afternoon, getting toward dusk, the time of the mosquitoes, and their buzz filled the air after days of rain. I'd gone to fetch Z at the beach and told her we had to get home in time to see Anna hack down the bananas. She was not pleased, so wrapped up was she in her beach activities. Now, though, she watched in awe. Anna stood on top of the wall separating ours from the property below, a not altogether safe position, given the ten-meter drop on the other side. She used a chopper to hack at the top of the bunch. I grabbed the bottom. When Anna delivered the coup de grace, I hung on and managed to pull it over to our side of the wall. Small flies buzzed around it. It was very heavy, about waist-height.

Anna hacked row after row of bananas away from the main stem. I gave a banana to Z, and she opened it herself. They were not the slender bowed commercial bananas, but thick and stout, as if about to burst their skin, like a fat man in a too-tight suit. I'd expected them to be tasteless and starchy, but they were nearly too sweet. Over the coming days, Anna turned the kitchen into a banana processing factory, making banana jam, banana lassi, banana popsicles, dried banana chips, banana bread. We gave away bunches of bananas to just about everyone we knew. And still it was hard to get rid of them all.

Then Anna disappeared, or began to disappear, the final disappearance coming at the end of a long string of extraordinary misfortunes that most certainly rivaled our own.

The string began with Anna finding out that her husband had another woman. (I thought to myself: If you had to choose between your spouse disappearing and your spouse going off with another, which would you prefer?)

One morning, Anna arrived and said, *I have some bad news to tell you.* Hardly ever did she share her personal life with me; she'd been more eager to do so with you, searching for some sister solidarity. Her husband's sister had told one of Anna's daughters, who had told her. After she found out, she confronted her husband by phone. He neither confirmed nor denied what she had heard, which she took as confirmation. She said she had suspected something like this for a long time. He was, she said, never good to her. Several times he took money she had given him and did things with it that she didn't know or didn't agree with—she'd always insisted that most all of her money go toward her children's education. He was the one who had control over several bank accounts that were supposedly in both their names. She feared that now she would be left destitute or without means to fight for what was hers, if her husband so chose to claim that all the money, the land, the farm were his alone. The farm was in his native village, far from her own. It had been given to him through a government scheme for landless farmers. Anna and he had built the house on the land together, with money she'd earned. She was intent on breaking up with him, but she didn't know how she could extricate herself while keeping what was rightfully hers. Without the farm and house to go back to, the place to which she'd planned to retire, she would have no place in the Philippines. It was as if, after twenty-some years in HK, her life in the Philippines was evaporating before her eyes, with her children grown, two of them overseas (besides the daughter helper in HK, there was a son in the Gulf), and now her husband betraying her.

A few days later, through negotiations brokered by her children, she spoke with her husband again. This time, he admitted he was with another woman, but he claimed it had been going on for only two months. Anna suspected a much longer time. She had also spoken with her pastor, probably the most powerful person in the village. He sympathized with her, expressing indignation at her husband's behavior, and said the whole village would be against a man who went behind his wife's back. But then Anna asked the pastor about the possibility of an annulment (she considered divorce beyond the realm of the admissible, given the religious proscription), and the pastor replied that even an annulment would be "against religion". Anna's children supported her, though some questioned whether an annulment, or any form of legal separation, was not excessive or unnecessary. Anna, though, was adamant about that course of action. She wanted nothing to do with the man anymore, and that break had to be formalized. So that was how it was: In "spirit", everyone was on her side, but in practice, it was not hard to see the forces aligning against the woman.

Then Anna's husband was cast out of the village and told he could not return as long as he was together with the other woman. The woman, it transpired, was also from the village, indeed had been a friend of the family. She was also told to leave. Many of Anna's husband's own family members, who were numerous in the village, were against him and supported Anna, at least according to what they told Anna, though if the dispute came down to a matter of property, I imagined they might think differently, at the prospect of some of it vanishing from their family's hands. Several people suggested that Anna get a separation, but she wanted a more final and definitive break. The husband went to stay with one of their daughters in the provincial capital.

The main thing Anna wanted decided was the status of the house and land. One morning, Anna arrived for work an hour late. She had been standing on the steps leading up to the house crying and talking on the phone with her sister-in-law. She came in ranting about how it was her who had supported the family all those years, supported him as well—he'd been unable to work for years due to an injury of some kind—, and he took her money, and the more money he took, the more his expectations of her grew. He put her down in front of others. She was a human being railing at the cosmic injustice of it all, railing to someone who hadn't the power to overturn the injustice, to issue a new ruling. Over the following days, Anna became understandably distracted. Her hours became less regular. I told her she could take time off if she needed to, but she decided against it; among other things, the work provided some distraction from the situation at home. She could not simply sit and fret all day, and she often seemed to enjoy being with Z. The place got messier and messier. She got tired more easily. A very hearty woman, she began to show her age. More lines of silvery-grey appeared in her black hair. Over several evenings, after her working hours, she made phone calls to her husband from our home. She roomed with other helpers; there was nowhere else she could have the privacy to speak with her husband. It was after Z had gone to bed. I sat elsewhere in the flat and heard her voice in the kitchen or your office, long pauses during which she listened to her husband (with what seemed to be extraordinary patience) punctuated by her voice rising in consternation, anger. She told me he expressed remorse but refused to accept responsibility. The question of eschewing the relationship with the other woman never even arose. He seemed surprised at the turn of events and basically just wanted things to return to the comfortable way they were before, and in that sense, seemed deluded, for that would entail the un-revealing of the affair and its continuation, with him once again ensconced in the family home in the village from which he'd been removed.

I had heard many stories of that sort: the husband supported by the wife who lives far away in a foreign country and returns for two weeks once every two years ends up with another woman. Living almost permanently apart put great pressure on relations—the woman's sacrifice to make money that couldn't be made at home, men fooling around behind the backs of the breadwinners. These Filipinas, heroines and chumps. They kept the economy afloat with remittances. Meanwhile, their lives lived elsewhere made their lives at home slip between their fingers. And they were left with, well, themselves in the end. And for what? for what? To take care of other people's children in a place far far away. Because it paid better than anything their own country could offer. Their own pathetic excuse for a country that pimped them out abroad.

The evening phone discussions with her husband culminated in Anna's decision to go home. (I had told her straight off that if she needed to, she could.) She had to be there to sort things out. It couldn't be done over the telephone. But when she looked, her passport was gone. She had lost it. She went to the Philippines consulate to get a new passport but was told it couldn't be prepared before her scheduled departure.

She could, however, get a travel document that would allow her to return to the Philippines, and she was assured by the consulate that it would not be a problem procuring a new passport at home. At that point, in retrospect, she should have known better, and I should have known better and told her to postpone her departure until she had the passport in hand. Once she'd left and began to encounter difficulties, I told several Filipinas about them and they all laughed and scoffed at the promise the Philippines consulate had made. *It's hard to get a passport in the Philippines*, they all said. But she sensed her property being taken from her with every moment that passed and was desperate to get back. In the meantime, her two-year work visa was about to expire, and she went to HK Immigration to get her new work permit. Since she didn't have a passport, a provisional re-entry visa was stamped in her travel document, with a deadline for re-entering HK just after the return date of her air ticket, which in turn was five weeks after her departure from HK. So she went back to the Philippines, the beginning of a very long odyssey.

Although the village assured her she could return to her home, which they had forced her husband to vacate, she stayed with another one of her daughters in the provincial capital. It was easier from there to visit the relevant authorities on a daily basis, but the passport was not forthcoming, in spite of repeated assurances from authorities that it would be. Just trying to recall the many twists and turns of the saga nearly gave me a headache: One document after another was required, without end, and every time she thought she had fulfilled requirements, she was asked for a new one. Each one required a trip to a different government office. She rushed about the city to get each. Eventually, she was told the passport would be delayed, past the date of her return air ticket, and even past the date her HK re-entry visa would expire. By this point, she had collected a bookthick packet of documents. As expected, she missed her return flight. The HK re-entry visa expired.

I was advised by HK immigration authorities that she could still re-enter HK on a tourist visa and then, once here, apply for a new work permit. Finally, after I made inquiries with the Filipino authorities in Manila, she was promised a passport by a certain date. It didn't come on that date, of course, but indeed was given to her a few days later. She booked a one-way ticket to HK (her original return ticket had to be forfeited). She went to the airport on the departure date and was prohibited by the airline from boarding the plane because the Philippines had a law that said Filipinos going to places like HK on tourist visas had to have a return ticket, the ostensible justification being to combat human trafficking, though it seemed that any self-respecting human trafficker could easily circumvent the requirement by purchasing a round-trip ticket and not using the return leg. From the airport, she had to travel six hours back to where she was staying. A round-trip ticket was purchased but when this time she was given a boarding pass, she was stopped by Philippines immigration officials at the airport, interrogated, and prevented from departing, without any clear reason given. She was simply told that further investigation was needed and she would be contacted. By phone, she reported this all to me, her voice filled with exhaustion and dismay. I said, *Whatever. Go back to your daughter, for now, and settle what needs to be settled.* With all the time spent trying to get the new passport, very little progress had been made on securing her rights to her home and property. And so the matter remained, and in a way, I had stopped caring about it, lacked motivation to do anything about it, had too many other "things on my plate", as they say.

Whenever I spoke with Anna by phone during that time, she kept repeating the phrase, *Too much pressure*, like a refrain after narrating each new episode in the interminable struggle. She was required to show the passport-issuing authority a voter registration record to prove she was resident in the area of the country where she was applying for the passport (because that office was only for residents of that area). She couldn't get a voter registration record because she hadn't voted in her home province since 1991 because she had been in HK since 1993, and the voter registration authorities deleted records of all voters once they had become inactive for a certain period of time. She went back to the passport-issuing authority and asked, What to do? The official replied, *Use your common sense.* Anna's daughter, who had been helping her throughout, taking time away from her own job to do so, turned to her mother in tears and asked, *What in the world does he mean, 'use your common sense'?*

He means money, daughter, Anna replied, *he wants money.*

In this part of the world, when officials were trying to shake down their own citizens, they rarely did so by openly demanding money (though sometimes they mentioned certain "fees" that had to be paid). They were, as a rule, more polite, more subtle than that. In fact, more often than not, corruption happened with a smile. *...meet it is I set it down, / That one may smile, and smile, and be a villain...* That phrase had come to mind with ever-increasing frequency in recent years, in this part of the world where all sorts of malfeasance had been normalized, and perpetrators spoke with a straight face as honorable people, having undemocratically obtained and secured their positions of power. To put it simply, they had power and you did not, and that meant they did not have to be nasty to get what they wanted from you; if you didn't give it, you didn't get what you wanted from them, as simple as that.

Her absence grew in length, from days to weeks; it appeared ever less likely she would return, as if her case had through alchemy metamorphosed from physical to metaphysical. I couldn't help but think of Anna's predicament as much like that of Odysseus, one barrier after another interminably preventing the homecoming, with the significant difference that she was trying to escape from home and return to HK, was being held back not by alien gods and goddesses and creatures and forces but by the tentacles of a home country that would not let her go, not out of love but out of a petty official desire to milk her for whatever she was worth, which was all the more pathetic or reprehensible, depending on how you looked at it, given how precious little she had.

At the same time, I had the impression that, deep down, Anna did not want to return and that we would never see her again, that somehow the passport problem was part of an elaborate scheme to not return. (Then again, often in that period I had thoughts that bordered on the paranoid: I also wondered whether or not you had somehow engineered your disappearance, in order to never have to return.) The most likely reality, of course, was that Anna was a victim of her country's corrupt, minimally competent bureaucracy, to which she, a citizen, meant nothing, over which, she, a citizen, had no power, and this one tiny incident was illustrative of the epic, on-going struggle, whose outcome was by no means certain, in this region of the world and elsewhere, of people to go from being subjects to citizens, from being ruled to rulers, from having to abjectly grovel before officials to telling them who was the boss and holding them accountable. And here, it should be mentioned, we were regrettably speaking of an ostensibly democratic state, the Philippines, unlike the one in which we lived.

Of course, her struggle to return was only part of her struggle. The other part was the small matter of her husband's infidelity and how to respond to it, and in her struggle to leave the country, her original reason for going could at times almost be forgotten. I actually heard less about that, presumably since there wasn't anything I could do, than about the passport and visa situations, about which I could do something. What little I heard was that she continued to attempt to get an annulment but was rebuffed. When push came to shove, even though people—pastor, villagers, in-laws, sons and daughters—said they supported her and that she was in the right, almost everyone was against her doing anything drastic, especially if it involved her going "against religion". The only exceptions were one son and one daughter. So there was a stalemate. On the one hand, villagers lead by the pastor wouldn't allow her husband to return to the village or to their home as long as he was together with the other woman. On the other, Anna couldn't get an annulment and had no allies in procuring a legal decision regarding division of property. Up against those forces, especially without money, she was powerless. Their house stood empty, looked after by in-laws and their children. Anna could have returned but refused to. She remained in the provincial capital at her daughter's place.

Then, just when I had stopped thinking about it and simply assumed we'd never see Anna again, she bought another return ticket to HK, the Philippines immigration authorities inexplicably let her out (did she finally relent and give them what they wanted? I could not see her doing so), she flew to HK, was allowed to enter on a tourist visa, and magically appeared again one day at our door. Not for long, though. It was the sort of saga you had the sneaking suspicion would never end; it had to do with permanent and incontrovertible misalignment of the stars, or, to put it less astrologically, a person squeezed between inadequate protection of rights without recourse in two different places.

She re-applied for a renewal of her work visa with HK immigration, which told her that 1) she couldn't apply for a new work visa while in HK and would have to leave in order to do so, contradicting the previous advice it had given me, 2) since her previous contract with us had expired, she had to apply not for a renewal of work visa, but an entirely new visa, even though she had originally applied for a renewal of work visa before returning to the Philippines, while her previous contract was still in effect, 3) it was illegal for her to work as a helper in the meantime, and 4) while waiting for the response from HK immigration, she had overstayed her tourist visa and was in violation of the law.

After several phone calls getting passed up the hierarchy in HK immigration, I managed to find a relatively sympathetic official, who insisted that whatever advice HK immigration had previously given us, Anna indeed had to leave HK, but that he would extend her lapsed tourist visa for a few days in order to allow her to do so legally and that once she had left, her application would be expedited. So Anna left again, this time to Macau, just across the border, and stayed somewhere she'd found through church connections. Her application was then approved, and Z and I went into the immigration department to pick it up. It had already been processed, so we didn't have to wait long, a good thing with a two-year-old in tow. Still, it took some fifteen minutes, with no statement as to how long we would have to wait, giving a brief taste of what I'd experienced on numerous occasions before, staring into the gaping mouth of bureaucracy, the indefinite wait. Since we were picking up the visa for Anna, it was on a floor of the immigration department dedicated to handling foreign domestic worker visa applications, and everyone else there was Filipina. The HK immigration people, being HKese, were swift and efficient, but at the same time, you couldn't but help detect a bit of an undercurrent having to do with the fact that the applicants were at the mercy of the HK government, that they were subjects, not citizens—that constant refrain that followed them wherever they went, whether in their own country or abroad. While waiting that short time, I thought, Welcome to the endless wait of the underclasses! The world could be divided in two—those for whom it works, and those who work for it. For many of us, the world was one of great convenience, for many others, of indefinite waiting, often for things that never came, whether one had a right to them or not. This tale might be boring—one had heard it so many times before—, but at the start of the twenty-first century, it was still the way the world worked.

We sent the visa to Anna in Macau, and two days later, she reappeared again.

Then Typhoon Haiyan/Yolanda, estimated to be the strongest typhoon to ever make landfall, hit her home near Tacloban. Phone networks were down. She couldn't reach her family to find out whether or not they had survived. In the first days after the storm, estimates were that it had killed upwards of 10,000 people. *You have to go back*, I said, even though it wasn't clear how or when she would be able to travel to the affected area since overland transport was impossible and inbound flights were dedicated to relief aid. So I sent her on her way with a year's salary in severance pay to help her family, for surely even if they had survived, they had not escaped without damage to their homes and property.

It was the first global event to register on Z's consciousness. Anna had told her about it before she left, in order to explain why she was leaving. It made an impression. She kept wanting to see photos of the destruction. For days afterward, Z repeated, *The typhoon blew the houses down. Siupengyao* (the Cantonese for "children"—literally "small friends") *don't have houses. They are sad. We can help them build new houses. Then they will be happy.* She drew houses in water-crayon on the sides of the bathtub and the wall above it, then smeared them out with her hand and a wet washcloth, signifying the typhoon and its effects, then drew them again, rebuilding the damaged and destroyed houses.

Fortunately, estimates of casualties were revised downward, from ten thousand to two to three thousand, but then they climbed and climbed up to over 6,000. Whole swaths of human habitation had been all but wiped out, more than eleven million people affected and hundreds of thousands displaced. Overall, it was a catastrophe that in scale and severity made our personal catastrophe, mine and Z's and yours, the disappearance of a single woman, pale in comparison.

That was the thing about routine low-grade persecution—the continual harassment, intimidation, house arrest, collective punishment of family and acquaintances, frequent detention of various kinds of people who pushed the envelope of rights and citizenship even slightly and calmly and moderately in China: There were always far worse or more dramatic things happening elsewhere that grabbed the headlines, things like downright loss of life, sometimes on a massive scale. The persecution was so habitual that most of the time, it flew beneath the radar, at least most people's radars, with only an exceptional case every so often rising to general public awareness, and that only outside of China, since within, media censorship prevented widespread awareness. The assertion that your disappearance was more emblematic of a national catastrophe at a much deeper and more pervasive and long-lasting social, political, historical and psychic level than a freak storm could bewilder many, if not strike them as exaggerated at best, perverse at worst, out of proportion; but it was the nature of the catastrophe that most failed to recognize it as such.

We did not hear from Anna again. Did she make it back to Tacloban, did she not? Did her family survive, did they not? She had disappeared, in the sense that sooner or later, most people disappear from one's life, a sense considerably different from that of your disappearance. Regardless, Anna's absence contributed to my not altogether rational feeling of abandonment. While she was there, I found her presence intrusive, however helpful, indeed at times indispensable, she was; now that she was gone, I, we had been abandoned.

Without her around, Z's grandparents' visits, which had become bi-weekly, sometimes even more frequent, to make up for the disappearance of first mother and then helper, were the only chance I had to do the things one can only do when not looking after a child, and that was only for a few hours a week. At first, I thought Anna's departure a disaster. But after a while, apart from the not-insignificant fact that I couldn't do anything else but care for Z, I got used to it and thought it was o.k. The case was filed away in the folder, All of the things that you think you need but you don't, a folder which by necessity appeared to be growing ever thicker. After all, if I'd wanted to, if I had been sufficiently motivated, I could have found a replacement for her, but I didn't even try.

•

We had such good times together. Whatever we did, we enjoyed ourselves, reading, jumping on the bed, drawing and painting, taking a walk, going to the playground, or the library, or the beach, rock-climbing, collecting rocks and shells, going on an "adventure" to the village on the north end of the island, where we would feed the fish in a big cement pond overgrown with vegetation and play in a deserted playground. It was a precious time in her life, and it hurt whenever I thought of you missing it, of Z missing her mother. She seemed to know very well how things stood, that the two of us had to look after each other. Every evening, I helped her to fall asleep, tired pals lying side by side.

It took Z a while to wind down. She had to process the day. We lay and discussed whatever she wanted—death (of the dinosaurs, of the little bird whose corpse lay outside our gate, of the gecko whose corpse lay behind the toilet, of people), growing up (*I'm getting bigger and bigger and bigger, soon I will be a big girl, I will be bigger than Teacher*), friendships (she especially loved stories about her and her friends' exploits and adventures, and in particular, their escapades once they'd grown up—they became delivery people, they played guitar and cello, they went on trips around the world), catastrophe (typhoons, which we talked about endlessly, Tacloban, Anna and where she might be, people having accidents), Mommy's absence (*I like mommy so much* was the plaintive refrain).

She drank a bottle of milk while I told stories based on topics she requested. *Story!* she demanded.

What do you want a story about? I asked.

And then she suggested a topic. She was never at a loss. That night, it was about a giant cup of coconut juice that she and her friends had to figure out how to drink using stepstools and straws, a favorite of hers in that period. Once the milk was finished and she could open her mouth for something else, Z reflected on the events of the day, if in a somewhat elliptical, obscure, indeed haiku-like fashion that required interpretation. She had become a fountain of language, gushing words.

I put polka-dots on the giraffe, she reported in reference to a nursery school activity. They'd made paper giraffes, and then, when they dried, put brown dots on them, which she referred to as polka-dots.

I cried when you left. She didn't like it when I dropped her off at nursery school. I stuck around for a while but then snuck away when she got to the point of sufficient engagement in the activity at hand. She wanted me to know that after my departure, she noticed I was gone, expressing attachment and perhaps reminding me of my responsibility to her, of how much she depended on me, of how little else there was between her and, what?, the abyss, especially with her mother gone. Don't think that you don't matter, baba. Don't think I don't know how little we have besides ourselves. It reminded me of another recent moment:

Yao mo wash hands, baba? Have you washed your hands yet, daddy? Not only was the statement typical of her mixing of Cantonese and English, but it was a sign of her feeling the need to take responsibility for me, just as she expected me to do for her, this being a question I often asked her before eating. She knew that life was not that easy for me either, and I too needed looking after.

Are you o.k? she would sometimes ask, if I happened to be lying on the sofa or the rug resting.

I was impressed by her ability to think about the day just passed, by her sensitivity to what was happening around her. I teased out what she was trying to say, repeating it back to her in my own words with a comment or two of my own that she could elaborate on if she so chose.

Once Z finished reflecting on her day, there was a silent pause. The next stage of the bedtime ritual went like this: *Let's go to sleep now*, I said. *Let's close our eyes, be quiet, not move. Sleep well, lovely girl. Sweet dreams. I love you very much.* And then a kiss, on the cheek or forehead. She rolled on top of me, we hugged, she kissed me, pressing her face up against mine—she had not yet grasped the concept of puckering one's lips and pressing them against another—, she rolled off and tried to settle.

I want you to sleep well, baba, she murmured.

What?

I want you to sleep well, baba. Then more flopping about, trying to find a comfortable position. Then, eventually, the silence that said sleep was near. I listened for her breathing in the darkness.

It would still be a while before I heard the deep breathing that signified sleep.

In that waiting silence, a story came to mind. You had told it to me not long before your disappearance. It was a story you had heard from someone else. A 27-year-old man finds his biological parents after 22 years of separation. At the age of five, he was abducted by child traffickers in the poor inland province where he was born and sold to a childless couple in a relatively prosperous coastal province where children, especially boys, could fetch a good price. And so he was raised for a time as the son of the couple who purchased him, but they died when he was still quite young, and their parents, his "grandparents", took up the burden of raising him, developing a deep attachment. Maybe because of the early deaths of those new parents, you surmised, he was able through the years to preserve something like a mindmap of his origins, whereas it seemed most other children abducted or adopted before the age of five ended up with nothing but a blank as far as their original parents were concerned, a prospect that always struck you with horror, thinking of Z: *If she were kidnapped today, she would most likely come to remember nothing of us*, you'd said before you were kidnapped. The 27-year-old had a vague recollection of a tarmac road that passed in front of a home made of brick, and behind the home, a school. He remembered an old woman in the village into which he was sold remarking shortly after his arrival that he spoke with what sounded like a Sichuanese accent, and from this, he surmised that he was from Sichuan. Someone suggested to him that if the road had been tarmacked already 22 years ago, at a much earlier stage of development, it was most likely a major thoroughfare. And so began his search on Google Earth, covering stretch by stretch of trunk road in the huge province of Sichuan, until he found an area that bore some resemblance to the fragmented images of his memory. An emissary was sent: Did someone from here lose a child years ago?

Yes, one couple said. A reunion was arranged. The mother fixes the long-lost son a bowl of noodles. The son weeps. Now, now, the mother consoles, no sense dwelling on the past. We are lucky that, at the end of it all, I can serve you noodles and you can eat them. And with that, 22 years of separation were washed away.

The baby thieves of China were prolific. Anything could be bought or sold. Had there ever been a purer form of capitalism, a freer market? Even in HK, one had to always keep an eye on one's child. You, who specialized in nightmares, taking up the burden for the both of us (I never remembered dreams of any sort), had dreams about Z disappearing, in various situations, one of the most frequent being that the two of us were arguing so vehemently with one another, we forgot about Z, and then when we looked, she was gone. After the dreams, you spoke with urgency: Please look after her well! Please keep your eye on her at all times! At all times! But Z did not disappear.

Others were not so lucky. Tens of thousands children had disappeared in China in recent years, presumably abducted. One estimate put the number at a difficult-to-believe 70,000 per year (versus about 100 per year in the US). Parents of disappeared children received little to no help from police. Then, when they tried to organize on their own to support one another and publicize their plight, they were harassed by the police, the same entity that refused to help them.

The father of a missing daughter said, *They say China has human rights, but this isn't the case at all, not a single bit. Before this happened with our child, we thought everything was great, just like we saw on TV. Now, we know it's all fake.*[1]

The words of another father rang in my ears: *This is what I want to say to my son: Son, your dad and mom were not good. We*

---

1 "Agonizing, lonely search for missing kids in China", Jack Chang, Associated Press, December 27, 2014

didn't watch you closely enough. That's why you were kidnapped. Son, daddy and mommy are sorry. No matter where you go, as long as we're alive, as long as we have breath, we'll be trying to bring you home.[2]

I, by contrast, had only a wife missing, Z only a mother. I hadn't been good enough by half either. The people thieves, whether traffickers or the Partystate, were always only a step away, lurking around every corner. The world was, as my parents-in-law never tired of reminding with nearly every comment, simply by their vigilant presence, a dangerous place, and anyone who didn't heed that admonition, constantly and without fail, had no one but themselves to blame. No one but themselves to blame. No one. But themselves. To blame. Being a parent was an experience, or better, an exercise in deep vulnerability. Of course, such was the case before the child came into the world as well, such was always the case in life, but it didn't seem that way: I could look out for myself, you could look out for yourself, we could look out for each other, and if anything did happen to either one of us, terrible, yes, but so be it, it came with the territory. But a parent seemed to be not so much swimming as swirling in contingency, randomness, having forces much greater than ourselves ranged against us. Uncontrollably. And there is no one but yourself to blame if you don't contend with them, fight them off, stave off the worst, continually and forever. The infinite fragility out of which either beauty or terror or suffering or some combination of the above emerged.

While some children were abducted, others were abandoned. "Baby hatches" had been recently opened in several mainland cities. Unwanted children could be dropped off, or disposed of (depending on how you looked at it). The logic behind the baby hatches was that they reduced the risk of the children

---

[2] "Living with Dead Hearts", a film directed by Charlie Custer and Leia Li

being killed or dying of exposure since they would presumably be abandoned anyway. It was better to be left in a baby hatch, a place dedicated to abandonment, rather than in the usual places, a public restroom, a train station or worse. The vast majority of the abandoned children were mentally or physically disabled or had a serious health condition. Often the parents left messages apologizing for abandoning their children but claiming they could not take care of them. Giving birth to a disabled child was regarded as a catastrophe. Parents in China received little to no support in coping with raising a disabled child, and medical treatment for a child with a chronic illness or disability was prohibitively expensive.

So, boys, who were marketable, were kidnapped and sold. Girls, who were not, were delivered to orphanages, which made a tidy profit sending them abroad for adoption. And sick and disabled children were abandoned. An altogether efficient sorting process. Tens of millions of other children were left by their parents in the care of their grandparents in the village while the parents went off to cities and coastal areas to work, a situation that greatly resembled that of HK foreign domestic workers. There were no easy choices for a poor rural parent in China.

Ever since Z had come along, I could not stand to hear or read the stories of unfortunate children, I who always thought of myself as able to face just about anything, more able than you, who had a long list of things you didn't want to hear about or see, who in downtime from work insisted that all stories you read or watched had to have happy endings. Anything else just reminded you too much of work. But here I was, turning away from headlines, from taking notice of stories in which things did not turn out well for the child, the unloved, abused, exploited, harmed, killed, disappeared, diseased or disabled child. In Syria, bombs and guns had killed 11,500 children so far;

764 children had been executed, 112 of whom appeared to have been tortured first. The six-year-old Chinese boy whose eyes had been gouged out. The Sacramento ten-year-old suffering from neuroblastoma, with bruise-blackened eyes and distended belly like that of children with kwashiorkor. How much suffering could a small body endure? The seven-year-old HK girl whose mother, after a fight with the father, apparently over how to raise the child, took her and, hand-in-hand, to spite the husband, jumped off the top of the public housing estate highrise where they lived.

Where were you that night as I lay in the dark listening for the deep inhalations and exhalations that signaled our child slept? Were you thinking of me, of us, imagining us lying in bed, Z on the verge of sleep? I prayed no harm beyond your disappearance had come to you or would, prayer the harmless weapon of the powerless.

Z's turtle lamp cast green stars and crescent moon upon the ceiling and walls of the dark bedroom. Didn't people use to think that the world sat upon a giant tortoise? At the start of *A Brief History of Time* Stephen Hawking tells the anecdote, perhaps apocryphal, of a public lecture Bertrand Russell once gave on astronomy: *He described how the earth orbits around the sun and how the sun, in turn, orbits around the center of a vast collection of stars called our galaxy. At the end of the lecture, a little old lady at the back of the room got up and said: 'What you have told us is rubbish. The world is really a flat plate supported on the back of a giant tortoise.' The scientist gave a superior smile before replying, 'What is the tortoise standing on?' 'You're very clever, young man, very clever,' said the old lady. 'But it's tortoises all the way down!'* Tortoises all the way down, I found myself thinking on many occasions.

Up in the clouds, beyond the green stars and crescent moon, appeared images of children, like angels insofar as they were celestial, but persecuted angels, angels chained to the earth, subject to the arbitrary cruelty of which human beings sometimes seemed dark masters.

There were the stolen children:

Gedhun Choekyi Nyima, the Tibetan boy who at the age of six was recognized by the Dalai Lama as the reincarnation of the Panchen Lama and days later was kidnapped, along with his whole family, by the Partystate, never to be heard from again. Where was he? What was he doing at that very moment, if indeed he was still alive since no sign of his existence had ever come light? He would be 23 years old by now.

And Dejazmatch Alemayehu Tewodros, son of Emperor Tewodros II of Ethiopia, who committed suicide after military defeat at the hands of the British, who then, out of the goodness of their hearts, took his son under their wing, bringing him, age 7, back to England, his mother dying en route, rendering him an orphan. There, he was subjected to the Victorian charity of the great and good, including the Queen, but nevertheless died of pleurisy at the age of eighteen. Was the death of the silent boy a kind of protest against the charity imposed upon him? The Queen arranged his burial at Windsor Castle, where a plaque remembering him bore the words, *I was a stranger and ye took me in*. The bitter irony of those words: First, he was taken from his homeland as a young boy. Then, eleven years later, he died. Then, his epigraph was chosen for him, a nugget of Christian charity. The last thing his homeland's invaders did was to ventriloquize his voice, putting words in the mouth of one who could no longer speak, portraying him as an object of pity, aggrandizing themselves as the ones who *took him in*, whether he liked it or not, and of course, he would never be able to say for himself now. If ever we were to have a boy, I thought of calling him Alemayehu, *he who has seen the world*, and, I hoped, he would talk back.

Or, if another girl, Alem, the *world* itself, based on a promise I'd made several years earlier and had yet to keep, having met an Alem in Addis Ababa, a bright-eyed eternally smiling girl of seven who lived at an orphanage run by the Sisters of Mercy, Mother Teresa's order, about which I was ambivalent, to put it mildly, vaunting as they did ignorance in the form of strict reliance upon "God's will", a perverse version of fate that meant in practice, let whatever happens happen for it was bound to occur. Alem had a twin sister. Their parents had almost certainly died of AIDS, though in the course of the rapid deterioration of their health, they had never been diagnosed, so little access to health care had they had. Beyond that, I knew nothing about the girls' past, not even where they were from. The orphanage had separate sections for HIV-positive and HIV-negative children. Alem's sister was HIV-negative. She had been segregated from her sister at the orphanage and then adopted by an American couple, taken to a place far far away. Alem was HIV-positive, though she appeared as healthy as any other child, if perhaps a bit on the small and frail side. She would almost certainly be adopted by no one. I visited her weekly and took her out on excursions together with other children; otherwise, they hardly ever got a chance to leave the orphanage, the sisters were so understaffed. Over the months, the question emerged: Should I adopt Alem? She was adorable. We had a rapport. With the Sisters of Mercy, she received inadequate medical care. Adopting her, taking her away from there would almost certainly save her life, or at least substantially prolong it. Was there, would there ever be any more concrete chance to do good in my life? Though I could not adopt all HIV-positive orphans, at least I could one I had gotten to know. But I didn't. Why not? Why did I leave Alem to die, as she surely must have by now? My home life was a mess. My long-term partner was breaking up with me; I would have to raise the child alone. As ever, there was virtually no stability in my life, no place to which I could bring Alem and say, This is home, where you can stay and be safe for the rest of your childhood. But at bottom, those were excuses—no home situation was perfect, and whatever the flaws of mine, it would be an immense improvement over hers in the orphanage. Wasn't the real reason selfishness? Or that it would require sacrifice, it would require me upending my life and reorienting it toward her? That it would confer upon me an absolute responsibility about which I was deeply ambivalent? Years of low-grade regret were the result of my non-decision. I never decided not to adopt Alem; I just never decided to do so. And then events took me away from Addis, away from Alem. And though I intended to stay in contact, it was hard to do so, and eventually it dwindled to nothing. If, by some miracle she was still alive, she would be 18 by now. Her face stayed fixed in memory, Alem, the one who would never let me go, who clung and smiled and clung. I promised myself if ever I had a daughter of my own, I would name her Alem, but then my daughter came, and got a different name.

Not all of the images up in the sky between the clouds, above green stars and crescent moon projected from the back of a turtle, were those of lamas or scions or adoptable orphans.

Some were those whose lives had been blown apart by circumstances, conflicts, political acts far beyond their control, the dirty-faced displaced children, Halima Gisa, a Nuba of Sudan, the Afghan refugee children of Islamabad, Abdulrahman Bahadir, Aktar Babrek, Awal Gul, Basmina, Gullakhta Nawab, Hayat Khan, Hazrat Babir, Ibraheem Rahees, Khalzarin Zirgul, Zaman, Laiba Hazrat, Madina Juma'a, Naseebah Zarghoul, Nazmina Bibi, Noorkhan Zahir, Robina Haseeb, Safia Mourad, Shahzada Saleem, Satara, Waheed Wazir, Zarlakhta Nawab, for they did all have names, yes, that at least, if not much else. I learned their names because I had downloaded their photos from the internet and named the files according to their names. A Palestinian photographer, Muhammed Muheisen, who lived in Islamabad, befriended the children while taking photos in their neighborhood. The portraits were straight-forward, direct, nothing fancy about them. Muheisen knew that was the best way to convey the dignity of the kids: You didn't have to do anything fancy; they were who they were; that would come through. I'd scrambled the photos into a collage, mixed with photos of Z, which became a screensaver. All of those siupengyao and Z together. I recited their names in alphabetical order when I went running. After a few weeks, the litany of names came almost automatically, and with each name, the image of the child.

And some were the formerly nameless who emerged out of obscurity. Their fate was to become synonymous with infamy. Mohammed Al-Durra, killed at the age of twelve on a street in Gaza and immortalized only because his murder was captured on video. The video still—the image that appeared before me now—was grainy: Mohammed's face, eyes closed in a grimace of fear, partially visible beneath his father's arm attempting to shield him from the bullets. His victimhood iconic, like Kim Phuc's, the Vietnamese girl fleeing naked from a U.S. napalm attack, her skin burning, and like that of the Warsaw ghetto boy, hands raised in surrender, whose identity had never been ascertained despite much posthumous investigation. A pageant of the massacre of the innocents, *all the boys in Bethlehem and its vicinity who were two years old and under*, children the receptacles of pain, their suffering emblematic of a world out of joint.

A scene from "Shoah": A passenger in a skiff on a quiet, small rural river, the very image of provincial insignificance—nothing of world-importance could happen here. Weathered-looking, he sang a song whose tune floated out across the stillness of the surrounding countryside. He was one of three people—three people!—to have survived the Chełmno extermination camp where hundreds of thousands were murdered. He was now 47 but looked older. He had been persuaded to return from where he now lived in Israel to this now-serene, then-horrific place. He was singing the song, or one of the songs, that saved his life, kept him alive while wave after wave of his counterparts were massacred. He was thirteen and the killers allowed him to live because they liked his voice and he could sing tunes in German, familiar tunes that filled them with bittersweet homesick nostalgia. As the Russians closed in, the order went out to shoot all remaining Jews. The boy was shot in the head but miraculously survived, rescued from a field of corpses by a Polish peasant, treated by a Russian doctor. The figure singing on the boat thirty-four years later was the child in the man.

Until my dying day I shall refuse to love a scheme of things in which children are put to torture. A Camus character said that, a doctor, responding to another character who tried to justify the "mysterious ways of god" after the death of a child.

Then amongst the constellation of images were also those of children in no discernible way victims of violence, child not only victim, not only receptacle of violence, but child as raw, fragile, dignified, vital: Bruce Davidson's almost naked skinny shaggy-haired kid half-silhouetted on a New York fire escape; Peter Doig's girl in white standing high up in the thick bare branches of a tree; Michael Andrews' portrait of himself teaching his young daughter Melanie to swim, both naked except for barely discernible briefs, pale white skin in black water.

And then there were also images of the child lying next to me in the dark:

Her face at Wang Fu, where we got takeaway dumplings, something we did not infrequently after your disappearance. We stopped by at offpeak hours, diners few and scattered at the few tables in the narrow place, their faces hidden by bowls from which emerged the sound of slurps. After placing our order, we peered into the kitchen through the open window where the cook set the orders for the waitress to fetch. Z loved to watch the cook work, scooping the *jiaozi* out of a vat of boiling water with a large spoonlike sieve in one hand and placing them on the plate he held in the other. I loved, in turn, to watch Z's face, illuminated by the fluorescent kitchen light, animated by awe.

And: Sitting together in the open-air stern of the ferry as it went around the back of a gigantic port-bound containership, its hulk looming over us. I pointed out the highrise hospital set against the steep green hillside on the southwest corner of the main island. *That was where you was born*, I told her, *where you came out of mommy's tummy*. She was familiar with this story. I often told it at bedtime, beginning with how she started out in her mommy's tummy and ending with when she grew up and got on a plane and went far away with her best friend (*Come back?* she'd ask, in slight alarm. *Yes, and then you came back, and mommy and baba were happy*). It made an impression on her: There, in that building, she came into the world. She sat pensively staring at the tall building. Or perhaps she was groggy, having just awaken from a nap.

Then: The last July 1 demonstration for universal suffrage, hundreds of thousands of people marching in the street. Long Hair and his sidekicks carried a coffin at shoulder height, as they always did, their longstanding prop symbolizing those killed by the army in Beijing on June 4, 1989, reminding of what could happen in HK if we didn't fight for our rights while we still could. I sidled up to the coffin, holding Z, who grasped the handle that ran along its side, helping to hold what was actually an empty plywood box painted black (how many had been smashed or confiscated by the police through the years!), becoming one of the pallbearers. She smiled: How cool, holding the handle of the coffin that symbolized, on the one hand, the decades-long and continuing oppression of the Partystate, and, on the other, the desire for freedom and democracy that would not die no matter how many they killed. Of course, that wasn't what she thought was cool about it; she was carrying the coffin with those other guys, those cool guys, marching together with them.

The breathing was steady now, slowing, deep, bordering on snores. How fortunate we were there, Z and I, lying in that warm, comfortable bed, in spite of what had happened to her mother, in contrast to her mother and many other children around the world. I picked up the empty milk bottle and ever so gently lifted myself from the bed. Before I closed the door, I turned back. In the dim turtle light, I could discern a figure lying on the bed, spread-eagled, her limbs stretched in all four directions, her pink pajamas against the dark sheets.

How big she has grown, I thought: She takes up nearly the whole bed. It was only then, turning to the light outside the door, I noticed my face wet with... what... tears? I who never cried—you always accused me of being unfeeling because you had never seen me cry. If you could see me now. But then, one of the reasons my face was wet was that you couldn't see me now, shedding tears for Z's beauty, our impossible situation, the injustice of a child forcibly separated from her mother. Ever so gently, with the care of a thief, I shut the bedroom door, the doorknob slightly squeaking. Where did we go from here? In that answerless silence, Z's haiku filled the ears.

I put polka-dots on the giraffe.

I cried when you left.

I want you to sleep well, baba.

4

What had I been thinking, taking the "Air Train" into the city? That evening, it was a train in name only. From the airport, there was a shuttle to Jamaica Station; from there, an express train into the city, except the express train wasn't working. To enter the city, instead, required taking two local trains, changing from one to another by going up and down a series of mazelike staircases. With a child. And two suitcases. Trapped in someone's bad joke. In what seemed the middle of the night, but was really just evening, not too long after dark. Riding with night people, amongst whom we must surely have stuck out, passing through a ring of gloomy poverty to reach the glittering jewel at its center. This was the introduction to the great metropolis of capitalism and democracy (to the extent the two could go together, and perhaps that was precisely the problem), its crumbling infrastructure paling in comparison to the supercleanefficientcomfortableconvenientaffordable Airport Express and MTR of HK. Disheartening. Wealth ringfenced from the rest of society. Hardly a good advertisement for democracy. You can keep your democracy if we get supercleanefficientcomfortableconvenientaffordable public services and transport, I could hear the masses shout all the way from HK to Singapore to China.

It had been a long flight. Z had weathered it well. In fact, it was this final struggle to enter the city that was doing her in, and not only her. She wanted to be carried. Along with two suitcases. Up flights of stairs. Poor girl. As usual, she had been so good. I'd wondered whether to take her on the trip at all. Gong-gong and Po-po had offered to look after her while I was gone. I would have got a lot more done that way, and more swiftly. (I was always amazed at how much longer things took with her. I did things fast. I was addicted to speed. She made me slow down. Since we'd had her, I'd gotten even better at doing things fast, as I had even less time to do them than before.)

But it felt harsh to leave her behind, wrong. We were in this together. We should do it together. I asked her whether she wanted to come. She did. And so she came.

Well, I said to her, after the fifteen-hour flight, trying to climb the stairs of some dark decrepit station in Queens up to the platform for the train that I swore would bring us into Manhattan, *you wanted to come on the trip, you gotta help me out a bit.*

To which she replied, *I'm so tired, baba, so tired.*

On the flight, arcing over the northern end of the largest ocean in the world and down through the cold wastes of upper Canada, I was struck by a strangely palpable fear that the plane would crash, killing us all. There was nothing about the mundane flight to give reason for such a fear, except for the sheer unnaturalness of hurtling halfway around the world in the upper reaches of the atmosphere in a tin can, but then that went for every transcontinental flight. After all, it was rather seldom, wasn't it?, that planes went down above oceans, simply vanishing out of the sky, disintegrating mid-air at 30,000 feet, or dropping suddenly and plunging into mid-ocean. Takeoff, landing and flying low amidst difficult topography presented the greatest danger of crashes, no? In recent years, whenever you or I had ventured into the evil empire, only one of us went, never both together, so that if we were apprehended, there would be one parent left behind to look after Z. But Z and I weren't following the same precept now. We could both go down. You would be left with no one. You would get out. There would be no one there to greet you, to say, Welcome back! Such were my thoughts on that flight.

Apart from that fear of falling out the sky and disappearing, there was also a sense of just how counter-intuitive the trip was—going away from you in order to find you. It wasn't as if I had been making any progress there in HK, but still, to go to the other side of the world from where you were, well, it just felt wrong. In that period, I could hardly do anything without tying myself in contradictory emotional knots, guilt vying with, well, what? Guilt we were going farther away from where you had to be, guilt at the sense of liberation and relief at getting away from "the scene of the crime". It almost felt like a vacation. And accompanying the guilt, a deep physical sadness that pervaded the body. As if I were betraying you. Even if the trip was ultimately, I hoped, for your benefit.

While Z slept splayed across two seats—a relief, for I had feared she would have difficulty sleeping on the flight, her newly gangly body used to sprawling spread-eagled across a mattress—, myself sitting on the armrest abutting the aisle to make room for her, a refrain kept going through my mind, as if on a loop.

When someone disappears, it's as if you're supposed to put your life on hold, or as if your life has been put on hold whether you like it or not. Part of you does not want anything to happen, wants time to freeze at the moment of disappearance, not only for yourself but for the whole world, and not resume until the disappeared is returned to you. But at the same time, life must go on, as they say; you have to carry on, you have no choice, again whether you like it or not.

It's as if you should do nothing, or perhaps you feel you can do nothing, you've been rendered incapable by the disappearance, all power and agency robbed from you, some vital internal organ removed, or you don't want to do anything except sit in this eternal waiting room, and yet, you must, you must.

Sometimes, you want to do something else, anything else. You find there is still desire, and appetite, and things attract you back to life, to the moment, the present, in the absence of the disappeared, and you feel guilty about that: It is wrong to desire, it is wrong to want anything else but the return of the disappeared.

Sometimes you think it is worse than if the person had died. With the dead, at least you know they are dead, but with the disappeared, there is indefinite uncertainty, the long tunnel without sign of end. You think constantly that something terrible could be happening to her at the very moment that you're taking a warm shower, shaving, combing your hair, having breakfast, and so on through the course of the day. You worry constantly that she is in danger, abused, and at the same time, you are the constant victim of deluded hope, that all is o.k., that one day she will return, that all will, eventually, be as it was before, though even if she does return some day, nothing will again be as it once was.

The shower, the grooming, the daily chores can at least be justified to some extent by the necessity of hygiene, or of presenting yourself to the world, or of doing what needs to be done to get by, to continue to survive, maintaining your self-respect, trying to carry on with some semblance of normality, for the sake, even, of the disappeared, as a kind of carrying of the flag, their flag, a type of loyalty: I shave for you, I shower for you, I drink this cup of coffee for you; all that I do, day in, day out, I do for you.

But what about visiting an art museum, or taking a swim in the ocean? Should not pleasure be forbidden to lovers of the disappeared? How can you enjoy yourself when the disappeared is almost certainly suffering, even if of nothing else than deprivation of freedom? Enjoyment, pleasure is betrayal.

Going elsewhere, too, if it is in the opposite direction of where she is. (And at that moment, I had the sudden urge to ask the pilot to turn the plane around and head straight back to HK.)

You think of all that she is deprived of, beginning with her freedom and working your way down to the creature comforts.

You think, sometimes, that life is worth little more than its creature comforts, the small freedoms, making a cup of coffee for yourself however you want, whenever you want, when it is raining and you want to sit inside with the steam rising from the cup and watch the rain and think about life, about the past.

It is not like longing for the distant beloved: As I write, outside the rain is pelting down, and where are you, dear one? No, because even *though you do not know where the beloved is, you are almost entirely certain that the beloved has not freely removed herself from you, that the beloved is not in possession of her freedom. No, it is not like that because you cannot make plans to meet again.*

●

The trail, which never was warm, had gone cold. Colder. Efforts to find any solid information at all had come to a dead end, water seeping into the sand before it reached the sea. This was worrying: Usually so many months after a Partystate abduction, there was a sign of some kind. The fact that there wasn't was itself a bad sign: Perhaps, like Gao Zhisheng, the person had been so badly mistreated (I couldn't even bring myself to use the word "tortured"), the regime didn't dare show him and was waiting for him to sufficiently recover and for telltale signs of the abuse to disappear. Or perhaps the captive was especially recalcitrant and the continuing incommunicado detention was a form of both punishment and pressure; of this there was a high probability in a system that placed such a premium on (coerced) confession and (coerced) cooperation.

I had finally hired a lawyer. It had taken me some time. I'd consulted people I trusted, Chang Boyang and Chang Pingan in particular, rights lawyers both. Chang Boyang had left Beijing and had a fellowship at an HK university, from which perch he still spoke out with regularity. Just as the HK fellowship was coming to an end and the prospect of having no legal means to remain outside of the mainland loomed, you had helped him to line up a fellowship at a prestigious US university with a reputation for taking persecuted dissidents under its wing. Chang Pingan, on the other hand, had remained in Beijing and somehow managed to retain and renew his lawyer's license, unlike many of his colleagues in rights defense work who had been disbarred, Chang Boyang included. But he had kept a decidedly low profile—until recently that is: He was representing Ilham Tohti, the outspoken Uighur academic, who, like you, had been spirited away, though at least in his case, his wife knew the Partystate had him—he'd been nabbed from their apartment while she was home.

Independently of one another, both Chang Boyang and Chang Pingan insisted we needed someone big, established, an insider with integrity, someone with contacts in the corridors of power who could snoop around and hear whisperings. That was Ma Lianshun. Ma had represented Liu Xiaobo and many others, somehow without ever having fallen foul of the regime himself. To the contrary, his law firm flourished. It was reckoned that this was because he was from an older generation, many of whom were on the route to power within the system before eighty-nine hit. Those who sided with the demonstrators had their official careers destroyed or went into exile, unless they had a profession such as law which provided some independent means of survival. Even though the careers of their counterparts who supported the regime flourished in the aftermath of eighty-nine, there were still contacts kept across the divide, a divide which Ma apparently had managed to straddle, being held in high regard by government critics and those in the rights defense movement while also retaining the respect of people inside the regime.

Ma was happy to take the case, though, he added, *I am expensive.* You and I had met him once, in his old-style law offices in a corner of the park bordering the Forbidden City (from which he'd since been evicted, not for political reasons, though; presumably because the grounds were coveted by someone much better connected than he). He took us to lunch at a nearby restaurant, which he made a point of saying belonged to the man who was once Mao's personal chef. The owner played off that reputation: Old black-and-white photographs of scenes from Mao's life lined the walls. (If there were ever décor to induce loss of appetite …) He had fond memories of you. In particular, he was impressed with how much baijiu you drank at that meal at Mao's chef's restaurant. *Few women can drink like that,* he said. Yes, of course, he was willing to take the case.

He put to work his informal network of contacts at various levels and in various parts of the Partystate bureaucracy but heard nothing. The silence, he himself admitted, was chilling: Usually some word, some indication trickled out. After that initial reconnaissance, Ma put one of the younger lawyers in his office, Lawyer Ni, on the case. Lawyer Ni dug and dug, scuttling about with aplomb, never afraid or put off by the dirty work, digging into dark corners, of which there were many—it was a country of dark corners. He was a mensch through and through with a softish build that suggested it had been years since he'd had any physical exercise. I was confident he would do his very best but skeptical that he would be able to do much, at least not until your whereabouts and circumstances were ascertained. He also happened to be a highly enthusiastic amateur astrologer and promised to do his best for you in that capacity as well. I didn't have high hopes Ma or Lawyer Ni would be able to make much progress legally speaking—it was clear already that the Partystate had decided to handle this case outside of the law, to dispense with even the pretension it was following it. I was not surprised by that, but it worried me that they couldn't even find a trace of you in the system. I thought of Ma and Lawyer Ni largely as conduits, who, when needed, could make use of their contacts inside the bureaucracy, pass messages back and forth. It was good to have them in place though they hadn't managed to come up with anything yet.

Journalists also came to our aid. You had good relations with quite a few who over the years had relied on you for information, tips, sources, quotes, advice. They liked you, felt strong sympathy with you, and agreed not to report (yet) on your disappearance. They said they would keep their ear to the ground for any word on what had happened.

Meanwhile, as Ilham's recent enforced disappearance showed, the situation continued to deteriorate. Everyone, it seemed, was fair game. Under the guise of cleaning things up, with highly publicized crackdowns on official corruption, prostitution and organized crime, the regime was consolidating its power. Behind that screen of propaganda, anyone who might remotely pose any sort of threat — and that seemed to include just about everyone in independent civil society — was being targetted.

Besides Ilham, and the trials of Xu and others associated with the New Citizens Movement, there were other persecutions. Cao Shunli had just been brought from a detention center to the intensive care unit of a hospital, the culmination of months of medical neglect by prison authorities. Her health had now deteriorated to the point that her life was in danger. She had been kidnapped at the Beijing airport on her way to a training workshop in Geneva and held incommunicado for a month before being formally arrested on charges of "gathering a crowd to disrupt public order", the same charge leveled at Xu. Her crime in particular was to organize people to demand civil society participation in the upcoming Universal Periodic Review of China at the UN Human Rights Council, a role that according to the terms of the UPR was supposed to be guaranteed.

And then, on top of it all, it looked like Hu Jia was going down again. Hu Jia did things Gandhi-style. Everything out in the open. He was one of the few who said exactly what he meant, exactly what he thought. I loved him for it, but China was an exceedingly dangerous place to do that. He'd been recently interrogated all night long on suspicion of "provoking and stirring up trouble". In particular, the interrogators were interested in his Twitter posts (in spite of the fact that Twitter was blocked on the mainland and therefore reached an exceedingly small audience of tens of thousands, exiles and those within China who circumvented the Great Firewall), which, among other things, called for a rally in Tiananmen Square to commemorate the 25th anniversary of the massacre, urged people to wear masks to protest Beijing's bad air, and called on fellow citizens to follow Ukrainians in rising up against the Partystate. He'd also expressed concern about Ilham and the Tibetan self-immolators. With public statements like that, the wonder was that he'd not been arrested already, and the only reasons I could think of were that he was already under (extra-legal) house arrest and therefore couldn't really do much *except* express himself online, it was fairly easy for the Partystate to block those expressions within the Great Firewall, and he had a high enough profile that the Partystate thought twice before doing anything too nasty to him. The persecution of Hu Jia made me particularly sad. It had something to do with the way the regime had already destroyed his relationship with his wife and the fact that the two of them had a young daughter. Not only that, but he was pure, and his thinking was radical in that it was consistent—compassion for all, including the environment, animals, all people, including Tibetans and Uighurs. There were few public figures in China (or, for that matter, most places) who were so rigorously consistent in applying their life view. Of course, on every count, that put him at odds with a Partystate that was almost as consistently hostile to freedom of expression.

In the face of this deteriorating situation, and having had no word on your disappearance, Opal decided she had to act. She would enter the mainland under an assumed name. That would reduce the risk of attracting attention and being followed. A false return-to-the-motherland pass was forged. She didn't exactly have a plan; she would just see what she could find out. She would track down contacts, see what she could piece together. There were advantages to being on the ground, she said. *The worst that can happen is that I will come back with nothing*, she said.

You can't really believe that, I replied. *The worst that can happen is that you end up like Y and BY.* (Just as in your case, nothing more had been heard of BY either.)

Still, I grudgingly went along with Opal's plan, or non-plan, grateful that someone was taking some initiative on your behalf when it seemed things had reached an impasse (or, really, had been at an impasse ever since the time of the disappearance), but guilty about the fact that she was putting herself in danger and skeptical that anything could come of the mission.

I still hadn't told your organization all Opal had told me about the exact circumstances of your disappearance or what you were up to at the time. I didn't see how it might have helped and was worried the information might alienate your organization from you or make them feel less responsible to you. I felt a bit guilty about that too, as if I were playing a double game. My upbringing said if you wanted people to help you, you had to be straight with them. On the other hand, your organization had never contacted Opal, either, even though it knew that you had tried to enter the mainland together with an accomplice. I didn't know whether to take this simply as sloppy investigating or limited interest; probably the latter—while strong on traditional research, it was hardly the sleuthiest of organizations and had little appetite for or experience of skullduggery.

Although, then, we still hadn't gone public, following the advice of multiple actors, there were many people alerted to the situation—the lawyers, the journalists, the human rights community in HK, China and beyond—and doing whatever they could, which, unfortunately, wasn't much. What could they do? I didn't blame them. If the most powerful regime in the world was intent on hiding someone in one of the largest countries in the world, a country with many restrictions on independent investigation, extraordinary resources or luck were needed to find her. It was that, the fact that nothing was happening, that everything seemed stalled, that persuaded me to go to NYC, where your organization was headquartered.

Strictly speaking, your organization had done its duty. It was sticking by you, one of its researchers who had disappeared while conducting "field work" (you always chafed at the underlying colonialist/Orientalist/anthropological connotations of the term, as you did at "mission", as in "going on a mission", for example, to save the souls of the savages). But there was the small point that, like the others, there didn't seem to be much it could do. That said, after its initial efforts, it didn't seem to be doing much either. There was not great drive or initiative coming from those quarters.

I'd stopped hearing from them except when I called. I guessed the idea was they would let me know when there was something new, and there was nothing new. Venturing to NYC, I felt a bit like a gadfly pestering them. Their first reaction when I suggested a meeting in person seemed to be, What's the point? But they acceded to the request. A person in a position such as I couldn't be so worried about bothering people, for your sake, of course; in a sense, it was my duty to do so. I wondered whether you weren't discretely being jettisoned, perhaps not even intentionally, and then wondered whether I wasn't just being paranoid about that. I knew that the sort of thoroughly suspicious logic that was advisable standard operating procedure in dealing with the Partystate could easily bleed over into attitudes towards others entirely outside of that context and come off both paranoid and offensive. If there was a jettisoning, perhaps it was not even conscious; it was just, simply, the process of being forgotten. Time moves on; things change; people go about their business, their lives. Still, surely, at the end of the day, an organization dedicated to justice would stand firmly by the side of someone treated unjustly, especially when she was an employee, wouldn't it? What happens when those charged with not forgetting forget?

But how far could it go? It was a professional organization, after all. A highly professional organization, with highly competent people, very efficient, very focused, very purposeful and goal-oriented. It knew what it was about and did well what it did, was the best in the world in fact. But that also meant constantly trimming and cutting, ensuring focus, prioritizing, constantly saying, However much we might like to, we don't have the capacity to do that, we're spreading ourselves too thin. Sometimes "professional" could seem synonymous with "soulless". The ability to analyze and act rationally, at a certain emotional distance, was a necessary quality of the game, but there had to be something at the heart that motivated, something beyond or deeper than just doing your job well, or personal ambition, reputation, status, especially, perhaps, when searching for a disappeared person. You needed passion, tenacity, almost obsession; you needed to be the dog that just would not let go. Otherwise, there was calculation: when to cut your losses. You started thinking more in terms of the good of the organization, the organization's strategic plans and priorities, and your loyalties, potentially, split. After all, it was your professional responsibility to look out for the good of the organization, but perhaps something was lost in the calculation as well, perhaps the disappearance of an employee, especially after a period of time, became a matter less urgent, less central to the organization's concerns, preoccupations.

Then there were the small matters of your salary, legal costs and travel expenses that hadn't been so much as broached. I'd always been bad at raising the issue of money, thinking it beneath the dignity of the matter at hand, although I knew it was necessary to do. I preferred to assume your organization would fulfill its financial obligations to inquiring whether or not it would. And, as yet, it had not provided assurance it would do so; meanwhile, this business of searching for the disappeared, it wasn't cheap.

You were a nervous person generally, but you'd always viewed your tenure at the organization as precarious. You'd been hired largely because its China people had been enthusiastic about you. You'd always gotten the impression that their immediate supervisor was less so, indeed, hired you as much as anything else to show confidence and trust in the China people. You felt that he didn't have a very good understanding of China or the specific challenges of working there, and therefore, insufficient sympathy. A lot of his ideas and suggestions might have been in line with organization priorities but could sometimes strike you as bizarre or irrelevant in the Chinese context.

And he it was I met on our first day in NYC, an imposing man, highly intelligent, adept, refined. A charming man. He had a way with words. Presentable. That was it: He was eminently presentable, with the sheen gleaned from being part of the in-group for years. He fit into the institutional culture. He could run in establishment circles. One could easily imagine him interacting successfully with elites in government, the media, business. Whenever I met someone like that, I was reminded of why I'd never been successful (at least, in the conventional sense of the term). The head of the organization had graciously agreed to attend the meeting, to bestow his presence, though largely to keep informed and show moral support, and he mainly sat and listened. The communications director, who'd always been very well disposed towards you, was also there, as were the China people and a few others whose names and positions I didn't catch. (I wasn't always at my most observant in those days.) I was worried about my propensity to misbehave, to come on too strong, to lash out, to rub people the wrong way. I lacked the qualities my interlocutor possessed, the winning ways, the ability to address issues of potential conflict or rift in a non-confrontational, even agreeable, manner. I reminded myself I had to control myself, for your sake. I had a tendency to get lost in the moment, carried away, and end up damaging the cause.

What was there to talk about? That was what I wanted to see. Searching for a disappeared person was a matter of grasping at straws.

The main thing I wanted to discuss, that your boss and I had more or less agreed in advance would be the priority of the agenda, was whether or not the search had to enter new territory, namely, publicizing the disappearance, which would amount to upping the ante.

Up to now, there'd been all-around consensus that the quiet behind-the-scenes approach should be the first recourse, and patience was required. But that had yielded nothing, not even confirmation of the abduction. Among other things, some very gracious people at the US consulate in HK and the embassy in Beijing who knew you and were well-disposed towards you had made quiet representations on your behalf, though they could have argued they were under no obligation to do so, given that you were not a US citizen. They got nowhere, found out nothing. To the extent they got any response at all from the Chinese side, it was to the effect that there was no information, and anyway, the information they were requesting had to do with a Chinese national, and therefore, it was an entirely domestic matter irrelevant to the Americans. There hadn't even been a denial along the lines of "no, we do not have that person", which, based on past experience, was a strong indication they did.

At the meeting, there was agreement that going public was the next step, and there were no strong reservations or objections raised to doing so, but then the questions were how and what the timing should be. The second Universal Periodic Review of China was coming up at the UN Human Rights Council, one of the China people reminded everybody. This was a chance to formally get your case on the international agenda. Your organization could highlight it in its stakeholder report and perhaps also get some governments such as the US to raise it in the advance questions states submitted to the state under review, which the latter was expected to answer. The chances of the Partystate responding directly were close to nil, but at least it would be put on notice that its refusal to deal with the matter discretely had meant that it would now become an international issue. The thinking was that one reason the Partystate had kept its abduction of BY and you secret was that it didn't want anyone to know what exactly it was investigating, and the threat of publicizing the abductions could shift the Partystate's calculations. Not that the Partystate responded much these days to foreign pressure of any kind, especially when it came to human rights issues or individual cases.

Yes, that's a good opportunity, I said, grateful for the suggestions. I was desperate for any movement, anything "actionable", as the lingo went. But in the back of my mind, I heard your voice. You scoffed at anything having to do with the UN as a useless irrelevance, a sure way to get nothing accomplished. Whenever there was a session of the Human Rights Council, you referred to it as "the usual non-event". Still, I was at the point where doing something was better than doing nothing. How ironic it would be, I said to you during that meeting, if the UN turned out to play a role in your release. Not likely, came your response, loud and clear, so clear that I feared it would distract me from the meeting and my distraction would be noticed. I already suspected they didn't quite regard me as a serious person, and pulling a Macbeth would do nothing to change that. What are you smiling at? I nearly expected someone to ask.

Others suggested your organization could step up lobbying of friendly governments and place articles in the many wide-circulation media outlets with which the organization had good relations. *Yes, yes,* I said, *thank you and thank you.* Though I couldn't see that it all would amount to much, one never knew. Once one pushed the nuclear button of publicity, going from almost no one knowing to hundreds of thousands, even millions, it was hard to foresee the result. That was why, up to now, those who did know thought it a risk not yet worth taking.

We also discussed what other entities had or had not done. The HK government said it had lodged a formal inquiry, but it provided no details or documentation of having done so. It said no response had been forthcoming, and it didn't appear to be pressing or urging the Partystate to respond. The HK government was not aggressive in its approaches to the Partystate; it essentially played the role of a subject beseeching on bended knee, a petitioner. The EU, individual EU countries and the US all had a habit of adopting a preferred prisoner of conscience. It was not beyond the realm of possibility that we could get them to make representations to the Chinese government at different levels in regard to your case, to call for your release, perhaps even publically once behind-closed-doors representations failed. Your profile did, after all, resemble those of other adopted PoCs, with the significant difference that you weren't a mainland resident.

The meeting had the expected feel of an anti-climax. Oh, well, I thought, a long way to come for not much. Your boss was cordial, professionally concerned. I might have been wrong—that transposed paranoia acting up again—, but I detected a slightly critical or distanced attitude: well, she knew what she was getting herself into, was probably doing things we didn't know about and hadn't signed off on, and anyway, she was never really my top choice. I couldn't blame the organization for the way the world worked: It had to get on with its usual activities. There were new human rights abuses to address every day. It couldn't stand still, put all else on hold, let an unfortunate occurrence like this slow it down. The world kept spinning, it moved on, as it had to, while I, we stood in place.

On the way out of the office, I met a woman to whom you had once introduced me. She recognized me and expressed her sympathy. She was now one of the higher-ups in the organization. In passing, she mentioned her own "troubles" in China. Troubles, I asked, what were those? She had been a China researcher "once upon a time," she said, and had lived there undercover for five years, leaving only when the Chinese authorities did not approve an application for visa renewal, effectively barring her from the country. She'd been briefly detained on a couple of occasions in connection with investigations into lead-poisoning incidents but, being a non-ethnically-Chinese foreigner, was released with nothing but rebukes. Then her good luck ran out with the refusal to renew the visa. Had she ever told Y about this? I asked. Why, no, never. Why not? I wondered. Well, the opportunity had never arisen. I see, I said. Walking away, I wondered how strange that no one had ever thought to inform Y that a previous China researcher had been detained and eventually forced to leave the country. It was like a secret history and made me wonder how much other relevant information might have been withheld, however unintentionally, by people who were supposedly "on the same team".

In the elevator on the long way down, I met Sebastião, the other China researcher—had he timed it that way; did he wish to have a word; was it just coincidence? A tall, dashing, articulate man, he was just the sort your boss took to. He knew how to play the game, enjoyed interacting with the high and mighty, had the media at his fingertips. He pitched a message perfectly, framed an issue for the general public in an attention-grabbing way, pithy and serious, without dumbing it down. You had always admired his professional abilities and his China expertise while being somewhat suspicious of his motives, marveling at how, though you both did the same work, you came at it from vastly different perspectives.

I always thought that if we couldn't go into China, they would dump us, Sebastião said to me under his breath.

Sebastião gave the impression he was confiding in you while at the same time expertly withholding. And, I imagined, just as he might confide in you about someone else one moment, he might turn around and confide in someone else about you another. While Sebastião was one of those who'd advocated strongly that you be hired and probably saw your strengths more than most, while he was always helpful and courteous towards you, I'd advised you to hold your cards close to your chest as far as he was concerned, something that took some mindful self-discipline, as your tendency was always to be cheerfully open toward all, at least all who were supposed to be on the same side.

Are they dumping Y? I asked. Is that what just happened in there?
He shrugged noncommittally.
What do you think? I asked again.
Well, they seem to be with you this far, he said.
Yes. And for how much longer?
Hard to know, he said, *hard to know*.
True, but have you heard any rumblings one way or another?
Well, it's safe to say that the higher-ups are genuinely incensed that the Chinese have one of our people, but it's also safe to say they're always thinking first and foremost of the best interests of the organization.

That's about what I was thinking, I said. And we left it at that.
Where are you off to now? he asked.
I'm on my way to pick up Z.

After a pause, he said, *Children are prisons.* Was he trying to sympathize with me? It seemed so, though it didn't quite come across that way.

Yes, I said, *I suppose they can be. Goodbye, Sebastião, goodbye. See you in HK*, though I didn't know if I ever would.

Afterwards, standing alone on the sidewalk, the thought suddenly struck me: you're a vegetarian. What could they possibly be feeding you? It was hard to imagine your captors, having paid no heed to your rights or legal procedures, accommodating your diet. You got what they had; you ate it or had none. I imagined you were making do. I hoped, at any rate, you were fed well. A typical consequence of imprisonment in China was weight loss, if not malnutrition leading to other complications and diseases.

On the downtown train, it wasn't the meeting I mulled over but Sebastião's words. Children are prisons. It was something I'd thought a lot about. Sebastião was divorced and had a teenage son in Brazil whom he saw about twice a year. Perhaps his comment referred to his own experience, though I couldn't see how seeing a kid twice a year could constitute incarceration; it was more likely he was remembering back to the time before the divorce. Before I had a child, it had always seemed to me that the worlds of parents shrunk. They became less focused on the wide world out there, more on their own little world. Whereas earlier, I would have been too selfish to be a good father, now I had reached an age at which I didn't desire much, felt I had done and seen much of what I wanted to. There was still much left to do; it was just that I didn't have a need to go out searching for it. There were no jobs I wanted, no place I felt I needed to be, and I knew that the probability of realizing my visions was small. So the child didn't seem to be taking me away from any particular destiny. Basically the only things I wanted were the more abstract things that had not much to do with my own personal life, justice, rights, democracy, freedom for others, etc, and yes, whatever I might do to advance those in some small way, I should certainly try. And it was certainly the case that I could have done more without a child than with. So, yes, if you had children and you didn't want your world to grow smaller, you had to fight against the almost gravitational pull in that direction, and my world had grown somewhat smaller since Z came along; there was simply less I could do, and I spent so much time with her. That meant that much less time spent on other things, with other people.

On the other hand, though I hardly swam in the romanticism of parenthood, there was some truth to the rhetoric that a child opened up a whole new world. I certainly didn't look at it as someone whose most ardent wish in life was to have children. It was all a matter of what one chose to commit to. Yes, children were prisons, but so, in a sense, were most things you decided to give your all to. Did true freedom consist of doing whatever you wanted whenever you wanted? Perhaps, but that could also be a form of emptiness, of something so light it just evaporated into the air. Did not much of freedom paradoxically consist in what one chose, truly chose, to commit oneself to, whether raising a child, or some other endeavor, as if one approached one's freedom through the decision to curtail it?

I appreciated Sebastião's comment, as I always appreciated the provocative, the sharp and cutting, though also found it a bit strange under the circumstances, given that you yourself could very well be in prison, a real prison. If children were a prison, then working on human rights in China could very well be, or lead to one, as well!

Before the meeting, I had taken Z over to the home of Marni. From the moment you started at the organization, Marni seemed to have a soft spot for you. I knew that now the decision had been made to go public, Marni would work hard to put your case prominently in the media spotlight, something she was exceedingly good at. Marni was, to put it simply, a person with a good heart, a person who wished the best for others, continually looking for ways to help and support them. She was also exceedingly well connected. It had always been a mystery to me how a person got to be that way; I regarded it as an almost magical talent. She loved to communicate, to talk to people, to connect with people, to please people, and she was good at all of that. She was one of those sorts who only had to pick up the phone and she could talk with anybody. It didn't hurt that her husband was a media mogul and former publisher of a leading business newspaper. Since leaving, he'd founded a start-up which he then flipped for tens of millions of dollars. How did these people do it? Well, I'll just start a company and sell it for mega-millions. It was as if they cooked up an idea and the next moment, that idea became a reality. They lived in a realm where things got done, progress was made, goals achieved, dreams realized.

They lived in a penthouse in a building that was the tallest in the world when it was built in the first decade of the twentieth century. They had three children looked after by two nannies from Sichuan—Marni wanted the kids to learn Putonghua from a young age. Ever gracious, ever generous, she had offered to have her nannies look after Z whenever I was busy. I'd gratefully taken her up on the offer, not least because I feared Z would be lonely without the company of other young children.

As I entered the lobby of Marni's building, got buzzed in, went up the elevator, knocked on the door and entered the sort of living space one usually only imagined—spacious, tastefully, simply but expensively furnished, with commanding views of both the East and Hudson Rivers—, I thought the whole while of what you had once written to me about an evening at the home of a financier in Brooklyn, opposite the house where Truman Capote wrote *Breakfast at Tiffany's*. There was a strange combination of guests. You and your boss were the first to arrive. The financier had shown a particular interest in human rights in China, and the informal meeting was to cultivate his support with a view towards perhaps receiving a substantial donation at some point in the future, a donation that could be put towards work that the organization otherwise hadn't the capacity to do. Then in came a socialite with one of the most illustrious family names in HK. The next to arrive was Chen Guangcheng's family, minus Chen who was at the UN Human Rights Council in Geneva—his two children, his brother and his mother, real country pumpkins, as you put it, straight from the Shandong soil. The children were quickly becoming NYC kids. The financier had funded their education at a private school. He and they took quickly to each other, had a rapport. Last to arrive was the financier's wife, very wealthy in her own right. She mentioned in the course of conversation that she had seven billion dollars invested in China alone. (I suspected you had gotten the figure wrong. No, you replied, she definitely said seven billion. I still didn't believe it; I was convinced she was rich, but not that rich. You often got numbers wrong; it was one of the few elements of English you'd never quite mastered). You were the only one there fluent in both English and Putonghua, so you acted as interpreter. After a while, the women left to attend an event organized by the alumni association of their women's college. Then the Chens left, and by the end of the evening, it was just the financier, you and your boss. The financier, you said, was a very nice person, but you felt uncomfortable.

When you have that much more money than others, it's just really difficult to communicate in any genuine way. It is as if we were different species. Our realities are so completely different. He mentioned friends like Soros and Kerry. He was a major fundraiser for the Democratic Party. *On the one hand,* you said, *he is very friendly, but on the other, he cuts you off and jumps in and presses his views. You left feeling angry. It's nice of him to support the Chens and perhaps he's going to help our organization, but should the world be so incredibly unequal such that we can't connect as human beings? He really couldn't believe that we don't fly first class (because he thinks human rights people should enjoy privileges like that because we work so hard for such a just cause). When you have so much money to make things happen, whatever you do to 'help' tends to get twisted into a show of your own power. He said he has been trying to push Guangcheng to learn English. His strategy is to get his kids and wife to become very good at it to motivate him. So far, so good, right? But when I commented later that Guangcheng's older brother and mother seem concerned that the children are losing their Chinese, he took little notice of what I was getting at, just repeating that was his strategy blah blah blah. He didn't understand the subtle dynamics of that family and the need for connections between the generations. It's all about what he wants to do. The Chens are an example of the power imbalances being so great that someone has to be very careful to be helpful, and he certainly doesn't see that. And we wonder why Guangcheng went bonkers!* (You were referring to the fallout between him and his original American benefactor, NYU, as well as to the rumors that he was being ill-advised by people with their own agendas.) *Being surrounded by all these people who want a piece of you and who are controlling and scheming to push you this way and that, in the name of helping you, because they are used to getting their way. At the end of the debate about why we don't fly first class, he said next time I fly I should call him so he can get his Delta executive friend to make sure I fly first class. When you have power dynamics like this, every single interaction becomes thwarted by it. There's no genuine conversation, there is no real exchange of thoughts because we aren't equal. What a fucked up world we live in. God created us equal. Yeah right.*

(On the other hand, you enjoyed talking with the Chens, felt perfectly at home with them. You related better to the salt-of-the-earth types. They talked about Kegui, Guangfu's son, Guangcheng's nephew, who was serving a three-year sentence for "intentional infliction of injury". He defended himself and his family, reportedly with a knife, when officials raided his home late at night looking for Guangcheng after the latter's escape. They talked about the dire lack of access to health care in villages, and you were inspired to consider that as a topic for your next major report, the one you were just getting around to at the time of your disappearance.)

I knew just what you meant. But I wondered: Your vague feeling of discomfort in the financier's home at the power imbalances amongst those present and how they played themselves out in the wider society—to what extent did that feeling lead to any useful or accurate social critique? Wasn't the world dialectical? For better or worse (better and worse?), wasn't capital needed for all sorts of things, including h.r. work? And if it took a bit of RobinHooding to pull it off rather than a complete upending of society or substantial efforts for greater equality, well, so be it. Some things had to be taken as givens or you could never get around to doing anything. The tendency was, the closer to the action you were, the more you saw things in black and white, no? But how to keep your sharp edge without devouring yourself, harming others or treating them unfairly? How to remain faithful to your vision when it contrasted so sharply with the world you saw that it sometimes seemed there was no ground for use of a common language? How did you withstand the tension between the two, a tension that could never be resolved?

Authoritarian governments, authoritarian corporations, authoritarian workplaces, authoritarian schools, any place where some tried to lord it over others, all unaccountable, opaque concentrations of power, gross power imbalances that left some much more able to exert their will than others. These we hated with a vehemence that threatened to corrode us over time. Because we saw their harmful effects. On real people. Whom we knew. This hate wasn't very Buddhist, was it? I'd never been able to master that Gandhian/Christian love-thy-enemy ethos, however much I agreed with it in principle. Compassion for all, including those whose actions harmed others, was central to any good life, good society, but it was equally necessary for self-preservation. It was you, yourself, who could eat yourself alive with gnawing resentment; you were as much a threat to yourself as anyone else, if you didn't watch it, didn't pay attention. For there was something else too. Justice. The trick was combining compassion with justice. The absence of justice was, sometimes quite literally, maddening. Yes, you could turn *your* other cheek, but you hadn't any right to turn others' cheeks for them; you wanted to stop them from getting slapped at all, stop others from slapping them.

It struck me often that we were more "radical" than most anyone we met, less able or willing to accept the world for what it was. I hated the way that word "radical" was used, to mean something like beyond the pale, beyond the acceptable, marginal, extreme. It could be adopted as an ironic badge of pride, like queer, dyke, the n-word. Its etymology—radix = the root, radical = forming the root, of the root, getting to the root of things, basic values, basic principles, how one wished to live, how one envisioned people living together fairly, honestly, equally, what a good society should look like. How strange that such a term had been misappropriated as one of opprobrium, had taken on overtones of condescension, disapproval. Did radical, then, when it came right down to it, simply mean being in the minority, and did being in the minority mean we were wrong, or if not wrong, deluded? You could swiftly answer no, but in practice, it was often hard to be sure.

Not long after your visit to the financier, you went to see Guangcheng himself, genial, charismatic, smiling, open, but also—it seemed to you—weighing uncertainly just where to put his efforts in this new world where he knew not the language nor the lay of the land, far away from where, his whole life up to now, he had a sure grasp, worked effectively, made an impact. The life of the exile is the worst curse, you couldn't help but think to yourself, at the same time recalling how unbearable the Chens' life had become back in Dongshigu, under indefinite (and illegal) house arrest, completely cut off from the world. Now, they were living in the light, airy highrise apartment the financier had provided with windows on three sides. It was furnished and decorated, as you put it, Chinese peasant style, which meant not very cozy. The one detail that struck you was the small lemon tree growing in an area near a window bathed in direct natural light. Guangcheng loved lemons. *Lemons*, you said, *lemons—the man is growing lemons in Manhattan.*

Standing outside Marni's door, waiting for someone to answer, I wondered, Could lemons be grown in Guangcheng's native Shandong? Isn't it a little cold there as well?

I arrived at Marni's before she herself did. Z was in her element, amidst all the toys in James' playroom, and had bonded with Mary, the woman with a lilting Caribbean accent looking after James that day (the Sichuanese nanny was out sick), who laughed at almost everything Z said—so cute so cute. Z and James played well together. James was an easy-going, accommodating and quiet boy. He was obviously used to children coming to a playroom bigger than 99% of the children in Manhattan had. Z was happy to be around another siupengyao her age, and also happy to play with his toys. She excelled at enlisting other children in acting out her fantasies; she and James spent a long time putting out fires, her latest obsession.

When Marni got back, she gave James a bath, Z kneeling at the side of the tub next to Marni while I looked on. She told the history of the place, spoke of its remodelling, then, after the bath, gave a tour of much of what I'd noticed already before she arrived. The views. Both rivers in the mid-distance, one on each side of the apartment. And almost directly in front, on one side, the new skyscraper that had gone up in place of the World Trade Center. At the level of Marni's apartment, some thirty floors up, the new tower looked elegant, dignified, more so than most any other skyscraper I, who was by no means a skyscraper aficionado, had seen. I was impressed in spite of myself. Marni said the basic structure had been completed, but the interior was not finished yet. It was due to open some time later in the year.

At the time of the destruction of the World Trade Center, her husband was shaving when he saw the reflection of the north tower going down in the bathroom mirror. After that, a debris cloud rose up to just below the thirtieth floor, where they were, so they continued to have an unimpeded view of the destruction of the second tower. When it went down, the area became blacker than night with the smoke and debris cloud rising. They eventually had to evacuate—all of that part of lower Manhattan was declared contaminated—and ended up living in New Jersey for six weeks. Then, one day CNN reported the adjacent building was unstable and could collapse. She sent her husband back to rescue the cats. Their own building held firm. When it was built over a century before, it was the tallest free-standing building in the world, and since at the time there was no experience to fall back on to determine what it would take to hold such a tall building up, its foundation was dug down to five floors below ground. This exceedingly deep foundation probably helped it to withstand the shock of the World Trade Center's collapse, measuring about three on the Richter scale. The apartment looked directly down on Zuccotti Park, a bird's-eye view. Marni said she was on maternity leave and writing a book about torture during the Occupy Wall Street demonstrations. They were noisy, she said, even thirty floors below. She made it sound as if their main significance, as far as she was concerned, was the distraction from writing.

James and Z blew kisses to each other in the hallway before Z and I boarded the elevator for the ride back down to the ground floor. *Thank you, Marni, thank you*, I said, morosely grateful to anyone who reached out the least little bit with a helping hand. We're pathetic, I thought. Z and I went back up to the Upper West Side, where your organization's apartment was. It was spare, without personality, in an exceedingly ugly building, not just average ugly—one of those buildings where you thought someone really had to go out of their way to make it that ugly. In its impersonality, the apartment had the feel of a safehouse, a place to hide someone away. It gave me a desolate feeling. I wanted to spend as little time there as possible.

Z and I walked over to the park. It was the tail end of a hard winter unwilling to release its grip. What should have been days of change were unusually cold, with a bone-chilling wind. NYers were yearning for spring to come, despairing that it ever would. Being an HK child, Z had, except for a brief summer visit to that Northern Paradise where she climbed her first mountain in winter gear and made a small snowman with the unmelted snow at the top, never experienced truly cold weather, and she was rather sensitive, to put it mildly. *I'm cold, I'm cold, carry me!* was the plaintive refrain of our NY sojourn. I'd thought that, whatever else, if I was at a loss for activities to entertain Z, the park was close by, but due to inclemency on the part of the meteorological gods, the park was almost empty. It gave me that same desolate feeling as the safehouse—these abandoned places in the middle of the teeming city. It took some encouragement to persuade Z to even give the park a try, in spite of the fact that she was a playground aficionada and wherever we went, was always on the lookout for new ones. Travelling with her had always been a matter of scoping out playgrounds; as long as we hit a playground a day, I could keep her in good spirits. And, while discerning, she embraced playgrounds of all different kinds, from the most basic and simple to the most grandiose and varied—she could see the good in every one, as they say. This one in Central Park, apart from being empty except for us, was surprisingly rundown. Z rather tentatively climbed swung slid jumped carouselled. She seemed rarely affected by my dejection, but her unusual tentativeness was a kind of statement to the effect that this was not as good as it could be. Or maybe just meant she was cold. The one highlight was the daisiupengyao swing, the swing for big kids. With longer chains hanging down from a high crossbar, you could swing gleefully high and long—weeeeeeeee!

Almost all of the snow was gone, the result of previous thaws. A few sad patches subsisted here and there. (The concept of "yukky snow" had entered her vocabulary during our NYC stay. Z was constantly on "yukky snow" patrol, suddenly exclaiming as we walked down the street, Look, there's some yukky snow! pointing toward a crystallized patch covered in black street grit up against a sidewalk tree.) All was muddy and gray. I reminded Z of the summer snowman she'd made on the top of the mountain in that Northern Paradise out of the unmelted snow patch. If that snow hadn't melted yet at that point past mid-summer, perhaps it never would; the snowman we made might still be there; might always be there, the eternal snowman. (Periodically, I'd remind her of it: *Remember that snowman we made? Do you think it's still there?* And she would always say, *Yes*.) Now, in the park, I said, *Let's make a snowman!* The suggestion enthused Z enough to distract her from how cold she was. We went about gathering snow from the surviving scraps and patches and assembled a scrawny tilting off-color snowman on grass, paltry perhaps but Z was proud and happy. *Your second snowman*, I said. *But this one, I think, will melt, probably quite soon.*

Z was upset by the prospect. *But I don't want it to*, she said.

It's a beautiful snowman, I said, *and even when it melts, it will remember us.* After some time regarding our creation, I said, *Come on, Z. It's time to head down to Dmitri's.*

The safehouse was in a perfect location, not only due to its proximity to the park but also to the dinosaurs and the dioramas of the Natural History Museum. Z was fascinated by one in particular: A sambar under attack by wild dogs. The tips of the sambar's antlers are blood-stained. A dead dog, apparently the victim of an antler thrust, lies off to the side. The sambar's legs and underside are covered with bloody bite marks. The Children's Museum was also only a few blocks away. Z could spend endless hours there. But once the meeting was finished and there was no more business with your organization to speak of, I preferred not to stay in its apartment, though no one had ever so much as intimated we couldn't stay longer. Sometimes it seemed organizations of substantial resources showered people like us with generosity in order to escape from doing much about the matter at hand. Oh, how unfair that was, I scolded myself: Their resources did not stretch so far as to have any effect on the richest, most powerful dictatorship in the world; why blame them? One should be vigilant about one's sadness becoming bitterness, the bitterness then seeping into the creases of one's life until it eventually becomes inseparable from it, life and bitterness one. Everywhere I turned, my ressentiment was there.

A fellow resident at the safehouse was the woman who ran the organization's Russia office. She'd flown in from Moscow for a top-level security meeting to decide what to do with the office. In the wake of the invasion of Crimea and with nationalistic sentiment stoked, the climate in the country, which had been bad for some time, continued to worsen for independent civil society organizations, especially those working on human rights and with foreign links or funding. Should they keep the office open, close the physical office space but keep the workers in country, close the office and, for their safety, move the workers out of the country? She hoped the organization was going to be as committed to the four workers' best interests as she was. She had a one-year-old. While pregnant, she had received death threats that referred to the pregnancy. In response, the organization took the unusually brash step of holding a news conference in Moscow to denounce the threats and call on the government to protect it, calculating that bringing them out in the open was the best defense. Now the general situation in the country was even tenser, even if she had not personally received threats against her and her family this time around. So it was not only China. Neo-authoritarianism appeared to be gaining ground, evolving into a model of its own; could it possibly be the wave of the future? What was the world coming to? Where had it taken this wrong turn? The Russia office had particular symbolic significance, since it was opened in the wake of the demise of the Soviet regime and represented hope and expectation for the future. To close it now would definitely be a sign of the times, of unrealized hopes and expectations, of things going backwards.

•

Z and I took the subway downtown to Dmitri's. I'd already deposited our suitcases there, after having dropped off Z at

Marni's and before the meeting, and just returned to the safehouse to pick up our bags and a precious toy of Z's I'd forgotten. (Magna-tiles. You had often dreamt of getting them for her, but they couldn't be found in HK. I knew you'd be happy I'd gotten them for Z in NYC. They were a big hit with her.)

Adam the Clarinetist opened the door. Dmitri was still at work. I had never met Adam the Clarinetist before; I only knew it was him because Dmitri had said a man named Adam would be there, and then said, in passing, of all possible particulars he might have given me about the man, that he was a clarinetist. What a nice instrument, I thought; would I recognize him by that? I had a sudden image of a man who walked around, always, holding his clarinet. When Adam opened the door, he held no clarinet. I would be happy if Z learned to play the clarinet. Then again, I would be happy if Z learned to play any instrument at all, so utterly lacking in musical talent was her father. Adam the Clarinetist was a sweet, proper, instantly likeable young man. Well-scrubbed, pleasant-looking, gracious, the sort who knew how to act in all situations. Dmitri could do much worse.

I was filled with melancholy awe to think how long I had known Dmitri now, how many years it had been. Some dozen. He had originally been my student. Now, we were friends, though I had visited him several times and he had never visited me, making me sometimes wonder whether I wasn't imposing myself upon him and he, as an ever-filial former student, felt obliged to receive me. Whatever the case, he was always a wonderful host, a balm. Apart from Z, it had been some time since I'd had what felt like a truly human connection with anyone.

Dmitri was from Russia. He came to the school in the Northern Paradise where I taught. I was assigned to be his advisor. Dmitri, like all of the students at the Northern Paradise school, was on a full scholarship and had gone through a rigorous competition to be selected as the Russian representative in his year. Like many eastern European students, he was a math and science whiz as well as having multiple other talents. In particular, he was a dancer. He came from a provincial town not far from St Petersburg, and his family was relatively well off. His parents had started a soft drink company in their basement and named it after him and his brother. Dmitri went on to get a full scholarship to an Ivy League school. He majored in engineering, a safe choice, a field in which he had talent, in which there were many jobs, for which he had no passion.

He was smart and ambitious and flexible and charismatic enough to do well just about anywhere he went. He ended up working for a consulting firm, then hopped from that to finance. Whenever I saw him, I asked questions about what he did. He responded obligingly, but I still found it difficult to figure out exactly what it was. He was currently at a secretive, publicity-shy company that worked like a hedge fund, leveraging, as the jargon went, information technology to give it a trading edge of a matter of milli-seconds. It was essentially IT guys (for they were almost all guys) showing they could outdo more traditional financiers, and it was the trend of the industry, another area in which he had talent, and had made very good money, though again without passion. It was simply what a bright young man with a foreign passport could find to do that paid good money. And crucially, the employer sponsored his green card. Foremost among his ambitions was to never go back to Russia.

While I saw the work to be of dubious if not negative social value (the argument in its favor was that it made markets more efficient, which was of net benefit to the vast majority even as huge profits accrued to the precious few), I was happy for him and admired his success. Coming from an oppressive country, a country he wished to escape, not so much because it was oppressive as because of its prevalent backward attitudes and lack of opportunities, he felt he hadn't the luxury of spoiled Western kids to just follow his desires, had precious little margin for error. This was the situation of many of the students from developing or less fortunate countries who came to the Northern Paradise school. According to official school doctrine, they were expected to go on to be a force for peace and justice in the world, but in reality they had to look out for themselves. Frequently their families, often extended, were depending on them as well, and since they were so conspicuously talented, they were able to get scholarships to top schools in the US and then get recruited by top-paying firms in finance and consulting. So the supposedly idealistic school ended up being a force more for brain drain than peace and justice, a feeder to Ivy League schools and the corporate world.

Dmitri was savvy, the sort who always seemed to be in the right place at the right time, who made lucky breaks happen, who knew the right people to meet and how to meet them; indeed, I, who was poor at exactly that, found his talent uncanny. He'd just gotten his green card and had taken advantage of the economic downturn and static-to-falling housing prices to buy an apartment in Manhattan. The green card and apartment were his declaration of independence. He was finally his own man, a self-made man, a sooner-or-later-to-be American; his fate was his to make. He had worked hard to make it.

Having achieved all that by the time he was thirty as well as being wealthier than the vast majority, he went back to the school where we'd gotten to know each other for his ten-year reunion. The place, on the edge of a beautiful fjord, remained in the memory of most alumni as a primal image of safety, refuge and joy, a place where no truly bad thing could ever happen to you, all the more so for the substantial number of students who came there from rather precarious situations. It was also fondly remembered by most as the place where they had made the best friendships of their lives.

At the reunion, Dmitri had a one-night stand with another former student. Irony of ironies, he had not even really been interested—the other party was the initiator, but somehow, it happened. And irony of ironies number two, for one such as he who had always been exceedingly careful, the condom broke. He thought of immediately going to the nearest hospital, which was over an hour away, to get emergency prophylactic treatment, but he wasn't sure the hospital would have the drugs and, having been told by others that he was being paranoid, decided against it. Several weeks later, he became ill, went to the doctor, and tested positive for HIV.

Understandably, Dmitri struggled to come to terms with this new dispensation. His old boyfriend, Joshua, supported him and also helped him to find the best treatment available, including from doctors who had been in the forefront of research into treatments for HIV and AIDS for decades. Dmitri was perfectly healthy now, taking his regular drug cocktail. He had been diagnosed early, and as long as he continued as he was, he expected to live normally and remain healthy into the foreseeable future.

Nevertheless, his new status changed Dmitri in many ways, or perhaps it is more accurate to say it brought on changes that had been immanent for some time. He considered leaving finance and going to med school, something he eventually decided against when he figured how long it would take him, how expensive it would be, and how difficult it was even then to get into the sort of work he might want to do. Joshua, his ex, was already investing in medical technology companies, and Dmitri came to do much research in the area, both to assist Joshua and out of his own interest. He became an expert on many aspects of health care and on cutting-edge technologies, treatments and drugs. He thought of eventually starting his own organization to promote research on HIV/AIDS and adequate treatment of people with the virus/syndrome but in the meantime spent a great deal of time outside of his job investing in emerging medical technologies, which essentially involved placing bets on what would work. In this way, he figured, he would eventually have a much bigger impact on improvements in health than if he had become a doctor.

His positive status also drew him back to Joshua, a surprising turn of events given that he'd managed to extricate himself from that relationship after many turbulent years. Joshua was considerably older than Dmitri, by about a quarter of a century, and he was a peculiar person. Both had seemed to have come to terms with the break-up and already grown used to the new relationship, according to which Dmitri was Joshua's right-hand man when it came to investing in emerging medical technologies. I imagined that if Dmitri stuck with this, he would eventually become an immensely wealthy man, as, indeed, Joshua already was.

Dmitri estimated Joshua was worth about a billion dollars. I didn't know whether he was exaggerating, but it was probably safe to say hundreds of millions at least. His parents were Holocaust survivors. His father hid out during the war, then immigrated to the US afterwards. His mother had come to the US before the war, though she lost almost all of her family to the catastrophe. Joshua was a high-flyer. He went to Harvard, and then straight on to Harvard Law School. Even before he took the bar, Goldman Sachs recruited him as a trader. He was able to do calculations exceedingly quickly at a time when that still mattered, before the industry was completely computerized, and so he made the firm and therefore also himself a lot of money. Nearly before he knew it, he was made a partner. Then the firm decided to go public, turning the partners into instant, not millionaires, for they were already that, but multi-millionaires, hundreds-of-millions-millionaires. Joshua left Goldman and went to work for Soros, where he made hundreds of millions more. Then he left Soros and for over a decade invested on his own. He took an intellectual interest in researching and then becoming a major investor in a promising enterprise. He had a preference for the health and medical industry, especially potential breakthroughs in cures and treatments of diseases. Joshua was extraordinarily bright and talented, but Dmitri said that as much as anything else, his career demonstrated the importance of good fortune and timing, for he had entered into trading during that window of opportunity when it was still not computerized, before deregulation and the boom when many investment banks grew exponentially, often going public. Today people with Joshua's mathematical dexterity enjoyed no great competitive advantage, as computers could calculate much faster than they could.

It was not their age difference that made them something of an odd couple. While Dmitri loved people and was abundantly endowed with social graces, Joshua had been diagnosed—I do not know at what age—with Asperger's. Obviously, he was a high-functioning type but with noticeable difficulties connecting socially and emotionally with others. It could not have been easy, I thought, being in a relationship with such a person, and I'd wondered what it was that had attracted Dmitri to Joshua or brought the two together for what had been, if I recalled correctly, over five years, if not longer. And now they had this funny post-relationship relationship, which was, on the surface at least, largely business.

Joshua lived all but ostentatiously. He owned a townhouse on Gramercy Park and therefore had a key to the gate of the only private park in New York off-limits to the public (there were others such as Zuccotti which were privately owned but in practice operated much as public parks, except of course when authorities wanted to clear them; then, suddenly, the laws governing private property became all-important). But he didn't live there; he rented it out. Instead, he lived on Union Square, in a building with a long history including renown as the headquarters of Warhol's Factory from 1968 to 1973. Joshua lived on the very floor where Warhol had been shot. Back then, it was a rundown building in a rundown part of town. By the early nineties, it was vacant and purchased in a foreclosure auction by a construction company, which, in turn, hired a revered restoration architect, coincidentally the same who had also restored Marni's tower in the financial district. Now, Joshua's building was a desirable, stratospherically expensive address.

Dmitri had agreed to introduce me to Joshua. It felt a bit like an audience. We entered the top-floor flat via a separate purpose-built elevator that went to that floor only. Joshua's home was also his workplace. Papers were spread all over multiple tables in the big, open main room. Three men worked for Joshua as his assistants in various capacities. They were all gay and, Dmitri later told me, HIV positive. Dmitri showed me around the flat. He took me out on the roof, which looked north to the Empire State Building. It had a tower that prior to restoration was a minaret. Yes, the place was pretty amazing but not what one might expect of a probable billionaire. It was dim, poorly lit. It hadn't been remodeled in ages and had the air of a crashpad from the seventies, a temporary quality, as if it might be vacated at a moment's notice. Joshua had little sense of, or interest in, interior decorating.

Dmitri prepped me for the meeting, warning that Joshua could come off as abrupt. I shouldn't take it personally or as a sign of lack of interest. When I introduced myself, he, staring at papers on a table where he sat, merely nodded without looking up. Then something in him said, What you are supposed to do when you meet a person is to stand up, face him, look him in the eye, introduce yourself and shake his hand. Which is what he then proceeded to do. He attempted to make small talk, stiff, unnatural, exceedingly uninterested, as if he couldn't be bothered. I myself was poor at small talk; a silence ensued. I could imagine how he and Dmitri got along: Dmitri had all the social skills to compensate for Joshua's awkwardness and set the latter at ease.

Dmitri had told me that Joshua liked no-nonsense proposals, so that's what I put to him.

Dmitri has said that I might be able to run my idea for a school by you.

Yes, he said, *please do. I don't know what I can say, though. I don't know much about education.*

Nor, I imagined him thinking, am I much interested in it. It was a bit of an awkward fit: I knew in advance that education wasn't one of his main interests, neither in a business sense, nor for philanthropy, nor personally, though he was a generous donor to his high school alma mater. But it wasn't that often I had a chance to speak with a person of such great wealth that he could realize with one decision a project that otherwise would take years of struggle to find funding for. Not only that but he knew other, equally wealthy people. I didn't expect he'd be interested in the project himself, but I hoped he might mention some others to me, or vice-versa.

We sat down. Half-listening, restless, he glanced here and there at papers scattered about the messy desk that doubled as the dining table, being closest to the open kitchen. He and Dmitri were scheduled to have a conference call later that evening, a board meeting of a firm on the west coast that was developing ways to detect and treat re-emergent cancer in people who had gone through chemotherapy and whose cancer was in remission. The crucial question of the board meeting was the timing to release the new product. Information about a competitor had come to light, forcing them to decide whether or not to act fast, since they already had a patent and their competitor, apparently, did not.   Joshua was probably more interested in that, wanting to pass through this moment sitting across from me and get to the other side.

Even as I was presenting to him, I found myself thinking, Joshua is only a little older than I, by five or ten years. His example makes me wonder what I have been doing my whole life. Whatever value one might or not assign to his accomplishments, he has succeeded immensely at what he set out to do, far more than one could expect in one's whole life, let alone in the first half of it, as he had. His challenge was now to figure out how to give meaning to the second part of his life. Mine was as ever to accomplish something solid, something to stand by, something that would not just melt into thin air. That was partly the idea behind the school, to consolidate my experience and ideas and put them toward building something concrete and lasting. But you needed money for that, of which I had none and he had lots.

Yes, the school, I said. *Well, first maybe I can tell you what brought me to you, what made me think it might be useful to talk.*

No, no, tell me about the school itself first.

It's a secondary school. To be precise, students would attend for the last two years of their secondary education, complete it there. It would be college preparatory and provide an excellent academic education. But that's only the starting point—lots of schools do that. (Well, actually, not many do even that well, but that's another story; the better ones do, at least). The students would live there together for the two years. And—this is what makes it unique and would justify its existence and the amount of funding it would need to make a go of it—it would be a kind of 'activist training camp'. I actually hate that phrase, highly problematic, but it's the best shorthand I've found so far to get the idea across in a way someone else might grasp. So not only would the students get an excellent academic education, a large portion of their time would be spent on extracurricular activities, and these would focus on giving them the knowledge, experience and training needed to be effective activists in whatever area of civil society they chose to work in. The school would be based in Asia, and the majority of the students would come from countries across mostly South, Southeast and East Asia. The thinking behind that is the world hangs in the balance, and in the coming decades, it could go in several different directions. It could become more democratic and rights-respecting, or it could become more authoritarian and repressive. The direction it takes will depend to a large extent on Asia because it is the part of the world with the largest population, and it is growing most rapidly economically and becoming more influential globally. Not only that, but just as the world as a whole hangs in the balance, so do many Asian countries—they could become more democratic and rights-respecting or, just as easily, more authoritarian. Education has a big role to play in deciding the direction of these countries and the world. Most education these days is non-progressive; it reinforces the status quo. Its purpose is to prepare young people for the world as it is. It tells young people, You will succeed to the extent that you conform and please those in positions of power. Progressive education, on the other hand, prepares students to recognize deficiencies in the ways the world works and to go out and address those. Its aim is improvement, progress, not conformity. Our attention should be focused on making public education across the world more progressive, but I don't see that happening any time soon, and it's much too big a challenge for someone like me to take on. In the meantime, there is a particular, strategic role to play for a school such as the one I envision. Central to its mission would be promotion of democracy, human rights and justice; commitment to these particular values alone would make it different from most schools most places. Students would be chosen based on their existing interest in and commitment to progressive social and political change in their communities and further beyond as well as their future promise. At the school, not only would they learn from excellent academic teachers in their subjects but from older activists in various fields, some of whom might be permanent faculty but many others would come for semester or month- or year-long fellowships, to take time out from their stressful work and do things they don't ordinarily get time to do, and others still might come simply to run workshops of a matter of days or weeks in length. The students, of course, would also learn a great deal from one another, coming as they would from countries very different culturally and linguistically but also with striking similarities in terms of level of development, political structures and histories, challenges faced, and so on. They could compare and contrast, find out what works in specific places and what works almost anywhere, as well as eventually becoming the core of what would develop into a strong trans-national Asian network of activists who would continue to learn from each other and coordinate and collaborate in the future. The students would have an impact far beyond their numbers. They would go back and act as multipliers in their communities, their societies, their countries.

If this is in Asia, Joshua asked, why not find funding in Asia? God knows there are lots of rich people there these days, a lot of money sloshing about.

Good point, I said. But then again, to my knowledge, there aren't that many progressive people with money. And the practice of philanthropic funding of education is not so well developed. True, plenty of money goes to existing universities, or alma maters, or local schools in poor areas, or flashy, marquee projects, but there's little if any creative funding readily available for specific, unique projects such as this one. I'm not opposed to funding originating in Asia, as long as it didn't compromise the project; it's just that I don't know of any ready source.

Where are you thinking of in Asia?

I'd originally thought of Taiwan because it's a new democracy, only a couple of decades old, but one that in many respects has made a strikingly successful transition from dictatorship and has much that students from elsewhere could learn from. But the big hitch with Taiwan is that it's pretty isolated due to its political situation. Not only that, it's hard for mainland students to get permission to study there, and however this school would turn out, it would have to have a significant number of mainland students, given that China is the biggest dictatorship in the world and will in itself play a major role in determining the future direction of Asia and the rest of the world. If China remains authoritarian, the world could very well become a scarier place. So the recent thinking is India. India is the oldest democracy in Asia, even if it is a democracy that continues to be compromised by all sorts of problems like corruption, caste discrimination, one of the world's highest rates of absolute poverty, grossly deficient public education, and extreme inequality. I am even thinking that studying the challenges India faces in living up to its promise as the biggest, most diverse democracy in the world would be an excellent opportunity for the students. It also happens to be a relatively cost-effective place to run a school. I've been to India now a couple of times looking at potential locations and partnerships.

Who's going to run this school?

I have a network of progressive educators and activists. The core team would be drawn from that, most of whom are people I've worked with before and trust. The school would be run democratically, and the core team would function as a collaborative leadership.

I could ask you a lot of questions about your background and what makes you well suited or qualified for this, but I think I'll leave that for later and assume you are. I know you're Dmitri's teacher, and if you produced him, you must be doing something right.

Well, nothing's produced Dmitri but himself. I can't take any credit for that.

Don't schools along these lines already exist?

No, not really. There's the network of colleges that I taught at and Dmitri studied at, but in their set-up, the way they are run, and the people who run them, they're actually pretty conservative and *traditional. In terms of where their students end up and what they end up doing, their impact is negligible. That's where I met Dmitri, and look at him*, I said turning and grinning, *—very successful but he used the school to escape his society, not to return to it and be effective there as a changemaker. They have virtually no demonstrable record of impact over more than half a century of existence, and that's because they really don't take their mission seriously, a mission which is itself weak and watered down. In a way, the idea for this school grew out of frustration with those colleges. They're not progressive places; they're conventional places. A large proportion of their students, regardless of where they come from, go on to top US universities, which lead them to conventional careers, more often than not far away from their own societies. They're just private boarding schools with kind of a cool, unique recipe. Besides that, colleagues and I have run all kinds of workshops on human rights down through the years in Asia. They're great experiences and confirm the legitimacy of the theory and strategy behind the school, but they are ultimately rather superficial, lasting as they do maybe only two or three weeks each.*

What's the financing plan?

We need someone to cover the capital costs of start-up and the operating budget for the first five years, during which time we would diversify sources of funding as we establish a successful record. My research has shown that the best source of funding would be an individual or small number of individuals who believe in the project and are committed to it. That's what I'm looking for now.

What sort of money do you have in mind?

The easiest part to calculate is annual operating costs. There, I figure about six million per year, 30 million for the first five years. The capital investment would depend greatly on exactly where the school would be, whether there would be a new purpose-built facility or it would move into an existing location—variables like that. So that figure could be anywhere from five million to thirty million. So, overall, 35 to 60 million.

Leave me the blueprints, and I'll see what I can do. If I come across anyone who might be interested, I'll pass them on and ask them to contact you.

Thanks very much. I appreciate it.

That was it. It was over, the interview, the audience. I appreciated Joshua's time and attention. I was actually surprised he listened as intently, and as long, as he did. I had expected to be interrupted more frequently. I saluted him and Dmitri, who was staying behind for the board meeting and might not come home that night (he and Joshua often strategized late into the night), descended alone in the elevator to the square, and headed the dozen or so blocks back north to Dmitri's place, where Adam the Clarinetist was keeping watch over Z, whom I'd put to sleep before I left.

For better or worse, it had been years since my mind had been full of dreams. If I still had any dream at all, it was to start a school along the lines of what I'd told Joshua about. The vision had developed out of my experiences as an educator in dozens of countries. I had had the idea for ages and was skeptical it would ever become a reality. Three years before, I'd made a major effort, reaching out to a lot of people to see if I could bring it about. I was confident the idea was right, but I hadn't been able to convince others, neither potential colleagues nor funders. Perhaps, I told myself, I just hadn't found the right people yet. My thinking now was that if I happened to find those people, great, but I wasn't about to go it alone; I wanted it to be a collaborative project. Several teachers and activists had indicated interest, but none were prepared to jump from what they were doing as long as the place continued to exist only as an idea: They wanted a reality to arrive at, while I wanted comrades to create a reality together with. At the same time, as long as the place remained theoretical, it was hard to draw funding from people I didn't know (a group which included all rich people) to the project. So my new approach was to meet rich people and talk. If that lead somewhere, great; if not, well then, it wasn't meant to be. I was o.k. either way. I was very attached to the idea and believed it would succeed if it ever had the chance, but I knew I couldn't realize it on my own and was resigned to it never being realized if I didn't meet the right people to make it happen.

Besides that dream, I was at the end of the line when it came to education. After eight years in that Northern Paradise, then working freelance on various education projects in several different parts of the world, including human rights education in dozens of countries all around the world, I'd had one other full-time job as a teacher, in HK. It was greatly dispiriting and convinced me that, as far as education went, I had all but rendered myself unemployable—there were few existing schools I could work at in good conscience, and there were perhaps equally few that would put up with me, my ideals, ideas, expectations, demands, big mouth. I'd gone into that last school telling myself it was just a job. We'd come to HK for other reasons, to be near your parents, to work on China, and after a year of my being unemployed, we needed income. All I had to do was do the work, take the money, and shut up. Of course, it didn't turn out like that, and I was eventually all but hounded out by the school leadership.

I sometimes thought there was something quite sad about this state of affairs, given that in terms of experience, energy, ideas, innovation, ability to gain an overview of and analyze the state of education globally and the roles it did and could play, when I looked around, I saw that I had much to offer that few other educators did. But that was the way it was: I'd worked myself right out of a career. There was no demand for someone like me. In business, there was demand for people with certain skills, skills that were seen to contribute to maximization of profits, and people with those skills were sought after and recompensed accordingly. In education, it seemed, it was all about sterile bureaucratic qualifications, and as long as one had those, one's actual qualities were of little concern; it was all about plugging pegs into holes.

Now, at what might be the end of a decades-long career as an educator, I was left with ideas and aspirations I had no way of realizing. If I found the deep pockets, then great; if not, then nothing. It was strange to contemplate the prospect that my last few decades might not have anything to do with education. This was the dead-end of the idealistic, progressive educator; there was little to no room in formal education for such a person, at least not if you weren't willing to put up with a lot, and I no longer was.

And what was meant by "idealistic", "progressive"? In lieu of having any place where I could actually attempt to bring progressive ideals to life, I'd been ruminating, the result of which was something I'd come to label, a Discourse on Education, Freedom, Democracy and Infinite Responsibility. (Don't laugh at the title. Perhaps my problem was I couldn't avoid the pompous-sounding in an era in which self-irony was obligatory. You had to take yourself absolutely seriously, treat yourself as the most important thing in the world, in order to succeed, but at the same time act as if you didn't.)

I was a sucker: my whole life I'd bought the idea, an idea that had degenerated into an enduring cliché, about the importance of education, the essential role of education in realizing, maintaining, perpetuating any decent society. In fact, my experiences lead me to believe ever more, not less, in the idea, even as I realized how far most schools, most school systems were from anything approaching the ideal education.

There was the idea of the school, yes, the one I pitched to Joshua and hoped to pitch to others with the ability to fund it, but beneath that even was a vision much wider and more comprehensive in scope: I had come to see the need for a thoroughgoing democratic education, of a kind that could be found as of yet in only a few places. The idea of the school was just the tip of the iceberg because, after all, it was just one school. The need was to change education systems across the world, in virtually every country.

What was "democratic education"? To use such expressions, one had to recover overused, misused, abused terms such as democracy and education; they had become so hollow. The vision was this: A school was a microcosm. The way it was designed and run was essentially what the students learned about society, given that they spent so much time at school and school was their first, most substantial experience of society, lasting all of their formative years. If the school was designed and run on a democratic basis, students would learn to be active citizens able to cooperate, collaborate, compromise and constructively manage conflict; they would be prepared to leave formal education and enter society as "multipliers", people with the skills, interest, and experience to promote democracy. Democratic education would foster values of fairness and equality, respect for rights, political consciousness (of the role that power plays in human affairs) and the necessity of acting politically, knowledge of and interest in civic, social, economic and political affairs, appreciation of diversity, difference, tolerance, and the importance of understanding the other.

What might this look like in practice? Some years before, I had been involved in piloting a so-called "human rights friendly schools" project at about a dozen public schools in a dozen different countries around the world. The parameters of the definition of "human rights friendly school" were deliberately set wide: We said that efforts to integrate the concept, practice, knowledge and history of human rights had to occur in four separate areas of school life: the curriculum and the classroom, extracurricular activities and events, school governance, and the physical spaces and environment at the school. We made basic suggestions and then we left it up to the schools to decide what goals they would formulate and what plans they would make to reach those goals in each of those areas. We were interested to see how much diversity and similarity there would be in these schools in very different countries and cultures. Some of the basic elements were the following: Human rights should be taught in the curriculum, whether across a range of subjects or as a separate subject. Classrooms should be run in a democratic manner, and schools as a whole should be run democratically. Students and staff should participate fully in formulating and implementing disciplinary procedures. We hoped the schools in the pilot project would eventually act as models, concrete examples of the possibility of such a type of school not only existing but excelling in that country, that culture. Democracy and respect for rights were really as much a culture—a way of thinking, a way of acting, a way of living—as a formal political system and set of laws. And schools, being microcosms, were just about the best places to be steeped in that culture. Of course, a country like China would look very different if its schools were run in that way, if students received that kind of education, but so would a country like the U.S.

Now with considerable institutional experience, I looked back on the Human Rights Friendly Schools Project as one of the few initiatives I believed in. If I could create any job for myself, it would be to grow and administer that project. I would flit about the world, meeting human rights educators and administrators, teachers and students of schools involved in the project, deepening it, broadening it. But alas, that was not how things turned out. I had come across one or two opportunities in my life to realize a vision, and they passed me by because I could not penetrate the core of power that would have given me the chance to do so.

Was it not paradoxical that I would argue for the necessity of democratic education, education for freedom and infinite responsibility, from a position of such deep skepticism about—even suspicion of—institutions, such as schools, educational systems? I realized I was something of an anarchist at heart. I constantly found institutions deeply dissatisfying, disappointing, constraining, often suffocating, gratuitously limiting, with a tendency to exist just to perpetuate their existence. I usually wished to break free from them. At the same time, while I had an emotional (and perhaps also aesthetic) aversion to institutions, I believed they were necessary. Building fair, functional, effective institutions was essential to the success of any democratic society, and not only that, but institutions had significant achievements to justify their existence. So the position at which I arrived was that rules were needed, they should be decided as democratically as possible, and generally, there should be as few rules and institutions as necessary—rules and institutions should justify themselves in terms of their necessity, fairness, functionality and effectiveness or they should reform or cease to exist. Educationally, this meant teaching young people to regard institutions critically, to analyze them, to ensure that they were justified, to hold them accountable, to reform or do away with those that weren't, to create new rules and institutions where necessary. Hopefully, this would lead to the preservation, improvement, creation and maintenance of institutions that people believed in, felt invested in, felt they had a say in, knew how to act effectively in and use to realize, maintain and perpetuate fair, democratic, rights-respecting societies.

But democratic structures and institutions, while desirable and necessary, were insufficient. Within strongly capitalist or casteist or authoritarian or discriminatory or otherwise unequal societies, they had a way of becoming co-opted by the most powerful who by force or wealth could corrupt those structures and institutions and bend them to their will. What was needed, then, to complement such structures and institutions was democratic culture. That would entail an understanding of and respect for human rights, a desire to broaden and deepen freedoms for everybody, and the knowledge, will and ability to act as a citizen.

Was the concept really too utopian, too idealistic? Did it refuse to recognize some element of human nature or the way things were that could not be overcome? Was it really too big an ask, too difficult to bring about? When it had a solid philosophical basis as well as a solid foundation in international law and custom, why was there great ignorance about it, great resistance to it? Why had it never sufficiently come about, apart from in exceptional institutions and small pockets of the world?

There was a reciprocal relationship between society and education: Society influenced education and education influenced society. Few societies were so permeated by democratic culture as to see the patent need for democratic education. Despite rhetoric to the contrary, most societies were more invested in control, conformity and obedience than they were in the realization of the potential of children and young people, as individuals and as a collective. And this left a distinct mark on the type of education they gave their children, their young people: As I'd told Joshua, schools became bastions to protect and promote the status quo, to turn children into useful fodder for the economy. Not that I had anything against giving young people skills that would allow them to get jobs per se, but if the educational system were fixated on that purpose, it, and the society it was a part of, would remain exceedingly limited and do a disservice both to its young people and society as a whole.

In contrast, progressive education had as its purpose to help individuals to realize their potential through living and developing in freedom, and this would in turn help society change for the better, to become freer, more democratic. Progressive education recognized the so-called "baser" instincts of human beings; it didn't think human beings were perfect or only good. But it saw that there were many human virtues—creativity, compassion, rationality and critical and analytical acumen, curiosity, joy—, and it helped people to cultivate and develop them, not to squash or forget them or regard them as irrelevant.

Education for the status quo, even of the better kind, was largely engaged in encouraging students to conform. It told students, largely implicitly but also often explicitly, that success consisted in pleasing people in power: If you pleased your teacher, you would be rewarded and eventually be able to attend a competitive university, and if you pleased authorities there, you would eventually be able to get a well-paid job, and before you knew it, you were on your way in life. The ultimate objective of the student in this type of education was to fit in. One could say that this type of education appealed to what might be called the "lower instincts".

Instincts of self-preservation and self-promotion were not necessarily wrong, but when they were reinforced as paramount, they tended to create selfish, segregated societies in which people often regarded their interests as opposed to others' rather than focusing on common interests and ways of working together. Systems that had a tendency to focus on metrics and measurements such as student test scores in a limited number of subjects as the best indicators of success were of this paradigm.

Education for the status quo of the worst kind was simply engaged in oppressing students, the oppression often mirroring general kinds of oppression present in the society at large. In this context, individuality, freedom, true independence—while perhaps rhetorically lauded—were actually considered either as threats or signs of deviance, even failure.

It was not an exaggeration to say that a significant part of most people's formal education entailed learning how to be unfree—*all men are born free, but yet live in chains.* I didn't agree with much of Rousseau: It was disputable that people were free at birth, and it seemed simply untrue that one could only be free in a state of nature or that "savage man" was free. But I did think Rousseau was on to something in saying that the only true purpose of a state was to secure freedom for its citizens, that the worst system of government was one in which the most people were not free. Likewise, his famous statement implied that an effect of a great deal of education was to chain people mentally, socially, spiritually, economically to certain ways of being which were probably more in others' interests than their own and from which they might never escape.

The prevalence of education to preserve and reinforce the status quo was not surprising given that a society's educational system was a reflection of the society and that in even relatively democratic societies, the majority of people spent much if not most of their daily lives in relatively undemocratic spaces and institutions. These included the family, schools, workplaces, religion, corporations. All of these could be quite rigidly hierarchical and authoritarian. In them, people learned to listen, to take orders, to be passive objects formed by the larger entities, as opposed to active subjects shaping and controlling them. Most people spent a large portion of their days in situations in which their rights were circumscribed, curtailed, restricted, in striking contrast to what their full rights as citizens in democratic societies were supposed to look like outside of those contexts.

Apart from the simple fact that most people spent much of their daily lives in contexts that were hierarchical and authoritarian, there were of course pervasive social and political forces that militated against democratic education and culture, such as gross economic and social inequalities and the domination and exploitation of some people by others.

In contrast, the true purpose of an education worth the name was freedom, liberation. Liberation of the individual. Liberation of the individual's mind and actions. A good education helped the individual to become sovereign of herself, of her life, and to act as a sovereign individual in the world. And it did this for the society as a whole regardless of wealth and privilege. This entailed developing the ability to think and act creatively, critically, compassionately. It meant developing a sense of responsibility not just to oneself but to others, and to not just those with whom one had personal contact but with more abstract communities as well, such as society, and distant people and groups who were affected by one's actions as a citizen and consumer. And that meant learning to cooperate, collaborate, share, think of the big picture, construct and live in a community, consider and work for the common good. Thus was the individual educated to be a force for liberation in society. Liberation, then, was both an individual and collaborative, a social and political educational project.

I used to tell whoever appeared the least bit interested that the true goal of a good education was individual, social and political liberation. I was struck by how many people seemed surprised or taken aback at this vision of education. One reason for the reaction was that education had come to be seen to a great extent as an individual endeavor—yes, the individual should strive for excellence and betterment, but beyond that it was up to each individual to decide for himself about the endeavors to which to put one's efforts. Or education was regarded largely from a narrowly utilitarian or instrumentalist perspective: It was meant to provide the necessary skills and knowledge to get by and perhaps even flourish in society.

I also began to detect something I had overlooked: There was an undercurrent amongst both intellectuals and non-intellectuals that seemed to identify the desire and search for freedom with selfishness. Having spent much of my time down through the years with people who suffered due to lack of freedom, or insufficient freedom, due to multiple constraints on their actions, in places where the value of freedom was entirely self-evident, I was astounded that freedom, a term which to me had exclusively positive connotations, was getting such a bad rap. It was as if freedom had ceased to take on any of its, to me, obvious social and political inflections and was being regarded almost exclusively as personal freedom, freedom to do whatever one wished in one's private sphere, without regard for any "externalities", any effects beyond that or, even more narrowly, freedom to consume whatever one wished. According to this view, there was a kind of worship of unlimited personal freedom, no matter at what expense.

George Packer, in his book, *The Unwinding*, seemed to think Americans had gone mad on freedom, and this was at least partly to blame for what he saw as the "unwinding" of the society that was taking place in slow motion before his eyes, the unraveling of the social contract, loneliness, atomization, alienation, decreasing levels of solidarity: *The unwinding brings freedom, more than the world has ever granted, and to more kinds of people than ever before—freedom to go away, freedom to return, freedom to change your story, get your facts, get hired, get fired, get high, marry, divorce, go broke, begin again, start a business, have it both ways, take it to the limit, walk away from the ruins, succeed beyond your dreams and boast about it, fail abjectly and try again. And with freedom the unwinding brings its illusions, for all these pursuits are as fragile as though balloons popping against circumstances....*

This much freedom leaves you on your own....

To me, it seemed strange that a surfeit of freedom was being blamed for all this, and I wondered to what extent that blaming of "freedom" for America's ills was a specifically American phenomenon.

Jonathan Franzen tried to avoid discussion of the meaning of his novel's title when *Freedom* came out, though he was on at least one occasion provoked to make a statement: *And I will say this about the abstract concept of 'freedom'; it's possible you are freer if you accept what you are and just get on with being the person you are, than if you maintain this kind of uncommitted I'm free-to-be-this, free-to-be-that, faux freedom.* He also said that perhaps somewhat without knowing it, he was involved in a Proustian search for that sense of freedom he felt in adolescence, and that this occurred to him suddenly during a radio interview in New York, when he realized how long it had been since he'd felt that adolescent rush of freedom. One reviewer said that a surfeit of freedom was the main problem of the novel's characters. Again, freedom seemed to be regarded primarily in terms of personal freedom, as in the freedom to re-invent oneself, to be whatever, whoever one wished. This seemed like a highly insulated and apolitical conceptualization of freedom, a form born from living in a society, in a part of that society that seemed cushioned from the everyday brutalities, restrictions, constraints endured elsewhere. At the end of the day, was this all one had left to worry about? It seemed a distinct problem of luxury.

And at the end of an article called, "Why you can't buy a first class ticket to Utopia": *One day, perhaps, a kid will ask her mother: 'Mom, is it true that in the olden days they used to let rich people get on the plane first while everyone else had to wait? And that the rich people got to sit in especially comfy seats in a special part of the plane where no-one else could go?' And the mother will be able to say, 'Yes, sweetie, it's true. But that was at a time when everyone was focusing on liberty—which they understood rather simplistically as maximizing consumer choice in a free market—and had rather forgotten about equality and fraternity. Eventually they realized that these values mattered as well.'*

With such limited conceptions of freedom prevailing at least in the US, amongst the comfortable and complacent ("oh, we have too much freedom, what a terrible fate!" when what they really meant by freedom was selfishness, greed and narcissism), I saw that I would only get so far proclaiming that the goal of education was freedom, liberation. To many, an excessive focus on the value of freedom could appear as the promotion of selfishness, of extreme individuality, every man for himself, a potential threat to the social fabric. What came to mind was Vaclav Havel's gnomic statement in a message to young people of the world, to the effect that we are all, ultimately, infinitely responsible for everything, a belief I clung to almost as an article of faith, like the boddhisattva vow:

> As long as space endures,
> as long as sentient beings remain,
> until then, may I too remain
> and dispel the miseries of the world

Or Bakunin: *Freedom without socialism is privilege and injustice; socialism without freedom is slavery and brutality.*

I understood infinite responsibility to be implied in freedom. Taking responsibility for oneself, for those one knew, for the communities to which one belonged, for the wider society, the world, for people on the other side of the world who worked under exploitative conditions in the factories that produced the consumer goods one used on a daily basis— all of this was the mark of a free person. But I couldn't assume others saw true freedom and responsibility as inextricably linked. So I had to change the title and emphasis of my discourse, from "on Education, Freedom and Democracy" to "on Education,

Freedom, Democracy and Infinite Responsibility". It was getting clunkier by the day.

Mental, spiritual, social, political and economic freedoms were intricately inter-related, just as one's own well-being was to others, all others, everywhere, and this should be both subject and substance of a genuine education. Such an education would have to combat the powerful cultural inclination to over-identify oneself as a consumer and under-identify oneself as a citizen. It would have to stress the rights and responsibilities that came with being a citizen, a concept which in many respects was radical if taken to its logical conclusion, for it conferred upon every individual an obligation to social leadership. Education had to be a way of recovering one's own dignity, recognizing and respecting the dignity of all others, akin to the Gandhian idea of swaraj, the deep concept of self-rule—all must be sovereign over themselves, changing oneself being the foundation of the broader revolution, which although it might oust the oppressor will be superficial if the oppressor is not replaced by those with a different way of operating, a different culture, a different morality.

I often thought of how naïve, or unrealistic, or deluded this way of thinking about education must appear from other perspectives, the Marxist, for example. It would remind that the possibility of realizing such an education on any kind of systematic level was slim to non-existent, given the ideological and economic forces ranged against it, the relationship between "base" and "superstructure", to employ the correct Marxist terms. I accepted the point: After all, it was hard enough to bring about significant changes of this sort in individual schools, and I had tried and failed on more than one occasion. I hadn't even gotten to the point of attempting to change whole school systems or cultures of education. Or Gray's perspective, deeply skeptical about the idea of human progress as embedded in "liberal humanist" thinking, regarding it as essentially utopian, deluded at best, simply a different form of authoritarianism or imperialism at worst. Yes, I granted that as well. But there were strains of modest optimism with which to counter them. One shouldn't adopt human progress as a religion or take it as a given, but one should strive to improve the things that aren't so good, knowing full well the chance of failure is high. A record of progress in certain areas over the past century gave some cause for hope. I thought of Critchley's recognition of powerlessness in the face of the state, multinational corporations, international finance capitalism. He posed the question, What can be done when nothing can be done? And answered that what can be done is to embrace the powerlessness and work from there, from that position. Its great virtue was its realism, but it risked consigning the struggle to the margins, the cracks and crevices of the system. I thought of Scott's lovely phrase, the "art of not being governed", of creating spaces of autonomy. Education from that perspective became a way and means of finding or creating free spaces, community, culture, alternatives.

And anyway, you had to try. Determinism had a lot of good arguments in its favor, and yet, and yet, things did change, sometimes, in some places, always far too few, not fast enough. There was a critique of human rights thinking—which would include this concept of deep democratic education—as pie-in-the-sky, but I had always thought of the philosophy or theology or vocation of human rights not as utopian or revolutionary but as inherently conservative: It sought to prevent people and governments from doing the worst and told people and governments to respect some basic things, to get out of others' way, to let them lead their lives. Yes, it envisioned a better world and had an idea of what that would look like, but at the same time, it didn't necessarily expect it, at least not overnight, and it didn't attempt to force or coerce it into being. It was ameliorationism rather than utopianism. It believed in the incremental, gradual improvement over time, much hard work to get just a little way... as long as indeed—and this was a potentially big sticking point—things weren't actually going backwards, which often seemed to be the case, rather than forwards. In fact, it had an almost-as-bleak outlook on life, on human beings (you need to protect yourself, be protected from them), but it had an in-spite-of ethos: Even knowing that, you had to persevere, for what was the option otherwise?

Sometimes I wondered whether or not my rage against tyranny in its hydra-headed forms and manifestations constituted its own kind of neurosis. What was so bad about muddle-along schools, which was what most were, with muddle-along teachers, which was what most were, teaching muddle-along students, which was what most were? Didn't I understand that while one might strive for perfection on a personal, individual level, to do so society-wide brought with it its own risks, of fascism, totalitarianism? Just let people be, I thought, let them be less than what they might be; it's o.k. And when and if people are ready to rise up against tyranny, they can. I was skeptical about the capacity of people to use democracy effectively, constructively; there were plenty of instances of them failing to do so. I bordered on misanthropic in my low opinion of most people. Misanthropy and a belief in democracy did not exactly complement one another. Then again, my belief was not that democracy was invariably the most effective but that it was the fairest and on aggregate the least worst. And all the more argument for the necessity of democratic education: People had to prepare themselves to take on tyranny, so that, when they were ready to do so, they would have the capacity to do so. Resistance, revolution didn't just happen, or when they did just happen, the chances of them being effective were lessened if those undertaking them were unprepared. But what was so great about freedom anyway? Most people, it often seemed, didn't want it, or wanted only a modicum of it, a facsimile, something that looked and felt like it, or a highly restricted form of it. And what was so great about democracy? Most people could hardly manage themselves, let alone a polity.

So there were plenty of practical and philosophical arguments against deep democratic education. And yet the idea persisted.

There were also plenty of cautionary tales regarding progressive education. Indeed, its history was checkered, to say the least. Apart from looking for money for the school while in NYC, I also conducted research on a topic that had interested me for some time. Projects in progressive education had a tendency to start out promising and then degenerate, and there were a number of prime examples in NYC alone. In particular, they became captive to an exclusivity, or, to put it more simply, they came to serve the interests of a very narrow socio-economic class, this in spite of the fact that many were originally set up to serve an entirely different class. Montessori was a good example of this. While having started out serving working class children with no other access to quality education in Rome as well as children with disabilities, these days most Montessori schools were so expensive few could afford them. The Little Red Schoolhouse in NYC started as an experiment in public education, inspired by John Dewey. During the Great Depression, the public school system could no longer afford to fund it, and it was privatized by supportive parents. These days it cost nearly $40,000 a year, and although there was financial aid available and children from all socioeconomic backgrounds were encouraged to apply, the overall socioeconomic composition of the student body was skewed strongly to the upper class. Not only that, but there was little of discernibly progressive quality about the school any more; it simply seemed upper-class liberal, probably a pretty good school within that paradigm, but no more no less. Then there was the Ethical Culture School, a name I loved. It would eventually become the Ethical Culture Fieldston School, which now charged close to Little Red Schoolhouse's tuition and boasted one of the biggest financial aid programs in the country, though that boast was somewhat deflated by the fact that only a third of the students received full or partial aid. Again, it had become a rather ordinary private school, if of a somewhat more liberal bent. It had started out as a free school for the children of the working class; indeed, its first name was the Workingman's School. One of its early teachers had been Lewis Hine, who went on to become the photographic documentarian of his time of the poor working conditions in the US, especially for child workers. The projects for which he later became famous started with taking students of the Ethical Culture School out to photograph the lives of recent immigrants. Perhaps the last to fall was Cooper Union, the school that its founder said should be "as free as air and water". But that very year for the first time in its 150-year history, it had begun to charge tuition. The Marxist view would apply well here: Excellent alternative progressive education was doomed first of all to be marginalized and then to be captured sooner or later by class interests.

It was discouraging to regard the limits and failures of progressive education when mainstream education appeared so barren.

While most societies were full of high-flown rhetoric regarding "children as our future", rhetoric that more often than not they failed to realize to any measurable degree, what was striking about most education systems was their lack of vision and ambition; they were stagnant. The achievement of universal primary and in many countries also secondary education, and the widespread increase in basic literacy and numeracy that went along with that, were of enormous significance and rightly venerated as a milestone of social, political and economic development. But then it was as if once that was achieved, the thinking and ambition of formal education never went much further in any but a few cases. Once you got all the kids in school, got them to read and write, what should you do with them? The question had never really been taken seriously. And the achievement of universal education came at some cost. In order to scale up, the factory model was employed; universal education became a matter of "mass production". As an initial means of getting kids into schools and teaching them to learn to read and write, this had its advantages, as well as its downsides, but it should have been regarded as a starting point rather than a destination. Instead, what was still essentially a factory model (despite rhetoric of liberal aspirations) predominated most places, even those that clearly had the resources to do otherwise. Children simply marched from class to class to class, subject to subject to subject, on a fixed and rigid timetable as if once the die had been cast, nothing could be changed.

I regarded democratic education as essentially the last frontier. If education didn't move in that direction, then, essentially, it wouldn't move. And if education didn't, what were the chances society would? Of course, it was always possible: The relationship was dialectical—society could influence education as much as the other way around. But if education didn't significantly contribute to the development of democracy, freedom and respect for rights, that represented a failure to harness one of the most powerful social forces in the modern world, and it could easily end up doing the opposite, promoting authoritarianism, obedience, bigotry or worse.

Since you and I had become parents, the question of what sort of education Z would get was a frequent topic of conversation. You dreaded the prospect of Z attending HK schools. You said they'd damaged you for life. And you were one of the successful ones, excelling in the system. You received scholarships for secondary, university and graduate studies abroad. Still, you found the HK education humiliating and degrading. It stole your childhood. It was meant to plug children seamlessly into the grossly unequal, hierarchical economic structure of HK.

Your education had robbed you of creativity, imagination, joy in learning. You told an anecdote from your last years of secondary education abroad, in that Northern Paradise. Being from HK, you did better at math (how could you claim HK education did not prepare you well, to compete, to excel in the modern labor market?! You were a perfect example of why HK did so well on those horrible PISA rankings) than most others and found yourself in a Further Maths class along with two of your good friends, a girl from Japan and another from Åland. You noticed the sheer pleasure they took in trying to solve mathematical problems; in contrast, whenever you received an assignment, your primary emotional reaction was anxiety—all you wanted to do was get it right as fast as you could. HK education was still stuck in a colonial mentality, according to which decisions were made elsewhere (previously London, now Beijing), so they were nothing for me to worry about, I just had to keep my nose to the grindstone and plug away, and that didn't even really require thinking, just problem-solving in the most narrowly technical of senses. Its assumption was that life was a matter of cut-throat competition, you either succeeded or failed, and you had better buckle down and cripple yourself to get through. Education was to provide the requisite skills to at least survive if not prosper in that hostile rule-or-be-ruled world out there. You wanted to do whatever you could to avoid your effervescent, joyful, fun-loving, curious, imaginative, spontaneous child suffering a similar fate. At the same time, you hated the idea of opting out of the public school system, especially as the private schools in the city were extremely socioeconomically segregated (few had financial aid programs of any kind) and elitist in attitude.

As pre-school approached, you and I (in a supporting role)

hatched the idea of a cooperative pre-school run by parents of children Z's age, of which there were a considerable number on the island.

We called a meeting of the parents, some twenty or so. While there was some disgruntlement with existing educational offerings, and some excitement at the prospect of starting something new that corresponded better to the parents' vision of the sort of education they might want for their children, right from the start I also noticed a certain discomfort. The parents immediately focused on practical details such as how much it would cost, where to find premises, level of parental involvement required, who the teacher would be and how the teacher would be trained. All of those questions were important, and you and I had already calculated and had answers to them, simply to demonstrate that a go could be made of it if the will were there. But from my perspective, the important thing was first to decide whether or not this was something we wanted for our children, and to decide it collectively, to make a commitment to the project. After that, all those details could be addressed; of that I had full confidence. But people easily became lost in the details. It was as if they had to know exactly what it would look like before they could decide whether or not they were interested.

I tried to convey the idea of a cooperative—that we all paid into it and we all ran and supported it, not least of all by contributing work, that we as parents owned the school and were responsible for it. This, I thought, was one of the more exciting aspects of the project, but for many parents, it was forbidding, even something of a turn-off. For me, it was a new and interesting way of working together with people I liked and respected. For them, it seemed burdensome, a potential black hole of effort. Though I understood the misgivings and apprehensions, I had limited patience with them: At the end of the day, either you made the leap or you didn't.

I was disappointed in my insufficient ability to inspire people and suspected that at bottom, it was because my ideas and thinking were a little too far off the beaten path—often he who inspires is he who taps into people's way of thinking and is able to pull them to a slightly different place —, but I ultimately blamed the parents. It seemed to me they suffered from a general malaise I'd noted in many advanced economies: Their identities as consumers were strong; their identities (and abilities, and sense of responsibility) as citizens were weak. They were used to comparing and contrasting the products on offer and making a decision, and the market had proliferated to such an extent that more often than not, they had quite a few choices, even if they weren't terribly wealthy. If someone does it and offers it to them, they will evaluate it and decide whether to take it, but as for doing it themselves.... They weren't used to looking at social problems, or virtually any common problems for that matter, and figuring out what to do about them, and then doing it. There was a reluctance to take collective action. This was across the board, whether the parents were Chinese or not, but as you said in reference to the Chinese parents you'd spoken to, everyone liked to complain about existing institutions but did nothing to establish alternatives. You were especially hard on the Chinese, though to my mind, they were no worse than the others: You said that in speaking to them about the school, you thought of all that had not been achieved in Chinese culture, society and politics, and you could not help but think that that had something to do with deeply ingrained tendencies to social passivity and skepticism if not downright pessimism about social endeavors—it was futile to try to improve the world; the most one could do was arm oneself against it, and that was what a good Chinese education helped one to do.

Again, James C. Scott's lovely phrase, the art of not being governed, came to mind. If you didn't like something about the way a society, a government was, one option was to attempt to change it. That could be very difficult, especially in non-democratic societies such as HK. Another option was, rather than trying to change it, simply stepping outside of it, or as far outside of it as one could. That was what the cooperative preschool idea was about: The HK education system was in great need of reform, but no one on the inside was going to do that—they had neither the ambition, the motivation, the vision nor the capacity, and worse, they were impervious to suggestions and pressure from outside. So one was left with the option of the parallel system, which to me seemed a great idea, an obvious idea, but then I realized when talking with others that it struck them as radical—where would that leave their kids, would they be outside of the system, and if so, would that put them at a disadvantage? Again, the tendency was to think you had to get inside of the system at an early age and stay within it in order to succeed. To me, at preschool level, the risks were few if any, the potential benefits great; if the parents wished to enter their kids into the system at a later date, not only should they be able to make the transition but they would be well positioned to excel. But even where the risk was minimal, the trepidation was great. Sometimes it seemed it to me we simply lived in a deeply conservative era.

Needless to say, when push came to shove, the initiative failed to get off the ground. We figured we needed at least eight, ideally twelve children to make a go of it, and we couldn't convince that many parents. So, right at the start of our child's education, we were faced with the prospect of sending her to a school we didn't fully believe in, one that fell short of our ideal. There were many good sides of this: Most of the children on the island went to the school, so Z would be going to school together with her friends and a cross-section of the island's population. Because of the laid-back influence of the island, the school was not nearly as hardcore, competitive or driven as schools elsewhere in the city (though it did seem to us that it shared some of the rigidity, inflexibility and lack of creativity in instruction that we associated with the HK system). And perhaps most important, the parents of most children reported their kids liked it. So it wasn't as if we were condemning the child to hell, but at the same time, we felt we could have done much more, much better.

Not only could I not get my own visionary school off the ground, we couldn't even start a simple cooperative preschool on the island. What did all these ideas about education amount to? A bunch of ideas about education, that's what. Active citizenship basically meant a lot of work for not much gain. No wonder most people didn't bother.

What came to mind more than anything else just then was not, however, a formal school or educational system or philosophies about the relationship between education and democracy or society, but Xu Zhiyong and the New Citizens Movement. The trials against them on spurious criminal charges such as "gathering crowds to disrupt social order" had recently concluded. I thought you could argue that what the NCM was, first and foremost, was an educational campaign, an attempt by Xu and others to educate ordinary people about what it meant to be a citizen, an active citizen claiming one's rights and fighting for the rights of others. And that was precisely what the Partystate found so objectionable, such an affront, even a threat. (That and the fact they were calling for public disclosure of officials' assets!) This is what Xu said in his final statement at the trial.[1]

---

1 Actually, the judge did not allow him to make the statement in its entirety but interrupted him after about ten minutes, telling him that what he had to say was irrelevant to his case. The full text of the statement he had prepared and wished to give was released afterwards by his lawyer.

What the New Citizens Movement advocates is for each and every Chinese national to act and behave as a citizen, to accept our roles as citizens and masters of our country—and not to act as feudal subjects, remain complacent, accept mob rule or a position as an underclass; to take seriously the rights which come with citizenship, those written into the Universal Declaration of Human Rights and China's Constitution: to treat these sacred rights—to vote, to freedom of speech and religion—as more than an everlasting IOU.

And also to take seriously the responsibilities that come with citizenship, starting with the knowledge that China belongs to each and everyone one of us, and to accept that it is up to us to defend and define the boundaries of conscience and justice.

What the New Citizens Movement calls for is civic spirit that consists of freedom, justice, and love: individual freedom, freedom without constraint that brings true happiness, will always be the goal of both state and society; justice, that which defines the limit of individual freedom, is also what ensures fairness and preserves moral conscience; and love, be it in the form of kindness, tolerance, compassion or dedication, is our most precious emotion and the source of our happiness.

Freedom, justice, and love, these are our core values and what guides us in action. The New Citizens Movement advocates a citizenship that begins with the individual and the personal, through small acts making concrete changes to public policy and the encompassing system; through remaining reasonable and constructive, pushing the country along the path to democratic rule of law; by uniting the Chinese people through their common civic identity, pursuing democratic rule of law and justice; forming a community of citizens committed to freedom and democracy; growing into a civil society strengthened by healthy rationalism.

> *Common to all those who identify themselves as citizens are the shared notions of constitutional democracy, of freedom, of equality and justice, of love, and faith.*

Amen. Yes, that was democratic education.

And yet. And yet. Xu was in prison. You were disappeared. That's the way those things go, I supposed. Easier to be a banker, all things considered.

Walking back to Dmitri's from Joshua's that night, all I could think—besides all that—was how nice it would be to have the money to live in a place like NYC without worries. Then again, the problem was what you had to do to get the money. But it wasn't as if Joshua and his kind looted and pillaged. They were opportunistic: They understood the way the system worked and used their talent and savvy to take advantage of it, benefit from it.

And anyway, what was I doing, leading my life, furthering my projects, pursuing goals that weren't directly related to that of your release, when you were still in captivity? It seemed the height of frivolity, like enjoying breathing deeply the late-winter air while walking the beautiful NYC streets, imagining that one day I was destined to live there. But the difference was that at least you needed to breathe to live, so if you had to do it, you might as well enjoy it, right?

The lobby, the doorman, the elevator, the door—back to the life of the father of the half-orphan, the husband of the disappeared.

●

Our final days in NYC were an aftermath, empty though full, full of time that had to be filled, like being in a much too big waiting room where even the slightest sound echoed, tainted by being in the wrong place. I couldn't explain a dull hurt or ache in my chest. I had visions of suddenly dying of a heart attack and leaving Z parentless but immediately brushed them off, telling myself it was as if, in your absence, I had adopted your hypochondriac tendencies, as a form of solidarity or a sign that I missed you, or, more likely, simply due to your influence. *No, I said, I'm not going to die, not today at least,* the words I used to speak to reassure you when you asked, as you did so often, *Am I going to die?* And then I didn't. Die, that is.

There wasn't much to do but hang out with Z. That was fine. We went to places I thought she might like, the zoo, playgrounds and parks. We gathered sticks and pinecones, climbed trees with low-hanging branches. It continued to be too cold for comfort, and wherever we went was abandoned. Z was not pleased: *I'm cold I'm cold carry me.* It was physically taxing carrying her around the city, so big and heavy was she now. At home, she always took the scooter. When she was tired, I pulled her by the handlebars. We had a pact I would not carry her, a pact temporarily broken while in NYC, with no access to a scooter.

Dmitri was busy. We hardly saw him in those last days. Busy with work, evening investment meetings with Joshua, love affairs. (He liked Adam, who was a nice guy and treated him well, but there were no sparks. Meanwhile, he was drunk on Marat, a fellow Russian, though Marat was together with another man with whom he swore he was about to break up, except that he never got around to doing that and was still living with him. Dmitri began to suspect that, however wonderful Marat was, he was perhaps less than honest. Why couldn't Dmitri just fall for a nice boy like Adam?)

One morning, Adam again graciously looked after Z, and Dmitri and I went for a long run all the way down the length of the island along the East River. We argued loudly about the financial crisis. Dmitri said there was no way the government could effectively regulate the financial industry—it hadn't the resources and couldn't afford the expertise. Thus, most any regulation was bound to be ineffectual and misguided: rather than achieving the intended end, it would simply hamper people in doing legitimate business and possibly have a retarding effect on economic growth. Dmitri told about the flooding of Lower Manhattan during Hurricane Sandy as we passed the Con Edison plant that was knocked out, causing a black-out for days, and forcing Dmitri into uptown exile at a hospitable friend's place. We ended our run at the Blind Pig to watch the Arsenal match, Dmitri, who scorned football, humoring me.

One early evening, Adam, a very useful clarinetist, volunteered to look after Z again, and Dmitri and I took a walk. I loved to walk and walk and walk aimlessly around the city—in that period, it was probably the thing I enjoyed more than anything else, and Dmitri indulged me. Only half-intending to, we ended up standing in front of the Stonewall Inn, magnificent in its inconspicuousness, its ordinariness. I thought of Edmund White's memory of Stonewall: *... even I got excited when the crowd started battering down the barricaded door with a ripped-up parking meter and when someone tossed lit garbage into the bar. No matter that we were defending a Mafia club. The Stonewall was a symbol, just as the leveling of the Bastille had been. No matter that only six prisoners had been in the Bastille and one of those was Sade, who clearly deserved being locked up. No one chooses the right symbolic occasion; one takes what's available... GLBT leaders like to criticize young gays for not taking the movement seriously, but don't listen to them. Just remember that at Stonewall we were defending our right to have fun, to meet each other, and to have sex.* I liked that: *No one chooses the right symbolic occasion; one takes what's available.*

I thought of Bob Rafsky, who came out when he was 40. Previous to that, he had been married to a woman. They had a daughter. He and his wife divorced but continued to raise their daughter in harmony. Rafsky pushed indefatigably, vehemently, passionately, and, most important, effectively for adequate treatment for people with AIDS, giving vibrancy and thrust not only to that campaign but to the longer-term gay rights movement. He died of AIDS in 1993 at the age of 47, two years before the discovery of the combination drug therapy that might have prolonged his life, that, in much improved form, now allowed Dmitri to continue to lead a healthy, productive life into the indefinite future. *Thanks to all of those who came before*, I said quietly, nearly under my breath, the words swallowed up by streetnoise.

Dmitri was by inclination the jaded, apolitical sort, but he had become less so in recent years, and it wasn't hard for him to see that he was a beneficiary of "those who came before." Strange how things change, I thought, with no plan. They just sort of happen, with people deliberately pushing them along sometimes, often to little effect, and then movement occurs where you might not expect it, Stonewall being the perfect example, which just goes to show youneverknow, youneverknow, youjusthavetokeeptrying. It was such moments, such places that gave hope. You had always said what you admired about the US was its seemingly limitless capacity for change, a capacity you often found hard to detect in China, weighed down by far too much history and oppression. Of course, the chances of progressive change were lower under dictatorship, but still, the successes of the LGBT rights movement in recent years showed it was often the case that you push and push for years without seeming to get anywhere, and then, suddenly, you start progressing in leaps and bounds. Then again, China had changed immeasurably in recent decades, just not always for the better or in the ways it most urgently needed to; still, change was possible. And then again, sometimes you pushed for years and years and never got anywhere; there were no guarantees.

Standing on the sidewalk in front of Stonewall, that ordinary extraordinary place, I thought of just how far democracy, rule of law, human rights had come in the last one-hundred years, and also of just how far they had to go in China, here in the twenty-fifth anniversary year of junefour, your disappearance just one sign amongst many of the lack of progress. By contrast, since Stonewall and the AIDS Treatment Campaign and Rafsky, both equal rights for LGBT people and treatment for people with HIV/AIDS had seen substantial improvement. And the tide continued to roll in the right direction: Dmitri told of the thousands who had gathered in front of Stonewall to celebrate Obama's announcement that the federal government would no longer defend the Defense of Marriage Act. It was becoming increasingly uncool to discriminate openly against gay people, to make openly homophobic statements, just as in a previous era, the sea change had occurred which made it unacceptable in polite company to utter racist comments. (Of course, that didn't mean the definitive end of racism or discrimination, but it was a clear sign of a change in the Zeitgeist, in what were considered the normative values of society.)

But Dmitri and I paused there only briefly. We wandered over to the Hudson, walked along the river, and cut back to the city, passing the Joyce Theater just as the crowd spilled out onto the sidewalk for intermission. We ducked in for the second half of the show, pretending we were part of the ticketed crowd. Dmitri's enthusiasm for modern dance was infectious.

Being with him made me want to live in NYC, to lead that kind of NYC life, so far away from the danger and insecurity and instability and pressures and stress we faced in HK, in China, in a police state. It was hard to remember our reality back there while we were here. NYC was so far away that the things you didn't want to remember, you could easily forget, or at least push to the back of your mind. You knew they were haunting you, lurking in some corner, but they seemed much less looming and ominous.

Still, those last days were mournful, a doomed reprieve. I found it hard to keep up my spirits around Z, while Z was cold and needy. Just when spring should have been coming, NYC decided to stay unseasonably cold. Z missed her friends, the familiar. She liked NYC, said she wanted to move there (she said that about most places we visited), but it wasn't yet her place. And her mother was beyond far away.

She cried at the chill in Central Park Zoo until I got her to feed the goats, the sheep, the llama, and their rough tongues tickled the palm of her hand. But it was only when we came to the enclosure confining the snow leopards that she forgot she was cold. No one was there, not even the snow leopards. Two cubs had recently been born, the first snow leopard births at the zoo. We waited a long time. Tour groups came and passed. No one had the patience to wait. I was surprised Z did. I told her that snow leopards were hard to see. They could camouflage themselves in the rock and snow of their natural mountain habitat, and you could be staring right at them without seeing them. *Maybe one is staring at us right now! They see us but we don't see them*, I said.

But there's no snow here, Z noted.

Good point, I allowed. *So maybe they'll be easier to see when they come into view.*

I told her of George Schaller, who had spent years tracking and studying the snow leopard and other species in the Himalayas and Tibetan Plateau. *He has worked his whole life to protect them*, I said. *Many of those species are at risk, endangered even*. I didn't tell her that the whole reason the snow leopards were here at the Central Park Zoo (if they were!—we still hadn't seen proof) had to do with the cooperation between it, the Bronx Zoo and Schaller's Wildlife Conservation Society, which had over the years bred eighty-some snow leopards distributed to

American zoos. Since the snow leopard was so difficult to find let alone study in its natural habitat, much had been learned about snow leopards from observing them in captivity and, arguably, this had been put toward better protecting them in their natural habitat. I generally hated zoos, hated seeing animals in cages—it was a sign of my desperation to find things to do that Z would enjoy that we came to the zoo at all—, but that project promised to justify itself.

At that moment, in a whisper (how did the child who usually spoke loudly know to whisper?), Z said, *There they are!* And there they were, the two cubs shambling shyly over the ridge of their enclosure and coming down the hill towards us, followed laconically by their mother. No one was there but us and them; suddenly, we were all alone together.

They're even younger than you are, I said, *just babies.* They came right up to the glass separating us. We talked with them, and they seemed to talk back. When other zoo visitors approached, the cubs vanished again, back up over the ridge. As we were leaving, we passed a sign with the Tibetan mantra, om mani peme hung. The zoo recognized this animal had something to do with Tibet, though its range was broader, extending to Nepal and Pakistan. The snow leopard spoke to endangerment, all that could be lost, both human and animal, if one was not careful, if one let thoughtless or arrogant power or people simply have their way.

Z had of late become obsessed by numbers and counting. *There were three of them and two of us*, she said. I was waiting for the other foot to fall, and then, after a brief pause, it fell: *Those babies had their mommy, but I don't.*

Yes, that's true, I said, then added, *But they don't have their baba and you do.* I refrained from drawing her attention to another point of similarity: Their mommy, like yours, is in a cage; at least you're not.

After seeing the snow leopards, I suggested to her we get a toy snow leopard, but Z held out for a stuffed monkey at FAO Schwartz, not far from the zoo. Hairy and long-tailed, it was nearly as tall as she. She immediately took to carrying it wherever we went, garnering the attention of strangers, much to her unease: *What a nice monkey you have!* Her look said, Keep away from it! When I carried her, she had a propensity to hold the monkey by the tail. When I put her down, she still held the monkey by the tail and it drug on the ground. *Your monkey will get dirty very quickly that way*, I'd say, and she'd immediately snatch it up and hold it to her breast. Still, that monkey swept up more than its fair share of NYC sidewalk dirt.

At bedtime, Z asked for a story about George Schaller (I was impressed she remembered his name) and herself going to Tibet to save animals. She envisioned them collaborating. I reached back into my memory of the books of his I'd read and the animals he described, and I told her about the chiru (or Tibetan antelope), the Tibetan wild sheep, the blue sheep, the Marco Polo sheep, the kiang (or Tibetan wild ass), the Tibetan brown bear, the pika, describing each as best I could. In the story, Z met all of these animals. They told her their plight. She sympathized with them and promised to protect them.

At Asia Society, the security guard came on too strong, teasing her that he liked the monkey so much he wondered if she would give it to him. He then actually lunged to grab it, a play-lunge but of the kind not easily interpreted as such by a child: A big stranger looms over little you with intent to dispossess—how often men showed affection for children through teasing! Z was not pleased and ran away in alarm.

We had come to see an exhibition on Densatil, a monastery in Tibet that had been destroyed during the Cultural Revolution along with thousands of other Tibetan religious institutions. The Society had pieced together an exhibition by borrowing from various collections into whose hands remnants of the obliterated monastery had fallen. To assemble all those pieces in one place given their provenance, the circumstances of their dispersal, and the fact that many came from private collections was a curating feat. How strange that these pieces that had been taken from a demolished medieval monastery in Tibet should reunite at this slick gallery in the prosperous Upper East Side of Manhattan some five decades later. What was once used in religious practice was now displayed as art. Words like plunder and dispossession came to mind, as did the term the Dalai Lama had used to describe what had happened, and was happening, in Tibet, cultural genocide. So was this exhibition rescuing culture from genocide or benefitting from it? An even more interesting exhibition would have fully documented the story of how this exhibition came together, although in doing so, it most likely would have revealed things about the global art and relics market that some of the collectors might have preferred to keep under wraps. It could be argued that the black market in art hadn't destroyed the monastery; the Red Guards took care of that. Illicit trade had in fact preserved what was left. But the political circumstances of the monastery's destruction and the items' dispersal were only tacitly alluded to, which might also make the destruction appear to a less-than-well-informed visitor little different from, say, that caused by a natural disaster.

    The gallery was dark. Small spotlights focused on the individual works. Whether intentional or not, the effect was to accentuate the mystical aura of the items. Because many of the pieces were displayed at adult eye level, I held Z in my arms and walked about, narrating under my breath. The ambience compelled reverent whispers, about the objects, about crimes committed for which still, to this day, not a single soul had been brought to justice.

How was the monastery destroyed? Z asked.

Bad people tore it down, I said.

What happened to those bad people who tore it down? she asked.

I don't know, I said. *Nothing happened to them for destroying the monastery. The government wanted them to do that. It happened a long time ago. Probably some of them are dead now, but probably some of them are still alive.*

But why did they do it? she asked.

They wanted to destroy everything old, I said. *They thought old things were bad. They wanted to destroy everything that was different from what they believed in.*

I could see her trying to make sense of such a strange idea. What *did* you say about such evil absurdity? Of course, you could say similar acts had occurred since time immemorial, so repeatedly that you could posit the urge to destroy was somehow programmed into human beings. Z fell into a hush, an unusual state for her, influenced by the somber atmosphere of the darkened gallery and by what she had just heard.

We came to a two-foot-high statue of Virupaksha the Worldly Protector who guards the west, according to the caption. Certainty struck: This was the statue from which a small turquoise stone had come that I had carried in my pocket for several years, a remembrance, a good-luck charm. The Worldly Protector was made out of copper or bronze. There were inlays where semi-precious gems were to sit, but many of them were missing, around the figure's breast in particular.

Four years before, I had been in Beijing, tailed by shadowy figures. I feared I endangered whomever I met, like a contagion. I took elaborate precautions to arrange meetings outside of normal forms of communication (phone, internet) and to ensure I wasn't tailed whenever I went to meet someone. Among others, I met a former Tibetan student. The last time I'd seen him, he'd been down and out and begged me for money. This time, he took me to restaurants, showered me with gifts. He never said it in so many words, but it became apparent from allusions he made that the source of his newfound wealth was some kind of smuggling he'd gotten involved in through his brother, who had started out as a black market currency trader on the Tibet-Nepal border. From what I could gather, the brother had gone into the more lucrative business of smuggling art out of Tibet, and he had become his brother's assistant.

The last time I saw him, he gave me the turquoise stone. I should always keep it, he said, it was very powerful. He didn't say precisely where it had come from; perhaps he didn't know himself; he only surmised that it was from a temple statue that no longer existed.

But here it was; it still existed.

I had left the turquoise stone at Dmitri's, wrapped in a scrap of newspaper at the bottom of my toilet kit. Something within me had warned against taking it to the exhibition. If I had, perhaps I would have been stopped by that very same guard who had lunged at my daughter's monkey and branded a thief. I sized up the holes around the breastplate- they were the size of my stone; I was certain this was where it had come from.

When my former student gave me the stone, I deliberated ever so briefly whether or not to take it. I thought of asking whether it had been pilfered or acquired illicitly, but decided against it—to do so would be graceless, especially toward someone who had been down so long and was now giving this stone to me not only as a token of gratitude, for having been his teacher, for having stuck with him through thick and thin, but also with pride that now finally he could give something to someone who had given to him. How could I reject it, or even ask questions of it? Also, in a sense, it was better to know as little as possible about it. It came into my possession, and *I* was the one to smuggle it out of the country.

I imagined that when the monastery was pillaged in the sixties, some of the vandals, while outwardly exhibiting great political fervor, sequestered anything that looked to be of particular value. They probably kept their theft secret even from one another. Who pried the turquoise stones out of the breastplate and kept them hidden for years until certain political winds had passed and they became safe to sell?

As my former student placed the stone in my hand, I remembered the last time I had seen him on the roof of a cement building in McLeod Ganj where he was living in a former chicken coop. He did not look well then. He was not eating properly. He was going back to Tibet to help his family and work with his brother (who had already spent time in prison for black market currency trading). He asked for money to return.

The next time I heard from him, his family and all of the villagers were being forcibly evicted from their village along a river in Kham (Qinghai to Chinese) in order to make way for a dam. They were moved to a remote location several hundred kilometers away where, he said, there were no clear ways to make a living. They were being given compensation, but it was not enough to reconstruct their village at the new site. He asked for money to help his family.

After that summer in Beijing, I had not heard from him again. Had he avoided calamity?

Staring at Virupaksha the Worldly Protector I thought that my student had made me complicit in the crime, and I had willingly embraced the complicity in accepting the stone and, not only that, had compounded the complicity by carrying the stone around with me wherever I went these last four years. Talk about bad karma. I imagined going back to Dmitri's apartment, digging it out of the bottom of the toilet kit, marching back to the museum and "turning it in", insisting that it be immediately re-inserted in Virupaksha's breastplate. But what sense would that make? The only people who deserved it, perhaps, were the heirs of the tragedy of Densatil who were now being allowed to rebuild the monastery, to the extent that it could be rebuilt, in much reduced size.

Z must have wondered why I lingered so long. I said a brief prayer to Virupaksha: *I believe I am a beneficiary of your having been damaged and removed, but you still look dignified even without your precious stones. I ask that you confer upon me and my daughter your protection and that it extend to my wife, on the other side of the world, in the land that conquered yours, who has fallen victim to the same oppressors as you yourself. I promise you I will take good care of your stone, and that one day, if possible, it will be returned to you, or to the place from which you come.*

What does that mean? asked Z.

It means I will help to rebuild the monastery, I said.

The gallery juxtaposed the items with prints of black-and-white photos of the monastery taken in 1948 by Pietro Francesco Mele, a photographer in the expedition of Giuseppe Tucci, who had come to study the monastery. Only two years after that, the country was invaded by the People's Suppression Army, and the monastery was cut off from other foreigners until its eventual destruction in the sixties. In other words, these were the last known extent photos of the monastery before it was torn down. So much, I thought, so much has been destroyed!

In a separate room, there was a sand mandala created by monks. Z was fascinated by it, and by the fact that after making it, they would destroy it, collecting the sand and pouring it into a river—all is change, nothing lasts, we should not attach to anything, least of all that which we have created, for it will all be destroyed.

What river will they put this sand in? Z asked.

I don't know, I said, *maybe the East River, maybe the Hudson River. Those are the closest ones.*

Before leaving the city and saying goodbye to culture, there was one last exhibit I wanted to see, at the Morgan Library about the origins of *The Little Prince*. I had not yet told Z the story, nor shown her the book, thinking she was still a bit too young. So she had no point of reference from which to enjoy the exhibition, which centered on original watercolors Saint-Exupéry had made that did not make it into the eventual first edition of the story. I had not known that it was in the US during the second world war that Saint-Exupéry wrote the story and did the watercolors. After he finished the manuscript, he went off to rejoin the Free French Air Force in North Africa. His plane disappeared on a reconnaissance mission a few weeks before the liberation of Paris, and he was never heard from again.

The caption of one watercolor was, *Tu deviens responsable pour toujours de ce que tu as apprivoisé...* (You become forever responsible for what you have tamed...), the fox's message to the Little Prince. It echoed Havel's words about being responsible for everything. It was also the caption of a drawing Tatyana had given me decades ago. The relationship between the fox and Little Prince reminded her of ours. She also gave me a miniature copy of *The Little Prince* in Serbian.

Inspired by thoughts of Tatyana, she of the Shard in London and the Renzo Piano Building Workshop, I schlepped Z off to the site of the new Whitney, downtown on the Hudson, at the lower end of the High Line Park, on Gansevoort. It was still under construction, due to open the subsequent year. Much progress had already been made. I didn't know exactly why I'd come; there wasn't much to see just standing on the street outside of the building site. I just wanted to know what it felt like to be standing there. A pilgrimage. I marveled at all of the capital that had gone into it, hundreds of millions of dollars. I marveled at the accomplishment, the capacity to marshal money, power and beauty all to this end. And it looked good: You could tell already it would be a successful project, an architectural gem. I'd heard that after Hurricane Sandy, which had hit during construction, the museum's steel frame had been redesigned so as to bend instead of break in the face of the next major storm. As with the Shard, I imagined Tatyana was Piano's right-hand woman on the project. She was all over the place, ensuring these icons, the Shard, the Whitney, got built. I was amazed but not surprised at how far she had come, all she had done, at the bold, independent, successful career she had made for herself, testimony that talent, will, ambition, hard work won out in the end.

That evening, after Z had gone to sleep, I did something I had not done in years, something most probably highly inadvisable, something I could find lots of reasons not to do but did anyway. I wrote to Tatyana. The message was simple, short:

Dear Tatyana, Just came across this email address and wonder whether it's yours. Travelling in New York and wondering how you are. Whether you reply or not, I send my best!

Amazingly, the very next day, I received a response.

It was a surprise to see your name in my inbox. I hope you are well. I now live in B, very happy, very rooted.

I have to ask you something that has been on my mind for a while, and I hope you will appreciate how difficult it is for me to do that. Before I left Norway I gave you a book of my drawings (the one with Maeda balancing on the pole). It is a black book, about A4 size, that looks just the same as the books we used for art classes. I am sure you know what I am referring to.

Can you please send it back to me?

Please understand that this is really difficult for me to ask, but also incredibly important to me.

All my best

And she provided the address to which the notebook could be sent.

When I first saw the unbelievable reply in the inbox, I felt joy. How could I be so fortunate to receive a response from her? It was like an answer from the gods. Reading the message, though, was like being hit by a punch. There was a gap between blow and pain, a delayed reaction. I reread and analyzed the text.

There was no "dear" in the salutation. That could not be a mistake. OK, these days people often dispensed with the traditional salutations of correspondence as too stuffy, formal, artificial, but still....

Then, *It was a surprise*—not a pleasant surprise, just a surprise.

Then she says that she's in B, to ensure I know that she is nowhere near NYC, so there is no question of a meeting. She probably thought that I thought she might be living somewhere nearby and was checking, just in case, though the thought had not occurred to me.

Then, she assures she is very happy, very rooted, that is to say, not without anything she would want; in other words, "stay away, don't even bother".

The message was methodical, leading step by step up to the knock-out blow, the request for the notebook. She had given me the notebook full of her art—paintings, drawings—before departing the Northern Paradise. It was the best present I had ever received. Not only was it beautiful in its own right, but, having been given to me, it was like a marker, testimony on my behalf—we had known one another, I was somebody, I had lived, this had happened to me; whatever else might be said about me, I was worthy of receiving something of that quality from someone of that caliber.

I had stored the notebook and not looked at it for years, not wanting to be reminded of it, but happy to know that I still had it somewhere, that this had happened to me at one point in my life, and through all the changes in my life, which involved leaving almost everything and everyone behind at one point or another during upwards of two dozen relocations, retaining almost nothing from previous periods, I had managed to retain it, most everything else having fallen by the wayside.

It hurt physically to re-read the message and to think of giving back the notebook, though she had every right to demand it, and simply because she was the one requesting it, my immediate and unqualified response was, well, yes, of course, if you wish.

I was reminded of Ophelia (she of *Nymph, in thy orisons / Be all my sins remember'd.*) giving Hamlet's letters back to him: *My lord, I have remembrances of yours, / That I have longed long to re-deliver; / I pray you, now receive them.* Except in that case, she is returning something rather than requesting that something be returned to her. Hamlet feels deeply offended, rejected, hurt, and lashes out in anger. Ophelia seems to imply that she is giving them back, breaking up with him, because she has felt rejected, felt that the sentiments for her expressed in the letters are no longer felt (*words of so sweet breath composed / As made the things more rich: their perfume lost, / Take these again; for to the noble mind / Rich gifts wax poor when givers prove unkind.*) But one still wished to believe that Ophelia still felt something for Hamlet.

In Tatyana's case, it was more like a simple, unemotional cancellation: All that happened with you was a mistake. I was deluded when I made the gift to you of the notebook. I want to cancel the giving, and I want returned a part of my past that is important. This shall be the final excision of you from my life. That notebook has to do with me, not you.

It was a brilliant stroke, betraying no residue of emotion or attachment, simply an act of tidying up her life, recovering something she wished she had never given away.

The message hurt all the more for being so perfectly polite, business-like and terse, saying no more than what had to be said for the purpose of making the request.

But what else should I have expected? From her point of view, her experience with me had threatened at one point to ruin her life. And, testament to her strength, she had recovered from that. It was out of sheer sentimentality I had written to her: In feelings of tenderness, I had forgotten I was someone else's worst experience ever, or not even that—I should not flatter myself—, simply a bad experience, the kind from which one awakes and thinks, What could I possibly have been thinking? I was a symbol of her foolish youth.

Not that she intended to (in fact, I was sure she did not intend to; she was too noble, too dignified to stoop so low), but she knew how to cause pain, to inflict; she was nothing if not steely, a wrathful if not vengeful goddess, implacable; and confronted by her, I was reminded of my infinite faults and culpability to kingdom come. Served me right: I was getting no more than I deserved. Tatyana was like stern reality: Things are not as you wish them to be; just your wish that they be so so does not make them true. You regard the time we knew each other as blissful if tragic; I regard it as a terrible mistake.

So it was. Joy and tenderness shot through to pain and shame.

That she had gone so far as to give me her address, to allow me to know where she lived (if indeed that was her residence) was a sign of how keen she was to receive the notebook, for doing so might allow me to track her down. She was the sort who thought of every eventuality: If she gave me her address, next thing she knew, I'd be showing up on her doorstep. Indeed, for a moment, I was tempted to hatch a crazy plan, to tell her I would give the book back as long as I could deliver it myself, in person, in order, of course, to ensure its safe arrival; one could not entrust something so pricelessly valuable to even the best delivery service.

While I did not follow through on the crazy plan, I could not, of course, resist searching the address on Google Maps. It wouldn't find the street number and would only find the street when searched in Cyrillic. There was no street view. But still, there it was, more or less. It was impossible to tell whether it was a home address or some other kind. There seemed to be a lot of businesses in the area. In the satellite image, it just looked like row after row of nondescript apartment blocks, a typical urban neighborhood in a post-Communist eastern European city.

But just that grainy satellite image from high above piqued the imagination. It was comforting to think of her living her life in that city, her hometown, to think of her living life elsewhere in the world as I lived my life in HK. Maybe she was walking down that street with a child in her arms or by her side, a daughter, I liked to think, or, perhaps more likely, driving her in a small car, to the supermarket, or a friend's, or her grandparents'. The street name followed me around like an echo in a city far away, a magic key.

Happy, rooted, she said, (actually, *very happy, very rooted*) and yes, I could imagine that. She knew all the people in the architecture community, the arts community, and she was herself a person to know. She lead a well-rounded, full life in a place she could truly call home.

I didn't think I would ever be able to say I was *very happy, very rooted*. *Rooted* definitely not. I had never stayed anywhere long enough to become a part of a place. *Happy*—well, there were more important things than happiness. Happiness was a by-product of other things, like the experience of meaning, of the feeling of living life as one should. Who knew what she meant by happiness. I imagined she meant that she lead a life she had chosen for herself, and she enjoyed it, felt comfortable and content in it.

Her terse message provided a second lesson. This was the woman whom I had imagined at the right hand of Renzo Piano working on the Shard, the new Whitney, leaving her mark on the cityscapes of world metropolises, on modern architecture, but, assuming the story was no more complex than the email, here she had been the whole time in her hometown, having turned her back on the world of high-flying international architecture. I found this all the more ironic given that at the idealistic school where we'd met in that Northern Paradise, students had been exhorted to return to their own societies and contribute while all the forces at play lead them to continue studying abroad and become a force of brain drain, and at that school, Tatyana had been highly skeptical of the idealism preached to her. She'd hated the US, where she'd gone to top architecture schools, so it was not altogether surprising that she'd returned. I admired her all the more for it. (Then again, it was hard to imagine her doing anything I wouldn't admire.) The difference between where I imagined she was and where she actually was said a lot about how I created images that were more projections than based in reality.

I wrote back immediately, giving basic news: I was married, had a daughter—those bits also to imply I was not "after her" or "probing for availability", as I had taken her statements that she was happy, rooted (very happy, very rooted) to imply that she suspected. I also mentioned *The Little Prince* exhibition and said it was what had made me think of her.

> *Of course, I'll send you the book. The only catch is whether I can find it. I've moved so many times since leaving that Northern Paradise that my stuff is scattered all over the world. I'm almost certain, though, that it is in HK—I can envision the plastic box it's in. If it's indeed there, it will be easy to find and send. If not, then it's probably in a cardboard box under the stairs, a bit of a nightmare to get to, but do-able. I'm leaving*

NYC soon. It could be a while before I get around to it, but I will as soon as I can.

I received no response to my message. Presumably, she was waiting for actual news, whether I found the notebook or not.

Even before leaving NYC, the dream returned, the dream that had first appeared upon seeing the Shard. And as before, when she asked, my immediate response, without thinking of any of the complications or potentially divided loyalties, was, Of course! Whereupon she asked again: Would I be able to abide by the no-strings-attached recourse she required? Of course, I said, whatever she wished. The vision ended there. I sometimes tried to spool it out further, imagining different scenarios—how we actually met, how exactly she became impregnated. One version involved my going to deliver the notebook. The vision sometimes went beyond that, to the child. It was a boy; she raised him lovingly; she was a good mother. Did I ever meet him? A convincing scenario had not yet occurred.

Oh, and then did I remember that my wife was missing?

•

Or worse, much worse echoed over and over on the morning I heard of Cao Shunli's death. *Or worse, much worse. Or worse, much worse.* Namely, you could be killed. I shuddered just to think of Cao Shunli's death, and not only for the sake of Cao Shunli but because it reminded of you, what had happened to you, what could be happening to you, in that very moment. Shunli had, after all, herself been disappeared for a month before anyone knew what had happened to her.

She'd been spirited away from the Beijing airport as she was about to board a plane to Geneva to attend a training workshop on UN human rights mechanisms and their relevance to China. Eventually, about a month after the abduction, Partystate authorities notified her family that she was indeed detained, on suspicion of "picking quarrels and provoking trouble". Over the subsequent months, her health deteriorated. She had tuberculosis, liver ascites, fibroid tumors and cysts. In short, she was a sick woman, and prison made her sicker, as it did to many in China; permanently damaged health was a frequent outcome of imprisonment. Shunli reported to her lawyers that she was consistently being denied adequate medical treatment. Requests that she receive treatment or be released on medical grounds went repeatedly unheeded. It had been known for the past month that her health had taken a serious turn for the worse. From prison, she had been taken to an emergency room and then transferred the next day to a military hospital, by which point she was in a coma and her organs were failing. The hospital managed to stabilize her condition for some weeks but too late for her to recover. Subsequently, doctors said anonymously and off the record (for fear of reprisal) that she was in such bad condition when she arrived that they suspected her ailments had gone untreated for some time. During her weeks of hospitalization, it was very difficult for her family to see her. Her lawyers were not allowed to see her. Many supporters were detained for attempting to visit her. After her death, family members were allowed only a cursory viewing of the body, which was emaciated and bruised. An independent investigation into her death had been called for, and her lawyers submitted freedom-of-information requests to the government to get specific evidence about Shunli's medical condition at time of abduction; which, if any, doctors treated her; which treatments she received; and any records charting the deterioration of her health.

This strong, courageous woman had been all but murdered by the Partystate. Whether or not it had intended to kill her was in a certain sense beside the point; it was responsible for her death. That was how they did it these days: They no longer just took you out and shot you; they punished you by making you feel the full weight of their power. They ground you down gradually over time until eventually you were no more than a shell of your former self, if that even, health or soul or both destroyed.

Almost immediately after news of Shunli's death emerged, governments, UN special rapporteurs, even the UN Secretary General expressed dismay and concern. All of their attention, in the short run at least, had amounted to nothing: Shunli was dead. There was no response from the Partystate. Complaints had been made about her detention, requests had been made for her release on medical grounds, alarms had been sounded when her health seriously deteriorated, concerns had been expressed at her death by many different parties. Apparently it all made no difference.

Shunli's death put the debate about whether or not to go public with your case in a certain light. If it made no difference whether one did (as in hers) or not (as in yours), then what? Keeping your case secret was becoming ever more excruciating. I had a sickening sense we'd made the wrong decision and lost time. I wondered why I listened to others and did not just trust my instincts. It was only because I needed them, couldn't do it on my own; not because I trusted their judgment.

I felt depressed about Shunli, fearful about you, and well and truly stuck. That I had spent time doing anything but thinking about and acting on your situation filled me with anguish and guilt. I could have, for example, gone to Washington and met the politicians who took a special interest in China, I could have spoken to the international media, I could have used the trip to make a big splash. Instead, I was going home with nothing to show for it.

After Ilham Tohti, that most moderate of Uighurs, was detained and held incommunicado on the ludicrous charge of "separatism", RFA released a statement he'd made beforehand. Knowing that detention could very well be imminent, feeling the space around him slowly constrict, he'd asked that it be published if he was detained. He stated *there are no marks on my body*, and he had recently undergone a thorough physical check-up, which determined he was in perfectly fine health. He went on to say that he didn't want a government-appointed lawyer and had already designated his own lawyer, that he had never advocated violence nor worked with any terrorist or terrorist-affiliated organization, that indeed he had only ever preached peaceful resolution of conflict, and that he would never make any statement that went against his morals and principles (in the advent that the authorities tried to put words in his mouth or coerce a false confession through torture). Now, in the ever-lengthening silence of his incommunicado detention, those words hung heavy.

●

It had been weeks now since Opal had vanished across the border on her secret mission into the heart of the evil empire. The news of Shunli's death made me all the more worried about not only you and BY but also Opal. It was our plan that she would contact me regularly, if only to check in and let me know she was safe, but we had a strict security protocol that made it difficult to do so: No phone calls of any kind, new email accounts exclusively to communicate between us, encryption of messages, use of Tor, and a code to discuss key people, places and issues. She could not use a device of her own, nor one belonging to someone she knew, and she could not contact me from the home of someone she knew. These days one had to register at internet cafes, so that option was out even though Opal was using a fake ID. The result was that days would go by and I would hear nothing, and just as my concern for her safety grew to the point that I contemplated sounding the alarm, I would hear from her again.

Opal was not the best communicator, and it was not only to do with the fact that her English wasn't great. For as long as I'd known her, her mind had acted in mysterious ways. She was entirely reliable, fiercely brave and committed, yet it was sometimes hard to get a straight answer to a simple question out of her. What I really wanted to know was not what she actually told me. When I asked questions, they often went unanswered, or were answered indirectly, or elliptically, or partially. The few messages I had received since the beginning of her descent into the underworld were easily decipherable (meaning the code we had agreed on was functioning well): *The situation is bad. Everyone is frightened. No one wants to talk. People are going deep underground, remaining inactive for the time being, ceasing to associate with those they formerly worked closely with.*

I had more or less resigned myself to not getting substantially briefed until her return to HK, scheduled to be just after mine. Then I received the following from her, on the same day I heard of Shunli's death:

Dear George, Animal Farm is good book. Napoleon suspect Snowball of windmill. He use dogs. True or no I not sure—must read more. Then I will tell you my thought. Let you know dont worry bout me, I enjoy book. Yours, Xun

To decipher: I found out something new. The government suspects BY of being a ringleader of the NCM. It's the Beijing Guobao running the show. I don't know whether or not the suspicion has any substance. I'll investigate more and let you know what I find out. Don't worry about me; I'm actually enjoying the search.

If true, that would explain why BY had been held secretly for so long: She was regarded as a major security threat and no determination would be made on how to proceed with her case until they had extracted from her and others held in connection with the case whatever intelligence they were believed to possess.

The logical inference, then (not that any form of logic necessarily obtained in the matter), was that you were suspected of being a black hand, a conduit for influence or perhaps even funding from abroad, and establishing that would make it easy to characterize all of NCM as a foreign plot. The involvement of the Beijing Guobao, again if true, was a bad sign—it was one of the most ruthless and unscrupulous, carrying out orders directly from the top. If it had taken the lead, it was most likely that BY and you were being held in the vicinity of Beijing.

After having received that message, all I wanted was to get back to HK, to meet Opal, to see if anything more had been or could be discovered. What Opal said seemed plausible, and yet still, it did not quite add up. And in itself, the new information took us nowhere nearer finding or extricating you.

I wrote to Lawyer Ni. Did others, I asked him, at Ma Lianshun's firm know anything about detention facilities where the Guobao might hold someone like you? How likely might it be that you were being held at a known, recognized detention facility, as opposed to a secret, unofficial location? It was not inconceivable that Ma's firm had some contacts in the Guobao from whom they could informally glean information. And did they know of any private investigators who might be able to snoop around?

●

On our last day in NYC, Z and I took the Long Island Railroad out to Auburndale, outer Queens, beyond the Chinese enclave of Flushing, to visit Wenxiu and Churan. You and I had last seen them four years previously, at a hotpot restaurant on the outskirts of Beijing, at a time when they were being constantly harassed by the Partystate. Since then, all of us had acquired children, we Z and they two boys, now four and three. In fact, that last time we saw them, Churan was in the early stages of her first pregnancy. She reminded me it was I who had given their first child his English name, Luke. Wenxiu and Churan were new Christians, and, as many recent converts, fervent. They wanted a Christian name for their child, one that sounded good in English. Any of the Evangelists would do, she remembered me saying, but of the four, I thought Luke sounded best. Their younger child was named Jesse. I had nothing to do with that. In fact, by the time he was born, I had fallen out of touch with them. Before your disappearance, you'd told me they'd made their way to NYC, but it was only from going through your old messages that I was able to deduce how to contact them.

The family lived in the dim, dirty and dilapidated basement of a house owned by someone from Fujian. The upper floors were inhabited by Fujianese and Taiwanese. Only recently, Wenxiu and Churan had been granted political asylum in the US, an enormous relief: They could stay in the country and would not be forced to return to China; their new life had begun. They were not like other persecuted Chinese who, having fled the country, regarded their time abroad as simply exile, believing their fated mission and duty were to return to their homeland. Wenxiu and Churan knew it was time to start over. As things stood at home, there was nothing they could do there. They looked to the future. They were intent on becoming Americans through and through, on raising their children as Americans. With some help from you, Wenxiu had applied for and received a fellowship at Columbia to give the family an entry into, a foothold in the country. Almost as soon as they arrived in NYC, they applied for asylum. Now, in a matter of months, they would be granted green cards and be on the path to citizenship. The US was their future, China their past.

Their living conditions were poor, their financial situation precarious, their English (especially his) almost non-existent, their prospects and plans uncertain at best. It didn't matter. The US was so much better than China. Just the fact they felt safe made a huge difference. They could breathe; the air itself was freedom. The only problem now, said Churan, was that they were still too close to Chinese, near Flushing, renting from Chinese, living in the same house as Chinese. Churan had always had a low opinion of her compatriots. They were cruel, brutal; the dog-eat-dog society in which they lived made them that way, which was a way of saying they made each other that way. China was not a place for human beings to live if they wanted to remain human.

Churan's English was improving rapidly. Wenxiu's was not. He worked six days a week, ten hours a day, for less than minimum wage at a bakery owned by a man from HK. These Chinese sure knew how to exploit each other. You'd think they'd say, Here's a man who's had to flee his own country; let's support him and help him out where we can. Instead, it was, Here's a man with no English and no marketable skills; he has nowhere else to go; he is at our mercy; we can treat him as we wish. Wenxiu didn't mind, at least not for the time being. He had work, he could support his family, if just barely, he was learning to make cakes. As for what the future held, it was too soon to say.

They were living very much in the now, not out of choice but out of lack thereof. Wenxiu seemed to have given up any ambition to do any of the things for which he was trained and qualified in China. Here, you needed English for anything, and that was something he didn't have, and something he wasn't getting working in a bakery where all the other employees were Chinese. As far as I could tell, he never really did anything with

Columbia. The fellowship came without a stipend or financial support of any kind, which I found hard to believe: How were these people expected to support themselves in one of the most expensive cities in the world? As soon as they got to the US, they moved to Flushing, later to Auburndale, a different world entirely from Manhattan. When I told Churan about Z and I playing in Central Park, she said she'd never been. Celebrity dissidents got cushy, if temporary, appointments at academic institutions. Nice digs in Manhattan came with the package. I was always impressed by how savvy some were at taking advantage of the system. They appeared on panels all over, pronouncing on the situation in China. They basked in the glow of transitory admiration for their commitment to their principles, their courage in the face of oppression. That was all a far cry from Wenxiu and Churan's life.

Wenxiu came from a poor remote region of Sichuan and was the first in his family to go to university. He studied chemistry, which he hated, at an agricultural university in Beijing. He spent all of his spare time reading and developing his IT skills. Reading was his political awakening. He especially remembered the impact of Mandela's autobiography. After university, he worked briefly for a pesticide company, which, again, he hated. He gradually got to know people who shared his political interests and ended up offering his IT skills to activists and civil society organizations, amongst whom they were in high demand. This, he found, was his true calling; he felt needed, useful, and purposeful. But it didn't pay the bills, for none of the people he helped had any money to help him, so he continued designing and maintaining websites for media organizations in order to make ends meet. The spells of employment never lasted long, since each employer was eventually visited by the Guobao, which "suggested" that his employment be discontinued. The Guobao had also made it impossible for them to live in Beijing, warning a series of landlords against renting to them. They kept getting evicted. Initially, they moved to the desolate far peripheries of the ever-expanding metropolis, where we met them for hotpot, in the hope the Guobao would lose interest in them, but they were driven even from there and ended up in Churan's Hebei hometown.

When the anonymous call for a Jasmine Revolution went out in 2011, the government took the opportunity to crack down hard, striking out in many different directions. Wenxiu was swept up in the widely flung net, though, like all others detained, he had played no roll in the call, nor had he been in any way involved. (No one ever knew from whence it had come. Some even suspected it was planted by the Partystate itself to see whom it could smoke out.) For reasons no one quite fathomed, Wenxiu was treated particularly harshly. It may have been precisely because he was a nobody—such harsh treatment would arouse little concern beyond his immediate (and powerless) circle. In protest, Churan camped out on a blanket outside the town hall-cum-police station together with her at-that-time one-year-old first-born. She was pregnant with her second. Long after many of the others who had been rounded up in the crackdown were released, some to great fanfare, Wenxiu was finally let go in complete obscurity. After that, they dropped out of sight. We suspected they'd been warned against any contact with erstwhile colleagues. Rumors circulated that Wenxiu had given his interrogators information about the network and was now too ashamed to be in contact. It was hard to know how to take those rumors: To breed mutual distrust among activists was one of the objectives of the crackdown. It had in this respect been quite successful. You always complained of the cattiness of Chinese activists, of their inveterate backbiting. *If these people could just act together...* was one of your standard refrains. But the Partystate's primary objective was precisely to prevent that eventuality.

When we next heard from them, Wenxiu asked you for a recommendation for the Columbia fellowship, at exceedingly short notice, much to your annoyance. Of course, you wrote it for him. (It was almost a staple of your work, helping endangered rights defenders get out of the country. You wondered sometimes if you were actually doing them a service.) Wenxiu and Churan were surprised the Partystate gave them passports and allowed them to leave the country. The hitch was not their rights work but the second child, for which infraction they had to pay a hefty fine before the Partystate would issue a passport to the child. Others were also surprised Wenxiu and Churan were so readily granted passports, spurring further rumors that Wenxiu had cooperated with interrogators in exchange for being allowed to exit the country.

Wenxiu and Churan had heard about BY's abduction (I wondered how—it had been kept so quiet), but I was the first to tell them of yours. Afterwards, looking back, it struck me as an uncomfortable moment. Churan was anguished. She was a very warm person who had taken to you from the start. The two of you always had an excellent rapport, a deep trust. Of course, they had wondered when I had contacted them why you weren't coming to see them as well. So the news of your disappearance was one of the first things I mentioned when Z and I arrived. Rather than anguished, Wenxiu appeared more troubled, startled, taken aback, though that reaction may have had more to do with his character than the news per se.

I wanted to know what Wenxiu had been asked about under interrogation. That was my main reason for visiting, but it was a hard question to put. He didn't offer the information freely, and when I managed to ask, he said the only thing the interrogators were interested in was the network. They wanted to know who its leader was, who the main people were. They appeared to know very few names, but they did ask specifically about BY by name, and about you as well, though under a pseudonym you no longer used. There was a pause. *And what did you tell them?* I asked.

Nothing, Wenxiu said, looking nervous, though I couldn't be sure whether it was because he was being less than candid or he detected an implied accusation in my question or the tone of my voice and wasn't sure how to respond to it, being a non-confrontational sort by disposition. He was a nervous person, with constantly blinking eyes, on top of which he had about him the air of someone who'd been interrogated under strenuous conditions, and any situation or occurrence such as intrusive, aggressive or challenging questioning that reminded him of that triggered the old symptoms. *Nothing*, he repeated, *nothing at all*. And then, after a brief pause, sensing I wanted more: *I never even admitted I had anything to do with the organization, only that I knew some of the individuals mentioned, but I told them I didn't know what they did for the organization, or even that they worked for it, and knew nothing about the organization at all. I pretended I had never even heard of it.*

I didn't know whether or not to believe Wenxiu. Why should he divulge to me exactly what occurred during detention? When I gave him an opening, he didn't exactly take it and run with it. My impression was just the opposite: He said as little as possible. That was understandable: It was traumatic and it was the past. The detention had been a bruising experience (both literally and metaphorically) for the young couple, convincing them of the necessity of getting out of the country once and for all. And anyway, what, apart from a feeling of guilt or perhaps a desire to help you, would have been sufficient motive to confess that he had provided information in return for clemency or leave to go into exile? I suspected Wenxiu was less than entirely forthcoming because on at least two occasions he had left the country to attend meetings arranged by the organization at which Partystate informers were almost certainly present. The Partystate interrogators most likely had evidence that he not only knew about the organization but had worked for it.

The conversation moved on. We talked of other things, but it was as if there wasn't much more to say. Your disappearance and the implication that Wenxiu might be to some extent responsible for it hung over every word spoken, every slight action. I wondered whether I was no longer welcome. Did they resent me now? Were they afraid? They had escaped what they were afraid of. Was I a sign that maybe they never quite could, at least not yet? Was I like a tentacle of the past reaching out to grab them and haul them back? There was a slight chill, a distance in the air. We talked about mutual acquaintances and issues of once-shared interest, but they had put all that behind them; it was the past. The lines of conversation inconclusively trickled away into silence.

Their boys were rough and wild, shouting, running about, throwing and tugging and pushing toys, jumping on bed and sofa. The walls were covered in looping lines of crayon. The noise in the low-ceilinged basement was cacophonous—at points, I had difficulty hearing Wenxiu and Churan speak. About the elder boy, there was an air of uncontrollability—how would his parents be able to manage him, I wondered, especially as he got older, bigger, stronger? Then again, he was kind to Z, and I was impressed with how well she coped with him and his brother, bigger, louder, stronger than she.

I'd thought the youngest was just shy, retiring—he'd said almost nothing. But at dinner, when Churan asked what he wanted, it took him great effort to force out of his mouth an approximation of the first syllable of the food he desired. The boy, though older than Z by half a year, had almost no language. I wondered whether his hearing was impaired. Had Wenxiu and Churan ever had it checked? They seemed oblivious to the problem. I did not ask that evening but made a mental note to contact them later to ask. Watching him try to get a sound out was excruciating. My heart went out to the boy.

I left Wenxiu and Churan's none the wiser about your disappearance, with virtually all possible sources of information having been exhausted. On the platform of the Auburndale train station where they saw us off, I was distracted, searching my mind to see whether I truly had left no stone unturned. On the train, holding tired Z on my lap, gazing out the window at nondescript Queens passing by, I kept thinking, You are trapped there, they are free here.

5

Returning from NYC, we felt the contrast in climate immediately on our skin as we climbed the hill to home, humid air, verdant plants and flowers exuding moisture, and, as we entered the flat, the unmistakable smell not only of mustiness but mold. The pages of books curled nearly before your eyes. The bedsheets were uncomfortably damp.

As I made dinner, the water heater burst, spraying boiling water all over the bathroom, creating fog. The internet was not working. The façade of the house was crumbling, chunks of tile and small concrete slabs falling off the neighbor's balcony into the yard. Kitchen cabinet doors were coming off their hinges. This shoddy place! I thought. Will we ever live in a decent place?

Such thoughts often occurred upon return, reminding of our circumstances. You reacted to the almost physical sensation of loss of freedom: You felt a net closing in on you. It seeped into the home, as if it couldn't be kept at bay, and if you weren't careful, it got inside of you.

On our first day back, the sky turned so eerily dark, I was reminded of the scene of Christ's death: *At noon, darkness came over the whole land....*

My brother called to tell me mother had died. It was not unexpected. Seriously ill for years, she weighed seventy-eight pounds at time of death. Z and I had visited her a month before, on our way to NYC. She was doing poorly, but she had been ill so long, one never knew. Every time I saw her, I thought it could be the last. Still, something in me had suspected that might truly be the last time.

That night, the weather broke, the sky came down, lightning, thunder, heavy rain, strong wind. Elsewhere in the city, giant hailstones fell; rain flooded a shopping mall after the ceiling collapsed. 2,041 strikes of lightning were counted within one hour. Who counted them? How? Painfully jetlagged, Z slept through the cracks of thunder that seemed to be sounding right over our heads. I stayed up late, listening to the rain and making yogurt and bread. Those moments were the happiest, most peaceful in some time, in spite of your absence, mother's death, the feeling that the net was closing in.

Z woke at four in the morning, only two hours after I had gone to bed. Her first words were, *I want a story about the plane that comes home.* She was referring to what I had told her about the Malaysian airliner that had vanished without a trace. It was one of the last things we'd heard before leaving NYC. Just as we were taxiing to the runway for takeoff, Z blurted out, *How did that plane disappear?* If our fellow passengers heard her, nobody said anything. I whispered something to the effect of, I'll tell you later. Now, apparently, she wanted a reassuring story about the plane having been found and the people on it returning home.

Some people didn't tell those absent, imprisoned or otherwise separated of the deaths of family members, didn't tell children or students preparing for exams. I recalled the story of a university student accused of participating in the gang rape of a friend of a friend. He was held in detention without formal charge or trial for ten years. He was tortured repeatedly, and when he was finally released, he had chronic health problems that he expected would last the rest of his life. At the time of his arrest, he was engaged, and throughout his detention, his parents—the only ones from the outside he was allowed to have contact with, and even then, rarely—told him his fiancée was waiting for him. Only when he got out—on bail, no less! the charges still had not been formally dropped and would most likely hang over him indefinitely—did he discover she had long ago married and had a child. *It's o.k.*, he said, *they tortured me so bad on my genitals, I fear I'm impotent anyway.* If I were his parent, would I have told him? If you had asked me that before you disappeared, I would most likely have said, Yes, of course;

you can't keep something like that from someone; they deserve to know. But now, I was less sure.

The voice in my head that always spoke to you, that corresponded with you, conversed with you, stopped when mother died. I didn't turn it off intentionally; it just happened of its own accord. Something seemed wrong about telling you mother had died. It wasn't so much the desire to avoid dispiriting you, and it wasn't that it was the sort of thing I thought I should wait to tell you face to face. It was more that it was a mark of mortality, a reminder of time passing, of life (or death) going on without you, and yes, in that sense, it was a question of morale: I imagined you thinking, While I am here, all that is happening out there. I suppose that could go for just about everything I told you. But death was different. When someone dies, you abandon them, whether you want to or not; you abandon them by going on living; the living abandon the dead. And I didn't want to tell you anything that might raise the prospect of abandonment, that might allow the idea to enter your head that one day you could be treated as dead.

So I did not tell you about mother dying, or about the eerie midday darkness or the storm that came that night. I did not tell you about flying back for mother's funeral. I left Z with Gong-gong and Po-po because I could not bear messing up her internal clock again just as she was beginning to readjust to HK time, and anyway, we'd been there a month before and Z had had a chance to see grandma before she died. She didn't need to see her dead. My brother had sent me a photo taken moments after she died; it was not the sort of thing to show children. But I felt torn: it seemed just wrong to not take her to my own mother's funeral. And anyway: my mother had specified cremation; there would be no open casket, nothing but an urn to see. I stayed at mother's place, sleeping in her bed, sheets unchanged from when she had slept there last. I found two hairs on the fitted sheet, wrapped them in a tissue and put them in a Ziploc bag. In the bathroom medicine cabinet, I found three teeth in a Ziploc bag. I remembered her telling me about her teeth falling out. Relics. On her bedside table was Dorothy Day's *Loaves and Fishes: The Story of the Catholic Worker Movement*. Mom herself had told me the only books she could read anymore were thrillers and the Bible. What was she doing reading Dorothy Day in her last days? I turned to the bookmarked page near the end of the book (did she really get that far? Her pain was so intense she could not concentrate for long) and found a passage reflecting on a spell in prison: *...all we give is given to us to give. Nothing is ours. All we have to give is our time and patience, our love.... I realized again how much ordinary kindness can do.* And then, a few pages later, *'Use your common sense as far as it will take you,' Father Roy used to say, 'and when you realize you can do nothing, bow your head to the storm and pray—pray without ceasing. If that fails, rejoice that you, too, are accounted worthy to suffer and to realize your weakness and keep on praying like the importunate widow.'*

I buried two of Z's paintings with mother's cremated remains. One was made before she died. It was the last thing Z ever gave her, a representation of an enormous mango tree near where we lived on the island, sponge-painted yellow blotches surrounded by green. The other was made after mom had died, specifically to place in her grave. It was a "deep dark wood", as Z put it, of maroon and dark green paint inspired by leaves collected on a walk along a shady path to the northern tip of the island.

I did not cry (though I gasped, and choked, and shook). I thought of you scolding me for never crying. You equated not crying with not feeling. No, I objected, the two are not the same! And yet I wondered: Had I become less feeling, less compassionate, more severe, more merciless in my judgments? Had I made myself too hard?

Mother's death felt like yet another detour, yet another obstacle placed in the way of finding you. I had that dream-like feeling of struggling toward a goal while some powerful force pulled me further away from it.

When I came home, Z and I had one of many conversations about death in that period, as usual while lying in bed in the dark before going to sleep.

How do people die?

Well, usually it's because they get really old or they get really sick or they have a really bad accident.

Mommy is getting older and older and is going to die, and then there will be no more mommy.

Everybody dies, but I think mommy will live for a very long time still. She is still very young and healthy.

Is mommy dead now? As if she'd somehow suspected I had been withholding this information from her.

What do you mean?

Mommy isn't here. She hasn't been here for a long time. So I'm wondering if mommy is dead.

No, of course mommy's not dead.

How do you know? (Wise child: How could I be sure if I didn't even know where she was?)

I just know.

A pause, and then she said, *I just know too.*

Good, I said, *good.*

I last saw mother eighteen days before she died. Early the morning Z and I were to leave, I realized I'd forgotten to return to her some things she'd leant us. We had already said goodbye the night before and were staying in another apartment in her building. Z and I rushed up to her apartment. She'd left the door unlocked, and I burst in without knocking, expecting she would still be asleep. But she wasn't. She was sitting in a chair near the door, resting from the effort it took to get out of bed and walk to the kitchen. We were surprised to see each other; I startled her, and she startled me. I quickly put the things back I'd come to return. We had to hurry to catch the taxi to the airport. The morning light streamed in through the window, enveloping mother in a glow. *Goodbye, mom,* I said. I bent down and kissed her on her forehead—she was so small by then. In that moment, it was as if all of her life and all of mine appeared before me: I was kissing a frail but determined old woman close to death, but also a vulnerable, joyful little girl full of hopes and dreams—in fact, I was tempted to call her by her first and middle names; perhaps no one ever had called her that; it sounded like something to call a little girl—, and at the same time, I felt like a little boy and she was my venerated mother who had brought me up and given me everything I needed for life. Both of us were all of those things in that moment, she a little girl, a mother, a frail old woman struggling to make it to the kitchen, I a grown man with a little girl of his own but also, still, a little boy. And that person, who was my mother but who was also a little girl, a dazzling young woman who had grown up in a small, remote town, educated herself, and had the wide world of possibility spread out before her, a friend, a wife, looked up and said, as she had said so many times down through the years, *Have a good trip. I love you.*

Z fell asleep, leaving me to dwell on the memory and the feeling most associated with it, guilt that I had been able to do so little to alleviate her suffering. Even if I were incapable, I might still have just stayed by her side in her dying days, instead of being in NYC or HK.

Of course, at the time one could not be sure those were indeed her final days. I could be forgiven for not realizing as much, since it didn't seem to occur to anyone else either, so chronically had she been at death's door. She died alone, no one at her bedside in her last moments. *Did an angel whisper in your ear*

/ hold you close, take away your fear / in those long last moments? I hoped so because no one else did, myself included.

Knowing her, she would have preferred it that way, preferred to be alone, to not bother anyone and not be bothered.

Even so, if I had it to do over, I would have at least been there, to let her know I was there, if she needed me.

But then again, I had a wife who was surely suffering as well, elsewhere in the world. I could not be two places at once. Pulled in different directions, I ended up in between, nowhere.

Guilt at my inability to alleviate others' suffering was one of the primary feelings of my life, most of which had been spent in the company of people who suffered considerably more than I. And being familiar with it, I had also learned to contend with it, not just wish or whisk it away with false or superficial self-consolation ("you did the best you could"), to live with the constant tension between the negligible effects of actual deeds and ideal results, without allowing it to grind me down or discourage me. In awe at the irreconcilable immensity of others' suffering, I had always the awareness that what I had to contend with in my own life was, by contrast, perfectly manageable. I had noticed that in situations in which others became overwhelmed by fear, frustration, indecision, doubt, impatience, anxiety or a sense of inadequacy to the task, I remained composed, concentrated, undeterred. Experience had taught I was not up to the task but had to attempt it anyway; this amounted to a kind of faith.

But no matter how resilient and unflappable I considered myself to be, I flinched at the mere thought of torture, starvation, serious illness or injury, impending death, anything that threatened physical integrity, not least of all because I had seen that when the body is under assault, even if and once the assault has passed, the damage remains, not only physical but psychological, often irreparable. Some things cannot be repaired, undone. I seemed, these days, to be surrounded by people who in one way or another, to one degree or another, faced such prospects, were currently enduring them, or, in the case of my mother, had just put an end to them.

And the suffering that went on in great obscurity seemed at times limitless.

Tiina called and told of the beatings of three lawyers in Heilongjiang. They were investigating a report that Falun Gong practitioners were being held in a black jail when they themselves were taken into detention. We'd heard they'd been mistreated, but now that they had been released, details of the extent of their mistreatment were only now emerging. Ruan Weifeng was in hiding. He still suffered from his injuries but was afraid to go to hospital for proper treatment. Security officials had broken five of his ribs. After his release, he returned to his home in Beijing but immediately realized the Guobao were pursuing him, so he effectively disappeared himself, from them he hoped. The broken ribs came on top of a severe case of pneumonia he contracted during his detention in 2011 in the crackdown following calls for a Jasmine Revolution, something he had absolutely nothing to do with but was made to suffer for regardless. He had been beaten on the occasion of that detention as well, but the beating was less serious than the pneumonia in terms of its long-term consequences. After that release, it took him a full year to recover. And now the new beating. Damaged lungs on the inside, damaged ribs around them, his torso a living history of the Partystate's abuse. Tiina worried about him.

I called Tiina the Original Solidarity Lawyer. A law professor at an HK university, she spent considerable time and effort tracking the situations of at-risk rights defense lawyers on the mainland, quietly campaigning on their behalf. You and Tiina had bonded, not least of all because you were young women in a male-dominated field. Tiina missed the confidences she shared with you and, in your absence, sometimes called me to discuss her worries about this or that lawyer. *But then*, Tiina would suddenly say, interrupting herself, *why should I bother you with this? You have more than enough of your own worries.*

No, no, I objected, *I very much want to hear from you, and to know what you know. And Y would appreciate us staying in touch.*

In fact, Tiina had tirelessly worked on your behalf; hardly anyone in touch with Tiina in any professional capacity was lacking in information about your case.

It was Easter when I returned from mother's funeral. The next day, Z and I went on the annual island Easter egg hunt. How striking the contrast between the aliveness of the island's children, shrieking joy in their search for eggs, the feeling of community amongst the families gathered and, on the other hand, the solitude of death. Z found her quota of six eggs right away, then had to rehide the surplus she found after that, leaving them for other children to find.

It was also the festival of Tin Hau, goddess of the sea. An enormous bamboo theater was erected on the concrete football pitch for Cantonese Opera. The area was closed off for weeks to all other uses, much to the children's general dismay. Z was a fervent Cantonese Opera fan. Every day of the four-day festival, we would go and watch from empty seats one could invariably find near the front. At intermission, we peaked backstage at the musicians sitting off to the side and the actors applying makeup in front of mirrors. At night, as Z fell asleep, the singing and music across the bay drifted in the bedroom windows. Z said she wanted to be a Cantonese opera singer. We would take colorful old silk scarves I had gotten for you in Cambodia and wrap them around Z, who then danced and sung, the scarves flapping and flowing behind her like the sleeves and gowns of the opera singers. Her favorite part was to take a long, deep bow at the end, her head nearly touching the ground.

We'd been reading *Madeline*, a book we got in NYC. Z knew the story so well that I recited the first part of a couplet and left the second for her to complete. *But the biggest surprise by far*, I'd say, and Z rounded off, *... on her stomach was a scar!* Sometimes she said it in a small shy voice, sometimes she belted it out. The accompanying picture showed Madeline standing on her hospital bed proudly holding up her shirt. The eleven visiting girls look up in admiration. (The reader can't see the scar itself since Madeline is turned away.) Z was fascinated by the idea of having one's appendix out. We watched appendectomies on youtube. Z was able to describe in quite impressive detail the various stages of the procedure. She especially liked the instrument that simultaneously cut the appendix off and stapled the place from which it was severed. We had a book about the human body. Flaps could be opened to see under the skin, then under the bones, to the heart and lungs and the blood vessels. We made a paper skeleton and connected the joints with fake-brass fasteners. It hung from a bookcase with an entirely impassive face, the fanbreeze gently animating its limbs with every rotation, flutter-dance and repose, flutter-dance and repose.

We went into the sea for the first time of the year. It was a half-year already since we'd last gone swimming. Z didn't remember. The joy this time was as if it was the first.

●

Dear Tatyana,

Just to let you know: I haven't forgotten the notebook.

The past month has been crazy: Less than 48 hours after I got back to HK, my mother died. It was not unexpected: She had been very ill for a long time. My daughter and I had spent two weeks with her earlier in the month. At the news, I turned around and went back to the funeral, from which I've just returned.

I checked the 'easy' spot under the desk where I thought the notebook might be, but that just made me recall that last summer I moved the whole plastic box I think it's in to under the dreaded staircase. Next step: check there. That's a major project. It means taking out all the baby things, suitcases and assorted other plastic boxes full of winter clothes and who-knows-what-else that block access to the space under the staircase, then going through the boxes there to find the right one. I'll try to get around to this soon, though there are a million and one things to catch up on and attend to. Please bear with me!

The Little Prince seems to be following me wherever I go: A new exhibition in a shopping mall (very HK!) is opening this weekend. I'm planning to take my daughter to it. Last week, a friend gave me the 'Deluxe Pop-up Edition'. It will go to my daughter at her next birthday.

No answer came. Why should it, there being no practical reason to respond? After all, she wasn't interested in correspondence. And I had told her nothing more than, There is no news.

Perhaps I avoided putting the search for the notebook at the top of my list of priorities not only because I genuinely dreaded digging everything out but also because I knew that the closer I got to actually releasing the notebook, the more painful it would be. Not only that, but it would cut the thin (if largely illusory or imaginary) thread re-linking me to her, constructed of what I could spin out of a single terse response to my initial message, a response with the very practical purpose of requesting a gift be returned.

In the meantime, there were images: the downy moustache on the upper lip that she dyed blonde so that it would not be visible; a rough patch of skin about the size of an orange where her buttock met her leg. But which leg? I couldn't recall with certainty whether left or right.

And while I'd mentioned mother's death, I hadn't mentioned your disappearance.

The exhibition was small and plastic and tawdry in the center of an HK mall typical in that it could nearly asphyxiate with artificiality. The Little Prince was lost in, swallowed by the temple of consumerism, his surroundings hostile to all he stood for (authenticity, the search for meaning and love). Perhaps, though, this was his natural state, to be alienated, and the HK mall a more appropriate exhibition venue than the stately, elegant, elitist Morgan Library where we had seen Saint-Exupéry's original drawings in NYC. *Le petit prince*, after all, was hardly an elitist text; it was a commercial master of the universe, having sold in the tens of millions worldwide (estimates varied wildly, from 80 million to 200 million), ranking up there with the Bible, the Koran, Harry Potter and Mao's Little Red Book amongst the most widely disseminated texts. What strange taste the world had!

If I had been alone, I would have passed through the mall exhibition in five minutes, sniffing in disdain, but Z loved it. She wandered about, asking the same questions over and over and talking about the same things again and again. She liked being out and about, in a crowd, where the action was. She had a talent for enjoying herself and finding interest in just about any situation. She was grooving. There were plastic statues replicating the drawings of the sheep the narrator made at the Little Prince's request, the rose under the glass the Little Prince made to protect her from the wind, and the fox and the Little Prince together on the Little Prince's planet, the latter an apocryphal scene—the fox never goes to the Little Prince's planet. Was I just being a conservative stick in the mud, a snob, to wonder why, at the very least, the curators couldn't be faithful to the story?

All sorts of HK Little Prince fanatics had come out of the woodwork. Not a single one was male. Some brought boyfriends or children. They wore Little Prince dresses, Little Prince t-shirts. They took photos of themselves next to Little Prince statues and images. The place meant something to them. In HK, it was all they had, of dreams, of literary idols.

Z stood next to the lamplighter and, together with him, held the long pole at the end of which was the torch and douter that he used to light and extinguish the street lamp over and over for eternity. On his tiny planet, night and day lasted moments each. Z didn't get the existential critique of indefinitely repetitious, meaningless labor. Who did get it? If many did and followed the line of thinking to its logical conclusion, it would mean changing jobs. But maybe, as much as anything else, Saint-Exupéry's depiction showed aristocratic disdain for the little guy. At any rate, Z shone with joyful self-importance; indeed, she turned the lamplighter into a symbol of empowerment. I told Z that if I were the lamplighter, I would say, *No need to light the lamp. And anyway, how do I get off this planet? Little Prince, take me with you!*

We began to read *The Little Prince* together night after night. I was surprised at how much she enjoyed it, given its high ratio of text to illustration. After her bath in the evening, she would shout, *Little Prince! Little Prince!* In the middle of the day, Z would, apropos of nothing, burst out, *Draw me a sheep!* As visitors departed, she would warn, *Watch out for the boa constrictor!* She also discussed exploding volcanoes, which she had already been studying prior to her introduction to the Little Prince, and the importance of digging up baobabs while they were still small, which she compared with great acuity to our situation with the proliferating banana tree in our yard. We had on-going discussions:

Why is the Little Prince sad?
He is lonely.

Why is he lonely?

Because he doesn't have friends. He's looking for friends.

Why doesn't he have friends?

Because he comes from a small planet where he lives all alone and he left the planet because he wasn't getting along with his rose.

Where is his mommy-and-baba?

I don't know. We don't know where his mommy and baba are.

Maybe he's lonely because he doesn't have his mommy-and-baba. He's like Pippi. Pippi doesn't have a mommy-and-baba either.

Well, it's said Pippi's baba is a sailor and he's away at sea. So maybe he'll come back, but we never see him. (I didn't add that the implication was that he was lost at sea.)

Pippi's baba is like my mommy. They'll come back.

That's right: They'll come back.

But how should I know if they ever would, Pippi's baba, Z's mommy?

Whenever we parted, Z and I always said, Come back soon! It was more often than not me saying those words to her, since one of Z's favorite games, inspired partly by the Little Prince, was "going on a trip". Not a light traveller, she packed her many bags, said she was going, and waved goodbye, to which I was obliged to respond, Come back soon!

●

Hello, I'm here!

Oh, so you're here! So good to hear! Come out and see me!

Yes, I will. How's tomorrow?

Tomorrow's fine, perfect.

See you, then!

When Opal arrives, Z is happy to see her. It had been some time since they'd last met. I thought she would have forgotten her, but every now and then, she'd ask, *When can we see Opal again?* They are good friends.

A rainstorm had just passed. Water splashed onto the metal plate roofing the air conditioner on the side of the house, dripped from the banana fronds onto the patio. Everything was literally dripping wet.

To avoid any bugs, of the electronic rather than entomological kind, we went to the nearby beach.

Through the whole ordeal, no one had been more loyal, more committed to you than Opal. She stood by me, by you, by us throughout. Who knew whether her loyalty was to you personally or to the cause, the principle? I suspected both. She had just returned to HK from her secret mission to find you and BY. She had been gone weeks. I could only imagine how much I'd put her through, how difficult that time had been for her. I was happy to hear her voice when she called to say she was back, called on a normal mobile phone, her mobile phone, without the million and one security precautions we'd been taking for even the briefest of communications; this time, only one, Red Phone. Knowing she had returned safely to HK was almost as good as if it had been you.

It really wasn't too bad, Opal said. That was her phlegmatic summary of the trip. And she looked good. Opal always looked good, up for something, up for a fight, up for life. It was good to see: A trip like that could knock anyone out, leave you spooked, jumpy, cast a shadow over your whole demeanor.

I couldn't resist: *How do you mean 'not too bad'?* (Everything was "not too bad" to everyone these days: Pingan and Lianshun said the situation in the country was "not bad". I should just be happy to know that these people weren't going to get hysterical at the slightest provocation.)

I just had to know when to lie low, when it was o.k. to come up, who I could talk to, inquire with, who I couldn't. And it didn't take too long to size things up. You just had to hope you didn't talk to the wrong person because once they get you on their radar, it's all over. *As long as you stay off the radar, you can do quite a lot, get quite a lot done.*

About your case, I was a little disappointed. Or a lot, maybe. One just kept wanting a magic wand to be waved. Opal didn't have much more to report than what she'd already relayed in her cryptic email messages. She just expanded and elaborated. She'd spent most of the time in the town where BY lived in Hebei prior to her abduction. She learned that shortly before her abduction, BY had received an eviction notice from her landlord, who had been pressured to act by the local Guobao. It was always hard, she said, to determine the exact extent to which the various security organs in China were collaborating versus acting on their own, sometimes seemingly even at cross-purposes. Did the local Guobao, for example, know that the Beijing Guobao was casting its dragnet wide in the New Citizens Movement crackdown? Was the eviction notice ordered by the Beijing Guobao and carried out by the local Guobao? Or was the local Guobao harassing BY without even knowing that the Beijing Guobao was coming to "collect" her? Whatever the case, even before she could move out or fight the eviction order, she was kidnapped. Her landlord complained to Opal that she just disappeared; he didn't even know what to do with her possessions. He was not a bad man, Opal had to understand: When the authorities told you to do something, you didn't want to get on their bad side. And so, he put BY's things in a storage area in another building he owned, in case BY should return. Meanwhile, he's already rented her place out to a new tenant. He emphasized to Opal that it was he himself who had incurred the cost of the move. He laughed when she suggested he should send the Guobao the bill. After the abduction, surveillance of her place and the area of town it was in seemed to evaporate, and Opal could move around quite freely without fear of detection. She found out from people in the local security apparatus that it was indeed in relation to NCM that BY had been taken away and that she was not being held locally. So at least there was that: confirmation that she had been disappeared by the Partystate.

While Opal could find out quite a lot about BY, she learned almost nothing about you—you had no connection to the town. The only scrap she got was from her contact in the local security apparatus, who said they had been told to keep an eye out for any interlopers snooping around after BY. That was presumably in case you had somehow managed to cross the border and make your way to the town. But beyond that, nothing. The Beijing Guobao, which most likely handled your case directly, was impenetrable. Opal asked me if I'd relayed her message to Lianshun and Lawyer Ni asking them to see if they could find anything out from their contacts in Beijing. Yes, I had, I said, though I hadn't heard back. They seemed skeptical they would, since their initial search had yielded nothing.

To tell you the truth, I said, *they seemed a little... well... distracted.*

Opal just nodded.

Why, I asked, *do you think the Partystate has kept quiet about the disappearances for so long?*

They consider the case still open, the investigation on-going, Opal said, *the whole New Citizens Movement crackdown, I mean.*

But most of the key trials have been held now, haven't they?

Maybe they think there's more to discover, or that BY and Y still have things to tell them that they haven't told yet.

I remembered you often imagining that you'd crack in a second under coercive pressure, not to mention actual physical torture. I agreed with you—I'd be the same. So it was hard to think that you hadn't told them everything you could, unless of course you found some deep pool of resistance within you that you hadn't suspected existed, or, more likely, you simply didn't know something they thought you knew and they were still trying to get it out of you.

You know, said Opal, continuing, *there could very well be disagreements between different departments on this. The Guobao is probably the most ruthless: It initiated the NCM crackdown and wants to see it out to its conclusion, it wants to be thorough, it wants to crush it completely. And it probably feels it has the upper hand in any disagreement, and has had the upper hand up to now, because its actions are in harmony with the message coming from the top. The Man himself is for crackdown, in all areas, the Party, civil society. It's all about tightening the reins. If you're working in that direction, you've got the leadership's support in any turf battles. The central Guobao sees links and connections and conspiracies everywhere. The others want to do just enough to cover their butts, but not too much. Partly because they don't see the need, partly because they're lazy, partly because they wonder what they're getting out of it, how they're going to benefit personally. So the Partystate itself is probably still undecided what to do with them.*

OK, to put it another way, if our reading is right, the take-away is that something has to be done to further drive a wedge between them, to damage the Guobao's pursuit of the crackdown to its logical conclusion, to isolate the Guobao, to make the Man take a few more things into consideration, make it seem as if it makes a bit more sense to go easier, come clean with these cases. Ironically, the Guobao's own success in cracking down on NCM could swing things against it and in our favor. It could be argued that it's done its job, NCM's neutralized if not destroyed, it can let up now, especially if difficulties could be made for elements of the Partystate elsewhere; HK, for instance....

O got a big smile on her face. She was always up for making things difficult for the Partystate in HK. It was, you could say, her specialty. Even as I spoke with her, I mentally went over the counter-arguments: The hardliners held such sway at the moment that nothing could puncture their armor. And they had other big cases coming up, like Ilham. They'd want to see things through and push this hardline as the best, the most effective modus operandi all of the time—you had to be consistent, show people you meant business and would police the bottom line rigorously. Better to always be on the safe side and crack down hard on dissent, among other reasons for the deterrent effect: It sent out a strong warning to others who might consider dissenting.

What are you thinking? I asked.
What are you thinking? she replied.
What do you think about going public?
Having just returned from the mainland, Opal was not yet aware of the meeting I'd had with your organization in NYC. When I told her, she nodded in agreement.

I think it's time. I don't think it can hurt. Nothing's moving otherwise. It was typical Opal, I thought, to throw caution to the wind. *Or wait,* she said, just having a new thought.

I liked this side of Opal, this analytical side, and it was developing quickly. She'd always been slighted by the big players in h.r., partly, I was sure, because of her diminutive stature, partly because of her less than fluent English, partly for class reasons—she'd never gone to university, came from a working class background, but also because she never seemed to approach issues with that analytical acuity that was most prized in the highly professionalized world of paid h.r. workers, the ones who drove the agenda at the big organizations. She was always met with condescending admiration of her passion and courage, then duly ignored. But she was more streetwise than most, detected trends that others missed.

Then again, she said, *you could try once more through the backchannels. Ma Lianshun and Lawyer Ni would be the best-placed. Use them to convey to the relevant authorities that Y had nothing to do with whatever they are investigating, that it is time to let her go, and that if they don't—and this point is crucial: the Partystate understands no message, or at least takes no message seriously, without an accompanying credible threat—, this could all blow up in ways they might find difficult to control. It doesn't only have to do with their image abroad (they don't care much about that); it has to do with the political situation in HK. If HK people find out that one of theirs has been abducted and is being held incommunicado, it could have an effect similar to the chopper attack on Lau.*

O was referring to a recent incident: an editor of an esteemed daily was attacked with a cleaver on the street. A thug hopped off the back of a motorbike, struck the victim from behind, and hopped back on the motorbike, which continued on its way. HK people were appalled at the attack and believed it to be connected to the editor's work. The incident was regarded as one of many recent ominous threats to freedom of the press. The Partystate was believed to be behind the attack in one way or another. There was a history of the Partystate enlisting triads to do their dirty work in HK, and it was hardly the first time that a journalist had been attacked by thugs. A few months before the attack, the editor's newspaper had participated in an international investigation by a consortium of journalists into the moving of assets out of the mainland through offshore shell companies by Partystate elites, including some related to top leaders. It wasn't hard to imagine the attack was retribution for the editor's participation in the venture.

It could cause outrage, be seen as part of the on-going erosion of freedoms in the city, and make people see what could happen if there is not true universal suffrage to act as a bulwark against the worst that could happen here. Maybe it would swing the opinion of a lot of those people sitting on the fence, make them less inclined to accept a less than satisfactory package, the sort of fake democracy Beijing is cooking up even as we speak. Wouldn't it just be better, under the circumstances, to release her quietly? One less thing to worry about in contending with HK. That's what Ma and Ni have to convey.

I like it. It makes sense…. And we could get the big players abroad involved, to publicize it along the lines of 'Beijing kidnaps HK citizen'. (Here I was thinking primarily of the well-connected, savvy, amenable, big-hearted Marni.) Of course, in the end, I'm skeptical Beijing will bend to any pressure at all, but it's worth trying. Because, as you say, there seems so little else that can be done. And it's not as if quietly quietly has worked up to now…. But what about BY?

BY, unfortunately, they can do what they want with. There's even less leverage there. I imagine there's quite a few in the regime who look at Y and just want to get rid of her, get her off their hands. The best we can hope for with BY is that they don't see any political benefit any longer in portraying her as a black hand, a ringleader, and she'll be let off on lesser charges; 'gathering a crowd to disturb public order' seems to be the favorite at the moment. That's what a lot of the other NCMers got. There are examples of small potatoes just being let go, once they squeeze what they want out of them. So you never know.

We were skipping stones on the surface of the placid sea. Z was collecting "treasure" in a cracked plastic faded yellow bucket—shells, flotsam, rocks, seaglass.

Staring out across the bay, I thought of the ferry accident. Less than two years previously, we had been on our way home. It was evening. The full moon was rising. The sea was calm. Good sailing weather. It was the anniversary of the start of the Partystate dictatorship (referred to by the Partystate as National Day). Ours was the second-to-last ferry to the island before service would be suspended for the annual fireworks display in the harbor. Without warning, the ferry hit something with a big bang, sending Z and me flying through the air. I landed on my back and, luckily, she landed on my chest. I handed her to you and went out the cabin door to the area at the back of the ferry. It was strangely still—there wasn't a sound, and no sign of what had caused the crash. I could only see the moon's bright reflection on the waveless water and the shore of the island several hundred meters away—a swimmable distance, I thought at the time. I returned to the cabin. A big hole burst in the front. Passengers screamed and ran towards the back. Water gushed so quickly into the cabin, we thought we were going to have to go overboard. You were the better swimmer, so we agreed that you would go into the water first, I would hand Z to you, and then I would get in and stay as close to you as possible. I fumbled with my life vest—it was as if my hands had stopped working; I couldn't tie the straps. We found no child life vest for Z. A woman handed me an adult life vest, and I slipped it over Z's neck. Then the ferry started moving again. Fifteen minutes later, we were at the pier. The ferry crew were most intent on ensuring we didn't walk away with the life vests; otherwise, it was as if nothing unusual had occurred.

Not until we returned home and checked the internet did we find out that the ferry had hit a boat chartered to take workers and their families from the local power plant to the fireworks display. By the middle of the night, it had become clear there was enormous loss of life on the other boat. The eventual death toll was thirty-nine, including eight children aged three to eleven. It was HK's worst maritime disaster in forty years. The last had occurred in a typhoon. This had happened in calm seas.

How could it be—two boats collide; thirty-nine die on one, none on the other? On such a placid night?

Most of the people who died were not able to get out of the cabin of the swiftly sinking boat—less than a half hour after the collision, only its prow protruded from the water. After the rescue operation, the sunken boat was lifted onto a barge and pulled into the bay where we were now skipping stones. There, it seemed so large; it filled the harbor. For days afterward, orange life vests with the sunken boat's name stenciled in black floated up on shore. We had often swum in the water, played on the beach, but you now refused to go near the bay, even after the boat was taken elsewhere—for you, it was permanently haunted.

You said, *It could just as easily have been Z, us.* Amongst the 39 deceased, there were cases of both members of a couple dying; in others, one died, another survived. In some cases, children died, their parents survived; in others, parents died, their children survived. You said the accident made you realize deep inside how precious life was, how fragile; how precious our family, how vigilantly life and family had to be defended, protected, appreciated, cherished, how life had to be lived to its fullest every moment—all of those clichés that, once you feel them deep inside, are clichés no more. Our child is still alive. We are still alive. It is a miracle. Every day is a miracle. A miracle, over and over again. I was struck by your transformation from thoroughgoing skeptic. Can't you just believe in something for once? I'd sometimes thought. And now you did.

We finished skipping stones and just stared at the sea. Z came up and grabbed my leg, held onto it.

I turned to Opal: *How is your hostel going?* Some time ago, Opal had moved from an urban slum to a remote fishing village on the city's biggest island. After a girlfriend left her, she began renting out the extra room in her flat to travellers and gradually had taken on other rooms in the house and neighboring houses. Before long, without really having planned it that way, she was running a de facto hostel, entirely unlicensed. As so often in Opal's life, the unplanned bits, the things that arose—the secret mission, the hostel—threatened to swamp the formal bits, the paid employment.

It's going great. People are coming from all over Asia. It's a real scene. I love the girls, all of them. It's like having a commune that changes all the time. I couldn't stand a permanent commune where you learn to hate each other; you have to flush it out, get new blood.

Whoever's there cooperates, cooks, helps each other out. And it's a money-spinner too. If I could keep this up, I'd be able before long to patch together a proper income. But it's only a matter of time before the government finds out and shuts it down.

O could never afford the investment required to get the place up to code, and she didn't own any of the property. Some rooms she rented; others, she just had informal arrangements with the owners to rent their places and take a cut. Anyway, she wasn't the sort who had any desire to spend a lot of time "normalizing" operations. To her, things were good while they lasted; there was no expectation they would last for long, or that they should. I liked thinking of Opal out there running her own pan-Asian lesbian camp. More than just about anyone else I knew, it seemed to me she was leading a free life.

Come and visit, she said. *Come and see. The girls will love Z.*

Do you think there are any good babysitters amongst them?!

Well, me, for instance!

Z, in the meanwhile, had climbed into a deep hole freshly dug by a big dog and was busy burying herself in the sand. When she got up to her arms, she asked me to cover her, up to her shoulders. She sat there for some time, shifting slightly to produce giggling cracks in the sand, and then burst out with a gleeful laugh.

On ne peut pas simuler la liberté, Opal said with a sigh, a smile and terrible Cantonese pronunciation.

If I had not heard her say it before, I would not have understood what she was saying. It had become her motto, ever since we had seen its graffiti on a wall near the central train station in Geneva during one of our visits to the Human Rights Council. *Ha, I said, look at that! On ne peut pas simuler la liberté* , and translated for Orange, who had no French. She liked it and repeated it after me until she had committed it to memory. In the following days, I often noticed her uttering it under her breath. She even got a

Geneva acquaintance to provide her with an extended version: *Chine peut simuler tout, mais on ne peut pas simuler la liberté.* Then, on various occasions she would triumphantly make that declaration. She said it now, apropos of almost nothing, to remind of our shared history, a code word, a secret salute.

You can't fake freedom. I liked the sound of it, but freedom can be faked, can't it?, I thought, just like everything else. Freedom can be faked, and is being faked, all the time, every day. Some of the fake freedoms are perhaps real. The increased freedom in China in recent decades was largely confined to the realm of personal life, the freedom to get the job you want, to wear the clothes you want, to be with the people you want, the freedom to travel where you wish, the freedom to get rich. Those were real freedoms, even if, arguably, ultimately facsimiles of deeper, more basic ones that were withheld. The challenge for authoritarian regimes these days was to figure out how little freedom their subjects would consider sufficient.

I thought of Billy Bragg's lines, *You keep buying these things when you don't need them / but as long as you're comfortable it feels like freedom*, and, juxtaposed to those, the long lines of mainland shoppers outside of HK luxury shops, Louis Vuitton, Prada, Gucci. But Bragg was singing to a through-and-through affluent consumerist society. If you hadn't had such freedoms before, and they were all you were offered, all you could get, the savor of them had indeed a real taste to it. I remembered Wu'er Kaixi once saying that the freedoms the students of eighty-nine wanted were to wear Nike shoes and go on dates. If that's what they wanted, then, ironically, the ones who weren't killed got them.

I told Opal I'd recently seen her motto at Art Basel in HK. *On ne peut pas simuler la liberté* was stenciled in white block capital letters against the background of a huge silkscreened front page of *Libération*, the work of some globetrotting cosmopolitan artist. Of course, I thought, now it is really faked. Everything can be appropriated. What a bunch of posers these people were! People wrapped up in their own little worlds. Still, it looked cool.

That show, she told me, turned out to be the inspiration for yet another project of hers. *My girlfriend and I went to Art Basel, and we were laughing, looking at the paintings and saying most of them were too big to even fit on the walls of most HK apartments. And of course, Art Basel was too expensive for most HKese—the only way we got in was through someone my girlfriend knew who worked for a credit card company sponsoring the event. And HKese aren't the sorts who ever go to museums. So we decided we would take art to the masses. And we called up artist friends and friends of friends and friends of friends of friends and asked them to make art with one single proviso: it must fit in a public housing estate apartment of 350 square feet. So they made lots of small paintings, small sculptures—really interesting stuff, often with HK themes, as we encouraged them to do art on HK social, political and cultural issues. One of my favorites was a photographer went around the city and took photos of the views from the windows of apartments in different public housing estates and then put them all together, side by side along one whole wall of a housing estate apartment. And then we did the same with people we knew who lived in public housing estates or who grew up there and whose parents still lived there. And we said, Can we hang the art in your places and then invite people to come around and see it?*

And so the whole thing was performance art, an installation, whatever you want to call it. And since the old name of Art Basel was Art HK before it was taken over by Art Basel and rebranded, we called it AHK, short for Art HK. And the slogan was, See the art, see HK how most people see it, live it. We give guided tours and take people around to the different places. And we print maps so people can do it on their own if they want. We encourage people to leave tips at each apartment they visit, so that the residents can get something out of it. Most of the residents make hundreds and some even thousands of extra dollars a month. Plus, they say they like having the art on their walls. One of the rules is that the art the artists make is donated to the people who hang it in their places. So they can keep it or sell it or do whatever they want with it once the exhibition is finished. Since it seems to be going well, maybe we'll make it an annual thing. Of course, the public housing authority and the police found out and said that use of public housing estate flats for art exhibition to the public was unauthorized. They even put up flyers in the entrances of many buildings to warn both residents and visitors of that. So it became guerrilla art, and we had to take down the location map from the internet and distribute it only by hand to people who asked for it directly from us. Who knows? Maybe some of those people were undercover police, but so far no police have approached us directly.

Z and I walked Opal down to the ferry pier and saw her off. We waved goodbye from a distance as she entered the bobbing watercraft and disappeared from view.

I felt exhilarated by Opal's visit. *Thank you, Opal, thank you!* I said to her, to the sea, to the direction of the large island where she lived out across the water (on less hazy days, it was visible from our island) after she'd departed. How it helped to have someone on your side, fully and completely and assuredly on your side, morally above all else, but also intellectually, in the sense of being fully mentally engaged in trying to solve the problem. I knew it was a drug that would wear off, but still, it was nice to be high for a change.

I contacted Ni and Lianshun, Pingan, everyone else I could think of who might have Partystate contacts, who might swim through the opaque world of officialdom, or the even more opaque world of the security apparatus: *Get the word out! We're looking for Y. If we don't find her soon, we go public. Everyone will know. It will change the public mood in HK: They will think this could happen to them if they don't stand up for universal suffrage. This is your last chance.* I contacted Marni and asked her to get the final, formal go-ahead from your organization. *If we don't find Y soon, if she is not returned, we want to go public, and we want you on board, we need you on board, we need your support. Y's story needs to be in every international publication of record. We want the blow-up effect.*

•

And then Arsenal won the Cup, their first trophy of any kind in nine years, as if to remind that there's always this thing called hope. OK, it was just the Cup, and they had to come from two goals down to beat a second-rate team. In short, it wasn't pretty. But they won. And when it was nine years since the last time you'd won anything, your heart savored it, even if your mind told you it wasn't such a big deal. Nine years was a long time: Think of all the things that happened in the average person's life in the course of nine years—love, marriage, divorce, children, jobs, promotions, demotions, dismissals, accumulations, adventures, disasters, boredoms, pleasures and sorrows large and small, fortunes won, fortunes lost.

When the game ended, I was happy for the players, a very likeable bunch, though I knew they were millionaires many times over who, financially, had no need of this victory and most definitely could not be counted amongst the true underdogs of the world. An 87-year-old woman turned out for the North London parade to celebrate the victory, saluting the players at Highbury Fields as they waved from the open-top bus. She remembered going to the parade in 1930, the first time the team won the Cup. She was three years old and watched from her father's shoulders. Football always made her think of the smell of his hair cream.[1]

---

1 "Arsène Wenger faced ultimate penalty if his extra-time gamble failed", *The Guardian*, 18 May 2014

And something in me cracked, the way a burdened sky breaks and the rains come pouring down. I knew then all would be all right: You would return, somehow, someway, sooner or later, and yes, some day, some day, some day, all those things we ever wished for, well, it was hard to even say they would be realized, but something would occur—things would not stay as they were. My reaction caused me to realize just what resistance there was within me to believing that some desired thing was possible. I was so used to fighting for things that never happened.

●

Don't give up. Good will happen soon.

Everything is involved in seeking you, finding you, securing your release.

Don't give up.

Don't give up.

I say that even though I am quite certain you will never be able to read these words.

I remember we saw them on the walls of the canteen of a hostel for refugee Tibetan university students in Delhi: *Never give up. No matter what is going on around you. Never give up.* The Dalai Lama's words. Coming from him, someone who has never given up even in the face of impossible odds, the words meant something.

I know you will remember them too. Maybe they have even occurred to you there where you are.

Remember speaking about what a difference it would make if wisdom such as that was emblazoned on the walls of every school the world over? And while the exhortation may slide into cliché in other contexts, directed to young people whose homeland has been occupied, whose culture is at threat of destruction, it definitely speaks to the matter at hand.

O.k. well, yes, sometimes you should give up, admit defeat, but that's another story, not this one.

And yes, sometimes it is no more than a cliché, but this is not one of those times.

Don't give up. Good will happen soon. Everything will be o.k.

I remember your insistence on happy endings, on only watching films, reading books with happy endings.

But, I objected, most good stories do not have happy endings; there are not many good comedies.

For you, the happy endings were compensation for the way things usually worked out. You came across so much hurt and suffering in your work, you didn't want more of it in your off-hours. So I kept on the lookout for good happy endings, but rarely found them. Perhaps the saving grace was that they appeared less often in fiction than in life.

This story must surely have a happy ending, in order to meet your requirements, as any story with you at its center must.

So, never give up.

Communism, chiliastic as it is, has a happy ending too—the fulfillment of the revolution, the workers' paradise—, so surely your captors will see nothing against complying with the ending I am constructing for you. Then again, I'm not sure dictatorship, gross injustice, massive abuse of human rights, and turning the nation into a large-scale racketeering enterprise have happy endings.... But, well, yes, the two of us always did have a way of tempering our optimism; the difference is, it always seemed to get to you more than it got to me. Well, believe me, it's getting to me now.

And anyway, the Communists don't believe their own story anymore. Nor does anyone else believe it, though it is still repeated ad nauseam in public discourse, the supreme fake in a country of fakes—fake histories, fake products, fake speech. Indeed, its ideology is the primordial fake, the fake spring from which all other fakes originate.

And here we are, willing ourselves to believe the proposition that things will get better in the face of insufficient evidence.

Or, at least, I assume that's what you're doing there, wherever you are.

Most prison correspondence that ever gets published—usually long after the prisoner's release and the downfall of the regime that imprisoned her—is from the prisoner to someone on the outside. You don't come across much of the opposite, from someone on the outside to the prisoner. It's usually the prisoner who's famous, I guess. (And that reminds me: I've been trying to decide whether or not to make you famous, to publicize your case. If you've got any opinion on that, let me know, fast! Via telepathy, perhaps.)

I've found myself thinking Havel must not have had it so bad in prison, after all, since he was able to receive and send all those letters, those wonderful letters (in spite of frequent censorship and refusal by prison authorities to send some letters due to transgressions of prison regulations on permissible and forbidden topics of correspondence). It's hard for me to imagine you being allowed to write any letters at all, let alone send or receive them, given that your detention is entirely secret. It's hard for me to imagine your conditions being very conducive to letter-writing either: I think of how much even slight physical discomfort affects my mind, my ability to think, let alone write.

After Mandela died, there was much commentary and reflection. One thing I read which struck a chord was the following: *It is hard to remember now how unlikely this* [the end of apartheid and the not entirely but relatively peaceful transition to majority rule] *once appeared to many observers. The Washington Post correspondent Jim Hoagland wrote in 1972 that 'when I arrived in South Africa, it seemed as if Luthuli, Mandela, and Sisulu were perceived dimly, as if they belonged to another time, long past, and long lost'. The apartheid state appeared strong and ruthless, and it had foreign friends, including the United States.... Then, what Steve*

Biko called the 'paper castle' of white power crumbled in a very short period.[2]

Yes, things can change so quickly. What appears hard and fast reality today can simply dissolve tomorrow. Not that it definitely will, but it can; the possibility is there, even when it seems impossible. But there I go again, I can hear you saying, with my cheap optimism. By your criterion, Gandhi was a cheap optimist, if ever there was one (at least if you only listen to his words and forget all he sacrificed for what he believed in, also all that he accomplished even if, according to his own standards, he was a failure—failed to avert partition, failed to make Indians truly self-governing in the sense of swaraj, failed to liberate the Harijans, much to Ambedkar's sniffy disapproval). His words came to mind when I read about Mandela. Now what were they exactly? Oh, yes, something about tyrants always falling in the end: *When I despair, I remember that all through history the ways of truth and love have always won. There have been tyrants, and murderers, and for a time they can seem invincible, but in the end they always fall. Think of it—always.* I've always found those words deeply heartening; they echo through my consciousness, even when I am not aware of them. Then again, well, yeah, I always thought, because even dictators die (though their embalmed corpses seem to take longer to disappear, and their ill effects longer still). But how many people actually outlive the tyranny? *In the end* can be a very long time. After all, in the end, everything ends. In the meantime, many suffer.

See, there I go again: My optimism lapses into despair. I'm sure you would approve, or if not approve, concur. I swing constantly back and forth between optimism and, well, not despair but skepticism. Think of the unexpected collapse of

---

2 "Nelson Mandela: a leader above all others", editorial, *The Guardian*, 5 December 2013

the Soviet empire. No one saw that coming, on either side of the iron curtain. The point is not that dictatorial regimes are destined to fall, but that it is very hard to predict the future. People have a tendency to just assume that things will continue to be as they have been. That can lead to a near inability to envision a different reality.

I suppose I shouldn't even mention Mandela to you; he was, after all, in prison for twenty-seven years. He did triumph, though, *in the end*! I'm sure you won't be there nearly that long. I'm not nearly so sure you'll triumph *in the end*.

But anyway, we're not trying to topple anyone at the moment; all we're trying to do now is get you out of prison, or wherever you are. We'll start thinking about toppling them when you come home.

I remember on the evening of the day Mandela died, I was in a restaurant with friends. (Don't worry: your parents were looking after Z—they've been a great help, believe me, indispensable). I stood up and raised a toast: *To Mandela! To the end of apartheid! To the downfall of Partystate dictatorship! To freedom in China! To freedom in HK! In the spirit of Mandela, may it happen before long!* This was in one of those typically stuffy upper-middle-class places. The other diners looked bemused, embarrassed, perturbed. A few smiled politely, patronizingly—those weirdly fake smiles. Others looked as if they were thinking, If you don't react, the crazy man will just go away. Still others were coldly disapproving—how dare you foist your politics on me while I'm trying to eat. No one seconded me. Well, maybe, I thought, sitting back down, it won't happen after all, certainly not if this crowd is anything to go by. I recalled that Amnesty started when Peter Berenson heard that two Portuguese students at the time of the dictatorship had been sentenced to seven years in prison for having toasted to liberty in a bar. How could those students have known that their toast would lead to the foundation of what would go on to become the largest human rights organization in the world? And, of course, *in the end*, the Portuguese regime eventually fell, though that would take more than a dozen more years, not so long in the broad scope of time.

●

And just as Opal had said, things were starting to heat up in HK in ways that were exceedingly unacceptable to the Partystate. It had a problem on its hands. Its problem was HK. The natives were restless. It wouldn't take much more than a spark to set them off. But the Partystate was never one for giving an inch, not to mention backing down. A showdown loomed: which side would blink first?

HK had always had a way of pulling us into its mess, often against our better judgment. You tried your best to keep at arm's length what you regarded as the increasingly depressing political situation. There were many roles for you to play; you were much needed, sought after; but you eschewed them in favor of retaining the bits of time you had to do things you loved; things that reduced your anxiety level and took you away from where we lived, what we did; things like gardening and doing projects with Z.

Now, as things heated up in HK, I was increasingly drawn into the vortex, and I asked myself frequently whether or not I should be getting involved, given your situation. The longer you were gone, the more I was drawn away from keeping vigil for your return. Was that a betrayal? Sometimes it felt so. Sometimes I tried to justify my other pursuits by telling myself they were in your best interest as well, telling myself that they were what you would have wanted me to do. Beneath your ambivalence about political involvement in HK, you cared deeply about the place. And then there was what Opal and I had agreed on: The situation here could be used as leverage in your case. Yes, the Partystate was determined to show who was boss in HK, but at the same time, it didn't need anything to complicate matters further, such as headlines about its kidnapping of an HKer, born and bred in HK, and a human rights worker, no less. It was the sort of news that would signal the definitive beginning of the end of "one-country-two-systems" to even those in the city without a particular political bent, the sort of news that could become a decisive factor in determining just how things would play themselves out over the coming months, for the situation was such in the city that one felt just a little push one way or another could set off a chain of events that, once underway, could be difficult for anyone to control.

So even as it drew ever more of my attention, I justified my increasing involvement in the situation in HK by telling myself it would work in your favor. That was, I liked to think, at least partly true. For me, the pro-democracy campaign was intensely personal: it was all about getting you released, setting you free. I knew the eternal skeptic in you would have scoffed at the almost magical thinking of that belief, but to me, the two objectives were related, intertwined, and the way things went in HK would have at least an indirect bearing on the way things went with you. But wasn't there some chance that my involvement in the pro-democracy movement could hurt your cause, damage your chances of release, endanger you further? Perhaps, though I thought it was small. Perhaps I was throwing caution to the wind; perhaps I would regret it. Then again, in a sense, I took up the cause for you, in tribute to you, in solidarity with you, on your behalf, because you could not be here to see your city rise up; you had always wished it would; despaired it wouldn't. Indeed, the rumblings were everything you might have hoped for, and yet, when they came, you were gone.

Then there was the bit I rarely acknowledged even to myself: The disappearance was wearing on me, taking its psychological toll. Even while the plan Opal and I had devised gave me a sense, however illusory, that things were starting to move and perhaps even looking up, even while I threw myself into the HK pro-democracy movement, I sometimes noticed the strains. Most of the time, I didn't notice, but every now and then, something would occur to remind me. When I walked the streets of HK, I began to experience something bordering on momentary hallucinations. I would suddenly have the sense I was about to be attacked. Out of the corner of my eye, I detected someone about to lash out at me, a random person, a shopkeeper standing in a doorway, an approaching passer-by. I flinched and put up my arms to ward off the blow. Then I would turn and see that person had not even noticed me, or if they had, it was because of my strange behavior, and they regarded me quizzically: What's wrong with you? Indeed, what *was* wrong with me? I had at times in the past seemed to thrive in adversity. But now? I'd had my fill of it, but it just kept coming. One thrives on adversity, I decided, only when it comes in manageable measures.

I felt intensely isolated. Looking about, I wondered, Why didn't the whole city get behind us, support us? What was wrong with that shopkeeper, that passer-by? I forgot that they did not know; hardly anybody knew. If everyone did, I imagined, the injustice would clearly manifest itself to all and be magically redressed. But I knew that even if they did, our fate would still have met with a good deal of indifference in the midst of people's ordinary worries and anxieties, the daily challenges they faced, and the cynicism on the part of a good many. So what? One more ordeal amongst many. As if we don't have our own problems. In one way or another, she probably got what was coming to her. What business did she have fooling around there? Just as I imagined publicity would somehow magically save you, so I could almost hear the rebukes issuing from the lips of the indifferent. I sometimes had the sinking feeling that I had already waited too long, listened too much to counsel in favor of moderation, the "quiet approach". I, who was once a crusader, now reduced to flinching at apparitions, and this in the safest of cities—whatever else you said about it, the chance of being physically attacked on the street was exceedingly low.

In a way, my own psychodrama mirrored the situation of the city. That was the thing: It was hard to know what was real, what was not. Maybe my feeling didn't come out of nowhere, or only out of my head, maybe it was more than a sign of my exhaustion and mental depletion in the face of your disappearance, but was a sign of the times, a reaction to the tension in the city, a tension I couldn't help but soak up just from walking around the streets. Rarely had I seen HK so tense. It was never a relaxed place, but now there was a feeling in the air that something had to give before long. Then again, I'd had that feeling before, and then things would blow over without hardly anything happening, without hardly any change, or with things actually getting worse, and still people would bear it—they wouldn't grin, but they would bear it—and I sometimes would find myself walking around humming some variation on that famous line, now how does it go again?, oh, yes, *this is the way the world ends, not with a bang but a whimper*, except in HK's case, it might be more like, This is how HK succumbs, not with a bang but a grimace and a barely audible groan.

I had never lived in a place I'd liked less, found less charming. Well, that's not quite true: I'd lived in a long line of miserable places, and ended up in them precisely because they were miserable, and I didn't expect them to be otherwise, but, to correct myself, I'd never lived in such a miserable place for so long that I felt myself almost trapped there, could simply not pull away, hit the eject button, nor a place that presumed to be so modern, so developed, so prosperous, and yet at the same time presented such great challenges to attaining a psychological disposition resembling anything like well-being. I'd come to have affection for it in spite of itself, in spite of myself. Or had I? Well, it depended when you asked. Perhaps I had just acquiesced, slipped into the water and no longer noticed where I was. "Affection" sounded too sentimental where cruelty and indifference had become so entirely institutionalized, laundered much like the tycoons' wealth, that they were merely routine, passing largely unremarked, unnoticed. To take just the example that came most immediately to mind because it had become something of an obsession with me, there was no law on maximum work hours. Seventy-two-hour work weeks—twelve hours a day, six days a week—were common in a place that considered itself a modern, developed society. Sometimes it felt like living in a time warp—the place had never seen the basic labor rights attained a century ago in other developed societies. It was hard to have "affection" for that. Elderly people, often bent over double, collecting cardboard to sell to recyclers were a common sight in a city that was built by people of their generation, a city where one in three elderly lived in poverty, a city with no social security or pension scheme. It was hard to have "affection" for that.

It was a place where you found yourself (where I found myself) asking, What's it all for? It must be something more than, different from, besides, beyond *this*—long working hours, the struggle to survive, the constant and increasing consumption needed to keep the place afloat. I knew what *my* life was all for, but I looked around and wondered, What do these people think it's all for? And most of the time, my answer (and yours) was, Most of the time, most of the people don't think; they just do, they just work. People looked unhappy, constantly jostled up against one another on the streets, tolerating each other in the cramped places where they lived. It was not a place where you looked around and said, This is what it's for, this!, where the grace and actions of the citizenry were obviously self-justifying. And I'd been in a few places like that, so I knew the difference. Sometimes the faces were so glum and doleful it was comical.

There was such an enormous gap between the official rhetoric—"Asia's World City", often praised for its "competitiveness" and welcoming attitude to business—and the lived reality of the majority of the people that I came to think that whatever it was, it was the opposite of what was said. Among other things, it was the most unequal developed economy in the world according to some measurements and placed number 1 twice running on *The Economist's* crony capitalism index. Upwards of twenty percent of the population lived in poverty, including one in three elderly people and one in four children. About half of the population lived in public housing estates, unable to afford shelter at market rates. Things looked bleak to many young people—poorly paid jobs, poor working conditions, housing too expensive to marry, having to live with their parents into the indefinite future; affording children of their own appeared an even more distant dream. On top of it all, many aspects of society were deteriorating, including rights and civil liberties, with steady and increasing efforts by the Partystate to assimilate the territory, to mainlandize it.

But, one might note, no one was throwing bombs. No one was blowing himself or others up. No one was suddenly walking out in the crowded street and spraying the multitudes with automatic weapon fire. There was no fear of violence. There was no breakdown of law and order. There was no social collapse. It wasn't Syria or Central African Republic or the latest basket case du jour. It didn't have anywhere near one of the more corrupt governments or societies. Many people might not have a lot, might just be getting by, but there was no hunger, there was no deprivation. There was something to be said for basic peace and order, after all, for walking out your door without fearing you would be robbed or worse.

Ah, how true! And one should always count one's blessings. But besides comparison with the worst, another valid comparison would be between where the place should be, given its wealth, given what it could afford in terms of investment in the well-being of its people, and where it was. And according to that comparison, it failed. Just as one should always count one's blessings, one should never forget one's ideals. One should compare oneself to the best as well as the worst, especially when one had the resources to be amongst the former.

It was a place that, like the country of which it was a part whether it liked it or not, simply wore you down. That was the way it worked, the intent of the malicious gods, such that, now, when I had to bring myself to describe its existential struggle, summon what little energy and concentration I possessed to portray its climactic do-or-die moment, at which either the people took matters into their own hands or continued to be subjects molded by the will of distant others who most definitely did not have their best interests at heart, to describe a cause worth dying for, one that should matter deeply to the city, the country, the region, the world (and I was not hyperbolizing, not at all), I just felt tired. *Do I have to explain this all now?!* I said to myself. *I'm so tired of it all, so very tired. It's so boring. There's so little progress. It's the same things over and over again.* It occurred to me that the situation of the city had an effect very similar to that of your disappearance: It just wore you down over time. It was as if that was the Partystate's whole strategy: Be a big gorilla that sits on everything all the time, lets nothing move. *And yet,*

I must, I said to myself. *At the end of the day, what other option do I really have? My duty as a citizen compels me to.* Also because it was your city, where you grew up, from which you yearned to escape, to which, once having escaped, you returned and then felt trapped. And because, throughout all of what was to come, you were not there.

It was a place where, over the course of its 170-year history as a formal territory—ever since it was colonized by the British in 1842—, the people had never been their own rulers. There had never been democracy, neither under Britain, a democracy, nor under the Partystate, the largest dictatorship in the world. And it was still a colony, having been handed over by one power, Britain, to another, China, in 1997, with the people who lived there having had no say in the matter. Not only were they ruled by others, they were ruled from afar, this in a supposedly post-colonial era, and the people struggled with the same issues that the colonized world faced some half-century before. Again, it was that disorienting sensation of living in a time warp, surrounded by modernity, post-modernity, skyscrapers and state-of-the-art transport infrastructure, the best underground, the best airport in the world, a colony, a colony still, somebody else's place even though it's yours. How could it be? Whooshing about through comfort, convenience and efficiency, where most things worked and worked well, it was easy to forget that the people made none of the decisions governing their society.

The place was like a box that a giant picked up and shook. Living there, you were tossed about one way and another, and all you could do was orient yourself as best you could to being tossed about, for the tossing about itself you had absolutely no control over. And the funny thing was how quickly you got used to this state of affairs and came to regard it as normal, if you regarded it at all, for it was a bit like the air you breathed, just something you didn't notice so very often. And when you did notice, there was little that could be done about it—or so the thinking went—, so you just had to get on with things, make the best of them. That was the colonial mentality in a nutshell (or in a giant's box, as it were)—what can I do about it? These decisions are made by people far away over whom I have zero influence. All I can do is get on with things.

I had long had the basic theory that a person's, a people's greatest strengths were often their biggest weaknesses as well. HK people were exceedingly pragmatic. They didn't flee into realms of the impossible or improbable, let alone the ideal or utopian, or even simply things-not-as-they-are-at-this-very-moment. They said, This is the way things are; how can I best accommodate myself to reality so as to profit? They got on with things, worked hard, found a way to make things work. But the flipside of this was that they could at times seem so lacking in initiative, in any belief that through collective action a better society, a better world could be achieved, that they appeared trampled down, cowed, reactive, atomized, alienated from one another, simply the playthings of much larger powers and forces—the Partystate, global capitalism, oligarchic control. Their pragmatism was their fatalism—this is the way things are; nothing can be done about it; it's futile to even try to change anything. Their pragmatism/fatalism might have once been an approach to life that made some sense back in the days when the economy was rapidly growing and there was greater social mobility, but these days it seemed ever less justifiable, and it wasn't hard to see the crowds thronging the streets as cattle on their way to the abattoir.

Of course, this created tension, social tension, political tension, psychological tension, spiritual tension. Sometimes HK could feel unbearably tense, a place slowly, inexorably splitting at the seams beneath a veneer of normality, modernity, efficiency, a seemingly solid structure built on shifting sands.

Indeed, impermanency was the very essence of the place: After 2047—when the fifty-year "one country, two systems" period was set to officially end—, no one knew what would happen, right down to whether or not existing laws protecting, say, property rights would continue to exist, and how the territory would be governed. So everyone who could afford to do so, and had enough assets to protect, made exit plans, to ensure that if they had to, at a moment's notice, they could move themselves and as many of their assets as possible out of the territory. No one with enough to lose was foolish enough to gamble that everything they owned would be secure. And while waiting for the unknown of post-'47 to arrive, there was an inexorable steady both visible and invisible creeping mainlandization. The Partystate's end game for HK appeared to be to so entirely mainlandize the place before 2047 that when that day came, there would be little difference from the day before. HK was the oblivious frog being slowly boiled alive, or, even worse, maybe the frog who knew full well it was being slowly boiled alive, but for some reason, continued to do little to nothing about it, so limited did it see its options.

I found it strange that more people didn't think that having such an unresolved political situation, and one in which people lacked the basic political right of electing their own government and being adequately, fairly and equally represented in formal political processes and institutions, was an urgent problem, and even a potential threat to their property and livelihoods. I was surprised at the extent to which the Partystate, the colonial ruler, was able to peddle its propaganda successfully. People so often just seemed willing to opt for the status quo, the devil they knew.

The unstated philosophy seemed to be, When the ship goes down, it's everyone for himself. Get what you could while you still could and then get while the getting was good. Except that that option was available only to a small minority. Most people were trapped, readily exploitable captive labor. What would the workers do? Would they stop working for a moment to say, hey, we need to do this now so things will be better for us later? Would they have solidarity with one another? People were pitted against each other, pitted themselves against one another, acquiesced, among other reasons because they had no intellectual defense, no way of making sense of the situation they were in that helped them to do anything about it.

It was hard to know what happened to the tension created by the injustice. If anything, it turned inward, upon the self, upon the family, more often than outward. Even someone with his hand on the pulse of the city could hardly detect whether or not anything was brewing, so subdued could the place seem, even when it was stirred up, even when it seemed as if it had reached a breaking point, so adept were HK people at hiding their thoughts and emotions. Several times over the course of the years, I found myself thinking, This is it. How can people take it anymore? Something's gotta give. And then, without much of anything happening, tension would subside, if only temporarily.

•

Now, I thought, finally, things must come to a head. There was a clear objective, genuine universal suffrage. If it was not reached, if it was once again denied them, would HK people finally rise up and demand what was theirs, affirm that this was their city and they would be the ones to run it? You'd think so, you'd hope so. But you never knew; you never knew with this place.

At the time of the handover, already some seventeen years before, the so-called Basic Law came into effect, a kind of constitution for the territory during the fifty years, until 2047, that it was supposed to remain a separate jurisdiction from the mainland. The Basic Law was highly imperfect, a hodge-podge, cobbled together, apparently self-contradictory in places, the sort of document you could fob off on a people when you didn't bother to ask them what they wanted, when you believed they shouldn't have a say anyway, which was the case with both Britain and the Partystate. HK people were children to be handed from one guardian to another, and you don't ask children what they want because you know what's best for them, or, to put it another way, you deliberately confuse your own preferences with what's best for them.

Among other things, the Basic Law said the territory could have universal suffrage. It didn't say when or how or what exactly that meant; indeed, all of that was up for grabs. Since then, the Partystate had put immense effort and resources into going back on the promise, moving the goalposts and changing the rules of the game, right down to redefining "universal suffrage" which had clear international legal definitions and standards, postponing its introduction as long as possible, indeed if possible indefinitely, and to making it as hard as possible to introduce. It should have become abundantly clear to everyone in HK that the Partystate had no intention of living up to its promise and legal obligation.

A typical bully, the Partystate was playing chicken with the territory: How much could it get away with? Just how little could you force HK people to accept? To what degree would they allow themselves to be cheated? It had already managed to put off the promise for seventeen years. Would HK people blink again? When push came to shove (and there was some pretty heavy shoving coming from Beijing), would the majority back down? I hoped they wouldn't, I feared they would. The thinking amongst the HK establishment, most of whom had interests linked to Partystate rule, was that the HK economy was so inextricably linked to the mainland's that HK was entirely dependent on the mainland for its economic well-being, and so, at the end of the day, could not afford to displease the Partystate, which might seek to punish HK economically. The other side of the coin was that however powerful the Partystate had become economically, it still needed HK. As a local paper put it, *HK remains a vital gateway for money and business in and out of the mainland and Beijing relies heavily on the city's financial markets as the main medium through which state-backed and private sector firms raise money from international equity and bond investors. More goods pass in and out of China through HK's ports as a proportion of the total than any other gateway, with two-way trade between the city and the mainland valued at US$401 billion last year, according to China Customs Administration Data. Analysts say Beijing requires stability in HK during the mainland's long-delayed programme of economic reform.*[3] Others believed Beijing had more at stake in showing HK who was boss. Having staked out very clear positions, it couldn't afford to lose face. If it backed down over HK, who was next? Tibet, East Turkestan, Taiwan? The empire could begin to fray at the edges. As so often with dictatorships, once you started tugging the first loose thread, the whole sweater could unravel. The dictator relied on obedience, needed complete control, ruled through compulsion rather than consent. HK was a test case, and a special case, because it was semi-free, the only place under the Partystate's jurisdiction in which it could not simply directly impose its will without at least the pretense that someone in HK was behind the decision. The current Partystate leadership appeared even more loathe to appear "weak" than previous ones.

The struggle was as much within each HK person as between HK people and the Partystate. There was contention between,

---

3 "Financial Secretary John Tsang calls for compromise on electoral reform", *South China Morning Post*, 5 May 2014

on the one hand, the pragmatist, the realist, the cynic, who said one was simply not in control of the larger forces of society, of history, and one should not pretend to be, one should remember one was no more than a small potato and the best one could do was to accommodate oneself to the world as it was, and all told, HK had done pretty well playing by those rules, and, on the other hand, the part that wanted more, that felt her city deserved more, that looked at the city as it was and saw that it was unjust, that there was a small number of people profiting enormously, in whose favor the rules of society were rigged (in the case of HK, this was tycoons, business interests more generally, Partystate officials, their supporters and loyalists and their business interests more specifically), and a majority of people who no matter how hard they worked were condemned to no more than just getting by (HK people often reminded me of *Le petit prince*'s Lamplighter, living in a very small place, condemned to constantly lighting and snuffing out his lamp as the place spun so rapidly that night and day lasted moments each. When Z and I were at the exhibition, I'd wondered whether anyone else saw the similarity), who saw that the basic rules by which society was run had to be changed so that they worked in favor of the majority's best interests, not the interests of the few, so that they were responsive to the needs and demands of the general populace, not those of a very few. This was the wrestling match that went on behind each and every impassive face one saw walking down the street, whether that face knew it or not. The Partystate was betting on the pragmatist/cynic in every HK person. I feared the Partystate was right; hoped it was wrong.

People most places just wanted peace, which in practice meant the freedom to be able to get on with their lives without undue interference. You had to really immiserate or drastically provoke them before they got out and did something to change their situation. As long as things were o.k., well, then, what was the fuss? Was it all really worth the effort (and sacrifice) to change something that could be worse? And as long as the worst wasn't upon you now, why worry about it? Didn't you just risk upsetting the existing apple cart for something that did not exist and you did not know what it was? I was reminded of Hamlet's reasoning as to why more people didn't just commit suicide—that dread of the undiscovered country... as well as of the price to pay to get there. The constant reactionary argument against justice framed it in terms of refraining from doing anything that could damage HK's economic "competitiveness," that could lead to "instability". It was an argument that, examined rationally, didn't make much sense but seemed to have a powerful emotional, almost visceral appeal, playing as it did more on people's fears than hopes. That was, after all, the cynic's eternal gambit, to seek to motivate by fear, to bet on that as the primary motivating force of the lowest common denominator.

Meanwhile, HK had to contend with a highly dysfunctional political system and perpetual political crisis. The Basic Law stated that "the ultimate aim is the selection of the Chief Executive by universal suffrage" (why not "election"? one might ask), and this would be "in accordance with the principle of gradual and orderly progress". The Partystate often stressed the need for "gradual and orderly progress", which was its way of saying, Let's put it off indefinitely. Neither the Partystate nor its factotum, the HK government had ever articulated a road map to universal suffrage, against which one could measure the extent to which "gradual and orderly progress" was being made. It was, like so much else in dictatorship, whatever the dictator said it was. International human rights law allowed for "progressive realization" only of social, economic and cultural rights (those that required substantial resources to realize, such as universal education), not of political and civil rights which, requiring no substantial resources to realize (ie, allowing people to speak freely didn't cost a penny), must be realized immediately. The Basic Law also stated that the International Covenant on Civil and Political Rights, to which HK was party by virtue of having been a UK colony, would remain in force after the handover. The ICCPR specified the right "to vote and to be elected at genuine periodic elections which shall be by universal and equal suffrage". To put it mildly, there was clear tension between the legal obligation to immediately fulfill this right and the fact that, after seventeen years, it still did not exist. Indeed, according to its own pseudo-constitution, the HK government was illegal, illegitimate, and would continue to be until the day it was elected by genuine universal suffrage. So much for "stability".

Just on a practical level, the current political system had proven unworkable. The Chief Executive (itself a horrible title for the head of city, as if the city itself were a corporation, and that's probably how those on top saw it) was selected by a committee of some 1,200 delegates representing for the most part various industrial, commercial and financial sectors along with some professional and political sectors. Only 150 of the delegates could be said to be popularly elected. So there was no substantial popular representation on the committee, and the vast majority of its members were, by design, loyal to the Partystate. In other words, it was thoroughly rigged to ensure the Partystate's will prevailed. That meant the Chief Executive selected by the committee had no popular mandate. On top of that, he could belong to no political party. He was isolated both from the electorate, the population as a whole, and the political establishment, or, to put it in other words, he had no political base whatsoever, except of course that he was the Partystate's man. So it was no secret whose bidding he did. He was supposed to represent HK to the Partystate but instead represented the Partystate to HK. He was supposed to be responsible for the well-being of the HK people but was politically and structurally beholden to the Partystate. At the same time, without a political base, he had little real power in the city. As a result, there was little he could actually do. And, politically speaking, the city simply stumbled from one thing to the next. The only things that kept it going were a well-functioning if stiffly bureaucratic civil service and, of course, the hard-working, orderly, law-abiding, disciplined HK people. Those who selected the Chief Executive were grey yes-men with little talent or vision. From the point of view of the Partystate, the main purpose of the government, of the Chief Executive, was to simply fill a space so that no one else, someone elected by the people for example, could. He was not supposed to make anything happen; he was there simply to make something not happen. This system might have worked well in its own unjust way when the territory was a British colony and there was no question but that the Governor was appointed by and answered to London, but it was entirely inadequate and dysfunctional, except from the point of view of ensuring that the Partystate's will was carried out.

But all that was about to change. Or was it? In order to head off calls for direct election of the Chief Executive by universal suffrage in 2012, the Partystate ruled in 2010 that the Chief Executive "may" be elected by universal suffrage in 2017. Now 2017 was just around the corner, and the HK government had just finished a so-called "public consultation" on methods to "select" (it seemed allergic to the word "elect") the Chief Executive in 2017 with an eye toward implementing what it called "universal suffrage". It was pulling a typical propaganda stunt: On the surface, its aim was to consult the public in order to find a means of "selecting" the Chief Executive by "universal suffrage", but in fact, it was taking its marching orders from the

Partystate, and ominous voices emanating from there had made regular-drumbeat statements making it clear that the Partystate had no intention to allow anything remotely resembling genuine universal suffrage (though it would insist on calling its subterfuge "universal suffrage", in the hope, presumably, of fooling or confusing some people, its cynicism knowing no bounds). It was set on ensuring that whatever "selection" took place would be a fake.

The way it had decided on dealing with the inconvenience of the promise of universal suffrage in the Basic Law was to deny it once and for all by foisting upon the city something called by its name that was anything but. In other words, it had decided it had avoided the issue long enough by indefinitely postponing it and instead would turn it to its advantage and make it a central piece in its efforts to establish ever firmer control over HK. In the meantime, it would continue to pursue its United Front strategy of systematically co-opting and undermining key institutions and sectors of HK society. It would resolve the question of HK's formal political structure once and for all while cementing effective control over other areas. It was a savvy strategy on the part of an organization that had over the years shown a certain genius when it came to control.

While it was prepared to allow a general election based on the principle of one-person-one-vote, it insisted on controlling who could run. Its objective was to get the people to vote for their own dictator: You can choose between dictator A, B and C. It insisted that the Chief Executive had to be "patriotic", a Partystate euphemism for loyal to the Partystate (one of its propaganda fundamentals was to consistently conflate Partystate and nation), a requirement that just about everyone agreed was inconsistent with international standards as well as law on universal suffrage. There was no stipulation in the Basic Law that the Chief Executive had to be "patriotic", but the Partystate said that it was an obvious prerequisite. It also insisted that the nominating committee stipulated in the Basic Law had to be essentially the same as the current misnamed election committee, stacked as it was with Partystate loyalists, in order to ensure that any candidates eventually presented to the "selectorate" were Partystate-approved.

The HK government was supposed to come up with an "electoral reform" package to be vetted by the Partystate. If the Partystate passed it, it then had to be approved by two-thirds of the Legislative Council, HK's pseudo-parliament, which was 50% elected according to principles of universal suffrage and 50% controlled by so-called "functional constituencies" the majority of which were—surprise surprise—Partystate-loyalist in the same way the Chief Executive election committee was. Then it had to be sent back to the Partystate for final approval. It was an absurd situation: An explicitly anti-democratic dictatorship assumed the position of final arbiter on democracy in HK. When was the last time a Communist dictatorship allowed genuine universal suffrage in any territory under its jurisdiction?

For the six-month "public consultation", supposedly to solicit views from the public, which it then would proceed to misrepresent to the Partystate, essentially just echoing the positions the Partystate had articulated, the HK government put out a so-called public consultation document that was intended to be the basis for the consultation. It adopted a chummy rhetoric, the slogan on the title page being, "Let's talk and achieve universal suffrage". It was meant to give the impression that we're all in this together and all we have to do is sit down and discuss in order to figure something out. But the public consultation period involved no talking at all, no open public meetings between government officials and the public. And the document did not so much as refer to the article in the

Basic Law that said HK had to follow the ICCPR, as if it were entirely irrelevant to the issue, nor did it make any reference whatsoever to international standards. When criticized for this, the Justice Secretary responded, *It may not be helpful to discuss an international standard [of universal suffrage] ... because there is no international standard as such.* Jaw-dropping: How could anyone, especially someone who presumed to be an authority on law, say such a thing with a straight face when, just for starters, Article 25 of the ICCPR was staring him in the face, in HK's very own Basic Law?

The whole process was a choreographed charade. Those who were used to the HK government's way of doing things were not surprised.

Opinion polls going back many years had consistently shown that over two-thirds of the population wanted genuine universal suffrage as a matter of urgency. And there was no shortage of creative ideas. Yet virtually any model proposing some modicum of genuine universal suffrage had already all but been ruled by the HK government and the Partystate in propaganda that attempted to portray entirely sensible proposals as "extreme" or "radical" or not in keeping with the Basic Law and to accustom public expectation to a result that would fall far short of genuine universal suffrage. There was a constant drip drip drip hectoring and bullying. The sub-text went like this: We'll give you universal suffrage as long as it doesn't look anything like that. And if you demand it, you are a "radical", an "extremist" bent on bringing "instability" to HK, "unpatriotic", undermining the authority of the central government. Up was down, black was white.

●

For years, I had believed that the only way HK people could ever get their basic political rights was by rising up and demanding them en masse. That was the only thing the Partystate, which understood nothing but power, could not entirely disregard. Only power could change the situation, and about the only power HK people had was the power to embarrass the Partystate in the eyes of the world, the power to make the territory virtually uncontrollable if the Partystate continued to refuse to grant the people what was rightfully theirs. (The Partystate didn't really care whether the territory was ungovernable, just if it was *uncontrollable*—two different things.) Whether or not HK people would actual do so was the eternal question.

They had not so far, or, perhaps, only on a single occasion, in 2003, when, six years after the handover, the Partystate and its underlings in the HK government tried to ram down the throats of the people security legislation which would have brought HK into alignment with the mainland and potentially infringed or drastically restricted many civil liberties. Ignoring protests, the Partystate and the HK government forced the matter, leading to a demonstration of 500,000, one in every fourteen HK people, against the draconian measures. At the time, there was still raw fear HK would quickly become just like the mainland. The Partystate appeared taken aback—it had been a long time since it had been so spectacularly, unequivocally and widely defied (fourteen years, to be precise). The demonstration made a pro-government party change its mind about backing the legislation, rendering it impossible for the government to pass it, and that lead to its shelving until an unspecified later date, which more than a decade later still had not arrived, as well as to the eventual resignation some two years later of the territory's first post-handover Chief Executive, supposedly for "medical reasons", though the man had been in perfectly fine shape ever since.

Since then, there had been demonstrations of hundreds of thousands on multiple occasions, and it had become clear that one-off one-day demonstrations were no longer enough to make the Partystate and the HK government heed the call of the people. From the debacle, the Partystate had learned not to provoke HK people needlessly, not to give them a clear target by, for example, waving a red flag like the draconian security legislation in front of their faces. Most of the time, it could get its way by taking far less provocative measures that flew beneath most people's radar, and indeed, since 2003, it had focused on building up its supporters in the territory through infiltrating various associations and organizations and funding front parties. Indeed, the largest political party in the territory in terms of members and funding, was the main Partystate-loyalist party. An indication of HK's perverse political situation was that it was the only place in the world where the ruling party was underground, the party which on the mainland had over 80 million members, trillions in assets and the largest military in the world as its own private militia, directly answerable to it. Technically, legally, it did not exist, and yet it was everywhere. It was often thought that, post 2003, with its redoubled and diversified efforts to control HK, the Partystate had managed to erode the will of HK people to assert their basic rights. When push came to shove—and what was coming up was definitely a push-comes-to-shove moment, the first time since 2003 that the Partystate was attempting to force the people to accept infringement of their basic rights—, would they? Would they assert themselves in sufficient numbers, in a variety of ways that went beyond one-off one-day demonstrations, over an extended period of time?

Colonial and immigrant mentalities were still predominant in HK. Decisions regarding the society were made by others a long way off and one had nothing to do with them and had no influence over them, so one should just keep one's head down and stay out of the way. Most everyone in HK had come from somewhere else, mostly places in the mainland, over the course of the last century, making HK an immigrant society par excellence. The immigrant thought, This is not my place. I have no claim to it. It does not belong to me. I have come here to work and get ahead. Both mentalities militated toward political passivity. Both mentalities said, Keep your head down, keep your nose to the grindstone, avoid political and civic affairs; they have nothing to do with you. Getting involved will only get you in trouble, and it will change nothing, or you might even end up making things worse, for yourself if not for others as well.

The question of whether or not HK people would stand up and demand what was theirs was tied to the question of whether or not HK had reached, or was about to reach, a tipping point regarding the colonial and immigrant mentalities that had affected people's attitudes so greatly up to now. It was sometimes said, HK will never attain democracy until all the old people die. Yours was one of the first generations in which over half of the people were born in HK. From your generation onward, these young people identified first and foremost with HK, thought of HK as their city, if for no other reason than because they knew nothing else. Unlike your father and his generation, they did not maintain ties to the mainland village from which they came, even decades after having left, and there was not a part of their identity that was forever related to their place of origin. This was their place, for better or worse; like it or not, most of them were stuck here. They tended to see things differently from their elders. They tended to regard the HK government and the Partystate with skepticism if not downright suspicion, to feel alienated from the powers that be, to feel they lacked a voice, to feel trapped in a society that was theirs but in which they had no say. In the decades in which HK was not yet a fully developed society and the economy grew rapidly, when there was still a burgeoning manufacturing industry in the city, there was substantial social mobility, which acted as a safety valve. Your average young person, if she studied hard and worked hard, expected to get ahead, to join the middle class, to lead a life better than that of her parents. But that was ever less the case; social mobility had decreased. And most young people had nowhere to go: there were few opportunities to go abroad for most, and they could not move upward. They felt stuck, and with that came frustration.

●

There was not a general political consciousness amongst young people, nor were they especially politically active. While many might feel jaded, disaffected, alienated, they, as young people elsewhere, lost themselves in consumerism, mobile phones, computer games, make-up. Looking at most young people in HK, one did not have much hope that things would get better. The girls seemed intent on being pretty, passive and helpless: Save me, rich man, take care of me. I may not have a thought in my head, but I make a nice pet. The boys had an autistic quality about them, obsessed with computer games and gambling. But looking at *some* young people, one did.

Apart from the 2003 demonstration against security legislation, the only other time when "people power" got the government to back down on a matter dear to the Partystate was in 2012, only two years previously. It was another Partystate pet project that the HK government attempted to foist upon its population, this time its children and young people no less. The whole thing began with an "imperial"-style visit to HK by Hu Jintao, the red emperor at the time. He made what appeared to be a rather off-hand statement to the effect that HK young people didn't know enough about China and he wished they would learn more. Who knows what actually lay behind the statement (perhaps from the moment he uttered it, there was a plan), but at any rate, in the old imperial tradition (your wish is my command), his simple pronouncement was taken as diktat, and out of it, the HK government spun plans for a new subject at primary and secondary levels called "national and moral education". I was certainly amongst the considerable number of educators and parents who thought that HK young people could stand to learn a great deal more about China. It was one of the most fascinating societies in the world, with a rich culture and history, and it was essential that HK young people know about its recent history and its politics. I was amongst the first to criticize HK young people for knowing and caring too little about HK, about China, about the world. But the question was what HK young people should learn about China and how. First of all, there was the problem of the educational authorities collapsing "national" and "moral" education into one subject: What did the two have to do with each other? The clumsy name of the proposed subject was a tip-off, intimating that it was "moral" to be "patriotic", and indeed, a lot of the purpose of the subject appeared to be to inculcate "patriotism" in young people from a young age, before they could really think. (One of the more notorious sample questions on tests of primary school students was, When a foreigner criticizes China, what should you feel? Amongst the choice of answers on the multiple-choice test were "shame", "indignation" and "pride". A lesson encouraged primary students to identify China as their "mother".) Given that a staple of Partystate propaganda was to equate "patriotism" with loyalty to the Partystate, it didn't take much of a stretch of the imagination to think that the subject was in effect a kind of indoctrination and the method and purpose of the subject would be similar to the sort of political indoctrination that was at the heart of education on the mainland. As it was, there was little faith in HK educational authorities to design quality curriculum of any kind, and their introduction of this subject seemed particularly ham-handed, lacking in pedagogical foundation and subtlety, to put it mildly. It was yet another piece of the boiling-the-frog-slowly strategy, gradually assimilating HK to mainland mentality, undermining the principles of the one country, two systems policy that was supposed to be in place until 2047. Still, in spite of the (to an educator) shocking ineptness of preparations for the course by educational authorities, it looked quite likely that the HK government would be able to sneak it through. And they would surely have been heartily congratulated by their mainland masters for the success. But at the last hurdle, they tripped.

Young people had been grumbling about their schooling for as long as I or anyone else could remember. HK education was still stuck in the colonial era and had never advanced from the initial accomplishment of achieving universal enrollment. There was much learning by rote, memorization, teaching to the exam. It was all about getting the right answers and interminable homework. Competition was ruthless, even at primary level students had hours of daily homework, scores on exams were published and students were ranked from best to worst. Unsurprisingly, HK was one of those places that perennially scored well on the PISA test, one of the most negative influences on global education out there. HK students were as a rule obedient and hard-working, and HK people valued education greatly. But you couldn't say that the system produced much more than literate, numerate graduates, fodder for a job market that would exploit them with low salaries, poor working conditions and poor labor rights and protections. They were poor at creative problem-solving, at envisioning different scenarios, at taking initiative, at examining issues critically. They lacked curiosity. They remained immature insofar as they were generally unengaged with the social and political issues that surrounded them. They were trained to take up low- and mid-level jobs in the strongly hierarchical capitalist, corporatist system that dominated the HK economy, to enter into the system without complaint or nuisance.

Or so it seemed and so it was thought.

At the time, students in secondary schools were beginning to organize. They were a minority, but they were an impressive bunch—passionate, dynamic, active, savvy. They constantly bumped up against school authorities, who were, as a whole, ambivalent, to put it mildly, about autonomous student groups in their midst. HK schools were rigidly hierarchical; in the way they were run, they expected a certain type of behavior from young people, which could fit quite neatly under the dictum, Shut up and listen. The groups were expanding; you could always expect to find a few dozen interested young people at any given secondary school. And this was at a time when the issue of national education arose. There was much grumbling amongst the students. Well, one said, why don't we do something about it? And they did. And what they did was a success far beyond what even they had imagined.

A handful of them formed a new group with the awkwardly (and brilliantly) unidiomatic English name, Scholarism. It denounced the new moral and national education subject and called on the government to cease plans to introduce it. The government, in typical fashion, refused to countenance the demand and simply went full speed ahead. Scholarism organized a sit-in at HK government headquarters, surrounding the main buildings. Before they knew it, before anyone knew it, a movement was born. The sit-in drew ever greater numbers of young people as well as parents, teachers and supporters from other walks of life, eventually growing in number to tens of thousands. Several young people went on hunger strike, in deliberate homage to the Chinese student demonstrators of eighty-nine. Scholarism had ignited an infectious carnival atmosphere.

A new HK government administration with no sense of ownership over the project, and therefore little stake in defending it, had just taken power. It did not want such intense focus on this one government initiative to draw attention away from and potentially derail its other priorities, and so, after weeks of occupation of the grounds around government headquarters, it ditched it, announcing in a semi-face-saving measure, that the subject would be introduced, but now it would not be mandatory for schools to teach it. The uptake amongst the hundreds of schools in the city turned out to be in the single digits, showing how little enthusiasm for the subject existed amongst ordinary school administrators and teachers.

The anti-patriotic-education young people represented, I hoped, the new generations. They had shown they were a new force to contend with, existing as they did entirely outside of established power structures, including those of the existing pro-democracy political parties. And they didn't go away. After torpedoing the national education subject, they turned their attention to the struggle for genuine universal suffrage, and would come to take a place at its very center.

●

The rise of Scholarism dovetailed with another initiative that came about not long after. The new HK government administration that had backed down on the issue of the national education subject had uttered virtually nothing about its intentions regarding "electoral reform", even though the supreme authority on the matter, the National People's Congress Standing Committee, in rejecting calls for universal suffrage in 2012, had ruled back in 2010 that election by universal suffrage of the Chief Executive "may" be introduced for the 2017 election. Democracy advocates began to express disquiet about the HK government's silence on the issue: Top priority it clearly was not; it was probably awaiting instructions from the Partystate on how to proceed. The fear was that it would try to get away with doing as little as possible, and leaving whatever it did as late as possible, to the very last minute.

At the start of 2013, a law professor by the name of Benny Tai published an article called "Civil Disobedience as a Weapon of Mass Destruction" in a low-circulation newspaper read by HK intellectuals. In it, Tai said that if the HK government did not introduce an electoral reform plan that included election of the Chief Executive by universal suffrage in compliance with international standards, HK people could "occupy Central", the main business district, in protest. Something about the timing of the article, perhaps—in the wake of the successful occupation by Scholarism and others of grounds surrounding government headquarters and in light of the lack of substantive democratic progress in previous electoral reforms dating back to the handover, with widespread dissatisfaction with the new, unelected administration from the outset—, made the idea take off in a way that previous proposals for civil disobedience hadn't. Out of it, a month or so later, a new movement was born, christened, again rather awkwardly in English, Occupy Central with Love and Peace, as if it were to be an anachronistic gathering of hippies, though if you looked at sober professor Tai and his comrades, you would see that nothing could be further from the truth.

Implied in the name of the group was an emphasis on Gandhian nonviolent spirit and action as well as a retort to anticipated smearing of it as illegal, or destabilizing, extremist, radical, even potentially violent—all of which were descriptions very predictably and quickly employed by the usual suspects, the HK government, the HK police commissioner, the Partystate, and pro-Partystate establishmentarians, the sorts who had forever been lurking in the shadowy corridors of power. Some of the critics of the proposed civil disobedience were those who supported the idea of universal suffrage in theory but seemed to think it could be brought about simply by elites sitting down together and hashing out an agreement. In other words, they were in favor of universal suffrage as long as nothing but nothing was disrupted, as long as business as usual prevailed. Which was to say, they weren't really at all in favor of it, since genuine universal suffrage would seriously disrupt the privileges the elites enjoyed. The prevention of genuine universal suffrage was so intricately tied to defense of elite privilege as to be synonymous with it. Ever since its inception, Occupy Central, as it quickly came to be known for the sake of brevity (but also because words like "love" and "peace" sounded peculiar in most HK mouths), had bent over backwards to emphasize its non-violent nature and its place in a long history of civil disobedience for just causes.

The three who started it, Benny Tai, another professor (of sociology) and a reverend who had been active in the democracy movement for decades, were all intensely moderate people, in fact, as it turned out, obdurately, exasperatingly so (again, the whole thing about strengths also being weaknesses and vice-versa, in this case, moderation). They constantly stressed the rational, deliberate nature of the initiative. The act of civil disobedience, the occupation of the central business district, was the last straw and would only be undertaken if the HK government failed to table an electoral reform plan that included election of the Chief Executive by equal and universal suffrage in compliance with international standards. The movement would start with a series of "deliberation days" that gave participants the opportunity to examine and debate different models of universal suffrage and to promote democratic culture, culminating in an online referendum to select a preferred model of genuine universal suffrage.

At the end of a months-long process, on the last scheduled deliberation day in mid-2014, a vote was held to choose three of the various models that had been advanced to put on the referendum ballot. The only criterion for consideration of a model was that it comply with international standards of universal suffrage. The plans had been vetted accordingly by a group of academics from around the world convened by Occupy Central. Occupy Central would stand by whatever plan got the most votes in the referendum in its demands to the HK government and Partystate, and that plan would be the standard against which to measure the HK government's eventual proposal: If it fell far short of the main demands of the chosen plan, Central would be occupied.

There was much criticism by so-called 'moderate' pan-democrats of the three options deliberation day participants voted for because all three contained the element of public or civil nomination, that is to say, that the public be allowed to nominate candidates as a means of ensuring that the "right to be elected", a crucial component of the international legal definition of universal suffrage, be respected. The moderates believed public nomination was not the only way of ensuring genuine universal suffrage, and they feared that demanding it was to risk confrontation with the Partystate and damage the chances of compromise. The Partystate and HK government had said on numerous occasions that public nomination of candidates would not be in compliance with the Basic Law, which according to their interpretation reserved that right exclusively for the Nominating Committee. But the Basic Law did not expressly rule out public nomination nor give any directions as to how the Nominating Committee was to function. The Partystate and HK government simply rejected public nomination out of hand though there were reasonable interpretations of the Basic Law that would allow for it.

The judgment that since public nomination was nowhere in the Basic Law, it had to be ruled out was all the more galling considering that the Partystate allowed itself the freedom to add requirements that weren't anywhere present in the Basic Law, such as that the Chief Executive had to be "patriotic" and not confront the Central Government. This coupled with the fact that neither the Partystate nor the HK government had made any assurances regarding how the right to be elected would be safeguarded without public nomination fueled fears that the Partystate and the HK government simply intended to rig the election: Yes, you can all vote, but only for the people we pre-select. The only difference they foresaw between the way the Chief Executive was selected now and the way he would be after the electoral reform was that the "selectorate" would rubber stamp one of two or three candidates selected by the Nominating Committee. It was diabolical ingenuity, to get the people to participate in and formally approve by ballot their own subjugation, to deny a people a right by superficially offering it to them. Was this the future face of "democracy"?

Even the Occupy Central founders, moderates themselves, appeared embarrassed by the results of their deliberation day vote. In pale imitation of their Partystate adversaries, "moderates" claimed the vote had been hijacked by "radicals". But "moderates" had no one but themselves to blame for that because the people who voted were the ones who turned up, and the moderates hadn't turned up, for fear of being branded—eegads!—"radicals" themselves by association with the "radical" Occupy Central. The tensions revealed generational differences: The "moderates" belonged to the older generations, and those who voted in the deliberation day were student organizations like Scholarism (theirs was one of the three plans chosen for the referendum ballot) and political parties with large numbers of young members. These generational differences in turn had as much as anything else to do with approach and attitude towards the Partystate. Young people were impatient and indignant, fed up with the endless deferral of fulfillment of promises made ("justice delayed is justice denied"), whereas older people feared needlessly provoking the Partystate and searched for a compromise that had eluded them for years (dictatorships, and perhaps politicians in general, don't compromise with those they consider weaker than themselves). In the eyes of "moderates," to present a proposal the Partystate had already signaled it would reject was counter-productive. Young people regarded the moderates' approach as spent, exhausted, invalidated by the experience of constant failure. The moderates had largely decided to take the Partystate at its word regarding universal suffrage (that is to say, that it would eventually get around to implementing it), and the result was that the latter was about to renege on its promise. How could those older people have been so naïve as to believe that a Marxist-Leninist party would ever allow genuine democracy? And even now that it was clear it wouldn't, how could they persist with the same approach as before? It was as if they'd never fully understood the nature of the beast they, and all HK people, were dealing with, not even now.

The "moderates," believing they spoke for a significant number of HK people, said that in putting only options that demanded public nomination on the referendum ballot, Occupy Central was essentially denying many people in HK a voice. They overlooked the fact that one of the three plans chosen in the Occupy Central deliberation day was by the Alliance for True Democracy, which was made up of 29 of the 30 pan-democratic legislators in the Legislative Council, thus representing the pan-democratic mainstream. The "moderates" crying foul at the deliberation day outcome threatened to decrease the turn-out for the upcoming referendum, and people feared that disunity in the pan-democratic camp could make it a less effective force in the fight for universal suffrage. Indeed, you could argue that in recent years the Achilles heel of the movement was its continual reflex to fracture, to magnify the differences within its own camp.

The Partystate and HK government were predictably making hay out of the squabble, taking the opportunity to try to brand Occupy Central "extremist" and "illegal". The anti-OC propaganda escalated and appeared coordinated. The HK government was made up of the most mediocre people one could imagine, careerists, opportunists, bureaucrats. Indeed, mediocrity seemed the main job requirement; well, that and fealty to the Partystate. I often wondered whether HK government ministers could really be so ignorant or were cynically deceitful—one could never tell which. The Chief Secretary, the government number 2 under the Chief Executive, warned HK people against participating in the referendum, declaring it, like Occupy Central itself, "illegal". The Justice Secretary stated mysteriously that the referendum could not make something illegal legal, though no one had undertaken any illegal action so far. The Secretary for Constitutional and Mainland Affairs warned that anything having to do with public nomination almost certainly would not be included in the government's eventual electoral reform proposal (at least that warning, unlike the previous two, was reality-based). All of these statements were attempts to dissuade people from voting in the referendum. Even the Education Secretary was getting in on the act, urging schools not to encourage their students to participate in Occupy Central. He even threatened teachers with potential dismissal if they participated. His statements were perhaps the best clue of the coordination behind the government interventions, since he had said something quite different only a year previously, namely, that schools should let students "develop their own thoughts" and his department would not "take any retrospective action against teachers" who brought students to Occupy Central events. None other than the Chief Executive had apparently appointed himself representative of business and finance (which, of course, was really what he was, but most in his position tried to hide that fact), for he declared that if Occupy Central went ahead, businesses in Central would sue its leaders for loss of revenue.

The quality of politically appointed HK government officials was exceedingly poor and getting worse. The ideal official was obedient, obsequious, competent but not so competent as to be threatening to their medium-competent superiors, never believing in anything for belief was a career liability, and therefore never voicing any sort of opinion that ranged outside the realm of the acceptable/respectable/conventional/elite-consensus, being as gray as possible, blending in, conforming, speaking a weird mixture of an amalgamated language which combined Partystate-speak, bureaucratese and corporatese, all three being made up of phrases repeated ad nauseam as positions, undefended by logical argumentation, until they one day found themselves in the bewildering position of being on top, bewildering because they were essentially bottom feeders who had floated upwards while others around them sank or drifted off, and the more these bottom feeders rose to the top, the lower the quality of government officials became, as almost the only criterion—or the most important criterion, the first hurdle—for appointment was blunt stupid loyalty. Upon reaching the top, they simply did not know what to do, being effectively programmed, so they continued robotically acting the same as before, unable to mentally make the transition in role from servant to politician, and being conditioned to always take orders and now being on top, they looked around for another master, and to their great relief, found that the Partystate, in its great wisdom, was more than willing to "guide" them.

So it was they harped on and on about the illegality of Occupy Central before Occupy Central had done anything illegal. True, it threatened a campaign of civil disobedience if the government did not come up with a plan for achieving universal suffrage that complied with international standards, but why wasn't more of their rhetoric, more of the words they spewed out to the public, focused on how they were going to achieve that, on how it was legally their responsibility to the people of HK to do so? If they did so, then there was no need to worry about any potential "illegality". And while on the topic of illegality, they could also note that, technically, according to the city's pseudo-constitution, their own government was illegal and the longer they failed to come up with a plan that fulfilled the promise of the constitution, the longer they themselves prolonged the city's political crisis of having an illegitimate government. It was strange—no, it wasn't strange; it was entirely predictable—that they spent so many words vilifying Occupy Central when its proposals, in contrast to their predispositions, were in line with international standards and its proposed action was nonviolent and inspired by some of the great leaders of the last century such as Gandhi and King, people who were often vilified at the time but came to be revered as icons of political morality (as well as being on the right side of history). I never ceased to be amazed that in every era, in every struggle for freedom, there was never any shortage of lackeys to do the oppressor's dirty work.

And anyway, I thought, if anything, HK could do with a bit more nonviolent, principled, and spirited illegality. It wasn't as if HK was on the edge of chaos; just the opposite: HK had just about the most law-abiding, orderly, disciplined, hard-working, responsible people I had ever seen. The image that came to my mind when these officials droned on and on about the illegality of Occupy Central was of the hundreds of thousands essentially self-policing demonstrators that turned out year after year at the June 4 candlelight vigil commemorating the democracy movement of eight-nine and the victims of the massacre that put an end to it. Where else in the world could hundreds of thousands gather in a political demonstration without any violence or destruction of property? In the vigil's aftermath, many ordinary demonstrators who were not amongst the organizers stayed behind to scrape wax from dripping candles off the concrete football pitches where the crowd had gathered. It was not a city that had to fear any breakdown in public order; it was not a people that would suddenly engage in a frenzy of violence. It was a place that had to break free from deadness of thought, political amorality, and the oppressiveness of the lockstep conformity represented by these officials. What they really feared was citizens taking the running of their city into their own hands.

It was a most suffocating environment, and the claustrophobia wasn't caused by the physical density of the city, the fact that one was hemmed in by crowds on all sides, that people lived in such small cramped places, but by the narrow-mindedness and pig-headed lobotomized unthinkingness that prevailed in places of power and pervaded so many areas of society. As a cultural force, the government was insidious, and the only hope was that it existed at such a great distance from the people that it ended up infecting them less than I feared. In contrast to the image of the civic-minded demonstrators scraping wax off the pavement after the vigil, when I heard these officials speak, what came to mind was the slogan of their public consultation document on electoral reform: *Let's talk and achieve universal suffrage.* But the consultation period involved no talk at all, no discussion, no debate, no dialogue arranged by the government or between the government and the population, no public meetings, nothing of the sort. The slogan about talking was ironically the defeat of language, for the real implicit message was, Language means nothing, therefore, your words mean nothing, and this exercise is no more than a charade. Language, in the minds and mouths of those officials, was no more than a tool of deception. While the public consultation supposedly involved solicitation and exchange of views, the officials responsible dictated to the populace, telling the people how to behave, what to think and not to think, what was "illegal" and not, what was acceptable and not, without any "talk" at all. Their cynicism or stupidity—again, I could never figure out which part each—was so astoundingly brazen that, mouth agape, I found myself thinking, There must be a special place in hell reserved for this sort of trespass. We were on the terrain of the banality of evil. Ultimately, their only real argument was power: We have it, you can't take it from us. It was, at bottom, as simple as that.

    I thought of my discussions with Z. *We want real universal suffrage*, I told her, *but the government doesn't want to give us real universal suffrage.*

    Why doesn't the government want to give us real universal suffrage?

    Well, I said, thinking carefully of how to phrase it, *they want to keep all the power for themselves.*

    Why do they want to keep all the power for themselves?

    Well, because they're greedy.

    Later, Z dictated a letter to the HK government: *Dear Government, Stop keeping all the power and give it to us.*

    Did these officials shake in their shoes at the insecurity of their position? Did they ever fear they could be held accountable for their actions? The answer circled back to the eternal question I asked myself: What part cynical and what part stupid were they? They knew HK was a potentially sinking ship; they were hedging their bets: Their children studied abroad, they parked their fortunes abroad, they had properties abroad; they could get out fast if they had to.

In comparing the discourse of the two sides, you realized there was little point of contact, little common ground upon which to even conduct a debate. It was principle versus power. The one side discussed in terms designed to answer the basic questions of the matter at hand: What is universal suffrage? What are the international standards? How can they be applied and realized here? The other side was interested in power: How can we ensure that we maintain power? The power discourse disguised itself behind euphemisms exhorting people to be "rational", "realistic", "pragmatic", code words for doing what the Partystate deemed acceptable. And that side had an array of lackeys whose purpose in making logically indefensible proclamations was to normalize the discourse of power, condition people to it. *There is no international standard as such.* If you heard that day after day and nothing else, and didn't bother to find out for yourself whether it was true, it had an effect on you.

To me, the controversy around the plans chosen for Occupy Central's referendum was a tempest in a teacup. Part of the deliberative process in a democratic culture was disagreement. Disagreement was not cataclysmic but necessary, and in democratic processes, disagreement is out in the open, transparent. If anything, if indeed the "moderate" pan-democrats hoped for a compromise (their own plans didn't include public nomination, instead focusing on making the Nominating Committee more diverse and representative, thus hopefully ensuring that a diversity of candidates could be nominated), I didn't see how they could get it without pressure from groups like Occupy Central, which threatened to step outside of the (rigged) system, to not play by the rules. The Partystate, understanding only power, would not simply say, Well, let's compromise, unless it felt compelled to. The "moderates", if they stood any hope of success, needed Occupy Central. My impression was that, as establishmentarians, they were simply used to having their way, having their voice heard, and they hated the prospect of their position being usurped by upstarts.

It seemed to me that much of the criticism directed at Occupy Central, whether by "moderate" pan-democrats or the HK government or the Partystate, was really an expression of animosity towards the young. They liked to talk down to young people, couldn't countenance regarding them as equals. The voice of the young was marginalized and went under-reported in the media because they were not among the establishment, the elite, the types who organized press conferences that journalists attended to get their convenient sound bite. The opinions of the young and the marginalized were inconvenient and would be ignored unless they forced the issue. They were learning to play politics. Because of its lack of democracy, HK politics had always had a polished, polite, packaged, entirely unspontaneous veneer, beneath which it was, of course, vicious. Anyone who traduced that unspoken agreement and exposed the city's politics for what they were—exceedingly undemocratic—, was excoriated by those complicit in maintaining the façade. All I could think was, Thank you, young people! Please keep up the good work! You are our hope! It was always more likely to be young people rather than old who would put their bodies on the line if civil disobedience ever occurred.

By the time of the referendum, you had already been gone for some time, but in the early days of Occupy Central, you and I were both excited when enthusiasm for it spread. Finally, we thought, perhaps HK people will stand up. It was hard to imagine how they might otherwise gain democracy without the sort of unequivocal demand that came from civil disobedience. It was certainly not going to be handed to them on a platter. We had long advocated civil disobedience without anyone being much interested. And now, Benny's article had struck a chord and things started to take off.

But it didn't take long for us to realize there wasn't much of a role for us in OC. They weren't nearly as inclusive or receptive to ideas as one might expect from an organization that not only was fighting for democracy but made a point of promoting democratic decision making and culture. I just couldn't understand why they wouldn't want to involve you, this amazing, young, articulate woman who, among other things, was good in front of crowds, projecting just the image they wanted, and a great strategist and thinker. Like so much else in HK, OC's organizational culture was dominated by hierarchy and control-freakery. I'd often been struck by this unresponsive element in the HK character. It was never, Hey, what can we do together? It was always the skeptical if not suspicious look one encountered. Given how pervaded the society was by mainland spies and informers, suspicion was not necessarily unfounded, but still, it was as much a matter of attitude toward collaboration as of secure operating procedure. When you offered your services, and I saw they didn't recognize what they had in you, or simply weren't interested, I started to suspect—and this was still early on—that OC would amount more to a small organization to serve as a platform for its three leaders than a true movement. Not that they intended it that way. It was just that OC, rather than being a great departure from standard operating procedure, was emblematic of a problem that the HK pro-democracy movement had faced for years. It was poor at organizing, mobilizing, scaling up, reaching out beyond the base of naturally ardent supporters to those who would be interested if anyone took the time to appeal to them, and it didn't even seem to recognize this weakness.

The two academics who played the lead roles in OC knew the history and theory of civil disobedience back to front. But that was one thing, and quite another to be a seasoned practitioner. Their lack of experience was somewhat balanced by their activist pastor counterpart, but he was also aging, in his seventies, and maybe not exactly on the cutting edge any longer. They ran the "movement" as if playing chess, but whatever else it was, civil disobedience was not chess. In order to succeed, the movement had to appeal to the grassroots, the fifty percent of the population who lived in the public housing estates. A civil disobedience campaign succeeded to the extent that it could demonstrate to those in power that it had sufficient power. The power could come from various sources, but in the case of HK, the only hope was the power of numbers. If you don't have money, then your power is people, and people organizing. They had to enlist thousands if not tens of thousands of active volunteers. They had to have a presence in every public housing estate, and a small committee in each responsible for communicating, for recruiting, for holding events, for getting people involved. Among other things, this empowered people to take responsibility: Either this was their movement, the people's movement, or no movement at all. That way, when the Partystate and the HK government and Partystate loyalists criticized OC, instead of standing on the sidelines and being their usual judgmental selves, people would say, Hey, you're criticizing us, you're criticizing me—back off! They would understand things from the inside, as participants, as citizens; they would understand how it felt and what was at stake. They would be making the city theirs even as they demanded it back. Political leaders in HK were just too concerned with control and they strangled their own initiatives with their control. OC leaders didn't appear to recognize their own strengths and weaknesses, nor the need to draft in others to complement their strengths and make up for their weaknesses. Not enlisting the masses left them isolated when attacked by the

Partystate. Whatever ordinary public housing estate residents might think (and they had a tendency to blindly criticize anyone who stuck their neck out—who does he think he is? He thinks he's so important!—as you often said, HK people had a penchant for "bitchiness"), they hardly identified with OC and therefore weren't sticking up for them because they didn't see themselves as part of it all. Yes, the OC leaders were deliberative and rational and measured, but they also had to realize that whether they liked it or not, what they were doing was inherently confrontational. The young people pouring in and "hijacking" the last deliberation day brought that home to them in a way that left them feeling uncomfortable, and it ended up being the beginning of a parting of the ways between young people and OC, a constituency they had to have on board to succeed. When I laid this all out to OC, I didn't so much as receive a response.

You agreed with me, but your main critique was a little different, if related. You thought, perhaps because OC was lead by academics, it was making things too complicated, with all these "deliberation days", and in so doing, playing into the Partystate's hands. Universal suffrage, you said, was really quite simple: Virtually everyone should be allowed to vote, virtually everyone should be allowed to run for office and be elected. It was not so complex as to need constant deliberation and debate, discussing the ins and outs of all the different models and possibilities. The Partystate's ploy was to make the HK political system so entrenched and complicated that people would just throw up their hands in despair at figuring it all out. Hog-tying, I called it, binding in so many knots and snags they can't be loosened; indeed, the more you twisted and turned, the tighter it got. You said OC needed to keep it simple, keep its messaging direct and to-the-point, something everyone could understand and get behind: We wanted *real* universal suffrage, and what you are offering is *fake*. We will do what we have to do to get what is *our basic human right*.

I agreed with you but could also see OC's point of view: Their deliberation days were meant to encourage the development of democratic culture. Their message was that democracy wasn't all about running out in the streets and shouting slogans, nor was it about doing nothing but voting and leaving everything else for others to do. It was about participating, learning to talk with each other in constructive ways, solving problems together, and the structure of their movement was meant to demonstrate this by experience to those who took part. But, yes, I also agreed with you: past a certain point there was little to say. The Partystate wasn't interested in dialogue, or in figuring out solutions. It was a dictatorship; it was interested in dictating. In that circumstance, you had to stand up and say, No, I won't be dictated to by you; you will listen to me, the citizen, in whom sovereignty, ultimately, abides.

•

But what did it matter? Why should people anywhere else care about one little place that could hardly make a case for being amongst the worst off in a world full of poverty, war, collapsing and failed states, and plenty of other places with much worse human rights records?

Whenever I had the opportunity to speak about HK to outsiders (not that this occurred all that often—HK was hardly a place people were dying to hear about), I had my stock argument: HK mattered because China mattered. As HK went, so went China. As China went, so went the world over the coming decades, the coming century, maybe longer. Democracy in HK mattered because democracy in China mattered. Democracy in China mattered because democracy in the world mattered. If

China didn't become democratic, the prognosis for democracy in the world was poor. The stakes were high. No wonder Beijing was determined to deny HK the democracy it was promised. You should care. You should all care. So I said.

Asia—South Asia, Southeast Asia, East Asia—in particular hung in the balance. The most populous, fastest growing part of the world, it could go either way. There were the solid democracies, Japan, South Korea, Taiwan; the largest democracy in the world, India, flawed but occasionally inspiring and not yet a lost cause; Indonesia, which looked to be going in the right direction, and maybe Mongolia too; Bangladesh which seemed to get some things right but also had major challenges; the Philippines which were easy to give up on but still stood a chance; Nepal eternally on a knife's edge; Pakistan which was just a mess; Thailand, which had suffered a major setback with the military coup; and then a slew of authoritarian countries like Vietnam, Laos, Cambodia and Burma, as well as Singapore, thoroughly neo-authoritarian, and Malaysia with much the same model. The region could easily become more democratic and just as easily more authoritarian. China would be influential in determining its direction.

HK mattered because democracy mattered. HK was on the front line of what I saw as a, if not the, major battle of the time to come, between, on the one hand, democracy and respect for the full panoply of human rights and, on the other, neo-authoritarianism of the sort best exemplified by China and Russia. HK was one of the few developed societies without democracy. People yearned to be their own rulers, to be sovereign, to make decisions for their own society, their own lives. But HK was controlled by the largest dictatorship in the world, which, quite rightly, saw democracy as an existential threat.

Sometimes I thought people elsewhere should regard Partystate neo-authoritarianism as an equally urgent existential threat. In the West, to the extent that anyone paid attention to anything outside of the West at all, heads were turned towards the Middle East, towards "Islamic extremism". To the extent that China was a story that mattered, it usually had to do with business, finance, economic growth. While amongst Western policy-makers, China was seen as a competitor and perhaps a military threat, it wasn't regarded as the major ideological adversary in the way that the "evil empire" of the Soviet Union had been back in the days of the Cold War. But in terms of democracy, China was arguably a bigger threat than most anywhere else in that it presented the alternative model of neo-authoritarianism, which not a few saw as attractive or compelling. Neo-authoritarianism had little ideological pedigree, usually consisting of some bastardized Confucian, Platonic mish-mash of an argument to the effect that wise, benevolent rulers were better guarantors of a people's prosperity and well-being than irresponsible democracy, even if and when it meant certain restrictions on "rights"; indeed, the premise of the model was that the centrality of human rights to a decent society had heretofore been overstated. The argument became more convincing when you recalled that most institutions in democratic societies (corporations, many other workplaces, schools) were run to a large extent along not altogether different principles. Don't get me wrong: The fault line wasn't only between democracies and dictatorships; it was also between democratic and authoritarian forces within most societies. In that sense, rather than countries operating according to an on-off toggle switch, either democracy or dictatorship, it was most accurate to consider them on a spectrum, with democracy and respect for rights on one end and dictatorship and abuse of rights on the other. The world could easily slide in either direction on that spectrum. It depended on places like HK, on the decisions and actions of people in such places.

But what was so great about democracy? Hadn't democracy fundamentalists like myself just unthinkingly adopted it as some kind of dogma? Democracy mattered not only because it was the fairest system of governance that had yet been widely realized and implemented (ie, it was road-tested) but because it was the world's best hope for a decent future. And there was reason to worry about democracy's future.

In recent years, various reports had characterized democracy as "in retreat", "at a standstill", "in decline", demoralized, deteriorating. The thinking went, first of all, the number of democracies was not growing as it had in previous periods, especially in the aftermath of the collapse of the Soviet Union; secondly, many of the countries that had formally become democracies or had looked to be moving in that direction got stuck in transition and had regressed into semi-authoritarianism or flat-out authoritarianism; and, thirdly, even the more mature and more firmly established democracies were facing challenges and setbacks, perhaps even decaying, in the wake of the so-called "war on terror" and the economic crisis. So there were weak democracies, troubled democracies, corrupted democracies, fake democracies. The number of out-and-out fake democracies (places where elections were clearly rigged and/or unfair; places where the institutions of, culture of and government commitment to democracy were insufficient or lacking), in particular, seemed to be multiplying. (Why even bother put such effort into being a fake? one wondered. The idea was that you were supposed to be democratic, it had become the reigning paradigm, so you had to pretend that you were, even if it was patently fake.) According to the Economist Intelligence Unit's *Democracy Index 2012*, in that year, there were 25 full democracies, 54 flawed democracies, 37 hybrid democracies, and 51 authoritarian regimes. Only 11.3% of the world's population lived in full democracies, while 37.1% lived in authoritarian regimes. Of course, China skewed the figures, given that something like one in six people in the world was Chinese, and if India shifted categories from flawed democracy, where it was now, to full democracy, that would improve the percentage of people living in full democracies considerably. But still, even if you compared the percentage of people living in full or flawed democracies to those living in hybrid democracies or authoritarian regimes, the latter won out slightly over the former, 51.5% to 48.5.

I agreed with these assessments of democracy's troubled times. It was hard to find encouraging news. In my view, the West had simply and spectacularly fluffed it in the two decades since the collapse of the Soviet empire. It didn't recognize the great value of its democratic traditions, though it thought it did because it constantly speechified about them, believing its own rhetoric with too little underlying commitment. It often seemed it didn't really understand how its own societies worked, what was valuable about them, or why they had been so successful for so long. And it didn't really put much effort, or the right sort of effort, into ensuring that the transitions that were supposed to occur, not only in the Soviet empire but elsewhere in the world—for the end of the Cold War set off political chain reactions the world over—actually did occur. It had a very superficial understanding of what democracy was, what it actually entailed, the institutions needed to realize and support it, the types of culture that had to be fostered, the political investment and solidarity needed to bring it about. For whatever talk there had been in the nineties of the supremacy of democracy, of liberal democracy being the "end of history", there was far too little follow-through.

When push came to shove, capitalism was more important to the powers-that-be in the West than democracy, and that's where most efforts went, into creating more markets, into globalizing capital, internationalizing and deregulating finance, shifting ever more production to the cheapest (read: those with the fewest labor rights and environmental regulations) places they could find. At its moment of truth, when it had a once-in-who-could-guess-how-long window of opportunity to truly flourish and expand, democracy was hijacked by capitalism. Imagine if as much effort went into a world democracy organization (or even a world trade, labor and environment organization) as into the World Trade Organization.

It appeared that for the most part, the democracies didn't even notice this happening, or if they did, they didn't care much. To use the American expression, they took their eye off the ball. The balls they were focused on were mostly trade (in the nineties) and terrorism (in the early years of the new millennium). And anyway, free markets would lead to free politics before long, by necessity, right? A false and intellectually lazy equation was made between democracy and capitalism, when in fact, rather than being in league with each other, there was great tension between the two. The relationship was at least as much conflictual as complementary. Capitalism resembled authoritarianism more than it did democracy, as a look at most corporate workplaces would show. It was democracy's duty to so regulate capitalism as to ensure that the benefits that accrued from the economic growth it had a pretty good track record of bringing about were widely and fairly distributed, to the good of society as a whole.

HK was a typical example of a place where capital and democracy seemed the fiercest of adversaries, the tycoons and their minions firmly allied with the Partystate in the struggle to deny to the people their basic human right to genuine universal suffrage. It was not for nothing that two times running HK ranked first on *The Economist*'s crony capitalism index. Hardly a rabble-rousing anti-capitalist rag, it also reported that 15 families in HK had assets equal to 84% of GDP.

And so, while you now read of democracy being in retreat, in deterioration, in decline, demoralized, you rarely read the same of capitalism, even after the economic crisis, when if there ever were an opening for alternatives, it was then. The domination of the economic and financial powers that be had even contributed to a partial hollowing out of strong democracies like the U.S. and E.U.

There was no better example of this turn of history than the China story. Post-Tiananmen-Massacre, China was a pariah. But not for long. There was too much money to be made there. China was well-placed to capitalize on globalization. One thing the Partystate had done relatively well in its early decades when it was also killing tens of millions was to provide basic education and health care, and the result was that compared to many developing countries, it had a relatively well-educated, healthy, and—not least important—huge population. And it had an authoritarian government which, while nominally communist, did not respect the most basic labor rights. All at a time when capital and corporations were being freed up to roam the world looking for the best returns. And so China became the world's sweatshop, a sweet deal for dictators and capitalists. As much as you could say that the Partystate had relatively sensible macro-economic policies (which was true, with the emphasis on "relatively"—the job that so many other countries did being pisspoor), you could also say it simply got lucky, the timing was right. Global factors beyond its control came together to make it the best placed to take advantage of the changes. And the money poured in so fast, the people in whose pockets it ended up didn't know what to do with it. And whatever you thought of its political system, it was a force that had to be reckoned with. Its economic growth had rendered China indispensable. This economic growth fueled largely by exports made possible by neoliberal globalization helped to solidify the Partystate's power, both in the sense that most people were leading markedly better material lives than in eighty-nine with more freedom in their personal lives and so were more willing to put up with the "externalities" of dictatorship (thought it was constantly a question of how long this could last, given the myriad ways that corruption, injustice and environmental degradation impacted a large percentage of the population directly and concretely) and in the sense that both the Partystate and the powers-that-be within it became immensely wealthy, operating the country like a Mafia syndicate, an extortion racket, where, in exchange for outward loyalty you were, at the very least, left alone to get on with your life or, in the case of Party members and fellow travellers, allowed to benefit from political connections. This turn of events was accompanied by some of the most insipid (and often self-interested) political theories and analyses in the West, such as the policy of "engagement", according to which, economic integration would necessarily lead to a flourishing middle class that would demand political change, bringing about, eventually, an open political system. When this failed to occur, when indeed the urban middle classes that benefitted most from the economic growth were amongst the most conservative supporters of the system, Western analysts were baffled. Some even began to think that there was something to be said for an authoritarian system that produced economic growth on the scale of China's because, so the thinking went, those who did not have to face an electorate could plan long-term, concentrate on the big picture, though it was hard to see how, even if you assumed it was a good thing, it could be replicated or sustainable. So, instead of the wave of democracy sweeping over China, economic changes brought about by political decisions in the West had led to the prospect of China being able to exert an authoritarian influence abroad. The joke was on who? Me, I often thought. Since, it seemed, a great many were perfectly content to live with this state of affairs that drove me to distraction.

There were of course places of hope, places that had made or were in the process of making impressive transitions. There always were; hope was always there if you looked for it. Taiwan was significant as the only majority-Chinese society that was democratic. For you and me, Taiwan was a revelation. The last trip we made before Z was born—we had just learned you were pregnant; what would soon become Z, or was Z already, was already you, so it was her first trip, and our last as what we called in those days "free people"—was to Taiwan. Somehow, not just the people but even the air was freer there. Tunisia had fought through many challenges and looked poised to establish itself as the only country thus far able to make a transition from dictatorship in the Arab world. South Korea was another East Asian neighbor that had made impressive progress. And I'd been impressed by South America: A wind of democracy blew across the continent. It was hard to imagine Argentina, Chile, Brazil returning to dictatorship. A few of the eastern European countries were in the process of successful transition. These places— Taiwan, Tunisia, South Korea, Argentina, Chile, Brazil, Estonia, Poland—geographically and culturally diverse, showed that democracy was possible everywhere, as did, hopefully, Indonesia, the biggest majority-Muslim democracy.

But while there were some up-and-comers, the historically strong democracies of North America and Europe appeared to have lost confidence in themselves, and it seemed you could only find truly thriving, healthy democracy in small pockets. Even paragons of democracy like that Northern Paradise had shown signs of tripping. Nothing represented to me the West's lack of democratic self-confidence and the way that business interests continued to prevail over other considerations more than the recent visit of the Dalai Lama to that Northern Paradise. The occasion of the visit was a celebration of the 25th anniversary of the awarding of the Nobel Peace Prize to the Dalai Lama. Ever since it was awarded, both the people of that Northern Paradise and their government had been staunch supporters of the Dalai Lama and the Tibetan cause, and on every subsequent occasion when the Dalai Lama had visited, he had met with government representatives. On this particular occasion, though, no one in the government met him. Ever since the award of the Nobel Peace Prize to Liu Xiaobo, the first Chinese to ever win, the Partystate had punished the Northern Paradise government by cutting off all high-level governmental contact. A new Northern Paradise government was desperate to re-establish relations and had been warned by the Partystate against meeting the Dalai Lama. It caved, even though some members of government had previously been members of the parliamentary Tibet Committee and outspoken supporters of the Tibetan cause. There was not even any immediate reward for being a good little country. And there was little evidence that Northern Paradise businesses exporting to China had suffered from the Partystate's temper tantrum. Nevertheless, it caved. While in the big scheme of things, the Dalai Lama's visit was not the most momentous of events, I wondered whether the whole sorry episode couldn't be seen to be symbolic of a potential historical shift in power relations. It was hard to imagine back in eighty-nine, when the Dalai Lama received the prize and the Partystate massacred its own people in the nation's capital that such a thing could ever occur. And now it had. One of the world's internally strongest and deepest democracies had caved to its largest dictatorship, over pretty much nothing at that.

Since then, a new democracy, South Africa, had refused a visa to the Dalai Lama (he'd become a kind of shibboleth) to attend a conference of Nobel Peace Prize laureates. In protest, some other laureates boycotted the conference, the result of which was postponement and relocation to Rome, where the Pope refused to meet the Dalai Lama, in the hope that the refusal would help the Vatican (all right, no democracy that) to improve relations with the Partystate. Elsewhere in Democracyworld, after getting spanked by the Partystate for meeting His Holiness, David Cameron took a pass on the next opportunity and was supposedly rewarded with fat contracts for UK businesses.

So the world spun. It seemed at a kind of impasse. It was hard to know which way it would go. There were plenty of grounds for pessimism, if one so chose.

When it came to belief in democracy as the sine qua non of a fair, just, decent society, by no means did I assume I stood on the side of firm consensus, as I might have a couple of decades earlier. Indeed, when looking West, what was most striking were the jaded, skeptical, relativistic if not downright cynical and often very pessimistic attitudes towards democracy, on the part of not only cultural critics, political pundits and journalists but also large sectors of the populace.

And not without reason. In the US alone, according to one commentator, *This is what democracy looks like: grotesque inequality, delusional Tea Party obstructionism, a vast secret national-security state, overseas wars we're never even told about and a total inability to address the global climate crisis, a failure for which our descendants will never forgive us, and never should.... In America, democracy offers the choice between one political party that has embraced a combination of corporate bootlicking, poorly veiled racism, anti-government paranoia and a wholesale rejection of science, and another whose cosmopolitan veneer sits atop secret drone warfare, Wall Street cronyism and the all-seeing Panopticon of high-tech surveillance.*[4] And that was just for starters: the political system was corrupted

---

4 "This is not what democracy looks like: The long slow death of Jefferson's dream", Andrew O'Hehir, *Salon*, May 18, 2014

by money. Crazy campaign financing laws equated money with free speech. When you factored in the influence of business and financial interests on politics and the gerrymandering of electoral districts, you could be forgiven for wondering what was left of democracy.

Across the water, Europe wasn't doing much better. The E.U. had always had its large democracy deficits, to put it mildly. Its institutions existed at a great distance from its citizens, especially the overly powerful and opaque Commission. It had its accomplishments. It ensured peace (no mean feat, to say the least) and, to some extent, enhanced material prosperity (though the case for this was certainly less clear in the wake of the financial crisis) at the price of weaker democracy. Relatively passive citizens were willing to hand over the reins to it as long as their economies did well and they benefitted materially, the old Consumer Syndrome. But in the wake of the crisis, the E.U. had done even less well than the US in recovering economically and its leaders had lacked the ability to respond to citizen concerns and European problems or to reform the system in any substantial way. In terms of quality of life, security and deep democracy, many northern European countries were still far and away the best in the world, but the people there didn't necessarily see it that way. There was the rise of right-wing, anti-immigrant, hyper-nationalist parties in Sweden, Denmark, the UK, France and even the Northern Paradise (indeed, its anti-immigrant far-right party had just, for the first time ever, entered into a coalition government, a state of affairs that was impossible to believe could ever occur only a decade before). There was a sense of malaise. In recent years, I had met a significant number of Swedes (Swedes!) and Danes (Danes!) in their twenties to fifties who expressed skepticism about their social democracies. My invariable response, which I didn't always voice, was, You don't know how good you got it; you should appreciate all of your accomplishments, cherish them, protect and cultivate them. If you don't, they could indeed disappear. But these skeptics were looking at their societies from the inside, and they didn't look as good to them up close as they did to me from afar.

I didn't have any airtight response to the disillusionment with current-form democracy in the West, the logical conclusion of which was the prospect that the struggle for democracy was chimerical, a fool's errand. Democracy was certainly imperfect, by nature, and that, along with its accomplishments, was an important part of its history. All I could say was that democracy was a continual struggle everywhere, always had been and always would be; people should have no illusions that it could be otherwise. Exactly when was the golden age of American democracy? The century of slow-burn genocide of Native Americans? The era of slavery? Or the following century of institutionalized racism? The history of democracy in the U.S. was the history of the continual struggle of groups and individuals for equal rights and participation in the political process. I had recently come across the following words of Nehru, written decades before the Indian freedom struggle was won, decades before he became the first prime minister of the largest democracy in the world (another which struggled to live up to its promise, with its deeply entrenched casteism, corruption and poverty): *Present-day democracy manipulated by the unholy alliance of capital, property, militarism and an overgrown bureaucracy and assisted by a capitalist press has proved a delusion and a snare.*[5] How much and how little had changed!

Cliché it may be, but democracy was only as good as its people. In Rudolf Rocker's words:

Political rights do not originate in parliaments; they are, rather, forced upon parliaments from without. And even their enactment

---

5 From an unpublished review of Bertrand Russell's *Proposed Roads to Freedom*, as quoted in *The Life and Death of Democracy*, John Keane (p605)

> into law has for a long time been no guarantee of their security. Just as the employers always try to nullify every concession they had made to labor as soon as opportunity offered, as soon as any signs of weakness were observable in the workers' organizations, so governments also are always inclined to restrict or to abrogate completely rights and freedoms that have been achieved if they imagine that the people will put up no resistance. Even in those countries where such things as freedom of the press, right of assembly, right of combination, and the like have long existed, governments are constantly trying to restrict those rights or to reinterpret them by juridical hair-splitting. Political rights do not exist because they have been legally set down on a piece of paper, but only when they have become the ingrown habit of a people, and when any attempt to impair them will meet with the violent resistance of the populace. Where this is not the case, there is no help in any parliamentary Opposition or any Platonic appeals to the constitution.[6]

And anyway, what was better than democracy? What was the alternative?

I was under no illusion that democracy would be a panacea for HK; nor was anyone else. On the contrary: I imagined that if and when it came about, its inception would be followed by a period of disillusionment, as was often the case elsewhere, and it would face multiple challenges, including its capture or compromise by anti-democratic forces, whether Partystate or business. But I thought that as a governing principle and system, it might be fairer; it stood a better chance, or no worse, than the current system. But what kind of endorsement was that from one of its biggest supporters, especially in the face of its detractors? All I could say was that genuine universal suffrage was a basic right, both legally and morally speaking; freedom, equality, fairness and rights were worth fighting for;

---

6 *Anarcho-Syndicalism: Theory & Practice*, 1947

and democracy, overall, had a better track record of protecting and advancing those than any other system of government.

Often, exhibit A in my defense of democracy was its inspirations, its heroes, people doing amazing things to further the cause of democracy in just about every society, in just about every crack and crevice of society, in schools and criminal justice systems and health care systems and bureaucracies and formal politics and social movements and service delivery organizations. The list went on and on, of ordinary people doing extraordinary work for the good of their communities, societies, polities, practicing what had been aptly dubbed "trench democracy"[7]— people down in the trenches doing the unglamorous work that put flesh on the skeleton of democratic theory and aspiration. However compromised or dysfunctional democracies might become, as long as they provided the space for people like this to operate, to innovate, to improve, there was some hope.

●

So that was my long and not entirely convinced or convincing argument for democracy, for democracy in HK, and for why the rest of the world should care about democracy in HK. But the rest of the world was largely uninterested, or only intermittently interested, distracted, had other, more pressing concerns. Things were always more urgent, more dramatic and/or worse elsewhere. When I spoke, the reception was polite, no more, no less. The most you could expect was to get the world to train its eyes on the territory at key moments, so as to let the Partystate and HK government know the world was watching and they couldn't pull a fast one, though they would still try. To the extent that other countries had HK on their radar at all,

---

[7] *Boston Review.* See "Trench Democracy: Participatory Innovation in Unlikely Places", Albert W. Dzur, October 11, 2013

it was low priority on their China policy. Trade was top priority; indeed, it overwhelmed all others.

So HK was more or less abandoned by the "international community". It was on its own. What chance did it have when it came to that?

HK's only chance was to stand up en masse in a campaign of civil disobedience, which was by definition outside of the existing system, for that system was compromised and rigged, meant to contain and neutralize opposition, not channel it.

Predictably, in response to Occupy Central, which was as yet more a prospect than a reality (I often joked it would hold the Guinness world record, if there were such a record, for being the civil disobedience campaign that existed the longest without committing an act of civil disobedience), there had been rumbling threats of violence like far-off thunder. The threats were almost always oblique, along the lines of, If Occupy Central occurs, violence could result. What? Out of thin air? What was meant by that? Not only was Occupy Central an explicitly nonviolent campaign and its participants would be trained in the practice of nonviolent civil disobedience, but it was hard to imagine any considerable number of HK people turning violent. It just wasn't in them. Through years and years of demonstrations that sometimes reached the hundreds of thousands in number, there had never been any violence (apart, of course, from the demonstrator convicted of assaulting a police officer by whistling too loudly), not since 1967, when leftists inspired by the mass insanity of the Cultural Revolution across the border set off bombs and fought pitched battles with police on city streets. (One of those leftists was now the pro-Partystate president of the Legislative Council, HK's pseudo-parliament. Another, his brother, was a minister in the government—they had been "domesticated" and brought into the fold of establishment power in exchange for their loyalty.)

Violence, this abstraction. As if it could dispense with an

agent, a violator. This was violence as nothing but specter. Stupidity reigned, and it was hard to tell how much was intentional (ie, propaganda, meant to make people stupider) and how much not (ie, stupidity, the genuine article). Violence the specter was convenient to trot out whenever people demanded their rights. Was it supposed to mean they shouldn't? Or to suggest that somehow they were wrong to demand their rights if there was the potential of a violent response? That, perhaps, even they would be responsible for the violence inflicted upon them, since, obviously, if they hadn't demanded their rights, the violence never would have occurred?

Given that the chances of demonstrators turning violent were exceedingly slim, the allusions to violence had to do with the presence of the People's Suppression Army, which happened to have its HK garrison headquarters right in the middle of the city, a few hundred meters from the heart of Central, and, significantly, right next to the new HK government headquarters.

Indeed, some Partystate stooges were more explicit and had intoned rather loudly, full of the paranoid and belligerent rhetoric that was the Partystate's hallmark, that the People's Suppression Army would stand at the ready and act if called upon to do so. *Anti-China forces are using the Occupy Central movement to try to seize control of HK's administration. The People's Liberation [sic] Army will intervene if riots break out in the city. We cannot allow HK to turn into a base to subvert China's socialist regime under the guise of democracy.*[8]

I liked that: "anti-China forces". Who were they? Foreign, homegrown? No evidence was provided. This was a standard Partystate rhetorical trope, to invoke "anti-China forces" as an all-purpose bogeyman, partaking of nationalistic discourse whenever it suited. When the Partystate henchmen employed

---

8 Paraphrase of comments made by Zhou Nan. See "Occupy Central being used by anti-China forces to try to seize power, warns former Xinhua official", *South China Morning Post*, 8 June 2014.

the term, "anti-China", they meant anti-Party. In adopting the rhetoric, the Partystate lay the foundation of justification for any eventual intervention or crackdown. For, of course, any country would protect its sovereignty at all costs, would it not?

Also "under the guise of democracy". Democracy was, after all, nothing but a Trojan horse. Here, the Partystate was right: Democracy in HK could very well mean the beginning of its end.

It was striking that in the run-up to the referendum, the Partystate calculated it would be more effective to scare people away from participating with the distant threat of violence than to just be quiet and ignore it, pretending it didn't exist, consigning it to non-existence. It was a strategy that suggested the Partystate was either worried or over-confident, and it carried with it significant risk, for another possible outcome was that it would provoke people to see the Partystate's true repressive, bullying nature and convince them they needed to stand up to it. As ever, the dictator was cynical, calculating that people would be more motivated by fear than principle.

This rhetoric was especially brazen in the twenty-fifth anniversary year of the Partystate's massacre of its own citizens, when last they rose up en masse to demand their rights. Eighty-nine threw a long shadow across all events, inflecting every word spoken, every action taken on both sides. Back then, when the People's Massacre Army mowed down its own people, liberating them from their lives, all of HK was horrified, regardless of political opinion. Indeed, some of those most worried were the capitalists themselves, and those who worked for the capitalists. The agreement to transfer HK from the UK to the Partystate had already been made. Everyone knew the "handover" would occur in ninety-seven, only eight years into the future, and all they could imagine at that time was that at midnight on the first of July (the anniversary of the founding of the Chinese Communist Party, the "return of HK to the motherland" being the Partystate's birthday present to itself), the tanks would roll over the border and into the streets of the city. All those who had the means and connections procured for themselves citizenship and residence in other countries. They made sure they could move both their capital and their persons at a moment's notice. Only the captive masses would remain. So it was with a collective sigh of relief that the first of July nineteen ninety-seven came and went without hardly a soldier in sight except at the official ceremonies attended by all manner of villains.

And ever since, the People's Suppression Army had remained exceedingly discrete, never emerging from barracks in uniform. Indeed, it was said that the soldiers were not allowed to leave their compound and mingle with the people at all, whether in uniform or not. The PSA was an invisible presence. The headquarters was so silent, regarding the city with an impassive, inscrutable stare, it was hard to detect any life within at all, which, of course, made it all the more sinister: What were they doing in there? What could they be plotting? An estimated 6,000 troops were stationed in the city, a great many, it seemed to me, given that the garrison had much greater symbolic than military significance, there, essentially, ostensibly, to assert sovereignty. I never entirely shrugged off the horror that the very army that had massacred its own people in the empire's capital city (and had never been held accountable for its crimes; in fact, just the opposite—it was rewarded for protecting the Partystate from the people—hey, someone's gotta do it) had this invisible presence in the heart of the city. I wondered whether, unbeknownst to virtually everyone, the garrison included troops trained in crowd control, in handling riots. One of the reasons the People's Suppression Army was so brutal in eighty-nine, the thinking went, was that the troops sent into the city were very young, predominantly from the countryside, and trained for combat, not for dealing with large numbers of unarmed nonviolent civilians in urban areas.

So they approached their mission the only way they knew how, combat style. Since then, the Partystate had significantly beefed up the People's Armed Police, the entity charged with defending the Partystate from the people. This entity was supposed to be trained to deal with crowds. Were there any of these soldiers amongst the garrison of some 6,000?

Just a few years before, during the enforced disappearance of Ai Weiwei as part of the Partystate's widespread crackdown in the aftermath of anonymous internet calls for a Jasmine Revolution, "flash graffiti" of a stenciled image of the artist with the caption, "Who's afraid of Ai Weiwei", was video-projected onto the outer walls of the barracks. A spokesperson for the People's Suppression Army HK Garrison, which rarely said anything at all (speak softly and carry a big stick), was provoked to issue a statement: *Military facilities of the garrison and walls are not usual public areas but military restricted zones or protected areas according to the HK law. No one can paint or project pictures and images onto the outer wall of the barracks without the garrison's permission. Such an offence is a breach of HK law. The PLA [sic] reserve its legal rights*, presumably to act as it saw fit to "defend" itself against this "attack". It was laughable to hear the People's Suppression Army interpret the law, and indeed, most legal and political authorities, eventually even including the HK police, said that no law had been broken. It must have been a source of great frustration for the People's Suppression Army that people they would usually mow down mercilessly were untouchable except through some mysterious mechanism called the law, which, outside of the mainland, could not necessarily mean anything it wanted it to.

It was a sign of just how nervous HK people were at the possibility of the deployment of the People's Suppression Army that a very brief incident of trespassing on the grounds of PSA headquarters by four or five young people waving the old colonial flag got substantial media coverage. They simply entered an open gate and waved the flag until the police came and took them away. The soldiers stood nearby watching them. They obviously posed no security threat, but that a few kids waving a flag in a military compound could cause such a stir showed how edgy the city was. The elitist, establishment English-language daily intoned hysterically against "radicalism", again, the sub-text being, Do nothing to provoke the troops! I couldn't help but laugh out loud at the warning against "radicalism": in the heart of the city was an army that had slaughtered hundreds if not thousands of people to protect its political master, an illegitimate government insofar as it ruled through the barrel of a gun—how "radical" was that? And this august publication was worried about a few kids running around waving a flag? A great many were thinking, without saying so, that the stupid kids were lucky they didn't get shot. Virtually everyone thought it highly unlikely that the People's Suppression Army would take to the streets and terrorize the population, but the mere possibility cast a shadow over everyone's consciousness and calculations.

It was a strange place that way. Violence constantly lurked on its edges but rarely erupted. It was the safest, most nonviolent city in which I'd ever lived. This was even more remarkable considering it was in a very violent part of the world. For starters, it was part of a country ruled by the Partystate whose defining feature was violence, maintaining as it did its monopoly on power "through the barrel of a gun" as the Great Helmsman himself so aptly put it. It was an oasis of peace and safety (not least of all for women— many other cities were distinctly uncomfortable or downright dangerous places for women to walk, especially unaccompanied) thanks to its disciplined, repressed, orderly, law-abiding populace. To the extent that it was violent, its violence was more often than not turned inward, on oneself, on one's family. Violence was latently present; the constant question was, could it, would it erupt any time soon?

The fear of violence, chaos, disorder sat deep in the bones of any Chinese of a certain age, since much of twentieth-century China could be characterized by those features, and HK as a city in its current form was arguably shaped above all else by people seeking refuge from that violence, chaos, disorder as well as tyranny. They understood that life was fragile, that one should never underestimate the possibility that it could very quickly be taken from you, along with all else. Pro-Partystaters played on these deep-seated fears by raising the prospect of violence in connection with Occupy Central or, indeed, anything the Partystate would not countenance. The sub-text of the message was: You do not want to be like those many places in the world where violence, chaos, disorder reign, do you? And so it was that HK's standards and expectations were lowered: It was constantly comparing itself not to any vision of the place it could be (for according to those standards, it failed quite miserably) or to other places of a comparable level of development and prosperity but to places experiencing the calamities it had avoided, just as the Partystate had managed to retain its monopoly on power up to now because most people compared their lives materially today to those of just three decades ago, rather than comparing the current state of affairs to the way things really should be. Thus the specter of violence constantly hung over the most nonviolent, safe, peaceful city in a violent, dangerous, belligerent part of the world. And occasionally things occurred like the cleaver attack on the newspaper editor as if just to remind HK people what could happen if they didn't behave themselves.

In this sense, what obtained in HK, in the Partystate's China, was "negative peace". There was not justice, there was not freedom, there was not respect for and protection of basic rights, there was not rule by consent let alone democracy and effective popular oversight of the government, but there was not the senseless violence that could erupt at any moment and therefore was the most terrifying of all. It was not Pakistan; it was not those parts of Mexico most affected by the drug war. But China was just a step removed from that, from the chaos of the earlier part of the twentieth century when the state was too weak to impose its will, from the terror of civil war and Japanese occupation, from the state-inflicted mass violence of so much of the Communist era, insofar as rule was backed by implicitly threatened violence.

This was at a time of increasing militarization of the country as a whole, and not just in the most obviously occupied areas of the empire, Tibet and Xinjiang, but even in the capital. To supposedly guard against terrorism, APCs rolled through the streets of Beijing in the days leading up to the 25th anniversary of the massacre. Every year at that time, a variety of "suspect elements" were placed under house arrest or taken on trips away from the capital or very closely monitored, but the usual June 4 crackdown was harsher this time around, with hundreds rounded up, and quite a few charged with actual crimes, "creating a disturbance" being the one the Partystate was currently most fond of. Indeed, some people meeting in the confines of their own homes to commemorate the anniversary in private were arrested and charged with that crime. Violence, the threat of state violence, lurked everywhere.

●

As the 25th anniversary approached, commemorative articles, reflections, statements, photographs, videos appeared, ceremonies and demonstrations took place everywhere except where the events of eighty-nine occurred—*that* place continued to be a black hole of memory.

As much as I consumed the words, the moving images, participated in the commemorative activities, there was a part of me that remained aloof. Everyone had good stuff to say, profound stuff, important stuff, but the words lead nowhere, lead to no action, changed nothing, were facing backwards, towards the past. I found myself more concerned with what had not occurred. Elsewhere in the world, on the very same day, an equally important anniversary was to occur, also the twenty-fifth. On the very same morning that People's Suppression Army troops were mowing down the citizens, the first-ever free parliamentary elections were held in Poland. Solidarity won. Five months later, the Berlin Wall fell. Two years later, the Soviet Union collapsed. Just as Communist dictatorship was coming to a definite end in one part of the world, it was being reinforced in another. Contrast of contrasts, irony of ironies, our failure brought into full relief by the success of others, a failure that continued every day, day after day, perhaps even unto our death.

Twenty-five years have gone by, we have all grown old. But Tank Man in these pictures is still so young. From far away, his white shirt looks like a lily in summer, pure and unblemished. Tanks stopping in front of a lily. A historical moment, a poetic moment.... You are made of steel, I am flesh and blood, come on down, shithead! said Liao Yiwu, paraphrasing Tank Man from the former's exile in Germany, Liao that most Chinese of writers driven abroad, having eluded the Partystate's clutches in a dramatic escape after his friend, Liu Xiaobo's imprisonment. The soil of Europe, I thought, must be desolate for one such as he who had found continual inspiration, and trouble, in his native land.

Z and I visited the new June 4 Museum. Though it had been open for some time and I'd done some work for HK Alliance, the organization behind it, I'd not yet been. The occasion that finally brought me there was the book launch of *Closed Gate*, a story by Sayed Gouda, an Egyptian who'd been studying in Beijing in eighty-nine.

"Museum" was a rather grand name for the 800-square-foot space in a nondescript old office building. It was billed as the first permanent exhibition on the events of eighty-nine in the world. HK Alliance had been able to purchase it thanks to the many small donations made at June 4 candlelight vigils over the years. Under what was surely political pressure, the building's owner's corporation was suing the museum for improper use of space. I was made to sign in with the building doorman and show my ID. He rather apologetically claimed the rule only applied on weekends, but also said in passing that only twenty visitors are allowed at any one time, due to safety concerns, of course. The location was strategic: Though the building was hardly a prestige address or even prominent—you had to search for it in a side street—and the museum didn't have any street sign to alert casual passers-by to its presence, this in a city where neon proliferated like tropical foliage, it was in Tsim Sha Tsui, a part of town frequented by mainland tourists, not far from the gaudy jewelry shops and electronics stores where they shopped. In its first month, it had seen 7,000 visitors. If you divided the number of visitors by hours of operation, it was slightly over the limit of 20 at any one time.

Of course, mainlanders were its main target audience, since their access to information about the events was blocked. For me and others who knew what had happened, it contained little new. But for Z, it was new. We saw video of the Goddess of Democracy being destroyed by troops, looked at night images, dramatically illuminated by flash, of bloody young bodies being carried frantically to medical assistance. Z was not upset by the images of violence or of people in pain. She had already in her short life witnessed enough suffering and death to know that they existed. She was not like the Buddha exiting his palace for the first time at the age of 29, shocked to see old age, illness and poverty. She was just saddened. She asked why the soldiers killed the people. Exactly, I thought, that's the question, but said to her, *The soldiers did what their leaders told them to do. Their leaders didn't want democracy, didn't want to share power, so they told the soldiers to kill the people who wanted democracy.*

Afterwards, Z said that for Halloween that year, she would dress up "as the government", her friend Ramona would be "policemen" and another friend Nahanni "soldiers". Her "Halloween song" would be, *Leung Chun-ying* [the incumbent HK Chief Executive], *soldiers and policemen are in a tank, trying to find people to kill. Out came the sun and dried up all the rain. Democracy, democracy, no democracy. I want real universal suffrage! People fight really hard for democracy. Leung Chun-ying, soldiers and policemen are in a tank trying to find people to kill.* She sang it over and over, and I would often find her absent-mindedly sing-songing it while trying to construct a building out of magna-tiles or painting a picture. The combination of the current Chief Executive and the June 4 massacre, the collapsing of the eras of Beijing circa eighty-nine and HK circa fourteen, and the itsy bitsy spider all in one ditty was pure genius. Z hadn't even known the word "tank" before visiting the museum. She had been especially intrigued by the famous image of a couple on a bike hiding from tanks in a bridge underpass. She asked to see it again and again on my computer. She wondered if they eventually managed to avoid them. I don't know, I said, but I think they did.

I had thoroughly indoctrinated my child.

Once *Closed Gate* was published, Beijing Normal University revoked its invitation of Sayed Gouda to be a visiting professor. It had come perilously close to welcoming a subversive into its midst.

Gouda, for his part, was caught between a rock and a hard place, which is to say, two dictatorships. He described his most recent visit to Egypt as the scariest of his life. Arriving after midnight, from the airport to his parents' home, he was stopped at four military checkpoints. At each, he had to unpack his suitcases before the soldiers' eyes. None of the checkpoints had any light. It was pitch dark and the soldiers were threatening. The only light available for the search was from Gouda's own mobile phone. By the time he arrived at his parent's place towards daybreak, he'd decided he never wanted to return.

At the annual June 4 march, always held on the weekend before the candlelight vigil, there was a smaller turnout than usual, perhaps due at least in part to it being the hottest day of the year, some thirty-three degrees. On the pavement, under the sun, it felt even hotter than that. Still, I thought more would have felt the need to come out and be counted, especially given the fact it was the twenty-fifth anniversary.

The march had something of the stale feel to it that many HK Alliance-organized events had come to have in recent years. Perhaps I'd just grown too familiar with them, but they changed so little, they were like time capsules, had become ritualized, for better and worse. Even the slogans shouted were the same year after year: Vindicate June 4!—what the hell did that even mean? I didn't even agree with that, as if we should care about the dictator's version of history; we should simply repudiate it. Democracy in China! End one-party rule! Free Liu Xiaobo, Free [fill in the blank—whichever human rights defenders had been most recently detained]! Granted, the repetition was a form of determined constancy and perseverance, of not allowing memory to fade, not allowing forgetting to occur, a sign we would never give up. But it had lost some of its passion and nearly all of its spontaneity over time. It was underwhelmingly unimaginative, like a horse circling the mill, a donkey treading an ever-deeper rut on its accustomed path. Especially in the 25th anniversary year, I thought, there should have been something special. Of course, the new special thing was the museum, and a lot of effort had gone into that. Also, people to whom I expressed this criticism said that I shouldn't allow the fact I'd been around for a while to cloud my view; it was easy to forget how moving the vigil was to just about everyone who experienced it for the first time.

I helped Citizens' Radio solicit donations at its usual place along the march route on the corner of Tang Lung Street and Hennessy Road, rattling a donation box in front of passing marchers. It felt good to once again be amongst the ranks. Occasionally, I missed the old days of the weekly human rights radio program you and I had hosted in the years before Z was born. The Bull was up on the platform shouting slogans about Gandhi and the duty of civil disobedience. I was always impressed that so many older people, obviously people without a lot of money, dropped twenty-dollar bills in the donation box.

When it came to civil disobedience, Citizens' Radio was the HK veteran. It had now been broadcasting eight years without license, in defiance of the government which refused to issue one to the station. The HK government claimed there was not enough bandwidth for it, even though HK had fewer radio stations than almost any other major city in the world. It claimed that Citizens' Radio was not a viable operation, even though they had proven they were, continuing to operate all those years in the face of constant government harassment. In fact, the government had a prejudice against any independent, non-commercial community radio, and in recent years, other stations had simply circumvented it by launching online. Citizens' Radio had outlasted the police, who appeared to have just given up on raiding them and confiscating their equipment, as they had done regularly in the station's early years. I remembered its bare-bones studio on the top floor of a Chai Wan warehouse, surrounded by the little of what was left of the HK manufacturing sector; the rag-tag group that kept the station running year after year, voluntarily putting in long hours, virtually all of their free time, I guessed. When I asked the main technician how it was going, he chuckled and said, *No one listens to us any more; the government stopped raiding us because we're no longer a threat.* The station used to have the most eclectic programming in the city, and all sorts of programs that couldn't run on mainstream stations: young people on youth affairs, LGBT people on LGBT news and issues, radio hosts who'd been banned from government-funded radio and who were too "controversial" for the private stations, and us, with the city's only weekly program dedicated to human rights.

The march came and went before I knew it, so small was it this year—several thousand, as opposed to the tens of thousands I would have expected—, and I chatted with the usual Citizens' Radio gang, most of whom I hadn't seen in a while. They were strikingly friendly. The emotional solidarity was a refreshing balm. HK was not a town of ebullience; people tended to be standoffish, reserved, even those with whom one might expect to have the most natural affinity. The Citizens' Radio people were different. They made me nostalgic for what seemed a simpler time in our lives.

Where's Ying-Ying? they asked, calling you by your radio pseudonym (they knew neither your actual name nor your work pseudonym). It sounded like the name of a panda, and just hearing it again made me laugh. The question reminded me there were still many whom, even after all that time, I hadn't told. Your disappearance was such an all-encompassing reality, I often forgot how closely the secret had been held, for how long. Even before you had been disappeared, for security reasons, your life had been so compartmentalized that often one group you worked with didn't know about your work in other areas. The Bull was one of the few Citizens' Radio people who knew what your "real" job was, for you had helped him file a complaint with the UN Special Rapporteur on the promotion and protection of the right to freedom of opinion and expression. I suspected news of the complaint was one of the main reasons the HK government had decided to shift from actively harassing the station to just ignoring it. (I was often struck by the number of people I came across whom you'd helped in one way or another big or small.)

I told them what had occurred. They were shocked, and predictably outraged, to learn you had been disappeared. *I am still hoping she'll come back soon*, I said, even as they excitedly hatched plans to launch their own rescue mission. *Don't do anything yet*, I advised. *I'll be sure to let you know how it goes.*

Those people were like Opal, spirited, fearless. I had no doubt that if given the word, they would make an attempt to save you. But they were used to dealing with the HK government, an entirely different (that is to say, largely toothless if petty and nasty) beast from the brutal Partystate, and like so many activists focused on HK, even though they knew the dictatorship across the border influenced virtually every aspect of HK life, they were naive about it; they didn't entirely understand, to put it simply, the sheer depth and power of the evil. (Something about the Partystate had a gravitational pull on language, constantly tugging toward the fantasy genre. I would normally resist using that metaphysical descriptor, evil, but it was the first word that spilled out of my usually reticent mouth to describe the phenomenon of such a powerful entity that would stop at nothing to retain its monopoly on power.) During the years of "Get Up, Stand Up", our radio show, "Ying-Ying" and I would frequently discuss mainland and global issues that I assumed all those at the station would be familiar with—they were active citizens, after all—, only to be told on a regular basis how much they learned just from listening to us. It was a weakness of the HK activist community, its parochialism, its exceedingly partial knowledge of what went on just beyond the tiny territory's borders. I could understand they didn't know the specifics of events in, say, Syria, but they weren't even particularly well informed about the situation on the mainland. Then again, these were street activists. They had no fancy degrees. Their English was poor to non-existent. They worked blue-collar jobs or ran small businesses on slim margins and spent all their extra time at the station.

The Citizens' Radio people had made a plywood tank painted to resemble those used by the PSA in the eighty-nine massacre. Walking alongside the slow-motoring vehicle, we hurried to catch up with the tail of the demonstration. At intervals, especially when media cameras descended upon the tank, the Tank Man scene was re-enacted, a solitary man with plastic shopping bags in hand standing in front of the plywood tank. It looked so quaint, so different in scale from the epic scene on which it was based, the effect was comical; people smiled, charmed by the contrast. Nothing brought home to me more clearly how those already-long-ago events and images had become mythic, larger than life. It seemed, too, a good analogy to the relationship between the eighty-nine demonstrations across China and the current struggle for real universal suffrage in this tiny corner of that vast land—everything here happened in miniature.

I came across Chang Boyang. I'd consulted him about your case, and he'd recommended your eventual lawyers. He'd been on a fellowship at an HK university over the past year, more than any other reason to get away from Beijing, the epicenter of the ongoing crackdown. During the first part of the fellowship, he and his family had actually lived in Shenzhen, and he commuted daily across the border. Then Xu Zhiyong was arrested. The two of them had known each other since law school and worked together on some of the initial rights defense campaigns, such as the successful one to abolish the custody and repatriation system more than a decade before. Many considered that a milestone marking the beginning, or at least the first major accomplishment, of the rights defense movement, and it had fueled some optimism that peaceful gradual change could occur. Being ever-vocal, Chang Boyang spoke out against the Partystate's attack on his friend. Indeed, throughout the seemingly never-ending series of crackdowns on the multitudes of moderates, especially lawyers and academics, Chang Boyang had been one of the few who had, on a consistent basis, openly, loudly and freely denounced the Partystate in no uncertain terms. With Xu Zhiyong's conviction, under pressure from his friends, he decided it would be safest to stay entirely away from the mainland for some time, and he and his family moved from Shenzhen to HK. He hadn't tried going back across the border in months. His fellowship at the HK university was about to end. For some time, it had been unclear where he would go next. The HK government would surely not allow him to remain in the territory without a connection to a university. Fortunately, he had recently landed another fellowship at a prestigious US university for another year, thanks not least of all to a recommendation from you.

Is your family going with you? I asked.

Yes, he said.

Oh, that's good, I said. *That's very good.*

His wife and two young daughters were also on the march. I'd never met them before. He was excited, a bit distracted. He hadn't been on many HK demonstrations, wasn't as jaded as I. You couldn't do this stuff on the mainland, after all. He ran up to the front of the demonstration to meet the leaders; he wanted to see whether he could arrange to give a speech at the vigil. One could hardly devise a more certain way of incurring the wrath of the Partystate. Always off after more, I thought, as I watched him run ahead, and realized he hadn't asked about you. He was scattered, frenetic, had other things on his mind. To him, perhaps, you were just one of the many he knew being held hostage by the Partystate. Looking at his daughters next to their mother, I couldn't help but feel a bit sad, for Z, for you, for myself. Take good care of them, I thought. Don't go running up to the front of demonstrations and leaving them behind.

The march terminated at the gleaming new, forbidding, people-unfriendly and quite hideous government headquarters on the harbor, cut off from the rest of the city by a highway (with deliberate intention, buffering itself from the people), next to the PSA headquarters (symbolism obvious). Shouldn't it be *there*, I thought, the demonstration terminates? After all, that's the institution that killed the people we're remembering now.

Even before the obligatory declaration concluding the demonstration was finished, the march organizers on the rostrum not attracting much attention or enthusiasm, I noticed a commotion at the back of the crowd. Scholarism, the HK Federation of Student Unions and League of Social Democrats (LSD for short), with plywood tank and coffin in tow, were peeling away. The police initially looked set to prevent them from proceeding, as they had on previous occasions—these things all had a pattern and often seemed rehearsed, choreographed—, but eventually, not only did the police let them through but facilitated their progress along the three-kilometer route to their destination, the Central Government Liaison Office. The police had obviously received orders from their political superiors to, if at all possible, avoid confrontation or provocation or anything that could provide media fodder in these weeks preceding not only the twenty-fifth anniversary vigil but also, this year, the Occupy Central referendum.

They had a track record of doing stupid things leading up to the vigil, actions so reprehensible that they motivated even more people to turn out than otherwise would have, an effect their political superiors wanted to avoid at all costs in this crucial year. Perhaps the zenith of their buffoonery was the confiscation one year of not one but two replica Goddess of Democracy statues, under the claim that the exhibiting group did not have the relevant "entertainment license" to display them in public and that they were a danger to public health—they could fall over and injure someone. It was unwitting performance art—the police carting off by truck not once but twice the very figure that had been destroyed by PSA troops on the morning of June 4. The police seemed like puppets in someone else's show. Could they really be so oblivious of the ironic symbolism of their actions, or did they just not care? It was the old blurry line between stupidity and arrogance amongst the governing elites that I could never quite parse. The pro-democracy press, what little there was left, had a field day, with headlines like "Goddess of Democracy Arrested by Police", "Goddess of Democracy Kidnapped Again", "Police Hold Two Goddesses of Democracy Hostage", "Goddess of Democracy Forcibly Disappeared by HK Police".

In a demonstration brilliantly conceived by The Bull against the confiscations, you posed as an all-white Goddess of Democracy, dressed in a white gown, face and hands painted white, along with several other women in similar Goddess garb. You each stood stockstill, holding torch—which resembled more a soft-serve ice-cream cone—aloft in twenty-minute relay shifts. Everyone waited with baited breath: Would the police confiscate the live Goddess of Democracy statues as well? If not, why not? The police, outed, cornered, but of course refusing to admit they had been wrong, eventually returned the kidnapped statues in a face-saving compromise that HK Alliance allowed them—HK Alliance could have them back as long as they weren't displayed publicly before the vigil. A newspaper photo of you as Goddess of Democracy, torch lifted to the sky, still hung above my desk. I looked at it often, these days especially when you, and not just a statue, actually had been kidnapped. I remembered you complaining of how strenuous it was holding the torch high, though it was made of styrofoam, for your twenty-minute shift. At the end of the evening, after several shifts, your arm was sore. The vigil turnout that year was the highest ever, surpassing even the years immediately after the massacre. The police were determined to avoid such an own goal in this, the 25th anniversary year.

I followed the "radical" contingent. The proceedings at HK government headquarters had been so rote and dull, I wanted to be with the energy, and be a witness in case of any untoward behavior on the part of the police. (I could hear you say, even as I walked, You get too excited by anything with even the whiff of trespass and confrontation. Whenever I got in altercations with the police, it was always *me* you would criticize!) Several hundred strong, the young marchers electrified the air. They had patiently followed their elders and were now going their own way, literally. Some of the slogans they shouted were the same—they didn't disavow their elders (though they did have a preference for some of the more assertive, such as, End one-party rule!, which had somewhat fallen out of favor with some of the vigil organizers in recent years, a sign of the air leaking from their balloon)—, but others were different, much more with-it, incisive, politically savvy, forthright, in keeping with the moment: Keep the spirit of the demonstrators of eighty-nine alive! The eighty-niners were civil disobedients! You won't get public nomination without civil disobedience! Stand up; don't beg for universal suffrage on bended knee! In eighty-nine, they weren't fighting for the Basic Law!

Yes, I thought, and yes. *These* were the people keeping the spirit of eighty-nine alive, for they were not "well-behaved" (in spite of being, just like the eighty-niners, very polite and upstanding and proper, towards the police and all others), not doing what their parents expected of them, but taking up the responsibility of being citizens, which could at times include—as they well understood—the responsibility of civil disobedience. When it was a question of unaccountable government, it was up to *them*, these young people, to hold it accountable. It was young people taking responsibility for confronting the misbehavior, the lack of ethics and principle of the old.

Their slogans reminded me of how circumscribed the ambitions of the long-term struggle for democracy had become, even as it was characterized as "radical" by its enemies and by the establishment. Or, to put a more positive spin on it, how very moderate, patient, forgiving and forbearing the democracy struggle had been, perhaps too much so. Many of the older pro-democracy figures had actually been initially enthusiastic about HK's "return to the motherland" back in the eighties. From this point in history, it was often hard to imagine how they could have been so naïve as to conflate patriotism with recognition of legitimacy of the Partystate government. (Then again, back then, many thought the Partystate wouldn't be around for much longer.)

Apart from that, the starting point of most of the pro-democracy movement was acceptance of the flawed Basic Law, already a concession. The debate surrounded its interpretation: Was this proposal in line with the Basic Law, was it not? The more fundamental issue, though, was that HK people had never had any say in the handover from the British colonialists to their new colonial masters, the Partystate, never had any say in the Basic Law; it was never put to a referendum, nor were the people consulted in any way. (The Partystate would counter that there were some HK people, including even some pan-democrats pre-eighty-nine—after eighty-nine, they all resigned—, but these functioned in their capacity as private citizens, not as representatives, and once drafting was completed, the document was never put to the populace for so much as consultation, let alone formal approval by referendum.) And yet this was the document to which they were supposed to refer, the authority on constitutional matters. It wasn't *HK people's* constitution. So if you really wanted to be "radical", to get to the roots of the matter (as opposed to what was called radical in the establishment media, meaning, simply, that you demanded genuine universal suffrage, not the fake variety), you would say, Hey, wait a minute here; let's back up: First we have to decide whether the Basic Law is o.k. or we want to come up with our own constitution. Questioning whether or not the Basic Law was legit was tantamount to sedition in the eyes of Beijing. (Indeed, it most likely would have legally constituted sedition in HK if 500,000 people hadn't come out on the street in 2003 to protest against the proposed draconian security legislation that would have aligned HK with mainland security law.) This history had been obscured by subsequent events. And these young people, who were too young to experience it themselves, were the ones rescuing it from oblivion. One should not forget that history, which had disenfranchisement at its roots, whatever one adopted as one's bargaining position.

These young people had no illusions about "patriotism", the Partystate or the Basic Law. Watching them, I thought of what Hu Jia, in his typically delightful and also, for his own security, worrying way, said: *If this country really wants to change, well, if two million people went out onto the streets of Beijing, the CCP would start to shake. If five million went out, just in Beijing, they would fall. Right now we're lacking a desire to get on the street, to feel that this society is their responsibility.* Yes, both in the mainland and HK, the situation looked dire because the governments were determined to deny their subjects their basic rights, but at the end of the day, it was because people were not willing to do what these young people were doing, stand up and be counted. Occupy Central's declared aim was 10,000 participants, which from one angle seemed pathetically low. I'd like real universal suffrage, a great many seemed to think, as long as it's no skin off my back.

Godbless these young people, I thought, as I walked alongside them, these very ordinary-seeming, ordinary-looking young people from ordinary backgrounds with fire in their belly, righteousness in their hearts. These people are the future. If anything is to change for the better in HK, it will be down to people like these. I wanted to kiss them all. If only, I thought, they could ever reach critical mass.

I was reminded of Ahdaf Souief's recent comment about young people in Egypt at what was by then a very depressing juncture, dictatorship having returned with a vengeance, turning the clock back to Mubarak's time or worse just three years after the revolution had got off to a promising start. Many of the young people who'd played integral roles in the revolution were now sitting in prison. Soueif said, ... *the political system is built on the... idea... of people coalescing around leaders in hierarchies. The struggle is to invent a new system while the old one is attacking you, bad-mouthing you, murdering and imprisoning you. Watching the young and listening to them during these last few days of untrammelled deceit, vulgarity, inefficiency and jingoism, I brimmed with admiration: friends jailed and murdered, dreams mutilated, exhausted beyond limit, they were still astute, clear-eyed and funny. They may have lost this round, but they're no losers.*[9] What did it mean that I identified with them, that I continually identified more with such young people than with my agemates? Did it mean I just refused to grow up, was perennially immature, couldn't see the bigger picture, let emotion get the better of me, could not

---

9 "Egypt's revolution won't be undone: the people still have the will," Ahdaf Soueif, *The Guardian*, 30 May 2014

think strategically, insisted on living in a dream world? Or that I had retained passion, idealism, independence, some sense of what really mattered?

The police facilitated the raucous procession all the way to the Liaison Office, and then, predictably, as on so many other occasions, the stand-off began. They said the plywood tank could not pass; it was too big. This was standard police practice at this flashpoint, the invention of some excuse to prevent protesters from proceeding. An elevated flower garden had been built out front of the headquarters to reduce the amount of already meager space to demonstrate, and the police had further reduced this by erecting a kind of corridor with metal barriers through which all had to pass as if running a gauntlet, or like cows through a chute. It was a clear restriction of the right to freedom of assembly in the name of security, even though there had never been a serious security incident of any kind in front of the building (apart from Opal inadvertently spraying a security guard with champagne, for which she was charged with assault, a case the prosecution later dropped as quietly as it could). But the savvy tank-makers had been here many times before and had measured the width of the police corridor to ensure that the tank could fit. They were trying to demonstrate this to the police, insisting that it be allowed to pass along with the rest of the demonstration, including the coffin, which on previous occasions had not been allowed to pass for the same reason, although on this occasion the police had no objection to it. Such inconsistencies merely fueled perceptions of arbitrariness.

When the demonstrators tried to shove their way through the phalanx, they handed the police their opportunity on a silver platter (or, to put it another way, tricked them into committing the very sort of act they'd been ordered to avoid): The police converged upon the plywood tank like a pack of jackals on wounded prey, and with amazing swiftness and efficiency smashed it to bits. It was the surreal irony of the kidnapping of the Goddess of Democracy all over again: HK police smash a tank modelled on the kind used to terminate demonstrations in Beijing in eighty-nine, plywood pieces flying left and right. When they were done, all that was left was the young man who had been the tank driver with green helmet, standing there bemused, smiling, denuded of his plywood armor. But the joke was on the police: The press had gotten their front-page photo for the following day.

As I watched the pieces of plywood flying up into the air and descending to the ground, the police retreating from their frenzy, all as if in slow motion, scenes from the past, all having to do with the defacement and destruction of political art, overlapped like old film newsreels, as if history were a series of Russian dolls, one episode encased by another.

I thought of the words of a PSA commander in eighty-nine recalling the moment when, on the night of June 3 going on June 4, the soldiers attacked the Goddess of Democracy in Tiananmen Square: *We used iron bars to smash it several times until our hands hurt. I looked closely and saw that the statue's head had already been shattered beyond recognition.*[10]

And then I thought of the three young men from Hunan who in eighty-nine threw thirty-some eggs full of red paint at the infamous portrait of the world-champion murderer hanging on Tiananmen Gate. Student demonstrators, wishing to distance themselves from the vandals, turned them over to the police. The three were convicted of sabotage and counter-revolutionary propaganda and sentenced to sixteen years, twenty years, and life. Two were eventually paroled in 1998, one of whom escaped the country in 2004 and was given asylum in Canada in 2006. The third was released in 2006. He and the other still remaining

---

10 "The Rise and Fall of the Goddess of Democracy", Chris Buckley, *New York Times*, June 1, 2014

in China managed to escape in 2009 and were granted asylum in the US the same year. The mental health of the last of the three to be released had been destroyed by years of solitary confinement, beatings and electric shock. He stared vacantly and could not answer direct questions. It was hard to imagine he'd ever recover. Hours after the vandalism in eighty-nine, a new portrait of the arch villain replaced the defaced one. Who knew, with all the pollution, how often the portrait had been replaced since then, but after all these years, there the image still hung.

Then I thought of the police smashing up an LSD coffin on a pedestrian bridge near the HK government offices when Li Keqiang, the at-the-time anointed but still-to-be-appointed premier, visited. There weren't as many people about, or media, and the police were emboldened by the paucity of observers. I didn't hear it myself but was told later that the police had warned LSD that the coffin was too big for the bridge and it was unsafe to have it there. But there was plenty of room for it, and it seemed far more unsafe for the police to provoke an altercation on the bridge. Suddenly, at some signal I had not detected, the police attacked the coffin in a frenzy, and within an instant smashed it to smithereens. And then, as if embarrassed by their actions, they swiftly retreated, gathering up as many pieces of "evidence" as they could on the way, trying to pretend it had never happened, there had never been a coffin, neither before or after, there had been no before or after, no incident had occurred. One large piece had fallen on the ground near my feet. Without otherwise moving, I placed a foot on top of it. Two officers attempted to pull it out from beneath my foot, but I clamped down hard. They looked at me in consternation for a moment and then, seeing that their colleagues were already a good distance removed and receding further, scampered away. I picked up the piece and handed the "souvenir" to the LSD people who had been carrying the coffin. As ever, they laughed. One must be jolly in this line of work, this vocation, I thought, and the words of Socrates, the captain of the Brazilian national team at the eighty-two World Cup came to mind: *Victory is secondary; what matters is joy.* I wasn't sure about that, but joy was, under the circumstances, a kind of victory as well as a vocational necessity. (Brazil didn't win the eighty-two World Cup, by the way, and Socrates' philosophy fell decidedly out of favor amongst the powers-that-be in Brazilian national football.)

And then I thought, at my age, every experience, every observation, every occurrence, is overlaid with so many others that nothing is as it is, nothing was as it was. How could I possibly communicate with anyone anymore, tell anyone what I really thought about anything, about what something meant? It meant so much, I would have to go on and on like a book. I remembered how often you interrupted me. That annoyed me.

Hey, I'd say, *you interrupted me.*

But you take too long to make your point, you'd reply.

I have become too pensive for the world, I thought, too full of thought.

After the police smashed the tank, they receded, acting as if nothing had happened. As ever, the Citizens' Radio and LSD people who'd made and accompanied the tank laughed their good-natured laughs and directed good-natured shouts of protest at the police. *Hurray!* they yelled ironically. They expected to be treated this way. I was often struck by the humor and forbearance of the HK democracy movement; in many situations in which I would have lost my patience or temper, they smiled and laughed. While they thought the police were acting ridiculously, and being used politically as a tool to prevent people from exercising their right to freedom of assembly to demonstrate outside of the Liaison Office, they didn't hold it against them. In fact, it seemed a perfect climax, tricking the police into engaging in performance art. Next day, the images that would blanket local papers were of the police smashing the tank replica. Up to then, the government had done such a good job of lying low and not giving the media the chance to manufacture headlines about stupid actions against the movement. Now, in the days before the vigil, it stumbled. In spite of repeated police warnings not to throw objects over the gates of the Liaison Office, a storm of white chrysanthemums and paper "hell money" of the kind burned at gravesites swirled in the air and landed in the courtyard to the chant of "the people will not forget".

•

Then the perennial heaviness descended, the heaviness of June 4, a heaviness I'd felt virtually every year since the actual events in eighty-nine. It was a physical heaviness, in the chest, the shoulders, the throat, at the memory of those who died, all of the lives that were ruined and all of the hopes and dreams that were crushed, regret at the vision of China that died—at least in terms of it being an obvious, open presence in the life of the nation—over a quarter-century ago. Yes, that much time had passed. We had gone from youth to middle age.

If anything, I would have thought the world would do more to mark the quarter-century anniversary. In the course of the preceding year, there had been a lot of talk but not much action. Plans such as a round-the-world relay hunger strike had been hatched, but few, it seemed, had come to fruition. And there was not much new being said, but then, what was there to say?

It all made me weary. The tragedy of June 4 became in me a generalized grief about the state of the world and its various injustices. It was an emotional, spiritual symbol. Except for anniversary-related activities, I rarely scheduled anything else on that day. I was just too emotionally distracted, incapacitated. The heaviness of having the world on one's shoulders, of the prospect of it not getting better. And grief, grief, grief, undiluted, unremitting grief.

I thought of Emerson reflecting on his son's death:

The only thing grief has taught me, is to know how shallow it is. …souls never touch their objects. An innavigable sea washes with silent waves between us and the things we aim at and converse with. Grief too will make us idealists. In the death of my son, now more than two years ago, I seem to have lost a beautiful estate, — no more. I cannot get it nearer to me..... So is it with this calamity: it does not touch me: some thing which I fancied was a part of me, which could not be torn away without tearing me, nor enlarged without enriching me, falls off from me, and leaves no scar. It was caducous. I grieve that grief can teach me nothing.... Nothing is left us now but death. We look to that with a grim satisfaction, saying, there at least is reality that will not dodge us.

Caducous. A new word to me, a botanical metaphor. "Easily detached and shed at an early stage."

Emerson was right: Grief didn't change anything. It was just grief. It could be channeled, of course, to productive ends. But in itself, it was just grief, as much illusion as reality. (Then again, that could be said of most any emotion.) And yet my heart rebelled against his words of truth: Something had to mean something, didn't it? Grief became anger, anger became belief, belief became action. Were that action's origins delusion, "unreal", and if so, did it matter? *Grief too will make us idealists.* I wasn't sure how Emerson meant it—wasn't "idealist" here synonymous with delusive? But the way I interpreted it, I was sure it was true, in my case at least. The essay in which those words appeared ended, *Never mind the ridicule, never mind the defeat: up again, old heart!* …

there is victory yet for all justice.

It was a strange double experience. The international media did big commemorative stories on the anniversary. Inside China, nothing appeared. The internet was scrubbed clean of even the most oblique references to eighty-nine, though a few cryptic messages appeared long enough for others to see them before they were removed:

I remained silent all night. I don't dare look straight at the rising sun. I remember the sun that day was blood red, blood red, like a wide-open, bloodshot eye.

I was there on that day. I saw a lot, but cannot say much even after so many years. I keep thinking of a poem by Lu Xun: I lower my head. How can I write out these lines? / Moonlight like water shines on my dark garment.[11]

In Beijing and elsewhere in the country, nothing happened. Pu Zhiqiang, who had been apprehended at a private June 4 commemoration the previous year, was still in detention, without formal charges, without trial. In HK, people were gearing up for the evening.

At the candlelight vigil, the heaviness lifted. It was like a leaf or petal unfurling, a release. One day a year we allowed ourselves to imagine a better world together, and for those few hours, it seemed possible, within our grasp; indeed, achieved. The largest crowd ever gathered for the twenty-fifth anniversary, some 180,000; including all those who weren't able to get into the park, the large crowds that flooded the nearby streets, the number probably exceeded 200,000. Sea of people, sea of candlelight. For the first year ever, I did not volunteer at the media booth but instead wandered freely through the crowd, observing, feeling the atmosphere like a balm. I had always found it both deeply moving and cliché: People holding up their candles to the darkness. It was spectacular. And then

---

11 "Live-blogging the Tiananmen Square Anniversary", Amy Qin, *New York Times*, June 3, 2014.

everyone went home and things went on the same as before. It was like a staged drama, a production; it had the effect of preserving memory, but apart from that, it changed nothing; afterwards, everything was the same as before. If this was all we could summon up, I thought, the regime had nothing to fear. But while it lasted, it was deeply moving. A brilliant and beautiful evening that by the next day evaporated into thin air.

The vigil's best moment was Chang Boyang's speech. There he was, up on stage, denouncing the Partystate, characterizing the situation as dismal. He exhorted the vigilants to take part in Occupy Central as a way of carrying on the legacy of the demonstrators of eighty-nine. He sounded off-script; he had definitely not passed that part of the speech by the organizers who had not been able to bring themselves to endorse Occupy Central and encourage those gathered to join. Again, I sensed their age, their weariness, their caution, their lack of imagination: They were shouting into the abyss of the past. What were people, especially young people who weren't even alive in eighty-nine, to do with their feelings that night? How were they to be channeled? Chang Boyang's was the eloquent, fiery speech of someone who had simply had enough, who had seen his friends, one by one, being detained and persecuted, and felt it was his duty to speak up. And someone who had decided he wouldn't be returning to the mainland any time soon. Indeed, he said later that he had been warned by mainland officials about a week beforehand not to attend the vigil, with threats of unspecified dire consequences if their warning went unheeded. His response? *We must occupy Central with love and peace. We also look forward to occupying Tiananmen Square with love and peace one day, just as we did in 1989. That year, two things happened—the peaceful democracy movement of '89 and the bloody massacre of June 4. Let's have another '89, but not another June 4. That day will come because we have been and will be fighting for it.* I loved the man.

In this part of the world, working on these issues, it could so often seem that we spent all of our time fending off the worst, adopting defensive measures, taking rearguard actions, and hardly ever had the time or the resources to focus on advancing the best, actually trying to realize a positive vision of the way we wanted things to be. (I had always objected to the term "human rights defenders" as too narrow a descriptor, for, I thought, as much as anything else, such people were also human rights promoters, human rights practitioners, human rights realizers.) In HK, the two biggest victories, over Article 23 and the national education subject, were, however impressive, simply staving off the specters that haunted the land. The struggle for universal suffrage was about going on the offensive, attempting to realize a key plank in the vision of the society we wished HK to be, and Occupy Central was, well, central to that. And yet, on the 25th anniversary, the organizers failed to make the link. People's ability to miss an opportunity never ceased to amaze. Sometimes we had the capacity to sleepwalk through the most dramatic events, the most crucial issues of our time and not even notice them.

•

With the vigil over, all attention turned toward the referendum, scheduled to start eighteen days later. The posters and t-shirts advertising it said simply 6.22. When I first saw them, I thought they were another creative allusion to June 4 (6.4) to circumvent Chinese censors, à la May 35. As far as the Partystate was concerned, the date was nearly as sensitive. In the lead-up, it tried to discourage people from taking part.

The central plank in that strategy was a so-called White Paper put out by the State Council, *The Practice of the "One Country, Two Systems" Policy in the HK Special Administrative Region*. It was only the second White Paper on HK, the first appearing back in 1997, the very year of the handover. The Partystate occasionally published such documents on a range of issues to clarify basic policy. The fact that it was publishing one on HK at this point in time was interpreted by just about all concerned as an act of emphatic self-assertion, to put it mildly. The phrase "laying down the law" would be apt, if not for the fact that the document, and the Partystate, stood above the law, put paid to the whole concept of "rule of law", a phrase it soberly intoned ad nauseam even while the Partystate's very existence trespassed against it.

Up to then, the Partystate had been torn between not giving HK people a clear target to attack (its lesson learned from its 2003 defeat when it tried to foist draconian security laws on the territory) and nipping things in the bud (its lesson from '89). The White Paper was the clearest sign yet that it perceived the situation in HK as so grave that it needed to throw caution to the wind and put its foot down, regardless of the backlash.

About 20 to 30% of HK people were pro-Partystate, rarely out of conviction, most often out of perceived self-interest or habit or the fact that they belonged to some organization affiliated with the regime, or simply had been conditioned to obey, a rather deep instinct in some human beings that, if cultivated from a young age, was almost impossible to break. This group included those who benefitted economically from ties to the Partystate, first and foremost the tycoons who had made or substantially increased their fortunes from being politically connected, first to the British and now to the Partystate, and others who arguably did not benefit at all economically (indeed suffered from an undemocratic system with poor labor rights protection) such as working-class leftists, and then others such as indigenous villagers whose privileges were protected by the system.

Another 20 to 30% were adamantly and actively pro-democracy.

Of the remaining 40 to 60%, most would choose democracy if they could do so risk-free and without having to do anything themselves to bring it about, but since democracy could not be brought about so easily, the question was what side would they take when push came to shove. The Partystate was gambling that a significant proportion of them could be frightened into toeing the Party line. Without enthusiasm, to be sure, but it wasn't really since the Cultural Revolution that the Partystate really cared what happened deep in your soul. Hypocrisy and cynicism suited it fine; indeed, were preferable to genuine fervor, easier to control and manipulate. Up to now, the fear campaign consisted mostly of insinuating that supporting democracy could hit HK people's pocketbooks, as the Partystate could withdraw certain "favors" it bestowed upon its favorite jewel. But it now appeared that the prospect of OC had so alarmed the Partystate that the latter decided it could take no chances; thus, the White Paper. The Partystate, like most dictators, was betting on the worst in people winning out—they would calculate according to their narrow self-interest, as opposed to the general good of society or some higher ideal. Its own interpretation of its track record lead to the conclusion that if you tried to bring out the worst in people, you were often remarkably successful.

In one sense, there was little new in the document. Just about everything in it had been uttered before by one official or another, in one context or another. The news was that it had been published in black and white as official policy. Its message could be summed up as follows: HK is ours and will be governed however we want it to be. Any understanding that departs from ours is wrong.

It appeared only a little over a week before the referendum. The timing was significant. The Partystate trotted out the Chief Executive of HK to present it to the world, a telling choice: The document was published by the Partystate Council, but the Chief Executive announced it, as if he were an emissary from the Partystate rather than a representative of the HK people. (Indeed, he was, and always had been, but up to that point, a fiction had been maintained.) What better way to communicate the message of the Paper that "one country" took precedence over "two systems"? The Paper in timing and substance constituted an abrupt, unceremonious shoving aside of the HK government—"no more pussyfooting—we'll take care of things now"—which was reduced to no more than an inconsequential messenger boy. It put paid to any pretense that the HK government had any substantial role in the matter, a pretense that the HK government, up to that point, had worked assiduously to maintain. The Chief Executive had already turned being faceless, colorless, invisible, saying nothing whatever he said, into a strange kind of art form. Watching him announce the White Paper reminded me of videos of kidnapping victims that their kidnappers trot out in front of the camera in order to show they're alive and convey their demands: You hear the words coming out of their mouths, you see their mouths move, but you know they are not their words. They appear fearful, but it is a kind of controlled fear, a fear they attempt to keep hidden, if for no other reason than that their captors do not want to send a video of them losing their composure. Whether in his head or some less conscious spot, the CE had to have known he was betraying HK.

The White Paper stirred up a hornet's nest. It had managed to alarm just about everyone. Reaction was swift and strongly negative, even from those who tended not to pay so much attention to such things. On Facebook, the social medium par excellence in HK, I noticed your secondary school friends, who had never exhibited the least interest in politics, expressing a range of responses, from unease to condemnation.

The Bar Association issued a terse rebuke in legalese to specifically rebut the claims in *The Practice of the "One Country, Two Systems" Policy in the HK Special Administrative Region* that the judiciary had a duty to be "patriotic" and to work together with the executive to achieve common aims as well as to criticize a characterization of judges as administrators. This was followed by a silent march of barristers, only its second ever, the first having been fifteen years before, in protest against the National People's Congress Standing Committee overturning a decision made by the HK High Court—to protest against the White Paper's statements about the role of the judiciary. Dressed all in black, hundreds of lawyers solemnly walked from the High Court to the Court of Final Appeal in Central, the very district OC threatened to occupy. Protesters gathered in front of the Liaison Office. Once again, the police were facilitating, going out of their way not to provoke confrontations. This was all the more surprising given that the acts of protest involved burning copies of *The Practice of the "One Country, Two Systems" Policy in the HK Special Administrative Region*. (Over a year later, four prominent leaders of the pro-democracy movement would be charged with obstructing a police officer in relation to that act.) I was generally ambivalent if not opposed to the burning of the written word—it did not have an altogether illustrious history—, but in this case, it seemed an apt critique.

Things were beginning to spin, developments occurring so quickly they were hard to keep track of. The Partystate and the HK government were on the move; they too regarded this moment as decisive. The key lesson learned by the Partystate from eighty-nine was to not let events snowball beyond its control—nip things in the bud while it was still possible to do so. If the referendum succeeded, momentum would build, and who knew what might come next? To all appearances, their movements were coordinated. The conviction of one of the key pan-democratic politicians on a charge of disorderly conduct during a demonstration was upheld in an appeals court. He was immediately remanded into custody to begin serving a term of four weeks. The next day, in the newspaper, a photo appeared of his distinctive waist-length hair being cut, and a highly symbolic photo of his new do was circulated. He'd asked to be released on bail to be allowed to complete the current session of the Legislative Council, due to go on summer recess in a month, but the judge had denied the request. He would be out of action, sitting in a prison cell, during the referendum and July 1 demonstration.

There were so many condemnations of OC by HK government officials and chambers of commerce (even three foreign chambers of commerce, Canada, India and Italy—from three democratic countries no less—thanks a lot, brothers and sisters!—businesses everywhere these days were their own separate nation, decidedly un- if not downright anti-democratic) that one wondered about the extent to which they were intricately coordinated right down to the exact timing. Listening to them, you would have thought the apocalypse was at hand—OC would mean the collapse of the HK economy! Did they themselves not hear the hysteria, the overkill in their voices? Were they not inwardly ashamed of themselves?

The mud was raining down on OC, poor little OC. As Opal said, you had to love it even if you didn't; you felt maternal towards it, wanted to protect it. Or, to put it another way, she said it was like a girl you wished you liked more than you did. You felt you should like her, so you tried your best to. OC had made itself a target and now the good old academics and reverend were standing up and taking the hits, bravely, patiently, too patiently many believed.

It was strange: There was an obvious governance crisis in HK, but the Partystate preferred to ignore it rather than doing the unthinkable—actually engaging in real negotiations towards resolution of the crisis, for to engage was to recognize a counterpart as in some way equal or at least worthy of a hearing, and that was something that the dictatorship could not countenance; it would regard such an act as stooping, a sign of weakness—or feared that others would. Accordingly, the all-powerful dictatorship backed itself into a corner, and then it wasn't so much as if it made decisions but that its prerogatives made decisions for it: Imposition was all it knew, all it could do. The Partystate signaled it would allow, at most, cosmetic changes: All voters could cast a ballot for the Chief Executive, but it would vet candidates beforehand to ensure that all were "loyal", "patriotic". In effect, this gave voters virtually no choice and ensured that the current problem would continue to exist, that the Chief Executive had little to no legitimacy because s/he had no popular mandate. While the Partystate's legitimacy ultimately came from the barrel of the gun, and that was understood by all, whether consciously or unconsciously, the Chief Executive had no mechanism of violent enforcement at her/his disposal, and the result of that was that s/he was isolated from everyone in the city except the few Partystate allies and so had to depend on his role fulfilling the will of the Partystate as his only source of legitimacy, one that was not respected in the city; indeed, amongst a large section of the populace, just the opposite—it was detested, despised, resented. But better that than anything else, as far as the Partystate was concerned. The government of HK would, if the Partystate had its way, continue to act as little more than a place-holder and water-carrier: there to act on the Partystate's will and otherwise ensure that no one else could take its place, certainly no one who rode to power on the popular will, and in the meantime, it would continue to assimilate the tiny territory to the massive mainland, a project that would take years but would be eventually accomplished.

And one day, people would look up and no longer be able to distinguish HK from its neighbor across the border, Shenzhen.

With the Partystate having elbowed the HK government out of the way, the confrontation was more direct—between it and the HK people. Having built a fearsome reputation on brooking no dissent, it couldn't afford to look weak. It was reckoning it could stare HK down—a sufficient number of HK people would blink, forcing the pro-democracy movement to back down in quivering, humiliated capitulation. But what if it didn't?

While the noose tightened on HK, it was clear what most of the rest of the world would do—close to nothing, or even less. The EU was showing it was as irrelevant as ever. Right after the White Paper came out, it held a meeting with "civil society representatives" to discuss press freedom in HK, an altogether legitimate topic, but under the circumstances, hardly the most urgent. When one of the civil society representatives asked the EU consul general to HK whether or not the EU would make a statement defending HK's autonomy and right to universal suffrage in response to the White Paper, the consul general first responded that the question was "irrelevant" because what was under discussion was press freedom in HK, and then said anyway the EU already presented its position clearly, making reference to a recent report it issued that stated its support for universal suffrage, a report that was not publicized and none of the civil society representatives present had ever heard of. It most likely sat buried on an obscure page of some website or other. When pressed that that was quite different from making a public statement, the consul general deflected the question and said it was important to get back to the matter at hand. But then why would such an official stand up tall for democracy when there was such a gaping democratic deficit in the EU, a deficit that even after the resounding victory of foes and critics of the EU in recent EU parliamentary elections the commission simply couldn't bring itself to even consider addressing? The powerful commission, which seemed more often than not to operate largely by virtue of inertia, was full of paper-pushers, careerists, bureaucrats, diplomats content to spend their lives on the cocktail circuit, the dregs dressed up in suits; very well-educated, intelligent and socially sophisticated dregs, but dregs nonetheless. They couldn't be bothered to even so much as stand up for one of the EU's supposed core values, democracy. As far as they were concerned, there was only one core value, and that was trade. At the roundtable, they said they were looking for "innovative, technical solutions". The mere utterance of the phrase induced cringes. It meant things they could throw money at to look like they were doing something but were entirely uncontroversial because innocuous. A hedge fund manager who wanted to create a data-crunching website to monitor the performance of Legislative Council members received heaps of praise. In contrast, a former journalist's report that former colleagues of his had been approached by the Partystate's Ministry of Public Security and offered HKD 100,000 dollars a month to spy was met by silence. Meanwhile, during a break, an EU rep snuck up to a friend, an NGO worker, one of those "civil society representatives" and reported that the EU was carrying out a collaborative EU-Partystate police training project on the mainland. No EU officials except the ones directly involved in the project were allowed to participate or even know what was going on. Calls by some EU officials to include human rights in the training were rejected as "unhelpful".

The UK, which was responsible for getting HK into its current mess, issued perfunctory six-monthly Foreign Office reports that portrayed everything in HK as peachy, though of course with a few problems (grave furrowing of earnest brow and downturned mouth) that could be overcome. It said what it expected in any upcoming electoral reform was "genuine choice", but like the HK government, it refused to acknowledge international law or standards in defining what that meant. When Li Keqiang visited the UK a week or two after the publication of the White Paper, the UK uttered not so much as a peep on the subject.

Meanwhile, the PSA headquarters had taken to erecting a light show on the side of its building facing the harbor. It was a tradition of tall buildings on HK Island to kit themselves out with lights that flashed in different patterns. Still other buildings were topped with big neon signs. From the Kowloon side, it had the cumulative effect of a light show. The glum PSA headquarters had always been silent and dark up to now, but it decided to join in the show, blinking the five characters for the Chinese People's Liberation [sic] Army—中国人民解放— in quick succession on its façade. The character for "people", 人, was missing one of its strokes; whether it had burned out or been forgotten was hard to say, since information from inside the building was not readily forthcoming. The army had become just another brand on the harbor, like any other—Nike, Samsung, PSA. It didn't matter whether you peddled shoes or electronics or death.

I'd been trying to convince your father to vote in the OC referendum. Whenever I brought it up, he just glanced away with a sheepish smile and shook his head. It had been a while since I'd had a political discussion with him. Back in the early days of our acquaintance, we had them frequently, and he seemed to enjoy them. We often disagreed, but he pursued them always in good nature, without a hint of antagonism or perturbation. But it seemed the older he got—he was now in his mid-seventies—the less inclined he became to think or to take an interest in intellectual or political matters.

It was right around the time of the seventieth anniversary of D-Day. He liked to watch history documentaries on television and had recently seen one on D-Day. He spoke of it with great interest. There were scenes of the commemorative celebrations, which included Putin. Whether or not Putin would attend had been a matter of speculation and dispute, since the anniversary followed hard upon his invasion and annexation of Crimea. Your father praised Putin.

What a good guy, he said. *What a nice smile. And he's making peace with Ukraine. It takes a big man to offer the hand of peace to those who have wronged him even when he is in the right. Everyone needs a good leader like that.*

But what about the invasion of Crimea? I asked.

He did a good thing to protect the Russians of Ukraine.

Why did they need protection?

Ukraine treated them badly.

How so?

Well, just so, of course.

I think you're getting too much of your news and views from Xinhua.

Oh, no, he said, *I never watch CCTV.*

Conversations like that reminded me of what we were up against, the mindset of a great many—False Consciousness personified. It wasn't so much the dictators who presented the greatest resistance, who were the hardest to overcome, but the mindsets of a great many people, many of whom were decent, kind, generous like your father.

He admired Mao as well, though he himself had fled Mao's Great Famine, in which some thirty-five million people had died as a direct result of political decisions made by the Partystate in full awareness of what was occurring. Mao's infamous statement in regard to that catastrophe, the largest famine in modern history: *When there is not enough to eat, people starve to death. It is better to let half of the people die so that the other half can eat their fill.* On the occasions your father voiced approval of one action or statement or another by Mao, I wanted to ask him what he thought about those words, but I never had. You said your father suffered from Stockholm syndrome, the victim's admiration for, identification with his oppressor.

You'd think he'd be haunted by what he had seen, but he seemed blind to it. Where he came from, when he came of age, you had to be blind in order to live. If you managed to get on with your life, to not perish, this counted as success. Now, near the end of his days, the Partystate, the very same that had ruled in Mao's days, had taken his daughter, reclaiming her like an unpaid debt he owed them for what? for escaping its clutches, for not succumbing? And he stood before me praising a dictator.

I had always been fond of this pleasant, helpful, gregarious man, even as his daughter found his constant anxiety, his fear that the worst was about to happen, his life lived according to the priority of evading its myriad dangers, his obsessiveness (all traits she'd inherited from him), his hyperactivity, his busy-body-ness, his complete (and unconscious) disregard for privacy difficult to tolerate. *Come on,* I'd say, *give your father a break. He is who he is; you're not going to change him.* But in reaction to his praise of Putin, I felt contempt boil up in me. I tried to suppress it, telling myself I had no right; he was an old man, he didn't know better. Contempt was cheap, the easiest thing to feel. But the impulse to slap him was nearly uncontrollable. What's wrong with you? I said to myself. I felt ashamed. And what good would a slap do? He would stare at me dazed and dismayed: What was that for? What had he done to deserve that? Only trusted me, looked out for me, looked after Z whenever I needed him to, always bringing her some cheap plastic made-in-China toy or trinket you'd roll your eyes at, provisioning fruit and nuts and other foods he'd gotten at the wet market on the other side of the city where he lived and transported to us by trolley, each time telling me how much cheaper they were than on the island. I managed to put down the slapping urge like a rebellion, but in its place came sadness, weary sadness, for you, for him, for myself, for us all.

•

While your father was resisting any involvement in the HK democracy movement, even one as minor as casting a vote in a referendum, another old man was taking a different approach. 83-year-old Cardinal Zen had decided that in order to unite the pro-democracy movement, encourage people to vote in the upcoming referendum, and counter the Partystate's anti-referendum campaign, including the White Paper and massive propaganda, he would walk 20 kilometers per day for seven days through each of the 18 districts of HK in the week leading up to the referendum, for a total of 140 kilometers in all. He had originally considered a hunger strike, but his friends talked him out of it for health reasons. And anyway, a hunger strike seemed more anti, a walk more pro; a walk was much less grim and set a more positive and optimistic tone in the lead-up—onward and upward and so on. He'd invoked Gandhi in announcing his decision and made mention of the salt march. I couldn't help but laugh thinking of the differences: For starters, what Cardinal Zen proposed—walk around the city—was not illegal, as making salt was under the British, and therefore, not civil disobedience. True to their nature, these HKese were moderate and law-abiding. More than Gandhi, what Cardinal Zen reminded me of was Christ carrying the cross. The implicit message of the act was, If I at 83 am willing to suffer, to take up the cross, even if only in this small, physical way, can you not yourself make some small effort to bring about the end we desire?

Cardinal Zen was one of the few icons of the democracy struggle left, persevering through the decades, not yet succumbing to death. I suspected he recognized this exalted status and wanted to "leverage" it. He was one of the few figures left who was so revered across the pro-democracy establishment that he could effectively call on them all to unite. He must have been dismayed to see all the petty bickering in the lead-up. He gave the moderates a face-saving way to return to the fold and support the OC referendum since they could turn out for the referendum-promoting walk to pay their respect to him, in reverence of him.

At the start of the walk, they crowded around him and in turn the media crowded around them. The diminutive old man was swallowed up. I could hardly see him. They were claiming him as their own, wrapping themselves in the aura of sanctity and purity that comes from selfless decades-long dedication to the cause. He, in turn, was allowing this transaction to occur as long as its end—unity—was achieved. Virtually none of the groups of young people who had energized, even transformed, politics of late were present. Perhaps, at 8 am, the Cardinal was starting too early for them; they were all still in bed. But it was more likely they realized this stunt was arranged to bring the older moderates who had been behaving like tantrum-throwing children back into the fold, and they kept their distance for fear that if they came too close, they might say what they really thought—that the moderates were conservative and spent old farts—and re-open the wounds the Cardinal was trying to heal.

So you had the strange situation of the people who had given the most recent manifestation of the movement its energy so far staying away from the highest-publicity event encouraging the populace to vote, and the people who had kept the movement at arm's length encouraging people to come out and vote in the referendum they'd criticized. Perhaps the fact that it was a moderate exercise would encourage some of those in the middle who were sitting on the fence to participate in a project lead by people who had been demonized as "radicals". I was walking with a young woman who was part of Occupy Central's core group of volunteers. She put the large turn-out of moderate pan-democrats down to the behind-the-scenes work of one of the Occupy Central leaders. He reached out to them even as they criticized him, and they responded.

Throughout the long walk that first day and the other long walks over the following days, Cardinal Zen was mostly silent and grim, surely due to the physical effort required to walk such distances in the intense summer heat and humidity, though I also imagined him thinking, Here I've spent my life on this, and look how far there still is to go (20k a day to be precise!), and I'm surrounded by these knuckleheads and numbskulls who can't figure out how to cooperate to reach a common goal. What's going to happen when I'm not around anymore?

•

In that period, life was phantasmagoric. At night I watched three World Cup matches, sleeping in between for a total of three to four hours: two hours' sleep, a match, one hour's sleep, a match, one hour's sleep, the final match. Z would get up and we'd make breakfast and eat it during the second half of the final match. In daylight hours, I walked twelve hours with Cardinal Zen. That was nothing: Some others walked all through the night. I would have as well if not for the World Cup matches—one can only sacrifice so much!—and Z. Her grandparents were already doing overtime on babysitting duty. The sleep deficit, watching a spectacular tournament in a dynamic country, Brazil, on the other side of the world where much was far from perfect and yet there was the football-energy and the protest-energy and the burgeoning-culture-energy, the heat, humidity and walking all combined to give the sensation I was no more than a block of wood carried along by the fast-flowing stream. I just looked up now and then to see where I was going and even then often could not get my bearings. The list of errands undone piled up, and there was the constant guilt of not attending to anything properly, or in a timely manner.

Not for a moment did I forget you. While I felt guilt in the pleasure I took watching the World Cup (were your guards doing the same? I wondered), the Cardinal Zen walk felt like penance for whatever had occurred between us in the past that was not so pleasant. I found myself looking forward with greater urgency to your return and believing that some way somehow it would occur, and when it did, through all of this work, I would have prepared myself to receive you, to be worthy of you and your suffering, and to make all better between us. At the same time, just imagining the reunion, I had the fear that before long we would fall into old ways and fight and I would show that I really could not change at all.

It was during that intense period that Alec and Matthieu visited for not even twenty-four hours. I had known them in the Northern Paradise. They were my upstairs neighbors the first year I lived there and the last. In between, they left, went elsewhere, and then came back. But even though our time there overlapped for only two years total, we became fast friends. We shared an interest in football. Alec, a decades-long long-distance runner, got me running when I quit playing football myself. He needed someone to pace him; I needed a new way to stay in shape. We were both teachers, and we shared a tendency to antagonize those in power. We went on many runs together in cold, rain, snow. At the end of a long day, when I was too tired to do anything and it was already getting dark, Alec would pop around and say, *Up for a run?* in such a way that I knew it was futile to resist. *Not really, but....* I would reply, and go get changed.

Alec was fifteen years older than I. His son, Matthieu, was only a few months old when they left the Northern Paradise. When they moved back, he was six. He and his mother had visited us on the island in HK three years before. Then, he was thirteen. And now, when I saw Alec and him both, he was, amazingly, nearly seventeen. Our acquaintance spanned the entirety of his life. Alec's wife, Matthieu's mother was Chinese. Intelligent, ambitious, efficacious, talented, she had left the Northern Paradise because she had gotten bored. She returned to China to try to start a school. She'd been at it for four years. Through ups and downs, we stayed in touch, and she kept me updated. But then she stopped communicating. Now, I'd heard through others, after many mishaps and plans falling through, things had come together and the school would open the following year.

Liu Wei was an economist by training, and her personality resembled the cliché of the profession—hard-headed, pragmatic, not given to idealism. She was good at getting things done. During his visit, Alec hardly mentioned Liu Wei. One of the few times he did, he said how nationalistic she'd become. According to him, she bought into the propaganda narrative about incipient Chinese greatness, and she saw the school project as part of it, as her way of participating in the resurgence of her country. I'd originally been interested in Liu Wei's efforts to start a school, offered my help (an offer she didn't take up), and had spent the previous World Cup, when both of us happened to be in Beijing, talking to her about it. But then, as said, she ceased communicating. A mutual friend had put her finger on it, with an explanation that I found myself reluctant to accept: You're too disruptive, especially in the Chinese context. Your emphasis on rights, indeed on political and social ideals of any kind, is threatening to the realization of such a project.

I came to see Liu Wei's school project as the antithesis of my vision, a perfect brew of everything I loathed: 1) funding from nouveau-riche Chinese tycoons; 2) a cozy relationship with the Partystate, which had agreed to host the school and—a huge coup—grant it an exception to a law forbidding Chinese nationals to attend international schools on Chinese territory. That would make the school, as far as I knew, the only international school in China where Chinese students and foreigners would study together; 3) support from the network of visionless old boys who held the power over the system of schools of which the school in the Northern Paradise where she, Alec and I had all worked was a part, and had basically turned it into a franchise operation not much different from McDonald's, with a strong emphasis on branding and virtually none on principles or ideals. I knew Liu Wei: If she were to defend herself in my court, she would tell me this was how things got done: You didn't just create something out of nothing, you had to make use of the powers that be and the money you could find to do it, and, if you really wanted to make it happen, you couldn't always be so particular. Of course, the question was, whether or not that approach risked corrupting from the very start the heart of the enterprise you set in motion, but then, in her case, perhaps it didn't because the main objective was to make it happen, without being overly concerned about what exactly "it" would eventually be. What it would be was a reality, not a dream, and, if Alec was right, it would be part of the Chinese Dream. I did not envy her success or respect that sort of school, but I did regard it as a symbol of my own impotence: She was able to realize a school; I was not. As simple as that.

Alec was no correspondent, and our contact had been intermittent. He and Matthieu had followed Liu Wei to Guangzhou. They had already been there for three years. During that time, we hadn't seen each other once. Liu Wei had moved on two years previously to the city near Shanghai where the school was to open. I sensed that she and Alec had become estranged, but I hadn't actually asked and no one had told me. Alec and Liu Wei were both stubborn and opinionated, a recipe for conflict (not too different from us, actually), and during my time as their neighbor in the Northern Paradise, I'd seen a few fights, big fights, serious fights. On top of that, I sensed that as they got older, their interests diverged ever more, taking each in different directions. Perhaps they had accepted this. Still, I always felt a little sad when I thought of them. Maybe it was just the melancholy awareness of time passing, that nothing lasts; maybe it was for the best if they went their separate ways. Alec was just a couple of years from retirement, and in the few comments he made on the subject—what he might do, where he might go—, she was not mentioned. Now Alec and Matthieu were about to return to the Northern Paradise without her. She would stay in China to run the school. Three years previously, when I'd heard they were coming to Guangzhou, I thought we would see each other regularly, but now, somehow three years had passed without them ever having visited us. (It was too difficult for us to visit them, for security reasons.) Now, Alec had decided, in the last moment, to come down for a quick visit before they were to leave China for good.

It was only while I stood in the arrivals reception area of the train station waiting for them that it occurred to me that I hadn't seen Alec since I'd left the Northern Paradise nine years earlier. It seemed amazing that it could have been that long ago, that so much time could have passed. Matthieu was even more the "fine young man" than he had been three years before— kind, intelligent, approachable, with a sunnier disposition than either of his parents. Alec was his old self, but older, a little heavier.

I met them at the station, having come straight from the Cardinal Zen walk. I was still wearing the t-shirt (6.22—get out and vote!) and carrying a large placard emblazoned with the words, Stand up for real universal suffrage, don't accept a fake! Alec asked about them, and on the ferry back to the island, expressed skepticism about my activities. This was not unexpected. Alec was never a great activist. He was always first and foremost a thorough-going individualist. This didn't mean he never got involved, just that he thought for himself. He did things his own way. At times, his interests overlapped with causes, such as that of the Sahrawis, who were from the last colony in the world recognized as such by the United Nations, Western Sahara, and that was largely through meeting people from there—he identified with them on an immediate and personal level and was motivated to become involved in their cause, organizing runs in support of them, running in their incredible Sahara marathon (yes, through the desert).

He didn't buy my "As HK goes, so goes China; as China goes, so goes the world" shtick about HK as a bellwether in the global struggle for democracy, against neo-authoritarianism. Surely I must realize that HK was inconsequential, peripheral, that its conditions were so different from those elsewhere in the country that it could hardly be regarded as in any way crucial to determining the country's future. All of my investment in what he called "local politics" might be a colossal waste of time, based on an illusion. I couldn't possibly think that the Partystate would ever allow anything approaching genuine democracy in HK as long as it governed. And it looked like it could and would govern for a good long time to come.

He was playing devil's advocate, as was his wont, and also expressing the sort of views many foreigners who had spent time living in China had. To them, life there was pretty normal, and they believed what they saw, and "the other China" was all but unimaginable, or, if they had heard about it, very difficult to believe, the China of 98% conviction rates based largely on confessions, many if not the great majority of those in turn coerced, through torture and mistreatment of various kinds; the China of multiple injustices, though they knew generally of issues like internet censorship and encountered them themselves when they tried to access globally popular sites like Facebook and Youtube that were blocked by the Great Firewall.

The sub-text of Alec's criticism was that he suspected me of being a sentimentalist, of just supporting people because, well, it seemed the right thing to do and made me feel good about myself, about life. My conviction was a substitute for careful hard-headed strategic calculation. A math teacher, during the course of the visit, he lamented that, with few exceptions, Euclidean geometry was no longer being taught. He found that fact indicative of a general decline in the teaching of mathematics. Technology, such as calculators, he believed, was being used too much as a crutch, to the detriment of what he saw as the biggest benefit of the study of mathematics to the ordinary student—learning a certain way of thinking, logic, deductive and rational reasoning. And that's the way he was, priding himself on not accepting anything at face value, at questioning everything, at eluding ideology. That was all fine and well, but, I wondered to myself, what would be his own coherent, positive vision, of the world, of life? Did he have one? Alec was nothing if not a committed, consummate teacher. He had taught students all over the world for decades. That's what he wanted his students to learn: Don't rely on assumption, prejudice, however fashionable, influential and even persuasive it might be; think for yourself. Beyond that, he took pleasure in getting to know his students, mentoring them. He never really seemed to have grand projects he was working on, but he was always up to something, and he pursued it with vigor and purpose, whether organizing people to go on a run or a hike or to watch a football match—he was good at getting people involved, and I was always one of those who most willingly joined in on his schemes. He was good at making you feel that whatever you participated in was an important event.

He mentioned the children's park that had just opened across the street from where he lived in Guangzhou. He watched the grandparents take their grandchildren there and thought of what rough lives those grandparents must have lead, but now, near the end of them, they could take their grandchildren for walks in the park, and they lived and ate much better than they ever had. He had a friend who'd grown up poor in the countryside. Now, the friend owned two apartments and a car outright, bought with cash. He still considered himself poor, though he was probably better off than most middle-class people in Canada, where Alec was from, who were mortgaged and indebted to the hilt. Chinese people, he said, appeared to him in the following way: The government dictated to them what was allowed and what was not, how they could entertain themselves and how they could not, and the vast majority of the people simply complied, and, for the most part, could see no harm in that, did not even recognize it as an issue. This came close to the oft-heard views that 1) as long as most people were living better material lives than ever before, there would be no great demand for change and those pushing for it would remain in the vast minority, and 2) the Chinese people simply lacked "the democratic gene".

I hadn't yet told him that you had been disappeared. Since he lived in the mainland, it was too risky to tell him by email, and I didn't think this was the right moment—in the midst of a debate, it would seem like pulling a trump card. Indeed, from a certain angle, it would weaken my argument, making my political activity appear all the more like part of a personal grudge, emotionally motivated rather than the result of deduction, rationality, a grand objective strategy. At any rate, introducing the personal element would change the tenor of the debate. At the train station, I'd merely mentioned in passing that you weren't around. I'd planned to tell him more when we got home, but whenever the right moment looked to be approaching, we got interrupted, or our attention was diverted, and I never got around to it.

All that Alec said was at least partially true. I didn't have the energy to summon up a complete response. I simply said, *Yes, that might quite possibly be true. I might be wasting my time.* I did add some qualifications: You could see from the Partystate's heavy-handed treatment of HK, a lot was at stake, and not just what would happen in HK. In this sort of work, there were many battles, and you won some (hopefully) and lost some, but along the way, whether winning or losing, you were also doing other things, such as gradually and surely developing a democratic culture, a democratic consciousness among participants and a wider circle of citizens as well, and this was a foundation for subsequent success as well as an important end in itself, for it changed society for the better now, and wasn't dependent on what the dictator did far away. It was a powerful and emboldening experience, I said, for people to emerge from the atomized society and participate in something larger than themselves. You could see the scales fall from people's eyes: I am not alone, there are others who feel the way I do; could see how transformed they felt to just contribute in whatever way they could. That in itself was the overcoming of the sort of mentality, the colonial mentality, that was holding HK back as much as the external oppressor. Yes, things often looked bleak, but one should keep in mind Mandela's words about it always seeming impossible until it is done. There was something about dictatorship that was inherently fragile. From a certain point of view, the Partystate was constantly juggling elements (the combustibility of injustice in the society, including the small injustices that the majority experienced in their everyday lives, the need to keep the economy chugging along at a high rate of growth, the polluted environment) just to stay afloat. So, I said, it's perfectly possible it could all be for naught. But then, the same could be said about a great many enterprises with uncertain outcomes—they were potentially a waste of time.

Throughout my life, I'd been criticized for spending too much time on supposedly lost causes. But then wasn't that what solidarity was all about, standing side by side with the politically weaker in order to shift the balance of power? It was done as an end in itself and not just to achieve the end. The least one could say about it was that it was no more a waste of time than the million and one trivial ways people managed to fritter away their lives. Could not watching football, something the two of us did quite a lot, fall in the category of waste of time? I thought of asking Alec, but did not.

In the less than twenty-four hours Alec and Matthieu visited, we went running/hiking (like many road runners before him, Alec had a hard time handling the steep hills of the island, and it was also there where his age most showed; he said he had hardly run in Guangzhou in the last three years; I was amazed to see him out of shape; out-of-shape just did not match my image of him), swimming (they loved being in the sea so much they didn't want to get out; it was nearly dark when we finally emerged), and watching football. In the morning, we saw the England-Italy match in a crowded pub full of England supporters. It was raining and grey. On the television screen, the T1 signal was hoisted. Typhoon season was on the way. Even while watching what was up to then the most engrossing match of the tournament, I found myself thinking, We are now heading into the dead blankness of summer, skies washed out by heat and haze.

Z and I saw them off at the train station where I'd met them. In the wake of the visit, I felt a gaping, disproportionate sadness (which any rational person would probably attribute largely to sleep deprivation, though it seemed much more than that). The brevity of the visit made it all the more intense—they were there and then, just as quickly, they were gone, short enough to be a dream, and the aftermath was like waking from a dream.

What was that sadness about? Everything. But more specifically, about missing them, missing the relationship I had with them years before in the Northern Paradise, the long runs and watching football, missing my life there and half-envying their imminent return, re-experiencing that feeling of loss that came with being exiled from the Northern Paradise, missing mother and that feeling you have when you know you can turn to a parent, someone bigger than yourself, for support (and this, in a way, was an eternal loss, since I had rarely relied on my parents while they were alive, although somehow, just knowing they were there, made a difference), missing weekend calls with mother and watching her watch Z grow up, missing you and the thousand and one small ways we were together, thousand and one small things we did together. Once I got going, there was a litany of reasons to feel deeply, desperately sad. The loneliness of feeling that it all depended on me, Z entirely depended on me, your release depended on me—for who else could be expected to care as much?

Then I heard your voice say, You miss having friends. And I thought, it's true. It had been a very long time since I'd had a friend at my side. There were many friends far away, whom I seldom saw, with whom I corresponded all too rarely (mostly due to the general decline in correspondence—paper letters had been all but dead for years, and I'd even noticed a drastic falling off in email correspondence), but there were no friends who lived nearby, whom I saw on a daily or even regular basis, with whom I could do things like stay up all night watching World Cup matches taking place on the other side of the world.

Once the door opened a crack, sadness came in a flood. Moments usually came right after waking. Also, there was something about sitting on the sofa with Z after her nap, she herself not feeling well, and not knowing what to do next that opened the trap door to the abyss. I had to continue to function, but it was important to be aware of the abyss, to keep in touch with it, even if the general discombobulation that accompanied standing at its edge for any length of time did not feel right. I had to maintain some equilibrium, considering there was someone else, namely Z, who depended on me. Children can save you from yourself, for better and worse.

They should have never come, I thought, all the while being pathetically grateful they had. They reminded me too keenly of what a normal life is like.

The place was messy in the wake of the visit. It was so small that when someone visited, it was like setting up camp, unfolding the dirty pink sofa-bed that had been our raft through the night. I'd been so busy with the Zen walk and the World Cup that the place hadn't been put back in its place for some time. Z was actually getting worse at picking up after herself as she got older. *Do you want to make pizza?* I asked Z. After I'd made the dough and rolled it out, and cut the cheese, the tomatoes, the vegetables, she put them all on the surface of the crust, tomatoes, then cheese, then vegetables, dressed in her apron and chef's hat made by the mother of the woman who'd looked after my mother when she died.

•

On the day when Cardinal Zen was scheduled to pass through Kwun Tong, the working-class wasteland of public housing estate high-rises where your parents lived, I asked your mother to accompany us. She was a Catholic, and I figured her allegiance to the faith would oblige her to come along. But she was reluctant. I was always the sort who couldn't resist pressing people to see what they really thought, especially when it appeared they were attempting to hide a negative attitude or an aversion, and so I did with her.

You don't seem to be a very big fan of his, I said. *He's a great man, don't you think?*

She didn't have much to say about that; she could hardly criticize an authority figure in the church, even a retired one, even one the higher-ups in the current diocese had somewhat distanced themselves from. But she did venture to say that she wasn't too sure about this universal suffrage. She couldn't quite understand what the big deal was, why people thought it was so important.

Well, I said, *Cardinal Zen has always been a big proponent of religious freedom on the mainland. The church you belong to isn't even allowed to exist there. Its bishops have spent most of their lives in prison. Some were disappeared decades ago and no one knows where they are or even whether they're alive. There are only four officially recognized religions, and they're all controlled by the state, they're state churches, and the people who work in them are technically employed by the state. So what the mainland calls the Catholic church is not allowed to have anything to do with the Vatican, and the Partystate appoints its bishops. That's not the way it is in HK, but it very well could be in the near future if the people don't get to run their own government. Right now, there's a big Partystate campaign going on in Zhejiang to restrict religion. It includes tearing down churches, even state-run churches, and crosses on churches. If the Partystate has its way, it will gradually incorporate HK into the mainland, and who knows what will happen then.*

Your mother listened, and nodded. She didn't seem convinced. I wondered whether I should pull out the trump card: How could she think like that when the very same Partystate opposed to democracy in HK had disappeared her daughter? Enforced disappearances didn't happen in places with proper democracy. But I didn't have the heart to say so; it seemed too cruel.

Still, I was frustrated at the inability of people like your parents to connect the dots, even when the issue had a very personal, direct and immediate impact on their lives. (The loss of a child—how could you get more personal, direct and immediate than that?) For people like them, reality, what they referred to, was what they saw before them, whether they could make head or tail of it or not. Everywhere around you, you saw people working long hard hours, sweating, making things, "building buildings" as Z put it in one of my favorite songs of hers. "Building buildings... people building... people building people's buildings..." I would find myself humming in her singsongy voice as I walked about the city and saw the constant, incessant construction. In its compulsive industriousness, its density, its constant busy-ness, HK could remind of an ant colony. *This* was reality, what you saw, could clearly indubitably see before you, *this*, the physical world around you in constant unrelenting hustling perpetual change. The energy, the sheer energy and the undeniable materiality were intimidating, awe-inspiring. Up against that, what chance did an abstraction like democracy have?

The last day of Cardinal Zen's week-long walk was the opening day of Occupy Central's online referendum.

In the days preceding the referendum, Popvote, the website of the organization commissioned by Occupy Central to conduct it, was inundated and sporadically paralyzed by distributed denial-of-service attacks of such size and complexity that they could only have been organized by an entity with extraordinary cyber-capabilities, such as... hmmmm... a government, perhaps? Some called it the largest single cyberattack ever publicly reported.

It got the same amount of traffic in one second that Google's global search engine got in an hour. Popvote, with the help of a US cybersecurity firm, was eventually able to buttress itself against the attacks, but as a result, Occupy Central decided to extend the polling period from the initial three days to ten, hoping to ensure that it would have the site up and running for much of that time so that everyone who wanted to vote could. *Apple Daily*, HK's biggest and only firmly pro-democracy daily newspaper, also underwent cyberattack. It happened to be a big supporter of Occupy Central and had publicized the upcoming referendum. Both Popvote and *Apple Daily* reported the cyberattacks to the police. The police made no statement about investigating them. By contrast, Taiwanese prosecutors had announced an investigation into attacks on Next Media, *Apple Daily*'s parent company, there. In the first two days of the referendum, many reported being unable to vote, and there were certain periods that were rough, but by the third day, the attacks had been overcome. The sites stabilized and learned to fend off the attacks.

By the start of the last day of his walk, the 83-year-old cardinal had covered 120 kilometers, and by the end of it, the total would be 140. As on the preceding days, he was accompanied by a contingent of several hundred other walkers. By midday, reports began to arrive of the number of votes. Three hours into polling, it was already up to 100,000, and by five, in the late afternoon, it had reached 200,000. The mood of the walkers palpably lifted, and that was reflected in the demeanor of Cardinal Zen himself. Throughout much of the week, he had been grim and silent (someone later told me that was down to shoes that didn't fit, but I couldn't believe it was only that). Now, though obviously exhausted, he was happy, smiling, joking, full of joy and relief. A burden was lifting from his shoulders. With the preliminary vote counts already indicating large numbers and growing fast, the walkers began to realize something extraordinary, magnificent, historical was afoot.

It began to dawn on the city as well: smiles, waves, applause of people riding past on trams and buses, from taxi drivers, from shopkeepers and passers-by—we were all conspiring in some great endeavor. And the numbers kept increasing, and fast: by midnight of the first day of polling, over 380,000. On the first two days, the only way to vote was on-line. On the third day, actual physical polling stations opened, fifteen in all around the city, and at many, lines snaked out the door and down the street. By the end of the third day, over 700,000 had voted—more than 20% of the electorate, almost 40% of the number of voters who turned out in a typical Legislative Council election. 700,000 exceeded all expectations. One of the leaders of Occupy Central said in wonder, *At first I couldn't believe the voter turnout, but I reflected later: Why didn't we trust HKers?* A newspaper that had covered Occupy Central critically bore the grudging sub-headline, "Ninety per cent of people at Occupy Central's polling stations demand a say in who can lead the city, as even critics turn out to vote." In the days that followed, I kept recalling an image of Cardinal Zen at the end of the walk. His mission had been accomplished. He'd walked the 140 kilometers in seven days through all eighteen districts of the city. As the hundreds of others who'd accompanied him on the last day celebrated, he was forgotten for a moment. I caught sight of him fast asleep on the floor nearby. His head and shoulders were slumped against a wall, as if he'd originally intended just to sit down but then, before he knew it, had fallen fast asleep and slid down the wall. He looked like a slack doll, a puppet, a ventriloquist's dummy that had been animated by a spirit that, its mission now fulfilled, had departed. Or like a little boy with grey hair.

In the end, your family voted, your mother who was skeptical of the value of democracy, your apolitical brothers, all except your father, who'd decided to return to his native village in Guangdong to go biking instead.

When your mother matter-of-factly told me she voted, as if in passing, I responded with an astonished look, to which she gave a half-proud self-satisfied well-of-course-what-else-would-I-do nod. Z, who had been playing quietly on her own, looked up suddenly and pleaded, *I want to vote too!*

Then come here, I said. We opened the Popvote page and entered your HK ID number. *Now you have to choose what mommy would want since she's not here. You're voting on her behalf. Normally, siupengyao aren't allowed to vote, but I think this case is exceptional.* Z ticked a square next to a statement she couldn't read (for she could read nothing yet, apart from her own name), but I knew that was exactly what her mother would want. *Oday yiu zhen po xun*, she said—we want real universal suffrage. *Yes, indeed, we do*, I said. Through prison walls, you had voted, a true absentee ballot.

The elites didn't know what had hit them. They'd thought they had everything under control. Their displeasure flailed in all directions. The referendum was illegal. (Ha, I thought, if all of those eventually 790,000 had conspired to commit a crime, they really should be worried!) It couldn't possibly be representative of public opinion. It supported proposals that were illegal according to the Basic Law. They suspected the figures reported by Popvote, the most established and reputable polling organization in the city, were inflated but gave no evidence to support their suspicion. They said that "dishonest elements" had participated, thus rendering the exercise invalid, but it turned out that the only dishonest elements that could be located were members of a pro-Partystate group who had voted using false HK IDs. They tied themselves in knots with inconsistent and illogical rhetoric. They said everything must follow the Basic Law, but then claimed it was self-evident that the Chief Executive had to "love the country" (read: the Partystate), though nothing of the sort was in the Basic Law. They said the referendum didn't represent public opinion, though more than one in ten HK people had voted and their side had no comparable measurement or indicator of public opinion. They said it was illegal, though they could point to no law it broke (they seemed to confuse two concepts, one of illegality—a crime having been committed—and the other of legal standing—the fact that the referendum was not legally binding, and this confusion in itself was not very reassuring in terms of the Partystate's understanding of rule of law).

The HK government tried to keep its head down, pretending nothing was happening. No statements were forthcoming by any ministers, who up to then had taken every opportunity to warn the public against having anything to do with Occupy Central. It wanted to ensure it didn't further provoke but instead gave the impression it was superfluous, as if the whole issue had nothing to do with it.

China Daily, the Partystate's mouthpiece, garnered headlines for its over-the-top rhetoric, referring to the largely online referendum as "mincing ludicrousness", a plot, a game, a joke. But my personal favorite was its comparison of HK people and a greedy wife: *This situation reminds me of a fable I read as a child. It tells the story of a fisherman who one day caught a fish with magical powers. He was granted three wishes in exchange for the fish's freedom. The fisherman and his wife found their life was improved overnight after making their first wish. Life was even better after the second. Then, his wife got greedy and asked to be made a Queen with the fish as her servant. The fish became angry and punished the fisherman's wife. The couple's life returned to its previous miserable state. If the opposition camp has any political wisdom it should accept the current realities and behave appropriately*[12]. The analogy was a wonderfully toxic mix of politically reactionary sexism, almost its own form

---

12 "The opposition should accept reality", Leung Lap-yan, *China Daily*, June 16, 2014

of poetry. *Accept the current realities and behave appropriately....* What a wonderful motto to live by.

And anyway, they said, when all was said and done and they had thrown all the mud they could muster, the referendum didn't matter.

That was their best point. It didn't matter in the end, did it? It didn't change anything. On that last note, they were perhaps right. After the exhilaration of witnessing hundreds of thousands of HK people standing up and demanding real democracy, we were not one step closer to our goal, and it was unclear to everybody what would happen next.

I spent much of that intense week of the referendum out on the streets of HK leafleting. Entreating others to vote brought on a constant rush of impressions, thoughts and emotions. In the course of a leafleting session of a couple of hours at a time, I would come across hundreds if not thousands of citizens. I would look into their eyes, they would look into mine, or look away. I would approach them, and they would shield themselves, scurry past, or stop and chat. Though it was grueling, and one could argue that in terms of the bottom line, increasing the turnout, the returns were diminishing, I enjoyed the leafleting. It gave me a sense of common humanity. Most people, I thought, just wanted others to be kind to them. Smiling at them, greeting them, saying good morning, acknowledging their existence was one basic and not necessarily superficial way of being kind, even if, indeed, I was asking something of them.

A lot of people appeared entirely divorced from their social and political contexts and wanted nothing to do with them when invited to engage. Of course, those contexts had a profound effect on their lives; they could not avoid them but preferred to act as if they didn't exist. Leafleting was a constant reality check: Yes, 20% voted in the referendum but 80% did not, and I was meeting many of those 80% on the street day after day.

Some were friendly but uninterested, some were too busy (and always would be), some were apathetic, a very few were outright hostile. In others, there was a shyness, something in them that almost wanted to be drawn out, wanted to be invited, given the opportunity to participate in some small way, to rise up out of their selves and their immediate personal lives and orbits. Given that opportunity, some, not all but some, would take the leaflet and perhaps discover a new part of themselves that they rather liked. For them, taking part in the "greater matters" of their society, even in just a small way, was a big step, a paradigmatic shift in the way they lead their lives, thought of themselves, of their relationship to society.

Canvassing helped me to cultivate empathy toward all and to guard against dogmatism and entirely rigid intellectual positions. It was also an antidote to my ever-looming misanthropy. People were overworked and underrested. They did what they could to get by. How much more could be asked of them? Sometimes they struck me as valiant, heroic, bravely struggling in the face of the adversity that was their daily lives, the powerful economic, social and political forces they were up against, whether they knew it or not. Occasionally someone would approach to tell me she disagreed with what I was doing. Thank you, I would always reply, for telling me, and best wishes to you. I felt gratitude towards them for making the effort. To disagree openly without rancor was the beginning of something. All of this, sometimes, felt like the beginning of something, an opening, to what exactly was unclear. Meeting people on the street didn't change any basic opinions I held, but it reminded me that you had to meet people where they were, not where you wished they were, you had to be willing to meet them there.

And yet just as I admired all the people I encountered and entreated for being the heroes of their own lives (or the anti-heroes, if they were that), it was not just all the sleepy morning commuters that made the thought recur that most people sleep-walk through history. To them, I thought as they passed, history doesn't matter. They don't recognize it, don't see themselves as part of it, let alone as being able to shape it, or actually shaping it simply by their passivity if nothing else. One of my repeated exhortations was that HK was at a critical historical juncture. We all had to recognize that and play our role, even if up to now we'd been largely inactive. The "historical argument", I sensed, was not one with great popular appeal. *Remember, we are making history*, I would shout. *We have to stand up and be counted. We must take our fate into our own hands. We must let the Partystate know we won't be bullied.* If HK people didn't stand up, that would seal HK's doom. The bully would know that it could basically get away with anything, and the creeping assimilation and erosion of autonomy would continue apace. I had been trained to see certain moments as crucially influential of subsequent events, revolutions and the like, but standing there on the street corner, I realized that even at those times when there was mass involvement in uprisings that brought about great change, most people were just getting on, just living their lives, standing off to the side, uninterested, unaware.

Nothing could be taken for granted. Yes, the referendum turnout was magnificent, a form of resistance showing the best side of HK people, refusing to allow the Partystate to frighten them or to cynically manipulate their short-sighted money-grubbing narrowly self-interested tendencies. After all, it was more than one in ten people in HK, more than 10% of the population. It was more than one in five registered voters for a referendum that was not legally binding, could not in itself make anything happen, and on top of that, was linked to a movement, Occupy Central, about which many were ambivalent, to put it mildly, because of its potential element of civil disobedience. Astounding, yes. But in that 1 in 5 lay the catch too, for where were the other 80%? The referendum had been extended from the original three days in length to ten due to the cyberattacks. Organizers wanted to ensure that all who wanted to vote had the chance. But whereas 700,000 voted in the first three days, fewer than 100,000 voted in the last seven. In other words, the vote plateaued. What did it mean that the pro-democracy movement found it so hard to break through that 20-some-percent barrier of active participation? Opinion polls over the course of the seventeen years under Partystate sovereignty consistently showed that more than 60% of the populace wanted real universal suffrage. And yet, where was that 40% that didn't turn out? If they didn't get involved now, would they ever?

The Partystate and the democrats were contending for the souls of the 50 to 60% in the middle. 20 to 30% strongly supported one side or the other. All evidence indicated most of the rest wanted democracy, but where were they? How to get them out? After all, they were the ones who torpedoed the revolution in Egypt. First, they supported it, both actively and passively, and then they supported the coup against the Brotherhood, and then they supported a return to dictatorship in the name of stability. Their lives and society had been a mess since the revolution had occurred—for revolution was messy—, and so they opted for peace and stability though it meant returning to the past, when they were unhappy. It was easy to get frustrated with the short-sightedness of such attitudes of "the people in the middle", but from the angle of their own lives, who could blame them?

Perhaps one could only expect assertive push-back when the Partystate crossed the line and became too oppressive; in other words, the old negative defense— "we don't want that"—rather than the positive struggle to achieve a tangible end—"we want this". At all other times, people got lulled into complacency or simply had too much else to do, and other things, such as democracy, got deprioritized, especially when there was no clear route to that destination, indeed, when time spent on it seemed futile, destined to simply run up against an implacable force. Wasn't it more in your interest most of the time to *accept reality and behave appropriately*?

Your father came back from biking in his home village in Guangdong a day early, in time to vote on the last day of the referendum. Miracles did occur.

Since the referendum had been extended from its original three days to ten days due to the cyberattacks, the annual July 1 march followed hard on its heels, just two days later. It did not take long to see HK people would not disappoint. The numbers were huge, and I reckoned early they would meet or surpass the record of half a million in 2003. If that demonstration lead to the government eventually shelving the draconian security legislation that would bring HK laws into alignment with mainland laws on sedition, subversion, treason and the like, one wondered whether this one might have any effect. I suspected not. I suspected the HK people suspected not. The days of a one-day mass demonstration having any influence on the Partystate were past. And still, in spite of their lack of expectation that what they were doing that day would directly lead to a tangible improvement, they came. And came. In Great George Street, crowds were packed so tight that many people didn't even make it to the march starting point in Victoria Park and simply joined the march at another point along the route.

In 2003, due to the enormous crowd, you and I had been stuck in the park for hours, waiting to set off on the march. The heat was intense. It sickened you. When we finally did get out of the park, you had to sit on the curb to recover. You were wearing an oversize black t-shirt with the surname of the then-Chief Executive turned upside down ("down with Tung," it essentially said), light tan linen trousers, your old maroon NB sneakers, already quite worn. Your hair was in pigtails. You looked up at me with a forced smile that said, I'm ok, even though you weren't. Like thousands of others that day, I learned my lesson: Don't get stuck in the park. And so on this July 1, eleven years later, I flitted about, scouting: What were people up to, how many were there, what was the mood?

The date was as if designed for provoking protest. Not only was it the anniversary of the handover, but the handover occurred on the anniversary of the founding of the Party; in other words, HK's "return to the motherland" was the Partystate's birthday present to itself. Sick. From the Partystate's point of view, it was a milestone in its glorious history. It had come to power promising to "reunite the motherland" that had been dismembered by Western and Japanese imperialists. That entailed re-establishing control over East Turkestan, invading and conquering Tibet, and clawing back HK, Macau and Taiwan. Macau "returned to the motherland" two years after HK. Now only Taiwan was renegade.

There was a hideous VIP-only ceremony held in front of the hideous Golden Bauhinia Statue, nicknamed Golden Bok Choy, always up there on the list of the city's ugliest tourist sites, in Golden Bauhinia Square near the harbor. The spot had been propagandized on the mainland as a sign of sovereignty, part of the Partystate's unceasing efforts to make China great again, and mainland tourists flocked there as if on pilgrimage. It would never occur to any self-respecting HK person to visit such an evil place—it took a trick the Partystate was extremely adept at pulling off to make such a magnificent setting on the harbor so ugly. On this particular anniversary, the "dignitaries" arrived by boat. It was feared that if they came by road, they might have to encounter the people. The ceremony in the square was followed by a reception stage-managed in the best Partystate tradition so as to exclude anyone who might voice an opinion that departed from the Party line. In symbolism few could miss, HK people were effectively excluded from official events commemorating the "return to the motherland" because they couldn't be trusted to behave, to stick to the script. The official commemoration emphasized that the handover had nothing to do with HK people and everything to do with the Partystate's self-image, its narrative of history. How the Partystate could ever look itself in the mirror and see anything it liked—therein lay the mystery of tyranny.

The march had become the people's commemoration of July 1, and it was essentially, year after year, a rejection of Partystate control.

There was the usual atmosphere of celebratory defiance, but today it seemed even more so than usual. Hundreds of organizations came out. It was a festival of civil society and a vision of what the city could be. Being in the crowd engendered hope. People were warm, open, different from HK people's usual stony indifference towards each other, often the case when people lived so crowded together—you just had to ignore others to maintain your sanity. But here, everyone was responsible for everyone else, happy, impressed with each other. You could see it in people's eyes: They looked around, saw themselves, saw others, and thought, This is the way we could be. Our better selves.

Weaving through the crowd, about halfway through the march, I caught up with the lead truck. The going was slow, and in especially congested areas such as Causeway Bay, people were pressed up against each other. I feared at some points there was a risk of people being crushed, or of stampeding. The police had limited the march to three lanes out of seven on the main road, hardly sufficient for the hundreds of thousands marching. The joy of the rest of the march contrasted with the tension at the front, as organizers plead with police to open more lanes. Police appeared uninterested in listening, let alone negotiating. They simply tried to persuade the lead vehicle to move more quickly. My impression was that they were under strict political orders to keep half the main road open, as having to altogether close the road to traffic would make headlines. But the organizers didn't want the whole road, just one additional lane. They conveyed to police that they were receiving reports of bottlenecks in two areas congested not only by the demonstration but by shoppers, passers-by and by-standers. On top of the complaints of feeling crushed and fears of trampling, by that point, tens of thousands of marchers had been trapped in the park, the march's starting point, for two to three hours while other marchers were still trying to get into the park. The police had only one exit at the park and were asked to open others. Again, the police appeared uninterested in entertaining the request. Their sole concern was to make the lead vehicle move more quickly—in their eyes, that was where the problem lay. Then came reports that at one bottleneck, protesters unable to take the pressure of being crushed up against so many others had pushed through police barricades, and there had been tussles between protesters and the police. This would prove to be the one and only slightly or potentially violent episode to mar the whole day of the half-million people march, but the fact that marchers feared being trampled and were essentially trying to create some more room for themselves, some literal breathing space, was certainly an extenuating factor. Though there had been many previous demonstrations of hundreds of thousands that were largely self-policing and entirely free of violence, destruction of property and arrests, there was on this occasion an edginess in relations between police and demonstrators that had previously existed but was getting sharper.

Three hours after the march started, the first marchers arrived in Chater Road, Central, the designated end point. It would take those stuck in the park where the march began seven long hours to complete the seven-kilometer march, a sign of just how relentlessly heaving and congested the crowd was. They arrived at Chater Road just after ten in the evening, long past dark. That was when the organizers declared the march officially over and handed things over to the students.

The day before the march, two student groups had declared that they would conduct sit-ins following the march proper. This created a stir. Occupy Central had to clarify that this was the students' decision, not its own; Occupy Central itself would not be participating but expressed strong support for the students. The student groups were Scholarism and HK Federation of Students, the two I'd been impressed by on the June 4 march nearly a month before when they veered off on a march of their own, heading for the Central Government Liaison Office. I hadn't been wrong about their energy. After the referendum, Occupy Central had said that it needed to present the results to the HK government and await its response before deciding what to do next. But the HK government had given its response *before* the referendum had even taken place: It was illegal. In other words, it would refuse to recognize it even as a legitimate expression of opinion. So OC's approach seemed exceedingly formalistic and creepingly incrementalist. By contrast, the students said that it was time to step things up, and the July 1 march was the perfect opportunity. They declared that one group would sit-in outside of the Chief Executive's office, call for a meeting with him, and await his arrival at work the next morning. The other group would occupy Chater Road, a main artery of Central, the business district. Both announced in advance their intention to end the sit-ins at 8 am.

I wanted to stay with the students through the night, but I had to go home and relieve my dedicated parents-in-law, who had been caring for Z all day. I had been a bad father of late, spending little time with Z, and she had been acting up as a result. The grandparents and she, though, had had a good day. After I put Z to bed, I found several live streams of the Chater Road sit-in and followed it from home, staying up all night tweeting. I had been worried about the students and called for observers and journalists to keep an eye on police behavior. I needn't have worried: There were hundreds of onlookers and so many media people that the police ordered them on several occasions to move out of the way. They admirably ignored the police and clustered around almost every removal of a demonstrator, police officers having to disentangle the demonstrator from her fellows on either side and then haul her off, one officer per limb. After several hours, the police finally managed to push the media outward to the perimeters of the gathering and barricade themselves with metal barriers around the largest clusters of demonstrators. Even so, it took them the whole night to clear less than a block-long segment of the street.

The process settled into a strange routine, with all playing their role, the protesters shouting slogans and sitting locked arm in arm, the police dragging one demonstrator after another away after painstaking extraction. Both sides showed restraint and self-discipline. Of course, it was the demonstrators I was most impressed with even as I acknowledged that the police refrained from using disproportionate force. The demonstrators were young people who'd never before engaged in nonviolent direct action. Later, quite a few reported how scared they were. During my time in HK, there had never been an act of civil disobedience on this scale. And yet the young people pulled it off with great spirit, without rancor, in spite of fear. My heart swelled with gratitude to them. Yes, I was right on the June 4 march when I suspected that these people, the young people, would be the future of the movement, the future of the city.

Each side used the event as a trial run for what was to come, the threatened occupation of Central. Based on both sides' performance, the apocalypse did not await, as the fear-mongers had been prophesying.

Z woke several times during the night. She didn't sleep well when I was not in the bedroom with her; her sleeping self could sense my absence. When I went in to comfort her, she had strange requests. One time it was, *I want raisins from the müssli*, as distinct from raisins out of their separate bag. Another, *I want a balloon blown up and tied*. The third time she woke up, she sat up, cried and said she did not want to go back to sleep. I picked her up, brought her out to the main room where I was watching the sit-in, and held her.

Who are they? she asked, calmed now and pointing to the screen. *What are they doing?* She knew I had been at a demonstration earlier in the day. When I got home, I'd given her stickers from it, which she'd immediately stuck on her shirt, a little chair of hers, a glass door. So she understood when I explained they were part of the demonstration. *What are the police doing?* she asked.

They are arresting the demonstrators and taking them to prison, I said.

Why?

The police say the demonstrators shouldn't block the street.

I don't want the police to do that, she said.

I don't want them to either. The demonstrators are just students. They're not really doing anything wrong. In fact, I think what they are doing is right.

But why do the police arrest people who are doing something right? she asked.

Sometimes the people who are the bosses of the police tell them to do that because they don't like what the people are doing.

What do they not like?

They don't want to give the people democracy, and the students are telling them to give the people democracy.

She fell silent. My answers satisfied her for now, probably because it was the middle of the night. Eventually, she lay down on the pink sofa, from which I removed all the cushions to make room for her, and she fell asleep while I continued watching the demonstrations and tweeting. She didn't mind the screenglow; in fact, that and my presence calmed her, and she slept peacefully until the sky lightened and the first birds of morning sang.

As the 8am deadline approached and the police still had not finished clearing the street, the bystanders became vocal cheerleaders of the students, counting down the time. When the clock struck eight and there were still several dozen demonstrators to be cleared, the crowd erupted in cheers. The irony of it was that if the police had just allowed the demonstrators to sit in until eight and then go their way, a whole night's effort of clearance would have been saved. Instead, it took thousands of officers longer to remove them than if they had been allowed to remove themselves. Both sides declared victory. The police had managed to clear the street before the day really got moving. And that, presumably, was what they were under orders to do at all costs; they couldn't risk the demonstrators breaking their 8am promise. One had to think that thousands of police taking the whole night to clear a little over five-hundred demonstrators all congregated in one single area did not bode well for the future: Occupy Central had plans for at least ten-thousand occupiers. How could the police possibly cope with that? Tactically, it appeared that if it planned well and was able to summon the requisite numbers, Occupy Central had the upper hand. Based on the night's events, the government, the police had reason to worry, especially if the night was meant to show they would have everything under control.

Meanwhile, the police hardly disturbed the other sit-in outside the Chief Executive's office at government headquarters, probably because it didn't block a road and they had to concentrate their efforts on removing demonstrators from a main artery. Some of the ones outside the CE's office even got several hours of sleep. In response to the student call to meet with them, the Chief Executive's limousine arrived in the morning and swiftly entered the building via an alternate route, an anticlimactic end to the night that signaled the CE's disdain or, depending on how one looked at it, fear.

By 8 am, the police had announced 196 arrests, which seemed impossibly low given how many bodies I had seen drug away through the night. And indeed, by noon, they had revised the number to 511. The demonstrators were taken to a police training college, as the authorities had no other facility large enough to detain and process so many, another sign that they would have difficulty coping with the even larger numbers of OC. Reports began to emerge of significant delays in processing. Lawyers had begun to go to the college in the early hours of the morning to meet their clients, but they were kept waiting for as many as five hours. Eventually, 25 demonstrators were released on bail and 486 with warnings. This was interpreted as the police intending to press charges against the 25 they considered the leaders. The 486 let off with a warning were told the police reserved the right to prosecute them later. The charges were unlawful assembly and obstruction of a public thoroughfare, as well as, apparently, in some cases, obstruction of police officers in carrying out their duties. The police intended to apply the law selectively, since presumably either all those arrested were guilty of unlawful assembly or none of them were; none, after all, denied they had taken part. Why did they appear to be singling out a select few? Probably to avoid gumming up the courts. One of the possible effects of large-scale nonviolent direct action was not only overwhelming the police but also the court system, if the government intended to prosecute everybody. But it seemed the government's case against the 25 it appeared ready to prosecute would be weaker if it couldn't justify why those and not others. And of course, the longer the cases drug on, the more public opprobrium they would excite. The action, as intended, placed the government in a no-win situation. I wondered whether or not they fully understood their plight. They seemed in no hurry to prosecute the 25 arrested.

After their release, demonstrators complained of insufficient access to food and toilets, something that authorities tacitly acknowledged, claiming to have been overwhelmed, as if that was justification for denying detainees food and toilets for hours, but again, it did not bode well for their ability to contend with even larger numbers in the future.

The HK police next arrested five of the march organizers for failure to follow police orders and, most ridiculously, in the case of the lead van driver, "idling an engine", a relatively new law that had been passed with the intention of cutting down on pollution from vehicles standing at the side of the road. Police had up to then been criticized for not enforcing it, in particular when it concerned the limousines of the wealthy that could be seen idling in the business district on any given day, so it raised many an eyebrow that they suddenly had developed an enthusiasm for pressing the charge.

All the way back to 2003, in eleven years of marching on July 1, never before had organizers been arrested. There had always been disagreements between them and police about various aspects of crowd control, but through the years, the march had always been conducted peacefully, quite a remarkable achievement in light of the hundreds of thousands who participated. One assumed organizers and police would continue to agree to disagree. Until this year. What was different, undoubtedly, was the political situation, the extent to which the Partystate and HK government felt threatened. The police contended that the lead vehicle of the demonstration had been moving too slowly, and when the police ordered it to speed up, the vehicle moved even more slowly and stopped at times. In a sense, this was true, but only partially so: It was because the organizers were attempting to relay to police reports that there was not enough room and demonstrators were at risk of being crushed.

By coincidence, the Chief Executive's twice-annual Question-and-Answer Session at the Legislative Council, HK's pseudo-parliament, took place two days after the march and sit-ins. Democratic legislators protested against the Chief Executive's indifference to the people's desire for democracy. Two of them were expelled from the chamber and the rest exited in solidarity with them. The Chief Executive was asked whether he would step down if his government did not succeed in carrying out its responsibility to enact electoral reform. No, he said, he would not. The stage was set.

And what was the count after those whirlwind days? 800,000 voted. 500,000 marched. 511 + 5 were arrested. Once again, I could not avoid the feeling that it took so much to accomplish so little.

•

Not long after, Occupy Central held a banquet to thank volunteers. It was the pause before the next storm, the National People's Congress Standing Committee "verdict" on whether or not to allow HK to proceed with "electoral reform", to be handed down some seven to eight weeks hence. I went to the banquet, in spite of my ambivalence about this HK cultural phenomenon. But I thought I should show myself, show my support and appreciation; it was the least I could do. It had been a hard eighteen months for the three leaders and founders of Occupy Central and their many faithful assistants. They had been under intense pressure, including vilification campaigns unleashed by the largest dictatorship and propaganda machine in the world. They had withstood, and, thus far, come through, not just surviving but, lately at least, thriving—accomplishments worth celebrating. They had lead with equilibrium, grace, moderation, forbearance, courage, modesty, mindfulness, intelligence, determination and a sense of humor. And they wished to thank the hundreds who had been indispensable to making it all happen, all of those who worked behind the scenes in obscurity. It was a worthy occasion.

The reverend had a divine smile. It glowed. That was nothing new; it always had. Looking at him, I wondered when I had last smiled such an unguarded, unselfconscious, life-loving, pure smile.

The law professor looked relieved at the referendum turnout. In a speech, he said he didn't really want to occupy Central. He hoped it turned out not to be necessary. There was nothing new in that statement; he'd made comments to that effect several times before. And there was a certain humility in them too: I am just a law professor, not a street fighter, and the fact that a law professor like myself has brought himself to the point of threatening civil disobedience shows how desperate the situation has become. He was playing the reluctant activist. Because he was a reluctant activist. How these months had told on him! How he wished—so I sensed—to return to the quiet life of the academic! What in the world had he gotten himself into?

He was a deeply humane man. I recalled his recent letter to HK police in the aftermath of the Chater Road sit-in. The HK Junior Police Association, the union representing most officers, had come out with a statement criticizing demonstrators for "picking quarrels and creating a disturbance", which not only was not a crime in HK but was a term borrowed from the mainland (where it was a crime, of dubious validity), a possible sign of the mainlandization of the HK police. Rather than criticizing the police and calling for accountability, the law professor praised the police for their professionalism in clearing the road of demonstrators, saying that their handling of the sit-in met international standards of law enforcement, apologized to the police for any worries caused by the prospect of Occupy Central nonviolent direct action, and expressed understanding of the tremendous pressure they must be under. He hoped the police understood the ideas behind Occupy Central, which, he said, respected social order and was willing to take legal responsibility for violating the law. He reached out to the police, saying Occupy Central did not view them as the enemy and understood they were obliged to follow orders, and asked them not to see the demonstrators as bad elements who wished to challenge police authority. He emphasized that the police and demonstrators shared the city's core values of rule of law, human rights and democracy. We are on different sides, he said, but our hearts are the same. He asked the police when carrying out orders to think critically and ask themselves what pushed HK people to take the step of nonviolent direct action. He expressed confidence that front-line officers were wise and knew how to handle nonviolent direct action, but he advised that the law was not the same as conscience, that there were bad laws and also bad uses of good laws, and that in simply following orders and enforcing the law, the police could not guarantee to themselves that they weren't violating their conscience.

I didn't necessarily agree with a lot of that message—I regarded the police, especially its increasingly politicized leadership, more critically—, but that was the sort of leader one wanted, humble, open to communication and dialogue. And really, there was nothing objectionable in his reluctance to occupy: Virtually no one was truly chomping at the bit to invade the central business district. But still, something about his comment in that moment struck me wrong. It set off a reaction that bore strong resemblance to what I'd heard about panic attacks. They're not ready! I thought. They don't know what they're doing! The moment is upon us—a crucial moment in the history of HK's struggle for democracy, an opportunity that would not come soon if ever again—, and they're not prepared. Here we are at this stupid banquet congratulating ourselves, and around us, the battle is well on the way to being lost. Who could I share this sentiment with? I wanted to stand up and shout it: Don't you realize?! But I sat there silently gazing about the hall, feeling my spirit deflate by the minute, the second. These were the people who were going to bring this momentous struggle to its climax? They were good people. And good volunteers, good administrators, good at concentrating on their small tasks and doing them well, committed, responsible, dependable. But hardened activists? People who really understood what they were up against and had what it took to overcome it? It was one of those panicky "I'm-surrounded-by-amateurs!" moments. I thought of you and knew that you would understand exactly what I was feeling.

When I'd gone out to the bathroom earlier, I saw a poorly dressed older man of the sort that could be seen all over the city, a stock character, taking a photo with his smartphone of a piece of paper on the reception table next to the main entrance to the banquet hall. Boo! I said to the man. He scurried off. I asked him what he was doing there. He scurried faster. I went up to the table and looked at the paper: a guest list someone had left there. The amateurishness of leaving a list like that lying around for all and sundry to peruse! I picked it up and put it in my pocket, intending to give it to whoever was responsible for it. I thought if the Partystate and HK government knew what they were up against, they would see they had nothing to fear.

In their massive propaganda campaign, they had made Occupy Central into a bogeyman that would destroy the city. Ironically, they had done as much as anyone else to create OC.

Behind the scenes, the capacity of the movement was questionable; so was whether or not it was a movement at all. How did OC possibly expect to be prepared for the NPCSC's all-but-certain hardline decision on electoral reform? It had stated repeatedly that it needed a minimum of 10,000 people to effectively occupy Central, but last I heard, it had signed up some 2,000, and that was months ago. As far as I knew, it had not actively recruited more in a long time, so focused had it been on the referendum and aftermath. There were surely thousands more out there who were interested, but how did OC intend to get them involved? And how was OC planning to train them all? Again, to my knowledge, it had conducted no training in nonviolent direct action. And then once they had the numbers, they had to have a strategy for deploying them: How exactly was Central to be occupied? Presumably, there were discussions about these matters within the inner circle, but weren't we past the point of initial discussions? Wasn't it time to "operationalize"? In the sit-in that had followed the half-million-strong pro-democracy march, since there were only several hundred participants, the police outnumbered them and could, albeit with great effort and at great expense and after several hours, corral them, cut them off, and pick them up and carry them away one by one. Presumably, the advantage of 10,000 participants was that the police could not use that corralling technique, since the participants would disperse to different parts of the district. But then would police seek to corral the smaller groups? And if so, was the idea just to allow the police to do so? Would police seek to cut off "supply lines", and if so, were they to be allowed to do so? What about logistics of getting food and water to people sitting in, especially if they did so for many hours or even days on end? All of these questions swirled around my head. This was not going to happen, not going to get off the ground, and if it did, it would evaporate nearly as soon as it began. Or if it took off, it was a matter of chance and spontaneous appeal rather than the planning, the hard work, the laying of foundations of this group.

These people, I thought, were just leaving everything to chance! Didn't they know they were up against adversaries that left nothing to chance? I kept hoping things were going on in secret that I knew nothing about, but it was hard to keep things entirely secret from me, so I suspected that was not the case. A movement was broad-based, transcended any leaders; OC was an organization with three leaders and administrative volunteers to serve them.

I left early, not because I was disheartened—I was; I felt nearly physically sick—but because I had to relieve the grandparents who were once again looking after Z. I had an urge to run not walk out the door of the banquet hall and never come back. What had I gotten myself involved in? We are chained to our causes.

When I got home that night, I realized the guest list was still in my breast pocket. I'd forgotten to track down the person to whom I was supposed to return it.

●

Dear Tatyana,

This is turning into a monthly report!

I got a couple of free hours earlier this week to go through the storage area under the stairs. It is so packed and dark that I basically had to rifle through boxes, feeling with my hands for the notebook. Unfortunately, I wasn't able to find it. I didn't have time to actually take the boxes out and look through them one by one in the light. That's the next step: I've resolved to, at some point soon, take everything out, go through it, and reorganize it, and I'm sure when I do that, I'll find the notebook. Sorry for the long wait—patience, please!

I didn't describe how hot, humid and dusty it was feelingly perusing the boxes in the near-dark of the cramped storage area. Nor did I mention the papers in the boxes I rifled through with my one free hand (the other grasping onto another box or leant against the wall for balance as I bent and stretched) were so damp I imagined I would end up having to throw most of them out. If they were that damp, what shape would the notebook be in when I finally found it?

I didn't mention *The Little Prince* in the message either. I thought of doing so, but refrained, out of perhaps a misplaced sense of self-discipline: I didn't think Tatyana particularly wanted to hear from me, let alone my chatty news, so I kept the message to the minimum. She might have suspected appeal to our one-time mutual interest in *The Little Prince* was meant to charm or seduce her. Who knew? Perhaps it was.

I somewhat regretted not having mentioned it. There was a lot to say, but then Tatyana was perhaps not the person to say it to. I'd mentioned in the previous message that I'd gotten a pop-up book version of *The Little Prince* and was planning to give it to Z for her birthday. And since then, her birthday had come and gone, and she had received the book.

She would take it out of its protective plastic sheath several times a day, page through it, and ask me to explain the pop-up pictures. Within only a few days, she came to know the story well, or at least the bits of it related most closely to the pictures. She flipped from page to page, pointing to each picture, describing it perfectly, remembering everything I had told her, telling the story to herself. The elephant inside of a boa constrictor, the sheep, the rose, the fox, the baobabs, the snake, the inhabitants of the other tiny planets—it was uncanny sometimes how quickly she learned, how her mind seemed to register everything, take it all in.

One evening, after her bath and before going to bed, she sat naked on the pink sofa, the book open on her lap, and said, <u>The Little Prince</u> *taught me to read the other books.* I wasn't quite sure what she meant. I took her to mean that reading *The Little Prince* made something click for her in terms of reading other books.

I would be off doing something elsewhere in the flat and hear her narrating a story to herself. I'd peak in to see her leafing through a book in complete concentration. That must have been what she meant.

I imagined writing to Tatyana regularly, month after month, to give her updates on the indefinite search for the notebook, which was never found but always would be. The monthly updates metamorphosed into a one-way correspondence. There was never any response. She probably never even read them. At first, she might have, just to see whether there was any news on the notebook. But then, once she saw that in message after message the only news was that I still hadn't found it, she would develop the habit of scanning a message for news and then deleting it. It made no difference; I continued writing. That was the vision; I never followed through on it. I mentally composed several that were never sent, but just imagining gave me insight into what it was to have faith in a god to whom one's prayers might be addressed, a god in whom one might confide, a god from whom one seeks approval, a god to whom one might show the capacity for faith without any hope of response, a god who never answers.

Z became more concerned with matters of fate—what happened to people and places long after they had been forgotten by most others? Walking along, apropos of nothing, she would suddenly ask, *Did the man with the crashed airplane ever get out of the desert, or did he die because he ran out of food and water?*

I don't know, I replied, *but I think he got out of the desert; otherwise, he wouldn't have been able to tell us the story of how he met the Little Prince.*

She knew that people died from getting very old or very sick or having a very bad accident. But she kept pressing me: What was it exactly about being very old or very sick that made people die?

Well, I said, *if they are very old or very sick, some of their body parts start to not work so well.*

One morning I pulled her on her scooter up the steep hill to the village at the top of the island. The birds were singing in the trees. How beautiful the island was, how beautiful life was, despite (or because of) every argument to the contrary (and there were quite a few good ones). Z wore her pink t-shirt with four moose, identical except that each was a different color and, as she herself pointed out to me (I hadn't noticed), had different expressions: surprised, sad, happy and the last I forgot. The smallest size available, it looked like a tent on her when we got it; she had grown, and it now fit like a frock, coming down to just above the knees. She held a hand-puppet sheep in one hand. It was given her when she was a baby, and she had never had much interest in it. She had rediscovered it recently; she claimed she had found "her" on the way home one day and Sheep was lonely so Z invited her along. Now as we advanced up the hill, she was giving Sheep a lecture in a sing-songy voice.

There are snakes in the world.
There are clouds in the world.
There are trees in the world.
There are brown leaves in the world.
There are green leaves in the world.
There are acorns in the world.
There are cucumbers in the world.
There are eggplants in the world.

There are tomatoes in the world.
There are sunflowers in the world.
There are papayas in the world.
There are stars in the world.
There are holes in the world.
There are drainage pipes in the world.
There are beaches in the world.
There is sand in the world.
There is everything in the world.

That night, as we lay in bed, she asked, *Why does the earth spin?* And then, *Why are we humans?*

●

It was the first typhoon of the season. There were strong winds, occasional deluges. Z was fascinated by storms. In the library we came across Maya Angelou's poem, "Life Doesn't Frighten Me", set to paintings by Basquiat. The paintings were a bit too abstract for Z, but she liked the rhythm and rhyme of the poem. I said, *Of course, there are scary things in life, but most of the time, if something's scary but you bring yourself to do it, to work past it, to go through it, you find out it's o.k., and then you're not scared by it anymore. That's what 'Life Doesn't Frighten Me' means- don't let fear control your life or stop you from doing things you want to do.* Z nodded vaguely in half-comprehension.

You always complained about the deeply fearful orientation towards life your parents had unconsciously instilled in you by example, osmosis, and even more of how difficult it was to resist, how it seeped into you at an early age and made you the tense, anxious person you were. You wanted to protect your daughter from that fearful outlook that pervaded everything. You wanted your daughter to preserve her natural joy, creativity, fearlessness. You feared your own anxieties, inherited from your parents, would somehow, against your will, seep into your daughter.

I was sometimes proudly astounded at how brash and self-confident, nearly full of herself, Z could be. But she was also at an age when she began increasingly to feel small fears and anxieties. At night, she snuggled up to me and whimpered in a mock baby voice, *I'm scared.*

What are you scared of? I'd ask.

She would make something up, a slight noise she had just heard outside the window or the like. If she could articulate her fear, she might have said, By the immensity of all the terrible things that could possibly befall you. She was becoming aware of dangers, threats, of the fact that the world was not always a friendly place to small people like herself or to many others either. When meeting strangers, she would often hide between my legs. When encouraged to try something new, she would often turn away.

Z would be starting pre-school in the autumn. I hoped it would not be the beginning of a long excision of joy. I remembered your fears: your HK education robbed you of creativity, of imagination, made you depressed, though you got so used to that you didn't even notice until you left HK. You didn't want that for your daughter.

Z approached the world with fascination, delight, zest, confidence, curiosity, intelligence, relentless energy, open open eyes. My first obligation was a negative one, the same as that of the development industry- do no harm. Protect that amazing ability to thrill oneself with being alive.

I signed Z up for swimming lessons at the government pool. Against my better judgment. Because her friends had been signed up, and because I thought you would want me to, not because I was interested myself or thought it a good idea. I couldn't understand the point—here we lived on a beautiful island, surrounded by water, with a beach a five-minute walk away, and Z loved to be in the water. What was the point of travelling to town to get into a pool? Z would learn to swim in her own good time. But I signed her up.

Here was a water child who had always experienced water as pure joy, and on an island dotted with beaches, she had spent a lot of time in the water from when she was only a couple of months old. And yet, here, in this government pool, she began to exhibit fear and reluctance. It wasn't just that she was asked to do things that scared her, namely, putting her face in the water and blowing bubbles. It was that she was simply told to do these things without any suggestion as to how, and not in a context of play, of having fun doing it. Up to now, Z had associated learning with fun. If the child did not have a motivation (it was fun and interesting), how did one expect the child to learn at that age? The answer was, The child must learn, and given that the child must learn, it was simply a matter of telling the child to do it, and the child did it, regardless of how the child felt about it. I hated the prospect of Z going from loving being in the water to developing a fear of it. The teacher was a perfectly nice man, just someone who had come up through that educational culture of simply telling the child, Do this, and expecting the child to do it. There was some art to teaching a child how to do something challenging and perhaps frightening that you thought was good for the child to learn. But art didn't enter into the concept of education here. So I worried about Z starting pre-school. And I could just imagine what you would think.

I'd taken her to the orientation, had her measured for her uniform.

Z and I walked down the mostly deserted main street, shops still open but mostly empty, shopkeepers staring out at us, waving as we passed. Not much custom in typhoon weather. At the concrete football pitch, there were some low spots on its uneven surface that dependably collected rainwater in a heavy shower. Z wore her rain boots, bought by you shortly before your disappearance. (I had bought no clothes for Z since then; what she had was becoming small, somewhat threadbare, stained in places.) Z zoomed across the pitch on her scooter, jumped off, and splash-splash-splashed through the puddles, laughing delightedly.

On the far side of the pitch, just barely visible from the puddles, was the old pier, now used for cargo. A few days before, Z and I had climbed a pile of small rocks several meters high that was now diminishing rapidly, a digger scooping the rocks up and dumping them into VVs (motorized "village vehicles", specially constructed for the narrow paths of the roadless island) which waited in a queue to be filled and then zoomed off.

Look at that, Z said, *let's go there.*

Yes, I said, *let's go.*

Z hesitated. *It's kind of scary*, she said.

Life doesn't frighten me! I announced boastfully, my voice contesting with the strong wind.

Z smiled slyly. *Life frightens me!* she replied.

Unbelievable that this person was my daughter. That *this* person was her father.

Yuri Gagarin! she shouted with glee, in regard to nothing in particular. She had just learned about him in her space book. Something about the name struck her, stuck with her.

Who's Yuri Gagarin? I asked.

First person in space.

Who was in space before Yuri Gagarin?

A dog!

Good thing she never asked what happened to the dog: I could hardly countenance uttering the words, She never came back. But how else could I respond to such a question? Perhaps the dog's fate never occurred to her. Nor its name. Laika. A stray found on the streets of Moscow. Soviet scientists believed street dogs would be heartier since they had already shown they could withstand extreme cold and hunger. I remembered the musings of the boy in "My Life as a Dog": *What about Laika, the space dog? They put her in a Sputnik and sent her into space. They attached wires to her heart and brain to see how she felt. I don't think she felt so good. She spun around up there for five months until her doggy bag was empty. She starved to death.*

Little did the boy know Laika really died within hours of lift-off from overheating. This was not revealed until 2002. From a stray on the streets of Moscow to death by overheating as the first dog in space, none of it of her own volition.

We returned home. Later that day, I thought to myself, it seemed we had for so long now been living in an emergency situation, living emergency lives. Would we ever live a normal life again. (Then again, come to think of it, had we ever before?) It was as if we had been in a big empty room awaiting a train that had no schedule. It all felt claustrophobic, desperately sad: We would all grow old (if lucky) and die, I thought while staring at Z lying sleepily with her head in my lap, her body on my torso, her legs at my shoulders, after a nap. What came to mind were the heartbreakingly perfunctory last words of *Dr Zhivago*: *One day Lara went out and did not come back. She must have been arrested in the street, as so often happened in those days, and she died or vanished somewhere, forgotten as a nameless number on a list which later was mislaid, in one of the innumerable mixed or women's concentration camps in the north.* As simple as that.

That was the difference between then and now. These days, people rarely disappeared from the street forever, though they might for quite some time. These days, the Partystate didn't just kill you, not as freely or easily. Who said there wasn't progress, if only creeping, sideways, incremental, by degrees? If those degrees marked the difference between life and death, were they not substantial? Who was to say? But that anyone would regard the act of disappearing you as anything but out-and-out reprehensible was hard to swallow. For what kind of life was the life of the disappeared? How was it preferable to death? It was preferable to death because there was still the hope of freedom, however unbearable the secret detention may have been. It was people who committed that act, the act of abduction; it didn't just occur of itself. I struggled to refrain from regarding them as simply evil.

For all we knew, Lara didn't die. But for those left behind, what was the difference between death and disappearance? The only difference was the excruciating, unlikely possibility that the disappeared would return.

What if you were never to return? What would we—Z and I—do? Would we stay in HK, knowing there was always a slight possibility you might? Where else was there to go? What kind of life could we live? But what was there to do here? What kind of life would we live here beyond the indefinite holding pattern in which we'd been ever since your disappearance?

And if you did return? Go on living the same life as before, as if nothing had ever occurred? Unimaginable. But what, then?

6

Then Opal came good.

When it happened, it all happened so rapidly, after nothing happening for so long.

I've got something to tell you, but not on the phone.

Good news?

Well, yes, I suppose. As good as news can get in these dark days, she said cryptically, poetically, Opal-ly.

Then maybe we should take the opportunity to finally come out and see you.

Please do!

It felt like a vacation, going out there, and reminded me how long it had been since Z and I had even gone anywhere out of the usual. I hadn't been to Opal's island in years, though it could be seen from ours. It was not only the going away, the going to somewhere new that gave the holiday feeling. It was also that Opal's place felt like a summer camp, an eternal pan-Asian summer camp for girls, girls who liked girls. To think that it had all started with Opal "going into exile", so to speak, fed up with urban life and finding a place to rent for almost nothing in a hard-to-get-to village on the south coast of the big island. And from there, her encampment just grew and grew and grew, encompassing apartments in the same building and then nearby apartments, and now setting its stamp on the village as a whole, which seemed to be made up mostly of old people either ignoring or quizzically blinking at the new life Opal had brought to the dying place and girls girls girls who had found their way there from the four corners of Asia. There were HK people, of course, and Taiwanese, but also Indonesians, Filipinas, Malaysians, Singaporeans, mainlanders. The place had gained a reputation across a wide swath of East and Southeast Asia as a refuge, a sanctuary, a place where one could be oneself, and be accepted for that, with no apologies, no discretion, and meet like-minded people from elsewhere. Most came from places where they felt compelled to hide important parts of who they were. Some came for a weekend, or a short break, others had long-term rentals and were involved in projects lasting months, often having to do with art or writing. And, right at the center of the action, Opal basked in it all, all the while acting as if what she had created had nothing to do with her, had simply happened.

This is like a dream, I said.

Yes, it is like a dream, she said. *Sometimes I look around and wonder if it's real. It's how, without knowing it, I'd always hoped to live.* Then, looking at Z, she asked, *And how are you, little one? How are you, beautiful one?*

Z was already off exploring, getting herself temporarily adopted by the women who showered her with attention. She enjoyed it. Already at her age, she was less wary of strange women than of men.

Opal said, *Children rarely move in straight lines. That's why I like children. They're monsters, but wondrous monsters.*

After a pause, I said, *And...?*

Opal told a story. It was an Opal story. It had Opal all over it. She had a knack for hobnobbing with ordinary people, the sorts whom most would usually ignore because no gain could be expected from paying them any attention. But Opal paid everyone attention, and the most ordinary the most. One of her contacts in the provincial town where BY had been living before her disappearance, the town she'd snuck into, where she'd lived undercover during her secret mission, was a low-level Guobao. He came from that town and somehow had a heart. They drank a lot together, something else Opal was good at. He was impressed with how much liquor she could hold. When he got drunk, he would apologize profusely and repeatedly for what he was doing, saying, *It's just a job, it's just a job, everyone needs a job, I don't know how I fell into it, but I did, I can't get another, and because I hate it, I'll never be any good at it, and I'll never get anywhere. This is my fate.*

He'd gotten back in touch with her, out of regret, she thought. He had something to tell her: Those women she was looking for—for she had confided in him about that; Opal had a knack for doing things that could seem either incredibly reckless or prescient—, he had found them. They were being held not far from Beijing, about halfway between there and the provincial town, in a Guobao "guesthouse". He hadn't actually seen them, he'd been told about them by colleagues, but he was pretty sure the information was accurate. *I'm trusting you with my life*, he said. *This is the sort of thing that's the end of me if anybody finds out. And you know what I hear? I hear they don't really want them, especially the foreign one. They're trying to find some way to get rid of them.*

Wow, I said. *Some way to get rid of them?... And so, what do we do now?*

Well, as I see it, this gives us leverage. Now is when we play our only card, the threat to go public.

Yes, I said, *you're right. Now. We contact the usual people?* By whom I meant the lawyers.

Yes, the usual people. Tell them to be sure to phrase the message they convey not as an ultimatum coming from us but as a piece of news they'd heard and were passing on. I'll contact the security people I'm in touch with.

Marni has all the media lined up and is just waiting for the go-ahead. How long should I tell her to give it?

A week. And tell the lawyers to tell them that. I'll do the same with the security people. One week and then we go public.

A week. A week and then we 'launch'. The timing's right. There are three weeks before the NPCSC HK decision. I guess as hardline as that'll be, the Partystate won't want anything else to even further provoke HK.

You never know with them, but it's time to do something.

We then talked of other things. We'd been through this long enough together that we both knew what we had to do.

We watched Z playing with the women. They were down near the beach. I couldn't hear her, only see her. She appeared to have constructed an elaborate role play and was instructing the women on their roles.

Then Opal said, *I'm off to Taiwan soon.*

What? You mean for a trip?

No, to study, maybe to stay, who knows. I'm sick of this place. It's going nowhere. It's ruined, infested. I need to do something for myself. I'm sick of sacrifice.

But HK's just getting going. Something's going to happen soon. Big. You should stay and be a part of it.

You might be right, but it's not my fight to fight. I've been fighting for years; it's time for others to take up the baton.

What are you going to study?

Human rights. An MA. Two years. I'm surprised they let me in, makes me wonder about the level of education there, but I've heard the program is good. It will be my first proper education. I wonder if I'll be able to manage.

You'll manage. You'll more than manage.

Are you pleased?

About what?

About me studying human rights.

Yeah, it's great. But I wonder if it will make you better at what you already do. You're pretty good at it, you know. And the stuff you know, and the stuff you can do is not the sort of stuff you learn in school…. Isn't it a kind of escape?

Hey, she said in protest, *I have a right to improve myself, don't I?! I don't forever want to be the 'grassroots activist' that everyone steps on, that everyone uses, no one respects.*

Yes, I see…. I miss you already.

Oh, don't say that!…. Don't worry. I won't go before Y comes back.

It's not that I meant.

I know it's not, but still….

I looked around, and asked, *But why would you leave this? Why would you give this up? You have a good thing going here.*

Yes, but now this place will live without me. There are good people who will take over and take it forward. I can't stay here forever. Nothing lasts forever, you know.

Thanks for telling me. But some things should last a good long time, no?

Yes, like life and freedom.... Life. And freedom.

It isn't home?

It is. That's why I'm leaving.

So restless! You know, Taiwan was the last place Y and I went before Z came along. We knew she was in Y's tummy, so I suppose you could say it was Z's first trip as well. We loved it there. It was a revelation: a democratic majority-Chinese society.... We'll come visit you.

Yes, please do.

Through our intermediaries, we let the powers that be know that we'd be going public in two weeks' time, just a week before the NPCSC decision was due. We told them we'd notify the international press, the UN, foreign governments. We hinted that we'd publicize the case widely in HK, and the disappearance of an HK permanent resident would have the effect of scaring even more people about the Partystate's intentions regarding the city at a time when apprehensions were already high. It could have a crucial effect on the direction of the universal suffrage campaign, could even be a kind of tipping point, depending on how well we played it and what the uptake was. It was not the sort of notoriety the Partystate needed at what all expected to be a turbulent time.

Coupled with what I imagined was the Partystate's dawning realization that the two of you were worth relatively little in custody, the ploy seemed to have worked. The Partystate had already crippled if not killed the New Citizens Movement. It no longer posed a threat, nor did any other form of independent organization or movement, however loose-knit. Either they'd already gotten what was useful out of you or they hadn't. Whatever the case, your utility had tipped into liability.

Before long, messages were relayed to us through the intermediaries that a release was imminent. When, after that, we didn't hear anything for a while again, we reminded the matter was urgent, we needed something specific. We didn't say in so many words, but we hoped our intermediaries made clear that we couldn't hold off on going to the press much longer. We imagined you and BY had already been moved. Opal's contact had gone silent; who knew what had happened to him; he probably just thought it too risky to be in touch. But even if you had been moved, the Partystate had been put on notice that we were on their trail and would not let up. Then we were given a specific date, and a specific place, the Lo Wu border crossing at Shenzhen. The deal was sealed except for the last, all-important step.

It was hard to believe. Even if the Partystate no longer wanted to keep someone in custody, rarely did it simply let the person go, especially if it had already (illegally) detained the person incommunicado for months on end, and most likely tortured and/or almost certainly mistreated her as well. It had to show it was right in the first place before concocting a face-saving way to let her go. This usually involved a confession, which if not outright forced was at the very least presented as a condition of release, then a perfunctory trial, followed by conviction and sentencing. Only after the sentencing was a way devised that could at once superficially appear to follow legal procedure and show the Partystate as clement and merciful in the face of obvious villainy or disloyalty or ingratitude for such beneficence. But just letting her go?

If it were true, it seemed the only possible explanation was that the Partystate perceived the situation in HK to be sticky enough already; it didn't want to complicate it by any detention of an HK person causing a furore. Even if only a remote possibility, anything that could tip the balance in favor of "illegal forces" (read: the pro-democracy movement) in HK was to be avoided. Such a case could have the effect of outraging people who otherwise sat on the fence or weren't inclined to do much, actually provoking them to do something or actively support others who were.

●

So we go to where we are to meet you, hoping that something—the stars, the gods, your captors—will bring you there.

We have been promised nothing certain, given only vague signals, messages from the opaque netherworld.

You must guard against too much hope, I tell myself. Though it is sometimes the only force that keeps you going, I say in the same breath. How much is too much? Any at all?

On the train to the border, Z on my lap, Opal next to us. The ride seems long. I've made it only a few times before. There was the time I went with Opal, the time I went to meet Opal when she was released; before that, it has to have been many years, I can't even remember. The train cars are different from ones on other lines of the HK underground—extra-wide. TV screens show news and commercials. The train is packed with mainlanders on their way home. As we near the border, there is more Putonghua than Cantonese. HK's inevitable slide, I think, swallowed up by the billion to the north.

I don't mind the long ride. Part of me wants to always be going and never arrive. Is it the part that wants to avoid disappointment or the part that wants to avoid fulfillment, the fear of what comes afterwards?

All the way up, Opal is uncustomarily quiet, solemn. Perhaps she intends to leave me to my thoughts. Perhaps she senses the ceremonial aspect of the journey, the mission, my desire to pay attention to my thoughts right before I meet you so that I will remember it afterwards. If I meet you. She has, after all, been with me pretty much from the start, is part of the story that lead to your capture, understands the import of it all. She plays with Z, drawing her attention to passing sights, this child for so long weighing me down, this child who never gives up on me, who, every time I look at her, I think I don't deserve her, who, every time she looks at me, I think I don't deserve a look like that. She often comes up to me and wordlessly offers her hand: Here, take it, her gesture says, I need you to hold it, to let me know that all is o.k. in the world and that I am safe. Her request for reassurance is a reassurance to me: If I am here to offer you my hand, then all is o.k., even—especially—when it's not. Looking at her perpetually mobile hands in the train carriage, I marvel that someone thinks she can be safe and protected from the dangers and evils of the world simply by holding my hand.

It is good that she doesn't know it's not true, as this journey we are on at this very moment so amply shows.

In a flood of tenderness, all is absolved, the little girl a figure of intercession. Memories bunch up in an impatient queue; all of the moments you've missed, stored up inside of me for your return. All of this time, I have been thinking of things I want to tell you, and then it is as if I turn to my side and find nothing but empty air, a storehouse of memories that constantly leaks. With so much to show you, to tell you, I am afraid that when we actually meet again, I will be speechless, able to proffer nothing. You will ask me to tell you what you missed, and I will draw a blank.

●

Walking down by the little-used old pier one evening, we pass the deserted fish market, where there are usually only two or three vendors selling out of styrofoam boxes. We stop and regard a row of fish hung from their tails on a horizontal line to dry in the sun. Z stares for a long time. Then she says, *Look at their eyes—they can't see us.* An infinitely sad look passes like a shadow over her face. I think she is going to cry. But it is more like a cosmic wince, a recognition far beyond her years. *No*, I say, *they can't see us. You're right.*

She has a fever. I spend hours lying in bed next to her—the only way she can rest, fall asleep, be calm is by snuggling up to me. She is limp, eyes narrowed to slits. When I pick her up, her heavy body drapes over my shoulders, my chest. She clings to me.

Baba, don't go away.

I won't.

Please. Never.

Of course I won't ever go away.

Sometimes the only way to calm her is to go out and watch the moon. She stares up with sad feverish reverent eyes.

Are there any astronauts there right now?

No, they left, I say. *But they forgot to turn out the light.*

She smiles her first smile since the fever descended, not so much because she finds what I said amusing as to say, I appreciate the effort.

A deluge. Water cascades in mini-waterfalls down the hundreds of steps from our house to the village. Driven out of its hiding place by the flood, a large turtle scuttles across the village main street. People look on, amazed. I go to the turtle. It retracts head and legs into its shell.

What are you doing, baba?

Saving the turtle from these people, I say under my breath, hoping the people won't hear, voice drowned out by the cacophonous rain.

What will the people do to it? she persists.

I don't know, maybe nothing. Maybe toy with it. Maybe eat it. I don't know, but I don't trust them. I don't trust people to treat animals well.

I'll help you, baba.

We carry the turtle down to the dirty beach that rims the harbor and put it in what looks like a safe place out of the rain, out of human view.

At the seafood restaurants on main street, turtles are displayed in tanks. Buddhists buy them sometimes, put them in buckets, bring them up to a pond in the mountains, release them, to accumulate merit.

When we ascend to the village main street, Z turns and says to those still standing about waiting for the downpour to cease, *Don't touch the turtle, people!*

After that, she replays the story over and over.
And how did the turtle look when you went to pick it up?
Scared.
How did you know?
It retracted its head and legs into its shell.
Can a turtle see when it's in its shell?
I don't know—good question; I think so.
I want to see the turtle again. Turtles are cool, aren't they?
But we should leave the turtle alone, I say. *The turtle doesn't want to see us again.*

With giant banana leaves for wings, one in each hand, each leaf nearly twice her height, she is pretending to be a giant predatory bird circling high above on the slipstream, swooping over the yard's green grass. The sun glares only a day after the deluge that cleansed the air, vanquished the haze; the air dazzles. Something about the sharp, clear light on the circling Z makes me nostalgic for the moment even before it has passed.

She has just helped me to cut the fronds from the tree that was slowly but surely conquering the yard. I told her that first it would take over the yard, then the house, and then we would be living in a banana tree. It is the first time since Anna went that I have done anything to maintain the yard, and now only because it has obviously gotten out of control. A bunch of green bananas hangs over Z's inflatable wading pool; I have nightmare visions of it coming loose and landing on her while she is in the water. Another large bunch of bananas leans up against the house. The branch from which they hung broke off in the last storm. We wonder whether they will ripen.

After she is a predatory bird (that never caught any prey, just swooped and whooped), she takes the wings and makes a teepee on a frame of three long sticks propped up against one another, laying the banana fronds against them carefully for walls. Then she is a mouse. This is her nest. I am an owl. My nest is on top of the ladder in the corner of the garden, at the edge of the steep, terraced hillside, overlooking, directly below, the village and the harbor, and, off in the distance, the tallest mountain on the island, the blue water of another bay beneath it. Up there on the ladder, one does indeed feel above it all, and nothing but nothing in that moment can touch me, us; in that moment, we live a charmed life, owl and mouse. I swoop. She narrowly avoids the predator by scurrying inside her teepee-nest. Is it not a good sign that she identifies more with the prey than the predator? Or is it a bad sign?

She is such a fun-loving child; whatever she does, she does with joy. Where could she have got that from? Certainly not from us. Or are we more joyful than we think? Do we underestimate ourselves?

When she is pleased with herself or enchanted by something, she forgets herself and sometimes exclaims, *Look, mommy!* I don't correct her or say anything at all. Then, often, after a moment, something inside her notices, and she says, *Look, baba!* without letting on that she noticed the mistake.

The political situation has taken me away from home ever more frequently. Z gets upset at my every absence, at the fact I'm gone more often. She has crying jags and misbehaves in ways she never did previously. She throws uncontrollable, raging fits that remind me of nothing so much as yours. After pushing me away and saying all manner of nasty things, and just as it seems it will never stop, she flings herself into my arms and only calms down if I hold her for a good long time. I find it harder to cope with her. This new phase is shattering my preferred image of her as small companion in distress, fellow sufferer, exemplary child. Perhaps she is all that, but she is also a three-year-old whose mother has disappeared and who, ever since, has had to depend on a very faulty human being for almost everything material and immaterial. A three-year-old?! Three years old already?! I gasp. And you are her father, don't you forget that. Friend, maybe, as well, and all those other things perhaps, but father first and last. Before, our intimacy to some extent offset the hardship and gave me the strength to face it; now, it seems more often the case that on top of everything else, I just haven't the energy to deal with her fits and foul moods.

One evening, she throws a fit before falling asleep because I'm not lying in the exact place in her bed where she wants me to be. During the night, she wakes up twice shrieking and only settles when I come and lie next to her. In the morning, she throws a fit because during the night, her magnatile construction partly fell down. I am exhausted because she is exhausted. Exhausted by absence.

One night, she awakes, comes out of her bedroom (previously, your office—I've converted it in your absence, just as you had intended to do; I think you'll be pleased to see it now, Z certainly likes her room). I hear her coming, should get up and head her off. Often, in the middle of the night, if I get to her soon after she wakes, she quickly drifts back to sleep. She peaks into our room, sees you aren't in bed, and shrieks, *I want mommy, I want mommy now!* Has she had a bad dream? During your long absence, she has never done this. She won't let me close to her and seems to almost blame me for your absence, as if I am responsible for it. I try to reason with her—*you know mommy's not here right now, but she will come back*—, to no avail. The fit goes on, though gradually abates after repeated admonitions—she will wake the neighbors, the police will come and take her away (ok, I know—low). Finally, she becomes so exhausted that all that's left is the uncontrollable heaving sobs, and, in between the gasps, her pitiful words, *I can't stop, I can't stop*. She lets me pick her up. Her whole body collapses onto mine, head resting heavily on my shoulder. *Take me out to see the moon*, she says weakly. I hold her in one arm and unlock and open the sliding glass door with the hand of the other, stepping out into the moonlight. The moon is high in the sky. Her eyes follow the light; she turns her head upward, squinting into it. OK, her look seems to say, that is there; perhaps things are o.k. After a moment, she says, *We can go inside now*, in a voice as weary as any adult's. She wants to lie down on the sofa. I put her down there and lie down next to her. *I want you to hug me*, she says. Then, after some time, she falls back asleep.

We go outside after her bath. She's naked. It is dark. The moon is almost full. She climbs the ladder and stands on the next-to-top rung, my hands gripping the back of her thighs. She looks down on the village below, the brightly lit football pitch in the distance. *Arsenal is winning*, she says. She's said the same before, from the same vantage point, overlooking the same scene—it's become a habit. Actually, Arsenal's not doing so well, but I appreciate her confidence. She arranges matches between Arsenal and other teams. My favorite is Arsenal versus the Cantonese opera singers. Arsenal always wins.

Looking up at her standing on the ladder in the dark, the light of the almost-full moon shining down on her, I think of how much she's changed since she last saw her mother, since her mother last saw her, all that time passing, never to return.

●

The moments of greatest respite come after putting Z to bed. It is night and all is quiet. It is, I think, the closest I come to a feeling of freedom, the freedom of having been unburdened by a weight, however temporarily, not only the weight of caring for Z, but also the weight of your disappearance, and of spending every waking moment in solidarity with you, always imagining what you must be experiencing, denying myself any pleasures or comforts you almost certainly do not possess. The weight never disappears, but it lightens ever so slightly in that time after Z has gone to sleep. Often enough, without any particular intention, I listen to Gould's Goldberg Variations, the volume just loud enough to be audible but not so loud as to risk waking Z.

Wet cobblestones past midnight. Arriving on the bus from Stansted. Had it rained earlier, or was that just the nightdamp of a cold climate? At that late-early hour, the cobblestones appeared almost black, reflections of streetlights glistening off them. I made a mental note to check when I passed during the day to see if the cobblestones were really that dark, but I never remembered to. Sometimes to this day, I find myself wondering.

Past midnight, and no one there to meet me, no way to contact you. You were staying at a friend's. I didn't have the number, or a phone, or any coins for a telephone box, and there were no shops open nearby to get change. I just stood there waiting, hoping you'd arrive, wondering what I would do, where I would go, if you didn't show up at all. We didn't know each other so well at that point: Had I misunderstood? Did you really not want me to come? Then you came. Things were so new, I'd yet to understand that lateness was your modus operandi—always in a hurry, always trying to catch up with time, always arriving in time to avert a catastrophe, but just.

It was your term break. You had bought a cheap package for a long weekend in Fuerteventura and invited me along. After spending a short night on your friend's sofa, we flew out of Stansted the next morning. It was the first and only time in my life I'd gone to a typical tourist destination, stayed in tourist accommodation, surrounded by pale northern tourists. I would have hated it if I weren't with you.

The recording of the Variations was one of the very first presents I gave you. Purchased at Blackwell's music shop on Broad Street. Through the years, we have listened to the Variations hundreds of times, so often I wonder whether you have heard the music there where you have been all this time. It is the sort of music, of art, that maybe helps you through. It does me. It was almost always I who played the Variations. Can I remember a single time it was you? You seemed to enjoy them well enough, but perhaps not so much as I. That leaves me wondering if it was perhaps a gift the giver enjoyed more than the receiver. They have, in my memory, in my mind, become emblematic of the two of us together. I can't even remember how I came to choose the cd. I knew you played piano. I was almost entirely ignorant of classical music, and it was one of the few pieces for piano I knew and liked, though I can't recall how I might have first come across it. Through the years, I played it at all times of day, especially shortly after awakening in the morning, breakfast, especially on weekends when time slowed down and we didn't have to rush off somewhere but could sit and eat and listen, or half-listen, the music blending with the environment. Because of that, it evokes memories of the many interiors, climates, seasons we have shared. The period of your disappearance is the only I can remember when I have played it regularly in the evening, after Z goes to bed.

The music has meant to me the promise of renewal, the chance of starting over, grace, a cosmic impersonal mercy, the opposite of what nature and much of humanity have to offer.

You were unhappy there, in that wet, cool place, that age-old college town. You found the people cold and superficial. All they did was drink. They communicated mostly by means of cultural references almost entirely lost on you. You were lonely; you missed the good friends you'd made in the last place you'd lived, the best friends you'd ever made in your life. But I loved to visit you in that beautiful place. I was living amongst refugees in one of the poorest countries in the world, and just walking the centuries-old streets, passing the centuries-old buildings reminded me that some places in this world are truly peaceful and safe, a refuge from terrible unsolvable lives and situations. All was new and exciting for this fugitive in your room.

Then there was the person who one Saturday morning berated me for never wanting to go out on the weekends and stomped out, leaving me stunned, Z crying. When we tried to follow, she stomped back in, said we weren't going anywhere because I didn't want to. Z kept crying. At such times, I saw you as a soul tied up in knots, a specialist in constructing mental hells, making perfectly fine or not-so-bad situations terrible. Your utter emotional unfairness reminded me of a child's. I didn't know how to contend with it. I thought our best days were over. Two people together tend to just as likely make each other miserable as not. Terminal monogamy just wears people down, leaves both sides worse for wear. It's too great a price to pay for security. I yearned for solitude, the old Sartre hell-is-other-people rag coursing through me.

That tantrum-filled Saturday morning ended in us going out. Far too early. Nothing was open. We didn't know where we were going. You said it was up to me. I hadn't a clue where to go, was just going out because you'd initially berated me for not wanting to. We took the Star Ferry across the harbor. At least, I thought, that's a nice ride, Z likes it. On the other side, we could stroll along the harbor and see what was happening. As we got off the ferry, on the TST embankment usually swarming with mainland tourists, we saw three youths brutally kicking and punching an older man. I shouted and ran in their direction. You snapped photos with your phone. The youths bolted, leaving the beaten man curled up on the ground, covering his head with his arms to protect himself. I gave chase. The youths outran me, kept running until out of sight. The beaten man was hairless. The savage kicks and punches had opened wounds from which blood flowed. His arms and head were purplish red, indicating he had once been badly burned. He didn't want us to call the police, making me wonder whether there was more to the incident than met the eye. Thanks but no thanks, he said, and limped away. The gratuitous violence, highly unusual on the streets of HK, had jaggedly entered our morning as if not by coincidence, like an objective correlative of the earlier marital discord.

A few days later, you broke down after another futile fight that seemed to erupt out of nothing, and repeated your view, which I had heard many times, that I didn't really understand the stress you were under.

What do you mean? I asked. It had always been difficult to pry difficult thoughts out of you. I would ask you repeatedly to explain yourself while you sat silently or said, What's the point?

After some silence, you said, *I have bad thoughts.*

What sort of bad thoughts? I wasn't sure I wanted to know.

Of not living. You said the words so softly I wasn't sure I'd caught them.

Of what?

Of not living.

You mean suicidal thoughts?

You nodded.

Why?

Something approaching a torrent: *People are so bad, and there's no way to stop them being bad.... You can't change anything, everything is the way it is, nothing's going to change.... Everything's so uncertain. Something bad could happen at any time. I could cross the border and be taken away. Something bad could happen here. You can never feel safe.... The only joy has been Z. Now I'm polluting her happiness. I often feel I can't go on....*

I tried to be kinder after that. I always tried to be kind. I succeeded some times more than others.

At times we were on the same side, fighting the same thing together; at times, not.

If you felt this way when you were free, how must it have been in detention? It would take a miracle for you to come through in one piece.

Which of these variations on the same person were Z and Opal and I to meet now at the border, if indeed there was any there at all to meet?

Not long before your disappearance, you found two small hard painful lumps in one of your breasts. (I'm ashamed to admit now, on this train going, hopefully, to meet you, I can't even remember which.) A non-specialist did a mammogram and CAT scan. He said the mammogram showed nothing, and the CAT scan indicated there was no problem at all. The lumps were almost certainly harmless, he concluded, but to be on the safe side, you should keep an eye on them and get them checked in another six to twelve months.

With your hypochondriac background, you were not especially reassured. This was, in fact, your first serious panic attack related to your health since Z's birth. For some time, concern for Z's health had entirely displaced worries about your own. Before that, I had regarded your hypochondria as a refraction of anxiety about other areas of your life. In retrospect, I wonder whether this new attack was a premonition of the disappearance, or at least of the choice you soon found yourself facing, whether to risk crossing the border or not. As ever with your hypochondria, it was not that you entirely imagined maladies where there was none to be found, but that you took one piece of possible evidence (lumps in the breast) and constructed a compelling doomsday scenario out of it, which then cast a looming shadow over the whole of your life; to use what in this case might be considered a tasteless metaphor, it was concern metastasized.

Right after that initial examination, you met a friend whose mother had died of breast cancer. She urged you to get a biopsy. Due to your excellent health insurance with the US-based human rights organization, you were able to book an appointment with one of HK's best-known breast cancer specialists, a woman who over the decades had campaigned effectively for better awareness and treatment of the disease in HK, one of those amazing people who almost invisibly improves life for the population at large simply by plugging away in her own particular area of expertise. She was now an old woman and received patients at an exclusive private hospital on a part-time basis. There was a long wait for an appointment with her.

A researcher to the core, you studied all available information. What you were able to determine was that, without a biopsy, you could go two years monitoring lumps through regular check-ups and self-examination without being able to conclusively rule out malignancy. When you told me this, your face took on the most distressed expression. Two years was a long time to fret.

Look, I said, *either you say to yourself, I've done all the research and have not been able to discover anything the matter, so I will assume everything is fine unless I find out otherwise, or you worry the whole time.*

Just give me a hug, you said, collapsing into my arms.

Several times in the past, you would worry endlessly about some malady being life-threatening. You would get a doctor's opinion, and after receiving it, be unsatisfied, and then seek out an expert in the particular field of the illness for a second opinion. Only after the second doctor had told you that everything was fine and there was nothing to worry about, the storm broke and the skies were washed clear. You were relieved, you could breathe freely, you had been given, as they say, a new lease on life. Until the next illness cropped up.

I thought of just how many ailments you had had, and how frequently. Bronchitis, harsh menstrual cramps that had a profound effect on mood, excessive menstrual bleeding, anemia, multiple allergies, especially to dust stirred up in our apartment, migraines with vision so blurred you could not make out characters or letters on the computer screen—all this in what appeared to be a perfectly healthy body with a strong constitution. You had eczema of the hands and eyelids sometimes so severe you could hardly bear the pain and itchiness. Were you really more prone to illness than I or were the illnesses physical manifestations of unaddressed anxiety?

You told me you'd had the lumps ever since secondary school—I'd never noticed—, but now was the first time they hurt; you couldn't understand why. The first doctor you saw could think of no cause of the pain, nor did he think it was a cause for concern. He seemed to imply there was a psychosomatic element to it.

What worried you most was the prospect of dying and being separated from Z. You felt your mortality more deeply than I. For several nights in a row, we had an almost identical conversation:

Am I going to be o.k?
Yes, you're going to be o.k.
Am I going to die?
No, you're not going to die, not any time soon.

And then you began to weep. *I don't want to miss Z growing up. You won't miss Z growing up.*

Then the silent weeping, tears dripping onto the pink sofa, turned to sobs.

I accompanied you to the appointment. The breast cancer specialist examined you briefly, asked a few questions, and concluded there was no need for a biopsy. She gave the same advice as the first doctor: Check the lumps regularly and get another examination in six to twelve months.

The visit lead to a reprieve. The fits stopped, the fights stopped. We just enjoyed being together. I remember wondering whether things were getting better now, finally. You compared the feeling after the specialist told you there was no need for a biopsy (and, crucially, you believed her) to your feeling after the ferry accident in which 39 had perished: How fragile all life was, how vulnerable, precarious, and how precious our life together. The feeling was a physical sensation in your chest that sometimes felt it would burst with joy and sometimes constrict to the point of choking you with fear. You just wanted to spend all your time with Z and me. You didn't want to be away from us for even a few hours.

You called it a second honeymoon, compared it to what you referred to as our first honeymoon, the period we lived in London after getting married. You felt free and happy then; the future glittered.

That it was there I should have been, by myself, when you disappeared! When I came back from London after your disappearance, your office was a mess, as usual. In my absence, no one- not Anna, not your parents- had dared to touch it. It looked just as you had left it before vanishing. When I opened the office door and tripped over a backpack on the floor, I started to giggle, a response to your incurable messiness. It was usual to have to step over things on the floor in order to arrive at the desk. And then, once one made it to the desk, one had to push things out of the way in order to clear a space wide enough for, say, a book, or a laptop. There were several dirty plates and cups scattered about. Your robin's-egg-blue teacup was half-full. The milk had curdled on the surface of the tea. A plate with bread crumbs and a full egg yolk, now hard and dry, sat on top of the printer. Z's toys, which you had been culling, and materials for projects planned for Z were under the desk, where they had colonized so much territory there was hardly room for one's feet.

How much time has passed since then! In your absence, your office has been converted into Z's bedroom, as per your plans. Of course, I haven't been able to do it anywhere near as well as you would have, but I aimed at what I thought you would want. I rented an office space elsewhere on the island and moved the things from your office there. I also tried to organize them.

As I sorted through the piles on your desk to prepare for the move, I came across several small silver metal trays of seaglass scattered in different places. You had collected it over years from beaches around the island. I remember you saying that, unlike everything else, it was yours. Everything you got ever since Z was born was for Z; never anything for yourself. It was true; all of your clothes were old and worn. I, the family launderer, laughed at how ragged your underwear were; the elastic waistbands hung loose. But you collected the seaglass only for yourself. It made you feel serene. At some point, I imagine, you planned to do something with it. I don't know what. It just became part of the general clutter of your life there on your desk.

I gathered the seaglass. Z and I bent wire around it, twisting pieces together. Over months, we worked on the project at irregular intervals. A mobile emerged, and grew and grew. Now it is quite large. Very large, actually. So large as to become ungainly and present many challenges regarding balance, a problem with which someone with such low spatial/mechanical/engineering IQ as I struggled. In the end, it turned out quite beautiful, I think. Very beautiful, even. I tried to adopt Z's process of creation—to not to have a goal, to not think in advance of where I was going. Of course, it was impossible; but simply trying influenced the result, and Z's help was indispensable. I would stand on her black stepstool and hold the mobile up in the air with one hand, then ask her to walk around it and tell me what she thought from different angles, until it got too big. Then I screwed a fist-large hook into the ceiling and hung it from there, colorless and green and brown and even some blue pieces of seaglass clear but mostly frosted with what I take to be something like a salt glaze. Now it's waiting for you, hanging from the ceiling in the new office where you've never been.

Z usually loves to explore the use of new materials, to experiment, but she was initially reluctant to undertake the project with me. It was only when I repeatedly told her that this was for mommy (I didn't quite dare to raise her hopes by saying "for when mommy returns") that she began to take some interest. We constructed it in many small, incremental steps, adding just one piece of glass and one piece of wire per session. As she began to see the pattern emerge, the mobile being realized little by little, piece by piece before her eyes, she was impressed and her interest grew. By the end—there was no clear end, but by the time we came to a point where we didn't know what else to do or how to extend it, having still a good deal of seaglass that could have been added—, she was perhaps even a little proud.

Also amidst the flotsam on your desk, a curious, mysterious image, almost immediately recognizable yet so surprising that it took a moment to recall where exactly I'd seen its kind before. The small photograph poorly printed on cheap paper was almost entirely abstract, would be virtually indecipherable if not for its familiar black fan shape. I initially saw nothing, but then, whether through wishful thinking or worst fear or accurate perception, discerned a tiny white alien floating in that dark universe, and just then felt something I'd felt only once before, a sudden rent in the heart, with the difference that this time, in the absence of a medical expert, I couldn't be sure. There was no "caption", no date stamp, no name. When had it been taken? Was it even yours? How long had it been lying there beneath the detritus? I guessed you'd gone to the doctor while I was away; you didn't want to tell me over the phone; were waiting until I returned.

We hadn't been trying; it was the last thing we intended to do just then. You wanted another. I was of no particular disposition: If you did, I wouldn't stand in the way. But, we agreed, whatever the case, it was best to wait until a safer, clearer, more stable time. It was hard to foresee, though, when that might possibly come. One couldn't wait forever. You must have felt something to make you suspect. I knew you well enough to be quite certain that you would have taken a store-bought pregnancy test before visiting a doctor. The test, then, must have been positive, and those tests were highly accurate, were they not? You would have just gone to the doctor to confirm. So, even though, looking at the image, I couldn't be certain, surely the fact that I'd found the image, that it existed, was all but confirmation. If indeed, it was yours. But who else's could it be?

Taken aback, inundated by thoughts and errands related to your disappearance, and due partly to an assessment of priorities—hardly the most urgent matter, whether or not you were—, I set the matter aside for months, and I probably would not have gotten around to it even then, if not for the fact that I met a parent of one of Z's friends who was a doctor, and I showed her the image. It looked like a foetus, she said, in its very first weeks. At that early stage, the doctor was usually confident enough to affirm the pregnancy, but it wasn't conclusive, so a follow-up visit was routinely prescribed, just to be sure.

So, then, you weren't alone when you disappeared; you were not one but two? All that time in some room or cell forsaken by the world, new life grew inside you. Did your captors know? Did you tell them? If you didn't, at one point did they figure it out for themselves? Did they care? Did it result in any special treatment or attention? Was it possible that small fact getting ever bigger influenced their decision about what to do with you? It was one thing to disappear a woman, another to disappear a pregnant woman, no? And now, if it were true, you would be nearly to term. There at the border, should I be looking for a woman with a very large belly? Should I be looking for a woman with a newborn?

•

I look up and around the train carriage, thronged with homeward-bound mainlanders and their loot—trolleys full of their HK purchases, big suitcases, loud voices. Even for them, who previously had their movements tightly circumscribed and, especially when it came to exiting the mainland, had to go through strenuous, time-consuming procedures, crossing the border these days is a mere formality. They're going home; they probably feel free. 40 million of them visited last year—over five times the HK population. They can come and go nearly as they please. Do they know about Gao Zhisheng? Do they know about Ilham Tohti? Probably not. If they did, would they care? Probably not.

Gao has just been formally "released" after eight years of a combination of various forms of captivity that run the gamut—imprisonment, disappearance, house arrest. The persecution included severe physical torture. His immediate family—wife, daughter and son—are in the US, having escaped the mainland, and were unable to see him upon his "release". He was delivered as scheduled into his brother's hands at the jailer's gate in a remote town of East Turkestan. After having spent the past five years in solitary confinement—"all alone in a dark room" were the exact words his sister used—his mental state is so unstable, he would not have been able to make his way out of the prison on his own. His teeth are falling out. He has lost a lot of weight. He appears to have lost the ability to communicate with others, to hold a steady conversation. He responds with difficulty to questions. While formally "released", and though the Partystate has no legal grounds to restrict his freedom, Gao is not free, still followed and surrounded by police wherever he goes, his movements circumscribed, his family frightened into silence. His brother told those able to reach him by phone it was "inconvenient" to speak. Casually destroying a person is an effective warning to others. Those who need to be warned are well aware of Gao's case. We can crush you with our little finger, without so much as thinking about it. In fine calibration, the more directly you challenge us, the more you will be crushed.

Ilham's impending trial on separatism charges will certainly result in a guilty verdict, though there appears to be no evidence whatsoever to support the charges. The only question, the only suspense now is what the sentence will be. Death is the severest penalty, but not even the greatest pessimists believe the Partystate will judicially kill him. He will far more likely receive the Gao Zhisheng kill-him-slowly-by-neglect-and-mis-treatment. Judging by recent developments and the predilections of the current Parystate leaders, the sentence will be long indeed, as if in inverse proportion to the paucity of evidence. Seven of his students have been arrested as well, and disappeared—in months, their families haven't heard from them once, don't even know where they are. The main purpose of their arrests is to coerce testimony from them against their teacher. Of course, they will almost certainly stand trial themselves on trumped-up charges.

How strange, I think, looking at my fellow passengers, when the mark of nationality is that you know less about what is happening in your country than people outside of it; ignorance, a sickness, a disease, an epidemic infecting the majority of the population, seeping into the language, making it exceedingly difficult to say and think many things. The unfreedom is pervasive, linguistic, intellectual, spiritual. They are free to acquire, shop, consume. What more could they want?

The thoughts about Gao and Ilham occur against my will, produce a physical response—a wince, a cringe, a feeling of breathlessness as if having been punched in the gut and had the wind knocked out of me, a lament struggling to emerge from my strangled throat. The mind flees from thoughts of the conditions of your captivity, from the prospect that the reunion might not occur today. After all, I tell myself, I know so little about your abduction and detention, why speculate?

And then it hits me—how could it not have occurred before now? (What else hasn't occurred until now? What else have I overlooked? What else have I failed to see though it was right in front of my face?) Not long before your disappearance, you met a man who made a confession to you, a person you knew quite well, though you saw him only occasionally, hadn't seen him in a good long time. In the course of the conversation, he said, *Do you remember those documents I gave you? The ones I gave you to pass on to ____ in case anything happened to me?*

Yes, you said, you did.

At the time, I feared being disappeared, perhaps even being assassinated. Do you want to know why?

I'm not sure, you said.

I was the one who made the anonymous calls for the Jasmine Revolution. A contact in the Partystate security apparatus gave me an oblique warning. He said I should never meet anyone alone. He'd been at a meeting where I'd been discussed. He wasn't sure how they knew. They didn't really seem to know for sure. Probably just process of elimination—they'd detained and tortured everyone else by then!

You wondered why he told you, guessed he wanted to get it off his chest, to relieve himself of the burden of the secret. Maybe, in case he disappeared, he wanted at least one other person to know. He had expressly told you he'd acted alone and never told anyone else. You were the only one who knew.

I suddenly wonder if that intelligence could have had anything to do with your disappearance. Perhaps the Guobao had been conducting surveillance on him, on you, that lead it to believe you knew something. It had used the calls for a Jasmine Revolution to launch a wide-ranging crackdown, to strike far and wide, as if a form of collective punishment. At the same time, it had been frustrated at not having gotten to the bottom of the "plot" against the regime. It had never managed to arrest anyone who had any connection to the calls. Your acquaintance said that if he had known in advance of the extent of the crackdown, he would not have made the calls. That sounded disingenuous; he could not have been so naïve. Of course, your disappearance could have had nothing to do with the calls for a Jasmine Revolution. It's just that in recalling your acquaintance's revelation, I am struck that after all this time, and here, on the verge of hopefully meeting you again, I still know nothing. O and I and others have been working on the assumption that you were disappeared in connection with the crackdown on the New Citizens Movement, but we don't actually have any but the most tangential evidence, such as BY's disappearance, to support that supposition. So the disappearance could just as plausibly have nothing to do with NCM either. Strange, after all this time, to still be so ignorant.

Whoosh! Near Kowloon Tong, the train shoots out of the tunnel. *Found it!* I had been clearing out the storage area, going box by box, to remove most of it to the new office, when I discovered Tatyana's sketchbook in the most obvious of places where I had not thought to look before, nearly at the top of a clear plastic box. It was like coming across a magical treasure, one that a rather large part of me did not wish to relinquish. I couldn't bear to open it—too painful! Doing so would only make me want to keep it. I asked her for delivery instructions. For only the second time, she responded (the first was to my very first message, and that was to request the book in the first place, now many months ago). A series of messages discussing how best to get the notebook to her followed. Communicating across the years to someone I used to know well and now not at all. As if we were collaborating on a common project—how to send an object halfway around the world, an object of priceless value, and ensure it arrived at its destination.

Once I'd written her that I'd found it, the tone of her replies became friendlier—I imagined because she didn't want to do or say anything at that crucial moment that might make me think twice about returning the notebook, now that she almost had it in her clutches. Once that matter was concluded, the notebook safely in her hands, I imagined I would never hear from her again.

After I sent it, I wrote from a café near the express delivery office:

It's sent. Supposed to arrive tomorrow, Wednesday, your time.

I'm so nervous! I asked the woman at DHL whether she could personally accompany the package. She assured me many times that it would arrive safely, but the way she packed it didn't inspire confidence. It's in a small box. I put some wrapping around it but she didn't put any additional. All I can imagine right now is it bumping around in that box all the way to B.

> Would you please confirm when you receive it? And if for any reason, it doesn't arrive tomorrow, would you let me know that too? And when you receive it, please check whether it's in good condition and let me know. It's come through these years and followed me all over the world in excellent shape—want to make sure that it makes the last journey home as well as it's made the last (what?) fifteen years, right?
>
> If you want to, you can check at the DHL site. The waybill number is 60 3180 4741.

Then, as I had requested, she confirmed she had received it. And then nothing more.

The silence was accompanied by mourning, but also relief, relief that the "mission" was concluded, that communication could cease, that the past would cease protruding into the present, could return to being nothing but wisps of memory strewn across the days. Even the slightest contact, for whatever reason, felt like a betrayal (because it was!), especially at a time when you were in such a terrible situation and had no freedom to do anything you desired while I was using my freedom to do this, to betray. How we abuse our freedom! (How I abuse my freedom!) Incorrigible mind, incorrigible heart.

Why had I done it? Out of some great need to communicate, though rationally I could not have expected any satisfactory communication. But that was exactly it: the desire to do something for no other reason than to follow the dictates of the heart. The feeling of isolation recalled a time, a moment, a person with whom isolation was deeply overcome. I had to keep hidden the most important thing in my life from almost everyone. Of course, T and I made arrangements about nothing more intimate than the delivery of a notebook, but that felt more important than almost anything else.

If I had revealed to her the situation of my wife, of my family, would she have responded any differently? I had mentioned in a previous message that my mother had just died. She said nothing in response to that, probably thought I was just trying to trick her into communication beyond the bounds of the business at hand. Then again, parents die. It's not uncommon; it's the way of the world; whereas not every day is one's spouse disappeared by the largest dictatorship in the world.

Passing the stations of the New Territories towns, nondescript high-rises clustered around shopping malls, places I hardly know, have only heard of, never been, never had any interest in, we are approaching the border.

Once, years ago, we were returning from visiting friends in Jiangxi. We arrived at the Shenzhen train station so early that the crossing was not yet open. We had several early morning hours to kill in that desolate border area. We found a restaurant that was open and had breakfast, *youtiao* and *xifan*, my favorites. That was before Z—how free and easy that time appears now! Still, what remains is the memory of fear bordering on panic: we had come so close, were on the verge, and yet perhaps we would not be allowed to cross to freedom.

In the aftermath of the referendum and march, the Leninist machine utilized every dirty trick in its arsenal. Depending on your point of view, this showed either the immensity of its power or its desperation; perhaps both. There was a predictable barrage of propaganda equating the struggle for democracy with chaos and violence; smear campaigns against pro-democracy leaders; coordination of businesses, front organizations, allied political parties and the HK government to condemn OC; threats against pro-democracy media; an anti-OC signature campaign and march (participants were bused in and paid to attend). The atmosphere is grim, but ultimately the Partystate can't win; it is just postponing its inevitable demise. HK people will come to rule themselves in one way or another, at one time or another. You would consider that false optimism: To think anyone, especially the HK democracy movement, stands a chance against such a powerful machine dedicated solely to the perpetuation of its monopoly on power and the crushing of its enemies is wishful thinking.

The Partystate's anti-OC campaign is meant to send a message: You shall pay a price both individually and collectively for your involvement in the democracy movement. It is to make each person think: If it comes to the next step, nonviolent direction action, as it surely must, what will I do, what price will I have to pay? All things considered, if all were "normal"—if you hadn't been disappeared, if you didn't work in a "sensitive" area, if we weren't under surveillance, if we lived in a politically secure place—then of course I would join, without hesitation. But here, now, there are sacrifices to make. Throughout HK, people are making similar calculations, undertaking similar deliberations. Should I do this or not? It is always safer not to, and understandable, but if too many take the safe route, there is no movement.

What kind of person am if I don't put my family first?

If, at the end of this train journey, we do not find you, then how can I take part in civil disobedience? If I do and am arrested, Z's grandparents will be entirely shouldered with the burden of looking after her. And what about Z? Hasn't she already been through enough? How can I risk depriving my child of yet another parent? And even if you are allowed to cross over to the (relatively) sane side of the border, whether or not I join the occupation is dependent on how you are, whether or not you are capable of looking after yourself and Z, whether or not your mental state could tolerate the stress of more adversity in the face of the Partystate, of yet another member of the small family being incarcerated.

For long now, every simple decision has seemed complicated. Your doomsday scenarios used to irritate me. Yes, I said, you have to plan for the worst, hope for the best, but also keep in mind that the worst is unlikely, keep some perspective, some sense of proportion, don't let the prospect of the worst infect you. Take it into account, prepare for it, but don't let it cripple action; it should simply inform action. What if, you said in the early days of OC, I was arrested? Once they discovered who I was, who we were, who they had on their hands, their persecution would be unrelenting. They would try to deport me, and eventually succeed, overcoming whatever legal hurdles might stand in their way. Then I would have to leave. We would be separated. You would feel obliged to stay and do your work to the bitter end. What then? you would say. What then? These are the things we have to think about, plan for. What could I say to that? Some things you can't plan for, some things you just have to leave to fate. That was after OC was founded and before you disappeared. Now decisions seem even more complicated, involving even more factors, permutations, scenarios. Sometimes it makes me not want to do anything at all—easier that way, less to think about, less risk.

●

At Lo Wu, we exit the train, the hordes pushing and shoving as if their lives depended on being first to the immigration queue. Why in such a hurry to return to captivity? It is only when one arrives at the destination that one realizes it wasn't worth struggling to get to. But then again, for some people—more than a billion, to be more precise—it is home. And home is home.

This border, it has determined the fate of so many.

Pingan, who has provided advice on your case and acted as an intermediary, was stopped on the other side of the border and prevented from crossing. His family lives in HK. He deposited them here after the Jasmine Revolution crackdown. His children now go to school in HK. But he's not allowed to cross the border to see them. Hard to know why; perhaps his legal representation of Ilham. After sending his family to HK, he continued to work in Beijing but kept a low profile. Then Ilham was detained, thrusting Pingan back into the spotlight. Ilham had retained Pingan as his lawyer since long before his detention. If he had so chosen, Pingan might have decided against representing Ilham, especially when it became clear the latter was going to be charged with that most "sensitive" of crimes, separatism, carrying a potential death penalty. But Pingan couldn't just abandon Ilham in his time of need. He recently travelled to Urumqi and finally, for the first time since Ilham's detention, was allowed to meet his client. The event received a lot of coverage outside of the country since it was the first confirmation that Ilham was even still alive. After that, Pingan was not allowed to cross the border, though he had done so on a regular basis before, countless times. No reason given. Just no. Though he was a citizen, had a right to freedom of movement, to exit and re-enter his own country, and on top of that, had the pass required of mainlanders to cross the border to HK. Just no. Himself on one side, his family on the other. For how long, he did not know.

Your father himself, given all his family's meager savings, paid smugglers to take him across the border in order that one member of the family, the youngest, the strongest, the most promising, could escape the Great Famine then in full swing. Under the circumstances, it was the family's best possible "investment". While your father smuggled himself across the border half a century ago and these days can go back and forth between HK and his home village in Guangdong almost as freely and easily as anybody could make a four-hour commute anywhere in the world, his daughter's most recent attempt to cross the border resulted in a descent into a black hole from which she has yet to emerge (though perhaps at this very moment, she is on the other side of the border, just a few hundred meters away).

By the way, I haven't told him or your mother that I am coming to pick you up, for fear of disappointing them if you aren't handed over. The last time I saw him, only a couple of days ago, he said, probably influenced by all of the time he has spent with Z recently, that he wished he had not worked so much and had spent more time with you while you were growing up. I suppose that's a common sentiment, but his regret was nonetheless poignant.

I have told Z. I would have preferred not to, but it was the only way I could explain where we were going and why we would wait a long time if necessary. I emphasized to her that it is by no means certain you will come.

The crowd swarms about with its booty. Amongst the tourists are the parallel traders who avail themselves of the individual visitor multiple-entry scheme to cross the border day after day buying tax-free in HK and then selling their purchases on the other side of the border at a profit, due to high mainland tariffs. They also transport milk powder, drugs and other items in high demand because mainlanders trust their safety much more than that of their equivalents produced on the mainland. Last year, of 40 million who visited HK, 23 million were single-day visitors. With their trolleys piled high and their trademark white-red-and-blue carrying bags, the parallel traders are bonafide members of the precariate, eking out a living in a legal grey area.

All this commotion, all this life, where this one momentous event is hopefully about to occur, a momentous event of which no one around us is even aware.

Where should we stand? Where should we wait? I ask Opal.

I've never done this sort of thing before, wait at the border for the release of a loved one from extrajudicial captivity. For

Opal, crossing at Lo Wu went back to childhood. Her father lived in Shenzhen. He'd left her family, moved there, started a new family, for years hardly acknowledging hers. Opal resented him but visited him now and then. He was, after all, her father. For him, going to the mainland was a chance to start over, the border like the River Lethe where he cleansed himself of the past.

Let's stand over here, she says, motioning to a cramped corner. The border crossing area on the HK side has many tight angles. There are no places with a commanding view.

Inside the enormous immigration hall, where lines of border-crossers snake up to the immigration booths, one can see for some distance, but not here, where we stand, outside the doors from which, after passing through HK immigration, people emerge. Here, your eyes have to frenetically scan the crowd, zipping rapidly back and forth across bodies and faces only meters away. Still, there is but one set of doors through which those entering HK can pass, and we stand several dozen meters away from it, with a view across the expanse, glimpsing just about everyone passing through. As long as we keep our eyes glued to the area, the chances of someone passing without us noticing are not great.

There is no one we can contact, no phone number we can call to inquire about the situation. The arrangement for release and handover, since it has to do with an entirely extra-judicial process, is entirely off the record. Officially, it does not exist; strictly speaking, this is not happening. We were expressly warned against alerting the media. If their scouts saw the media, the release would be called off.

Having established our vantage point, I breathe. The wait has begun. It is one of those moments in life that seems exceedingly unreal. Perhaps all heightened moments have that aspect. Because they are more real.

I turn to Opal: *Am I dreaming?*

I don't know, says Opal. *I was wondering the same thing.*

What? whether I was dreaming or you?

Both, I guess.

Well, I hope at least one of us isn't.

A pause. Then...

But that wouldn't work, would it? If only one of us was not dreaming? Because that could mean that the one of us who wasn't dreaming was in the dream of the other, who was.

Hmm, yes, you're right. I don't know the way out of it. Hopefully, neither of us is.

How about this? Opal says with resolve, looking up at me for emphasis, not a trace of irony in that momentarily child-like face intent on solving a conundrum. *We are both both dreaming and not dreaming.*

That sounds about right.

Who's dreaming? interjects Z, who's been sharply half-listening in her usual way. And when her question isn't immediately answered, she repeats, *Who's dreaming?* in a demanding tone.

O is. And I am. And we are not, I answered. *Are you dreaming?*

No, I'm not dreaming.

Oh, that's good. But maybe you are in our dream.

That's silly! she exclaims with a big smile, suddenly in on the joke, but then, on second thought: *What are you dreaming?*

I don't know. I don't know. I can't say. I'm afraid that saying might make it disappear.

Z responds with a quizzical look: *That doesn't sound entirely logical, baba.*

She is in my arms. She's become heavy to hold for any length of time. Such a big strong girl, I exclaim every time I pick her up with an exaggerated groan. I make sure I can both see and touch her at all times. If this is a dream, I tell myself, fearing Opal and Z have tired of the conceit, at least I can feel and see her, and that is real, no matter what else might not be. She's my reality anchor.

But it's not because I need a reality anchor that I hold her tight. It is because of Yu Man-hon, the autistic teenager who went missing at this very border crossing fourteen years ago, never to be seen again. He and his mother became separated at the bustling Yau Ma Tei MTR station in the center of Kowloon. Somehow, he made his way from there to Lo Wu. To do so required changing train lines, something a child with a developmental disability as severe as his would not have been able to do deliberately. He inexplicably eluded HK immigration and crossed the border. Mainland immigration officials found him on their side and, assuming he was from HK, sent him back. HK immigration officials questioned him and assumed from his response (or lack thereof) and appearance that he was from the mainland. He was sent back, to the wrong side, from which he had never come. His mother has searched for him ever since, in the face of a combination of official indifference and incompetence on both sides of the border. Investigations were cursory and inept. As far as could be discerned, mainland authorities had done almost nothing. Not here! they said, and that was the end of the matter as far as they were concerned. There were rumors that Man-hon had at some point been taken into custody by mainland police and, as the story went, either been beaten to death or sent to a remote rural location. Every now and then, a new interview with his brokenhearted mother would appear in the press. She is poor, and in poor health. She let him out of her grasp for a moment, and he disappeared forever.

I am so concerned about keeping eye and hand on Z that, I fear, I am not as intent on looking out for you as I should be. It's all I can do to both hold on to Z and search for you at the same time. I don't want to lose the former in the search for the latter, but I don't want a chance to find the latter pass due to holding on to the former. It isn't exactly a conscious thought, but somewhere there is this: Losing one loved one is more than enough.

I stand here remembering your fondness for happy endings, your aversion to sad endings. After a long day of work, dealing with cases of torture and myriad other human rights abuses, you didn't want to hear or talk about China, you didn't want sad or tragic stories, didn't want to watch disturbing or "depressing" films. There are not, I told you, that many really good stories with happy endings. Now I wonder, Could *you* give *us* a happy ending? Can an individual author her own happy ending? It depends on where she lives, where she comes from, what she does, what she's up against, how much power she has over her own life. Seeking liberation, fighting for freedom, she is constantly reminded of her own powerlessness—so much lies beyond her own control, even as concerns her own life. In wishing to effect an outcome, you throw your fate to the wind.

After waiting hours, I am about to give up and return home, not for my sake but for Z's. I hesitate before the worst moment of all, to raise Z's hopes only to dash them. It was grossly irresponsible to bring her. I can cope with my own disappoint but not with hers. Moments after asking Opal whether she thinks we should go, I tell her I'd like to wait a bit longer, and to myself I add, if only to postpone Z's disappointment. She is impatient, asking incessantly, *When is mommy going to get here?*

I don't know, I tell her, *soon, I hope.*

I envision dragging her away from the border: But I want mommy! I want mommy! she cries, eliciting stares, until she can cry no more and collapses on my chest in exhaustion. There is within me an irrational anger towards you for not showing up. By the time we get home, Z is asleep, head resting on my shoulder. I lay her down in her bed. She awakes, sleepily insists, *Baba, lie down next to me.* I do. She drifts back to blessed sleep as I stare at her face just barely visible in the greydark.

I think of Opal's impending departure for Taiwan, her human rights program, her next step in life. I will feel lost without her. She's already told me that if you don't show up, she'll put off going. *That's out of the question*, I said. *You must go.* She wanted to stay until the "mission" was completed. But I said, *No, you must go, you can't put your life on hold indefinitely. The term is about to start. You can't miss the beginning. You've more than done your duty. We can manage on our own. And of course, you can still help out from afar, so no need to stay here.* Still, remaining at the border, waiting for you, feels like a magical way to stave off Opal's departure. Every departure these days feels like an abandonment.

And what if we were to leave and then you showed up, crossing the border to find no one there? Of course, you could easily find your way home on your own (assuming your mental state is better than Gao's), but still, the thought of no one meeting you here is too much to bear. Indecision keeps feet planted, stuck between staying and going.

I glimpse someone who, at a distance, might be you—same hair color, same skin tone, same eyes, something about the way she carries herself, recognizably erect and strident as well as newly burdened, with heavy shoulders, in the way that a person emerging from extrajudicial secret detention and probable mistreatment might be—an apparition drifting across no-man's-land, as if visible only to me. I don't ask Z, *Is that mommy?* for fear it's not. Distant but distinguishable, she floats across that space between places. Gaunt. Thinner. Pale. Noble. Tired. Strong. Resolute. But as far as I can discern, in the gust of possible first recognition, no "fellow traveller", new life neither inside you nor in your arms. Did it never exist? Was the sonogram not yours? Did you miscarry? For now, I can't bear the thought. Too many questions. Can't even be sure that, mentally, you'll be all there. Perhaps a shell, collapsed and shaken within—it might take a long time to recover; she might never. Or she might go on just as before, as if nothing, or nearly nothing, has occurred. You can rarely be certain of another's inner resources, even of someone close to you, someone you think you know well. This person, I think, whom I know so well. Knew. And now? This person approaching. Exclamations from melodramas: We did not know she was still alive! And yet, there she is before us, as if returned from the dead. Few ever make their way back from the underworld. But she has broken free, broken through. I send a thought out to her across that space: don't look back! But, I quickly catch myself: That was Orpheus who did so, and Eurydice disappeared forever as a result. And so I check: Is there something I am not to do now, or to do, a small matter upon which eternity hinges, a detail that might make all the difference? Z, I sense, is curious, eager, but also hesitant, shy, her cheek pressed to my cheek, her chest to mine. The person I think is you has not yet seen us. I wonder as that person approaches whether I will be able meet her eyes. I lack confidence in myself, in you. But another voice says, exclaims, declares, We have done this. We have come through. You are still alive. I am holding Z, you are approaching. This is us, for now. For now, this is who we are.

www.ingramcontent.com/pod-product-compliance
Lightning Source LLC
Chambersburg PA
CBHW031717230426
43669CB00007B/173